THEORETICAL MODELS
OF COUNSELING
AND PSYCHOTHERAPY

THEORETICAL MODELS OF COUNSELING AND PSYCHOTHERAPY

Kevin A. Fall, Ph.D.
Loyola University — New Orleans

Janice Miner Holden, Ed.D.
University of North Texas

Andre Marquis, Ph.D.
Northeastern State University

Brunner-Routledge

New York and Hove

Published in 2004 by
Brunner-Routledge
29 West 35th Street
New York, NY 10001
www.brunner-routledge.com

Published in Great Britain by
Brunner-Routledge
27 Church Road
Hove, East Sussex
BN3 2FA
www.brunner-routledge.co.uk

10 9 8 7 6 5 4 3 2 1

Library of Congress Cataloging-in-Publication Data
Fall, Kevin A.
    Theoretical models of counseling and psychotherapy / Kevin A. Fall,
Janice Miner Holden, Andre Marquis.
        p. cm.
Includes bibliographical references and index.
    ISBN 1-58391-068-9
1. Counseling. 2. Psychotherapy. I. Holden, Janice Miner. II. Marquis, Andre,
Ph. D. III. Title.

BF637.C6F324 2003
158.3--dc21

                                                              2003011781

To my grandparents John and Helen Fall
and Hugh and Rowena McKinney
KEVIN A. FALL

To my husband, Gary Boudreaux, for his patience and support
JANICE MINER HOLDEN

CONTENTS

PREFACE

I (KAF) am writing the preface, as I often do, at the end of the writing process. Therefore, for you the reader, what is your first taste of this book is for me a reflection process akin to what a chef does, surveying the table as the guests arrive for dinner. As part of this reflection my coauthors and I would like to acquaint you with four main pieces of information: why we wrote this book, what we hope you gain from using the book, what is contained in the book, and how to use the book.

Why write another theory book? A brief review of the theory bookshelf reveals more than enough titles from which to choose. Personally, my coauthors and I love theory, and the use of theory in our development as educators and clinicians has been essential. There is a palpable sense of depth and mystery in studying theory that is extremely appealing to us; it reflects the murkiness of the therapeutic situation. When I talk to students about their reasons for studying counseling or psychology, they often provide the standard answer, "I want to help." How do you help? To be an effective helper, one must be able to discern the human condition; so the issue of the nature of humanity is in essence both a professional and personal one. Nowhere is the convergence of personal and professional issues more notable than in the study of counseling theory. So, in the most practical sense, we chose to write the book because we enjoy the topic. The three facilitators in your journey (Jan, Andre, and I) bonded by one ideal that we kept alive during this whole process: the desire to make theory accessible and practical while not sacrificing any of the depth of the material.

That brings us to the question of what you can hope to gain from using the book. Our hope is that you learn about yourself and the various theories. As you will read in chapter 1, theory development is a process, and the first step is learning about the content of each theory, while also applying the concepts to your own personal philosophies and values. Because we believe that the more you are exposed to the content of each theory, the more you will have a personal reaction to the theory, we have taken great care to explore issues that are largely ignored by other texts. We hope that the depth of the material ignites some passion and helps you resonate with the philosophy of some theories over others; they are different for a reason. We hope you will discover the usefulness of theory. In an age where the motto seems to be, "Do whatever works," the mental health field risks forgetting that the primary tool of the counselor is the **self** of the counselor. Theory is an extension of the therapeutic self. Forgetting that point seems dangerous.

Contained in these pages you will find all the major theories of counseling as well as some new approaches. Most notably, we hope you enjoy the surprises—the obvious ones, such as the chapter devoted to an innovative approach, Integral Counseling, and the comprehensive overview of Systems Theory, as well as the more subtle ones, such as our attention to philosophy, spirituality, multicultural issues and other recent developments in the field. You will encounter case examples that illuminate theoretical concepts and philosophical underpinnings to help you explore your basic convictions. Theory development is a process, and to help you on your journey, we provide primary source reading and internet and video resources for further exploration.

Most of you are probably using this book as a required text in a graduate course on theory. We have been there, so we know that theory texts can seem abstract and distant, which can lead to you putting the book back on your shelf to collect dust until your comprehensive or licensure exams. We hope you use this book as a resource in your personal development as a mental health professional. We purposefully did not include a comparison chapter because we want you to compare and contrast the theories on your own. Explore! Get personally involved in the theories! The book is designed for you to literally work your way through the personal theory development process by reading the chapters, flipping back and forth and comparing sections, and using your class time to discuss the deeper aspects of the theory.

This has been a long journey for us and we hope you enjoy the end result. Like theory, this book is a process and we are open to your suggestions. I (KAF) would be remiss if I did not thank Whewellene Fischer for her tireless work editing and reformatting the figures of the book. I would also like to thank Jan and Andre for their hard work on this project. We all thank our first acquisitions editor, Tim Julet, for the vision to begin this project, and our new editor, Emily Epstein Loeb, for her courage and incredible patience in seeing it through to its end. Staying with the chef metaphor, we have prepared a lavish table for you. To learn, to develop your tastes, you must dive in and experience the offerings. Have fun, and good luck with your learning!

KAF, JMH, AM

CHAPTER 1

INTRODUCTION

There is nothing so practical as theory.
—Kurt Lewin, social psychologist

There is no therapy without theory.
—Earl Ginter, counselor educator

COUNSELING THEORY

What Is Counseling Theory?

Imagine this: You are conducting your first individual counseling session. You have oriented your client to procedures and to ethical and legal considerations in the counseling process. You are ready to turn the focus to your client and her reason for being in counseling. You might facilitate the beginning by saying, "Well, Kim, now that we have dispensed with the paperwork, where would you like to start today?" That sounds easy enough. No problem. We do not need theory to do that, right? Now the client begins to tell her story and the information begins to accumulate. Having begun, how do you proceed? What is your purpose, what are your goals, and how do you pursue them? How do you conceptualize your client's psychological dynamics? How do you determine what you can do to help her reach her counseling goals?

In a standard 50-minute session, you have a myriad of choices. How do you decide whether and when to follow your client and/or direct her? How do you decide whether and when to address the counseling relationship, assessment of the client, or strategies for change? With each communication, your client will provide you with additional information; how will you organize and interpret that information? With each client communication, you have a variety of responses from which to choose; how will you choose the one response you make? Your choices are crucial; they will influence the direction of the session and the experience your client has in the session. Under the pressure of limited time, how do you make these multileveled, multilayered decisions? If this sounds complicated, it is because the process of counseling is a complex inter- and intrapersonal journey. How do we answer all these questions and help our client?

It is these very questions that counseling theory answers. Good application of theory brings some sense of order and meaning to what, otherwise, would be a meaningless jumble of data. It consists of concepts, along with corresponding terms, that are related to each other and are internally consistent with each other, that is, that do not contradict each other (Patterson, 1973). It provides a rationale for action in relation to phenomena.

In essence, a counseling theory is *a story of a person.* It is the theorist's story of each human being's life, including yours. Like any good piece of literature, a good counseling theory provides good character development. In the case of counseling theory, this means an explanation of how each person developed: how one became who one is today. Good theory also provides an explanation for problems people face and develop in life and how someone comes to seek further development through counseling. Within this storyline of change a new character emerges: the counselor. Counseling theories provide various plot lines for counselors that outline responsibilities, functions, and techniques.

What Are the Advantages of Counseling Theory?

Almost certainly, you have had the experience of setting out on a journey to a place you've never been before. You probably appreciated any information you could get regarding what to expect and how best to go about the journey. If you ever have been—or could imagine being—a tour guide, then you know that your need to be prepared probably multiplied exponentially; you now have a contract whereby the members of your tour group pay you in exchange for your provision of a particular kind and high quality of service. How helpful it would be if someone had already done the legwork you need to provide that service and had put their collective wisdom into one resource book for you: a guidebook.

A tour guide using a guidebook can be compared to a counselor using a counseling theory. Counseling theory constitutes an organized, consistent way for you to understand and respond to the variety of clients and issues you will encounter as a counselor. Counseling theory is your *guidebook* about how to accompany and assist clients in the journey of change.

Why Are There so Many Counseling Theories?

A trip to the travel section of any bookstore can reveal that, for any travel destination, several different guidebooks exist. Compared with each other, the guidebooks have certain similarities and certain differences. Correspondingly, as the table of contents of this text shows, not just one but numerous counseling theories exist, also with certain similarities and differences. They are similar in their sharing of a few very core beliefs: that each person is born with certain innate tendencies and psychological functions; that each person's environment contributes to the kind of person one becomes; that, as a result of some interaction of innate tendencies, environment, and perhaps other factors, people develop; that some modes of functioning are preferable to others; that, once developed, people can develop further—can change in the direction of the more preferable mode of functioning; and that an interpersonal process called *counseling* can facilitate that change. Beyond these basics, each theory includes its own beliefs about *how* people are innately endowed, *how* the environment influences people, *how* people develop, *what* constitutes preferable modes of functioning, *how* they change, and *how* counseling facilitates that change—and the beliefs of each theory in some way contradict the beliefs of every other theory.

Why is there not one single theory of counseling upon which everyone agrees? The answer to this question may be illustrated by the story of the five blind men and the elephant (Das, 1996).

Five men from India, all blind from birth, met each day and passed the time by making up elaborate, amusing stories. One day, while visiting together, they heard a rustling. Unbeknownst to them, an elephant had wandered nearby. Sensing that the sound came from a harmless source, they each approached and reached out to the source of the rustling sound. Touching different parts, they immediately fell into disagreement in their attempts to explain what the thing was. The first man, feeling the elephant's body, interpreted it to be a mud wall and expressed confusion as to how it suddenly could have materialized in that location. The second, touching a tusk, interpreted it to be an ivory spear. The third, feeling the elephant's moving trunk, interpreted it to be a python hanging from a tree. The fourth, tugging gently on the elephant's tail, interpreted it to be a rope. The fifth, reaching around the elephant's leg, interpreted it to be a palm tree. Just then, a small boy passing by asked why they all were examining that elephant. At first, the men were uncharacteristically at a loss for words, but once the boy had passed, the first three men expressed a sense of foolishness and shame at having so boldly asserted their limited interpretations as the complete story or the whole truth. "'Perhaps it's better to be silent,' suggested the fourth man. 'But better still,' concluded the fifth man, 'is to learn the truth from one who directly knows it'" (Das, 1996, p. 59).

Another helpful analogy is the hologram. A regular photographic negative, if cut into pieces, shows only a part of the picture. By contrast, if a holographic negative is shattered, each piece contains *a dim reflection of the whole picture*. Each piece is accurate to the extent that it reflects the whole picture; simultaneously, each piece is inaccurate to the extent that it only dimly reflects the full richness of the whole picture.

The human psyche may very well be to counseling theorists what the elephant was to the blind men and what the holographic fragment is to the complete hologram. Humanity, the human psyche, and human behavior are so diverse and complex that no one person can completely comprehend them. What is left, then, is that each person who tries to grasp these phenomena holds a piece of the truth. Illustrated most clearly by the blind men and the elephant, the various pieces of truth appear to contradict each other. To the extent that a particular piece of truth resonates with some people, they become adherents to that perspective, and the perspective is affirmed and reified. Yet each piece of truth, if projected to represent the whole truth, is done so only erroneously, and no "small boy" has yet been recognized by all theorists and counseling practitioners as offering an integral theory of the entire phenomenon of human experience; no one person has yet put together the pieces of the hologram of human existence into its full richness.

What Are Some Disadvantages of Counseling Theory?

In summary, just as a guidebook is an invaluable resource to a tour guide, a counseling theory is an invaluable resource to a counselor. Nevertheless, just as every guidebook is limited in that it reflects the author's particular "take" on the travel destination, every counseling theory is limited in that it reflects the theorist's particular "take" on human experience and behavior.

To elaborate, based on what seemed most evident, each guidebook author highlighted some features of the territory and made little or no mention of other features. Consider the traveler whose purpose is to visit other countries' museums. On the journey itself, she sees a building in the distance, but because her guidebook does not mention it, she misinterprets an actual museum for some unimportant store, and she misses the exact kind of experience for which she undertook the journey. Or the traveler who is very focused on the features mentioned in the guidebook may not even have noticed the building/museum. In the extreme, when later encountering other tourists who claimed to have visited the museum, the traveler may doubt their veracity and disbelieve that the museum even existed, for surely it would have appeared in the guidebook if it existed and were of any importance.

Similarly, a counseling theory can become a perceptual filter through which important data about a client may be missed, dismissed, misinterpreted, or denied. For example, some theories have little to say about the meaning or value of dreams as an instrument of change. Others downplay the influence of biology in personality functioning. Yet others have little to say of spiritual experience or reduce it to a rationalization. A client who had a meaningful dream, who suspected a strong biological influence in one's lifelong struggles, or who had a profound spiritual experience runs the risk of being poorly served by a counselor bound to any of these respective theories.

How Can You Reconcile the Advantages and Disadvantages?

Counseling theory has its advantages, but it also is quite plural and has disadvantages. Considering all this, how are you, the student of counseling, to approach counseling theory?

One alternative would be to throw all guidebooks away. However, putting yourself in the role of a tour group member, would you want a tour guide who had no knowledge of, and no plan for how to make the most of, your destination territory? Probably not. Spontaneity has its place, but probably not as the guiding principle when someone comes to you in serious need—as most clients are—often paying, sometimes dearly, in time and effort if not money, to achieve improvement in their lives. You probably serve your clients best by having at least one guidebook—one counseling theory—to bring some internally consistent sense of order and purpose to the counseling undertaking.

Another alternative is to use all the guidebooks at once. However, as a tour guide, especially a brand new one, using this strategy, you run a high risk of feeling overwhelmed by the sheer volume of information. In trying to be comprehensive, you might run ragged both yourself and the people in your tour group. In addition, the sources may present options that are contradictory and even mutually exclusive: When you have only time enough left to visit one more destination, yet your collection of guidebooks present several seemingly equally attractive sites, how do you decide which one to visit?

To use a more human relations example, imagine yourself as a young, first-time parent. You have just spent a delightful hour bathing, dressing, playing with, feeding, and freshly diapering your infant. It is now his bedtime, and you put him to bed in his crib. As you close the door, he begins to cry. By every indication, he is completely healthy, and all of his needs have been appropriately met. What do you do? Do you go back in, or do you leave him to cry? What if one child development expert emphasizes the importance of you setting limits as a foundation for your child's mental health, but another expert emphasizes the importance of your avoiding abandonment and, instead, nurturing a close emotional bond as a foundation for your child's mental health? You must decide: You either go to your child or you do not, and you carry out your decision either in a state of ambivalence and inner conflict or with a reasonable sense of clarity and confidence.

We believe that you probably would rather be prepared to address the bedtime situation by having a clear sense of the alternative in which you most believe, so that you can carry it out with a minimum of uncertainty and a maximum of confidence. And so it is with counseling theory. We believe the best alternative is for counselors to identify one guidebook as their main resource and, to a lesser extent, to consult others' guidebooks for enhancements that do not contradict the primary resource.

To identify which guidebook you'll use as your main resource, you must first familiarize yourself with each one. One purpose of this textbook, then, is to present an introduction to each of the guidebooks that most current counseling professionals use. As you become acquainted with each one in turn, you will probably find that you resonate to more than one. This makes sense, considering that the elephant *does* have tusks, *does* have a tail, and *does* have a trunk—that each theory *is* an accurate reflection, albeit dim, of the "whole truth." The fact that each theory is at least partially correct, however, raises another crucial question that will be addressed next.

Which Is the Best Counseling Theory?

The next question might very well be which guidebook—counseling theory— is best to use as your primary resource. In fact, quite a bit of controversy exists in the field of counseling in this regard. We will address this issue by responding to several related questions.

Has research shown one theory of counseling to be more effective than another? In a nutshell, we believe the best answer is "no." As a result of the most comprehensive investigations, no one counseling approach has emerged as clearly superior to all others. Again, this is probably because the elephant *does* have a trunk, a tail, and so on. Research on the effectiveness of psychotherapy is, however, a crucial and somewhat more complex topic, one to which we will turn very shortly in a later section of this chapter. For the purpose of identifying one "best" theory, however, research gives little direction.

Are proponents of one theory any wiser than those of another? This question is somewhat more difficult to answer. As Richards and Bergin (1997) said regarding the three primary worldviews to which humans adhere (see Table 1.1), wise and thoughtful people align with each of these mutually exclusive perspectives. In other words, at the most fundamental level of how they see the world, intelligent, insightful people disagree. What Richards and Bergin said about worldviews can also be said of counseling theories: At the most fundamental level of how counseling theorists see people—people's nature, how they develop, and how they change—wise and thoughtful theorists disagree. Because the evaluation of what is "more wise" is a subjective one, you are encouraged to keep this question in mind as you sequentially explore each of the theories described in this book.

Assuming that popularity reflects collective wisdom, to which theory do most current practitioners subscribe? Research into this question yields a somewhat clearer answer (Bechtoldt, Norcross, Wyckoff, Pokrywa, & Campbell, 2001; Jensen, Bergen, & Greaves, 1990). It appears that the largest percentage of counselors who specify one guiding theory identify cognitive-behavioral and existential theories followed by psychodynamic, person-centered, and systems approaches. However, we encourage you not to allow yourself to be swayed too much by these outcomes. Throughout the history of Western psychotherapy over the past century, the answer would have been very different depending on when the question was asked. The most popular theory today may be in relative disfavor tomorrow.

Considering that a counselor does best to identify one primary theory from an informed knowledge of those that are most widely endorsed, but that no one "best" theory can be identified on the basis of research, relative

TABLE 1.1
Three Major Worldviews Among Humans

	Naturalistic (Scientific)	Subjective Idealistic (Western or Monotheistic)	Objective Idealistic (Eastern)
Metaphysical assumptions about the nature of reality:			
	Naturalism Everything is exclusively a phenomenon of nature.	**Supernaturalism** Phenomena exist that transcend nature.	**Naturalism and supernaturalism** Some belief, disbelief in transcendent phenomena.
	Atheism God is not real.	**Theism** God is real.	**Atheism and polytheism** No single transcendent God.
	Determinism Every event is determined by a cause.	**Free will** Humans have freedom to choose though often within biological and environmental limits.	**Free will** Humans have freedom to choose.
	Universalism Universal laws exist whereby phenomena are generalizable and repeatable.	**Contextualism** Some real phenomena are unique and unrepeatable.	**Contextualism** Some real phenomena are unique and unrepeatable.
	Reductionism Any phenomenon can be understood by reducing it to its parts.	**Holism** The whole is greater than the sum of its parts.	**Holism** The whole is greater than the sum of its parts.
	Atomism The foundation of reality is found in increasingly smaller parts.	**Holism** Reality is increasingly lost with successively smaller parts.	**Holism** Reality is increasingly lost with smaller parts.
	Mechanism The universe is like a machine.	**Mechanism** The universe is a manifestation of some intentional intelligence.	**Mechanism** The universe is a manifestation of intentional intelligence.
	Materialism The universe is essentially matter.	**Materialism** The universe is essentially spirit.	**Materialism** Some belief, some disbelief, universe is spirit.

(Continued)

TABLE 1.1
(Continued)

Naturalistic (Scientific)	Subjective Idealistic (Western or Monotheistic)	Objective Idealistic (Eastern)
Axiological assumptions about what is valuable, good, and right:		
Ethical hedonism	Ethical altruism	Ethical altruisim
Optimal good is a maximum of pleasure and minimum of pain.	Optimal good is foregoing pleasure and bearing pain to benefit others.	Optimal universal "good" and "rights" exist.
Ethical relativism	Ethical universals and absolutes	Ethical universals and absolutes
"Good" and "right" are never universal, always relative to a context.	At least some universal "goods" and "rights" exist.	Some universal "goods" and "rights" exist.
Epistemological assumptions about what can be known:		
Positivism	Noesis	Noesis
Observable facts are our only source of positive knowing.	Some source(s) of knowing transcend what is observable.	Some knowing transcends the observable.
Classical realism	Theistic realism	Theistic idealism
The universe is separate from human consciousness, which can know it.	God is separate from human consciousness, which cannot know it.	Where theistic, consciousness is a part of God.
Empiricism	Epistemological pluralism	Epistemological pluralism
Our physical senses are the only reliable source of knowledge.	Some source(s) of knowing transcend the senses.	Some source(s) of knowing transcend the senses.

Adapted from *A Spiritual Strategy for Counseling and Psychotherapy*, by P. S. Richards & A. E. Bergin, 1997, Washington, DC: American Psychological Association.

wisdom, or collective wisdom, how do you, a counselor in training, identify your own guiding theory? It is to this question that we now turn.

How Do You Identify Your Guiding Theory of Counseling?

This discussion may, so far, seem to imply that theory is "out there"—apart from you, a guidebook external to you that you consult as needed. This implication is partly true. It is equally true, however, and perhaps more important to know, that *you already have a counseling theory.* That is, you already have beliefs about what causes people to be as they are and what they need in order to continue in their development; in the process of living, you already have begun to develop your own fledgling guidebook. And the basic philosophy you have established probably matches one of the existing theories better than any of the others.

The problem is that you've probably developed your guidebook informally and without conscious awareness. If you are to find the best match, you must become aware of your own basic beliefs about how people develop and change, and you must subject those beliefs to scrutiny.

Let us first address the idea that you already have a counseling theory. One way to discover you already have a theory is to realize that, if you had to conduct a counseling session right now, you could do so. You would make choices about how to begin, how to proceed, how to respond moment-to-moment. You would make at least some of those choices based on your belief that those choices would be more effective than other choices. Although you couldn't say *how* effective your choices would be, nevertheless, you likely would have some rationale for at least much of what you do.

Another way to know that you already have a theory of counseling is to answer questions that theories of counseling address, such as those in the box.

As briefly as possible, give your current answer to each of the following questions:

Human nature

At the core, are people basically good, evil, or neutral?

How much of personality is inborn, that is, determined or influenced by biological and/or other innate factors?

What, if any, inborn drives, motives, tendencies, or other psychological or behavioral characteristics do all humans share?

How much of a person's individuality is the result of innate factors, such as heredity?

Role of the environment in personality development
How influential is one's physical and/or social environment in the
development of one's personality?
How does the environment influence personality development?
Model of functionality
What constitutes functionality/mental health in a person?
Dysfunctionality/mental unhealth?
How do innate and environmental factors interact such that a per-
son manifests relatively more healthy or unhealthy functioning?
Personality change
Once a personality has developed to a lesser or greater degree, how
does it change?
What conditions are necessary but not sufficient for change to oc-
cur?
What conditions are both necessary and sufficient?

You almost certainly had some ideas in response to the above questions.
Those ideas constitute your current theory of counseling. Now that it is clear
that you have a theory of counseling—whatever its degree of development—a
next question might be, how *good* is your theory? How might you evaluate
the quality of your theory? One way to explore this question is to put yourself
in the role of a counseling client.

The Seven C's

Think back to a time when you felt the most vulnerable, the most
in need of assistance in coping with some aspect of yourself or your
environment. Imagine that, at that time, you went to a counselor.
By placing an X on each continuum below, rate the qualities you
hope you would find in your counselor.

My ideal counselor would have a theory of counseling that is:
        Very complete 0——0——0——0——0 Very incomplete
(Indicates how comprehensive your counselor's beliefs about people
are, how well her beliefs prepare her to work effectively with a wide
variety of people and issues)

Very clear, straightforward 0——0——0——0——0 Very unclear,
                                                    complicated
(Indicates how easily you and others can understand your
counselor's belief system, how straightforward it is, how free it is of
an excess of complex terms and concepts, how "elegant" it is)

Very internally consistent 0——0——0——0——0 Very internally
inconsistent
(Indicates how much your counselor's belief system contains elements that complement rather than contradict each other)

Very concrete 0——0——0——0——0 Very abstract
(Indicates how easily the concepts in your counselor's belief system
can be perceived in real life, can be measured; especially how easily
your progress in counseling can be assessed and, thus, the effectiveness of the theory tested)

Very current 0——0——0——0——0 Very out-of-date
(Indicates how well your counselor's beliefs match what the best
contemporary research has shown to be true of people and to be
effective in helping people change)

Very creative 0——0——0——0——0 Very uncreative
(Indicates how well her belief system can accommodate new information and the extent to which it provides her with the foundation
to develop innovative approaches to unique people and situations)

Very conscious 0——0——0——0——0 Very unconscious
(Indicates how aware your counselor is of her belief system, how
purposefully she can access and utilize specific concepts and skills;
how well she can devise a course of action based on a rationale and
explain her rationale, when requested to do so)

If you are like many counseling theorists (Combs, 1959, p. 159), you
value a counselor whose guiding theory of counseling is complete, clear, consistent, concrete, current, creative, and conscious: the seven c's. (Perhaps
our next book will be titled Counseling Theory: Your Guidebook to Sailing
the Seven C's!) In other words, most people prefer a counselor that uses a
well-thought-out, up-to-date approach that is sensitive to individual needs
and can be understood by clients and counselors alike.

Now return to your own answers to the questions about personality development and change. How confident are you that your ideas fulfill the
criteria of the seven c's?

Personal Theory Development as Process

The process of identifying a guiding theory can, at first, seem a formidable
task. It is not a matter of *choosing* a theory, like you might choose whether to

eat strawberry or vanilla ice cream. Rather, it is a process involving several steps or stages. Watts (1993) developed a four-stage model to describe this process.

Beginning with the Exploration stage, students are encouraged to conduct an internal inventory of values and beliefs, as you began to do by answering the questions posed earlier in this chapter. From this foundation of self-awareness, you are in the best position to explore the major theories of counseling. You can learn about prominent theories through classroom study, films, consultation with practitioners, and texts such as this one. The goal of the Exploration stage is the ability to begin to compare and contrast your beliefs and values with those represented in the various theories.

Watts, like we, recommended that you enter the second, Examination stage by identifying from among all the theories the one that seems closest to your views: the single best candidate that will most likely serve as your guiding theory. Once you have made this tentative commitment, immerse yourself in primary resources—print and visual media produced by the original theorist or those who, themselves, identify the theory as their guiding theory. Recommended resources at the end of each chapter provide you with an opportunity to explore primary sources of each theory. As the immersion progresses, if you begin to feel that the fit between theory and self is awkward, then return to the Exploration stage to revisit personal values and understanding of existing theories.

If you continue to feel a resonance with the theory, you are ready to proceed with the Examination stage by beginning to apply your theory with clients under supervision in a prepracticum or practicum course. When beginning to counsel, as when beginning to develop any skill, a certain amount of awkwardness is natural. Remember when you were first learning to drive? You probably felt somewhat overwhelmed, whereas by now you have probably had the experience of driving from point A to point B without even thinking consciously of what you were doing! In driving, as in counseling, it is important to persevere in making initially foreign skills become "second nature."

Another factor to consider in this second part of the Examination phase is the enormous amount of anxiety that most beginning counselors feel initially. The stress of getting out of the classroom and into the counseling room can be very disequilibrating. Consider the following metaphor for this experience: During your academic preparation you are learning to create a set of filters, of glasses, that guides your view of self, others (clients), and the world. The better you are able to integrate personal values and theory, the better your glasses will fit. You walk into the clinical experience able to see reasonably well, and consequently you feel rather confident, even proud of your glasses and your ability to use them. During your first session as the counselor, and repeatedly after that, you begin to feel pressure to *be* or to do something you are not; it is as if a giant hand comes down from the sky and knocks the glasses off your head. You have difficulty seeing the client through your glasses. Anxiety steps in, and you feel you must desperately grasp for any technique that works. It might be helpful to know that the big hand of anxiety is normal at this stage and that your glasses cannot be completely removed (leaving you blind) because they are a part of you; they are your beliefs. In reality, the filters are only moved off their previous position, knocked sideways, and can be repositioned or altered as you gain more experience. Confidence in your abilities and your theory grow in the remaining stages. However, if you have persevered on the basis of a good understanding of the counseling theory you have identified, yet you continue to feel awkward or have trouble putting the theory into practice, it could mean that you do not have a good fit. In this case, you probably need to cycle back to the Exploration stage.

Assuming you experience an increasing sense of "good fit" with your guiding theory throughout the Examination stage, the third and fourth stages include taking the blending of theory and personal values to a level of Integration and Personalization. Integration occurs when you have assimilated the theory into a personal way of being. Technical eclecticism may become fitting, whereby techniques from other theories can be evaluated for compatibility with the philosophy of your personal theory and utilized as appropriate. Personalization involves a lifelong commitment to refining, expanding, and clarifying your personal values and their relationship to the process of counseling.

Whereas the first two stages are achievable within the structure of your graduate program, your achievement of the last two stages depends largely on your investment in the process. Many counselors never reach the Integration stage because they fail to develop the necessary level of self-understanding. Some therapists choose the path of, "I heard a workshop on hypnotism. I think I will try that with my 3:00 client"—using any new technique regardless of rationale. Exploring self and theory takes persistence and passion. This exploration is characterized not by blind devotion, but by intellectual and personal openness and curiosity. The payoff of the journey is greater self-understanding, clearer client conceptualization, greater effectiveness, and a reduced likelihood of burnout (Boy & Pine, 1983).

To return to our analogies from earlier in the chapter, in this process of coming to understand and work with the elephant that is the human psyche, each counselor is probably neither as ignorant as the blind men nor as omniscient as the small boy. Rather, each is in the process of perceiving the elephant ever more clearly and accurately—and working with it more effectively. Thus, the best any counselor-in-training can do is identify the guiding theory that best approximates her own beliefs about people, then commit to the ongoing process of refining those beliefs in light of personal experience and current, high-quality research. In the final section of this chapter, we will discuss yet more rationale in support of this approach to a difficult but important issue in your development as a professional counselor.

How This Book Is Organized

To help you approach each theory in the most understandable way, and to help you in your comparison of the various theories, we have organized the theory chapters with a particular format. By reading the following outline overview, you will prepare yourself to make the most of the chapters that follow.

I. Background of the theory

    Historical context. What was the historical and cultural context in which this theory developed?

    Founder's biographical overview. What were the major experiences of the founder's life, and how did his life relate to his theory?

    Philosophical underpinnings. What philosophical perspectives provided the conceptual foundation of this theory?

II. Personality development. How does personality develop, according to this theory?

    Nature of humans. What factors in personality are innate and influential across the lifespan?

    The function of the psyche. What inborn motives, such as drives, needs, or tendencies, consistently animate the person across the lifespan? What operating principles are fundamental to the psyche?

    The structure of the psyche. What psychological constructs exist at birth either actually or as potentials? Psychic structure typically is either aggregate, having parts that can operate in opposition to each other, or holistic, being a unified whole whereby any parts operate in the service of the whole.

    Role of the environment. How do factors other than innate factors influence personality development?

        Impact of the familial environment. What is the role of one's early familial environment, and how important is the influence of that environment throughout one's life?

        Extrafamilial factors. What is the role of one's environment besides one's early familial environment, and how important is the influence of that environment throughout one's life?

    The healthy/adaptive versus unhealthy/maladaptive personality. What characterizes optimal and less-than-optimal human functioning? How do the influences of human nature, the environment, and any other factors interact to result in optimal and less-than-optimal functioning?

    The personality change process. Each theory rests on the basic assumption that personality, whether partially, substantially, or fully formed, can develop beyond its current form, that is, can change. How does this theory conceptualize and promote personality change?

Basic principles of change. In general, how do people change, either in or out of the counseling setting? What is the "prime mover" of change: feelings, thoughts, and/or actions?

Change through counseling. In particular, what characterizes the change process in the counseling setting?

The client's role. What is the client's part in the change process?

(1) Motivation to change. Why do clients seek counseling? If a client is mandated to counseling, what influence will that fact have on the change process?

(a) The client's experience. From the client's perspective, what provokes a client to seek—or in the case of a mandate, not seek—counseling?

(b) The counselor's conceptualization. From the counselor's perspective, what dynamics underlying the client's experience provoke—or don't provoke—the client to seek counseling?

(2) Capacity for change. How much is the client's personality determined, and, consequently, how free is the client to change?

(3) Responsibility for change. How passive or active must the client be in the counseling process?

(4) Source of resistance. To what extent does the theory embrace the idea that clients in counseling sometimes resist change? To the extent that it does, how does the theory conceptualize the psychological dynamics at work in resistance?

The counselor's role. What is the counselor's role in the client's change process?

Goals of counseling. What does the counselor conceptualize to be the aim of the counseling process?

Characteristics of an effective counselor. What attitudes and behaviors characterize the counselor who is most likely to facilitate client change?

Stages and techniques

The therapeutic relationship. What constitutes a "good" therapeutic relationship, how important is it, and how is such a relationship established and maintained throughout the counseling process?

Assessment. To what extent is formal and/or informal assessment used, when during the counseling process is it used, and what form(s) does it take?

Change strategies. What specific techniques does the counselor employ to facilitate developmental change?

Addressing client resistance. In each theory that embraces the concept of client resistance, how does the counselor recognize and respond to resistance?

III. Contributions and limitations of the theory

How does this theory interface with recent developments in the mental health field? (These topics are discussed in depth in the next section of this chapter.)

The effectiveness of psychotherapy

The nature/nurture question

Pharmacotherapy

Managed care and brief therapy

Diversity issues

Ethnicity

Gender

Sexual orientation

Spirituality

Technical eclecticism

DSM-IV-TR diagnosis

What are the weaknesses of this theory?

What distinguishing addition has this theory made to counseling and psychotherapy?

IV. Current status. Since its original inception, how has the theory developed to its current status?

V. Summary

VI. Recommended resources

RECENT DEVELOPMENTS IN MENTAL HEALTH PERTINENT TO COUNSELING THEORY

In this final section of this introductory chapter, we will address in more detail one aspect of the outline that appears above. A crucial ingredient in the evaluation of a counseling theory is the extent to which the theory has incorporated, or could incorporate, information that has been discovered since the theory was created. The theories we describe in this text were, for the most part, developed prior to 1980. However, over the past three decades, research and practice in the mental health field, along with social change, have yielded new information and perspectives. It is no fault of traditional theorists that they did not consider these developments when they were formulating their theories; they cannot be held responsible for knowledge that did not exist at that time. You, however, a counseling student entering the 21st century, are in a position to consider these developments as you study each counseling theory. You are responsible for knowledge that exists at this time. The following discussion addresses several of these developments and their implications for you in your process of identifying your guiding theory of counseling.

The Effectiveness of Psychotherapy

How effective is psychotherapy, what factors play a role in its effectiveness, and, in particular, what role does counseling theory play? In their thorough review of the quantitative research on the effectiveness of psychotherapy, Asay and Lambert (1999) summarized several conclusions.

- Psychotherapy works. At least half of clients will achieve a beneficial outcome in 5 to 10 counseling sessions, whereas one-fifth to one-third will need more than 25 sessions to achieve a positive outcome. Counselors need to quickly identify and address client characteristics that contraindicate brief therapy or even predict a lower likelihood of success in longer term therapy: poor motivation, hostility, a history of poor relationships, and passivity in the counseling process. Most clients who achieve a beneficial outcome will maintain their gains, especially when counselors help them adopt an active role in their progress, help them expect the likelihood of temporary setbacks, and help them rehearse how to handle such setbacks.
- Forty percent of positive outcomes in psychotherapy can be attributed to extratherapeutic factors, that is, factors essentially out of the counselor's hands. These include client factors such as the severity and chronicity of the client's problem; the client's level of motivation to change; the client's capacity to relate to other people; the client's ego strength, that is, such characteristics as the ability to tolerate and manage emotional pain and the ability to create and follow through on plans; the client's psychological mindedness, that is, an understanding of psychological dynamics and insight into motivation and cause–effect aspects of behavior; and the client's ability to identify a focal problem. Extratherapeutic factors also include the quality of the client's social support system and the client's ability and motivation to access and use self-help and community resources.
- Fifteen percent of positive outcomes can be attributed to the client's expectation of improvement, a factor for which both the client and the therapist share responsibility. The client brings a history of relative optimism or pessimism, in general, as well as prejudices about the probable effectiveness of psychotherapy, in particular. The therapist can instill hope while avoiding the ethical breach of guaranteeing any particular outcome.
- Thirty percent of beneficial outcomes can be attributed to the therapeutic relationship, on which the counselor exerts the most influence. It is the

counselor's responsibility to establish and maintain, and consistently communicate, acceptance of, warmth toward, and empathy for the client. In this regard, certain counselors may feel challenged when working with certain clients, such as a previously emotionally abused counselor working with a client who reports emotionally abusing a child. Still other clients represent a challenge to virtually any counselor, such as clients who meet the criteria for certain personality disorders. In either case, it is the counselor's responsibility to establish and sustain accepting, warm, and empathic interaction with the client. If a counselor finds oneself behaving toward a client in a "critical, attacking, rejecting, blaming, or neglectful" way (Asay & Lambert, 1999, p. 44), the counselor has the responsibility to take action to remediate oneself or refer the client to another therapist. Counselors also need to integrate these qualities of a good therapeutic relationship with appropriate limit setting when therapeutically and ethically indicated. In addition to the counselor undergoing high-quality training to learn how to facilitate a good therapeutic relationship, a counselor should undertake self-care to avoid burn-out, continually collaborate with the client to maintain a sense of joint cooperation in the therapeutic process, and assess client progress at the beginning of each session.

- Finally, fifteen percent of beneficial outcomes in psychotherapy can be attributed specifically to the techniques the therapist uses. In 1993, the Clinical Psychology Division of the American Psychological Association created a task force to identify psychotherapeutic approaches validated by research to be effective or probably effective (Crits-Christoph, 1998). Members of the task force established criteria, including a minimum number of studies with acceptable research design that had involved the use of standardized treatment manuals and had yielded statistically significant results. Then they surveyed the vast psychotherapy research literature. Counselors need to be aware that critics have argued against both the empirically validated treatments in particular and the use of treatment manuals in psychotherapy and in the training of psychotherapists in general. Nevertheless, "keeping an open mind, but a balanced perspective, in considering the use of treatment manuals and empirically validated treatments will give clinicians more options" (Asay & Lambert, 1999, p. 45).

Near the end of each chapter, we will help you apply this information to the theory at hand by offering our answers to the following questions:

> To what extent does the theory, at least, address or, at best, incorporate these factors?
> To the extent that it does not, to what extent could the theory be modified to incorporate these factors without violating the theory's basic premises?

The Nature/Nurture Question

To what extent is personality a manifestation of nature, the influence of heredity, or of nurture, the influence of experience in the natural and social environment? In 1990, the American Counseling Association's *Journal of Counseling and Development* published a special feature on the genetic origins of behavior (Baker & Clark, 1990). They cited such researchers as Thomas Bouchard (Skovholt, 1990), director of the Minnesota Center for Twin and Adoption Research, whose research team has studied dozens of identical twins separated by adoption at or shortly after birth and reunited as adults for the first time at the center's research site in Minneapolis. These research participants have provided a unique opportunity to study concordance rates, the extent to which personality traits are shared, in two people who possess identical genes but who were raised in different environments. Findings from these and other studies have yielded several findings that contradict or challenge prevailing beliefs of the early to mid-20th century:

- For most personality traits, genes explain at least 30%, and up to 50%, of the variance in the trait (Gatz, 1990, p. 601).
- Environmental factors—all effects except genetic—explain the remaining 50% to 70% of variance (Gatz, 1990, p. 601).
- Of the environmental factors that explain the remaining variance, shared factors, such as growing up in the same family, have little or no influence on personality traits. Rather, nonshared experiences, those unique to the individual, have the greatest effect (Gatz, 1990, p. 601). Therefore, "parenting styles and traditional family variables may be relatively unimportant in understanding problem behavior" (Baker & Clark, 1990, p. 598). Rather, in understanding the environmental contribution to the development of a particular personality trait, counselors might do well to focus on a client's *unique* experiences with caregivers or other people or situations (Baker & Clark, pp. 598–599). Unique experiences include such things as illness, accidents, specific interactions with a specific caregiver, and receiving awards.
- Caregiver behavior may be the result rather than the cause of a child's genetically predisposed behavior, a kind of "reverse causality" (Rowe, 1990, p. 609).
- "Genes may be expressed at one age and not another" or only under specific circumstances (Baker & Clark, 1990, p. 599).
- "Biology is *not* necessarily destiny" (Baker & Clark, p. 599). When a genetic influence is known to exist, environmental accommodations often can maximize or minimize the genetic influence.
- Several phenomena that are the focus of counseling or are addressed in counseling have a known or a strongly suspected genetic influence: schizophrenia, depression, manic-depression, and Alzheimer's disease (Gatz,

1990); chronic anxiety and panic disorder (Carey, 1990); reading disabilities (LaBuda, DeFries, & Pennington, 1990); antisocial behavior (Raine & Dunkin, 1990); and extreme introversion (Ellis & Robbins, 1990).

• The prevailing view in the mental health field is that distressing psychological symptoms are the result of some combination of genetic vulnerability and environmental factors.

Near the end of each chapter, we will help you apply this information to the theory at hand by offering our answers to the following questions:

> What do people of this particular theoretical persuasion believe about the nature/nurture question?
> How do those beliefs compare with the recent developments described above?
> If they differ, could the recent developments cited above be incorporated into the theory without violating the theory's basic premises?

Pharmacotherapy

Psychiatrists and other physicians can prescribe any of a number of medications that reduce or eliminate distressing psychological symptoms (Holiner, 1998). Some research has indicated that psychoactive medication can be as effective as, or even more effective than, psychotherapy, at least in the short run; other research has indicated the superiority of psychotherapy over psychoactive medication; and yet other research has indicated that medication in conjunction with psychotherapy is often most effective (Holiner, 1998). An excellent source on the subject of pharmacotherapy is Preston, O'Neal, and Talaga's (2002) *Handbook of Clinical Psychopharmacology for Therapists.*

Evaluating the potential benefits and drawbacks of pharmacotherapy can be complex and value laden. For example, premature ejaculation abates with certain psychoactive medications, but the disorder recurs as soon as the medication is discontinued. Conversely, premature ejaculation is highly responsive to certain quite simple and easy sexual exercises; the symptoms abate for as many as 95% of men within just a few weeks, and the men then have a skill that will serve them for their lifetime (LoPiccolo, 1998). In cases such as this, counseling tends to value "skills over pills." However, some conditions require pills along with or in addition to skills.

Near the end of each chapter, we will help you apply this information to the theory at hand by offering our answers to the following questions:

> To what extent does the theory address pharmacotherapy, providing guidelines about if and when pharmacotherapy should be considered or used?

To the extent that the theory does not address this issue, how compatible is the theory with pharmacotherapy?

To what extent could pharmacotherapeutic considerations be added to the practice of this theory without violating the theory's basic premises?

Managed Care and Brief Therapy

Prior to approximately 1980, when a mental health practitioner worked with a client who received insurance reimbursement for expenses incurred from psychotherapy, the typical arrangement was for the client to choose the psychotherapist, for the psychotherapist to determine the length of therapy and therapeutic approach, and for the client or therapist to file directly to the insurance company for reimbursement. Since about 1980, managed care has changed that process. Managed care refers to health maintenance organizations (HMOs), preferred provider organizations (PPOs), and government-funded programs such as Medicaid and Medicare (Glosoff, Garcia, Herlihy, & Remley, 1999). Organizations such as these restrict which mental health professionals they will reimburse, determine how many sessions for which they will reimburse, require substantial paperwork describing treatment protocol and client progress, and reimburse only for certain favored psychotherapeutic approaches. The favored approaches are those that are brief and that have been validated, in particular, cognitive-behavioral. It has been said that managed care is more aptly termed managed cost.

Some counselors work in environments heavily dependent on managed care for reimbursement, such as the community agency or the private practice. If you anticipate possibly being such a counselor, near the end of each chapter, we will help you apply the above information to the theory at hand by offering our answers to the following questions:

Does this therapeutic approach constitute a form of brief therapy?

If not, have recent practitioners published guidelines for adapting the approach to a brief therapy format?

If not, could the approach be adapted to a brief therapy format?

How amenable is the theory to incorporating the counseling techniques favored by managed care?

Diversity Issues

The United States contains a diverse—and, regarding some domains of diversity, an increasingly diverse—population (U.S. Census Bureau, 1992). Consider the distribution in three domains of diversity: ethnicity, sexual orientation, and religious affiliation (see Figures 1.1, 1.2, and 1.3). These figures indicate that you inevitably will encounter issues of diversity in your professional counseling experience. In its *Code of Ethics and Standards of Practice*, the American Counseling Association (1995) upheld nondiscrimination and the respect of differences regarding age, color, culture, disability, ethnic group, gender, race, religion, sexual orientation, marital status, and socio-economic status. "Respecting diversity means that [counselors] are committed to acquiring the knowledge, skills, personal awareness, and sensitivity that are essential to working effectively with diverse client populations" (Herlihy & Corey, 1996, p. 295).

Contrast these facts about diversity with the fact that every theory described in this text was originally developed by a Western (European, European-American, or European-Australian), Caucasian, apparently heterosexual, male from a Judeo-Christian background. In addition, almost all the theories originally were formulated over 20 years ago, before diversity issues came to prominence in the mental health field. Existing counseling theories might reflect characteristics—values, beliefs, and practices—that are incompatible with the characteristics of certain diverse populations.

Near the end of each chapter, we will help you apply this information to the theory at hand by offering our answers to the following questions:

How, if at all, does the theory address diversity issues?
How flexibly does or could the theory accommodate specific characteristics of various diverse populations?

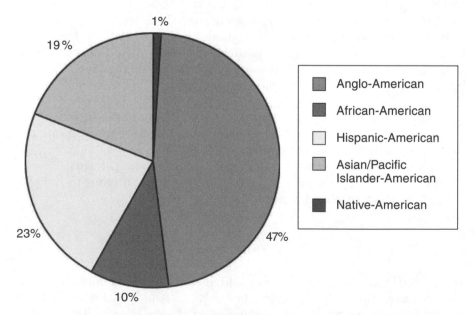

FIGURE 1.1
Projected U.S. population distribution by ethnicity, year 2003.*

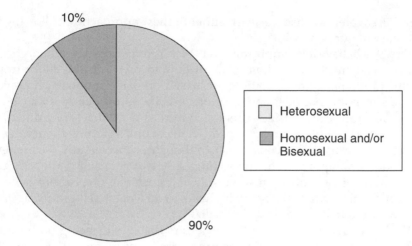

FIGURE 1.2
Sexual orientation among U.S. population (estimate based on information from http://www.indiana.edu/~kinsey/bib-homoprev.html).

Technical Eclecticism

Recent surveys reveal an increasing tendency for mental health profession-als to identify their theoretical orientation as "eclectic" (Becktoldt, Norcross, Wyckoff, Pokrywa, & Campbell, 2001). Eclecticism means "selecting what seems best from various systems" (Morris, 1976). This practice suggests an atheoretical or polytheoretical approach to counseling. As we discussed ear-

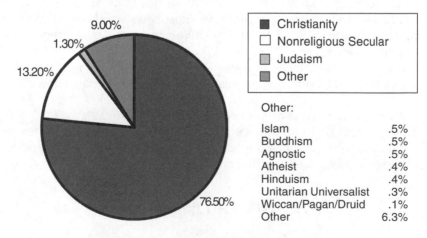

FIGURE 1.3
Top 20 religions in the United States, 2001.
(American Religious Identity Survey, 2001).

lier in this chapter, we disagree with either of these approaches. Following is a summary of our viewpoint.

First, we believe it is simply impossible for a counselor to be atheoretical. The counselor must make choices about how to respond to a client from moment to moment; those choices are based on some rationale, however conscious or nonconscious; and a rationale is based on beliefs about how people develop and change—theory. Whereas a counselor cannot be atheoretical, a counselor can be nonconscious of one's guiding theory.

Second, we also value consistency in thought; consequently, we eschew a polytheoretical approach to counseling. Any two counseling theories directly contradict each other in some way. For example, one cannot believe both that people's innate tendency is always to do what is self-gratifying and that it is always to do what is self-actualizing.

With these two points in mind (the impossibility of being both rationale-based and atheoretical and the impossibility of being both internally consistent and polytheoretical) the inevitable consequence is for each counseling student to identify the one theory that best reflects his or her own beliefs about how people develop and change. This process is supported by research results: The evidence in favor of certain psychotherapeutic treatments is outweighed by an absence of evidence for the superiority of any one psychotherapeutic approach over another.

Having stated the case for *theoretical purity,* we also endorse the concept of *technical eclecticism,* a term first coined by Arnold Lazarus (Lazarus & Beutler, 1993). Technical eclecticism involves the adoption or adaptation of a technique that grew out of a theory other than one's own guiding theory. In other words, the technically eclectic counselor uses any technique adopted or adapted from another theory that does not violate the basic tenets of one's own guiding theory. We believe counselors who subscribe to theoretical eclecticism are seeking flexibility, but they achieve flexibility at the expense of self-awareness and internal consistency. Those who are theoretically pure and technically eclectic find flexibility while achieving self-awareness and internal consistency.

Near the end of each chapter, we will help you apply this information to the theory at hand by offering our answers to the following questions:

How amenable to technical eclecticism is the theory at hand?
To the extent that it is amenable, what specific techniques from what other theories can be adopted or adapted for use in a conceptually consistent way with the theory at hand?

DSM-IV-TR Diagnosis

In 1952, the American Psychiatric Association published the first edition of their *Diagnostic and Statistical Manual of Mental Disorders.* The most recent fourth edition with text revision, *DSM-IV-TR*, was published in 2000 (American Psychiatric Association, 2000, p. xxiv ff.). The purpose of these publications was to identify categories of, establish nationally acceptable nomenclature and descriptions of, and determine incidences for the various mental disorders.

A complete *DSM-IV-TR* diagnosis includes five "axes." For Axis I, the clinician indicates any clinical disorders other than personality disorders and mental retardation. Axis I includes psychotic, adjustment, anxiety, mood, sexual, eating, and sleep disorders. Axis II includes personality disorders and mental retardation. If a general medical condition seems relevant to the mental condition specified on Axis I or II, it is indicated on Axis III. Axis IV indicates psychosocial and environmental problems potentially relevant to the mental disorder. Axis V indicates the clinician's assessment of the extent to which the mental disorder impairs the client's overall functioning, from 1 (extremely severe impairment) to 100 (no impairment) (American Psychiatric Association, 2000, p. 34).

The acceptability of diagnosis—and even of the concept of "mental disorder"—varies from one theoretical orientation to another. In the extremes, some theories eschew the diagnosis of clients, whereas others consider it essential. Even in those orientations in which it is considered vital, clinicians are often quite mindful of the power of labeling and, consequently, handle a diagnosis with requisite care. Community agency counselors are often required, and private practice counselors seeking third party payment from managed care providers are almost always required, to render a *DSM-IV-TR* diagnosis for clients.

Near the end of each chapter, we will help you apply this information to the theory at hand by offering our answers to the following questions:

How does each theory view the diagnosis, and even the concept of "mental disorder"?

If you will be dealing with managed care, which almost always requires the mental health practitioner to diagnose each client, how compatible is that requirement with the theory?

How might you reconcile any discrepancy between the theory's view on diagnosis and the pragmatic necessity of rendering diagnoses?

CONCLUSION

Your task as a developing counselor is to identify the theory that will serve as your guidebook in the practice of counseling. The purpose of this textbook is to help prepare you to do so. Each theory consists of a unique system of beliefs about how people develop and change. By coming to a good understanding of each theory, and by assessing how well the beliefs of a particular theory coincide with your own beliefs, you will provide yourself with the means to identify the theory that is a best fit for you. Because that theory offers a more conscious elaboration of ideas similar to your own along with a set of conceptually consistent techniques, it can serve you as you launch into your development as a counselor.

In addition, throughout your counseling career, your guiding theory can be a resource to which you turn when feeling challenged in your work with a particular client. As you develop, and to the extent that your theory embraces it, you may expand your repertoire of counseling techniques by—in a way that is conceptually consistent with your guiding theory—adapting or adopting techniques that grew originally out of other theories. By using your own experience of success and failure along with an ongoing awareness of current research, you can refine your approach, ultimately creating a theory—an internally consistent system of beliefs and techniques—that is both increasingly accurate and uniquely your own. In doing so, you become progressively less like the blind men and more like the small boy in your discovery of how to work with the elephant that is the human psyche; you incorporate ever greater clarity and depth in your understanding of, and workings with, the hologram of human existence.

References

American Counseling Association. (1995). *Code of ethics and standards of practice.* Alexandria, VA: Author.

American Psychiatric Association. (2000). *Diagnostic and statistical manual of mental disorders* (4th ed., text rev.). Washington, DC: Author.

Asay, T. P., & Lambert, M. J. (1999). The empirical case for the common factors in therapy: Quantitative findings. In M. A. Hubble, B. L. Duncan, & S. D. Miller (Eds.), *The heart and soul of change* (pp. 23–55). Washington, DC: American Psychological Association.

Baker, L. A., & Clark, R. (1990). Introduction to special feature. Genetic origins of behavior: Implications for counselors. *Journal of Counseling and Development, 68,* 597–605.

Bechtoldt, H., Norcross, J. C. , Wyckoff, L. A., Pokrywa, M. L., & Campbell, L. F. (2001). Theoretical orientations and employment settings of clinical and counseling psychologists: A comparative study. *The Clinical Psychologist, 54,* 3-6.

Boy, A. V., & Pine, G. J. (1983). Counseling: fundamentals of theoretical renewal. *Counseling and Values, 27,* 248–255.

Carey, G. (1990). Genes, fears, phobias, and phobic disorders. *Journal of Counseling and Development, 68,* 628–632.

Combs, A. W. (1989). *A theory of therapy: Guidelines for counseling practice.* Newbury Park, CA: Sage.

Crits-Christoph, P. (1998). Training in empirically validated treatments: The Division 12 APA task force recommendations. In K. S. Dobson & K. D. Craig (Eds.), *Empirically supported therapies: Best practice in professional psychology* (pp. 3–25). Thousand Oaks, CA: Sage.

Das, A. S. (1996). *Vedic stories from ancient India.* Borehamwood, Herfordshire, UK: Ahimsa.

Ellis, M. V., & Robbins, E. S. (1990). In celebration of nature: A dialogue with Jerome Kagan. *Journal of Counseling and Development, 68,* 623–627.

Gatz, M. (1990). Interpreting behavioral genetic results: Suggestions for counselors and clients. *Journal of Counseling and Development, 68,* 601-605.

Glosoff, H. L., Garcia, J., Herlihy, B., & Remley, T. P., Jr. (1999). Managed care: Ethical considerations for counselors. *Counseling and Values, 44*(1), 8–16.

Herlihy, B., & Corey, G. (1996). *ACA ethical standards casebook* (5th ed.). Alexandria, VA: American Counseling Association.

Holiner Psychiatric Group. (1998, October). *What's new in psychopharmacology for the 21st century.* Paper presented, Dallas, TX.

Jensen, J. P., Bergen, A. E., & Greaves, D. W. (1990). The meaning of eclecticism: New survey and analysis of components. *Professional Psychology: Research and Practice, 21,* 124–130.

LaBuda, M. C., DeFries, J. C., & Pennington, B. F. (1990). Reading disability: A model for the genetic analysis of complex behavioral disorders. *Journal of Counseling and Development, 68,* 645–651.

Lazarus, A. A., & Beutler, L. E. (1993). On technical eclecticism. *Journal of Counseling and Development, 71,* 381–385.

LoPiccolo, J. (1998, October). *Postmodern sex therapy.* Paper presented at the meeting of the American Association of Marriage and Family Therapists, Dallas, TX.

Morris, W. (1976). (Ed.). *The American heritage dictionary of the English language.* Boston: Houghton Mifflin.

Patterson, C. H. (1973). *Theories of counseling and psychotherapy.* New York: Harper & Row.

Preston, J. D., O'Neal, J. H., & Talaga, M. C. (2002). *Handbook of clinical psychopharmacology for therapists* (3rd ed.). Oakland, CA: New Harbinger.

Raine, A., & Dunkin, J. J. (1990). The genetic and psychophysiological basis of antisocial behavior: Implications for counseling and therapy. *Journal of Counseling and Development, 68,* 637–644.

Richards, P. S., & Bergin, A. E. (1997). *A spiritual strategy for counseling and psychotherapy.* Washington, DC: American Psychological Association.

Rowe, D. C. (1990). As the twig is bent? The myth of child-rearing influences on personality development. *Journal of Counseling and Development, 68,* 606–611.

Skovholt, T. M. (1990). Counseling implications of genetic research: A dialogue with Thomas Bouchard. *Journal of Counseling and Development, 68,* 633–636.

U.S. Census Bureau. (1992). *Statistical abstracts of the United States: The national data book* (112th ed.). Washington, DC: Bureau of the Census.

Watts, R. E. (1993). Developing a personal theory of counseling. *Texas Counseling Association Journal, 21,* 103–104.

CHAPTER 2

CLASSICAL PSYCHOANALYSIS

BACKGROUND OF THE THEORY

Historical Context

Sigmund Freud's life spanned the late 19th and early 20th centuries almost entirely in Vienna, Austria. When Freud was born, Europe was in the Age of Reason/Age of Enlightenment. The prevailing belief was that "the advance of science and the general extension of education assured the progressive perfection of society" (Huizinga, 1936, cited in Kreis, 2000a). Ironically, it was through science—empirical investigation—that Freud himself, along with other social and intellectual forces, advanced the Age of Modernism (Kreis, 2000a). Newton's concept of a mechanistic universe was shattered, irrational forces in humans were highlighted, and the existence of God was questioned and, by some, denounced. "Western civilization, built upon the twin pillars of faith and reason, of Christianity and Science, now faced its greatest challenge" (Kreis, 2000a).

With the conclusion of World War I came widespread disillusionment and an Age of Anxiety about the potential for human peace and the meaning of life. Europe saw an increase in fascism—the belief in government by power and authority, by "a special breed of man . . . a Philosopher/King" (Kreis, 2000b). This philosophy contributed to the development of World War II, at the beginning of which Freud died.

Economically, Freud's era was a time of industrial expansion, of general prosperity punctuated by periods of relative impoverishment, which Freud experienced both as a child and in the aftermath of World War I. Socially, one force until the death of Queen Victoria in 1901 was the Victorian value of sexual restraint.

Another social force with which Freud contended throughout his life was anti-Semitism. It, in part, prompted his family of origin to move before he was 5, and it was the sole motive for his family of creation to move at age 81, less than 2 years before his death, to escape Hitler's persecution. In between, anti-Semitism played a significant role in Freud's choice of vocation and his ability to exercise and advance in it.

Founder's Biographical Overview

"I am not a man of science at all, not an observer, not an experimenter, not a thinker. I am nothing but a conquistador by temperament, an adventurer . . . with all the inquisitiveness, daring, and tenacity of such a man" (cited in Gay, 1988, p. xvi).

Freud expressed a distinct distaste for the "lies . . . concealment . . . hypocrisies . . . and embellishments" (cited in Gay, 1988, p. xv) of the biographical enterprise. As early as age 29, Freud reported with glee that he had undertaken to frustrate his future biographers by destroying "diaries . . . letters, scientific notes and . . . [publication] manuscripts . . . [sparing] only family letters" (cited in Jones, 1953, vol. 1, pp. xii–xiii). However, over the ensuing years, Freud actually provided biographers with much more revealing—and potentially damning—material: his own extensive self-analysis, which he conducted and published in the service of his passion for the development of his theories.

His memories from his first few years included feeling jealous when his newborn brother deprived Sigmund of sole access to his mother's breasts, then guilt when, only months later, Julius died; seeing his mother naked, which aroused sexual feelings toward her; entering his parents' bedroom out of sexual curiosity only to be banished by his angry father; and displacing his resentment toward his father as rival for his mother's affection to his brother, Phillip. Having revealed his early childhood memories, as well as his dreams and innermost wishes, he later witnessed these intimate disclosures misused and abused by his detractors. In response, Freud and his family wholeheartedly endorsed one person, Ernest Jones, to present the most truthful account possible of Freud's life. Jones' (1953) three-volume work is the official biography of Sigmund Freud, authorized by "Professor"—as he was known among his friends—himself (Roazen, 1992).

Peter Gay (1988), widely considered the most reputable of Freud's contemporary biographers, offered the perspective on Freud's commentators that "every worshipper who has hailed him . . . has been matched by a detractor who has derided him . . ." (p. xvi). Gay continued:

> Unlike other great figures in the history of Western culture, Freud seems to stand under the obligation to be perfect. No one acquainted with the psychopathology of Luther or Gandhi, Newton or Darwin, Beethoven or Schumann, Keats or Kafka, would venture to suggest that their neuroses damaged their creations or compromised their stature. In sharp contrast, Freud's failings, real or imagined, have been proffered as conclusive evidence for the bankruptcy of his creation. It has become a common tactic to strike at psychoanalysis by striking at its founder. (p. xix)

Although "no statute of limitations pertains to unearthing flaws in Freud's character, there must be some point in the development of a discipline when questions about its founder no longer bring the whole structure into doubt" (Moore, 1999, p. 37). With these considerations in mind, we embark on a biographical sketch of Sigmund Freud.

Because Freud considered early parental influence to be formative of a child's—and, later, that child's adult—personality, we begin with his parents. At age 40 and already a grandfather, Jakob Freud, a merchant who primarily sold wool, entered his second marriage, to Amalie Nathansohn. Amalie maintained her vibrant personality throughout her life. Six weeks prior to her death at age 95, her photograph was featured in the newspaper, upon which she commented, "A bad reproduction; it makes me look a hundred" (cited in Jones, 1953, vol. 1, p. 3).

Amalie's and Jakob's first child, Sigmund, was born on May 6, 1856, at 117 Schlossergrassse, in the small, quiet, Moravian town of Freiburg, about 150 miles northeast of Vienna, Austria. Schlossergrassse has since been renamed "Freudova" in his honor. Although his middle class Jewish parents subsequently bore five daughters and two more sons, Sigmund's mother's intense love for and pride in him left an indelible impression: "A man who has been the indisputable favorite of his mother keeps for life the feeling of a conqueror, that confidence of success that often induces real success" (Freud, cited in Jones, 1953, vol. 1, p. 5). Freud (1949) came also to believe that, as a child's primary caretaker, the mother is "the first and strongest love-object . . . the prototype of all later love relations" (p. 70). Perhaps the doting he experienced from his mother influenced his later choice of a wife—Martha Bernays. Early on, Martha recognized and deeply appreciated her husband's greatness, and she enjoyed his fame. She went beyond the call of duty, even for those days, in assuring that Freud and his work were undisturbed—from keeping their home quiet and orderly to applying toothpaste to his toothbrush! A pupil of Freud's once joked, "If I had had such a wife, I too could have written all those books" (cited in Roazen, 1992, p. 57).

Freud also believed that a child "identifies with" caretaking and authority figures, taking on their characteristics as the child's own,which forms a template for later identifications. Jakob would have played such a role for Sigmund. Despite popular opinion, no evidence suggests that Jakob was any more stern that the average father. On the contrary, everything suggests he was gentle, kind, tolerant, and affectionate, as well as just and "objective." Perhaps Sigmund's identification with him facilitated Freud's later identification with men established in their professions who served to influence and even mentor Freud. There was Ernst Brucke, the physiologist under whom Freud studied in medical school and in whose research laboratory Freud worked immediately after receiving his M.D. There was another of Brucke's students, Joseph Breuer, whom Freud credited with the creation of psychoanalysis and with whom Freud published *Studies on Hysteria* in which Breuer's patient, "Anna O.," became the founding patient of psychoanalysis. There was Jean-Martin Charcot, the celebrated French neurologist whose use of hypnosis contributed to Freud's shift away from purely physiological explanations of psychopathology to more psychological ones involving mental processes, and whose valuing of empirical observation over theory contributed to Freud's lifelong willingness to revise his theories based on new observations. And there was Wilhelm Fliess, an M.D. ear, nose, and throat specialist and Freud's longtime and intimate friend, with whom Freud engaged for years in "an immensely revealing and scientific correspondence" (Gay, 1989b, p. xxxiii).

Freud's heroes also reveal his identifications. As a boy, Sigmund marked the backs of his toy soldiers with the names of Napoleon's marshals. Napoleon and Hannibal fulfilled Sigmund's martial ideals, and Freud's fondness for military language and imagery pervaded his later system of thought: conflict, struggle, enemies, resistance, defenses (Roazen, 1992). Also later in life, he enjoyed quoting the saying of Heine: "One must . . . forgive one's enemies—but not before they have been hanged" (cited in Roazen, 1992, p. 181). Freud also admired Shakespeare, for his understanding of human nature and his power of expression, and Nietzche, whom Freud believed had achieved an unmatchable degree of introspection (Roazen, 1992, p. 192).

Freud believed that human personality resulted from the interplay of innate disposition with environmental circumstances. No better example exists than the matter of Freud's intellect. Biographer Jones (1953) referred to innate disposition when he said that, unlike characteristics that could be traced to the influence of identification, "[Freud's] intellect was his own" (vol. 1, p. 4). Nevertheless, Freud's parents influenced its development by valuing intellectual achievement. When Freud was 3, and then again at 4, his family moved, finally to Vienna, in part to find better educational opportunities for their children. Both Sigmund's parents encouraged him to cultivate high ambitions and catered to him, which, he would probably say, provided him with a psychological ideal involving achievement. Year after year, he was first in his class. At age 9, Sigmund entered high school—a year earlier than normal for the time. He graduated summa cum laude at age 17.

One month later, Freud enrolled in the University of Vienna to study law. However, driven by his "greed for knowledge" (Freud, cited in Gay, 1989a, p. x), coupled with his recent reading of Darwin's *The Origin of Species* and hearing a lecture concerning Goethe's essay on nature, Freud's interest in science was sparked, and he shifted his focus to the only other profession available to Jews: medicine (Hergenhahn, 1991). Originally, Freud planned to pursue a career in research, so he might come to understand some of the great riddles that had puzzled him since childhood (Gay, 1988). His studies were so stimulating and vast that he did not graduate with his M.D. until 1881, after which he worked briefly in Brucke's laboratory.

In April 1882, Freud fell in love with Martha. To make the kind of money he needed to establish what they both considered a respectable bourgeois household, Freud reluctantly left the laboratory to become a physician. Freud first worked at the Vienna General Hospital, where he became a recognized expert in the diagnosis of brain damage and honed his skills as a neuroanato-mist. In the spring of 1884, Freud began "experimenting" with cocaine.

Freud found that the "magical substance" (Hergenhahn, 1992, p. 458) relieved his depression, helped him work, cured his indigestion, and seemed not to have negative side effects. As a result of his patients' apparent im-provements from cocaine, he published six articles in the following 2 years advocating the drug for its benefits. Gradually, reports of cocaine addiction from around the world proved Freud's advocacy unfounded. He was severely criticized, a development that both harmed his reputation as a physician and, later, contributed to the suspicion and skepticism with which the medi-cal community responded to his radical ideas (Hergenhahn, 1992).

Although Freud was never addicted to cocaine, the same could not be said of nicotine. He smoked, on average, 20 cigars a day for most of his adult-hood. Aware of the health risks of smoking, he tried several times to quit, but failed. Even when he developed cancer of the jaw and palate, and experi-enced almost continual pain and extreme difficulty with speaking, he would not cease smoking. He himself might attribute this situation to a rational mind insufficiently strong to hold rein over irrational impulses.

Freud once said that, "second only in intensity to his nicotine addic-tion" was his "addiction . . . for the prehistoric" (cited in Gay, 1988, p. 170). Over his lifetime, Freud collected in excess of 2000 objects of antiquity (Gay, 1988, p. 171). His consulting room and study overflowed with sculptures and statuettes. One of Freud's patients remarked that "there was always a feeling of sacred peace and quiet" (cited in Gay, 1988, p. 170) with an atmosphere more like that of an archeologist's study than a doctor's office. Such a pas-sion on Freud's part invited interpretations, and Freud himself told a patient that "the psychoanalyst, like the archeologist in his excavations, must un-cover layer after layer of the patient's psyche, before coming to the deepest, most valuable treasures" (cited in Gay, 1988, p. 171).

In 1886, five months after opening his own practice in Vienna, Sigmund and Martha married. The Freuds had six children together. The youngest, Anna, would become her father's confidante, secretary, disciple, and repre-sentative. Eventually, she achieved the stature of a leading figure in her own right in the field of ego psychology, a development within psychoanalysis (Gay, 1988). One of the mysteries of Freud's life was his decision, as part of Anna's training, to psychoanalyze her himself, despite his own writings ad-monishing analysts not to take on analysands with whom they shared a close bond.

Freud remained in Vienna for most of the remainder of his life. Perhaps the best way to understand that expanse of years is conceptually. Greenberg and Mitchell (1983, pp. 24–25) characterized Freud's development of psy-choanalysis in three phases. The first, from the late 1880s to 1905, began when Freud adopted Breuer's cathartic method to treat hysteria, in which physical symptoms, such as numbness or blindness, arise with no identifiable medical cause. Breuer had found that, by hypnotizing the patient, having her trace a symptom back to its original circumstances, usually a trauma, and facilitating catharsis, which is the release of emotion surrounding the traumatic experience, the symptom would usually disappear. Anna O. called the process "the talking cure," and Freud believed during this time that the original trauma inevitably involved sexual abuse: "childhood seduction." During this time he also found that hypnosis was not necessary; that the same outcome resulted from the conscious but unfettered reporting of everything that came to mind: free association. In 1900, Freud published *The Interpretation of Dreams* (1965) and was appointed associate professor at the University of Vienna during this phase.

The second phase, 1905–1910, began when Freud published *Three Essays on the Theory of Sexuality* (1949) in which he abandoned the seduction theory and asserted instead that *fantasies* of seduction were the source of neurotic symptoms. Controversy still rages around this development: Did Freud make this fundamental change in his theory more in response to empirical observation or to social pressure? During this five-year period, "he developed and articulated many of the concepts which define the drive/structure model" (Greenberg & Mitchell, 1983, p. 25) that we will describe later in this chapter. In 1906, the Wednesday Psychological Society first met. This group went on to become the Vienna Psychoanalytical Society, eventually including Freud's medical colleague, Alfred Adler.

During the remaining years between 1911 and Freud's death in 1939 at age 83, he developed his ideas about how relationships with others relate to innate biological drives. He made many of his theoretical revisions and expansions "in response to dissents, particularly those of Adler and Jung" (Greenberg & Mitchell, 1983, p. 25). These years also encompassed World War I and the beginning of World War II, which most likely contributed to Freud's application of psychoanalytic principles to societal phenomena. One of his more widely read volumes is the 1929 *Civilization and Its Discontents*. In response to the establishment of the League of Nations, Freud and Albert Einstein corresponded about "the possible prevention of war" (Gay, 1989b, p. xlv), and their correspondence was published in 1933.

Although both of Sigmund's grandfathers were rabbis, his only religious exposure was from the Catholic Mass he attended with his Nannie who helped raise him in his early years. By the time he entered medical school, he was an avowed atheist, and he remained so throughout his life. In 1927, he published *The Future of an Illusion*, his "most sustained psychoanalytic assault on religion" (Gay, 1989b, p. xliv). Despite his disaffiliation from the Jewish religion, he could not disaffiliate himself from his Jewish heritage, and he experienced anti-Semitism throughout his life, culminating in 1938 when, shortly after Hitler entered Vienna, the Freuds fled to London. Less than a year later, Freud's cancer returned and was inoperable. Nine months later, Freud's condition had so deteriorated and he was in such agony that his physician complied with Freud's request for euthanasia by morphine overdose. Though

Freud did not believe in personal or spiritual immorality, he nevertheless continues to live on through the pervasive influence of psychoanalysis on the field of psychotherapy and on Western culture in general.

Philosophical Underpinnings

Freudian psychology is based on a Newtonian view of the world, including concepts such as the conservation of energy, forces, and deterministic cause and effect. From his mentors, he became opposed to metaphysical explanations for phenomena, those based purely on speculation and abstraction. Instead, he became committed to positivism, focusing only on what could be "positively" confirmed and reconfirmed by observation through the senses, and to the scientific method of developing and revising theories on the basis of observation.

In time, as Freud developed psychoanalysis, he would be criticized for putting forth an understanding of human nature that reduced it to biological forces. What must be realized, however, is that "Freud's mechanistic metaphors and his technical vocabulary . . . were the language of his world. . . . His attempt to establish psychology as a natural science on the solid basis of neurology fits the aspirations of the positivists with whom Freud had studied" (Gay, 1988, p. 79).

PERSONALITY DEVELOPMENT

Nature of Humans

Function of the Psyche. Psychoanalysis begins with the concept of energy. Roget's II Thesaurus (1995) defined energy as the "capacity or power for work: animation, force. . . ." Energy is the animating force of the universe and of the human being. Energy is characterized by several principles. It takes a variety of forms such as "mechanical, thermal, electrical, and chemical" (Hall, 1999, p. 36). It can transform from one form into another. It can be displaced from one object to another. It can be free, or it can be bound, that is, trapped— and it can shift between the free and bound conditions.

From a psychoanalytic perspective, even prior to birth, an infant's source of energy is the nourishment it receives through the placenta, and after birth, the source is food nutrients. Throughout life, a human's expenditure of energy is through physical functioning, such as metabolism, growth, sensing, and movement, and psychological functioning, such as perceiving, remembering, imagining, and thinking, while both awake and asleep. Freud referred to the totality of mental life as the *psyche*, and the energy potentiating mental life as *psychic* or *psychological energy*. He assumed that physical and psychological energy is always present in a fixed amount and continuously transforms back and forth through some unspecified process.

According to Freud (1949), "the true purpose of the individual organism's life [is] the satisfaction of its innate [biological] needs" (p. 17). When a need arises, the body releases stored energy that activates the need-related *drive*[1] (Arlow, 2000, p. 28). The drive is experienced as a disturbing, unpleasant *tension*. More specifically, a drive has a *source*: the need; an *aim*: the discharge of tension through imagination or action, which results in regaining a relaxed state of quiescence; an *object*: some image of a thing, person, and/or activity that will achieve the aim; and an *impetus*: an urge to achieve the aim (Hall, 1999, p. 37). For example, in the hunger drive, the source is the need for nutrition; the aim is the discharge of hunger-tension through imagination or action that results in quiescence; the object could be, for example, the mental image of food or the actual eating of food; and the impetus is the urge to produce the object—the image or action. (How anorexia and obesity develop is the more advanced "stuff" of psychoanalysis that we will address below.)

Though Freud (1949, p. 17) hypothesized a myriad of drives, he concluded that they all could be reduced to two fundamental ones: a *life drive* and a *death drive*. Freud called the energy of the life drive *libido*. He believed that, during childhood and adolescence, libido invests itself in a particular sequence of areas of the body, called *erogenous zones*. This process gives rise to particularly intense needs at particular times of development, which, in turn, makes an important contribution to personality development. Libido could be *mobile*, moving from investment in one object to another as needs dictated, or could become *fixated*, that is, bound to a particular object of desire. Although Freud saw evidence of the death drive in aggression, destructiveness, and the ultimate fate of every person, he did not name an energy of the death drive or specify developmental stages for it (Arlow, 2000, p. 28).

---

[1] Arlow (2000) made the excellent point that "these impulses have been loosely and inaccurately referred to as *instincts*. The correct term in psychoanalytic theory, translated from the German *Treib*, is *drive*" (p. 28). However, he went on to say that because of widespread use of the term "instinct," he would use the two terms interchangeably. For three reasons, we will use the term "drive." One is that it is the accurate translation. A second involves modern psychology's distinction between instincts and drives. Instincts are innate, unlearned, complex behaviors that are stimulated by a sign stimulus, are carried out stereotypically by every member of a given species, and are impervious to modification. An example is the specific migration pattern of the peregrine falcon in response to seasonal changes. Biological drives also are innate and unlearned, but, unlike instincts, they are inferred, not directly observable, states shared by numerous species and carried out uniquely by each species and even within each species. An example is the hunger drive, which a fish might satisfy by eating fish food or its own offspring, a Kalahari bushman by eating live grubs or native roots, and an American by eating a hamburger, salad, or any of a myriad of possibilities. When Freud referred to hunger, sex, elimination, etc., he was referring to them as drives, in the way we have just defined them.

To the drive-related process, an individual brings the two types of functioning that characterize all of human mental life. *Primary process* comprises the mental functioning of a newborn and dominates the functioning of a young infant. Freud believed that infants are born with some fundamental images inherited from frequently repeated experiences of their ancestors, such as the image of food in response to hunger, and that they also can learn rudimentary associations based on their own experiences, such as generating the image of the mother's breast or a bottle in response to hunger. In primary process, images are fleeting and are not distinguished from reality; thus, the images themselves can momentarily satisfy the need. Through *predicate thinking,* a kind of association process, two similar objects are experienced the same, despite their differences (Hall, 1999, p. 40). Thus, energy can be *displaced* from one object to another: If a breast or bottle is unavailable, an infant might suck a thumb; later in life, if a repairperson does not show up for a third time, the frustrated customer might lose his temper with his child.

In the case of any drive, the underlying and most basic motive is that of the *pleasure principle*: to minimize the pain of tension related to an unmet need and maximize the pleasure of relaxed quiescence when a need is satisfied. As already indicated, primary process continues throughout life. Additional examples are the person who experiences momentary relief from stress by imagining oneself on a tropical beach, or someone sleeping who, needing to urinate, repeatedly dreams of doing so and feels momentary relief each time. Indeed, primary process can be most readily observed during the psychical function of *dreams*, a topic to which we will return.

Obviously, primary process has its advantages and its limitations. Thus, from the moment of birth, as one continually interacts with the "real" outside world, one develops one's ability for *secondary process*: to distinguish between inner experience and outer reality and to use thinking and problem solving to plan and enact a way to produce desired objects *in reality* (Hall, 1999). Secondary process also involves a phenomenon crucial to personality development, *identification*: the ability to incorporate "the qualities of an external object, usually those of another person, into one's personality" (Hall, 1999, p. 74).

So far, we have mainly used a simple example of the hunger drive that illustrates both the essential force of *cathexis,* the investment of energy in objects of gratification, and the smooth process of drive gratification. However, due to a variety of additional factors, psychological dynamics are rarely so smooth. For example, among the numerous drives, two or more can, and often do, conflict—as with the exhausted, famished person who is torn between sleep and food. In addition, conditions in the outside world, such as the unavailability of a cathected (desired) object, often result in what is termed *external frustration* (Hall, 1999). Within the realm of what is innate in the psyche is the infant's innate potential, beginning a few months after birth, to develop *anticathexis,* the withdrawal of energy from an object of gratification. Anticathexis results in *internal frustration.* We will explain below why a person develops anticathexis, but for now, it is most important to realize that primary process involves only cathexis, whereas secondary process involves both cathexis and anticathexis. Thus, for a variety of reasons, the actual dynamics of the psyche, or *psychodynamics*, range from relative harmony to profound conflict. Profound conflict from within can be as threatening as actual danger from outside oneself, resulting in the unpleasant emotion of *anxiety*. As you will see, anxiety is an important factor in psychopathology.

Anxiety is always perceived consciously, meaning that it is in a person's awareness (Hall, 1999). However, the cause of anxiety is not always conscious. *Unconscious* function involves psychological material that was never in one's awareness—or that *was* in awareness but, because of its painfulness, was relegated to unawareness—a process called *repression*.

Unconsciousness, repression, and other dynamics come into play with the innate function of sleep. Regarding the origin of sleep, Freud (1949) explained that "there arises at birth an instinct to return to the intra-uterine life that has been abandoned—an instinct to sleep. Sleep is a return . . . to the womb" (pp. 39–40). Freud believed that the innate function of dreaming enabled a person to remain for a prolonged period of time in the state of sleep. Because a complete understanding of the functions of sleep and dreams relies on an understanding of certain psychological structures, we will return to this topic in the next section.

Finally, it is an axiom in psychoanalysis that the function of the psyche is lawful and explainable. The principle of *determinism* asserts that every manifestation of a person's psyche is determined, that is, is caused by conditions and events from both the recent and distant past. The source of any aspect of a person's current mental life can be traced back to its roots: the interaction of one's *innate disposition*, or inborn resiliency or susceptibility to the effects of experience, with one's experiences, particularly the *experiences of infancy and/or early childhood*—hence the psychoanalytic term *infantile determinism*.

Structure of the Psyche. Over the years that Freud developed psychoanalysis, he formulated two models pertaining to psychical structure: the topographical and the structural models. The following discussion will explain both models and how they relate to each other.

The Topographical Model. According to the *American Heritage Dictionary* (2000), one definition of topography is a "graphic representation of the surface features of a place or region on a map, indicating their relative positions and elevations." In the psyche, the "elevation" is the availability of mental contents—sensations, perceptions, thoughts, memories—to awareness.

At the surface level is consciousness, containing material not only available to, but actually in, awareness. "We can be conscious of only one thing at a time" (Hall, 1999, p. 57). Thus, although consciousness itself—the process of being aware—is usually continuous, the contents of consciousness are quite fleeting. You can experience this fact by setting a timer for three minutes and tracking the contents of your consciousness by noting repeatedly to yourself, "Now I am aware. . . ."

Where do the contents of consciousness come from, and where do they go? The unconscious? Yes, although Freud distinguished between two domains of unconsciousness that actually represent a continuum of availability to consciousness. He called the domain of mental material that is easily accessible to awareness the *preconscious*. You can experience your preconscious right now, by turning your attention to your right foot. Just a moment ago, the sensation of your right foot was *available* to consciousness but was not *in* it, until you turned your attention to it. And once you resumed reading, that is, turned your attention back to this text and made it the object of your attention, awareness of the sensation of your right foot probably returned to your preconscious mind. Here's another experience of your preconscious: Think about your last meal. Again, that memory was probably easily available to consciousness, awaiting, so to speak, your bringing it "up" from the domain "just below" awareness. The vastness of the repository of the preconscious was brought home to one of us (JMH) recently when I attended a reunion: Lyrics to songs I had not sung in 40 years "popped" back into my conscious mind—in some cases, entire songs consisting of several verses. Material can lie latent in the preconscious mind for a lifetime. You've experienced the "deepest" level of the preconscious when you've had something "on the tip of your tongue." And if you think *that is* maddening, wait until you find out about the potential of the unconscious proper to madden!

An understanding of the unconscious can be clarified by understanding the two criteria for mental material to reside in the preconscious. First, the mind must be able to represent the material in language, that is, it must be describable in words. Thus, every infant's and young child's experience that developed prior to the child's having language to describe the experience exists in the unconscious. These memories are not forgotten; they exert their influence on the older person, but outside the person's awareness.

The second criterion involves the pleasure principle: The mental material must not be too painful. Experiences that are overwhelmingly painful are repressed—relegated to the unconscious mind where they do not represent an immediate, conscious threat—but, again, where their influence continues to be exerted on the psyche. Repression is like preventing a helium balloon from rising by holding one's hand over it: The task is a continuous one of opposing forces. And unlike in real life, where the helium disperses over the course of a few days, the energy of a repressed memory does not disperse but remains intact and bound—a force within the psyche that requires continuous opposition.

Freud believed that, as vast as the preconscious is, the unconscious is exceedingly more vast. This belief implies that, inherently and unavoidably, humans for the most part do not know who they really are.

The Structural Model. The psychical structure that Freud theorized somewhat later in his career, and the one that became the foundation of personality theory in psychoanalysis, brings together all the functions and structures described so far in this section on Personality Development. It is a three-part model of a phenomenon that does not correspond directly to the brain yet does, Freud (1949) believed, have "the characteristics of being extended in space" (p. 13).

The foundation of the personality is the *id*. Id is Latin for "it," implying a primitiveness so extreme as to be unnamable. The id *is* the entire personality of the infant at birth. It is biological in orientation, being made up of the drives, as well as drive-related phenomena such as inherited, rudimentary object images. The id's contact with the real world is extremely limited, consisting only of the sensing of external stimuli and the acquisition of rudimentary object images through its cortex, or outermost "surface." The id is capable of only two means of discharging drive-based tension: imagining objects, that is, need/drive-satisfying things, people, and actions; and reflex action, such as sucking, swallowing, urinating, defecating, squinting at bright light, pulling away from extreme pain, and numerous other simple, innate behaviors.

Operating entirely by primary process, the id has several characteristics. It knows only cathexis, the force of urging desire, and nothing of anticathexis, the force of inhibition. It is atemporal, living entirely in the "now," having no sense of past or future. It is irrational: In it, opposing drives exist side by side with no means to be reconciled; thus, a person can, at once, feel an urgent desire for two opposite and mutually exclusive things. Another aspect of id's irrationality is its predicate thinking, treating similar objects as if they were identical.

Without a sense of time or the ability to reason, and with numerous urgent, often conflicting desires and only minimal contact with reality, the id has no awareness of itself as a separate entity, yet it is totally self-centered—often referred to in psychoanalysis as *narcissistic*. It is insistent in its demands while, simultaneously, having no ability to execute voluntary action and thus no way to produce needed objects in reality—an apt description of a young infant. Also as a result of its limitations, it is amoral, with no sense of "right" or "wrong." Because the infant as yet has no language, the id is totally unconscious—as evidenced by the universal phenomenon of infantile amnesia: Who can remember the first two (or more) years of life? Yet this id is the source of all energy of the personality. It is the beginning of the story of personality development, but clearly, considering the range and complexity of adult personality, it is not the end.

Within the id lies the potential for the development of another, qualitatively different part of the personality: the *ego*. Ego is Latin for "I." Beginning at birth and continuing throughout childhood, as the id, at its cortex, is in contact with outer reality, some of its energy is "given over" to the formation of the ego. As a result of experience in the "real" outer world, the infant gradually comes to differentiate its inner experience from outer reality. Inner experience comes to comprise one's sense of a separate self. This sense of self begins to emerge as the child acquires language comprehension, even prior to when the child is actually able to speak. Thus the sense of self is capable of being preconscious, and thus conscious. In fact, the ego contains all three topographical dimensions.

As the sense of self consolidates, so does the motive to preserve the self, a motive of which the atemporal, irrational id is incapable. Also, as the self consolidates, so do a variety of psychological abilities. The child discovers increasingly that "If I do *this*, *that* will happen." Thus, the ego is able to employ secondary process to reason, plan, and execute voluntary action. The ego is the mentally oriented part of the personality that operates by the reality principle: Do whatever actually produces objects of gratification with a maximum of pleasure and minimum of pain. The ego learns through processes such as trial-and-error and identification.

Originally, the ego arises to serve the id. However, with development the ego realizes that, at times, to truly maximize pleasure and minimize pain, gratification must be delayed, displaced, sometimes even denied. To accomplish these feats, the ego creates anticathexes, the inhibitory forces that oppose urging desires. Through this opposition and the ego's other qualitatively different ways of functioning, it becomes increasingly—but never completely—differentiated from the id. As it does, it progresses in its ability to act in opposition to the id. It might be said that the ego begins as slave to the id but usually becomes, to one degree or another, but never completely, master of it.

Within the ego lies the potential for the third and final personality dimension: the *superego*. *Superego* is Latin for "above-I," suggesting images of both a judge in an elevated position above the courtroom and an ideal perched high on a pedestal. Superego develops because the pleasure principle is not served entirely by the id and ego alone. An ego strategy for drive satisfaction can be perfectly gratifying and perfectly reasonable, but not perfectly acceptable, such as one of our (JMH's) favorite examples: eating strawberry shortcake for breakfast. How different is the strawberry shortcake from a strawberry-and-whipped-cream-covered Belgian waffle? Yet eating strawberry shortcake for breakfast *just is not done*. To avoid the pain of punishment, a child begins to learn very early in life to restrict behavior within certain acceptable limits—limits that do not necessarily make sense to the reasoning ego.

Whereas the ego cathects objects that are most practical and expedient and anticathects those that are not, the superego, being socially oriented, cathects objects that are socially and morally appropriate and anticathects those that are not. The superego develops based on the punishments and rewards from anyone who has authority over the child: first, one's primary caretakers—usually the parents, then other authority figures such as teachers. Eventually, the child identifies with other powerful and idealized figures, like movie stars and politicians.

The superego has two aspects. One is the *conscience*, acquired through experiences of punishment, comprising what is "wrong" to do, and capable of self-punishment through guilt. The other is the *ego-ideal,* acquired through experiences of reward, comprising what is "right" to do, and capable of self-reward through pride. Because the processes of punishment, reward, and identification typically begin prior to language comprehension and continue well into childhood, the superego, like the ego, contains all three dimensions of mental topography: unconscious, preconscious, and conscious.

Just as, in the service of the pleasure principle, the ego arises out of the id, becomes differentiated from it, and develops the capacity to act in opposition to it, the superego follows a similar developmental course with respect to the ego. It operates on what might be called the "perfection principle," cathecting only objects that conform to its sense of acceptability and its high ideals and anticathecting those that do not. Though the superego may seem totally opposed to the id, their objects often coincide: Consider the high school student who gets a date with the most attractive, intelligent, popular person in class.

Yet even when their objects conflict, id and superego share at least one important characteristic: both are irrational. It is just as unreasonable to expect always and immediately to get exactly what is wanted, as it is to expect always to get and do what is perfect. In addition, Freud (1949) noted that "the super-ego often displays a severity for which no model has been provided by the real parents, and moreover . . . it calls the ego to account not only for its deeds but equally for its thoughts and unexecuted intentions" (p. 95). You may begin to realize the difficult spot in which the ego often finds itself: trying to satisfy, and survive in the face of, the often powerful conflicting demands of the id, the superego, and the outside world.

An illustration of the relationship between Freud's topographical and structural models is shown in Figure 2.1. With an understanding of these structures, you are now prepared to understand Freud's views on sleep and dreams.

Dreams. Sleep, you may recall, results from the drive to regress—to go back in developmental history—to the pleasurable state of prebirth existence in the womb. To whatever extent the ego and superego have developed, when sleep is desired, they relax, nearly ceasing functioning to allow the regression, which gives the id more play in the psyche. Both the more powerful of the unconscious wishes in the id and the unconscious roots of unsatisfied conscious wishes from the ego energize drives. That increased energy threatens to arouse the person from sleep. To safeguard sleep, the relaxed-but-not-completely-inactive ego fantasizes a fulfillment of the wish. Then it makes the whole process even less anxiety producing by distorting and transforming the entire "story" into symbols that disguise the original cause of the dream: an unacceptable, id-related wish.

This process makes sense in the case of the sleeper with a full bladder who dreams of urinating, the sleeper who dreams in the morning that she has awakened and gotten ready for school, or the sleeper who dreams of

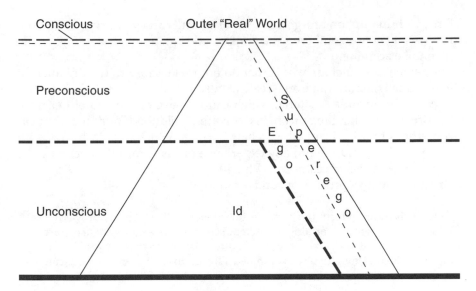

FIGURE 2.1
Relationship between topographical and structural models of personality.
Adapted from *Three Views of Man*, by R. D. Nye, 1975, Belmont, CA:
Wadsworth.

having sex with an anonymous partner. But what of nightmares? How can they reflect wish fulfillment? Freud explained that nightmares are the ego's *failure* to produce an adequate fantasy. In other words, a sleeper awakens from a nightmare of being chased by a bear, not because the bear is chasing him but because his ego was unable to generate a fantasized escape. The *wish* to escape from pain, to "master" situations involving the threat of severe pain, was still the cause of the dream.

Few chase dreams involve chasers—bears, criminals, aliens—that the dreamer has actually experienced. They clearly represent something or someone else that has made the person feel chased or threatened. Yet, upon awakening, it is the symbols that one remembers, not what they represent. These symbols—what one remembers of a dream—Freud called the dream's *manifest content*. What they represent—the hidden meaning of the dream—the original wishes that the symbols are disguising, he called the *latent content*.

Freud (1949) found in dreams the single best source of his understanding of the workings of the unconscious mind and its primary process:

- Dreams "may be confused, unintelligible, or positively nonsensical . . . , may contradict all that [our egos] know of reality . . . [yet] so long as we are dreaming," dreams feel absolutely real; indeed, they *are* our reality (pp. 38–39).

- Dreams bring up long-forgotten memories and can even bring up memories we had not remembered—had repressed—but, upon awakening, recognize to be accurate.
- They sometimes include words that do not make sense to the dreamer (at least initially) or are not even "real" words.
- Dreams can include "material which cannot have originated either from the dreamer's adult life or from his forgotten childhood" and, thus, appear sometimes to arise from "the archaic heritage which a child brings with him into the world, before any experience of his own, influenced by the experiences of his ancestors. . . ." (p. 40).
- Dreams employ a process of condensation,

> an inclination to form fresh unities out of elements which in our waking thought we should certainly have kept separate. As a consequence . . . a single element of the manifest dream often stands for a whole number of latent dream-thoughts . . . a combined allusion to all of them . . . and [can even] have the meaning of its opposite. (pp. 42–43)

- Dreams employ a process of displacement, in which psychical energy is shifted from one dream element to another. The result is that a highly charged latent element may appear as an unimportant manifest element, and a highly charged manifest element may actually represent an unimportant latent element.

The undoing of dream formation—the decoding of symbolic manifest content to reveal its hidden, wish-fulfillment meaning—is called *dream-work*. Below, we will describe how an analyst enacts this process.

Defense Mechanisms. The ego faces multiple pressures, often contradictory and unrelenting: id frustration, superego guilt, and the demands of reality. To survive these pressures, the ego employs defensive mechanisms. These defense mechanisms constitute the final topic of this section.

All *defense mechanisms* share two characteristics. First, they in some way *distort or deny inner or outer reality*—the actual demands of the id, the superego, and/or the real world. Second, they *operate unconsciously*: The ego can only "fool itself" into the experience that the pressures are less than they really are as long as it remains unaware of the true nature of those pressures. Nevertheless, you might recognize occasional *conscious* use of some of these mechanisms.

We have already described *repression*, in which the ego avoids pain by relegating extremely painful mental material to unconsciousness, such as the person who genuinely forgets a dental appointment to have a root canal. In *fantasy,* one avoids frustration by conjuring up in imagination what is unavailable in reality, as with the person who fantasizes a romantic liaison with a favorite movie star. Using secondary process, fantasy is more complex than, but draws upon, the id's primary process of mere momentary object imagining. In *rationalization,* one avoids guilt by generating a reasonable explanation for something that actually arose from an unacceptable motive, such as the parent who abuses a child "for the child's own good." In *identification,* one avoids frustration or guilt by taking on the characteristics of another person, as in the case of a victim of abuse who may take on the abuser's view that the victim deserves the abuse or, conversely, escapes the victim role by taking on the abuser's abusive behavior. In *projection,* one attributes the source of inner anxiety to the outside world, as with the miserly person who perceives everyone *else* as trying to cheat *her.* In *reaction formation,* one escapes guilt by strongly enacting behavior opposite of an unacceptable urge, such as the performer with a selfish desire for public attention and recognition who develops a performance phobia.

Two defense mechanisms relate specifically to development. In *fixation,* one avoids the frustration and/or guilt of inadequacy by not progressing to the next developmental level of functioning, as in the case of the student who feels unprepared to commence life after high school and, despite his seemingly best efforts, fails a course in the last semester, disqualifying himself from graduation. In *regression,* one reverts to an earlier mode of functioning to escape current pressures, such as the jilted lover who withdraws into her room for days to cry.

Three additional defense mechanisms involve the concept of substitution. In *displacement,* one avoids frustration by substituting a less desirable but available object for the desired but unavailable one, as in the popular song, "If you can't be with the one you love, love the one you're with" (Stills, 1970). In *compensation,* someone incapable of a desired activity avoids feelings of inadequacy by substituting a "lesser" activity, such as the person who didn't make the team becoming the team's equipment manager. *Sublimation* involves a socially lauded substitution, such as the channeling of socially unacceptable sexual and aggressive wishes and impulses into "intellectual, humanitarian, cultural, and artistic pursuits" (Hall, 1999, p. 82). For Freud, such pursuits are always an expression of sublimation: the redirection of more basic desires into more elevated outlets. A specific example that comes immediately to mind is the writing of a theory textbook which, Freud would say, is energized by the unconscious diversion of the authors' sexual and/or aggressive inclinations. Freud attributed the intellectual and technological advancements of culture to sublimation.

Defense mechanisms always leave a residual of anxiety. As already stated, repression involves a continuous anxiety analogous to persistently holding down a helium balloon. Mental manipulations, such as rationalization and reaction formation, hide original motives but do not alleviate them. Developmentally related defenses leave the person unprepared to deal with reality, prone to further frustration, guilt, and/or actual pain. Substitutive defenses allow for the partial, but never complete, gratification of a desire; the pressure of residual desire persists in the personality. We will return to the topic of defense mechanisms in the section on healthy and unhealthy personalities.

Summary. The human psyche consists of material at various levels of availability to awareness. Conscious material is what is momentarily in awareness. Preconscious material is available to consciousness. Unconscious material is relatively, and sometimes deeply, unavailable to consciousness. At birth, the psyche consists of the completely unconscious id. With practical experience, some id energy is invested in the development of the ego, which retains some unconscious aspects but also involves preconsciousness and consciousness. With moral instruction, some ego energy is invested in the development of the superego that also contains unconscious, preconscious, and conscious aspects. As the ego becomes differentiated from the id, it can act in opposition to it; similarly as the superego becomes differentiated from the ego it can act in opposition to the ego. The entire dynamics of personality arise from the ego seeking to meet and manage the urgent, sometimes conflicting demands of the id, the often oppositional and equally irrational pressures of the superego, and the necessities of the outside, "real" world. In the process of coping, the ego employs a variety of defense mechanisms.

Role of the Environment

"The child," Freud (1949) said, "is psychologically father to the adult. . . . [T]he events of his first years are of paramount importance for his whole later life" (p. 68). Though Freud's writings predominantly addressed the internal dynamics of the personality, he attributed to the environment, especially the social environment, a powerful role in personality development. Human children are, at first, totally dependent on their caretakers, and they continue to be dependent for years.

The fledgling ego is extremely vulnerable to damaging assaults from the environment, to which the ego can respond only with defensive strategies. Psychological assaults come in three forms. In *privation,* a desired object is simply unavailable in the environment. In *deprivation,* it is available but withheld or withdrawn by other(s). In *trauma,* internal drive demands from the id and/or external drive excitations from the environment produce more energy than the ego can manage. For example, in sexual abuse of a child, the child is likely to feel entrapment, physical pain, sexual arousal, death anxiety, and/or guilt in amounts too great for the fledgling ego to manage. Environmental assaults, whether small or large, are ubiquitous. They represent psychological obstacles, and "the ways in which a person meets and attempts to overcome or adjust to these obstacles shape his personality" (Hall, 1999, p. 75).

Hall (1999) asserted that "the ability to displace energy from one object to another is the most powerful [instrument] for the development of personality. . . . The same energy source can perform many different kinds of work" (p. 84). Other people, especially authority figures, powerfully influence the objects of substitution in displacement, compensation, and sublimation "by sanctioning certain object-choices and prohibiting others" (p. 80). For example, presumably Freud would have said of himself that he chose cigars, rather than his thumb or lollipops, as a means of *oral gratification* because cigars were an object that external authorities considered age-appropriate and socially appropriate. Note that values change in this regard, as evidenced by the current general disfavor in which cigars and cigarettes are held by society at large due to their now widely known, serious health risks.

Similarly, Freud might have considered his prolific writing to be an object—in this case, an activity—that compensated for feelings of inadequacy in other areas of his psyche and/or that sublimated frustrated sexual energy. The fact that he wrote prolifically rather than won recognition for productivity on a factory line or for skill at jai alai could be attributed, to his having been urged by significant others to "cultivate high ambitions" and to being unable to pursue jai alai due to its absence from his culture. Again, the influence on particular personality manifestations by outer circumstances is paramount and carries profound effects.

Regarding *familial* influence, the influence of primary caretakers—usually parents, and especially the mother—on a child's personality is paramount. In Freud's (1949) words,

> A child's first erotic object is the mother's breast . . . later completed into the [entire] person of the child's mother. [She also becomes important to the child] by her care of the child's body. . . . In these two relations [feeding and body care] lies the root of a mother's importance, unique, without parallel, established unalterably for a whole lifetime as the first and strongest love-object and as the prototype of all later love relations—for both sexes. (p. 70)

The child's ego and superego are formed through training and education by, and identification with, significant others: the mother, then the father, then other family members. In summary, family members constitute significant others who are the source of environmental gratification or deprivation and with whom the child identifies.

Regarding *extrafamilial* influence, around the time a child reaches school age, other people exert influence on the child's developing personality. The child is disciplined by, and identifies with, personally acquainted authority figures such as teachers and religious leaders. Not long afterward, the child extends identification to impersonally known public figures.

Interaction of Human Nature and Environment in Personality Development

If innate drives could be given free expression, an individual would be anxiety free, though perpetually primitive. However, for at least three reasons, this hypothetical situation will never happen. One is internal: The id often presses for opposite and mutually exclusive aims, which means that, at times, at least one drive must go unsatisfied. Another is environmental: Everyone experiences in the external nonsocial and social worlds the privations, deprivations, and traumas that make drive satisfaction impossible in the short term and/or the long term; "stuff happens," as the saying goes—natural and socioeconomic disasters—and in the social arena, people are inevitably both unintentionally and intentionally cruel. A third condition is also environmental: the universality with which authority figures exert their influence through moral training intended to curtail or redirect drive gratification.

Although Freud acknowledged all of these sources of frustration, he believed that the most influential sources of personality development—and, particularly, personality psychopathology—could be attributed to the conflict that arose when any drive was particularly targeted by moral training. The two drives he believed to be particularly targeted in this way were the aggressive drive, one of the death drives, and the sexual drive, one of the life drives. Furthermore, the aggressive drive could rather readily find outlet in a variety of displacements, such as watching or playing competitive games and sports. The sexual drive, however, being more suppressed in Western society and undergoing certain universal and inevitable family dynamics, as shall be discussed below, represented the single most conflictual experience for a young child that, consequently, exerted the most influence over personality.

In reading the term "sexual drive," you may have immediately thought of the drive that culminates in sexual intercourse. Although this was, in part, Freud's meaning as well, he also meant something broader: the drive whereby pleasure is derived from the manipulation of, and the discharge of tension from, any bodily zone, apart from any value to the survival of the individual or the species. The zones to which he particularly referred included the genitals, which provide pleasure not only in the act of reproduction, which is usually, but not always, beneficial to a species, but also in a myriad of nonreproductive activities. The zones also included the mouth and anus. For example, sucking and biting appear to be pleasurable in their own right, apart from the intake of nutrition, as evidenced by smoking, chewing gum, and overeating. The expulsion of feces—defecation—is pleasurable even when it exacerbates dehydration; and the retention of feces, which arguably has no survival value whatsoever, can be pleasurable. For Freud, the term "sexual" referred to any of these three bodily areas made especially sensitive to excitation by the concentration there of libido, or life energy. These, then, are the erogenous zones.

The interaction between the sexual drive and related environmental factors plays out in the process of *psychosexual development*. Though psychosexual development tends to occur in a series of five stages, the stages sometimes overlap or even proceed concurrently.

Freud believed that at birth, and usually for approximately the first year of life, libido is invested primarily in the mouth. In the *oral stage*, pleasure is derived first from sucking and then, with the emergence of teeth, from biting. The caretaking activity critical to oral gratification is feeding. How the mother (or other primary caretaker) manages feeding can have a lasting effect on the infant's, and later that infant's adult, personality. More specifically, sucking is associated with the infant's most basic experience of dependency on the mother. If the mother is withholding in her feeding pattern, the child is likely to develop oral dependency, which can manifest not only as straightforward general dependency but also in a variety of transformations: reaction formation into defiant independence, or projection into seeing not oneself but others in need and providing assistance through becoming a counselor. Oral dependency can take two forms: a preoccupation with taking in, as with the person who would rather observe than participate, or with holding in/holding on, as with the person whose hobby is collecting bottles. (I, JMH, just had an interesting experience: While trying to type the word "hobby," I at first kept typing and deleting "bo," "bo," as if through some unconscious pressure to type the word "bobby" or "booby." In the example, bottles represent the mother's breast. Thus, Freud would undoubtedly interpret this variation on a "slip of the tongue" as some repressed oral dependency in me.)

"Oral aggressiveness by biting is the prototype for many kinds of direct, displaced, and disguised aggressions" (Hall, 1999, p. 106). A child's desire to discharge tension by biting is almost universally met with a caretaker's admonition, "Do not bite!" Later in life, one might displace the urge by making a "biting remark," or might try to control such an urge by "biting one's tongue." One might aggressively undertake an activity by really "biting into it." Oral aggression has its sublimation in careers such as the law or politics that draw heavily on argument and debate.

Other gratifying oral activities include spitting out and closing up against what is distasteful. "The spitting-out type of personality is characterized by disdainfulness and contempt, the closing up type by a shut-in, guarded quality" (Hall, 1999, p. 106). Anorexia, or self-starvation to control body weight, is understood orally as a "closing up" oral fixation. Conversely, if a child is punished for these oral activities, he might employ reaction formation, becoming gullible, prone to "swallow anything."

Around the first year of life, and lasting less than 2 years, is the *anal stage*. To the extent that libido has been satisfied in the oral stage, it moves to the anus. Tension develops as fecal matter collects in the rectum, and pleasure is experienced as the tension is released with the expulsion of the feces.

"Expulsive elimination is the prototype for emotional outbursts, temper tantrums, rages, and other primitive discharge reactions" (Hall, 1999, p. 107). The crucial caretaking activity is toilet training, which usually represents the first time the child is required by external authority to bring a reflex under voluntary control. "A person naturally resists having a pleasurable activity interfered with and regulated" (Hall, 1999, p. 108). Therefore, if the mother (or other caretaker) is rigid and harsh in her demands, the child may fixate and become rebellious or, conversely, compulsive about cleanliness and orderliness. If she pleads with the child and praises her for her successes at bowel control, the child may become productive, even philanthropic. If she overemphasizes the importance of bowel control, the child may fixate, developing personality traits such as thriftiness. These traits are manifestations of the anal-expulsive theme.

As previously stated, retention of feces also is pleasurable. A fixation on retention can result in personality traits such as possessiveness and compulsive collecting. A reaction formation to the retentive urge can result in compulsive expulsion, such as overgenerosity and compulsive spending and gambling.

Beginning before age 3 and lasting until age 5 is the *phallic stage* in which libido, for the first time, becomes invested most intensely in the genitals. The crucial caretaking activity is the mother's (or other caretaker's) reaction to the child's genital preoccupation. Though "phallus" means "penis," this stage is experienced by both boys and girls. But because boys' and girls' genitals differ, their courses through this stage also differ.

As a boy's genital urges increase, he learns to manipulate his genitals for the pleasurable sensation, and, through accompanying fantasies, his mother—already his firmly established love object—naturally becomes his primary sexual object. In Freud's (1949) own words, "he becomes his mother's lover. He wishes to possess her physically in such ways as he has divined from his observations and intuitions about sexual life" (p. 71). He begins to see his father as a rival who stands in the way of his exclusive relationship with his mother; his rivalrous feelings reach murderous proportions. Freud called this state of affairs the *Oedipus complex* after the Greek legend of Oedipus who unknowingly killed his father and married his mother.

"Under the conditions of our civilization," Freud (1949) wrote, the Oedipus complex "is invariably doomed to a frightening end. The boy's mother has understood quite well that his sexual excitation relates to herself. Sooner or later she reflects that it is not right to allow it to continue" (p. 71). She first forbids him to touch his genitals; failing that, she threatens the boy with castration by his father. At this point the boy, either remembering or seeing female genitals that lack a penis, develops *castration anxiety*. To reduce this anxiety, he may renounce his attraction to his mother and identify with the aggressor, his father.

As with the other psychosexual stages, a variety of psychodynamics result in a variety of possible outcomes. The boy may remain to some degree fixated on his mother, resulting in a kind of excessive dependence and "bondage to women" (Freud, 1949, p. 73). He also may retain resentment of his father, resulting in a compulsively competitive attitude toward other men throughout life. Or, out of fear of the consequences of sexual attraction to his mother and, through predicate thinking, other women, as well as fear of the consequences of hostility toward his father, he may completely repress women as a sexual object and, instead, feel sexually attracted to men. This latter dynamic was Freud's explanation of homosexuality. He believed everyone is born bisexual and that most people, through the Oedipal resolution of maternal renunciation and paternal identification, develop a "normal [hetero]sexual aim" (p. 26). He saw homosexuality as a fixation, a "developmental inhibition" (p. 26) involving the inversion (Arlow, 2000, p. 31) of that aim.

A girl's course through the phallic stage is different. Acutely aware that she is lacking a penis, she feels inferior, blames her mother for the lack, "[wishes] to have [her father's] penis at her disposal" (Freud, 1949, p. 77), feels rivalrous toward her mother as a block to the fulfillment of that wish, and displaces her wish for a penis into "another wish—to have a baby from [her father] as a gift" (p. 77). Though she represses this wish, it need not be transformed through any other defense: Through predicate thinking, "she will . . . choose her husband for his paternal characteristics and be ready to recognize his authority" (p. 77), and through compensation for her basic sense of inferiority, she will want to bear children.

Freud (1949) concluded that "the whole occurrence [of the phallic stage] . . . may probably be regarded as the central experience of the years of childhood, the greatest problem of early life and the strongest source of later inadequacy" (p. 74). In both sexes, memories of the phallic stage are powerfully repressed such that all sexual urges become unconscious until puberty. Thus, between the ages of 5 or 6 and about 11, the child is in the *latent* stage, during which the child focuses on education and socialization outside the home. Thus, Freud saw sexual development in humans not as one continuous, monophasic process, but as *diphasic,* consisting of the pregenital phases and the later genital phase, interrupted by the latent phase.

Puberty provokes the onset of the *genital* phase, which lasts until senility (Hall, 1999). The first three pregenital phases were narcissistic—focused on self-gratification—and involved isolated drives that were, so to speak, disorganized in relation to reproductive sexuality. In the genital stage, the dynamics of those pregenital stages become organized into a pattern of not only other-focused, reproduction-oriented sexuality but of personality in general. Recall that every imaginable personality trait and pattern can be understood as having roots in those first three stages of life, the result of the interaction of the person's innate drives and constitution with the person's experiences in the natural and, especially, social world. We now turn to the subject of how well, and how poorly, that interaction can go, culminating, respectively, in healthy and unhealthy functioning.

View of Healthy Functioning. Healthy functioning begins with innate dis-position. Although Freud did not elaborate on the qualities of such a disposi-tion, we might presume that the person is endowed with at least normal cognitive abilities and with an absence of propensity for excessive anxiety. Hall (1999) succinctly described the environmental conditions that maximize healthy functioning, one in which

> the child [is offered] a succession of experiences that are synchronized with his capacities for adjustment. At no time should the dangers and hardships be so strong as to be incapacitating to the child or so weak as to be unstimulating. In infancy the hazards of existence should be small ones, in early childhood the threats should be a little stronger, and so on through-out the years of growth. In such a graded series of environments the ego would have an opportunity to shed its defense mechanisms . . . and re-place them by more realistic and more efficient mechanisms. (p. 97)

Thus, the ego develops through both moderate gratification and moderate frustration: enough gratification to experience that unpleasant tension can be discharged and pleasant quiescence achieved, and enough frustration to encourage the development of strategies to obtain objects in reality and in accord with social, moral guidelines.

Hall (1999) distinguished between the stabilized personality and the mature and/or well-adjusted personality. He asserted that it is possible to have the former without the latter. The primary feature of the stabilized per-sonality is that the ego meets its goal of survival with a minimum of anxiety. The ego is in executive control, so to speak, finding realistic ways to manage the demands of the id, the superego, and the external world. Defense mecha-nisms are used minimally or, at most, moderately. In addition, for Freud (1949, pp. 26–27), the "normal" person was heterosexual, having learned to cathect a whole object—a person—and, in particular, a person of the other sex for the ultimate purpose of survival of the species through procreation.

In the bulk of his writing, Freud addressed the sources of distress in people and how to alleviate that distress. Consequently, he wrote very little about his view of the well-functioning personality. One exception is a pas-sage from *Civilization and Its Discontents* (Freud, 1929/1989), which Freud wrote at the beginning of the last decade of his life. In it he asserted that functioning well and being happy are not synonymous: "The programme of becoming happy, which the pleasure principle imposes on us, cannot be ful-filled; yet we must not—indeed, we cannot—give up our efforts to bring it nearer to fulfillment by some means or other" (Freud, 1989, p. 733). He fur-ther mused that "work . . . perhaps . . . [comes] nearer to this goal [of a posi-tive fulfilment (*sic*) of happiness] than any other method." He continued, "I am, of course, speaking of the way of life which makes love the centre of everything, which looks for all satisfaction in loving and being loved" (p.

733). Hence it has been said that Freud's view of mental health is the capacity to strive relatively successfully for happiness through work and love.

View of Unhealthy Functioning. In the parlance of Freud's day, psychopathology was generally divided into two categories: neurosis and psychosis. *Neurosis* was characterized by impaired functioning and/or chronic subjective distress with an underlying presence of anxiety and an observable presence of self-defeating behavior. Neuroses included what are now called phobias (irrational fears of specific objects or situations; conversion disorders) loss of sensory or motor function, such as blindness or paralysis that follow a conflict or trauma and that have no apparent organic cause; and dissociative amnesia: "an inability to recall important personal information, usually of a traumatic or stressful nature, that is too extensive to be explained by normal forgetfulness" (American Psychiatric Association, 2000, p. 520). *Psychosis* involved more severe loss of contact with outer reality, as in what are now called schizophrenia, delusional disorder, and bipolar disorder. Though Freud's writings mentioned psychosis, he focused almost exclusively on neurosis. It appears that he viewed the normal state, neurotic disorder, and psychotic disorders on a continuum rather than as discrete phenomena. For example, he said that "the neuroses . . . shade off by easy transitions into . . . the normal, and, on the other hand . . . scarcely any state recognized as normal [does not contain] indications of neurotic traits" (Freud, 1949, p. 63).

Freud (1949) conceptualized the neurotic as having a "weakened ego" (p. 60). That is, the ego is not up to the task of managing the demands of the id, the superego, and external reality. This condition is the result of some combination of innate disposition—presumably, cognitive deficits and/or affective tendencies toward excessive anxiety—and certain kinds of experiences. Those experiences can involve excessive indulgence, in which the ego is not induced to fend for itself, so to speak, and/or in which a lack of discipline fails to provide for superego development. At the other extreme, those experiences can involve excessive trauma—extreme privation, deprivation, and/or abuse that overwhelms the ego and forces it to rely excessively on defensive strategies just to keep itself afloat, to avoid disintegrating back into the id from which it strives to remain differentiated.

In either case of environmental excess, the ego does not develop, and/or has impaired access to, memory and action capabilities. Thus, the ego employs coping strategies that manage anxiety in the short run but, in the long run, defeat the ego in its own goal of self-preservation. Consider, for example, the soldier who, upon seeing the horror of combat and experiencing acute death anxiety, goes psychogenically blind; he protects himself in the short term from the immediate source of anxiety, but he renders himself disabled and, therefore, actually more vulnerable to death. (Note that this conversion disorder involves regression to an infantile state in which sensory processes occurred without conscious awareness.)

Freud (1949) asserted that "neurotics have approximately the same innate dispositions as other people . . . the same experiences . . . the same tasks to perform. The 'weak points' in a normal organization [arise from] one instinctual demand . . . one period of life which comes in question exclusively or predominantly in connection with the generation of neurosis" (pp. 64–65). That demand is the sex drive, and that period is the phallic stage. Neuroses could appear in childhood as general anxiety, nightmares, tics, compulsions, or behavior disorders (Arlow, 2000). Commonly, however, though the roots of neurosis lie in childhood, the manifestation is latent until later in life. At any time in the genital stage, a marginally developed ego can "decompensate"—lose its ability to cope—if the demands of normal, daily life become too challenging, if one encounters profound traumas, or if a later situation resembles, and thus reactivates, an earlier unresolved conflict (Arlow, 2000, p. 34).

The Personality Change Process

Basic Principles of Change. Personality change occurs with *insight*: when one becomes conscious of the conflicts underlying one's distressing feelings and self-defeating behavior, when one understands the true nature of those conflicts, and when one is able, rarely, to resolve them, or, much more commonly, to learn to deal with them more maturely and rationally (Arlow, 2000). However, much of psychological life never emerges naturally from unconsciousness. Furthermore, the ego, the part of the personality that has the capacity for consciousness, maturity, and reason, strives actively to spare itself anxiety by keeping conflictual dynamics *out* of consciousness. For these reasons, insight is highly unlikely to occur in the normal course of life; it is likely to occur only in the special circumstance of the psychoanalytic situation.

Change Through Counseling. Before we address the topics at hand, we want to say a word about terminology. The profession of counseling did not exist in Freud's time. If we assume that counseling primarily addresses normal developmental challenges, psychoanalysis might better be referred to as belonging in the broader domain of psychotherapy rather than the more specific subdomain of counseling. Nevertheless, this distinction becomes foggy in the professional literature. For example, because Freud and most psychoanalysts have been medical doctors, they have made reference to their analysands as *patients*. The term *client* was introduced by Carl Rogers after Freud's death. Nevertheless, current psychotherapists who rely heavily on psychoanalytic principles make reference to their "clients" (Kahn, 2002). We also will use the term "client" and will make reference to counseling, trusting that you now are aware of the ambiguity around this matter of terminology.

Client's Role. Clients' motives to seek counseling arise directly from their basic motive: to maximize pleasure and minimize pain. They are in pain, experiencing moderate to extreme emotional distress and/or engaging in self-defeating behavior that produces the anxiety of frustration and/or guilt. They are inherently motivated to alleviate their pain; on this point, client and psychoanalyst overtly agree.

However, although clients may say they are motivated to *change* as a means of alleviating their pain, the process of gaining insight puts clients directly in touch with the sources of anxiety and, thus, with painful anxiety itself. In other words, change is an inherently painful process. For this reason, from the psychoanalyst's perspective, the client is consciously motivated to change and unconsciously resistant to that very same change.

The client's experience in psychoanalysis reflects this dynamic. The potentially successful psychoanalytic client is in significant—not minor—psychological pain that is due to subjective dynamics rather than objective circumstances. As Arlow (2000) so poignantly put it, regarding objective circumstances such as severe congenital deformity or crippling disease, "No psychological insight can compensate for the injustices of life" (p. 39).

> The potentially successful psychoanalytic client also is strongly motivated to overcome their difficulties through honest self-scrutiny . . . , in a position to commit the time necessary to carry the analysis through to successful termination . . . , [willing to] accept the discipline of the conditions proposed by the psychoanalytic contract . . . , [and] able to accept . . . frustration and to express thoughts and feelings in words rather than action. (Arlow, 2000, p. 38)

The successful client also has the financial resources necessary for the process, which usually involves two or three sessions a week over the course of at least one year—more typically, two or more years.

The client's primary role in psychoanalysis is to free associate. In *free association*, one reports one's stream of consciousness without interruption and without censorship. The client brings to the psychoanalytic session concerns and/or dreams, describes them, and then proceeds to free associate anything that comes to mind pertaining to the concern or dream—and any other topic where the process might take them. In the proper therapeutic environment, free association enables defenses to be relaxed and unconscious material to be revealed. The client also must be open to the analyst's interpretation of what the client reveals; even if the interpretation does not ring true, the client must consider the possibility, or even probability, that one's lack of resonance with the interpretation is due to the client's repression rather than any error on the analyst's part.

As the preceding material indicates, the client bears a great deal of responsibility for his or her own change through psychoanalysis. However, even the client best equipped to benefit from psychoanalysis is, according to Freud, limited in the capacity to change. Conflict, being inherent in the human condition, can never entirely be overcome, and the unconscious, with its vast reserves of irrationality, can never be understood or harnessed entirely.

The concept of psychotherapeutic resistance has its origin in psychoanalysis. *Resistance* refers to anything on the client's part that interferes with the achievement of insight. Resistance can take many forms. In all forms, the client's ego is seeking to protect itself from the threat of painful frustration or guilt that would occur if unacceptable impulses and their associated conflicts became conscious. Freud (1949) said that "the maintenance of certain internal resistances is a *sine qua non* of normality" (p. 33). Thus he considered resistance in psychoanalysis to be normal and expectable—indeed, inevitable.

In one category of resistance, the client may *avoid free association* by arriving late to a session or forgetting it altogether, or by failing to pay on schedule, thus forcing the analyst to spend session time on financial matters. Another category of resistance occurs *during free association*: The client may fail to bring in any focal issues or dreams, may skip superficially from one subject to another, or may fall asleep.

In yet another category of resistance, the ego *disbelieves interpretations* offered by the analyst. Freud (1949) explained that

> When we attempt to [make another person's unconscious conscious], we should not forget that the conscious filling-in of the gaps in his perceptions—the construction we are presenting him with—does not mean as yet that we have made the unconscious material in question conscious to him. All that is true so far is that the material is present in him in two records, once in the conscious reconstruction he has been given, and besides this in its original unconscious state. Our continued efforts usually succeed eventually in making this unconscious material conscious to him himself, as a result of which the two records are brought to coincide. The amount of effort we have to use, by which we estimate the resistance against the material becoming conscious, varies in magnitude in individual cases. (pp. 32–33)

Regarding this latter category, Freud (1949) noted particularly his clients' resistance to interpretations regarding the phallic stage of psychosexual development. The "reconstruction [of the castration complex] during the work of analysis is met in adults by the most decided disbelief" (p. 74). And, again, "if we ask an analyst what his experience has shown to be the mental structures least accessible to influence in his patients, the answer will be: in a woman her wish for a penis, in a man" the acceptance of feminine tendencies in himself, which he associates with castration and its accompanying anxiety (pp. 77–78).

Counselor's Role. Because the terms *analyst* and *psychoanalyst* are not legally protected, anyone can use them, even a person completely untrained in psychoanalysis (American Psychoanalytic Association, 2003). The ethical, appropriately trained psychoanalyst begins with a thorough understanding of psychoanalytic principles derived from both the intellectual study of psychoanalysis and the experience of one's own analysis. Beyond this, Arlow (2000) identified three critical analyst characteristics. The first is *empathy*, the ability to identify temporarily with both the cognitive and emotional aspects of a client's experience while simultaneously retaining a sense of separateness from the client. The second is *intuition*, whereby "the myriad data communicated by the patient are organized in the analyst's mind into meaningful configurations outside the scope of consciousness" (p. 44). The third is *introspection*, in which the analyst, in her own private process of free association, consciously apprehends the meaningful configuration, which constitutes the basis of an interpretation. For example, with a client who is in analysis for a pattern of leaving romantic relationships just as they verge on commitment, an analyst might empathize with the client's traumatic memory of her dear father's sudden death when she was young, might intuit that the woman avoids commitment out of fear of another traumatic abandonment, and might introspect to bring that intuition into consciousness.

The analyst understands that, at this point in the process of understanding the client's psychodynamics, a given interpretation may have more or less merit, and may even be downright wrong. Once the configuration first becomes conscious, the analyst elaborates it, that is, cognitively develops the idea, and seeks to confirm or deny it by examining how it fits with the analyst's repeated observations of the client and her overall understanding of the client. If the analyst has employed the crucial skill of *timing* the delivery of the interpretation when the client is most likely to be receptive, such as while the client is exploring a case-in-point on the very same theme as that of the intepretation, client denial is less likely to be the result of resistance and more likely to be an indication that the interpretation is somehow off target. If client response includes surprised recognition of the validity of the interpretation, further association of related material congruent with the interpretation, and/or the spontaneous emergence of forgotten memories congruent with the interpretation, the analyst considers that interpretation confirmed.

Throughout this process, the analyst strives to remain as detached and objective as possible. She holds the possibility that a given interpretation may be unconfirmed because of client resistance and may, therefore, still be correct.

Stages. *Opening phase.* In the first 3 to 6 months, the therapist works to establish a constructive therapeutic relationship and undertakes an assessment of the client. In the first part of this phase, the client and analyst meet for a few sessions of face-to-face talk in which the analyst purposely gives the client the lead in deciding when and how much to say. In this way, the analyst pieces together the client's history, identifies the client's concerns, and begins to develop a superficial understanding of the client's personality dynamics.

One of the analyst's early tasks is to assess whether the nature of the client's distress is appropriate for treatment with psychoanalysis. Freud (1949) asserted that "the neuroses . . . alone seem accessible to the psychological methods of our intervention" (p. 63). Consequently, the psychoanalyst would discontinue work with clients who are, at one extreme, "impulsive, willfull, . . . highly narcissistic . . . basically dishonest, psychopathic, or pathological liars, [or psychotic]" (Arlow, 2000, pp. 38–39). The analyst also would discontinue work with clients who are, at the other extreme, experiencing only minor difficulties, because she would consider them insufficiently motivated to endure the challenges of psychoanalysis. In addition to this assessment, the analyst also would continue only with clients who demonstrated the qualities described in the "Client's Role" section above.

Once the client's appropriateness for psychoanalysis is established, the analyst explains how psychoanalysis works. According to Arlow (2000), "the understanding of the analytical situation must be clearly defined at the outset and the respective responsibilities of both parties explicitly stated" (p. 36).

If the client agrees to the verbal psychoanalytic contract, he proceeds to the second part of the opening phase by reclining on the couch in the analyst's office, angled such that the client cannot see the analyst's face. Both the position of lying down, a position associated with vulnerability, regression, and relaxation, and the freedom from visual awareness of any response on the part of the analyst, are intended to facilitate the emergence of unimpeded and uncensored client psychological material—most importantly, of course, heretofore unconscious material. During these sessions, the analyst continues to learn about the client's psychological dynamics and offers occasional interpretations that mostly address the client's conscious conflicts and that, therefore, the client is most likely to recognize and accept.

Transference. Typically, somewhere between 3 to 6 months after the client has assumed the couch, a distinctive dynamic in the client–analyst relationship develops. According to Arlow (2000), as "the patient is just about ready to relate his or her current difficulties to unconscious conflicts from childhood, concerning wishes over some important person or persons in his life" (p. 37), the client begins to have feelings for and expectations of the analyst that are excessive, unwarranted, and inappropriate in light of the psychoanalytic contract and the analyst's unfailing fulfillment of it. The client has somehow come to distort the relationship with the analyst, and rather than focusing exclusively on his own dynamics and their roots in the past, the client's attention, reactions, and needs becomes focused on the analyst. For example, the client may feel desperately dependent on the analyst, may feel "in love" with her, and/or may feel profoundly betrayed by something she has said or done.

As untoward as this client shift may seem, the analyst is not surprised. She *anticipates* the development of transference, in which, through predicate thinking, the client unconsciously transfers onto the analyst his unresolved conflicts with significant others from his past, usually his parents. The word *anticipates* is used here purposefully for both of its meanings: The analyst both *expects* transference to develop and, professionally speaking, *looks forward* to it, believing that it alone offers the client the opportunity for the lasting, healing insight into his most basic conflicts that are most fundamentally responsible for his current distress.

Working through. Because unresolved conflicts usually developed and became entrenched through myriad childhood experiences over time, and because of the power and pervasiveness of amnesia for those childhood experiences, insight into those conflicts and their manifestation in transference and the resolution and/or development of more realistic management of those conflicts does not occur with just one interpretation. In other words, the analyst cannot realistically expect an unresolved conflict that was years in the making to be resolved in one analytic session. Rather, the client needs to repeatedly revisit the theme in all its pervasive manifestations. To facilitate this, the analyst takes every opportunity to elaborate and amplify the theme. In this process, the ongoing recall of additional memories and the understanding of the themes playing out in transference reciprocally facilitate each other.

> It would be a mistake to believe that . . . the actual emergence of a repressed . . . traumatic memory of childhood regularly takes place. . . . [More commonly,] many strands of evidence . . . coalesce into an inescapable conclusion that a certain event did actually occur and had specific psychological consequences that have persisted throughout the patient's life. (Arlow, 2000, p. 38)

Consider, for example, the client who felt traumatized by her mother's constant and inappropriate invasiveness throughout her childhood and adolescence: walking in while the client was bathing, reading the client's diary without the client's permission, listening in on the client's phone calls, and so on. Such a client might display a related pattern of responses. Although it is the analyst's job to offer interpretations of the client's dreams, the client might become suddenly and extremely angry at some "presumptuous" interpretation the analyst offers. Although it is the analyst's job occasionally to inquire benignly into the client's life, the client might express resentment at the "nosiness" of the analyst. And when the analyst makes a suggestion pertaining to the client's relationship with her husband, the client might protest that the analyst is "usurping my power" and threaten to discontinue analysis. In each case, the analyst would use empathy, intuition, and free association to hit upon an interpretation involving the theme of perceived invasion and disempowerment that had more to do with the client's mother than with the analyst, and she would use timing to offer this interpretation when the client seemed most receptive.

Resolution. In this final phase of analysis, when analyst and client agree that they have achieved the client's therapeutic goals and the transference has been resolved, they agree upon a date to terminate. At this point, to avoid separation from the analyst, the client is likely to experience a resurgence of symptoms. Also at this time, the client is likely to express disappointment that he has not achieved the fantasy of a conflict-free existence. The analyst anticipates both of these seeming setbacks as issues necessary to address for the client to avoid relapse, and he responds to them with the same approach as he has responded to all previous material: using free association and interpretation. When the client has made relative peace with the process of separation and the fact of the ongoing struggle inherent in life, the analysis is complete, and analyst and client part.

Techniques. The primary techniques of psychoanalysis are free association and intepretation. The analyst employs these techniques to address both the concerns and the dreams that the client brings to analysis. We will illustrate their use with regard to one of Freud's psychotherapeutic innovations: dreamwork.

You will recall that people engage in dream *formation* to *encode primitive wishes into symbols*, thereby creating the *manifest* content—the obvious, remembered account of the dream—that *hides the dream's true meaning*. Analyst and client engage in *dreamwork* to *decode symbols* into their underlying *primitive wishes*, thereby discovering the *latent* content that *reveals the dream's true meaning*. In the dreamwork process, the client tells the dream and takes time to free associate on each element of the dream, whether seemingly important or unimportant. The analyst and, hopefully, the client offer interpretations regarding the latent content and its relationship to the client's unresolved childhood conflicts.

An example is the adult female client who reported the following dream:

> This dream was very simple. It began with a baked potato with a lengthwise cut and the white part of the potato "plumped" up through the opening. A single green pea came and landed in the potato. The potato was dry, and the pea was supposed to moisten it, but the pea was completely inadequate to the job.

The client was completely mystified by the dream but remembered it so vividly that she was sure it carried a hidden meaning that she was eager to discover. Some of her associations to the dream were:

- The plumped out potato: a vegetable she liked; an outside that was somewhat rough that protected a smoother, "purer" inside; fullness; abundance; readiness and eagerness to be consumed; warm and inviting; open; innermost contents revealed and available to be taken; the word "pot"—a receptacle, in this case, for moistening agents like butter and sour cream.
- The green pea: a vegetable she felt neutral about, her husband's favorite vegetable, small, powerless by itself, sweet but dry.

As she said the word "pea" a few times, she said "pee-wee," then "pee-pee," then "penis." She noted that, in the dream, the potato was passive, and the pea was active.

A psychoanalyst might interpret that the potato represented female genitals, and the pea represented male genitals. The analyst might further interpret that the dream harkened back to the client's childhood-based feelings of inferiority, of envy for the penis she did not have. She might suggest that the dream arose from the client's id-wish to have the powerful instrument of connection that males have, and from the unresolved ego-conflict between that wish and the reality of her anatomy and its related powerlessness. She might inquire into any experiences the client had had the day before the dream—experiences carrying the theme of inadequacy or powerlessness, experiences that may have reawakened the old, unresolved conflict from the client's earliest years of life. The dream may have indicated that the client had unresolved feelings pertaining to this complex and might not have developed adequate strategies to compensate for her feelings of inferiority. By understanding the nature of this long-standing conflict, and possibly developing relatively realistic compensations, she might reduce the force of the conflict and free her mind to attend to other matters. (For an alternate understanding of the dream, see chapter 10 on "Cognitive Counseling.")

Because of predicate thinking, in which one experiences as identical something similar but not identical, symbols often reveal their underlying meaning by virtue of their physical characteristics or their word associations. Hence, a penis might be represented by a banana or an umbrella as well as by the word "pea." Thus, the analyst, again, uses her own intuition as well as the client's free associations to uncover the wish behind the symbol.

Addressing Resistance. The analyst's response to resistance depends on the type of resistance. He responds to avoidance by acknowledging it to the client and analyzing it, making it the focus of free association and interpretation. He responds to disbelief by temporarily discontinuing interpretation and watching for opportunities to restate an interpretation when the client seems receptive.

CONTRIBUTIONS AND LIMITATIONS

Interface with Recent Developments in the Mental Health Field

Research on Personality Development and Function. Because psychoanalysis is the oldest of psychotherapeutic theories, it is most prone to disproval by subsequent discoveries. Interestingly, time also has favored some Freudian concepts with an accumulation of confirmatory evidence. Though a complete review is beyond the scope of this chapter, we will address a few of these topics.

Research has disconfirmed some of Freud's beliefs. For example, Harry Harlow's research on infant rhesus monkeys exposed only to "surrogate mothers" made of wire or cloth demonstrated that the infant's bond to the mother is not based on the oral stimulation of feeding but on the stimulation of physical embraces that Harlow called "contact comfort" (WGBH, 1998).

Regarding aggression, Freud (1949, p. 20) proposed that hostility and aggression are inevitably bound up in the personality as a byproduct of socialization and that death is hastened when such feelings are not released through expression. However, current research has established that expressing anger promotes, rather than reduces, the subsequent experience and expression of anger, and that people who are high in the chronic experience and expression of anger are more prone to stress-related diseases, including coronary disease, that actually shortens their lives (Radio National, 1998). Consequently, current approaches to aggression deemphasize cathartic expression of anger and emphasize the reduction of aggressive feelings and actions through anger management (see chapter 10 on "Cognitive Counseling").

Research also has confirmed others of Freud's ideas. Freud's contention of childhood sexuality has been confirmed by sonograms showing male infants *in utero* with the sexual reflex: penile erection. It also has been confirmed through research on child sexual behavior, such as how masturbation, even among preschoolers, is normal and, if responded to appropriately by parents, healthy (Steele, 2002). In addition, every human is sexually aroused during dreaming, which dominates a newborn's sleep and constitutes about 2.5 hours each night in an adult, no matter how sexual, or seemingly nonsexual, the content of the dream. These latter facts could be construed as support not only of Freud's theory of infantile sexuality but also of the sexual basis and latent sexual meaning of dreams. Finally, regarding the concept of the unconscious mind, foremost brain researcher Antonio Damasio (1999) asserted that, "Throughout the century, and through work unrelated to the original proposals of Freud and Jung, the evidence for unconscious processing has not ceased to accumulate" (p. 297).

The Effectiveness of Psychotherapy. Psychoanalysis is not listed among the American Psychological Association's empirically supported approaches to psychotherapy. Lacking a treatment manual, it didn't even get into the running in that sweeping analysis of psychotherapeutic approaches.

Even among analysts themselves, appraisal of the effectiveness of psychoanalysis is contradictory, at best. For example, Arlow (2000) confirmed that "unfortunately, no adequate study exists evaluating the results of psychoanalytic therapy" (p. 40) and offered that "the claims of psychoanalysis must be modest at best" (p. 40) because, at most, it enables a client to achieve a stable equilibrium that continues to be vulnerable to distressing external circumstances in the client's life. However, he went on to conclude that "the fact remains that when properly applied to the appropriate condition, psychoanalysis remains one of the most effective modes of therapy yet devised" (p. 40). In the absence of adequate study of psychoanalysis, that conclusion should remain in the realm of opinion rather than "fact."

A controversy continues to rage as over whether psychoanalysis proper is an effective treatment. Kahn (2002) offered a perspective that probably represents most psychotherapists' views: that psychoanalysis includes some concepts that are not therapeutically helpful and others that powerfully inform the therapeutic process. Those latter concepts can often be very usefully incorporated or adapted into a therapeutic structure that differs fundamentally from classical psychoanalysis.

The Nature/Nurture Question. Beginning with his own early adherents, Alfred Adler and the Swiss psychiatrist, Carl Jung, and extending through the behaviorists and humanists of the second half of the 20th century, Freud was criticized for attributing too much to biological forces within the person. These critics attributed more influence on personality development to various factors: environmental, especially social, influences; innate strivings to actualize all of one's potential; even spiritual factors.

With recent research on the influence of genetics on personality development, the pendulum has swung back toward Freud's (1949) original conception. His attribution of psychopathology to "'traumas,' particularly if they are met halfway by certain innate dispositions," (p. 65) sounds amazingly similar to current views of genetic vulnerability in which unique experiences interact with an individual's genetic susceptibility to psychopathology (Gatz, 1990). Though Freud might have offered a higher proportion, even the new view in genetics that approximately 40% of variation in personality traits can be attributed to heredity seems not far afield from Freud's perspective.

On a related point, results from genetics research are prompting revision of a legacy of psychoanalysis: the tendency to point a blaming finger at parents for having "nurtured" their children's maladjustment. As this thinking goes, if a person is not functioning well, it must be due to parental deprivation, overindulgence, or induction of trauma. The greater attribution of children's behavior to the child's own hereditary tendencies tends to reduce the "blame" of parents—and, for that matter, of children—and tends to place all parties in a collaborative stance with the counselor to identify and respond constructively to a child's innate tendencies that may be contributing to an identified problem. This development is a far cry from the psychoanalytic perspective.

Pharmacotherapy. Pharmacotherapy came into being after Freud's death. However, one can hardly fail to be impressed by the sagacity of his musings on this topic as well as on the future regard in which psychoanalysis might be held overall:

> We are concerned with therapy only in so far as it works by psychological means. . . . The future may teach us to exercise a direct influence, by means of particular chemical substances, on the amounts of energy and their distribution in the mental apparatus. It may be that there are other still undreamt-of possibilities of therapy. But for the moment we have nothing better at our disposal than the technique of psycho-analysis, and for that reason, in spite of its limitations, it should not be despised. (Freud, 1949, p. 62)

Managed Care and Brief Therapy. Psychoanalysis might be considered the polar opposite of brief therapy. Rather than aiming at expedient relief from discrete symptoms, psychoanalysis aims at the deep restructuring of the personality, a process that is costly in both time and money. Combined with its failure to demonstrate empirical support and the limited number of disorders it was meant to treat, psychoanalysis is antithetical to brief care and is not covered by managed care. As previously stated, psychoanalytic principles have been incorporated into briefer forms of therapy (Broderson, 1994; Kahn, 2002), and many of the brief forms of therapy are outgrowths of psychoanalysis.

Diversity Issues. Regarding ethnicity, Freud was an upper middle class Caucasian Westerner who developed a theory from working with others of his own sociocultural background. Although he was fascinated with the archeology of more diverse groups, and believed the principles he developed applied at least to all Western cultures if not to others, he undertook neither to study diverse cultures nor to take members of those cultures as patients. Thus, psychoanalysis is frequently criticized for being extremely culture-bound.

Regarding gender, psychoanalysis has been denounced by feminists for reflecting and promoting the chauvinism of Freud's time. Concepts like the phallic stage, named for male genitals; penis envy, with its lifelong implication of not only feelings of inferiority but actual inferiority; and the readiness of a well-adjusted wife to submit to her husband's authority, reflect an inherently superior view of men and inferior view of women. However, not all of Freud's ideas were sexist; consider his basic drive theory and his psychoanalytic techniques and processes. Some contemporary psychoanalysts have attempted to put those such as Freud's ideas to good use.

Regarding sexual orientation, Freud is now viewed as being heterosexist by virtue of his belief that heterosexuality was normal and his reference to homosexuality as a developmental inhibition and a perversion. His views about the origin of homosexuality—and heterosexuality—have not been substantiated by research (Bell & Weinberg, 1978), and the fundamental assumption that homosexuality is inherently psychopathological, at one time reflected in its listing in the *DSM* as a mental disorder, does not reflect the prevailing view in the field of psychology, as evidenced by its absence from the *DSM* for the past three decades. It is interesting to me (JMH) that even before homosexuality was depathologized, people looked with profound skepticism at Freud's Oedipal explanation for the development of heterosexual orientation, but continued to hold fast to that same theory as an explanation for homosexual orientation. The current view of homosexual orientation as a normal variation of human sexual orientation is incompatible with the Oedipal aspect of Freud's theory, but not with other more general Freudian concepts.

Spirituality. Regarding spirituality, Freud addressed only religion, not spirituality, in his writings and reduced religion to psychological origins. He considered religion to result from the universal wish to regress to submission to idealized authority: a deity. In particular regarding monotheism, he believed not that God created humans, but that men created God, so to speak, to assuage their unconscious guilt over their unconscious wishes to kill their fathers (Brunner, 1998). The possibility of a spiritual domain inherent in human nature was alien to Freud's thinking.

Technical Eclecticism. Free association and/or interpretation are used or adapted in some form in virtually every approach to counseling. Adlerians, for example, conceptualize psychological processes differently than Freudians, yet they propose to clients their interpretations of client's unconscious mental workings, albeit in a less authoritative and more tentative way: "Could it be that you . . . ?" Every approach to dreamwork—Adlerian, Rogerian, Gestalt, cognitive, and others not mentioned in this book—relies fundamentally on clients associating to the remembered dream and on the counselor and/or client interpreting those associations: intuiting connections, themes, and patterns that elucidate clients' inner workings and potentiate constructive change.

DSM-IV-TR Diagnosis. Clearly, Freud did not hesitate to diagnose conditions in categorical terms of psychopathology, such as phobia and psychosis. Presumably, he would have had no problem with rendering *DSM* (American Psychiatric Association, 2000) diagnoses if the *DSM* had existed in his time.

Weaknesses of the Theory

Several weaknesses of psychoanalysis have already been implied. Among them are its questionable effectiveness, its unavailability to the masses in need of psychological help, its culture-boundedness, its aspects that have been invalidated by subsequent research, and its failure to consider and/or account for a genuine spiritual domain in humans, in general, and profoundly meaningful and constructive spiritual experiences, in particular.

Another potential weakness is inherent in the theory itself. Any specific content in the psyche can be simply itself; can, through predicate thinking, stand not for itself but for something similar; or can, through reaction formation, stand not for itself or for something similar but for precisely its opposite. This openness of interpretation, combined with the authoritative stance of the analyst, in which any failure of the client to agree with the analyst's interpretation can be attributed to client repression, has the potential to disempower the client as an authority on his own reality. This state of affairs has led more than one exasperated client to abandon psychoanalysis.

Distinguishing Additions to Counseling and Psychotherapy

Perhaps Freud's most distinguishing contribution to counseling and psychotherapy is that he is credited as its founder. Prior to psychoanalysis, no well-organized, psychologically based system of thought existed to understand the human psyche. Virtually every subsequent approach arose either as an extension of psychoanalysis or in opposition to it. As you proceed to read subsequent chapters in this book, you undoubtedly will recognize many concepts similar to those you read about in this chapter.

Another contribution is the extent to which psychoanalysis "psychologized" Western culture at large through the pervasion (some might say perversion!) of psychoanalytic terms and concepts into popular thinking. We all, knowingly or not, speak Freud's language. Freud's concept of infantile determinism—that early experiences have a lasting effect on personality—has, for many Westerners since Freud's time, achieved the status of an *a priori* assumption. It also is commonplace to refer to someone as "defensive" or "neurotic," or to speak of repression, rationalization, projection, sublimation, narcissism, sibling rivalry . . . The list goes on and on. A lay person uses such words, and another nods in glib agreement, unconscious that they are affirming aspects of Freudian thinking that resonate intuitively.

CURRENT STATUS

Psychoanalysis persists as a force in the field of psychology, though a decreasingly powerful one. However, Kahn (2002) noted that the number of psychoanalytic training institutes in his area have increased rather than decreased. Such institutes can be found around the world, psychoanalytically oriented journals continue to be published, and books continue to be written about the theory, practice, and social impact of psychoanalysis.

Arlow (2000) identified what he considered "the most significant and powerful trend concerning modern-day psychoanalytic technique" (p. 45): the movement among some analysts from a position of objectivity in relation to the client, to one of *intersubjectivity*. From this latter perspective, the analyst is not an all-knowing entity who can stand apart from the client and presume with certainty to know the client even better than the client knows himself. Rather, the analyst, like all humans, is limited in her knowledge and experiences client material in an unavoidably subjective way, based on her own wishes and defenses. Rather than fight these realities, the analyst accepts them. In the process, she becomes more collaborative with the client and self-disclosing of her experience of the client, believing that, through a more mutual search for the dynamics underlying the client's distress, they are most likely to find the best approximation of truth.

SUMMARY

Sigmund Freud wrote that, "My life has been aimed at one goal only; to infer or guess how the mental apparatus is constructed and what forces interplay and counteract in it" (cited in Hall, 1999, p. 15). It appears that, to the best of his ability, within the limits of his personal potential and the philosophical, social, and technological systems within which he worked, he met that goal. Many ideas that originated with Freud are pervasive in current Western culture. Some of his ideas have lost credibility in light of subsequent research on behavior, genetic influences on personality, and the use of psychoactive medication to treat psychopathology; others have been confirmed through empirical research on sexuality, sleep, dreams, and consciousness. Psychoanalysis as a form of psychotherapy continues to be practiced, both in its original form and as an adapted form in brief therapy. It has been extremely fruitful to the field of psychotherapy by spawning most other approaches that are either an outgrowth of it or a reaction against it.

RECOMMENDED RESOURCES

Books

Hall, C. S. (1999). *A primer of Freudian psychology.* New York: Meridian. Although a close reading begins to reveal holes and discrepancies in psychoanalytic theory, this clear and dense volume still represents the best introductory overview of the personality theory of psychoanalysis. It does not address the psychoanalytic psychotherapy process.

Freud, S. (1949). *An outline of psychoanalysis.* (J. Strachey, Trans.). New York: Norton. Freud did not complete this, his last work. However, because it was his last, it reflects in a fairly concise form his ultimate formulation of psychoanalysis as a theory of personality and an approach to psychotherapy. Though I (JMH) found his writing obscure at times, I also found it startling to read in his own eloquent words (albeit translated) some of his most outrageous-by-current-standards ideas as well as some ideas with which I agreed immediately and which resonated deeply with me.

Arlow, J. A. (2000). Psychoanalysis. In R. J. Corsini & D. Wedding (Eds.), *Current psychotherapies.* Itasca, IL: Peacock. Short on personality theory, this chapter provides a systematic explanation of the process of psychoanalysis as psychotherapy.

Gay, P. (1989). Sigmund Freud: A chronology. In P. Gay (Ed.), *The Freud reader* (pp. xxxi–xlvii). This listing condenses into 17 pages the most critical facts pertaining to Freud's life. The ambitious student who wants to read excerpts of Freud's work throughout his lifetime may proceed to read this entire volume; those who want to read Freud's biography in depth are referred to Gay's 1988/1998 *Freud: A Life for Our Time.*

Media

A&E Television Network. (1995). *Sigmund Freud: Analysis of a mind* [Television broadcast]. An excellent 50-minute biography. Available for about $20 at http://search.biography.com/print_record.pl?id=5112

Learning Corporation of America (Producer). (1970). *Sigmund Freud: The hidden nature of man* [Motion picture]. New York: Learning Corporation of America. An excellent overview of Freud's life and ideas. Although it is an older production, its content and production values have held up over time. At one internet source, http://socialstudies.com, the video can be purchased for about $70.

Probably because psychoanalysis is difficult to depict in one short video, we know of none that attempt to demonstrate it. However, videos are available that demonstrate psychodynamic approaches derived from psychoanalysis:

Broderson, G. (Producer/Director). (1994). *Short term dynamic therapy* [Motion picture]. (1994). Washington, DC: American Psychological Association. (Available from the American Psychological Association, 750 First Street, NE, Washington, DC 20002-4242 or at http://www.apa.org/videos/4310330.html) A mock therapy session with "Dorothy" conducted by Donald Freedheim is the focus of this 36-minute video. The video is available for about $100.

Strupp, H. (1986). Psychodynamic psychotherapy. *Three approaches to psychotherapy III,* Part 1 [Motion picture]. Corona Del Mar, CA: Psychological & Educational Films.

(Available from Psychological & Educational Films, 3334 East Coast Highway, #252, Corona Del Mar, CA 92625 or www.psychedfilms.com/ThreeIII.1S.htm) In this 46-minute video, Hans Strupp briefly introduces psychodynamic psychotherapy, conducts a 30-minute session with "Richard," and briefly debriefs the session. The video is available for about $400.

Websites

Rich with photos and information about Freud, the Freud Museum in London's website is http://www.freud.org.uk/

Rich with information about psychoanalysis in the United States, the American Psychoanalytic Association's website is http://www.apsa-co.org/ctf/pubinfo/about.htm

Several North American psychoanalytic foundations and research and training institutes are listed at http://www.astrolabio-ubaldini.com/link.html

A listing of psychoanalytic journals and publishers can be found at http://www.dspp.com/links/psapubs.htm

References

American heritage dictionary of the English language (4th ed.). (2000). New York: Houghton Mifflin.

American Psychiatric Association. (2000). *Diagnostic and statistical manual of mental disorders* (4th ed., text rev.). Washington, DC: Author.

American Psychoanalytic Association. (2003). *About psychoanalysis.* Retrieved from http://www.apsa-co.org/ctf/pubinfo/about.htm

Arlow, J. A. (2000). Psychoanalysis. In R. J. Corsini & D. Wedding (Eds.), *Current psychotherapies.* Itasca, IL: Peacock.

Australian Broadcasting Corporation. (2003). Hostility and cholesterol. *News in Science* (1998, October). Retrieved from http://www.abc.net.au/science/news/stories/s13934.htm

Bell, A. P., & Weinberg, M. S. (1978). *Homosexualities: A study of diversity among men & women.* New York: Simon & Schuster.

Broderson, G. (Producer/Director). (1994). *Short term dynamic therapy* [Motion picture]. Washington, DC: American Psychological Association. (Available from the American Psychological Association, 750 First Street, NE, Washington, DC 20002-4242 or at http://www.apa.org/videos/4310330.html)

Brunner, J. (1998). Oedipus politicus: Freud's paradigm of social relations. In M. S. Roth (Ed.), *Freud: Conflict and culture: Essays on his life, work, and legacy* (pp. 48–61). New York: Alfred A. Knopf.

Damasio, A. (1999). *The feeling of what happens: Body and emotion in the making of consciousness.* New York: Harcourt.

Freud, S. (1949). *An outline of psycho-analysis.* (J. Strachey, Trans.). New York: Norton.

Freud, S. (1949). *Three essays on the theory of sexuality.* (J. Strachey, Trans.). Oxford: Imago.

Freud, S. (1965). *Interpretation of dreams.* (J. Strachey, Trans.). New York: Avon.

Freud, S. (1989). Civilization and its discontents. In P. Gay (Ed.), *The Freud reader* (pp. 722–772). New York: Norton. (Original work published 1929)

Gatz. M. (1990). Interpreting behavioral genetic results: Suggestions for counselors and clients. *Journal of Counseling and Development, 68,* 601–605.

Gay, P. (1988). *Freud: A life for our times.* New York: Norton.

Gay, P. (1989a). Sigmund Freud: A brief life. In S. Freud, *An outline of psycho-analysis* (J. Strachey, Trans.) (pp. vii–xx). New York: Norton.

Gay, P. (1989b). Sigmund Freud: A chronology. In P. Gay (Ed.), *The Freud reader* (pp. xxxi–xlvi). New York: Norton.

Greenberg, J. R., & Mitchell, S. A. (1983). *Object relations in psychoanalytic theory* (Part 1: Origins, pp. 9–78). Cambridge, MA: Harvard University.

Hall, C. S. (1999). *A primer of Freudian psychology.* New York: Meridian.

Hergenhahn, B. R. (1992). *Introduction to the history of psychology* (2nd ed.). Monterey, CA: Brooks/Cole.

Jones, E. (1953). *The life and work of Sigmund Freud, vols. 1–3.* New York: Basic.

Kahn, M. (2002). *Basic Freud: Psychoanalytic thought for the 21st century.* New York: Basic.

Kreis, S. (2000a). *The history guide: Lectures on twentieth century Europe: Lecture 1: Random thoughts on the intellectual history of 20th century Europe.* Retrieved March 29, 2003, from http://www.historyguide.org/europe/lecture1.html

Kreis, S. (2000b). *The history guide: Lectures on twentieth century Europe: Lecture 9: The Age of Anxiety: Europe in the 1920s (2).* Retrieved March 29, 2003, from http://www.historyguide.org/europe/lecture9.html

Moore, R. (1999). *The creation of reality in psychoanalysis: A view of the contributions of Donald Spence, Roy Schafer, Robert Stolorow, Irwin Z. Hoffman, and beyond.* Hillsdale, NJ: Analytic Press.

Radio National. (1998). *The health report: Anger kills.* Retrieved March 30, 2003, from www.abc.net.au/rn/talks/8.30/helthrpt/stories/s10309.htm

Roazen, P. (1992). *Freud and his followers.* New York: Da Capo.

Roget's II: The New Thesaurus (3rd ed.). (1995). New York: Houghton Mifflin.

Steele, R. (2002). *Masturbation: Is this normal for preschoolers?* iVillage, Inc. Retrieved March 29, 2003, from http://www.parentsoup.com/preschool/behave/qas/0,,262551_501425-2,00.html

Stills, S. (1970). Love the one you're with. On *Stephen Stills* (record). New York: Atlantic.

Web.Xperts. (1998). *Summary of studies on the origins of sexual orientation.* Retrieved March 29, 2003, from http://www.gaysouthafrica.org.za/homosexuality/studies.asp

WGBH. (1998). *People and discoveries: Harry Harlow.* Retrieved March 29, 2003, from http://www.pbs.org/wgbh/aso/databank/entries/bhharl.html

CHAPTER 3

SELF PSYCHOLOGY

BACKGROUND OF THE THEORY

Historical Context

Self psychology is the most recent of the four main schools of psychodynamic thought that emerged from Freud's pioneering psychoanalysis, the
other three being *drive theory, ego psychology,* and *object relations.* Over the
last 40 years, most psychodynamic theorists have worked primarily in analytic institutes. Consequently, most therapist-educators in academia today,
even those who regularly teach the theories of Freud and Erik Erikson, know
relatively little about significant developments in psychodynamics
(McWilliams, 1994). Nevertheless, psychodynamic theories are the most frequently named exclusive or primary guiding theories among mental health
professionals (Jensen, Bergin, & Greaves, 1990). For this reason and others
that will be discussed in this chapter, it is fitting that counselors be knowl-
edgable about psychodynamic theories. This chapter presents a very brief
overview of the first three schools and a more in-depth introduction to Heinz
Kohut's self psychology. Because the historical foundation of self psychology
is relatively richer than that of other theories, this section will be somewhat
longer than comparable sections in other chapters of this text.

In the primary literature of psychoanalysis and psychodynamics, the
terms *psychoanalytic* and *psychodynamic* are often used interchangeably. "Psychoanalytic" usually refers to traditional psychoanalysis; however, after Kohut's
radical departure from traditional psychoanalysis, he continued to use the classical terms "psychoanalysis," "analyst," and "analysand/patient." In this chapter, we will use "therapy/counseling," "therapist/counselor," and "client,"
respectively, while quotations from Kohut will retain his original terminology.

Each of the psychodynamic theories retains significant similarities to
psychoanalysis. Each adheres to the central concept that a person's feelings,
thoughts, and behaviors are profoundly influenced by psychological processes
and mental representations that are, to some degree, *unconscious.* Each affirms the *formative impact of early caretaker–child interactions* on one's present
experience, the *development of personality through invariant stages,* and the
presence and importance of *defenses, transference, and the interpretation of the
client's psychic material in the therapeutic process* (Perry, Cooper, & Michels,
1986).

Psychodynamic theories can best be understood in relation to Freud's theory of psychoanalysis that evolved through three primary phases, each characterized by a model. His first phase involved the *topographical model*. This model accounted for the relative degree of access a person has to his psychic material: from completely unconscious, to preconscious, to fully conscious. It included the concept of *drives* along with *defenses* that repress intolerable emotions to some level of unconsciousness. Freud's second phase emphasized drives in the context of a *structural model* whereby the *ego* mediates the primitive desires of the *id* and the moralistic demands of the *superego*. In his final *relational model* phase, Freud highlighted how *early experiences with significant others* interact with a child's innate topography and structure to determine adult personality (Greenberg & Mitchell, 1983).

The current school of psychodynamics that remains closest to psychoanalytic theory is *drive theory*, which emerged quite early in the history of psychoanalysis. Because drive theory is nearly indistinguishable from psychoanalysis, no particular proponent of this school exists apart from Freud himself. The emphasis in drive theory is on libidinal and aggressive drives that energize psychological processes. Libidinal drives are not merely sexual but refer more broadly to impulses toward bodily pleasure, excitement, anticipation, love, or happiness (Greenberg & Mitchell, 1983).

For almost 50 years, only classic psychoanalytic theory and its very close relative, drive theory, existed. By the 1940s, however, a few individuals began to create alternative psychoanalytic perspectives: Harry Stack Sullivan, Melanie Klein, Karen Horney, Erich Fromm, Clara Thompson, and Frieda Fromm-Reichman. However, none of these theorists developed their theories sufficiently and/or attracted a sufficient number of proponents to warrant calling their respective approaches one of the four primary analytic schools of thought (Greenberg & Mitchell, 1983).

The second actual school to emerge was that of *ego psychology*, primarily associated with Anna Freud and Heinz Hartmann. Ego psychology was so named because it emphasizes not the drives themselves but the ego's capacity to regulate, control, and channel the drives. Anna Freud's foremost contribution to this school was a much more detailed elaboration of the mechanisms of ego defense. Hartmann's foremost contributions were the concept that, in the interest of adaptation, the ego could actually alter drives, that is, change what one experiences as pleasurable; and the conceptual separation of the self—which is largely a locus of the felt-sense of "I"—from the ego. For a succinct overview of clinical applications of ego psychology, the reader is referred to chapter 5 of Bellak, Hurvich, and Gediman (1973).

In the 1940s and 1950s, while ego psychologists were refining their model of personality, various theorists in Europe, such as W. R. D. Fairbairn, D. W. Winnicott, and Margaret Mahler, established the school of *object relations*; their work independently paralleled that of Edith Jacobson and Otto Kernberg in the United States. In this theory, the term *object* can be understood to mean object of desire, that which satisfies a drive, and usually refers to a person, most importantly one's primary caregiver(s) in early childhood, as well as significant others throughout the rest of one's life.

The object relations pioneers worked with clients who would now be diagnosed as psychotic or borderline children and adults without a well-developed ego. They found existing psychoanalytic and psychodynamic theories inadequate for their understanding of such clients because those theories proceeded on the assumption that a client already had a developed ego. To more thoroughly explain how the ego developed, object relations theorists focused on the quality of the primary objects (people) in a person's infancy and very early childhood, how the person had experienced and internalized those objects, and how the internal representations of significant objects persisted in the person's unconscious mind throughout life, greatly influencing the quality of the person's experience (McWilliams, 1994). All of these dynamics profoundly impact the development of one's sense of self. Object relations theorists acknowledged the often very real actions of the object but *considered the client's perception of the object even more important than the actual object,* because the client's pre-egoic, prerational perception was likely to have involved misinterpretations. For example, a 1-year-old girl whose mother had to be hospitalized for a year felt abandoned; that is, she misinterpreted that her mother had abandoned her. In later relationships with other objects, she was hypersensitive to possible abandonment and misperceived it where it actually had not occurred (McWilliams, 1994). Clinically, the fact that her mother had not intentionally abandoned her was unimportant; her perception that she had been abandoned and her feeling of having been abandoned were key in her later relationship difficulties.

Object relations theory is complex; even a competent introduction is beyond the scope of this chapter. Suffice it to say that the theory has made several unique contributions to psychotherapy. One is the elaboration of theory regarding stages of psychological development in very early childhood (Klein, 1948; Mahler, Pine, & Bergman, 1975). Another is the understanding and treatment of severely disturbed clients, many formerly considered untreatable, such as those with borderline personality disorder (Kernberg, 1975). A third is a new appreciation of and perspective on countertransference in the psychotherapeutic process; in contrast to Freud's perspective of viewing strong emotional reactions to the client as the analyst's failure to maintain psychological neutrality, distance, and objectivity, the perspective of object relations theorists such as Harold Searles and D. W. Winnicott was that such reactions provided them their best tools for understanding and treating their highly distressed clients (McWilliams, 1994). A fourth contribution is the shift away from the impersonal therapeutic relationship of psychoanalysis toward a therapeutic alliance characterized by the therapist's personal involvement, engagement, and even self-disclosure (McWilliams, 1994). A fifth is Hartmann's initial conceptualization of a self that is more than the ego.

Self psychology, the fourth school of psychodynamics, was born with

Heinz Kohut's 1971 publication of *The Analysis of the Self*. However, this book actually was a continuation of ideas he had been developing over the previous 12 years. Prior to 1971, not only had Kohut been deeply committed to the teachings of classical psychoanalysis and its technical prescriptions, but he had also been a prominent member and leader of the psychoanalytic community. It was, therefore, only with great difficulty that he gradually revealed to himself and the analytic community what ultimately became a radical reformulation of psychoanalytic theory. Reflecting on his career, Kohut (1984) wrote that "in 1971, I was simply trying to pour new wine into old bottles, attempting to make new ideas appear less radically new and more acceptable not only to my fellow analysts, but above all to myself" (p. 193). However, by 1977, with the publication of *The Restoration of the Self*, Kohut presented his work as superordinate to mainstream psychoanalysis. Today, most mental health professionals view self psychology not merely as an elaboration of psychoanalysis but as a genuinely new school of psychotherapy (Kohut, 1979; Masek, 1989).

Like the object relations theorists, Kohut never considered classical psychoanalysis and the first two psychodynamic schools invalid or unimportant. He did, however, view them as limited, particularly in the understanding and treatment of people with more severe psychological disturbances. Kohut termed the more severe disturbances *disorders of the self* that include narcissistic, borderline, and psychotic conditions (Kohut, 1979; Masek, 1989), all of which will be explained and discussed in a later section of this chapter. In particular, Kohut described narcissism far more completely and broadly than it was—and is—described in the *Diagnostic and Statistical Manual of Mental Disorders* (DSM-IV-TR; American Psychiatric Association, 2000). Consequently, he considered narcissism to be far more pervasive than did most other mental health professionals.

Before proceeding with a more in-depth description of self psychology, one last overview point deserves mention. Of the four theories just described, most psychodynamically oriented therapists resonate more with one theory than the others but, clinically, call upon all four—or at least the latter three—to conceptualize their clients (Perry et al., 1986; Ursano, Sonnenberg, & Lazar, 1998). In so doing, the therapist explores with the client the primary concerns addressed in each school of thought. This "psychodynamic listening" (Ursano et al., 1998, p. 35) is summarized in Table 3.1.

In summary, psychodynamic theories, having evolved from Freud's psychoanalytic theory, have emerged primarily through four schools of thought. The first school, drive theory, emphasized the role of drives in psychological life. The second, ego psychology, emphasized the ego's ability to manage drives. The third, object relations, emphasized how the person develops through early experience with objects. The fourth, self psychology, emphasized the development and treatment of the self, a larger, broader structure/function than the mere ego. Following is a biographical overview of Heinz Kohut, who developed self psychology.

TABLE 3.1
Psychodynamic Listening

Drive theory	What does this client want?
	Are the client's wishes and fantasies developmentally appropriate?
Ego psychology	What defenses does this client primarily employ?
	How does this client go about getting what she wants?
Object relations	How does this client recall the significant people from the various stages of development in her life?
	Whom does this client behave, think, and feel like?
Self psychology	To what extent does this client like, value, and admire herself?
	How does this client respond to events that insult her self-esteem?

Adapted from *Psychodynamic Psychotherapy*, by R. Ursano, S. Sonnenberg, and S. Lazar, 1998, Washington, DC: American Psychiatric Press, p. 35.

Founder's Biographical Overview

Heinz Kohut, born an only child in Vienna on May 3, 1913, was treated as an especially talented child. World War I took his highly cultured father, Felix, away for Heinz's first 5 years, during which time Heinz lived with his mother Else and her parents. Upon his father's return, Felix's physical absence was apparently replaced by a psychological one (Strozier, 1985).

In her relationship with Heinz, Else seemed to alternate between oppressive closeness and distance. Kohut reported a sad and intensely lonely childhood due to his parents' frequent socializing. Nonetheless, "there was something deep and abiding between Heinz and his mother, whatever the residues of ambivalence" (Strozier, 1985, pp. 4–5).

Even by the Viennese elite's high standards, Heinz's education was remarkable. Beginning with 2 years of private tutoring, he proceeded to the Doblinger Gymnasium where he studied Latin for 8 years and Greek for 8, in addition to French, history, athletics, and more. At the age of 19, he attended the University of Vienna, from which he received his medical degree in 1938.

Kohut enjoyed telling the story of his only encounter with Freud. It was June 4, 1938, and Freud and his entourage were departing from Vienna for England to flee Nazi persecution. As the train was leaving, Kohut could see Freud looking out the window. Kohut tipped his hat to Freud, who returned the gesture as the train departed. This contact with Freud left an indelible impression on the young Kohut, who sensed a certain mission he was to serve in the history of psychoanalysis (Strozier, 1985).

In 1940, Kohut also emigrated from Austria. Arriving in Chicago with only 25 cents to his name, Kohut secured an internship at a small hospital and, later, a coveted residence in neurology at the University of Chicago. In 1947, he began to focus exclusively on psychiatry. It appears that he was consciously modeling himself after Freud: "there was, in other words, an early sense of purpose in Kohut, an inner fire and lofty ambition to be Freud's successor, long before those thoughts had any basis in actuality" (Strozier, 1985, p. 7).

Kohut spent the majority of his life in Chicago, enthusiastically teaching and training analysts and maintaining a full clinical practice until he died in 1981 (Goldberg, 1989). Throughout the 1960s, he proudly bore the title "Mr. Psychoanalysis" and was the most eminent spokesperson for traditional psychoanalysis (Strozier, 1985), serving as president of the American Psychoanalytic Association (1964–65), vice-president of the International Psychoanalytic Association (1965–73), and vice-president of the Sigmund Freud Archives (1971–81).

However, after the 1971 publication of *The Analysis of the Self*, he tended to elicit extreme reactions from the psychoanalytic community—from abject devotion to contemptuous disregard (Strozier, 1985). While many colleagues simply withdrew from him, some viciously attacked his bold new ideas. This genuinely hurt Kohut, who never completely reconciled himself to it. The orthodoxy of classical psychoanalysis was a gargantuan opponent, and Kohut's fortitude was emotionally costly. However, despite his difficult struggles, Kohut always persevered with humor and playfulness (Strozier, 1985).

In formulating self psychology, Kohut created a new theory of how the self develops, how that development can go awry, and how to treat the resulting disturbances. Although he authored only three books, many mental health experts consider them to be among the most important recent contributions to the professional literature (Strauss, Yager, & Strauss, 1984). Even John Gedo, Kohut's first apostate, wrote that "Kohut's personal contribution to psychoanalysis was so important that in the past two decades all pioneering work in the field deserves to be called 'post-Kohutian'" (Gedo, 1989, p. 415). Prior to his death at the age of 68, Kohut also wrote on the application of psychoanalytic formulations to the understanding of a variety of phenomena: music, literature, creativity, humor, group psychology, charisma, and wisdom (Akhtar, 1989).

Kohut became increasingly humanistic at a time when humanism was on the rise in U.S. culture. However, Kohut actually worked in relative isolation and disclaimed most influence from other theorists or from the zeitgeist of the time. Like Carl Rogers, with whom Kohut was not affiliated but whose theory shows striking similarity to Kohut's, Kohut claimed to have developed his ideas out of his own professional experience with his clients.

Philosophical Underpinnings

"Kohut has been a theorist in perpetual transition," according to Greenberg and Mitchell (1983, p. 357). His work can be divided into three phases that correspond to his philosophical evolution. In his classical phase, prior to 1971, his ideas aligned with those of psychoanalysis, including philosophical concepts of determinism: people are at the mercy of their biological drives and childhood experiences that, together, determine adult personality; and objectivity: the best way to understand another person is as a distant, uninvolved observer.

In Kohut's second, transitional phase, from 1971 to 1977, he began to conceptualize the self and, with that conceptualization, to shift philosophically. That shift culminated in his third, radical phase, in which he departed from psychoanalysis and aligned philosophically with humanism. In this philosophical transition, he criticized psychoanalysis's mechanistic focus, which misses the vital aspects of human experience, and supplanted a belief in determinism with a belief in a fundamental human tendency to proactively develop one's full potential and to overcome developmental arrests—without denying the tendency to be powerfully influenced, but not determined, by one's biology and environment. He also supplanted a belief in objectivity in favor of subjectivity: that the best way to understand a phenomenon was to enter it; that knowing a phenomenon inescapably involves subjective perception; that, indeed, objectivity is impossible because the very act of observing a phenomenon changes the phenomenon; that both the clinical and theoretical domains of psychoanalysis are defined and demarcated by that which is accessible to empathy and introspection. He expressed this shift in his realization in the 1950s that "reality per se, whether extrospective or introspective, is unknowable; we can only describe what we see within the framework of what we have done to see it" (Kohut, 1982, p. 400). These shifts are reflected in his psychotherapeutic system, which emphasized not biological but social urges in humans, not clients' pathology but their developmental potentials, not a negative view of lifelong irrational drives but a positive view of lifelong legitimate psychological needs, not a therapeutic stance of distant objectivity but one of experience-near subjectivity, and not insight but empathy as curative of psychological disorders.

A feel for the shift Kohut underwent is reflected in his criticism that psychoanalysts' mechanistic view of the psyche missed the vital aspects of human experience. He contended that analysts should focus not on a client's drives themselves but on a client's experience of drives. He advocated a profoundly phenomenological approach, what he called "experience near," in which the therapist should be close to the client's subjective experience—in fact, enter into it—to avoid "experience distant," that is, killing that which is most human through the objectification of human experience (cited in Masek, 1989, p. 184). In his last paper, he likened the experience distant approach of drive theory with its focus on drives at the expense of understanding how the self experiences drives, to an attempt to understand a painting by merely analyzing its pigments. Kohut maintained that the *meanings* of drives and conflicts *emerge only from the perspective of the self* (Greenberg & Mitchell, 1983). Although Kohut still viewed interpretation of transference as essential to therapy, he believed that effective interpretation necessitated an empathic inquiry—experience near—as opposed to the neutral abstinence of the objective, distant scientist/observer.

PERSONALITY DEVELOPMENT

Nature of Humans

Function of the Psyche. From the perspective of self psychology, the primary function of each human being is to relate with other human beings. Kohut affirmed the existence of biological and psychological drives. However, like object relations theorists, he saw drives not as primary to psychological life but rather as secondary, serving to establish and ensure continuation of what is primary: *relationship*. Thus, self psychology is essentially a social psychology. It is based on the contention that humans do not relate with others as one means to reduce the pressure of drives; rather, humans have drives to ensure that they will continually relate with others.

Relating with others is not only the purpose of psychological life; it is the means for achieving the sole lifelong human need: to develop and maintain a self. The self actually is several interrelated functions that include organizing experience and restoring cohesion that has been jeopardized; validating subjective experience; maintaining homeostasis through tension regulation, the soothing of physical and emotional distress; and esteeming one's abilities and felt-sense of "I" (Bacal, 1990; Kohut, 1971). The infant, overwhelmed with a cacophonous onslaught of experience, does not have the ability to spontaneously develop these functions. He is, however, born with the ability to form bonds with selfobjects. *Selfobjects are external objects,* usually people, *that are subjectively experienced as providing intrapsychic functions.* Beginning in infancy and throughout life, one naturally feels an emotional connection and a desire for continued interaction with selfobjects, what Kohut called the self–selfobject bond/relationship.

Also beginning at birth, as the infant experiences needs being fulfilled through selfobjects, the infant has the potential to develop structural/functional capacities via transmuting internalization, through which *the functions of the (external) selfobject are slowly, gradually, bit-by-bit transformed into internal capacities*, establishing the structure/function of the self (Kohut, 1977). Kohut described this as a type of psychological metabolism, analogous to physical metabolism, in which food is broken down, and aspects of it are absorbed and integrated into the physical system, usually fulfilling physical needs. Analogously, in psychological metabolism, selfobject experiences are absorbed and integrated, becoming one's own internal capacities. Kohut contrasted this process with the psychoanalytic concept of identification, in which one internalizes an entire person.

Kohut elaborated on some specific selfobject experiences that constitute the "food" of psychological metabolism. Each will be discussed below with an example. It is important to keep in mind that just as physical food is initially taken in and metabolized nonconsciously, so does the metabolization of psychological food—selfobject experience—occur initially at a nonconscious, nonrational, organismic level. Then, throughout life, although intake usually becomes more conscious, digestion and absorption continue to occur at a nonconscious level. This does not mean that the process cannot or should not be understood: One can come to understand physical digestion and, as a result, choose foods more purposely and healthfully. Nevertheless, one continues to be mostly unaware of the digestion process as it occurs. Analogously, one can come to understand the metabolism of psychological nutrients and, as a result, choose potential selfobjects more purposely and healthfully. Nevertheless, people are often unaware of transmuting internalization as it occurs.

The first innate human selfobject need, which emerges at birth and lasts throughout life, is for empathic attunement and empathic mirroring. Empathy is "intrinsically [comprehending] the experience of others from their own unique perspective, which is often very different from 'what I would feel if I were actually in their place'" (Baker & Baker, 1987, p. 2). In empathic attunement and mirroring, the infant's caretaker accurately perceives the infant's emotional states and emerging abilities and responds with acceptance, validation, admiration, and caring action. An example is a father who always enjoyed the taste of bananas but finds that when he introduces his infant daughter to mashed bananas, she grimaces. Despite the fact that he himself has never disliked bananas, when he sees her grimace, he empathizes by looking at her; grimacing as if his face were a mirror reflecting her facial expression; saying "Oooh! You don't like that!" in a way that expresses understanding, affirmation, even pride in her knowing and expressing herself; and discontinuing to feed her the bananas.

Through transmuting internationalization in repeated similar experiences, the infant comes to differentiate certain aspects of experience that a more mature self might label as "not liking things," "avoiding things that aren't liked," and "the taste of bananas" and to organize these into a broader category of commodities and activities that are, and are not, liked. Another aspect of empathic mirroring occurs when the child perceives that her developing abilities, such as the ability to crawl, are met with delight and pride, which can be conveyed verbally or nonverbally. "The gleam in the mother's eye" (Baker & Baker, 1987, p. 3) is a nonverbal example of a parental response that communicates a sense of value and self-worth to the child. It is natural that, at first, the child will respond to such mirroring with grandiosity, a sense of unbounded esteem and omnipotence. It is as if the child thinks, "I am wonderful! I can do anything!" However, with ongoing empathic attunement and mirroring experiences, the child will develop a more moderate and realistic matrix that comprises one aspect of self, specifically, the self pole of nuclear ambition: the child's core sense of motivation and initiative to achieve goals. However, when parents respond with chronic indifference, hostility, or excessive criticism, the reflection of self received by the child is one lacking worth, resulting in a decrease in both one's sense of self-esteem and one's self-assertive ambitions.

A second innate selfobject need is idealization. Beginning in somewhat older infancy, the child needs to perceive in at least one other person an image of greatness, all-powerfulness, and all-knowingness with whom to connect and merge. Kohut called this image the "idealized parental imago." Kohut believed that children, being less competent to function in the world, tend naturally to perceive primary caretakers as omniscient and omnipotent. When they are not disabused of this perception, they have their need for idealization met, and the groundwork is laid for the child's development of the self pole of guiding ideals: the child creates an internal image of, and strives to become, more than she currently is, an image of an ideal.

A third innate selfobject need is for the experience of twinship. Also called alter ego needs, twinship needs refer to an individual's "need to experience the presence of essential alikeness" (Kohut, 1984, p. 194). Research suggests that this need emerges developmentally last, at approximately 18 months of age (Kriegman & Solomon, 1985, p. 245). When the child perceives opportunities to perform tasks and carry out responsibilities like her idealized parental imago, she feels her twinship need met. This may be as simple as a little boy or girl being allowed to help her parents rake leaves or dust furniture.

Kohut (1984) underscored the strength of the need to develop a self by asserting that, in the absence of mirroring responses, children will intensify their search for idealizing or twinship experiences. He likened this tendency to a tree's ability to grow around obstacles that prevent its exposure to the sun's life-sustaining rays. In addition, any of these needs that were unsatisfactorily met in childhood will continue to be sought for throughout adulthood and will emerge as the respective type of transference if the person seeks therapy.

It may at first seem paradoxical to learn that humans have one additional need that must be met for transmuting internalization to occur and, thus, the self to be formed: what Kohut termed optimal empathic failures. These occur, in the context of a well-established self–selfobject relationship, when a young child experiences the selfobject failing to empathize in some mild, nontraumatic way. In fact, in the temporary absence of selfobject, the child gradually acquires the ability to do for herself what formerly was done for her. For example, a little boy is routinely terrified by a monster in a certain commercial. His mother usually notices this and comforts, consoles, and reassures him that the monster cannot hurt him, that everything will be fine. Then one day, just as this commercial is broadcasting, the mother's attention is consumed by an urgent phone call. The young boy, in the absence of optimal empathic mirroring, is forced to comfort himself, which he is capable of doing to some extent. The more "optimal opportunities" he is provided—not chronically or traumatically—the more fully he will be able to intrapsychically perform tasks for which he previously relied upon his selfobjects.

In summary, through the selfobject's empathic responsiveness to the child's needs, and the child's participation in the selfobject's organized experience, the self gradually develops (St. Clair, 2000). Humans never outgrow their selfobject needs. Recall that selfobjects refer to any aspect of any thing or person that fulfills self functions. Thus, it is natural that, throughout life, external selfobjects evolve, typically from caretakers in one's infancy, to teachers during primary school years, to peers during later childhood and adolescence, and to spouse, boss, colleagues, even one's culture, in adulthood.

In addition to the innate tendency for selfobjects to evolve through various forms, the nature of the needs themselves, their form and intensity, also evolve. Selfobject needs in all very young children are absolute, archaic, and global insistencies for unceasing selfobject fulfillment. As transmuting internalization occurs, one becomes increasingly capable of doing for oneself what formerly was done for one by others, including the ability to organize, understand, and validate one's own experience; to respond nurturingly to one's own feelings, to celebrate when elated, to soothe oneself when distressed; and to esteem oneself. As the self thus develops, one becomes less demanding in the seeking after fulfillment by external selfobjects; one requires less frequent, intense, and blatant external response, although the seeking for selfobjects never completely disappears—nor should it.

In this section, we have addressed the inborn functions, the lifelong drives, needs, tendencies, and processes, that play a role in psychological development. Some specific innate conditions in an infant, such as temperament and physical or mental handicap, complicate the likelihood that the infant's selfobject needs will be fulfilled. These will be further addressed below.

Structure of the Psyche. In discussing psychic structure, Kohut (1984) admonished his readers to remember that theorized structures are not actual things but conceptual tools, useful for understanding and communicating. To increase the likelihood that readers would maintain this awareness, Stolorow, Brandchaft, and Atwood (1987) presented Kohut's theorized "structures," such as the self, as *functions* or *dimensions of experience*. To help you keep this disclaimer in mind as you read the following material, we use the term structure/function.

According to self psychology, at birth, the infant's psyche consists of a continuous onslaught of immediate experiences—disorganized, unmanaged, unregulated, and lacking cohesion. The infant is born with the potential to develop a psychological structure/function that Kohut (1977) called the self: "the center of the individual's psychological universe" (p. 311), a recipient of impressions and a center of initiative that provides a person cohesion, organization, and continuity in space and time (Kohut, 1984). The self is the consistent sense of identity, the "I" that brings a sense of organization to perception and action. Although each person has the potential for a fully developed self, that potential is realized to varying degrees, for reasons that will be explained below.

Beyond the basic ability to organize experience in a manner characterized by a cohesive and continuous sense of identity, Kohut's concept of self also included three poles. One's nuclear ambition is comprised of one's general desire and level of initiative to achieve goals. One's talents and skills consist of the resources one brings to the achievement of goals. One's guiding ideals consist of the final goals one aspires to achieve. For example, Jane is a young adult who has a cohesive, consistent sense of "I" that enables her to organize, regulate, and manage her experiences. She has a high level of nuclear ambition, desire, and initiative; her talents include extremely good interpersonal skills, psychological mindedness, and understanding of counseling theory; and, among several guiding ideals, one is to be of substantial service to others by becoming a highly effective counselor.

Kohut differentiated the self from the personality. The personality consists of relatively persistent feelings and actions. For example, if I feel anxious much of the time, anxiety is one of my personality characteristics. If I usually behave outspokenly, or quietly, that typical behavior is a characteristic of my personality. But chronic feelings and habitual actions are not as central to one's experience as one's sense of reality, of initiative, of identity. These latter features constitute the self that underlies personality characteristics.

Another way to understand the concept of the self is by contrast to Freud's concept of the ego. In psychoanalysis, the ego is an essentially reactive juggler constantly challenged to manage three balls with minds of their own: the id with its irrational demands for gratification, the superego with its irrational demands for perfection, and the environment with its demands of reality. Whereas Freud's ego was reactive, seeking merely to keep the balls under control, Kohut's self was proactively and creatively imagining and seeking to achieve goals, to do more than a basic juggling act. Another point of comparison is that whereas the idealistic superego was fundamentally different than and separate from the ego, Kohut's self included guiding ideals. Overall, whereas Freud's concept of psychic structure consisted of aggregates in conflict, Kohut's consisted of a single, more unified, purposeful structure/function, though not without its own internal tensions.

Role of the Environment

Familial. By now, it is probably clear that, from a self psychology perspective, a child's family usually plays the most central role in the development of the child's self. The child is most likely to perceive selfobjects among her primary caretakers—those who interact most frequently with her and actually fulfill her intrapsychic needs. The child can perceive empathic attunement/mirroring only in people who actually express it, can perceive idealization only in people who actually offer themselves as ideals, and can perceive twinship only in people who actually provide opportunities for the child to perform tasks and carry out responsibilities similar to themselves. The extent to which caretakers provide empathy, idealization, and twinship are crucial factors in the child's self development.

In addition, empathic failures are inevitable occurrences in a child's environment. However, the extent to which such failures are optimal (mild, minor, and occurring in the context of an established self–selfobject relationship, thereby facilitating the child's self development) or suboptimal (chronic, severe, and occurring outside the context of a well-established self-selfobject relationship, thereby hindering the child's self from developing) clearly plays a formative role.

Kohut observed and theorized in a cultural environment very different from that of Freud. Since the Victorian era, family structures had loosened and family interactions had reduced. These changes created the conditions for a higher incidence of what Kohut termed disorders of the self: narcissistic, borderline, and psychotic disorders. It may have been that Freud had not theorized about such individuals with these disorders because fewer such individuals existed. Conversely, Kohut, encountering more such clients, experienced the need to develop an understanding of them (St. Clair, 2000).

Extrafamilial. Any aspect of a thing or person that/who fulfills one or more of a child's self functions, whether within or outside of the family, is a selfobject. As previously stated, selfobjects tend to change as a person develops, moving from caretakers in the original family to include such people as peers and teachers in the wider social environment and then to include a spouse or partner in the created family. For many people, less personal aspects of culture can serve as selfobjects. Information from newpapers can help one make sense of events, and both fictional characters and public figures can provide idealization and even twinship for the ongoing structure/ function of one's self.

Interaction of Human Nature and Environment in Personality Development

Self psychology holds that self-selfobject relationships form the essence of psychological life from birth to death, that a move from dependence (symbiosis) to independence (autonomy) in the psychological sphere is no more possible, let alone desirable, than a corresponding move from a life dependent on oxygen to a life independent of it in the biological sphere. The developments that characterize normal psychological life must, in

TABLE 3.2
Sequence in Development of Healthy Self

Establishment of selfobject bond	Optimal empathic failures	Transmuting internalization	Formation of self structure/function

our view, be seen in *the changing nature of the relationship between the self and its selfobjects* [italics added]. (Kohut, 1984, p. 47)

When an infant or young child's innate needs for selfobject relationships and optimal empathic failures are met with an environment that meets those needs, then, through transmuting internalization, the young child will develop the structure/function of a self. Thus, she can increasingly meet her own needs, becoming less intensely needful, though never independent, of (external) selfobjects. This process is summarized in Table 3.2

Under ideal conditions, the child's mirrored grandiosity becomes more realistic and is channeled into plausible ambitions; the self is characterized by vitality for life and life undertakings. Similarly, the child's idealized parental imago is introjected, emerging as one's values and ideals (St. Clair, 2000). Following suit, the child's experiences of twinship transform into her talents and skills, which she enlists in the pursuit of her ambitions and ideals.

Kohut (1984) insisted that no one ever completely outgrows the need for selfobjects. To support this contention, he cited how the artist Picasso, the philosopher Nietzsche, and Kohut's own conceptual mentor, Freud, relied on selfobjects, particularly during episodes of intense creativity and intense self-questioning and self-doubt. With this contention, Kohut defied Western culture's tendency to equate mental health with physical and emotional autonomy. Rather, Kohut asserted, the *quality* of one's selfobject needs change from absolute demands to more moderate, mature, resilient, and realistic forms. A healthy self is one that, except in the midst of extreme circumstances, is relatively cohesive and experienced as balanced, whole, continuous, organized, strong, and harmoniously vigorous. In addition, a person with a well-developed self knows how to select, establish, and utilize relationships to fulfill his selfobject needs (Baker, 1991). Because he can, to a great extent, fulfill selfobject needs internally, and because, consequently, his dependence on external others to fulfill those needs is reduced, he does not need others to be continuously empathically attuned to him; he can, so to speak, psychologically "afford" to see others as separate and different from himself. Thus is born his own ability to empathize: "to intrinsically comprehend the experience of others *from their own unique perspective*" [italics added] (Baker & Baker, 1987, p. 2).

Anticipating a "so what" response from people learning about his theory, Kohut (1984) remarked,

What an anticlimax! The reader may well think. Indeed, what a seemingly insipid, everyday occurrence compared to the drama of the primal
scene, of the child's sexual excitement and death wishes, that Freud
wrested from the unconscious. Perhaps so, but I would point out that
dramatic excitement and truth value do not necessarily go hand in hand.
The self sustenance that a little girl might get from silently working in the
kitchen next to her grandmother, that a little boy might get from shaving
next to his daddy or from working next to his daddy with daddy's tools in
the basement; these are indeed undramatic everyday events. The drama
ensues or, more correctly, the tragedy ensues when a child is chronically
deprived of such experiences. (p. 197)

Hopefully, you can forgive Kohut for the sexist flavor of his remark and hear
his belief in the critical nature of selfobject need fulfillment for the formation
of the self.

It follows, then, that when an infant's or young child's caretakers are
neglectful and/or abusive, exhibiting physical and/or emotional indifference
and/or hostility, the child's self development proceeds quite differently. In
neglect and abuse, the child experiences chronic and traumatic empathic
failures and thus perceives little or no empathy, nothing/no one to idealize,
and little or no opportunity for twinship. Thus, the child does not bond with
caretakers, so selfobject relationships do not form or are tenuous. Consequently, optimal empathic failures are infrequent or absent because such failures, by definition, occur only in the context of well-established selfobject
relationships. In turn, the child's self remains undeveloped and/or its fledgling development is arrested or reversed.

Baker and Baker (1987) likened the psychological development of the
self to the physical development of muscles. Optimal empathic failures comprise a kind of resistance, and some resistance adds bulk, whereas chronic,
severe empathic failures are like extreme physical strain in the absence of
conditioning and strength, a kind of "excess [that] exhausts, or can even
tear, the muscle" (p. 4).

Kohut believed that when primary caregivers chronically fail to meet
the child's selfobject needs, the child will develop a less-than-optimal self
and will exhibit psychopathology. It is important to note that severe self disorders result only if all three selfobject functions are chronically absent. Yet
Kohut believed that the single greatest contributor to people's psychopathology was their primary caretakers' failures to empathize with them. Stolorow
et al. (1987) focused even more specifically on what they called "reliable affect attunement" (p. 87): even a person's most fundamental ability to experience and acknowledge her feelings, rather than dissociate from or disavow
them, depends on her having experienced, as an infant and young child,
primary caretakers who provided a steady, attuned responsiveness to her
ever-changing emotions. Thus it is that, later in life, people are emotionally
crippled *not* by "the unconscious fear of forbidden erotic love that generates

anxiety," wrote M. Basch in reference to psychoanalytic theory, but by "the anticipation of reexperiencing the devastating, potentially disintegrating disappointment of early empathic failures if they dare once again reach for emotional fulfillment" (cited in Baker & Baker, 1987, p. 7).

Kohut posited that the earlier and more extensive the empathic failures, the more severe the psychopathology. Thus, psychosis resulted from the earliest and most extensive empathic failures, borderline conditions from somewhat later and/or less extensive failures, narcissism from yet later and/or less extensive failures, and neuroses from even later and/or even less extensive failures. These mental disorders reflect degrees of self-development.

The person suffering from a psychosis has not yet developed a self. The person's contact with consensus reality, the reality shared by most people, is impaired by their delusions, "false belief[s] based on incorrect inference about external reality that [are] firmly sustained despite what almost everyone else believes and despite what constitutes incontrovertible and obvious proof or evidence to the contrary" (APA, 2000, p. 765) and/or hallucinations, "sensory perceptions[s] that [have] the compelling sense of reality of a true perception but that [occur] without external stimulation of the relevant sensory organ[s]" (p. 767). From a self psychology perspective, delusions and hallucinations are among the self-defenses generated by a person with a psychosis in response to the frequent, severe empathic failures he perceives.

The person suffering from a borderline personality disorder has only the most tenuous and remote sense of a self. Such a person exhibits "a pervasive pattern of instability of interpersonal relationships, self-image, and affects, and marked impulsivity that begins by early adulthood and is present in a variety of contexts" (p. 650). One symptom people with borderline disorders generate in response to the frequent, severe empathic failures they perceive is splitting the perception of a person as either all good or all bad.

People who suffer from narcissistic disorders have a vague and unstable outline of a self. Kohut's description of narcissistic clients is quite different from that in the DSM-IV (APA, 2000). Such clients may exhibit grandiosity, may lack empathy, and may desire admiration. However, more common than this grandiose form of narcissism is the fragile manifestation accompanied by feelings of emptiness and boredom—lacking feelings of worth, zest, humor, and meaning—none of which are mentioned in DSM-IV. Thus, Kohut (1971) included in his conceptualization "circumscribed defects in self-esteem or self-esteem regulations, or broad disturbances in the patient's systems of ideals" (p. 22). Narcissistic individuals are unable to esteem themselves and thus live ever archaically vigilant for cues from others as evaluations of their self-worth. What appears to an outsider as an inconsequential, minor insult may be experienced by such an individual as an overwhelmingly negative evaluation of his very being, resulting in either depression or *disintegration anxiety*, which Kohut (1984) argued was "the deepest anxiety man [*sic*] can experience" (p. 16). In this circumstance, these vulnerable people will employ any behavior that wards off this impending sense of annihilation, even if that behavior is ultimately self-destructive. The most common responses involve some form of withdrawal or rage.

Finally, with regard to those with neuroses, a self has developed, but it is characterized by internal conflict. Again, these disorders were the focus of traditional psychoanalysis.

In each of these disorders, the person somehow strives for fulfillment in relatively archaic, developmentally inappropriate ways (St. Clair, 2000). Self psychologists view most symptomatic behavior as the person's best attempt to avoid intolerable emotions and to regain some sense of self-cohesion, self-comforting, and self-worth (Baker, 1991).

Although Kohut blamed psychopathology predominantly on early and/ or severe empathic failures, he did not intend to blame primary caretakers for their empathic failures. He considered caretakers' chronic, severe empathic failures to occur under a variety of circumstances. For example, even relatively able caretakers will likely be challenged to maintain consistent empathic attunement if the child in their care is extraordinarily needy, having severe physical or mental disabilities; if the caretakers' and child's temperaments are extremely discrepant; or if caretakers are functioning under harsh environmental circumstances such as war or poverty. In addition, caretakers themselves may be severely limited in their ability to empathize due to their own psychopathology (Baker & Baker, 1987; Kohut, 1984). Kohut implied that primary caretaker's self resources frequently are challenged, and although they are responsible for the role they play in the psychopathology of the children for whom they care, they are struggling under some burden of their own and are, thus, not to be indiscriminately blamed or criticized. In summary, Kohut's purpose in theorizing about caretaker's roles in the psychopathology of their children was less to focus blame on parents than to cast light upon the understanding of the etiology of psychopathology in clients and the challenges counselors face in providing clients what they missed in their self-development.

The Personality Change Process

Basic Principles of Change. Kohut disagreed with Freud's view of the essence of change, to make the unconscious conscious, or "where id was, there shall ego be" (cited in Kohut, 1984, p. 103). Rather, from a self psychology perspective, change throughout life involves development of the self, and it occurs through the same process that occurs in an ideal childhood (Kohut, 1971). Therapeutic life experiences involve self–selfobject relationships in which one continues to experience optimal empathic failures and, through transmuting internalization, comes increasingly, but never exclusively, to meet one's own self needs.

The difficulty is that the individual most in need of this experience is least able to manifest it for oneself. For person A, with a poorly developed self, to establish and sustain a healthy relationship with person B, person B must have unusual insight, patience, and persistence—the characteristics of an unusually well-developed self—with which to meet person A's relatively demanding selfobject needs and her tendency to perceive any empathic failure. These empathic failures may be inevitable in even the healthiest relationship as a reenactment of the traumatic empathic failures of childhood. In addition, because person A is powerfully invested in her own selfobject needs, she is less able to perceive and respond to even the moderate and realistic selfobject needs of person B. The more severe the disorder of person A's self, the more well-developed person B's self must be for the relationship to endure. In addition, a manifestation of person B's healthy self is that she exercises discrimination in close personal relationships, involving herself only in those relationships characterized by moderate, reciprocal selfobject need fulfillment. Thus, she is less likely to establish or maintain the relatively more one-way relationship with person A. For these reasons, the more severe person A's immaturity of self, the less likely she will be to find and secure therapeutic life experiences for herself, and the more her hope for self-development rests in professional psychotherapy.

Change Through Counseling. For Kohut, the organizing principle of the psychotherapeutic process can be thought of as reparenting, whereby the therapist provides selfobject functions for the client that the client's primary caretakers did not provide. In this process, the therapist communicates consistent empathic attunement and mirroring. In response, the client initially perceives the therapist as a consistent selfobject, forms a self–selfobject relationship with the therapist, and allows the establishment of selfobject transference(s): seeking—in fact, demanding—that the therapist meet not only the reasonable, moderate selfobject needs of a developmentally mature adult but also the client's unmet archaic selfobject needs. The basic therapeutic process involves (a) reactivation of the client's need(s) (selfobject transference), (b) nonfulfillment of some of the client's needs by the counselor (optimal frustration/empathic failure), and (c) reestablishment of the empathic bond between client (self) and counselor (selfobject). *This sequence must occur many, many times throughout the course of therapy.*

Another important component in the therapeutic process is the therapist's interpretations: communications to the client about the therapist's understanding of the client's psychological dynamics. Unintentionally, but inevitably, some interpretations will be inaccurate and not match the client's experience. These misinterpretations constitute empathic failures, which the transference-laden client experiences as reenactments of traumatic empathic failures from early life, and thus to which she reacts with emotional intensity: the sum of the current pain plus all the associated pain of the past. If therapy is to be therapeutic, the therapist must respond to this emotional intensity by remaining empathically attuned. As a result, the client experiences reestablishment of the self–selfobject relationship. In addition, feeling understood, attended to, and nurtured even in his extreme emotional reactions, the client will likely take a step in understanding and nurturing himself the next time he is not so empathically attended to, thus enacting transmuting internalization whereby he fulfills self functions for himself that he previously had demanded the therapist and other selfobjects meet.

With numerous repetitions of the last step in the therapeutic process the client's self gradually develops. As his self develops, his behavior in relationships changes, marked by decreased insistence, a decrease in disproportionate emotional reactivity, and an increase in the capacity for selfobject reciprocity. This reciprocity occurs first in his relationship with his therapist, and then with other selfobjects in his life.

To separate the client's and therapist's roles in this process is difficult because, from a self psychotherapeutic perspective, effective elements of the therapy are intersubjective and involve the interplay of both the client's and the therapist's subjective perceptions. Nevertheless, in the following two sections, the two respective roles will be teased apart.

Client's Role. Most clients seek counseling for relief from suffering that, from the self psychologist's point of view, is a manifestation of one or more disorders of the self. The client's suffering may take any of a number of forms: feelings of emptiness—their lives seem to lack zest, joy, humor, meaning, and purpose; feelings of anxiety, depression, or fragmented instability; feeling satisfied or worthwhile only when others respond to them in certain ways; an inability to maintain intimate relationships; hypersensitivity to perceived slights; difficulties in concentration; consequences of addictive behaviors such as gambling, drugs, or sex used to ward off distressing feelings; or hypochondria, insomnia, irritability, phobias, or obsessive-compulsive disorders (Bacal, 1990). However, from the self psychologist's point of view, underlying all these symptoms is the client's central motive: the search for a selfobject with whom to have experiences that contribute to the development of the client's self.

Regarding clients' potential for change, Kohut was generally optimistic. He believed that, provided that their selfobjects are affectively attuned and empathically responsive, people with disorders of the self are capable of resuming their arrested development. Kohut (1971) referred to *the establishment of selfobject transferences as the client's primary responsibility in therapy*. The transferential relationship demands the client's willingness to allow the therapist to become psychologically important to her, as well as to persevere through the process of empathic failure and repair, which, in turn, allows the reactivation of the client's developmentally thwarted needs and processes.

Kohut viewed selfobject transference as the soil from which therapeutic progress could grow. Stolorow et al. (1987) described transference as "the tidal wave of the past that washes over the present, leaving its unmistakable residues" (p. 28). They also wrote that it refers to all the ways in which the patient's experience of the analytic relationship is shaped by his own psychological structures—by the distinctive, archaically rooted configurations of self and object that unconsciously organize his subjective universe . . . an expression of the universal psychological striving to organize experience and create meanings. (1987, pp. 36, 46)

As such, the client, à la Piaget (1970), *assimilates* the therapist into his existing conceptual structure, shaving off the therapist's uniqueness and perceiving her as fitting the mold of previous selfobjects, rather than modifying his conceptual structure to *accommodate* the uniqueness of the therapist as a separate individual, the latter process being a function of a healthy self.

Selfobject transference involves the reactivation in therapy of those needs that were not met by the client's selfobjects in early life (Kohut & Wolf, 1978). Stolorow et al. (1987) believed selfobject transference is not a type of transference but, rather, a dimension of all transferences.

In self psychotherapy, transference takes one of three primary forms. In *mirroring*, the client tries to elicit approval and affirmation—mirroring of his worth—from the therapist. In *idealizing*, the client idealizes and seeks to merge with the therapist. In *twinship*, the client primarily needs to experience the therapist as someone essentially similar (Kohut, 1984). Whatever the form, when the therapist fails to provide what the client seeks, the client often responds intensely.

Regarding client resistance, Kohut reframed the concept in a very humanistic fashion, as "the principle of the primacy of self preservation" (1984, p. 143):

The so-called defense-resistances are neither defenses nor resistances. Rather, they constitute valuable moves to safeguard the self, however weak and defensive [the self] may be, against destruction and invasion. It is only when we recognize that the patient has no healthier attitude at his disposal than the one he is in fact taking that we can evaluate the significance of defenses and resistances appropriately. (p. 141)

Thus, resistance is viewed as the client's best attempt to protect a fragile self so that this self may grow in the future. Such "resistant" behaviors were perhaps the client's greatest assets in early life. For this reason, self psychologists view resistance as "a welcome indicator that the striving to complete the development of the self had never been totally given up" (Kohut, 1984, p. 209).

Counselor's Role. The primary responsibility of the self-counselor is sustained empathic inquiry into the meaning of the client's experience of the therapeutic (self–selfobject) relationship, which fosters the overarching goal of self psychotherapy: the establishment, strengthening, and/or maintenance of the client's self such that his self–selfobject relationships are relatively mature, realistic, reciprocal, and resilient. The therapist's role in this process is to reparent the client, that is, to permit the client to dwell in and consolidate the transferential relationship, all the while experiencing and communicating consistent empathy to the client. She can communicate her empathy, her caring and understanding, by offering interpretations that mirror the client's point of view as well as offer him insight into the processes at work in his psyche. The therapist's consistent efforts to empathically understand the client offer hope that the client's present and future need not be repetitions of the past and that "the sustaining echo of empathic resonance is indeed available in this world" (Kohut, 1984, p. 78).

Ironically, it is equally necessary that the therapist at times offer misinterpretations. Such misinterpretations are inevitable, for "there is no analyst whose responses are so 'optimal' as to preclude the patient's recurrently experiencing frustrating and hurtful discrepancies between what he is after and what he gets" (Bacal, 1990, p. 258). Although the therapist can expect to misinterpret without intending to do so, when the client reacts to misinterpretations, her intentional response to the client's reaction constitutes the very essence of self psychotherapy. When an empathic rift in an earlier selfobject relationship failed to be repaired, the client's self-development was arrested. If the therapist succeeds in repairing the current empathic rift, the client's self-development will proceed once again. The counselor's responsibility is to acknowledge her very real role in the rift and resume an accurately empathic stance.

Therapists typically find it much easier to remain empathically attuned to a client when that client's disappointment is directed at someone other than the therapist. In the wake of empathic failures by the therapist, the client is likely to either withdraw from or attack the therapist. Such reactions may be clear and overt, such as concrete expressions of blame, criticism, anger, rage, or inordinate appeals for apology or reassurance, or they may be subtle and covert, as when the client briefly breaks eye contact with the therapist, crosses his arms, makes a sarcastic remark or joke, falls silent, or changes the subject. The therapist's responsibility is to remain empathic: to detect that an empathic failure has occurred; to nondefensively acknowledge to the client what she has detected; to acknowledge her error in whatever form, usually a misinterpretation (her very real role in the failure); to understand that any disproportionate intensity in the client's response reflects traumatic residue from past similar situations; and, if and when the rift seems to have been repaired and the selfobject bond reestablished, to offer the latter understanding to the client in the form of an interpretation, making sure to emphasize that only some of the client's response is rooted in the past, while some of it appropriately emerged in response to the therapist's actual failure.

To own her fallibility and to detect and respond constructively to client reactions requires that the therapist have a very strong sense of self. She may feel challenged in this regard because, in allowing the client to be important to her, in allowing herself to care about the client, she has opened herself to her own selfobject transference reactions. Therapists may react with countertransference: feeling her self threatened and responding with some self-defense, such as not noticing or bypassing the client's response; noticing it but failing to take responsibility for her error, perhaps by justifying and insisting on the reasonableness and correctness of her own point of view; withdrawing emotionally from the client, becoming emotionally distant or indifferent, or counterattacking the client with blame or with a subtly critical interpretation. In any of these cases, the therapist has abandoned an empathic disposition, and the potential for self-development from the experience is lost.

The more disordered the client's self, the stronger the therapist's self must be for her to be able to sustain the level of empathy required for the client's self-development. In other words, the therapist must be able to acknowledge her imperfection without loss of self-integrity or self-esteem. In the face of client withdrawal, the therapist must not feel abandoned or must be able to quickly and effectively self-soothe any such feelings. Likewise, in the face of client attacks, the therapist must not feel overwhelmingly threatened by annihilation or loss of self-esteem. Sustained by a strong self, in the wake of an empathic failure, the effective self psychotherapist attends empathically to the client's subjective experience and accepts her role in the failure. She abandons the misinterpretation that led to the failure, admits her mistake, and seeks to understand the client's reaction. Through her ability to rally her empathic resources, the rift in the self–selfobject relationship becomes the very foundation for an even deeper, stronger relationship bond and a strengthening of the client's self. Such occurrences, if handled constructively by the therapist, are blessings in disguise, the essential struggles that result in client self-development, the goal of therapy.

One interesting form of countertransference deserves particular attention: a therapist's rigid beliefs about psychological dynamics. Kohut (1971) urged therapists to resist the

> temptation to squeeze his understanding of the patient into the rigid mold of whatever theoretical preconceptions he may hold, be they Kleinian, Adlerian or, yes, self psychological. . . . [A]n observer needs theories to [help him] observe . . . [but] these theories must be the helpmates of the observer, not his masters. (p. 67)

In Kohut's theory, the most fundamental curative factor is the therapist's empathic attunement to the client; conjecture about the client's psychological dynamics is secondary. Putting herself in the position of experiencing what the disordered client experiences is much like placing one's hand very near a flame. The therapist who cannot take the heat may resort to the use of psychological dynamic constructs to create emotional distance and, thus, defend her own self against the threat of burning up and annihilation. Presumably, the effective self psychotherapist would be aware of the many ways she might manifest countertransference; if she perceived herself engaging in it, she presumably would work through it or, if unable to do so, would seek whatever consultation or even personal psychotherapy she needed to strengthen her own self such that she could resume and maintain an empathic stance with the client.

In summary, the counselor's role in self psychotherapy is to provide the client with a reparenting experience characterized most essentially by sustained empathic attunement. In relationship with a highly self-disordered client, a therapist's ability to maintain and communicate consistent empathy is no easy task (Baçal, 1990). Yet the capacity to empathize with others is an ability that one can develop with sustained practice (Nissim-Sabat, 1989). Effective self psychotherapists undertake this practice to develop what they consider to be their single most important therapeutic skill.

Stages and Techniques. The self–selfobject relationship that forms between the client and the self counselor is truly the medium, the "holding environment," in which the client's self emerges. Although Kohut never explicitly described the physical conditions of the self psychotherapy situation, it appears that, unlike the psychoanalytic situation, Kohut and his client faced each other, seated. The topics the self psychotherapy client and therapist address appear to generally follow a sequence from immediate symptoms and related concerns in the client's life; to the client's history, with particular attention on selfobject relationships; to the nature of the immediate relationship between client and therapist; to the manifestations and resolutions of the client's selfobject transference that is at work in the rift/repair cycle of the client–therapist self–selfobject relationship.

Transference does not occur immediately.

> After an initial period during which his analysand has responded with outside behavioral improvement as well as with a degree of gratitude toward the analyst and his interventions within the psychoanalytic situation, [the analyst] is suddenly confronted with a seemingly ominous worsening of the analysand's condition. Such deterioration is characteristically accompanied by a barrage of reproaches from the side of the analysand that the analysis is ruining him, that the analyst's inept, misguided, bull-in-a-china shop interventions are destroying him. Why is there this period of calm before the storm? Why can the patient at first tolerate the analyst's unavoidable mistakes and errors in empathy only to become suddenly intolerant of them? The answer is simple to the point of triteness: What happens is nothing else but the transference clicking into place. Thus, during the calm before the storm, the analyst and the patient have jointly explored the patient's traumatic past, allied in the shared pursuit of a goal; once the storm breaks loose, however, the analytic situation has *become* the traumatic past and the analyst has *become* the traumatizing selfobject of early life. (Kohut, 1984, pp. 177–178)

In pursuing the sequence of topics from the client's present life to past life to the immediate therapeutic relationship, self psychotherapists repeatedly employ two phases that Kohut explicitly identified: the *understanding* phase and the *explanatory* phase.

The understanding phase involves the counselor's efforts to empathically understand the client's experience and communicate to the client that, to some degree, the therapist has actually experienced the client's inner condition. Some clients do not require a great deal of this. In such cases, the therapist

> can employ the total understanding-explaining sequence from the start. Furthermore, in many instances, either ab initio or later, there is no clear operational separation between the two steps. Even though the division between them remains valid in principle, the actual activity of the analyst combines them or oscillates between them so rapidly that the operational distinction becomes blurred even with respect to a single intervention. But during particular phases of many analyses, especially analyses of certain severely traumatized patients, the understanding phase of treatment must remain the only phase for a long time. (Kohut, 1984, p. 177)

The explanatory phase is actually an expansion and deepening of the understanding phase. Although still necessitating empathy, this phase enlists the therapist's theoretical understanding of psychodynamic processes, especially her comprehension of selfobjects and how they relate to the client's experiences, both in childhood and in the transference. Still residing in a state of empathy, she formulates these understandings into interpretations and offers them to the client. "It bears stressing that the analyst's essential activities in each of [these phases], not only the first one are based on empathy" (Kohut, 1984, p. 176). In addition, the greater the therapist's theoretical understandings regarding psychological dynamics, the more likely it is that her interpretations will be deeply accurate, which provides more "proof" to the client that the counselor understands. Again, however, more important than the objective correctness of interpretations is the manner in which they are communicated: They should be expressions of optimal responsiveness that the client experiences as restoring the cohesion and resilience of his sense of self.

In fact, Kohut believed that even if the therapist's inference about the client's psychological dynamics is incorrect, as long as the therapist also communicates accurate empathy of the client's subjective experience of the (mis)interpretation, the process of interpretation would have a healing effect. So, for example, imagine that therapist and client are walking into a session, and the therapist small-talks the comment, "I see you're wearing bright blue again this week." The client immediately feels defensive and says, "Do you think I should vary my wardrobe more?" The therapist detects that her remark has triggered a transferential reaction. As they sit down, the therapist might respond with genuine empathy, "It seems that you felt criticized by what I said about your clothes. Perhaps you think I made that observation because I found fault with what you were wearing." After processing this occurrence to the point that the client feels understood, the therapist might offer an interpretation: "Perhaps my comment reminded you of your father whom, for as long as you can remember, you experienced as so critical." The part about the father could be wrong; it may, in fact, have been the client's mother who was vigilant and critical regarding the client's wardrobe, a fact of which the counselor had been unaware but that yielded yet another empathic failure. But Kohut believed that the accuracy of the therapist's empathy for the client's feeling criticized, perceiving the therapist as critical, and experiencing some residual reaction to perceived criticism from the past, would override the erroneous inference about the father. The client could correct the therapist regarding that specific point, to which the effective therapist would respond with something like, "I see. It was your mother by whom you felt so criticized. I was mistaken in attributing your reaction to your relationship with your father. Now I see it was your mother."

Then, client and therapist could explore the emotional residue from the client's relationship with his mother and how it was activated by the therapist's original remark. When the therapist perceived the client to be feeling quite understood and the empathic bond reestablished, the therapist could reaffirm that her intention was actually to observe and affirm a client preference rather than find fault with a client choice. Assuming the client's ability, unobstructed by further transference, to truly grasp and believe the counselor's self-described motive, the client would take a step in accommodating into his self a previously unaccommodated experience: "When people who are important to me make observations about me, they sometimes are empathizing rather than criticizing."

From a self psychotherapy viewpoint, this piece of therapeutic progress occurred despite the therapist's erroneous interpretation. Rather, the progress occurred because of all the aforementioned steps the therapist took in responding to the client's experience of the (mis)interpretation. Kohut believed that each time the client receives an interpretation or other communication that does not feel right, he experiences anxiety regarding whether or not the therapist, unlike previous selfobjects, will recognize the empathic failure and process it with the client. By recognizing and processing it, the therapist transforms a potential retraumatization into a "development-enhancing structure-building optimal frustration" (Kohut, 1984, p. 207). Kohut wrote that such failures occur hundreds of times in good therapy, with each attended-to failure resulting in enhanced resiliency and the firming of client self structure and self-esteem:

> Whether this pivotal transference is a mirror transference, an alter ego transference, or an idealizing transference, it is the repetition of the two-step interventions of the analyst, the experience, over and over again, of understanding followed by explaining, that leads to structure building via transmuting internalizations. (Kohut, 1984, p. 206)

It might be said that this process, which is central to self psychotherapy, is not merely a corrective emotional experience, but a corrective selfobject experience.

Kohut (1984) described his own experience of this process in an example of a client with whom Kohut cancelled several appointments in a short space of time due to several trips. When they finally had a session, the client expressed strong emotional distress, to which Kohut responded prematurely, before he had succeeded in fully empathizing with the client, with several interpretations. Kohut continued,

> The patient, as I finally grasped, insisted, and had a right to insist, that I learn to see things exclusively in *his* way and not at all in *my* way. . . . [T]he content of *all* my various interpretations had been cognitively correct but incomplete in a decisive direction. The patient had indeed reacted to my having been away. . . . What I had not seen, however, was that the patient had felt additionally traumatized by the feeling that all these explanations on my part came only from the outside; that I did not fully feel what he felt, that I gave him words but not real understanding, and that I thereby repeated the essential trauma of his early life. To hammer away at the analysand's transference distortions brings no results; it only confirms the analysand's conviction that the analyst is as dogmatic, as utterly sure of himself, as walled off in the self-righteousness of a distorted view as the pathogenic parents (or other selfobject) had been. Only the analyst's continuing sincere acceptance of the patient's reproaches as (psychologically) realistic, followed by a prolonged (and ultimately successful) attempt to look into himself and remove the inner barriers that stand in the way of his empathic grasp of the patient, ultimately have a chance to turn the tide. (p. 182)

For Kohut, this counselor process was central to psychotherapy, and he added that, "if some of my colleagues will say at this juncture that this is not analysis—so be it. My inclination is to respond with the old adage that they should get out of the kitchen if they cannot stand the heat" (p. 183).

Self counselors will offer interpretations about a client's resistance, although they also acknowledge their own role in the matter. Like transference, resistance involves the client's organization of experience, the fears and expectations that one's needs and emotions will be met by the therapist in a manner similar to the traumatic responses of one's early selfobjects (Bacal, 1990; Kohut, 1984; Stolorow et al., 1987). Following this conceptualization, resistance is seen as the result of the client's *not* experiencing the therapist as a selfobject. Therefore, resistance is not merely an intrapsychic function of the client, but rather, a product of the intersubjective field between client and counselor, with the counselor's actions always playing a role (Stolorow et al., 1987). Unless the therapist is able to empathically identify the client's sense of impending fear or danger, which results in the client's felt need to enlist resistance, analysis of resistance will be therapeutically useless. Conversely, the client's feeling understood in a moment of great fear reestablishes the self–selfobject bond and creates the image of an object (the therapist) that is *not* a repetition of the client's past parental imagos. Stolorow et al. (1987) summarized:

> Among the most noxious of early pathogenic situations are those in which a child's attempts to communicate an experience of being psychologically injured or undermined by a caregiver result in a prolonged disruption of the vitally needed tie. When the child consistently is unable to communicate such experiences without perceiving that he is damaging or unwelcome to the caregiver, a watershed in the relationship occurs whereby a painful inner conflict becomes structuralized. It is this pathogenic process that is repeated in [analysis when the analyst tells the patient he is resistant]. . . . Such ideas generally occur to an analyst when his own feeling of well-being is threatened by the patient's expressions, and interpretations of resistance under these circumstance serve primarily to reconstitute the analyst's own sense of self. (pp. 51–52)

In conclusion, the essence of the self psychotherapeutic process occurs in two phases: understanding and explanation. The therapist's repeated ability, in the wake of empathic failure, to take responsibility for her errors and to offer accurate empathic understanding and interpretation of the client's psychological dynamics, creates the conditions for the client's self-development through transmuting internalization.

CONTRIBUTIONS AND LIMITATIONS

Interface with Recent Developments in the Mental Health Field

The Effectiveness of Psychotherapy.   Psychodynamic research has focused more on developmental issues than on psychotherapy outcomes. From the pioneering research of Mahler et al. (1975) on the separation-individuation process to a host of analytic researchers (Basch, 1985; Demos, 1987; Stern, 1985) who studied patterns of early infant–parent interactions, it seems clear that *the intense emotions that infants experience in relationship with their caregivers are primary and pervasive organizers of self-experience* (Stolorow et al., 1987). In fact, experimental research with many different species has revealed that "even mild forms of trauma may cause significant biochemical and behavioral changes. . . . This experiment confirms the psychoanalytic insight that disturbances in early development can produce delayed psychopathological changes" (Gabbard, 1999, p. 4). Kohut's reformulations of transference and resistance as activities of self-organization also interfaces well with developmental research in cognitive psychology and constructivism (Piaget, 1977; Mahoney, 2002).

Psychoanalytic outcome research has often involved case studies, which can be traced to Freud's methods (Bornstein & Masling, 1994). Unfortunately, this information is merely anecdotal. The lack of experimental outcome studies might be due to the relative newness of self psychology, the absence of a manual defining its method, and its originally long-term nature, all of which make research more difficult.

However, research corroborating the import of the therapeutic alliance in positive outcomes is indeed relevant to Kohut's concept of the self–selfobject relationship between client and counselor. Moreover, findings from the Vanderbilt I and II process/outcome studies (Strupp & Hadly, 1979) offer "evidence that regardless of how much 'warmth', 'friendliness', and 'support' may be present, if expressions of hostility (direct or indirect) are not effectively handled, there will be repercussions on the development of a positive therapeutic alliance and on outcome" (p. 1129). This is exactly the issue Kohut (1971, 1977, 1984) addressed in his admonishment that therapists attend to and repair disturbances in the self–selfobject bond when clients react with hostility or even rage to the therapist's empathic failures.

Reports that clients tend to do better in therapy with therapists perceived as similar to them has corroborated Kohut's positing of the importance of twinship needs. Kegan (1982), whose seminal developmental research has awed many mental health professionals, wrote that "this special kind of empathy [á la Rogers and Kohut] is crucial at every phase in the lifespan because it is actually intrinsic to the process by which we develop" (p. viii). Finally, research by Martignetti (1998) found statistically significant correlations "between authoritarian fathering and the need to idealize" (p. 134), which corroborates Kohut's theory of the idealizing selfobject need and the corresponding idealizing transference.

Kohut probably would concur with Asay and Lambert (1999) regarding the factors in positive psychotherapeutic outcome. Self-psychological theory accounts for how the quality of the therapeutic relationship, specific interventions, extratherapeutic factors, and the client's expectations about therapy all play a role in positive outcome. However, Kohut probably would have viewed somewhat differently the relative proportions of these factors, believing that an exquisitely empathic therapeutic relationship, in which the therapist succeeds in maintaining empathy even in the face of extratherapeutic factors such as severe and chronic pathology, can overcome the potentially therapeutically detrimental effects of those latter factors.

The Nature/Nurture Question. Kohut (1984; Kohut & Wolf, 1978) posited that the self emerges from the interaction between the child's innate or genetic potentials and the empathic attunement of the child's selfobject environment, though he emphasized the influence of the familial environment over genetics. However, the reader should note that Kohut is referring to influences on the *self* (a *core* construct pertaining to a person's experience of relatively enduring identity, coherence, resilience, and feelings of worth), *not* to temperament or personality traits such as shyness, activity level, intelligence quotient (IQ), dominance, fretfulness, impulsivity, and so forth (Efran, Greene, & Gordon, 1998; Rowe, 1990).

Nonetheless, Kohut acknowledged that constitutionally inherited factors significantly affect a child's potential to develop selfobject relationships and, thus, a healthy self. Usually, infants' brains are prewired to cry, look for faces, and so forth; with subsequent neurological development, the baby will smile and coo, all of which function to encourage and enhance selfobject relations (Horowitz, 1988). If something is wired differently, caretakers may fail to respond as selfobjects. Moreover, a child's temperament, which is genetically influenced, most likely affects his ability to establish selfobject relationships; to evoke, maintain, and tolerate different types and intensities of emotional arousal; and to negotiate self-object failures. Both of these cases exemplify a conclusion offered by genetic researchers: that caregiver behavior may partly be the result, rather than the cause, of a child's genetically predisposed behavior, a kind of "reverse causality" (Rowe, 1990, p. 609). Finally, Kohut (1971) stated that parents' own inherited psychological propensities had a profound impact on their ability to effectively serve as selfobjects. Thus, Kohut (1984) did, both directly and indirectly, acknowledge a role of genetics in the unfolding development of the self, and he also acknowledged its influence to be far more complex than he was able to understand entirely.

Pharmacotherapy. The only mention Kohut made in this regard was to a case of a client with agoraphobia. He noted how tricyclic medication functioned as the precursor to psychological structure by providing the calming and anxiety-curbing required for the client's self to emerge (Kohut, 1984). However, Baker (1991), one of the most outspoken current self psychologists, stated more broadly that "careful assessment of possible biological factors is essential. Combined psychopharmacological and psychotherapeutic interventions may be ideal" (p. 297).

Managed Care and Brief Therapy. Kohut's psychotherapeutic approach tended to be long enough for transference to develop and for empathic failures and reparations to recur many, many times. However, Crits-Christoph, Barber, and Kurcias (1991) present nine brief psychodynamic shorter term self-psychological approaches to therapy that point out that the primary difference between brief and long-term therapy is that the former gives equal attention to the management of specific client concerns as it does to addressing the client's self–selfobject interactions both outside of and within counseling sessions. Thus, although Kohut's form of therapy was largely incompatible with current demands of managed care, Baker's approach is compatible. Another excellent form of brief therapy that incorporates self psychology is that of Levenson (1995).

Diversity Issues. With regard to diversity issues, Kohut made significant strides beyond psychoanalysis in honoring each client's unique experience. Because self psychology adheres to the constructivist and relativist notions that all meaning requires interpretation, and all interpretation requires an understanding of the cultural context in which meaning is being sought, it avoids many of the cultural biases of some other therapies. Engaging in the "experience near" approach, the self psychotherapist constantly strives to understand and experience what it is like to be a particular client, rather than trying to fit the client into the preexisting conceptual structures. This substantially frees the therapist from cultural preconceptions.

Altman (1996) proposed that the psychoanalytic model, in which one person's subjective experience is the focus of another person's supposedly objective analysis, is limited in its capacity to accommodate racial, cultural, or socioeconomic differences. He suggested that such differences could be adequately understood only by a two- or three-person relational model in which all participants' subjectivity is acknowledged and engaged. Kohut's self psychology and Atwood and Stolorow's (1984) intersubjective approach, an expansion of self psychology, are examples of the latter model.

Roland (1996) explored issues of the universality and variability in the construct of the self. He brought to attention the Pakistani we-self, an experiential aspect of the sense of self that includes inner representations of their extended family and community. Likewise, Takeo Doi's psychoanalytic work highlighted various aspects of dependency relationships (amae), public self (omote), and private self (ura) in Japanese culture that are not recognized by psychoanalytic theory (Roland, 1996). Roland concluded that a new psychoanalytic paradigm is needed and posited the following constructs as universal:

> developmental stages, selfobject relationships, self and object representations, self-identity, internal object world, affects and drives, transference, resistance, and dream-analysis, among others. One must then decontextualize them of their current Northern European/North American content and forms—the particular variability they are accorded by psychoanalytic theory—and then proceed to recontextualize them using the clinical data of persons from significantly or radically different cultures. (p. 86)

Kohut's reformulations also have relevance for *gender issues*. His redefinition of psychological health as a mature dependence on selfobject relationships reduces the stigma that has been associated with women's emphasis on relationship and communion, as opposed to men's emphasis on autonomy and agency (Chodorow, 1978; Gilligan, 1982; Jordan, Kaplan, Miller, Stiver, & Surrey, 1991). Whereas traditional analytic theory is rooted in the Western value of individualism and the "secularized Protestant values of independence and self-reliance" (Roland 1996, p. 80), the relational primacy of object relations theory and self psychology "lessens the press for the independent, internally structured adult" (Jordan et al., 1991, p. 2). Roland went so far as to assert that, from a self psychology point of view, the values of extreme American individualism and mobility are not ideals for which people should strive but actually pathogenic, contributing to problematic selfobject relationships and instability of the self.

Although Kohut never directly pathologized *homosexuality* as a disorder demanding treatment, he did counsel individuals who sought counseling because they were disturbed by their homosexuality. Moreover, he clearly viewed clients' homosexuality not as a primary disorder, but as a secondary manifestation of a narcissistic/self disorder and of far less concern than tendencies toward depression, sensitivity to criticism, lacking zest, and so forth (Kohut, 1971). In fact, in his final book, Kohut (1984) wrote that homosexuality, as well as sibling rivalry, voyeurism, mother attachment, and so forth, should be viewed as a healthy psychic activity because it functions to safeguard the self's future growth.

Spirituality. Kohut (1971) wrote that "the relationship between the true believer and his God . . . corresponds to the ancient omnipotent self-object, the idealized parent imago" (p. 106). In this way, he reduced mere belief in God, which is a form of *legitimate religion*—which is in contrast to *authentic religion*, which involves not belief, but contemplative and direct experience of God (Wilber, 1999, vol. 3)—to the self's projection of an ideal selfobject.

It is quite noteworthy that the vast majority of transpersonal and integral theorists, those who theorize a spiritual domain in humans that transcends the ego or self, draw heavily from psychodynamic theories such as object relations and self psychology. In fact, Boorstein (1997) described at length how self psychology interfaces with both Buddhist meditation and the Christian-based practices. Kohut's work is infused throughout with Boorstein's transpersonal approach to psychotherapy.

Affirming both Kohutian and transpersonal contentions regarding spirituality, research suggests that one's level of object relations development is positively correlated with one's image of God and that both positively correlate with spiritual maturity (Hall & Brokaw, 1995; Magaletta, 1996; McDargh, 1986). Self psychology and object relations theories posit that one's relations with other people constitute the foundation of one's experience. The highest realms of human experience and development, as reported in the perennial philosophy—the distillation of commonalities of the world's major spiritual traditions—are comprehensible only from a perspective that attends to the experience of the self's relation to others and, ultimately, to the self's identity as spirit (Wilber, 2000). This psychological perspective can be seen among contemporary spiritual teachers: "the ego that is to be transcended exists only in the context of relations. . . . [T]he most fundamental [spiritual] disciplines, are those in the domain of relations" (Avabhasa, 1993, p. 12).

Technical Eclecticism. Self psychology is particularly fertile with regards to the opportunities it affords relative to eclecticism. Since Kohut's death, self psychology has become increasingly cognitive and constuctivist in flavor, especially in its perspective on resistance and transference as pervasive ways people construct and organize their experience. The similarities between Kohut's therapeutic approach and the humanism of Rogers is also, hopefully, readily apparent. Finally, self psychology interfaces extremely elegantly with integral and transpersonal approaches to counseling, both in its concern for what may be the most core of all psychological constructs, the self, and also in its devotion to understanding how early developmental difficulties affect subsequent self-development.

DSM-IV-TR Diagnosis. Kohut (1971) responded to the question of how to differentiate narcissistic disorders from borderline and psychotic conditions by writing that "my approach in this area does not conform with the traditional medical aim of achieving a clinical diagnosis in which a disease entity is identified by clusters of recurring manifestations" (pp. 15–16). Although he did not favor diagnostic labels, he did attend to diagnostic *levels* of structural development. For instance, in the psychoses and borderline conditions, a nuclear self has not been established. However, Kohut (1984) also wrote that, "to my mind, the terms 'psychosis' and 'borderline state' simply refer to the fact that we are dealing with states of prepsychological chaos which the empathic instrument of the observer is unable to comprehend" (p. 9). In other words, when a client's deficit of self is so severe that a therapist cannot empathically grasp it, the therapist's tendency may be to label the client "psychotic" or "borderline" and thus untreatable. Clearly, this label expresses and/or interferes with the therapist's willingness to take the heat of empathizing with profound intrapsychic chaos and thus aborts any potential therapy. Presumably, Kohut would not have objected to the use of DSM-IV diagnosis for the purposes of third party payment as long as the diagnosis did not undermine the therapist's willingness to sustain empathy for the client's ongoing experience.

Weaknesses of the Theory

One weakness of self psychology is that, in formulating it, Kohut failed to acknowledge and integrate the ideas of predecessors, ideas from which his own theory might be construed as having originated. These include Fairbairn's positing of drives not as primary, but as manifestations of relational disturbances; Winnicot's "good enough mother" and "holding environment," both of which point to the profound influence of the familial environment on development and pathology; and Mahler's work on separation and individuation. Kohut has been repeatedly criticized for such, and other, omissions. He both quasi-apologized for and justified his method:

> Let me emphasize initially that my continuing lack of integration of their
> contributions with mine is not due to any lack of respect . . . but to the
> nature of the task that I have set for myself . . . an attempt to struggle
> toward greater clarity. . . . [M]y focus is not on scholarly completeness; it
> is directed to the direct observation of clinical phenomena and the con-
> struction of new formulations that would accommodate my observations.
> (Kohut, 1977, pp. xx–xxi)

A second weakness of his theory involves Kohut's use of the term and
concept of *restoration*. Kohut posited that humans are born whole, hence the
notion of the restoration of the self through psychotherapy. It is one thing to
view newborns as full of potential, which Kohut did, and quite another to
posit that they are born whole and complete. The latter scenario would suggest that the structure of the self is already established at birth, which Kohut
surely would not have argued. Moreover, nowhere else in nature does one
encounter a developmental sequence that begins with wholeness and is followed by a condition requiring restoration. The concept of restoration of the
self, therefore, appears to be internally inconsistent with the bulk of Kohut's
theory. Perhaps a more accurate, though less elegant, phrasing would be "re-
sumption of the self's development."

A third weakness, though arguable, is the view of some mental health
professionals that Kohut focused his attention too narrowly on narcissistic
issues. In so doing, they say, he neglected the full spectrum of development
(Gedo, 1989).

Finally, Stolorow et al. (1987) cited a weakness in the form of confusion
regarding the concept of the self as both a person and a psychic structure.
They gave an example of a typical self psychology sentence: "The fragmented
self strives to restore its cohesion" (p. 18). They pointed out that the "self" in
this sentence refers to both a psychic structure that has fragmented (after all,
the person has not fragmented), and an active agent, the person, striving to
organize its experience. They recommend restricting the use of "self" to psychic structure and function as the organization of experience and using "person" for the agent initiating actions. They would reword the sentence thus:
"The person whose self-experience is becoming fragmented strives to restore
his sense of self-cohesion" (Stolorow et al., 1987, p. 19).

Distinguishing Additions to Counseling
and Psychotherapy

Kohut (1984) wrote that his work "has supplied analysis with new theories
which broaden and deepen the field of empathic perception" (p. 175). His
primary distinguishing contributions to the field of psychology and psychotherapy were his *reformulations of narcissism*; his description of the formation

of psychic structure via *transmuting internalization*; the concept of *selfobjects* and the three *selfobject transferences*; and recognizing the profound importance of *empathy* and the *centrality of the client's self-experience*. With these four primary contributions, Kohut made possible the treatment of people suffering from severe developmental arrests.

Kohut (1971) radically *redefined narcissism* not by the object or target of the drive (à la Freud) but rather *by the nature or quality of the relationship to the (self)object*. Thus, narcissism is a developmental line that one never outgrows, much like cognitive or moral lines of development. Within this line, one's mode of narcissism develops from archaic, absolute, desperate demands on selfobjects to more mature, differentiated, flexible, and resilient relationships with selfobjects. Kohut's radical reformulation not only emphasized the developmental potentials latent in one's narcissistic (selfobject) transferences, but also brought about a reevaluation of Western culture's emphasis on autonomy and what constitutes psychological health.

The concepts of selfobjects and selfobject transferences allow clients previously considered untreatable to be understood and thus treated therapeutically. The simple realization that a client may experience a counselor's mere presence as a calming and esteeming component of the client's self-organization can forever alter one's view of therapy (Stolorow et al., 1987). Kohut and subsequent self psychologists revisioned many psychotherapeutic phenomena in a kind of positive reframe. Transference was no longer seen as an obstruction to therapeutic work but as the foundation for it. Clients' intense emotional reactions were seen not merely as symptoms of psychopathology but as prime therapeutic material and opportunities for client self-development.

For Kohut, consistent empathic inquiry replaced insight as the primary goal of analysis. The relinquishment of preexisting beliefs that makes such inquiry possible includes relinquishment of cultural preconceptions. This same process of inquiry characterized Kohut's process of theory development, rendering his theoretical framework

> exquisitely self-reflexive and potentially self-corrective . . . [T]he consistent application of the empathic-introspective mode not only to the psychological phenomena being studied but also to the theoretical ideas that guide our observations provides us with an ongoing basis for critically evaluating, refining, expanding, and, when necessary, discarding these theoretical constructs. (Stolorow et al., 1987, p. 17)

In other words, self psychology includes itself in the domain under investigation, thus preventing its adherents from idealizing it as a final, all-encompassing theory. "Kohut's ultimate legacy to his followers is therefore likely to be this warning from the grave not to congeal his writings into self-psychological dogma" (Gedo, 1989, p. 419).

CURRENT STATUS

Stolorow, Atwood, and Orange (1999) portrayed Kohut as "a pivotal transitional figure in the development of a post-Cartesian, fully contextual psychoanalytic psychology" (p. 381). Toward the end of his life, Kohut acknowledged that although his investigations and reformulations were significant, they "should be considered to be a progress report about the present state of a step in the evolution of psychoanalysis that is itself only in its very beginning" (Kohut & Wolf, 1978, p. 413). Moreover, Kohut (1984) wrote that

> Much remains to be done; we need investigations of the special needs of adolescents and the elderly, for example . . . [and of] those shifts to a new cultural milieu that deprive a person of his "cultural selfobjects," during his mature years or when he has to deal with debilitating illness, or the confrontation with death. (p. 194)

Self psychology is a relatively young discipline with many adherents carrying forward its flame. Since 1985, *The Progress in Self Psychology* series has published a volume each year. These edited books discuss the cutting edge of self psychology, which continues to be expanded, refined, and articulated. Such work has tightened Kohut's theoretical loose ends, of which there were few. Individuals like Goldberg, Stolorow and Atwood, Baker, Bacal and Detrick, among others, are breaking new ground—toward investigations of objects other than selfobjects, for example (Goldberg, 1989). The intersubjective approach of Stolorow et al. (1987) is an expansion of Kohut's self psychology and demonstrates how theorists' and therapists' own subjective worlds profoundly influence their experiences and understandings of others.

As stated at the beginning of this chapter, a 1990 survey revealed that psychodynamic theories are the most frequently named exclusive or primary guiding theories among mental health professionals (Jensen et al., 1990). It is likely that self psychology, in particular, provides a therapeutic framework for this majority of psychotherapists. Perhaps more than any other, this information conveys most clearly the current status of self psychology.

SUMMARY

For Kohut, the reason our finiteness and death were not to be equated with meaninglessness and despair is that we can empathize with each other's subjective experience (Nissim-Sabat, 1989). Kohut did far more than merely rejuvenate and expand psychoanalytic theory. With his emphasis on the centrality of empathy, he brought the counselor's humanity into the therapy room.

"If one will only listen," wrote Goldberg (1989), "what Kohut and self psychology have to say is very hard to ignore" (p. xviii). Regardless of whether one chooses a self-psychological orientation or not, counselors will better serve their clients if they are at least aware of Kohut's key contributions, especially how counselors serve as selfobjects for their clients. Kohut formulated a theory that both underscores the need for empathy and enhances our capacity to empathically access our clients' subjective experiences in more of their rich diversity. He also knew that his work had uncovered more questions than it answered. He therefore created an integrating framework capable of accounting for both clinical phenomena and self psychology itself (Stolorow et al., 1999). His approach is an important contribution to the continuing human search for self understanding and the realization of human potential.

RECOMMENDED RESOURCES

Print

Kohut, H. (1971). *The analysis of the self.* New York: International Universities Press; and Kohut, H. (1977). *The restoration of the self.* New York: International Universities Press. Good primary source readings give a comprehensive foundation to the theory. Somewhat of a dense read, but worth the theoretical information.

Stolorow, R. D., Brandchaft, B., & Atwood, G. E. (1987). *Psychoanalytic treatment: An intersubjective approach.* Hillsdale, NJ: The Analytic Press. Good discussion of the similarities and differences in the various psychoanalytic/psychodynamic approaches.

St. Clair, M. (2000). *Object relations and self psychology: An introduction* (3rd ed.). Pacific Grove, CA: Brooks/Cole. Excellent for the beginning counselor who is new to the theory. Good explanation of concepts and good case illustrations.

Websites

www.selfpsychology.org: This page provide useful information including definitions of relevant concepts and a fairly comprehensive bibliography separated by special topics. Information about conferences is also available.

REFERENCES

Akhtar, S. (1989). In D. W. Detrick & S. P. Detrick (Eds.), *Self psychology: Comparisons and contrasts*. Hillsdale, NJ: The Analytic Press.

Altman, N. (1996). The accommodation of diversity in psychoanalysis. In R. M. P. Foster, M. Moskowitz, & R. A. Javier (Eds.), *Reaching across boundaries of culture and class: Widening the scope of psychotherapy* (pp. 195–209). Northvale, NJ: Jason Aronson.

American Psychiatric Association. (2000). *Diagnostic and statistical manual of disorders* (4th ed., text rev.). Washington, DC: American Psychiatric Association.

Asay, T., & Lambert, M. J. (1999). The empirical case for the common factors in therapy: Quantitative findings. In M. A. Hubble, B. L. Duncan, & S. D. Miller (Eds.), *The heart and soul of change* (pp. 23–55). Washington, DC: APA.

Atwood, G. E., & Stolorow, R. D. (1984). *Structures of subjectivity: Explorations in psycho-analytic phenomenology*. Hillsdale, NJ: The Analytic Press.

Avabhasa, D. (1993). *The incarnation of love*. Clearlake: The Dawn Horse Press.

Bacal, H. (1990). Heinz Kohut. In H. A. Bacal & K. M. Newman (Eds.), *Theories of object relations: Bridges to self psychology* (pp. 240–252). New York: Columbia University Press.

Baker, H., & Baker, M. (1987). Heinz Kohut's self psychology: An overview. *The American Journal of Psychiatry, 144*(1), 1–9.

Basch, M. (1985). Interpretation: Toward a developmental model. In A. Goldberg (Ed.), *Progress in self psychology, vol. 1* (pp. 33–42). New York: The Guilford Press.

Bellak, L., Hurvich, M., & Gediman, H. K. (1973). *Ego functions in schizophrenics, neurot-ics, and normals: A systematic study of conceptual, diagnostic, and therapeutic aspects*. New York: Wiley.

Boorstein, S. (1997). *Clinical studies in transpersonal psychotherapy*. New York: State University of New York Press.

Bornstein, R. F., & Masling, J. M. (1994). Introduction: From the consulting room to the laboratory: Clinical evidence, empirical evidence, and the heuristic value of object relations theory. In J. M. Masling & R. F. Bornstein (Eds.), *Empirical studies of psychoanlalytic theories: Volume 5. Empirical perspectives on object relations theory*. Washington, DC: American Psychological Association.

Chodorow, N. (1978). *The reproduction of mothering*. Berkeley: University of California Press.

Crits-Cristoph, P., Barber, J. P., & Kurcias, J. S. (1991). Comparison of the brief dynamic therapies. In P. Crits-Cristoph & J. P. Barber (Eds.), *Handbook of short-term dynamic psychotherapy*. New York: Basic Books.

Demos, E. V. (1987). Affect and the development of the self. In A. Goldberg (Ed.), *Frontiers in self psychology* (pp. 27–53). Hillsdale, NY: Yale University Press.

Efran, J., Greene, M., & Gordon, D. (1998). Lessons of the new genetics: Finding the right fit for our clients. *Networker*, 27–41.

Freud, A. (1936). *The ego and the mechanisms of defense*. New York: International Universities Press.

Gabbard, G. O. (1999). Psychodynamic therapy in an age of neuroscience. *The Harvard Mental Health Newsletter*. January, pp. 7–12.

Gedo, J. E. (1989). In D. W. Detrick & S. P. Detrick (Eds.), *Self psychology: Comparisons and contrasts*. Hillsdale, NJ: The Analytic Press.

Gilligan, C (1982). *In a different voice: Psychological theory and women's development.* Cambridge, MA: Harvard University Press.

Goldberg, A. (1989). In D. W. Detrick & S. P. Detrick (Eds.), *Self psychology: Comparisons and contrasts.* Hillsdale, NJ: The Analytic Press.

Gomez, L. (1997). An introduction to object relations. New York: New York University Press.

Greenberg, J. R., & Mitchell, S. A. (1983). *Object relations in psychoanalytic theory.* Cambridge, MA: Harvard University Press.

Hall, T. W., & Brokaw, B. F. (1995). The relationship of spiritual maturity to level of object relations development and God image. *Pastoral Psychology, 43*(6), 373–391.

Horowitz, M. J. (1988). *Introduction to psychodynamics: A new synthesis.* New York: Basic Books.

Horowitz, M. J. (1991). In P. Crits-Cristoph & J. P. Barber (Eds.), *Handbook of short-term dynamic psychotherapy.* New York: Basic Books.

Jensen, J. P., Bergin, A. E., & Greaves, D. W. (1990). The meaning of eclecticism: New survey and analysis of components. *Professional Psychology: Research and Practice, 21*(2), 124–130.

Jordan, J. V., Kaplan, A. G., Miller, J. B., Stiver, I. P., & Surrey, J. L. (1991). *Women's growth in connection: Writings from the Stone Center.* New York: The Guilford Press.

Kahn, E. (1989). In D. W. Detrick & S. P. Detrick (Eds.), *Self psychology: Comparisons and contrasts.* Hillsdale, NJ: The Analytic Press.

Kegan, R. (1982). *The evolving self: Problem and process in human development.* Cambridge, MA: Harvard University Press.

Kernberg, O. (1975). *Borderline conditions and pathological narcissism.* New York: Jason Aronson.

Klein. M. (1948). *Contributions to psycho-analysis 1921–1945.* London: Hogarth Press.

Kohut, H. (1971). *The analysis of the self.* New York: International Universities Press.

Kohut, H. (1977). *The restoration of the self.* New York: International Universities Press.

Kohut, H. (1979). The two analyses of Mr. Z. *International Journal of Psychoanalysis, 60,* 3–27.

Kohut, H. (1982). Introspection, empathy, and the semi-circle of mental health. *International Journal of Psychoanalysis, 63,* 394–407.

Kohut, H. (1984). *How does psychoanalysis cure?* Chicago: University of Chicago Press.

Kohut, H., & Wolf, E. (1978). The disorders of the self and their treatment: An outline. *International Journal of Psychoanalysis, 59,* 413–425.

Kriegman, D., & Solomon, L. (1985). Cult groups and the narcissistic personality: The offer to heal defects in the self. *International Journal of Group Psychotherapy, 35,* 239–261.

Levenson, H. (1995). *Time-limited dynamic psychotherapy.* New York: Basic Books.

Magaletta, P. R. (1996). An object relations paradigm for spiritual development with highlights from Mertons's spiritual journey. *Pastoral Psychology, 45*(1), 21–28.

Mahler, M. S., Pine, F., & Bergman, A (1975). *The psychological birth of the human infant: Symbiosis and individuation.* New York: Basic Books.

Mahoney, M. (2002). Constructivism and positive psychology. In S. J. Lopez (Ed.), *Handbook of positive psychology* (pp. 745–750). London: Oxford University Press.

Martignetti, C. (1998). Gurus and devotees: Guides or gods? Pathology or faith? *Pastoral Psychology, 47*(2), 127–144.

Masek, R. J. (1989). In D. W. Detrick & S. P. Detrick (Eds.), *Self psychology: Comparisons and contrasts.* Hillsdale, NJ: The Analytic Press.

McDargh, J. (1986). God, mother and me: An object relational perspective on religious material. *Pastoral Psychology, 34,* 251–263.

McWilliams, N. (1994). *Psychoanalytic diagnosis: Understanding personality structure in the clinical process.* New York: Guilford.

Nissim-Sabat, M. (1989). Kohut and Husserl: The empathic bond. In D. W. Detrick & S. P. Detrick (Eds.), *Self psychology: Comparisons and contrasts.* Hillsdale, NJ: The Analytic Press.

Perry, S., Cooper, A., & Michels, R. (1986). The psychodynamic formulation: Its purpose, structure, and clinical application. *The American Journal of Psychiatry, 144*(5), 543–550.

Piaget, J. (1970). *The child's conception of movement and speed.* (G. T. Holloway & M. J. MacKenzie, Trans.). New York: Basic Books.

Roland, A. (1996). How universal is the psychoanalytic self? In R. M. P. Foster, M. Moskowitz, & R. A. Javier (Eds.), *Reaching across boundaries of culture and class: Widening the scope of psychotherapy.* Northvale, NJ: Jason Aronson.

Rowe, D. (1990). As the twig is bent? The myth of child-rearing influences on personality development. *Journal of Counseling and Development 68*(3), 606–611.

St. Clair, M. (2000). *Object relations and self psychology: An introduction* (3rd ed.). Pacific Grove, CA: Brooks/Cole.

Stern, D. (1985). *The interpersonal world of the infant.* New York: Basic Books.

Stolorow, R. D., Brandchaft, B., & Atwood, G. E. (1987). *Psychoanalytic treatment: An intersubjective approach.* Hillsdale, NJ: The Analytic Press.

Stolorow, R. D., Atwood, G. E., & Orange, D. M. (1999). Kohut and contextualism: Toward a post-Cartesian psychoanalytic theory. *Psychoanalytic Psychology, 16*(3), 380–388.

Strauss, G. D., Yager, J., & Strauss, G. E. (1984). The cutting edge in psychiatry. *The American Journal of Psychiatry, 141*(1), 38–43.

Strozier, C. (1985). Glimpses of a life: Heinz Kohut. In A. Goldberg, *Progress in self psychology. Volume one* (pp. 3–12). New York: Guilford.

Strupp, H. H., & Hadley, S. W. (1979). Specific versus nonspecific factors in psychotherapy: A controlled study of outcome. *Archives of General Psychiatry, 36,* 1125–1136.

Ursano, R., Sonnenberg, S., & Lazar, S. (1998). *Psychodynamic psychotherapy: Principles and techniques in the era of managed care.* Washington DC: American Psychiatric Press.

Wilber, K. (1999). *The collected works of Ken Wilber* (vols. 1–4). Boston: Shambhala.

Wilber, K. (2000). *The collected works of Ken Wilber* (vols. 5–8). Boston: Shambhala.

CHAPTER 4

ADLERIAN COUNSELING/ INDIVIDUAL PSYCHOLOGY

BACKGROUND OF THE THEORY

Historical Context and Founder's Biographical Overview

Born in Vienna, Austria on February 7, 1870, Alfred Adler was the second of six children born to Jewish parents. Adler's childhood was filled with episodes of serious health issues and interactions with death. At age 3, his younger brother died of pneumonia while young Adler was in the room. At age 5, Adler almost succumbed to pneumonia and later recollected hearing the physician remark on his slim chance for survival. Although he did survive, Adler was plagued with numerous health problems and was even run over in the street on more than one occasion. Despite these challenges, Adler persevered and channeled his life experiences into later ideas of compensation, organ inferiority, and courage. The medical problems also seemed to prompt a striving to overcome death, which could have led him to pursue and eventually receive his medical degree in 1895.

Adler's first practice, as a general practitioner, was in an office near a Viennese amusement park. His patients consisted primarily of the park's artists and performers, and Adler was impressed with their individual areas of competence despite their social status and histories of childhood physical and emotional obstacles. Perhaps Adler recognized in them the importance of compensation that he had experienced while growing up.

In 1902, after Adler publicly defended some of Freud's ideas, Freud invited him to join a group that met weekly to discuss new ideas in psychology. Adler attended and became an active and vocal member of the group, mainly using the forum to develop and debate his emerging ideas of the human condition. Five years later, in 1907, Adler published *Organ Inferiority and Its Psychical Compensation*, outlining the process of compensation and overcompensation based on the evolutionary principles of Darwin. In the years to follow, even though he became president of the International Psycho-Analytic Society, Adler openly disagreed with Freud's views of the importance of the

Oedipus complex and the essential meaning of dreams, and the view that humans were driven creatures at the whim of vague energy constructs. In 1911, Adler gave several lectures openly criticizing Freud's emphasis on sexuality as the basis of personality development. Soon after, Adler left Freud's circle with a group of colleagues including Carl Furtmuller and formed his own school, the Society for Free Psychoanalytic Research. Although the two traded verbal barbs in various publications, Freud and Adler never met again after the split.

Adler renamed his theoretical process "Individual Psychology," a term referring to his belief in the indivisibility of the personality. In 1912, Adler published his book, *The Neurotic Constitution*, further describing the core tenets of his approach and demonstrating that Adler had conceived of an original, comprehensive view of healthy and unhealthy behavior. Along with Furtmuller, in 1914 he founded the *Journal for Individual Psychology*, which is still in circulation today.

During World War I, Adler served as a medic on the Russian front. Always stressing the importance of social interaction and embeddedness, war was especially difficult for Adler. Confronted with the devastating impact of war on soldiers, and later seeing its disastrous effect on children, Adler focused on integrating social interest, a feeling of community, into his theoretical framework. To further this idea, in 1918, Adler founded several child guidance clinics in Vienna and began attracting and training other professionals to develop other programs across the world.

In 1926 Adler made his first visit to the United States. He accepted a visiting professorship at Columbia University, and in 1932 he assumed the first chair of Visiting Professor of Medical Psychology at Long Island College of Medicine. He lectured enthusiastically across the United States and in other countries. His family joined him in 1935 to escape the Fascists who had taken control in central Europe. Despite the fact that his followers were scattered geographically as a result of fleeing Fascism, Adler continued a tireless pursuit of teaching others about Individual Psychology. During this time, Adler enjoyed popularity, and the crowds seemed to relish his presentation format, which included both lecture and live demonstration. On May 28, 1937, while in Aberdeen, Scotland to deliver a series of lectures, he collapsed while walking and died from heart failure at the age of 67. For more information about Adler, consult biographies by Bottome (1957), Hoffman (1994), and Rattner (1983).

Philosophical Underpinnings

Unlike Freud, who attempted to develop a theory that matched the medical model of his day, Adler developed a theory based on philosophy. The following section details the main philosophical underpinnings of Individual Psychology.

Responsibility and creativity. One of the most basic tenets of Adlerian psychology is the notion that people are responsible for their behavior, thoughts, and feelings. People choose behaviors that they believe will secure them a sense of belonging and significance. One can choose to behave usefully, that is, with social interest, or ineffectively, that is, selfishly, avoiding the tasks of life. The turning away from responsibilities is an active choice to act inferior, to give up, and this choice has its own natural consequences.

It is important to note here that the Adlerian view of responsibility is not an attempt to blame but rather to reeducate and encourage change. As Mosak and Maniacci (1999) pointed out, "Choosing does not always mean wanting. Freedom to choose is not the same as freedom of choice" (p.18). These points have important implications for the Adlerian counselor. First, a client may choose to come to a mandated group, even though he does not want to, if not going means he has to go to jail. The second statement notes that life does present boundaries that people cannot choose, such as hair color, parents, and the occurrence of traumatic events. However, our perception and interpretation of those limits are always within our control. People can choose the response when they can not control the stimulus.

Because people are responsible for aspects of self, Adler believed that it is not what happens to you, but how you perceive and then use your experiences that truly defines the human condition. It is the creativity of the individual that perceives and molds experiences to fit a personal way of being. This conceptualization can then be used to explain why people can experience the same event and be impacted in different ways. If it is the individual who perceives and makes meaning of events, then it is the individual who must be responsible for these perceptions and any feelings, thoughts, or behaviors that arise.

Teleology. Teleology, derived from the Greek *teleos*, meaning "goal," connotes Adler's belief that all behavior is purposeful. To understand a person, one must understand the person's movement and the goal to which they are moving.

Adlerians believe that a striving for superiority characterizes the final goal of every individual. Superiority, in the Adlerian sense of the word, means that because there are countless ways to strive and find significance, people create personal strategies for achieving superiority. These consistent strategies are called the *style of life*. All the behavior in a person's life will be evidence of moving toward the individual's chosen path to achieve superiority. Because the goal and strategies are self created, they are known as fictions. Adler borrowed this idea from Hans Vaihinger (1965) who believed that a person's interpretation of truth was fictional, and all fictions serve a person's final purpose or goal.

A useful personal application of teleology for students studying counseling is answering the question, "Why am I pursuing a graduate degree in mental health?" There are many unique answers to this question. Some might say, "To help people," "Because my mom wanted me to," or "Because I am a good listener." Each answer provides insight into the individual purpose of getting an education to become a mental health professional. According to Adlerians, that answer also allows the person (or counselor) to consider other, deeper goals. For instance, the person who answers, "To help people," could have the underlying purpose of helping people in order to feel powerful, needed, or meaningful. The underlying purpose or goal is the focus of Individual Psychology.

Phenomenology. Phenomenology, a term that has its roots with philosophers Husserl, Heidegger, and Jaspers, emphasizes that each person perceives the environment in a unique and personal manner. While Freud postulated an objective view of behavior, Adler relied on the individual's perceptions of events rather than on the objective events themselves, for it is on the basis of perceptions and interpretations that people choose thoughts, behaviors, and feelings.

Let us consider John, a 16 year old with a history of aggressive behavior, as he details his most recent fight. John maintains he did everything he could to avoid the bully, but at the end of the day the other boy pushed him, and John hit him back. In an attempt to connect with John, the counselor reflects, "You feel justified in striking him back. It was self defense." John replies, "I feel horrible, I didn't want to hit. . . . I gave in. . . . I let him win. I'm disappointed."

The different views of the event demonstrate the importance of the subjective nature of the client interpretation. To fully understand clients, psychotherapists must see the world from each client's uniquely personal perspective. Zukov (1994) illustrates the concept of phenomenology:

> Reality is what we take to be true. What we take to be true is what we believe. What we believe is based upon our perceptions. What we perceive depends upon what we look for. What we look for depends on what we think. What we think depends on what we perceive. What we perceive depends on what we believe. What we believe determines what we take to be true. What we take to be true is our reality. (p. 313)

Holism. Unlike Freud, who compartmentalized the psyche, Adler believed each person to be greater than the sum of innumerable parts. Adler, influenced by contemporary Jan Smuts, who coined the term "holism," formulated a view of a unified personality that emphasized that a person can be understood only by observing interconnected patterns in thinking, behaving, and feeling. Dreikurs (1989) confirmed that " the doctrine of the unity of the personality gave Individual Psychology its name . . . derived from the Latin word *individuum*, which literally means 'undivided', 'indivisible'."

The concept of holism embraces a philosophical belief that mind and body are one intertwined process that is lost when separated. Without the mind, the body is but a shell; without the body, the mind becomes an impotent idea factory without a means to make real its abstract thoughts and dreams. Traditional holism honors the whole person and the integrated expression of the parts working as a whole. Ignoring the whole ignores the essence of humanity and blurs the true picture of the person. These elements traditionally included physical, biological, and psychological constructs (Dreikurs, 1997). Adler took it one step further and believed that our social interaction must be considered within a holistic approach, because it is in the social arena where our minds and bodies find an outlet.

Social embeddedness. One of the most important aspects of Adlerian theory is its focus on the social importance of humanity. Derived from his own experiences, from reactions to the objective sciences of his day, and from the writings of Darwin, Adler viewed the role of our social nature to be of vital importance to the development of normal and abnormal behavior. Adler saw that, in essence, we are social beings. From the works of Darwin, Adler concluded that species, including humans, that formed tight groups were more successful than those that preferred isolation. Thus, a sense of community has survival value. At birth, we join our first society, our family, and then branch out into the larger world where we struggle for significance and belonging within new groups. For Adler, the social aspect became the testing ground for all intra- and interpersonal phenomena.

PERSONALITY DEVELOPMENT

Nature of Humans

Function of the psyche. From the Adlerian perspective, human functioning can be understood in terms of two innate motives. The first is the innate *striving for superiority* that is involved in all human activity "from womb to tomb." The second is *social interest,* which exists at birth as only a potential that must be developed. In the following material, these two motives are discussed.

   Adlerians believe that we are born inferior: small, naked, visually impaired, and helpless, not yet having a place of belonging and significance in our social surroundings. Our most fundamental motive is to move from a sense of inferiority to one of superiority, which includes competence, belonging, and significance. Adler (1956) asserted the ubiquitousness of the "creative power of life, which expresses itself in the desire to develop, to strive, to achieve, and even to compensate for defeats in one direction by striving for success in another" (p. 92).

The first manifestation of this innate striving for superiority is that infants seek to survive by learning ways to elicit care from individuals in the environment. At first limited in their repertoire of skills, infants make use of what they have, such as crying, cooing, and fidgeting, and repeat whatever produces the sought-after care, such as being fed, held, and rocked. Dinkmeyer and Sperry (2000) discussed how infants with deaf parents quickly realize that crying is not functional. They subsequently cry less but increase visual communications, such as making faces, turning red, and moving arms and legs in an exaggerated manner, to attract parental attention and care.

According to Adlerian theory, as infants and young children face each new situation in life, they continue creatively to develop and modify strategies for achieving superiority. In this process, children subjectively perceive and interpret their environment and draw conclusions about how best to find significance and belonging. Because children's cognitive development is limited, the conclusions they draw become convictions that often conform more to private logic than to the common sense that characterizes the consensus reality of more cognitively developed adults. By the age of 5 or 6 years, each child has created a prototypical style of life that outlines general strategies to find superiority, to move from an inferior "felt minus" position to a superior "felt plus" position. All future behavior is characterized by movement for this purpose.

Social interest is the motivation to contribute constructively to others and to society. Adler believed that we all are born with the innate potential to develop social interest but that it must be fostered through training by our parents and siblings and through later interactions with others.

Ansbacher (1992) asserted that although Adler's term *gemeinschaftsgefuhl* has often been translated as "social interest," actually the term "community feeling" is much closer to Adler's intent. Ansbacher (1992) considered community *feeling* to be the felt sense that one is part of a larger community, and he considered social interest to be the *action* of participating in that larger community in cooperative ways. By contrast, Kaplan (1991) defined social interest through the components of behaviors, feelings, and cognitions. Behaviors associated with social interest include helping, sharing, participating, cooperating, and compromising. Feelings associated with social interest include belonging, faith in others, optimism, communality, and the courage to be imperfect (p. 84). Some cognitions consistent with social interest include, "My personal goals can be attained in ways consistent with the welfare of the community," and "I believe in trying to respond to others as I would like them to respond to me" (p. 84).

To summarize, Adlerians believe that all people are motivated throughout life to move from inferiority to superiority. Although all people are born with the potential for social interest, that potential is relatively more or less developed among various people. Therefore, each person's striving for superiority is characterized by a relatively lesser or greater degree of social interest.

Structure of the Psyche. The structure of the psyche is the style of life. The style of life consists of convictions, expressed through thoughts, feelings, and actions, about how best to strive for superiority. Each person has the potential to rather easily be conscious of his or her style of life, although because one forms one's style of life prior to formal operational cognitive development, one tends to be nonconscious of it until life circumstances promote one to become more conscious.

As previously stated, the style of life is based on private logic. One person's private logic may match fairly closely to the common sense, whereas another's may not match very well, containing mistaken beliefs and basic mistakes about how to strive for superiority. Whether relatively commonsensical or mistaken, according to Mosak and Maniacci (1999), private logic has three main components: life style goals, hidden reasons, and immediate goals.

At the core of the style of life is the lifestyle goal: a long-term goal of which a person is usually nonconscious. In the Adlerian literature, this is also sometimes termed the *fictional goal*, the child's perception of the ultimate condition that, when achieved, will finally secure the child's superiority. The goal is a fiction because it is created by the individual person. An example of a fictional goal is "To please others."

Hidden reasons are more specific principles that derive from the lifestyle goal. People tend to be somewhat more conscious of the hidden reasons for what they do. Examples include pleasing others and avoiding their rejection by being sensitive and responsive to their needs, by anticipating their preferences, by being eager to agree to their requests, and by agreeing—or at least not disagreeing—with their ideas.

Immediate goals operationalize our hidden reasons; they are our daily answers to our long-term striving for significance. People tend to be quite conscious of their immediate goals. Examples of immediate goals are to drop everything when a friend asks for help, to give the other person the choice of where you go together for dinner, and to say nothing when someone says something with which you disagree.

In the examples of the three levels of the style of life, notice how each component contributes to a holistically consistent way of thinking, feeling, and acting. The actions, feelings, and thoughts that are a manifestation of immediate goals can be traced back to hidden reasons and, ultimately, to the fundamental lifestyle goal.

In the above example, pleasing was the central theme of the style of life. In fact, Adlerians believe that style of life tends to be structured around one of five themes or lifestyle typologies, termed *personality priorities*, of which pleasing is one. Adler (1956) first described four main lifestyle typologies: useful, ruling, avoiding, and getting. Dreikurs (1972) adapted the typologies to apply to children: attention, power, defeat, and revenge. Kefir and Corsini (1974) modified Adler's original categories into personality priorities: pleasing, superiority, comfort, and control (of self or of others). Table 4.1 outlines the distinguishing characteristics of each personality priority.

Nield (1979) discussed four points related to personality priorities.

Everyone has a number one priority (p. 26). Each priority can be used in adaptive or maladaptive ways. Discovering one's number one priority sheds light on the purpose of behavior.

Everyone has access to the other priorities (p. 26). Although the number one priority is the most informative, some people use other priorities in the service of the number one priority. For example, Mary may appear to please people, but her pleasing may be designed to control. The controlling priority surfaces when the secondary priority, pleasing, does not work.

Under stress the number one priority becomes most apparent (p. 27). By observing oneself or someone else under stress, that person's number one priority is likely to be most clearly revealed.

No one priority is inherently better than any other priority. All priorities have their advantages and disadvantages; the disadvantages tend to be associated with an extreme rather than moderate expression of the priority. Though the priorities may differ in their proneness to include social interest, any priority can be enacted with social interest.

Another perspective on style of life is how a person meets the challenge of the five central life tasks that all people must confront: love, work, friendship, self, and spirituality. The tasks of love, work, and friendship were first discussed by Adler (1956), while the self (Shulman, 1965) and spirituality (Dreikurs, 1967; Mosak & Dreikurs, 1967) tasks were conceptualized later. Each is outlined below.

The task of love involves one's relative ability to establish and maintain mutually satisfying intimate relationships. According to Adler (1978), from the beginning of life the child is immersed in various examples of this task, primarily modeled by parents. How the child perceives love relationships will guide basic convictions expressed in future behavior related to intimate partners. As the individual grows, personal experiences with the task begin to occur, typically in adolescence in the form of flirting and dating. Adler believed that love is commonly attached to feelings of inferiority in the forms of embarrassment and vulnerability. The following case example illustrates one client's attempt to confront the task of love.

Bob, a 32-year-old attorney, was upset with his inability to form a lasting relationship. He reported, "I moved from town to town with my mother. She was married three different times. Although I liked my stepfathers, I remember her saying, "Don't you trust nobody Bobby. They will rip your heart out and leave you for dead." I never dated much in high school, but I had several sex partners. I would never call them back. I figured I better

TABLE 4.1
Adlerian Personality Priorities

Priority	Method of belonging/significance	Benefit	Cost	To be avoided	Body movement	Counselor's gut response
Superiority	Being competent, right, useful, martyred	Purposeful, competent, strives to be the best	Overinvolvement, over-responsibility, fatigue, stress, uncertainty about one's relationships with other	Meaninglessness	Listening, attentive, alert; intense eye contact; constant movement	Feel inadequate or inferior
Control	Being in charge of others, authority, rule maker, boundary enforcer	Take-charge, reliable	Emotional distance; others withdraw or attack	Vulnerability	None or minimal; challenging eye contact	Feel challenged (power struggle)
	Being "a rock in the storm," composed, reserved	Composed	Emotional distance, diminished spontaneity and creativity	Vulnerability	None or minimal; rigidity; impassive facial expression	Feel distanced
Comfort	Being adaptable, calm, not "rocking the boat"	Relaxed, easy-going	Diminished productivity, reduced positive social interaction	Stress	Slouch; easy, fluid walk; shrug or shaking head	Feel irritated, annoyed, and/ or impatient
Pleasing	Being able to fulfill the needs of others first, altruistic, caring, unselfish	Cooperative, eager to please	Stunted growth, alienation, retribution; extended relationship outcomes include rejection, disgust, frustration, despair, exasperation	Rejection	Constant eye contact; half smile; immediate forward movement when called; hands in prayer/supplication	Feel pleased

Adapted from *Practical Applications of the Personality Priorities: A Guide for Counselors* (2nd ed.), by J. F. Brown, 1976, Clinton, MD: B & F Associates.

dump them before they dumped me. I guess I do that now too. I can't seem to open up. Every time I feel myself getting close to someone, I get scared and run away. I guess to them it looks like I'm the bad one, but it's because I'm so scared that they are going to hurt me first.

The task of work involves how well a person uses one's abilities to make contributions to society. What occupation the person chooses indicates how the chosen style of life addresses the task of work. Equally important is what the person does within that occupation. For example, consider someone who chooses the occupation of a judge. In this position, the person could be fair and compassionate or vengeful and corrupt. Children confront the work task first through play and later through how they function in school.

The task of friendship addresses Adler's belief in the social embeddedness of human beings. Here, the fundamental question is to what extent the person is connected to those in the community. The quality of the relationships is more telling than the quantity. For example, a person may have hundreds of acquaintances but have no one in whom to confide meaningful aspects of self. This task is of vital importance to children and adolescents. As the child moves from family to the larger society, it is with friends that the lifestyle strategies, including any mistaken beliefs, become apparent (Manaster, 1977).

Although Adler never fully discussed the task of self, its importance is implied in his writings. Later Adlerians have fleshed out the task; it involves how well the person has achieved a clear sense of identity that leaves one feeling at peace with oneself and in harmony with society. Mosak and Maniacci (1999) included issues of survival (biological, psychological, and social), body image, self-opinion (how I feel about myself), and self-evaluation (perceived good and bad traits or aspects) in the task of self.

The following case vignette from an adolescent female group demonstrates various ways to struggle with the task of self. Notice how the members discuss views of self, and note the ambivalent feelings that often are associated with this task.

Andrea: I don't know. It seems like the boys just want one thing: pretty girls with big breasts. I don't have them so I feel ugly.

Gina: Who cares what boys think. It's what you think that matters. I feel fine about myself. I have braces and don't feel that pretty on the outside, but I feel good most of the time. You're lucky Andrea; you are pretty and popular.

Andrea: I don't feel that way. I don't like me. I hate to look in the mirror.

Melissa: I know what you mean. I judge myself so much harder than anyone else. I know I am smart, athletic, and fun to be around. I like that about me. I don't know sometimes, I guess I forget and start to beat myself up about little things, but at the time they seem like a big deal.

Gina: I'm not saying I block everyone's opinion out. That's impossible, but no one is going to like you unless you can like yourself, you know? I know that sounds dumb, but I think it's true.

For Adler (1979), spirituality was seen as concretization and interpretation of the human recognition of greatness and perfection (p. 276), a manifestation of an ideal. The task of spirituality involves the extent to which one uses a sense of "something greater" than oneself to support and enhance one's striving for a personally defined perfection. Mosak and Maniacci (1999) delineated five subtasks that involve one's views: one's definition of and relationship to a higher spirit or being, the role and purpose of religion or spirituality, one's relationship to the universe, life and death, and the fundamental meaning of life. The following statements demonstrate two ways of confronting the spirituality task. Based on your knowledge of Adlerian theory, which client is using spirituality in a healthy way? An unhealthy way?

Tom: I know my life is a wreck, but I can hang on. I really believe that whatever happens to me happens for a reason. It's all a part of a master plan. If I pray long enough, things will work out. I can't change until my higher power feels it's time for me to change. Until then, I am just riding the waves of life, living by faith.

Carolyn: There are times in my life when I feel so depressed, like the world is against me. In those times, I go to church and ask for some insight and patience to help deal with my issues. I feel a sense of inner peace. After those moments of quiet reflection, I often am able to tend to my duties. I can learn a lot from my religion's teachings, and the one thing I always try to remember is that I was given free will. I can choose to be good or evil. With help and support from my church community, I am trying to be a good person.

A final topic pertaining to the structure of the psyche is the role of genetics in a person's style of life. Adlerians acknowledge that genetics provide some practical limitations on individuals. For example, odds are that a person who is three feet tall will never pursue the life task of work as a professional basketball player. However, Adlerians focus on how, despite apparent limitations, a person perceives and creatively uses genetically influenced propensities and characteristics. Adler (1996) asserted, "Our objections to the teachings of the hereditarians . . . is that the important thing is not what one is born with, but what one makes of the equipment" (p. 353). Dreikurs (1989) noted that humanity's ability to rise above genetic limitations differentiated us from other species. A child who is born with a club foot may perceive this as a barrier to living and may become discouraged, operating from a mistaken belief that, "Because of my deformity I can't belong. I must have others take care of me. I am helpless." Conversely, the child may perceive the abnormality as a challenge and compensate for the problem, channeling energy into ways of belonging that do not necessitate two fully functioning feet, such as pursuing the life task of work through a career in accounting, computers, or counseling. Adlerians emphasize that people born with similar genetic traits will perceive and use them in a wide variety of ways. Consequently, Adlerians encourage people to strive beyond their genetics and use the tools they were born with to connect with others and contribute to society instead of isolating oneself or excusing oneself not to live life to its fullest.

From the Adlerian perspective, the structure of the psyche is the style of life. The style of life consists of one's convictions about how best to achieve superiority. It is expressed in feelings, thoughts, and actions organized around a central goal. It also is expressed in one's degree of accomplishment of the life tasks. The style of life is determined not by one's heredity but by one's use of what abilities one is given.

Role of the Environment

Impact of the Familial Environment. When Adlerians discuss the influence of environment on personality development, they emphasize the social environment of the family. The child is born into a society, and that society is the family—the laboratory for the development of the person's style of life. Although Adlerians traditionally have referred to the nuclear family, in the following discussion, "parents" can be understood to be any primary caretakers and "siblings" are any other people in the care of those primary caretakers.

Very early in development, children begin to seek to know, "How can I fit into this family? How can I belong and be significant?" As they proceed to answer those questions for themselves, children are sensitive to the perceived responses of parental figures and the perceived roles occupied by siblings.

Parents establish a psychological atmosphere that the child is likely to perceive and to which the child is likely to respond. This atmosphere includes values that the parents express in activities and in ways of relating to each other, to other family members, and to people outside the family. A three-year-old who remarks, "Look at me. I'm working on the computer just like daddy. I'm a hard worker, right?" is perceiving such work to be important in the family. By emulating the parent, the child strives to achieve belonging and significance within the family. In understanding the psychological dynamics of this situation, the Adlerian emphasis on social belonging and cooperation is very different from the Freudian emphasis on sexuality and competition.

The most important value that parents themselves can enact and can encourage in their children is social interest. As will be discussed below, Adler believed that parental nurturing of the child's innate potential for social interest is central to the child's healthy functioning.

Regarding siblings, Adlerians believe that one influence on personality development is one's psychological birth order. Contrary to popular opinion, Adler (1958) believed that ordinal birth order, which refers to actual birth position, is less important than psychological birth order, one's perception regarding one's birth position. The following, adapted from Dewey (1991) and Sicher (1991), represent common themes often associated with birth order.

Every oldest child was once an only child and, therefore, likely reaped the bounty of the family's attention. When the second child is born, the oldest usually is suddenly forced to share, and a dethronement occurs. If the child feels secure in the family, the oldest will often strive even harder to be the best, to be the star: responsible, achievement oriented, and the bearer of the family values and ideals. If the place is less secure, the child may be increasingly hostile or take on infantile characteristics of the new baby—a form of "acting as if"—to get care and regain a sense of significance.

The youngest child is born into a world where many places of significance within the family already have been chosen, but the youngest has a unique position: He never can be dethroned. Usually occupying a role opposite of the oldest, the youngest is most known for using the over-responsibility of the oldest to their gain. Youngest children are usually considered the baby of the family and are therefore pampered. With all the older people around, it is typical for youngest children to feel that they are entitled to constant care. In one case a parent brought her 4-year-old to counseling because the child rarely talked or walked. When the counselor asked the child about his day, the mother answered, "Oh, he went to the mall with me and then to the store with his brother." The counselor asked the child again, "So tell me about your brother," and the brother answered, "I'm 13 and I play. . . . " The counselor suggested, "Perhaps your son doesn't speak or do for himself because he doesn't have to. You all get so much out of doing it for him." This case demonstrates a characteristic, yet extreme, position of the youngest child.

Like the other positions, being an only child—a small person in a world of big people—can have its advantages and disadvantages. Only children are likely to be the center of the family and can learn to feel very competent without the distractions of competing with other children. The child can use this advantage to form responsible and helpful patterns of life. However, when only children attend school, they often have a difficult time socializing with peers. It is almost as if they feel threatened that, with other kids around, their significance has been lost. Often they withdraw or seem like adults trapped in a child's body.

Shulman and Mosak (1988) described another sibling phenomenon that contributes to the uniqueness of each child: the teeter totter effect. The sibling who finds one role space occupied will often find another, usually an opposite, role to fill. For example, if one child is athletic, the other child may choose to pursue drama or academics. Occasionally, when one sibling is quite successful, the other sibling believes herself incapable of competing and becomes discouraged. Out of discouragement, she may choose delinquent behavior to balance out the success of the sibling. This latter example illustrates how "belonging" is best conceptualized not as being accepted but as *finding a place* in the family. Being "the black sheep" of the family provides a child with a clear position and significance, even if the position and significance are achieved through opposition and conflict—a lack of social interest.

To summarize, several aspects of Adlerian theory help explain how brothers and sisters who grew up in the same family may have created styles of life that are similar in some ways and different in others. Genetic influences may be similar and family atmosphere may remain fairly stable over time, accounting for at least some similarity among siblings. Yet because of psychological birth order and the teeter totter effect, along with each child's subjective perception and creativity, children who grow up in the same family interpret the family atmosphere in unique ways, accounting for at least some differences among siblings. In the end, Adlerians emphasize that one's style of life is influenced less by the family environment itself and more by how each child perceives the environment.

Impact of Extrafamilial Factors. In Adlerian thinking, the first 5 to 6 years of life are considered formative. The child encounters extrafamilial factors during those first years almost exclusively through the family. For example, in the case of a child raised during a war, it is not war itself, and not even the family's response to war, but the child's perception of the family's response to war that is influential in the establishment of the child's style of life. By age 5 or 6, the child has mostly developed a style of life that she uses as a template with which to perceive and respond to extrafamilial environmental events. Although powerful events, such as trauma or psychotherapy, can modify a person's lifestyle, the tendency is rather for the child to bring the lifestyle to the events and interpret and respond to those events accordingly.

Definition of Health

Healthy Adjustment. Social interest is the hallmark Adlerian concept in that it is a characteristic that Adler alone specifically honored. Social interest is tied to the Adlerian concept of healthy functioning. Indeed, Adler saw social interest as the gauge for mental health and maladjustment. In his view, a mentally healthy person will courageously meet the tasks of life with adaptable problem solving strategies that always take into account the welfare of others. In an individual with a strong feeling of community, the striving to overcome inferiority feelings is a flexible, lifelong movement toward optimal development, akin to Maslow's view of self-actualization (Maslow, Frager, & Fadiman, 1987).

To maximize health, children need to perceive and develop a sense of significance through contributing to others, working through inferiority feelings with courage, and feeling that they are a part of the whole. Parents play a key role in providing an environment that maximizes the child's opportunity to perceive and develop along these lines, culminating in the child becoming a cooperative and adaptive adult. Healthy individuals recognize and respect their connectedness with the community and continuously use courage to meet the tasks of life, connect with others, and learn from personal mistakes, using the normal feelings of inferiority as a catalyst for future change. Healthy adults will strive for superiority over problems in life by including and cooperating with others instead of competing with them.

Maladjustment. Adlerians believe clients are not mentally ill but, rather, are discouraged. Adler described maladjustment as pursuing a goal on the useless side of life, that is, striving for superiority with a decreased sense of social interest. This striving can be in the form of creating symptoms to escape the tasks of life or achieving superiority at the expense of others.

A child who experiences pampering, neglect, or an inconsistent combination of the two is likely to perceive the world mistakenly, develop convictions that are discouraging and anxiety provoking, and develop an inflexible style of life. As the person matures, he is likely to continue to use private logic characterized by rigid, mistaken beliefs to cope with life tasks. These beliefs cannot cope with adult demands and will likely lead to increased discouragement and rigidity and a decreased likelihood of breaking out of the maladaptive feedback loop that Adler termed the inferiority complex.

To clarify, Adler believed in three forms of inferiority: *Basic inferiority* is an objective fact that can be measured, usually some physical immaturity or disability such as small stature or blindness. This concept was the basis of Adler's organ inferiority and compensation ideas. *Inferiority feelings* refer to a subjective evaluation of self. Feeling inferior is a part of the human condition and is a choice at any given moment. An *inferiority complex* is a behavioral demonstration of inferiority based on a conviction that one *is* inferior. Whereas feeling inferior is not abnormal, believing and acting as if one is inferior is problematic. The inferiority complex includes symptoms to avoid the tasks of life and escape responsibility for meeting them while safeguarding one's self-esteem.

Safeguarding mechanisms are the Adlerian answer to Freudian ego defense mechanisms, with a few important differences. Whereas Freud's defenses were intrapersonal, Adler's were primarily interpersonal. For example, whereas Freud believed the ego employed defenses to protect itself from the id and superego, Adler believed individuals use safeguards to protect themselves from physical, social, or self-esteem threats (Mosak & Maniacci, 1999). Clark (1999) outlined four patterns of safeguarding: distancing, hesitating, detouring, and narrowing the path.

People who use *distancing* withdraw from perceived threats and challenges in life. Doubting, indecision, withdrawal, and isolation are all ways to use the distancing safeguard. These strategies help the person feel a sense of superiority in acting aloof while seemingly absolving her from responsibility for solving the problem at hand. An example of distancing is a faculty member who removes himself every time a conflict arises in the department. The professor may present a holier-than-thou attitude, preferring not to bother with such immature matters. However, the professor may find himself out of the decision making loop, even when matters concern him. In fact, the safeguard might be used to protect him from conflict or the stress associated with making important decisions.

People who use the safeguard of *hesitating* will eagerly confront the tasks of life, but will then identify reasons why they cannot complete the task. Symptoms will develop as justification for avoiding the tasks of life. Within this safeguard is the approach to life, "If only I weren't so angry, I would have good relationships with my family," or "If only I weren't so sick, I would be a good father."

A person who uses *detouring* protects self from failure by focusing on other matters. Typically, these are lesser tasks that take an enormous amount of time and leave the person with little to no time to address the larger concern. Because the more significant matter cannot be attended to, the risk of failing is minimized, at least for the short term. For example, a man who agrees to do chores around the house but has limited aptitude for the tasks might feel anxious when his wife asks him to put up a ceiling fan on Sunday. Instead of facing embarrassment when he admits he does not know how, or experiencing failure if he tries, he sleeps late, encourages his family to go to church, takes them out to eat for lunch, goes by the park on the way home, and then feigns exhaustion when he gets home.

In the *narrowed path* form of safeguard, a person accepts only tasks that are easy to accomplish, thereby avoiding failure but also underachieving in the bargain. The client with the MBA who chooses to work in a bookstore as a clerk is one example. When he examines this choice, he discovers it is not that he likes the bookstore as much as that he is afraid he cannot succeed as a businessman. Another expression of this safeguard is the accepting of larger tasks but choosing to finish only pieces, never quite completing the whole task. By this strategy the person can claim the larger task is a work in progress and avoid final critique of the work.

Adler discriminated between the neurotic and the psychotic in the degree to which each denies personal responsibility and social interest (Adler, 1956). A neurotic has a "yes, but" attitude, acknowledging social responsibilities but using symptoms as an excuse for not meeting them. A psychotic has no social interest, completely cutting all ties with society, but does not experience failure because she does not even conceptualize the phenomenon of social interest. Additionally, a psychotic may create delusions, hallucinations, and other symptoms to meet tasks (Mosak & Maniacci, 1999).

Just as a lack of social interest is reflected in safeguarding strategies, it also is reflected in mistaken beliefs. Mosak (1995a) outlined the following common patterns of basic mistakes.

In *overgeneralization*, people often use one experience to contaminate future experiences. Examples include, "You can't trust women. They all just want you for your money" or "The world is a scary place. It is never safe to take risks." The underlying message in overgeneralizations is, "It's not my fault I am not succeeding in [fill in the blank]."

In *false or impossible goals of security*, individuals function under an "only if" absurdity: "Only if I can be perfect will I truly find happiness" or "Only if I can control my children will I be a good parent." People making this basic mistake set ridiculously high expectations of self and others. Often the person wants recognition for having such lofty goals, or they can feel justified in succumbing to hopelessness and discouragement.

Minimization or denial of one's worth is often a clear example of acting as if one is inferior. Examples include, "I'm just the vice president. I don't really make any important decisions. I'm not as smart as everyone else." The message here is a purposeful attempt to avoid responsibility.

The basic mistake of *faulty values* demonstrates a decreased sense or absence of social interest. For example, "You have to get people before they get you" or "The man has to make all the decisions in the family. There is no discussion." These beliefs circumvent any perceived need for social interest and often alienate the person from others which, in turn, leads to greater feelings of inferiority and discouragement.

To summarize, people develop maladaptive styles of life when their environments do not nurture their innate capacity for social interest. The lack of social interest is reflected in the presence of safeguarding strategies and mistaken beliefs. Although Adler believed humans were capable of health through cooperation, the negative effects of failing to develop social interest include inter- and intrapersonal difficulties at the micro level and possible species extinction at the macro level.

The Personality Change Process

In general, people change when they come to understand the style of life they have created, especially its mistaken aspects, and choose to modify their style of life, including thoughts, feelings, and actions. According to Adler, the typical course of life sometimes can facilitate this process, but more often the person needs the atypical process of counseling or psychotherapy to facilitate change.

Change Through Counseling
Client's Role.   Clients come to therapy because they are upset that life is not working out the way they expected. They themselves may report that they feel depressed, anxious, or guilty. Underneath these subjective client experiences, the Adlerian counselor sees discouragement: the strategies that have worked for them in the past are currently failing them.

Clients seek therapy to reinforce that they are sick and stuck or because they are confused about what to do next and believe they cannot figure out new solutions by themselves. In either case, Adlerian counselors believe clients have a great capacity to change, and they place the ultimate responsibility for change squarely on the client. Adlerians believe that pampering, as evidenced by viewing the client as an unwilling party to the formation of symptoms, is disrespectful of the inherent creativity and power of the individual. Although, as you will read later, Adlerian therapists see the therapy as collaborative, the client is the one ultimately responsible for either maintaining or changing the chosen strategies for achieving significance.

Client resistance results from a misalignment of counselor and client goals. Clients who are not open to being challenged by the counselor or to taking responsibility for personal thoughts, feelings, and behaviors will resist the counselor's encouragement that they do so. Clients must also be willing to explore past family-of-origin experiences and relate them to present functioning. As the counselor confronts the client's private logic, the client will often use safeguarding mechanisms to protect the style of life from change. This safeguarding is grist for the therapy mill, because it itself is a mechanism the client employed as a child and continued to use consistently throughout life to avoid the tasks of life (Dreikurs, 1989). Therefore, client resistance is not viewed as maladaptive, but as information about the client's goals and their methods of achieving them.

Counselor's Role. The Adlerian therapist's view of the goals of therapy differs depending on whether the client is seeking counseling or psychotherapy. Although the terms counseling and psychotherapy are used interchangeably in this text, a brief delineation of the terms from an Adlerian view is appropriate here. Dreikurs (1967) viewed *counseling* as dealing primarily with immediate concerns, usually impacting only one task of life. *Psychotherapy* was a longer process concerned with a more dramatic reorientation of the client's style of life. Thus the therapist chooses the goals, method, and depth of exploration based on the need of the client.

Although each client's experience in therapy is different, Adlerian therapists pursue some common goals in both counseling and psychotherapy. Mosak (1995a) outlined the following goals:

The fostering of social interest
The decrease of inferiority feelings, the overcoming of discouragement, and the recognition of one's resources
Changes in one's lifestyle, that is, perceptions and goals
Changing faulty motivation
Encouraging the individual to recognize equality among all people
Helping the person become a contributing human being (p. 67)

Another way to conceptualize the Adlerian counselor's goal is that the counselor seeks to uncover the cognitive aspects of the client, particularly the basic mistakes in the private logic that constitutes the foundation of the client's style of life, so that the client can bring basic beliefs more in line with common sense and act on those revised beliefs with social interest.

The effective Adlerian counselor is an educator, collaborator, and encourager. The role of educator is used to teach the client about social interest and the purpose of behavior. The role of teacher blends with the role of collaborator in that the counselor avoids assuming total control or responsibility for change. The discouraged person will readily act inferior to get the counselor to assume responsibility; however, the counselor must always ensure that the client is working as hard as the counselor at any given time. "The therapist must induce [the client] to face the problems [he came to treatment to resolve] while leaving him to make decisions for himself" (Dreikurs, 1989, p. 88). Additionally, the therapist encourages the client to courageously face the tasks of life with a renewed sense of social interest. The person of the counselor, imperfect, competent, and empathic, is used as a tool to model healthy interest in others. As Manaster and Corsini (1982) noted, "An ideal Adlerian therapist acts as a whole person, encouraging confidently with sensitivity and with social purpose" (p. 168).

Adler (1983) believed that within these three roles, therapists must attempt to: (a) see things from the client's viewpoint; (b) understand why a client does the things he or she does, that is, the purpose of behavior; and (c) illuminate the style of life for the client. Adler claimed that if the therapist followed these steps, she would never experience confusion about what to do next. The simple act of being interested in the client's world, understanding personal motives, and being willing to point out patterns while encouraging the client to re-approach life, often produces change (Adler, 1930).

Stages and Techniques. The Adlerian perspective on treatment emphasizes a comprehensive understanding of the individual seeking counseling. Toward this end, the counselor enacts four phases of the therapeutic process: (a) developing the relationship, (b) investigating and understanding the style of life, (c) insight, and (d) reorientation (Dreikurs, 1967). It is important to note that the term "phases" is used instead of "stages" because counseling is not viewed as a linear process; rather, the phases tend to overlap one another. The phases of the therapeutic process will now be outlined, accompanied by typical techniques and assessment tools used at the appropriate phases.

In the first phase of Adlerian counseling, developing the relationship, the counselor lays the foundation for an egalitarian working relationship. Adler disagreed with the psychoanalytic notion of the anonymous, omnipotent analyst. Adler believed that if the therapist constructed a cooperative environment, the client would more openly and actively challenge faulty assumptions and would experience the benefits of collaborating instead of competing. In essence, the therapeutic relationship serves as the retraining ground for the client's development of social interest.

The development of the relationship begins with the first contact between counselor and client. The Adlerian counselor is encouraging and supportive while emphasizing the importance of the client's active participation in the counseling process, including regular goal setting, discussing key issues, and following through on recommendations or plans. Watts (1998) noted the congruence between Roger's core conditions of empathy, unconditional positive regard, and genuineness and the Adlerian use of social interest within the therapeutic relationship. The following case excerpt is an example of how an Adlerian counselor encourages cooperation and client responsibility from the first phone contact.

Client: Hi, I was referred to you for counseling. So I was wondering about appointment times.

Counselor: I'm glad you called. What is it that you would like to work on in counseling?

Client: Well, I don't think I really need to come. My wife suggested it.

Counselor: Well, I certainly respect your decision to follow through on your wife's request, but I have found that counseling works best if you have some idea of what you would like to work on before you invest the time and money to come. Does that make sense?

Client: Yeah, it does.

Counselor: There must be something that you're considering; otherwise you could have declined your wife's suggestion.

Client: You're right. I have been feeling down lately. I just feel like I should be able to handle it on my own, you know . . .

Counselor: You are feeling embarrassed about the need to seek help and support, but at the same time it must take a lot of courage for you to make this call. Perhaps discussing feelings would be a good place to start. What do you think?

Client: That would be great.

The effectiveness of counseling depends on the maintenance of a caring relationship characterized by work between two equals: the counselor and the client. This first phase provides the foundation upon which later change is built and is the underlying structure for the counseling process.

According to Mosak (1995a) the second phase, understanding and investigating the lifestyle, is comprised of two important parts: the understanding of the style of life and the understanding of how the client's chosen style of life impacts the ability to meet the tasks of life. Like the development of the cooperative relationship, understanding a client's style of life begins with the first contact. What is the client's demeanor towards counseling? Toward the counselor? How does the client explain the presenting problem? Who or what does the client blame for the problem? What is the client's posture? Voice tone? Each of these bits of information is a piece of the client's consistent way of being and gives the counselor insight into the client's style of life.

Style of life assessment can be informal or formal. Although discussions in this text are primarily general and informal overviews, Adlerians have published formal style of life inventories (Shulman & Mosak, 1988; Wheeler, Kern, & Curlette, 1993). During this phase, Adlerian counselors use a wide variety of tools and techniques to illuminate the client's patterned way of being. As the counselor gets a clearer understanding of the client's style of life, the counselor can begin to interpret and, thus, move to the next phase. The following represents a discussion of some of the more common tools used for this purpose.

Family Constellation. The family is the first society people experience. It is here, in interaction with family members, that the style of life begins to crystallize within the first 5 years of life. Adlerians believe that how one perceives significance in the family becomes the blueprint for later beliefs about self and others. Therefore, exploration of the client's perception of her original family and her place within it can produce key information about the client's present functioning. Two areas of common assessment include psychological birth order and perceptions of parental figures.

The main strategy for examining the family constellation entails assessing one's psychological birth order. Psychological rather than merely ordinal position honors the perspective of the client and the unique interpretation of the situation. Attending to psychological positioning enables counselors to explain why some clients do not fit into the traditional birth order profiles that have been created for the various birth positions. Psychological birth order profiles can provide the counselor with information for tentative hypotheses regarding patterns in the client's style of life.

The method for exploring birth order can be varied in its formality. The client can give brief descriptions of siblings and any characteristics that stand out for each, any information regarding relationships between the siblings, and commentary on how the client feels about each sibling. Asking the client, "What made your brother, Bob, special in the family? What was his unique role?" can elicit places of significance among siblings and the client. From this information, the counselor can begin to see themes that pertain to the family group and can formulate some ideas about the client's perceived method for belonging. These formulations are important to the present therapy. As Manaster and Corsini (1982) noted, "Clients often describe themselves as children in a way almost identical to how one would describe them as adults" (p. 181).

Personality Priorities. Typologies are constructs that allow counselors to make tentative hypotheses about a client's style of life and that help a client gain insight into personality dynamics. While it might seem to an outside observer that typologies lump clients into catch-all categories, the Adlerian counselor is most interested in how each client is uniquely using the characteristics of the typology in the personal striving for superiority. In essence, the typology is the beginning, not the end of the assessment.

Exploring personality priorities can help the client answer the question, "What is the primary strategy I use in my striving for belonging?" Brown (1976) organized a systematic method for using personality priorities with individual clients. Her method has been updated and applied to couple counseling (Holden, 1991, 2000). As early as the first session, the counselor may begin to form a hypothesis about the client's number 1 priority. Sometimes the first clue is the "counselor's gut response" (see farthest right column of Table 4.1). Once the counselor has an idea of the client's number 1 priority, she then can move to the interpretation phase: explain to the client the rationale for exploring personality priorities, outline the different priorities, and collaborate with the client on which one best matches the client's way of being. Defensiveness can be decreased by assuring the client that no one priority is "best." Once the counselor and client agree on the best fit, the goal of the reorientation phase is not to change the priority but to make the expression of the priority more healthy and adaptive. For example, a client with a pleasing priority can learn to say "No" before the feelings of being overwhelmed lead to a choice to withdraw from others. Pleasers can learn to catch themselves (see the "Reorientation" section below) and use self-statements such as, "I don't have to do everything that is asked of me. I can set limits and still belong and be significant."

Early Recollections. Adler believed there are no accidental memories. Recollections from one's past represent capsule summaries of one's present life philosophy. At any given time, an individual recalls certain events out of the countless experiences of one's lifetime. Adlerians believe we remember events that reinforce our current ways of viewing ourselves, others, and our environment. Therefore, a client's early recollection can be a useful tool to uncover the client's style of life. Additionally, research demonstrates that as the person modifies the view of self, others, and the world, the themes of the memories recalled will also change (Eckstein, 1976; Savill & Eckstein, 1987; Taylor, 1975).

A collection of 6 to 10 early recollections is usually sufficient for patterns to emerge. Solicitation of the recollection can fit the personal style of the counselor. For example, "I would like you to tell me your earliest memories. Let's start with your earliest, single specific memory before age 6." It is important to start before age 6 because, as noted earlier, Adlerians believe one's style of life is formed by this age. Additionally, the phrase "single specific memory" addresses the need to differentiate between a recollection and a report. A report is a general memory, such as, "My mother often scolded me for things I did," and is not specific enough to illicit any useful information. A recollection is a snapshot of a point in time: "One time my mother found me climbing on the counter to reach the cookie jar, and she gave me a real spanking." Recollections have more specific information and, more importantly, allow the client clearer access to emotions surrounding the recollection.

Early recollections can be interpreted in a number of ways. Counselors do well to keep in mind that the purpose of early recollections is to illuminate the client's style of life and basic mistakes therein. The focus is not on what the client did in the past but, rather, on how they are repeating the same behaviors and thoughts in the present. To process the early recollections, write down the recollections verbatim. Focus on content and affect. Interpretation, like all Adlerian counseling, is designed to be a collaborative process in which both counselor and client are active. The interpretation process involves the counselor reviewing the collected memories and searching for consistent themes or patterns. The counselor presents the interpretations to the client and solicits client feedback on the interpretations. One method for reporting themes is the use of the syllogism (Allen, 1971): I am . . . Others are . . . The world is . . . Therefore . . . The counselor and client work together to fill in the blanks and, at the end of the process, the style of life is more clear.

The following case examples demonstrate a collaborative interpretation of a collection of early recollections (ER). As you read them, look for patterns and try to discern the client's presenting problem.

> ER 1, age 5: I am at a friend's party. His name is Riley. All the other kids are gathered around the present table. Everyone gets a plastic dinosaur, but by the time they get to me, all the toys are gone. I burst into tears and run all the way home. I felt so sad and alone.
>
> ER 2, age 5: I wake up on Sunday morning to the sound of laughter. I walk into the kitchen and my whole family is sitting around the table laughing and eating bacon and eggs. They were having fun and didn't bother to include me. I felt left out and sad.
>
> ER 3, age 6: My mom and dad went on some kind of trip. They said they were going to a meeting for several days. I had to stay with Aunt Lois. I remember them driving away and watching them leave. I cried and felt like they were never coming back. I felt scared.

Even with only three recollections, the pattern is fairly clear. The client was a 12-year-old boy who was complaining of feeling isolated and "weird," like no one liked him. He did not like being sad, so whenever he felt sad, he would get into a fight. His syllogism worked out like this: I am unlikable (his word) and left out. Others are mean. The world is cold. Therefore I must fight to not be alone and sad. The early recollection process provides insight and a place from which to establish understanding and goals for change.

Dream Analysis. Unlike Freud, Adler did not believe that dreams are the domain of a raging unconscious, that they are symbolic, or that they represent struggles with past issues. Instead, Adler considered dreams to be problem solving activities designed to deal with future challenges. The purpose of a dream is to create a mood that motivates the client into action upon awakening. For example, a client is facing the decision of proposing marriage to his girlfriend. If he does not want to propose, his dream will contain frightening material and, thus, he awakens with a lack of resolve. If he is sure about his choice of a partner, he will dream pleasant, happy dreams. The dream itself is an extension of the patterns chosen by the dreamer and helps shed light on the client's true purpose.

The Question. "The question" (Adler, 1956) is a technique designed to uncover the purpose of the client's symptoms. By asking "the question," counselors are able to assess what the client is avoiding by using the symptoms. The following vignette demonstrates the use of this process.

Melissa: I don't know. I just feel so down all the time. I can't eat. I can't sleep. I must be sleeping only about 3 hours a night. It wears me out. All I can do is keep thinking, "Something is wrong with me. You are defective." It drives me nuts.

Counselor: If you weren't so down and anxious all the time and you could sleep, what would be different?

Melissa: Well, I would feel much better.

Counselor: I bet you would. If you could feel better, what would be different in your life? What would you be able to do that you feel you can't do now?

Melissa: Well I could go to work. When I feel so bad, I call in sick.

With this information, the counselor and client have some clue as to how the client uses depression to avoid the task of work. Further exploration and reorientation can proceed once the purpose is revealed.

Identifying Basic Mistakes.   This piece of the second phase is not so much a technique as a result of the themes emerging from the family constellation, early recollections, personality priorities, and dreams. The summary provides the counselor and client with information about consistent strategies within the client's style of life that are incongruent with social interest. These self-defeating ways of being are known as basic mistakes, which typically take the form of overgeneralization, false or impossible goals of security, minimization or denial of one's worth, and/or faulty values.

Summarizing the Material. The above strategies are designed to illuminate the client's style of life. The counselor uses as many strategies as necessary to gather the information needed to help the counselor and client see the client's consistent way of being and maladaptive patterns within the style of life. According to Dinkmeyer and Sperry (2000), the exploration of the client's lifestyle has another vital role: It helps the client feel understood:

> This type of understanding transcends establishment of rapport. . . . [I]t creates faith in the counselor and stimulates hope that things can change. This kind of understanding goes beyond empathy and confronts you with the fact that you are deciding to display a particular emotion [or behavior] and therefore, you can respond differently. (p. 114)

The information gathered, combined with the client's faith in the process and the counselor's understanding of the client's consistent way of being, provides the necessary foundation to move forward into the next phase.

Insight.   The phase of insight is focused on helping clients discover the underlying purpose of their behavior through assimilating their style of life consistencies and their use of private logic. The counselor offers tentative hypotheses regarding the client's purpose of behavior. These hypotheses are culled from the information gathered in the last phase and are interpreted within the here-and-now context with an emphasis on consistent future-oriented movement. By focusing on the style of life information, the client can come to understand how strategies that, at one time, were seemingly adaptive are now causing problems when applied rigidly to present and future concerns. If a good working relationship has been established and if the counselor offers hypotheses in the spirit of collaboration, the client is most likely to receive the counselor's interpretations. To meet these criteria, it is best if the counselor presents the hypotheses tentatively and both solicits and welcomes client feedback. For example, hypotheses that begin with, "Could it be . . . ," "Is it possible that . . . ," or "I'm wondering if this fits for you . . . ," all demonstrate insight in a way that also invites client response. The tentative construction allows the client to agree or disagree and thus decreases the likelihood of defensive safeguarding reactions. If the client disagrees with the counselor's guess, then the counselor can glean the benefit of collaborating with the client on a better conceptualization. Additionally, by handling the client's challenge in a cooperative and understanding manner, the counselor can model social interest and the ability to be accepting of one's own mistakes.

The goals for this phase are twofold: the client begins to see basic mistakes in the style of life and then begins to demonstrate this insight by noticing thoughts, feelings, and behaviors that typify the maladaptive patterns.

Dinkmeyer and Sperry (2000) suggested that the counselor can facilitate the client's active participation by at times asking, "From what you understand about your lifestyle, how would you explain the current experience you have just been describing to me?" (p. 117). As the client begins to demonstrate an understanding of the purpose of behavior, new strategies can be explored.

Reorientation. Reorientation is the phase in which clients translate insight into action. Adler believed insight was good, but that it was meaningless if the person did nothing with the new perspective. Out of the clarity of understanding one's purpose of behavior, the client is now challenged to choose a different strategy to attain significance; to shed old maladaptive ways of being, characterized by a demonstration of inferiority, an avoidance of life's tasks, and a lack of social interest. This challenge is scary because to complete it, the client must step out of the familiar into the unknown. Therefore, although the counselor is an encourager in this phase, the decision to reorient rests with the client.

To help with the reorientation, Adlerian therapists have created and utilized a wide variety of innovative techniques including giving advice, task setting with homework, guided imagery, confrontation, paradoxical intervention or antisuggestion, and encouragement (for more on encouragement see Table 4.2). Often Adlerians challenge clients to act as if they were different. For example, a shy man may act as if he is assertive and then solicit feedback on how others perceive him. The perception of the feedback is then used to challenge old beliefs and patterns. Along the same line, the push button technique can demonstrate that each person can create different emotions and beliefs at will. An angry client may be encouraged to get angry in session, then asked to choose to remove the anger and feel frustrated, then calm, then angry again. Through this process, the client learns the power of choice and control over one's self.

CONTRIBUTIONS AND LIMITATIONS

Contributions

Adlerian theory has had a lasting impact on the field of psychotherapy. Initially proposed as a socially oriented cognitive therapy, the approach provided a more human alternative to Freud's mechanistic model. Adler's most unique contribution, social interest, equates health with contribution to a greater good and is optimistic in its thrust. Additionally, Adler's work with families and child guidance continue in many facets of our society.

The most notable contribution of Adler's work is that his ideas have been blended and incorporated into almost every school of therapy included

TABLE 4.2
Praise, Encouragement, and Discouragement

Praise	Encouragement	Discouragement
1. You cleaned up your room just like I told you to!	You really worked hard at cleaning up your room!	You left a sock out. I hope you do better next time.
2. You got an "A". That's my girl!	I can tell you are very proud of your grade!	You may have made an "A" in science, but what about math?
3. You make Daddy happy when you tell the truth.	It was brave of you to tell the truth even though you knew you would be grounded.	I can't believe you disobeyed me! I don't want to hear another word!
4. You don't need my help. You're the smartest one in the class!	I am confident that you will do your best.	Here, just let me do it for you.
5. I like you a lot better when you are wearing your smile!	You look very happy today. Would you tell me about your day?	It's nice that one of us had an easy day! [Sarcastically]
6. You're doing great! Growing up just like your old man!	You are looking forward to going to high school and trying out all the cool new opportunities.	All teenagers are the same. They think they know everything. I was your age too. I didn't know crap and neither do you.

Reprinted from *Alternatives to domestic violence*, by K. A. Fall, S. Howard, & J. Ford, 1999, Philadelphia, PA: Accelerated Development. Reprinted with permission.

in this text, mostly without acknowledgment. It seemed as though Adler could see this coming when he stated, "There might come a time when one will not remember my name; one might even have forgotten our school ever existed. But this does not matter because everybody will act as if he had studied with us" (Manaster, Painter, Deutsch, & Overholt, 1977, p. 33). Ferguson (2000) remarked that "contemporary psychology increasingly reflects important concepts of Adler and Dreikurs" (p.14). Watts (2000) made a case for Adlerian influence and compatibility with a wide range of modern therapies: constructivist, cognitive, systemic, brief approaches, solution-focused, and narrative. Mosak and Maniacci (1999) showed similarities of Adler's formulations with those of family therapy, existentialism, object relations, and integration theories.

Having concepts borrowed without recognition is ironically Adlerian, in that the importance lies with the contribution, not the recognition or glory. Watts (2000) asserted that Adlerian psychology, because of its inherent depth and applicability, was ahead of its time. He contended that its contribution and staying power rests on its flexibility: Adlerian practitioners can be both theoretically integrative, albeit consistent, and technically eclectic (p. 26). As the mental health profession moves toward integration of theoretical approaches, Adlerian theory seems well placed for future shifts.

Limitations

A review of this chapter reveals some apparent limitations of the Adlerian approach. With a theory of wide depth and scope, practitioners, especially those learning about the field, may become overwhelmed with the amount of material and concepts contained in the theory. Nebulous dynamics such as striving for superiority, inferiority, fictional goal, and style of life are difficult to operationally define. Even the capstone concept, social interest, is still causing confusion regarding its definition and meaning. Adlerians need to address this limitation by continuing to research and define key concepts.

Although Adler had ideas about how humans grow, he did not formulate a sound theory of development or learning (Mosak & Maniacci, 1999). For example, although Adlerians discuss how to parent, they do not have a consistently solid developmental model from which to draw conclusions and differentiate developmentally appropriate behavior. Perhaps Adler resisted formulating a developmental sequence in reaction to Freud's model. Whatever the reason for originally ignoring the issue, Adlerians have ample modern models available to integrate into Adlerian constructs.

The most debilitating limitation of any theory is stagnation. Manaster and Corisini (1982) noted that while doing research for their book, *Individual Psychology*, they noticed that almost nothing had been added in the literature that in any way contradicted what Adler said; everything new appeared to be additions to, supplements to, or further explications of the basic thoughts of Adler. Carlson (2000) admonished Adlerians to expand and integrate, to become more inclusive than exclusive. He remarked that, "if Adler were alive today, he would not be sitting around rehashing the same concepts developed 80 years ago. Instead, he would be out in the community and the world, trying to make a difference. . . . He would look at larger systems and how to influence them" (p. 9).

The literature is full of examples outlining the attempt to integrate other theories with Adlerian concepts. For example, *The Journal of Cognitive Therapy* (1997) dedicated a special issue to exploring the integration of Adlerian, cognitive, and constructivist approaches. The *Journal of Individual Psychology* (1998) devoted a special issue to the integration of narrative and Adlerian theories, and Watts and Carlson's (1999) text, *Interventions and Strategies in Counseling and Psychotherapy*, contains chapters on the integrative application of Adlerian theory with an array of theories and a variety of special populations and clinical issues.

To this end, Adlerians must continue to strive to reinvent the theory in the light of modern times by using the very principles of community involvement and curiosity to contribute as first outlined by Adler and Dreikurs. If Individual Psychology is to thrive, Adlerians must bring it out of the shadows by actively educating professionals and society about their ideas. They can achieve this aim through workshops, practice demonstrations, involvement in political causes, and cooperation with other theoretical approaches and disciplines, much like Adler did in his time.

Interface with Recent Developments in the Mental Health Field

Pharmacotherapy. As discussed in chapter 1, the use of medication is an increasing reality in the realm of psychotherapy. In Adler's time, psychotropic medications were not used, but his daughter, Alexandra, had this to say about her father's probable view of medication: "I would have loved my father to have seen the effects of drugs on psychosis. I am sure he would have accepted it. He was always open to progress" (Manaster, 1977, p.57). Adlerians have debated this issue. Many believe that the use of medication is an ethical adjunct to therapy. In many cases, pharmacotherapy can help clients achieve a mental state in which they can benefit from counseling (Sperry, 1990). However, honoring the thread that describes psychosis as purposeful, some Adlerians have demonstrated the usefulness of therapy alone with psychotic patients (Mosak, 1995b).

Managed Care and Brief Therapy. For Adlerian therapists, the application of brief therapy is similar to the process of long-term therapy. Adler believed the important aspects of understanding the client and the purposes or goals of behavior were the key elements of the therapeutic process and could be achieved in a relatively short amount of time. Adlerians adopt a therapy method that could be brief in time duration, but emphasize the need to take time to understand the subjective experience of the client. Bitter and Nicoll (2000) outlined an Adlerian approach to counseling (see Figure 4.1) that searches for functional solutions to the client's problem without sacrificing the tenets of Adlerian theory.

The emphasis of the brief model is on using the tools and techniques, in any order, to understand the lifestyle of the individual and encourage change. For example, In Bitter and Nicoll's (2000) approach, "the data base," "meeting the person," "the subjective interview" and "the question" are all ways to form a collaborative alliance with the client and assess the presenting problem. The objective interview and family constellation/tasks of life/early recollections phases represent a lifestyle assessment. The combination of these two steps leads the counselor to make tentative hypotheses about the purpose of the symptoms of the presenting problem. Insight and agreement on the part of the client can lead to change, while disagreement or resistance leads the counseling back to more lifestyle assessment.

Diversity Issues. Gender, ethnicity, and sexual orientation are three important diversity issues addressed by Adlerian theory. Adler, in today's terms, was a true feminist, not afraid to comment on how women should be accorded the freedom of equality. As early as 1927, Adler (1978) seemed to be commenting on modern culture by stating "that human culture is characterized by the overtowering significance of man" (p. 5) and that "the low esteem of women is expressed in far lower pay for women . . . even when their work is equal in value to men" (p. 7). Adler was sensitive to the impact of inequality on both men and women and saw the conflict as possibly devastating.

Dreikurs (1999) noted that the generally accepted war of the sexes was a self-fulfilling prophecy of useless behavior on both sides: men striving for superiority over women and women acting as if they are inferior or rebelling against men. Adler refused to accept or use the term "opposite sex," choosing to say always *the other* sex. He wouldn't concede that the two genders must, by nature, be in opposition. Instead he preached the doctrine of social equality for all, regardless of obvious differences. That type of thinking was unacceptable in his time and, unfortunately, remains too much so in ours (Edgar, 1996). Adlerians observe the striving of each individual through the life task of love, described earlier. For healthy relationships to occur, the common conceptualization of the relationship between men and women as a war must be reoriented as a relationship based on cooperation, equality, and respect.

The issue of respecting one's cultural identity through an appreciation of the subjective view of every client has long been a focus of Adlerian theory. Sherman and Dinkmeyer (1987) emphasized that Adler's sociocultural concepts and practical, commonsense approach make Individual Psychology a natural fit for various ethnic groups. Arciniega and Newlon (1999) proposed

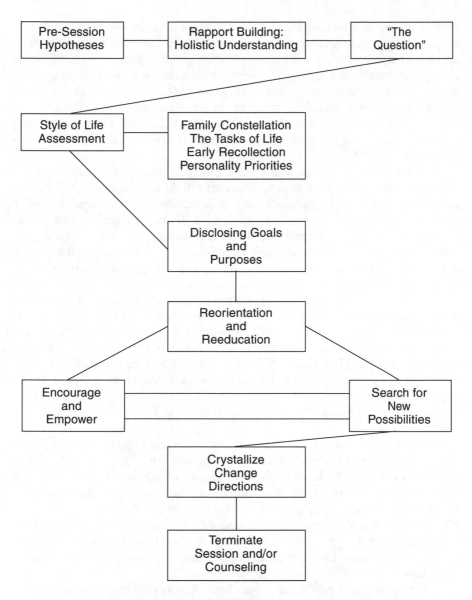

FIGURE 4.1
Adlerian brief therapy. Adapted from "Adlerian Brief Therapy With Individuals,"
by J. R. Bitter and W. C. Nicoll, 2000, *Journal of Individual Psychology, 56,*
p. 35.

that, of all the theories, Individual Psychology best suits the needs of minority groups by focusing on the importance of community, family, cooperation, and social interest, or contributing to a larger group. Mozdzierz (1998) noted that social interest is a unifying concept among cultures that encourage various groups to consider and respect the growth and striving of other groups. A review of recent Adlerian literature demonstrated a continuing effort to further explore the efficacy of the Adlerian approach with various cultures and multicultural applications (Duffey, Carns, Carns & Garcia, 1998; Watts & Henriksen, 1998).

The issue of sexual orientation is a good example of how a theory must adapt to changing societal views. Chandler (1995) reported that Adler originally conceptualized homosexuality as a deviation and a neurosis based on fears of failure with the opposite sex and a denial of social responsibility because of underlying inferiority. Today, the majority of mental health professions and professionals consider homosexuality to be a normal variation and a nonpathological orientation possibly resulting from genetic or other biological phenomena. Several professional associations, including the American Psychiatric Association, American Psychological Association, and American Counseling Association, have amended their ethical codes and standards of practice statements to encourage fair and equitable treatment of any sexual orientation. Adlerians have made efforts to reconceptualize homosexuality and bisexuality (Chernin & Holden, 1995). The issue continues to be a debated topic, but as Chandler stated, "Adlerian society must be more responsive to the needs of homosexual and bisexual populations if it is to maintain its applicability and respectability" (p. 87).

Spirituality. When most other mental health theories ignored or denigrated spirituality, Adlerians elevated it to the stature of one of the five tasks of life. Croake and Rusk (1980) and Leak, Gardner, and Pounds (1992) explored the integration of Adlerian, Eastern, and Buddhist concepts. Sweeney and Wittmer (1991) discuss spirituality issues as a means of moving beyond social interest, to a place of enhanced wellness. O'Connell (1997) wrote about the importance of spirituality in Adlerian counseling and its possible impact on personal growth. In this regard, Adlerians again appeared to be ahead of their times.

Nevertheless, the Adlerian view of spirituality remains quite ego-based. The Adlerian emphasis on rational consciousness disregards the entire contemplative domain characterized by transrational experience. Adlerians believe social interest must be nurtured by the social environment, while abundant documentation indicates that people experience profound transformations from self- to social interest in the aftermath of spiritual experiences (Ring & Valarino, 1998). It remains for Adlerians to integrate research on transpersonal phenomena into a truly comprehensive understanding of the human experience.

DSM-IV-TR **Diagnosis.** Unlike many psychological theories that emphasize pathology, Individual Psychology focuses on a person's unique use and meaning of symptoms, not the symptoms themselves. Some Adlerian sources indicate that, because labeling fails to tell the true story and movement of the client, Adlerians use diagnostic labels only for nontherapeutic purposes, such as completing insurance forms (Mosak, 1995a; Sperry & Carlson, 1996). Adler (1930) commented on the pitfalls of diagnostic labeling:

> If he stops at this point and believes that when he hears the word . . . "anxiety neurosis" or "schizophrenia," he has gained some understanding of the individual case, he not only deprives himself of the possibility of individual research, [he] will never be free from misunderstandings that will arise between him and the person he is treating. (p. 127)

Within the Adlerian framework, the primary axes of the *Diagnostic and Statistical Manual of Mental Disorders* (*DSM IV*; American Psychiatric Association, 1994) can be conceptualized in the following manner.

> *Axis I:* These disorders are classified as the "Yes, but I'm sick" neurotics (Mosak & Maniacci, 1999). Instead of confronting a life task, they create symptoms to safeguard and excuse themselves from meeting the given task. For example, an anxious man states, "Yes, I would love to meet a nice woman, but I am too nervous," or a depressed woman states, "Yes, I would like to work, but I am too sad and tired."
>
> *Axis II:* These personality disorders are characterized by, "Yes, but I'll do it my way." Sperry and Mosak (1996) illustrated that these clients respond to the tasks of life in idiosyncratic and inappropriate ways, usually failing to fulfill the task. "Yes I want to work, but I'm on a different wavelength than others so I must use caution" (schizotypal) and "Yes I want friends, but others hate me so I must demand reassurance or I will withdraw" (avoidant) are some examples.

Overall, diagnosis as classification is theoretically useless to the Adlerian. It tells the counselor how the client thinks they are sick, but Adlerians are more interested in what the client is doing with the symptoms, and how the client is using symptoms in the striving toward superiority.

SUMMARY

Alfred Adler created a form of therapy that emphasized the social nature of humankind. Opposed to Freud's negative and deterministic views, Adler focused on how every individual strives from inferiority toward a personal sense of superiority. The family plays an important role in development because it represents the societal training ground for the growing child. As the child interacts with the environment, a life plan is formed which guides the child in ways to be significant in the world. Although Adler viewed all behavior as purposeful, he distinguished healthy and unhealthy behavior based on whether or not the underlying purpose of the action was to contribute to society (social interest) or was for purely selfish reasons. The concept of discouragement as maladjustment is consistent with Adler's positive view of humanity; he described how maladjusted people have lost the courage to face life's tasks in socially useful and responsible ways. Thus, the theory of change emphasizes challenging the basic mistakes, faulty logic, and strategies of clients and encouraging them to find new ways of fulfilling their goals through socially interested methods.

RECOMMENDED RESOURCES

Books

Adler, A. (1956). *The individual psychology of Alfred Adler* (H. L. Ansbacher & R. R. Ansbacher, Eds.). New York: Basic Books. Excellent collected works of Adler. Difficult to read straight through, but a wonderfully comprehensive reference work.

Dinkmeyer, D. C., & Sperry, L. (2000). *Counseling and psychotherapy: An integrated, individual psychology approach* (3rd ed.). New York: Merrill. Easy to read and very practitioner oriented. The book also covers various treatment modalities such as group, couples, adolescent, and elderly applications.

Dreikurs, R. (1999). *The challenge of marriage*. Philadelphia, PA: Accelerated Development. This newly reprinted work is a must for applying the Adlerian concepts to couples. It covers a wide range of topics such as jealousy, sex, living together and parenthood.

Manaster, G., & Corsini, R. (1982). *Individual psychology*. Chicago, IL: Adler School. This is an older book but it covers just about everything. Nice case examples.

Mosak, H., & Maniacci, M. (1999). *A primer of Adlerian psychology*. Philadelphia, PA: Brunner/Mazel. The best new book on Adlerian theory. This book mainly addresses theory and is fairly light on the practice element.

Sicher, L. (1991). *The collected works of Lydia Sicher: An Adlerian perspective* (A.K. Davidson, Ed). Fort Bragg, CA: QED Press. This book has an informal feel and tackles concepts such as guilt, philosophical issue, early recollections, and generous case studies. There are even two question-and-answer chapters.

Sweeney, T. J. (1998). *Adlerian counseling: A practitioner's approach*. Philadelphia, PA: Accelerated Development. Easy to read and very practical. There is good coverage of spirituality.

Watts, R.E., & Carlson, J. (1999). *Interventions and strategies in counseling and psychotherapy*. Philadelphia, PA: Accelerated Development. Great overview of Adlerian theory with chapters on special populations and applications.

Websites

These websites supply good historical information, chat rooms, and book resources.

Alfred Adler Institute, San Francisco: ourworld.compuserve.com/homepages/hstein/
Alfred Adler Graduate School, Minnesota: www.alfredadler.edu
Adler School of Professional Psychology, Chicago: www.adler.edu

REFERENCES

Adler, A. (1907). *Study of organ inferiority and its psychical compensation* (S. E. Jeliffe, Trans.). New York: Moffat-Yard.

Adler. A. (1912). *The neurotic constitution.* New York: Dodd & Mead.

Adler, A. (1930). *Problems of neurosis.* New York: J.J. Little & Ives.

Adler, A. (1956). *The individual psychology of Alfred Adler* (H. L. Ansbacher & R. R. Ansbacher, Eds.). New York: Basic Books.

Adler, A. (1958). *What life should mean to you.* New York: Capricorn.

Adler, A. (1978). *Cooperation between the sexes* (H. L. Ansbacher & R. R. Ansbacher, Eds.). New York: Norton.

Adler, A. (1979). *Superiority and social interest* (H. L. Ansbacher & R. R. Ansbacher, Eds.). New York: Norton.

Adler, A. (1983). *The practice and theory of individual psychology* (P. Radin, Trans). Totowa, NJ: Littlefield, Adams.

Adler, A. (1996). The structure of neurosis. *Journal of Individual Psychology, 52,* 351–362.

Allen, T. W. (1971). Adlerian interview strategies for behavior change. *The Counseling Psychologist, 3,* 40–48.

American Psychiatric Association. (1994). *Diagnostic and statistical manual of mental disorders* (4th ed., rev.). Washington DC: Author.

Ansbacher, H. L. (1992). Alfred Adler's concepts of community feeling and of social interest and the relevance of community feeling for old age. *Journal of Individual Psychology, 48,* 402–412.

Arciniega, G. M., & Newlon, B. J. (1999). Counseling and psychotherapy: Multicultural considerations. In D. Capuzzi & D. Gross (Eds.), *Counseling and psychotherapy* (2nd ed., pp. 435–458). Columbus, OH: Merrill/Prentice Hall.

Bitter, J. R., & Nicoll, W. C. (2000). Adlerian brief therapy with individuals: Process and practice. *Journal of Individual Psychology, 56,* 31–44.

Bottome, P. (1957). *Alfred Adler.* New York: Vanguard.

Brown, J.F. (1976). *Practical applications of the personality priorities* (2nd ed.). Clinton, MD: B & F Associates.

Carlson, J. (2000). Individual psychology in the year 2000 and beyond: Astronaut or dinosaur? Headline or footnote? *Journal of Individual Psychology, 56,* 3–13.

Chandler, C. K. (1995). Guest editorial: Contemporary Adlerian reflections on homosexuality and bisexuality. *Journal of Individual Psychology, 51,* 82–89.

Chernin, J., & Holden, J. M. (1995). Toward an understanding of homosexuality: Origins, status, and relationship to individual psychology. *Journal of Individual Psychology, 51,* 90–101.

Clark, A. J. (1999). Safeguarding tendencies: A clarifying perspective. *Journal of Individual Psychology, 55,* 72–81.

Croake. J. W., & Rusk, R. (1980). The theories of Adler and Zen. *Journal of Individual Psychology, 36,* 53–64.

Dewey, E. A. (1991). *Basic applications of Adlerian psychology.* Coral Springs, FL: CMTI.

Dinkmeyer, D. C., & Sperry, L. (2000). *Counseling and psychotherapy: An integrated, individual psychology approach* (3rd ed.). New York: Merrill.

Dreikurs, R. (1967). *Psychodynamics, psychotherapy, and counseling: Collected papers.* Chicago, IL: Alfred Adler Institute.

Dreikurs, R. (1972). *Coping with children's misbehavior.* New York: Hawthorn.

Dreikurs, R. (1989). *Fundamentals of Adlerian psychology.* Chicago: Alfred Adler Institute.

Dreikurs, R. (1997). Holistic medicine. *Journal of Individual Psychology, 53,* 127–205.

Dreikurs, R. (1999). *The challenge of marriage.* Philadelphia, PA: Accelerated Development.

Duffey, T. H., Carns, M. R., Carns, A. W., & Garcia, J. L. (1998). The lifestyle of the middle-class Mexican American female. *Journal of Individual Psychology, 54,* 399–406.

Eckstein, D. G. (1976). Early recollection changes after counseling: A case study. *Journal of Individual Psychology, 32,* 212–223.

Edgar, T. E. (1996). Alfred Adler, a pair of plain brown shoes. *Journal of Individual Psychology, 52,* 73–81.

Fall, K. A., Howard, S., & Ford, J. (1999). *Alternatives to domestic violence.* Philadelphia, PA: Accelerated Development.

Ferguson, E. D. (2000). Individual psychology is ahead of its time. *Journal of Individual Psychology, 56,* 14–20.

Hoffman, E. (1994). *The drive for self: Alfred Adler and the founding of Individual Psychology.* Reading, MA: Addison-Wesley.

Holden, J. M. (1991). Most frequent personality priority pairings in marriage and marriage counseling. *Individual Psychology, 47*(3), 392–397.

Holden, J. M. (2000). Personality priorities in marriage counseling. In R. Watts (Ed.), *Techniques in Marriage and Family Therapy, vol. 1.* Alexandria, VA: American Counseling Association.

Kaplan, H. B. (1991). A guide for explaining social interest to lay persons. *Journal of Individual Psychology, 47,* 81–85.

Kefir, N., & Corsini, R. (1974). Dispositional sets: A contribution to typology. *Journal of Individual Psychology, 30,* 163–178.

Leak, G. K., Gardner, L. E., & Pounds, B. (1992). A comparison of Eastern religion, Christianity, and social interest. *Individual Psychology: Journal of Adlerian Theory, Research, and Practice, 53,* 33–41.

Manaster, G. J. (1977). *Adolescent development and the life tasks.* Boston: Allyn and Bacon.

Manaster, G., & Corsini, R. (1982). *Individual psychology.* Chicago, IL: Adler School.

Manaster, G., Painter, G., Deutsch, D., & Overholt, B. J.(Eds.) (1977). *Alfred Adler: As we remember him.* Chicago: NASAP.

Maslow, A., Frager, R., & Fadiman, J. (1987). *Motivation and personality* (3rd ed.). New York: Addison-Wesley.

Mosak, H. (1995a). Adlerian psychotherapy. In R.J. Corsini and D. Wedding (Eds.), *Current psychotherapies* (5th ed.). Itasca, IL: F.E. Peacock.

Mosak, H. (1995b). Drugless psychotherapy of schizophrenia. *Journal of Individual Psychology, 51,* 61–66.

Mosak, H., & Dreikurs, R. (1967). The life tasks III. The fifth life task. *Journal of Individual Psychology, 5,* 16–22.

Mosak, H., & Maniacci, M. (1999). *A primer of Adlerian psychology.* Philadelphia, PA: Brunner/Mazel.

Mozdzierz, G. J. (1998). Culture, tradition, transition, and the future. *Journal of Individual Psychology, 54,* 275–277.

Nield, J. (1979). Clarifying concepts of the number one priority. *The Individual Psychologist, 16,* 25–30.

O'Connell, W. E. (1997). The radical metaphors of Adlerian psychospirituality. *Individual Psychology: Journal of Adlerian Theory, Research, and Practice, 53,* 33–41.

Rattner, J. (1983). *Alfred Adler.* New York: Ungar.

Ring, K., & Valarino, E. E. (1998). *Lessons from the light; What we can learn from the near-death experience.* New York: Plenum.

Rychlak, J. F. (1981). *Introduction to personality and psychotherapy* (2nd ed.). Boston: Houghton Mifflin.

Savill, G.E ., & Eckstein, D. G. (1987). Changes in early recollections as a function of mental status. *Individual Psychology, 43,* 3–17.

Sherman, R., & Dinkmeyer, D. (1987). *Systems of family therapy: An Adlerian integration.* New York: Brunner/Mazel.

Shulman, B. H. (1965). A comparison of Allport's and the Adlerian concepts of life style: Contributions to a psychology of the self. *Individual Psychologist, 3,* 14–21.

Shulman, B. H., & Mosak, H. (1988). *Manual for life style assessment.* Philadelphia, PA: Accelerated Development.

Sicher, L. (1991). *The collected works of Lydia Sicher: An Adlerian perspective* (A. K. Davidson, Ed). Fort Bragg, CA: QED Press.

Sperry, L. (1990). Personality disorders: Biopsychosocial descriptions and dynamics. *Journal of Individual Psychology, 46,* 193–202.

Sperry, L., & Carlson, J. (1996). *Psychopathology and psychotherapy from diagnosis to treatment* (2nd ed.). Philadelphia, PA: Accelerated Development.

Sperry, L., & Mosak, H. (1996). Personality disorders. In L. Sperry & J. Carlson (Eds.), *Psychopathology and psychotherapy from diagnosis to treatment* (2nd ed., pp. 279–335). Philadelphia, PA: Accelerated Development.

Sweeney, T. J., & Wittmer, J. M. (1991). Beyond social interest: Striving toward optimum health and wellness. *Individual Psychology: Journal of Adlerian Theory, Research, and Practice, 47,* 527–540.

Taylor, J. A. (1975). Early recollections as a projective technique: A review of some recent validation studies. *Journal of Individual Psychology, 31,* 213–218.

Vaihinger, H. (1965). *The philosophy of "as if"* (C. K. Ogden, Trans.). London: Routledge & Kegan Paul.

Watts, R. E., & Carlson, J. (Eds.). (1999). *Interventions and strategies in counseling and psychotherapy.* Philadelphia, PA: Accelerated Development.

Watts, R. E., & Henriksen, R. C. (1998). The interracial couple questionnaire. *Journal of Individual Psychology, 54,* 368–372.

Watts, R. E. (1998). The remarkable similarity between Rogers' core conditions and Adler's social interest. *Journal of Individual Psychology, 54,* 4–9.

Watts, R. E. (2000). Is individual psychology still relevant? *Journal of Individual Psychology, 56,* 21–30.

Wheeler, M. S., Kern, R. M., & Curlette, W. L. (1993). *BASIS-A Inventory*. Highlands, NC: TRT Associates.

Zukov, G. (1994). *The dancing wu-li masters*. New York: Bantam.

CHAPTER 5

EXISTENTIAL COUNSELING

BACKGROUND OF THE THEORY

Historical Context

Existentialism grew out of a reaction, primarily from the philosophy community, to the dehumanizing forces at work in the scientific, industrial, psychiatric, and political arenas prominent during the 19th century. Most sources place the genesis of the existential movement at the end of World Wars I and II. However, Allers (1961) indicated that existentialism arose out of a prewar society that emphasized compartmentalization—family separated from work, religion as a lofty ideal far above the drudgery of daily existence, gender roles rigidly stratified, and industrial work involving humans as tools of production. Many people believed that such compartmentalization led to a surrender of self-awareness, to estrangement from self, and to the development of what Nietzsche termed "herd mentality." The seeds of discontent that were sowed before the war blossomed in the postwar environment of Europe. The prominent psychological theory of the time, Freud's psychoanalysis, mirrored a deterministic, humans-as-driven-automatons perspective, as did the theory that displaced it in the postwar decades: behaviorism. Both provided a natural point of reaction for the growing existential movement.

The ancestry of existentialism is deep and well documented. From the seminal writings of Gabriel Marcel, to the foundational work of Kierkegaard and Nietzsche, to the work of Heidegger and Sartre, existentialists developed a philosophy that, in turn, has been applied to counseling and psychotherapy. Unlike other psychotherapeutic approaches in which theory and treatment are of utmost importance and philosophy is considered a necessary but often ignored aspect, existential psychotherapists place the philosophy as the guiding force in both theory and treatment. Space limitations do not allow for a complete discussion of the proponents of existential philosophy, but Table 5.1 highlights the primary thinkers and their contributions.

Founder's Biographical Overview

We chose to present a biographical sketch of Rollo May, not because he is the only "founder" of existential therapy, but because his story provides the reader

TABLE 5.1
Major Contributors to Existential Thought

Philosopher	Contribution
Fyodor Dostoevsky	Work focuses on individual will, freedom, and suffering. Literary characters struggle with meaning of life in an intrapsychic manner.
Søren Kierkegaard	Considered the first existentialist. Kierkegaard reacted against Hegel and stressed the ambiguity and absurdity of the human situation. The individual's response to this seemingly meaningless condition must be to live a "committed life," as defined by the individual. Proponent of an individualized Christian way of life that, although the element of faith seemed impractical and irrational, could be one way of leading a committed life.
Friedrich Nietzsche	Ideas influenced Heidegger and Sartre. Developed concepts of will-to-power and overman (*Ubermensch*). Unlike Kierkegaard, who channeled individualism while staying connected to Christianity, Nietzsche rejected religion in favor of the individual will that lies in contradiction to the moral conformity of the majority.
Martin Heidegger	Writings on death, *Dasein,* and authenticity influenced existential psychological thought.
Franz Kafka	Literature exploring the human conditions of anxiety, guilt, and isolation. Explored meaninglessness by illustrating life as an "absurdity."
Jean-Paul Sartre	He noted that although human beings strive for rational explanations for existence, they will never find one. He viewed human life as a "futile passion," and his emphasis on human freedom, choice, and responsibility is well known in existential theory. He openly criticized the determinism of Freud and wrote about existential psychology (see *Existential Psychoanalysis*, 1953).
Simone de Beauvoir	Explored and applied gender issues to existential concepts. Could be considered the first feminist-existentialist.
Maurice Merleau-Ponty	Bridges phenomenology with existentialism. While phenomenology emphasizes the unique essence of the individual, existentialism is concerned with how the essence relates to existence.
Albert Camus	Explores meaninglessness through the view that life is absurd. Recognizing and resisting the absurdity becomes the balance of life.
Karl Jaspers	Coined the term *Existenzphilosophie* for his perspective on existentialism. Theistic approach that emphasized courage to face challenges of the human condition.

with a life that resonates with existential themes. Similar to other biographies in this text, the reader is encouraged to note how the theory of counseling was present within the practitioner, long before the theory was put to paper.

Rollo May was born April 21, 1909 in Ohio. May's early life was filled with family conflict. May's father worked at a job that required the family to make several geographic moves. May had five brothers and one older sister, who spent some time in a mental hospital (Rabinowitz, Good, & Cozad, 1989). At an early age, May sought refuge from the chaos of his family life by retreating to the banks of the St. Clair River, where he would sit, play, and watch the ships. One could conclude that the precursors to many of May's ideas about anxiety and ways to cope, both healthy and unhealthy, can be found in his early struggles within the anxiety-provoking environment of his home.

After an adolescence and college career marked by sparks of defiance, anger, and a love for the humanities, he graduated from Oberlin college and was soon hired by a Greek school to teach English to adolescent boys. Early on, May thrived in his new job. He found a connection with his students and enjoyed painting in the pastoral environment of Europe, but soon he became lonely. In fact, in the spring of his second year, May reported experiencing the beginnings of a "nervous breakdown" (May, 1985, p.8). Feelings of loneliness and intense fatigue forced May to bedrest for 2 weeks; there he gathered energy for a change in his life. May (1985) reported, after talking with some friends, that he began to walk. He walked approximately 10 miles to Mt. Horiati, where he then began to ascend the mountain. Six hours later, as rain soaked his body, he reached a plateau, where he stopped to think. As mountain wolves howled and approached his position, May took little notice, as he was thoroughly engrossed in his internal process. At dawn, May traveled to a small village in the mountains, where he began to write, "What is life?" and other thoughts on old slips of paper. May was confronting existential issues that would later be conceptualized as the core of existential theory: meaninglessness, isolation, freedom, and death (nonbeing). Answers were not found on that mountain, but the experience served as a catalyst for thought and a sense of being for May.

Shortly after his mountain experience, May expressed his self through art and further developed his interest in psychology. In the following spring, he chanced to see a flyer on a bulletin board about a seminar in Vienna conducted by Alfred Adler. May decided to spend the summer learning from Adler, a decision that became professionally and personally important to May's development. May commented, "I've often wondered to myself what would have happened had I never seen that little flyer" (May in Rabinowitz et al., 1989, p. 437).

May continued his interest in psychology by exploring doctoral programs in the United States. Much to his disappointment, he found many programs too focused on behaviorism and neglected to focus on other approaches, such as those of Adler or Jung. Fortunately, May discovered the program at the Union Theological Seminary aligned well with his interests, and he soon enrolled and met his greatest influence, Paul Tillich. Tillich's knowledge and ideas on religion, philosophy, and art provided May with a resource and friend who resonated with his own ideas. May's contact with Adler provided a rich foundation in counseling, while Tillich contributed the philosophical backdrop for May's search for a personal approach to dealing with life.

Due to family issues, May was unable to finish at the Union Theological Seminary, and instead moved back home, took a college counseling job, and began lecturing and writing about counseling. In 1939, he published *The Art of Counseling*, which reads like a primer of Adlerian psychology. The next few years proved hectic yet productive for May. He pursued a doctorate in clinical psychology from Teachers College of Columbia University. While finishing his dissertation on anxiety, he taught night courses, underwent psychoanalysis, and worked to support his mother. During this time, May contracted tuberculosis and spent the next 2 years in a sanitarium. May spent his time thinking about anxiety and not only completed his dissertation, but also wrote the book *The Meaning of Anxiety*, published in 1950.

Since the 1950s May has continued to expand and refine the art of applying existential thought to an approach to counseling. As an author and clinician, he has worked with Erich Fromm, Henry Stack Sullivan, Abraham Maslow, and Carl Rogers. For many, he represents the father of existential therapy in the United States. May's later career produced several important books, as he became a prominent force in establishing existentialism as a theory for mental health. After a lifetime of dealing creatively with the givens of life and its inherent anxiety, Rollo May died in 1994.

Philosophical Underpinnings

As mentioned earlier, unlike most other theories that include only a passing, obligatory reference to philosophy, existentialism's philosophy *is* the approach to counseling. This entire chapter reverberates with the philosophy of existentialism, but we begin with a few of the overarching philosophical principles of the existential movement, the common assumptions to which all existential philosophers and psychotherapists subscribe.

Ontology. Representing a radical departure from the mechanistic approaches of Freud and the behaviorists, existentialists developed a school of thought focused on the study of being, or ontology. Ontological issues address the spectrum of existence and the dynamic balance between being and nonbeing. From an existential perspective, being is not used as a noun representing an objective fact, such as, "I am a human being." Rather, it is used as a verb, connoting movement and process. This study of being encourages a deeper understanding of each individual's approach to existence. It examines the dynamic tension between being and nonbeing. In particular, it addresses the question of the extent to which someone is fully being, is authentic, is realizing his or her deepest nature through how he or she lives from moment to moment; or the extent to which someone is not fully being, is inauthentic, is untrue to his or her deepest nature.

Phenomenology. Existentialism holds that the only way one person can understand another is to appreciate the other's unique, subjective perspective on the world and self. Each human has the power to be aware or to not be aware, that is, to focus on or to ignore aspects of one's internal and external experience, and to integrate experiences into a meaning that is distinctly one's own. The philosophical roots of phenomenology rest with Husserl (1965), but his approach was too scientific and objective for existentialists, who modified his ideas to focus more on the ontological nature of the philosophy.

Responsibility. An approach that emphasizes the subjective study of being and how experience is interpreted by each individual naturally also places the onus of responsibility for being on that same individual. Themes of freedom, choice, and accountability are threads that run throughout all aspects of existential philosophy. Once again, this focus was largely in reaction to Freud's view that humans are driven by unconscious forces. Existentialists yearned to put the thinking, feeling human in the driver's seat of existence. They believed that, in addition to being responsible for one's own choices, one has a duty to one's fellow human beings with whom one is inextricably connected. As Sartre (1965) noted, "When we say that a man [sic] is responsible for himself, we do not only mean that he is responsible for his own individuality, but that he is responsible for all men" (p. 39). This social responsibility is best demonstrated by exercising one's freedom to choose alternatives that do not harm others or infringe on their own ability to choose and be free.

PERSONALITY DEVELOPMENT

Nature of Humans

The existential view of human nature springs from the ontological and phenomenological perspectives whereby human experience is best viewed through the eyes of the individual. As we discussed earlier, ontology is the study of being, and existentialists believe that each individual begins to understand another person and himself or herself by understanding the individual's subjective experience of being in the world (Binswanger, 1963).

Function of the Psyche. Each person is born with the potential, to some greater or lesser degree of consciousness, to have the core experience of the human psyche: the "I-Am" experience. This experience is the realization of one's being, one's existence. The presumably uniquely human I-Am experience is the awareness that, prior to any attribution of meaning to existence, one simply exists. This is what Sartre meant when he asserted that "existence precedes essence." Any "essence"—any feeling, thought, or action, any perception, desire, or value—is secondary to something that is absolutely primary: the simple, factual experience that one exists.

> Human existence, however, is never static. The existing person is dynamic, at every moment becoming. Existing involves a continual emerging, a transcending of one's past and present in order to reach the future. Thus *transcendere*, literally "to climb over and beyond," describes what every human being is engaged in doing every moment when not seriously ill or temporarily blocked by despair or anxiety. Nietzsche has his old Zarathustra proclaim, "And this secret spake Life herself to me. 'Behold' said she, 'I am that which must ever surpass itself.'" (May & Yalom, 2000, pp. 277–278)

This view of human nature implies that each person is innately endowed with a unique potential that the person will inevitably realize to some greater or lesser degree. Thus, the master motive throughout life is to preserve and assert one's existence, the process of "unfolding" one's potential.

Structure of the Psyche. Existentialists rejected the elementalistic psychology of their contemporaries, the psychoanalysts and behaviorists. Freud reduced the human psyche to the interaction of the id, ego, and superego, and behaviorists to the elements of stimulus and response. By contrast, existentialists asserted a perspective in which each human is understood to have a unique inner world that cannot be reduced to separate components and cannot be explained completely by natural sciences such as biology, chemistry, or physics. An analogy would be to describe a cookie as consisting of the elements of flour, sugar, eggs, and salt, formed into a shape and heated. But these elements do not capture the wholeness of a cookie. The same could be said of a piece of furniture or a nuclear power plant: the whole is greater than the sum of the parts.

Each person also is greater than the sum of his or her parts. Consequently, one must be understood in terms of one's potential for, and movement involved in, being in the world. In other words, from an existential perspective, the psyche of the individual is the whole of one's approach to existence, which existentialists term *Dasein* (Heidegger, 1927). Because *Dasein* includes structure, the whole of the person, and function, one's approach to existence, it is mentioned both here and in the section on the "Function of the Psyche."

In the context of the caveat of holistic nonreductionism, existentialists, like psychoanalysts, conceive of the human psyche as a spectrum ranging from complete unconsciousness or unawareness to complete consciousness or awareness. Relatively unconscious psychic material either never emerged into greater consciousness or emerged and was repressed.

One outgrowth of consciousness is the development of a self. "Each individual in the dawn of consciousness create[s] a primary self *(transcendental ego)* by permitting consciousness to curl back upon itself and to differentiate a self from the remainder of the world" (May & Yalom, 2000, p. 285). The levels of consciousness and self constitute the only psychic structures to which existentialists refer.

The Givens of Life. The master motive to preserve and assert one's existence is expressed in some more specific needs and wishes. Each of these needs/wishes, it turns out, are in direct conflict with the "givens" of life: conditions that are present in every moment of existence and that threaten existence. Each human is, thus, innately endowed with the potential to *perceive threats* to existence and, where threat is perceived, to *generate anxiety*. Although many existential writers have developed various lists of such givens, we have chosen to use Yalom's (1980) conceptualization because of its clarity and applicability to the therapeutic process. Yalom defined the four givens as death, freedom, isolation, and meaninglessness. With awareness of the givens of life inevitably comes anxiety. As you read the remainder of this section, you are encouraged to monitor your own sense of anxiety.

In conflict with the master motive itself, the need to preserve and assert one's existence, stands *death*. Consequently, existentialists consider death awareness and anxiety to play a primary role in human motivation. Death is the ultimate threat to existence, the ultimate threat of nonbeing. The potential for physical death begins the moment one is born; awareness of physical death begins early in life and reminds one that one's own physical existence is finite. Insults or potential insults to the physical body are, thus, innately perceived as threatening. With the early development of the self comes also the potential for psychological death: Insults or potential insults to the sense of self are threatening to the very sense of being. An example of such a threat is remarks by someone who is disparaging of one's self, attacking it, threatening its existence. Another is simply hearing feedback that contradicts one's sense of oneself: One feels threatened to realize that the self equated with one's very existence might, in fact, not be. Another example is entering an exam unprepared: Feeling the threat of failing to live up to one's potential, in a sense, that potential has died rather than been realized. Speaking of both physical and psychological death, Yalom (1980) noted how ubiquitous death is in life: "Life and death are interdependent; they exist simultaneously, not consecutively; death whirs continuously beneath the membrane of life and exerts vast influence upon experience and conduct" (p. 29).

I (KAF) was dubious of the existential assertion that death awareness and anxiety begin early in life. Then, while riding in the car with me one day, my 4-year-old son asked, out of the blue, "Daddy, will I die soon?" I was perplexed and a little nervous about this question, uncertain about how to answer. To reassure us both, I said, "No, you have a long time before you die." I hoped that would quell any more questions, but he thought about my answer and asked, "Why? What's a long time? Do you mean 10 minutes?" I was really nervous now, so I began to list all the things he had to accomplish before he died: play, go to school, teach his baby brother all sorts of things, go to high school, learn to drive, go to college, pick a career, date, get married, have kids, teach them stuff and play with them, and so on. I thought it was a good list, and even I felt relieved. He quietly thought about my list and asked, "How about learning to eat tacos?" I replied, "Yes, I guess that would be on the list." He summed up the conversation with, "Good. Now I know I will never die, because I don't think I'll ever like tacos!" As my son taught me, awareness of and concern about the finiteness of being starts very early, and each person responds to that concern in a unique way. If you feel any sense of increased tension as you contemplate the inescapability of your own death, you are experiencing the death anxiety that existentialists consider fundamental to human experience.

One specific expression of the master motive is the "deep need and wish for ground and structure" (May & Yalom, 2000, p. 284). Groundlessness and lack of structure feel innately threatening to existence because one cannot get one's bearings to preserve one's existence; some degree of ground and structure feels safer because it provides a stable foundation for making choices that can preserve existence. Standing in conflict with this need/wish is *freedom*. In fact, within the limits of uncontrollable circumstances, each human is completely free to do whatever he or she chooses. In fact, choice is not only a human capacity; it is a human inevitability. One cannot escape from this freedom, for even *not* to choose is a choice. For example, someone who chooses not to take action to right an injustice chooses to allow the injustice to continue unchallenged. Even when overt choices seem extremely limited—what May (1981) called "freedom of doing," alternatives always exist, if not in action, then in attitude, which May termed "freedom of being." Each choice either fosters or threatens one's existence, that is, the extent to which one realizes one's innate potential, hence the burdensome anxiety of freedom. The person who says, "I had no choice," really means, "I chose this alternative rather than another that I was unwilling to choose." For example, "I chose to turn my work in late rather than sacrifice sleep and put my health at risk," "I chose to comply with my boss's orders to repackage spoiled meat to be sold rather than lose my job," or "I chose to continue to be tortured rather than to cooperate with the enemy." Because one ultimately has the capacity to choose the attitude with which one meets even uncontrollable life circumstances, existentialists believe that each human ultimately is responsible and is the sole creator of one's own life.

Another specific expression of the master motive is "the wish to be protected, to merge and to be part of a larger whole" (May & Yalom, 2000, p. 285). Isolation feels threatening because one alone may not have the resources to preserve one's existence. In conflict with this wish is the given of *isolation*: despite the constant presence of others, each person is ultimately alone (Josselson, 1992). Because of each person's uniqueness, no one can be completely understood by someone else, can have exactly the same experience as someone else, or ultimately be rescued by someone else. Even with the advice or influence of others, a decision maker alone is ultimately responsible for the choice one makes. In suffering, even the extensive support of others cannot entirely or indefinitely alleviate pain that the sufferer ultimately endures alone. And in dying, even if surrounded by devoted loved ones, one ultimately proceeds alone. If you are feeling in any way distressed as you read this paragraph, you are experiencing the anxiety that accompanies the awareness of isolation.

Closely related to the need for ground and structure, the master motive expresses itself also in the need for meaning, evidenced in the innate human tendency to organize random stimuli into some meaningful pattern (May & Yalom, 2000, p. 286). *Meaninglessness* feels innately threatening to existence because no pattern exists in which to pursue a valued course of action; meaning feels safer because it provides guiding values for how to live, how to pursue the unfolding of one's potential. In conflict with the need for meaning is the given of *meaninglessness*, the fact that objects of our perception do not have inherent meaning but only the meaning that, through our perceptual organization, we impose on them, that we construct. Meaninglessness as a given stems from the first three givens. Namely, if one's death is inevitable, if one is responsible for how one chooses to create one's life, and if one is ultimately alone, then what ultimate meaning does life hold? Meaning involves a sense of order or coherence in life along with a sense of values—a way to prioritize experiences in terms of importance. The diversity of worldviews that exist on planet Earth exemplify the existential contention that life has no inherent meaning, or that if such inherent meaning exists, it has eluded humanity so far. Rather, meaning in life, what is valued, considered important or unimportant, considered to be worthy or unworthy of one's pursuit and one's efforts, is created by humans, both collectively and individually. May and Yalom (2000) posed the following question, which can serve as an assessment tool for understanding someone: "How does a being, oneself, another person, a client who *requires* meaning *find* meaning in a universe that *has* no meaning?" (p. 286; italics added). As you read this, you may be feeling anxiety and/or responding with ideas of your own regarding the meaning of life. The psychological functions of anxiety and response to meaninglessness and the other three givens are the foci of the next few sections.

May's Essential Aspects of Being. May (1961), in describing his six aspects of being, elaborated and expanded on the functions discussed above. The concept of *phenomenological centeredness* reiterates that human experience is best understood from the perspective of the individual: that all beliefs, feelings, and behaviors flow from the center point of the individual. On a related note, May (1961) contended that each person has the *potential to exist with other beings without losing centeredness*, that is, to interact with others without losing one's sense of being and identity.

May (1961) differentiated two aspects of awareness. *Awareness as self-consciousness*, the ability to sense and integrate information about oneself, itself has two dimensions: subjective and objective. For example, as you read this text at this moment, awareness of your inner experience of sensations, emotions, and thoughts is your subjective self-awareness. By contrast, awareness that you are reading—almost as if seeing yourself from the outside—is objective self-awareness. *Awareness as vigilance* refers to the ability to sense and integrate information from one's surroundings, in particular to perceive threat and safety. May (1961) considered this aspect of psychological functioning to be a type of alarm that informs individuals of the presence or absence of threats to being. Of course, from an existential perspective, all data is understood through one's subjective view of the world, so what one person considers a threat, another might not. For example, when driving in a car on a high and narrow bridge, one passenger's vigilance might register alarm while another's might register delight.

May (1961) described *anxiety as the struggle against nonbeing*; When one encounters the givens of life, one naturally generates energy to fend off death, isolation, and meaninglessness, as well as energy to deal with freedom of choice. In this process, May (1961) believed, each person has the potential to generate the *courage to self-affirm*, that is, to take courage and to affirm oneself in the process of addressing life's givens.

Dasein. *Dasein* (Heidegger, 1927/1962), loosely translated as "being there," refers to the fact that, at each moment in the process of existence, each person has a way of being. Dasein is "deep" in the sense that it reflects the cross-section fullness of a person in a given moment of the process of being.

A person's *Dasein* reflects several psychological functions, some of which are described above. The first is *awareness*, particularly a person's awareness of the inescapable "givens" of life and the extent to which one *perceives threat*. In response to the perception of threats to one's existence, physical or psychological, one inevitably generates *anxiety*. Thus, anxiety, the response to threats of nonbeing, is an inevitable product of living. Out of anxiety, a person naturally generates some *response*. How one responds, that is, how one manages anxiety and behaves, feels, thinks, acts in response to it, is characterized by some use of *defense mechanisms*. Like psychoanalysts, existentialists believe that each person unconsciously employs strategies to deny or distort reality to protect oneself from excessive anxiety. In addition to the psychoanalytic defenses, existentialists add *specialness*, belief in one's immunity from the givens of existence, and *belief in the existence of an ultimate rescuer*, some other being whom one can appease in exchange for total protection. Defenses used in moderation assist a person in moderating anxiety and thus in more successfully fulfilling the master motive to preserve and assert one's existence. Conversely, defenses used excessively become self-defeating in that anxiety is either largely denied or greatly amplified, blocking the person from effective fulfillment of the master motive. The more the person enacts the latter scenario, the more one will experience *existential guilt*. Other forms of guilt arise out of the innate potential to internalize an external ethical code and to violate that code. Existential guilt is the innate sense of malaise, either subtle or profound, that arises when one manages anxiety and generates responses defensively such that one fails to be, that is, fails to become, to realize one's full potential.

Role of the Environment

Several existentialists have written about the role of the environment in human development. We will summarize two main themes: the writings by Binswanger (1963) and Deurzen-Smith (1988), and those by May (1981).

The model that Binswanger (1963) and Deurzen-Smith (1988) offered consists of four interacting dimensions of environment: the *Umwelt*, or physical world; the *Mitwelt*, or interpersonal world; the *Eigenwelt*, or personal world (Binswanger); and the *Uberwelt*, or spiritual world (Deurzen-Smith, 1988). These authors asserted that the environment provides limits and is, therefore, an important factor in *Dasein*, one's being at any given moment. More important in existentialists' view, however, is that the environment is an influential rather than a causal force, affecting rather than determining an individual's being. One is not shaped by one's environments but rather subjectively perceives and creatively uses the environments in the struggle of existence. The four dimensions of environment are described in more detail below.

Umwelt (Binswanger, 1963), the "world around," is comprised of the natural world of physics, chemistry, biology, and ecology. It includes each person's biologically based needs, instincts, genetics, and neurochemistry. Each human is conceived in the physical realm through the act of sexual intercourse or in vitro fertilization followed by the complicated biology of gestation and birth. The *Umwelt* continues to be important throughout life as one comes to realize that existence in the physical world is bounded by the limits of birth and death and is limited by a variety of physical laws.

Mitwelt (Binswanger, 1963), the "with world," is the world of social interaction with other people. At birth, an infant begins to experience the *Mitwelt* as one relies on others to provide care and nourishment. Growing older, one typically forms friendships, intimate relationships, and work relationships, usually while maintaining ties with family and ancestors. These relationships are not defined by external variables or objective measures but, instead, are defined by each person's own subjective view. *Mitwelt* includes the important influence of culture on how one ascribes meaning to experience and on the ethical code that one internalizes.

Eigenwelt (Binswanger, 1963), the "own-world," refers to one's inner world or one's relationship with oneself; it could also be understood as a sense of "me-ness" or identity. It includes how each individual views self as well as how one perceives one's relationship to the external world. In the inevitable striving to overcome meaninglessness, one attributes meaning to experiences, thus developing unique likes and dislikes, opinions, and values. All of these attributions constitute the "me" environment: my sense of who I am, of what is meaningful and important to me—my sense of myself.

Until the 1980s, existentialism mainly emphasized the three dimensions that Binswanger (1963) had outlined. Then Deurzen-Smith (1988) introduced the concept of the *Uberwelt* to acknowledge the spiritual aspect of being. Literally translated as 'over world,' the concept of *Uberwelt* underscores that the universe is larger than humanity. *Uberwelt* also encompasses the individual's personal view of the ideal. "On this dimension of our existence we really come into the true complexity of being human, as we organize our overall views on the world, physical, social, and personal, and generate or are inserted into an overall philosophy of life" (Deurzen-Smith, 1997, p. 123). One's *Uberwelt* is influenced by religion as it is practiced in one's family and may be limited by what is acceptable in one's society. However, the Uberwelt can transcend social/cultural structures such as religion and, like the other dimensions, is dynamic in that it can be open and flexible to new information and ways of being, if the individual so chooses.

May's (1981) model of the role of environment in human development included three types of environmental limits imposed on an individual. The word "imposed" signifies that the environmental factors are beyond the individual's control; thus, he called these limits "destiny." *Cosmic destiny* refers to the limits imposed by the laws of nature, such as the climate into which one is born as well as one's heredity and biological processes. *Cultural destiny* refers to the limits imposed by preexisting social patterns, such as the language, economic system, technology, social practices, and values of one's culture. *Circumstantial destiny* refers to the limits imposed by sudden situations that include cosmic and/or cultural aspects, such as a hurricane, an accident, or a poor economy that leads to a cut in pay or unemployment.

Like his philosophical colleagues, May (1981) emphasized that even if a person cannot control the three aspects of destiny, each person is responsible for how one responds to them by virtue of the ability to recognize and exercise one's available options, actions, and attitudes. For example, Robert lost his job due to poor financial judgment on the part of his boss. Although Robert did not contribute to the failing of the company or the loss of his job, his life continued along with a new series of choices. He could choose to sit at home and collect unemployment, or he could choose to search for a new job. If he opted not to search for another job, that was his choice and not the fault of his boss. How one responds to destiny characterizes one's *Dasein—* one's unique way of being.

Familial and Extrafamilial Environments.   Clearly, both the familial and the extrafamilial environments involve all aspects of both May's (1981) and Binswanger (1963) and Deurzen-Smith's (1988) models. Both include phenomena with which each person must contend throughout existence.

In particular, the family is a crucial aspect of Binswanger's (1963) *Mitwelt.* However, existentialists have actually written very little about specific influences of the family on the individual. Maddi (1967) proposed that children are more likely to develop authenticity, the existential term for mental health, when parents create an atmosphere of respect and admiration for the uniqueness of the child and provide encouragement for the child to explore the givens of existence, both through the child's direct experiencing and through parental modeling. May and Yalom (2000) contended that people

> who lack sufficient experiences of closeness and true relatedness in their lives are particularly incapable of tolerating isolation . . . [A]dolescents from loving supportive families are able to grow away from their families with relative ease and to tolerate the separation and loneliness of young adulthood [whereas] those [from] tormented, highly conflicted families find it extremely difficult. . . . The more disturbed the family, the harder it is for children to leave—[they] cling to the family for shelter against [the anxiety of] isolation. (p. 293)

In summary, each individual encounters environmental limits throughout the struggle of existence. Whereas one cannot control these phenomena, one can control one's behavioral and attitudinal choices in response to them. How one responds reflects the quality of one's *Dasein*, one's being-in-the-world. Although it might appear to some that existentialism blames the victim or is unsympathetic in its approach, that conclusion would be inaccurate. Existentialism is a theory of hope in which limitations are acknowledged but also in which each person is considered capable of transcending limitations by being aware of one's options and accessing the courage to explore and, when chosen, exercise them.

Interaction of Human Nature and Environment in Personality Development

Most existential sources do not delineate stages of human development. However, Keen (1970) proposed four developmental stages congruent with existential theory.

In the first stage of *fusion*, the infant has little awareness of self as separate from other people. Experiencing existence primarily through *Umwelt* and through an extremely limited sense of *Mitwelt*, the infant responds to anxiety by clinging to parents and other caregivers. As early as the first year, the child enters the second stage of *separation*, beginning to recognize differences between self and others. This fledgling *Eigenwelt* experience of uniqueness can be exhilarating but also brings to bear the anxiety associated with the given of isolation. In the third *satellization* stage, the child responds to anxiety and creates a sense of security by acquiescing to adults in the *Mitwelt*. Parenting styles become very important at this stage. The extremes of overcontrol or indulgence foster a restricted *Eigenwelt*: too much punishment can restrict the *Dasein* of the individual, while an absence of discipline or limit setting will fail to prepare the child to confront limits and take responsibility for his or her actions. According to the existential perspective, parenting styles that encourage choices and consequences for one's decisions foster a more authentic and courageous child. At about 7 years of age, out of recognition of the balance between responsibility and choice, the child enters the final stage of *similarity*. In this stage, the child develops a sense of *Uberwelt* in which one is able to discern self from others and also to recognize similarity, a human kinship, with others in the *Mitwelt*.

To avoid contradicting the existential emphasis on a phenomenological view of being, Keen (1970) did not hypothesize the developmental stages as a rigidly sequential model. Rather, his stage model offers a view of the possible interrelationship between self and others and the possible role of the four dimensions of the environment in one's developmental experience. Again, according to existential theory, the environmental dimensions in general, and the family in particular, influence, rather than determine, one's development. These influences may constrict or enhance one's *Dasein*.

To summarize, existentialists, in their focus on the present *Dasein* of an individual, have not addressed in detail what environmental factors contribute to the way a person at any given moment participates in life. They have hinted that a person in a *Mitwelt* characterized by unhealthy functioning is likely to be poorly prepared to participate constructively in life. However, they are much less concerned with how someone *came to be* as they are than with the fact that the person *is* how they are and with the question of how a person can *become* more effective in preserving and asserting his or her existence.

Spectrum of Mental Health
View of Healthy Functioning. Mental health in existential theory is conceptualized as *authenticity*. Bugental (1965) noted that authenticity exists not as an achievement or objectively measured goal but, rather, as an ongoing striving, as one repeatedly confronts decisions over the span of one's existence. It also is not an all-or-nothing matter but a continuum, with authenticity at one extreme and inauthenticity at the other. Finally, authenticity and inauthenticity are not labels that one person can hang on another like an

evaluation or diagnosis. Although others may believe they perceive degrees of authenticity in someone else, it is that someone alone who knows his or her own level of authenticity. The degree of existential guilt that one experiences is the single best indicator of the authenticity of one's existence.

Authenticity involves a particular quality of awareness, of anxiety, and of response to anxiety. A person living authentically is aware of, that is, acknowledges, accepts, even embraces, the givens of life—death, isolation, freedom, and meaninglessness—as they play out in the four interrelated spheres of being: *Umwelt, Mitwelt, Eigenwelt,* and *Uberwelt.* Authenticity involves neither avoiding nor being preoccupied with any given or sphere. Authentic awareness facilitates normal, rather than neurotic, anxiety as one confronts choices each moment of one's life (May, 1977; May & Yalom, 2000). *Normal anxiety* is proportionate to the perceived situation, which, in turn, facilitates an authentic response. In responding authentically, one employs a minimum of defense mechanisms as one courageously addresses rather than avoids anxiety and courageously uses anxiety to make each choice. Authentic choices are those that express one's deepest nature, that involve the realization of one's innate potential. Some qualities that characterize authenticity are being fully present in the moment, being fully aware, and experiencing a kind of appreciation of being.

A ubiquitous example is an impending final exam. From an existential perspective, authenticity involves a realistic awareness of the situation. That awareness would involve a reasonable appraisal of the consequences of relative success or failure for one's future opportunities which, in turn, play some role in how one makes a living, all of which impinge on one's physical and psychological existence. Anxiety proportionate to a final exam situation may be experienced as recurrent thoughts of the exam along with concern, but not panic, about the possible outcome. An authentic response would involve planning a study schedule rather than procrastinating, adopting study methods that accommodate one's study strengths and weaknesses, and arranging to be on time to the exam. If an emergency arises, an authentic response would be to attend to the immediate demands of the emergency and, as soon as possible, to contact the professor to explore alternatives for making up the exam.

Thus, the existential model of mental health includes anxiety that one uses constructively. In a sense, the existential model also includes latitude for inevitable inauthenticity. Existentialists assume that, on the continuum of authenticity, each person strays from the ideal at least occasionally. In that instance, when one fails to live up to one's potential, one naturally feels guilty. Like anxiety, existential guilt is a normal part of being that neither can nor should be avoided. One may ignore or feel alienated from the *Umwelt,* let others down in the *Mitwelt,* violate one's sense of integrity in one's *Eigenwelt,* and fail to live up the ideals comprising one's *Uberwelt.* However, one can use even existential guilt authentically by regarding it as an early warning that can lead to humility and to future constructive choices. The mentally healthy individual uses anxiety, as well as the guilt that results from inauthenticity, authentically!

Deurzen-Smith (1997) asserted that authenticity involves accepting, and even welcoming, the fluid, changing nature of life circumstances. She added that someone living authentically is characterized by a sense of caring interest and psychological investment in one's physical, interpersonal, inner, and spiritual worlds.

Bugental (1965) elaborated on how an individual can create authentic responses to the anxiety that arises from the givens of existence. For example, in response to death anxiety, one can choose to have faith in one's existence and affirm that "I am." An authentic response to freedom is commitment, a willingness to make choices and be responsible for the outcome of the choices. Authentically responding to isolation involves engaging in relationship with others and accepting the fact that such connections are temporary. The authentic relationship is epitomized in the "I-Thou" relationship (Buber, 1970), in which both the connection between two people and the inherent separateness, uniqueness, and isolation of each is honored and prized. In a truly caring relationship, each person wants, in Buber's terms, to "unfold" the other, that is, he or she "care[s] about the other's growth and [wants] to bring something to life in the other" (May & Yalom, 2000, p. 298). Lastly, an authentic response to meaninglessness can be achieved by engaging in meaningful activities, with meaningfulness involving social responsibility but otherwise being defined internally by oneself rather than externally by others. In the case of vocation, an activity through which many people derive meaning, a person who collects trash, another who spends a lifetime researching the mating habits of the red squirrel, and yet another who counsels people, all may find authentic meaning in their work. Existentialists do not believe in fate or a great design or plan for one's life. The answer to the search for meaning lies in an individual's acceptance of the fact that the only meaning anything has is the meaning the individual assigns to it, and that some meanings coincide with an inner sense of fulfilling one's potential more than other meanings do.

Maddi (1976) poignantly summarized the authentic approach to life: "Only when you have clearly seen the abyss and jumped into it with no assurance of survival can you call yourself a human being. Then, if you survive, shall you be called hero, for you will have created your own life" (p. 136).

View of Unhealthy Functioning. Just as authenticity is the existential gauge of mental health, inauthenticity characterizes unhealthy functioning. Inauthenticity involves the excessive use of defense mechanisms: on the one hand, denial or avoidance of awareness of the givens of life or, on the other, preoccupation with the givens. Correspondingly, anxiety is disproportionate to the situation: It is either too low or too high to facilitate an authentic response. Consequently, the inauthentic response is characterized by a lack of courage, and by patterns such as avoidance, excuses, blame, and overreaction. Some qualities that characterize inauthenticity are being preoccupied with the past or the future, limited awareness, and a certain lack of ability to appreciate the fact of existence. Yalom (1980) remarked that "psychopathology is a graceless, inefficient mode of coping with anxiety" (p. 110).

Inauthenticity is characterized by retreating from the natural anxiety of being or transforming that anxiety into dread rather than using it as a catalyst for courageous choice. An individual blocked from existence by excessive defensiveness doubts his or her own potential for creation. In this condition of self-doubt, one is prone to relinquish one's inner authority and acquiesce to external authority. As Bauman and Waldo (1988) put it, "One takes on the values, ideas and beliefs of others and loses one's individuality . . . and falls away from the potential to express one's unique existence" (p. 20).

Because each person's most fundamental innate tendency is to preserve and assert one's existence, to continually become who one has the innate potential to be, a person experiencing inauthenticity, who has, in a particular moment, withdrawn from that process, is presumed to be somehow blocked. How the person became blocked is much less important than how the person *is* blocking the natural inclination to participate fully and effectively in the creation of one's life.

Returning to the example of a student faced with an impending final exam, inauthenticity might take one of several forms. One student may avoid thinking about the exam as a way to ward off anxiety about potentially failing, then procrastinate studying, then fail the exam, thus fulfilling the prophecy of the original anxiety. Another student may be preoccupied in awareness of the exam and generate so much anxiety about potentially failing that he wastes his energy in worry and dread, then, unprepared, fails to show up for the exam or drops out of the program. Another student may respond to anxiety by arranging for another, seemingly more capable, student to take the exam in her place. Yet another may reduce anxiety about his own sense of responsibility for less-than-desirable performance by blaming others, such as the teacher. And yet another may be so overcome with guilt for less-than-ideal performance that she becomes discouraged, morose, even depressed. From an existential perspective, each of these examples involves a lack of authenticity: a failure to meet the challenges and choices of life with courage.

Inauthenticity often is characterized by a disproportionate involvement in one *welt* at the expense of another. An example is the client who responds to the anxiety of isolation by neglecting her *Eigenwelt* and becoming immersed in an intimate relationship in her *Mitwelt*. This is how the client describes her situation:

> I am just so unhappy, but it hasn't always been like this. I used to have a job and friends and a life. When I met him, things changed gradually, yet dramatically. I felt so alive when I was around him. Sure, I played dumb and probably had sex with him sooner than I should have, but he said he

loved me. When he asked me to move in with him, I jumped at the chance. Who wouldn't? I mean, I was living alone and I hated that, but I sure miss my apartment. I moved in with him and put all my stuff in storage or sold it in a garage sale. He said it was his place and he didn't want to make it a "chick house." A few months later, I quit my job, and I just basically sit at home and wait for him. My life is now his life. He doesn't let me hang out with my friends because they are single and he calls them "whores." Maybe he's right. I don't know anymore. It's like I don't trust my instincts, you know? I am happy I am in a relationship. The singles scene is a nightmare. Maybe if we get married it will be better.

Inauthenticity can be seen in a number of symptoms for which people seek counseling. In the face of death anxiety, one person might manifest agoraphobia, developing panic symptoms and avoiding leaving the house for fear of dying, whereas another might manifest driving while intoxicated, and otherwise engaging in highly risky behavior that denies the potential to die. In the face of isolation anxiety, one person might withdraw from relationships for fear of experiencing rejection and loneliness, whereas another might manifest sexual addiction, seeking out numerous sexual partners to ward off isolation. In the face of the anxiety that arises from meaninglessness, one person might attempt suicide to escape a life that seems devoid of current or future meaning, whereas another might develop a compulsive disorder, engaging in repetitive, "necessary" behavior that distracts the person from questions of meaning. In the face of the anxiety that arises from freedom, one person might take a passive, defeated, "victim" approach to life by avoiding decisions, such as the man who, rather than proactively ending a stagnant marriage, instead complains of being trapped and manifests symptoms of depression, hoping the spouse will decide to file for divorce or have an affair to precipitate a divorce. In the face of the anxiety of freedom, another person might take an active, blaming, "persecutor" approach by finding fault with outside circumstances and other people outside for his or her own life situation. From an existential point of view, each of these seemingly diverse symptoms can be traced back to one underlying phenomenon: inauthenticity, a lack of courage to face the givens, experience the resulting anxiety, and proactively make realistic and creative choices as befits one's existential potential.

The Personality Change Process

Basic Principles of Change. From an existential perspective, change consists of increased authenticity. Increased authenticity occurs when one decreasingly makes use of defense mechanisms, that is, when one experiences enhanced awareness of the givens of existence as they manifest in each of the *welts*, when one generates anxiety proportionate to the threats in each of those domains, and when one creates courageous responses to that anxiety—responses free of either inactivity or overactivity, of either despair or blame.

Constructive change is most likely to occur within the context of an authentic relationship. The crucial dynamic in such a relationship is that one be supported in getting fully in touch with all aspects of living, both comfortable and painful. The goal is neither to exaggerate nor to eliminate anxiety but to acknowledge and experience it. In so doing, one drops defenses, affirms the fullness of living, and becomes unblocked to creatively use anxiety to achieve one's deepest potential.

Though rare, an authentic relationship can occur in everyday life. The reason for its rarity is that true caring, Buber's "unfoldment" that we previously described, can occur only when the caring person is relatively authentic, not needing the other to be a certain way to assuage one's own anxiety. For example, most friends and family members, when they see someone in pain, find that their own existential anxiety is provoked; seeking to escape from that anxiety, they rescue the person from pain through comforting and distraction rather than supporting the person in experiencing their pain to facilitate a more authentic existence. In addition, many people "use" others to assuage their own existential anxiety; in demanding that others be a certain way, one does not facilitate their process of becoming themselves. In light of the rarity with which authentic relationship occurs in everyday life, the individual seeking existential growth is most likely to find the necessary conditions for such growth in the special circumstances of the existential counseling situation.

Change Through Counseling. In existential counseling, goals follow the existential emphasis of gaining awareness and taking responsibility for courageously confronting the givens of existence. Through counseling, the client is encouraged to fully explore the givens of life and discover ways one could lead a more authentic existence. As Deurzen-Smith (1997) summarized, the goal of existential therapy is for clients "to learn to open up to what is there in our lives, no matter how hard the truths of our troubles, and see our own position and orientation towards all of this in order to reclaim our central role in our own lives" (p. 188).

Because the client's role involves certain requirements, existential counseling is appropriate for only some people. One must be willing to explore the givens of existence, be ready to face the anxiety that stems from them, and be prepared to experiment with new, more courageous responses to that anxiety. If the client is looking for instant relief or is otherwise not prepared to engage in the process of exploring one's personal world, of tolerating anxiety, and of taking greater responsibility in and for one's life, then the client is not ready for existential therapy (Deurzen-Smith, 1997).

The role of the counselor is to more systematically and purposefully provide a client with a change-facilitating relationship, that is, a more authentic relationship, than the client is likely to experience in everyday life. According to Moustakas (1994), this genuine relationship "is the essential condition that underlies all phases of therapy, the power that permeates all methods for facilitating meaning and growth" (p. 45).

The counselor's role can be summarized as an authentic "being there," a *Dasein* encounter (Bolling, 1995), an open experiencing of both the client and the counselor's self from moment to moment throughout the therapeutic process. The counselor attends both to what the client presents and to how the counselor experiences the client within the therapeutic situation. This "being there" is based on the counselor's genuine desire to understand the client's subjective perspective and approach to existence, especially the extent to which the client does and/or does not acknowledge the givens of existence, generate appropriate anxiety around those givens, and respond to that anxiety courageously, both outside of the therapeutic setting and within it. Upon sensing inauthenticity, the counselor sensitively points it out to the client, thus offering the client the opportunity for enhanced authenticity: increased awareness, anxiety proportionate to any actual threat, and courageous response to that anxiety. The counselor's role is not to provide clients with answers but to be there with clients as they struggle toward increased authenticity.

Two psychological processes assist the counselor in maintaining authenticity. One is a continuous searching attitude. The counselor seeks consistently to discover the client's unique humanity, his or her unique approach to existence. A continuous searching attitude prevents the counselor from thinking, "I know what this person is all about. I have seen this dynamic thousands of times in other depressed clients." Existential therapists understand that this client is different from all past and future clients. The consistent honoring of the individuality of the other is one hallmark of an authentic relationship.

Another process that assists the existential counselor in maintaining authenticity is resonance. Resonance begins with the counselor's well-developed awareness of his or her own struggle to be human: to be aware of, to generate proportionate anxiety about, and to respond courageously in the face of the givens of existence. On the basis of this awareness, the counselor then can resonate to the client's struggles. Resonance involves a kind of identification with the client's struggles, a feeling touched by one's commonality with the client, and a sense of connectedness based on that commonality (Deurzen-Smith, 1997). To resonate with clients, a counselor must authentically address not only the therapeutic encounter but also life outside the therapy session. According to Deurzen-Smith, "the existential therapist, rather than living some kind of holy, abstinent and devout life, needs to be immersed in the complexities of life as actively as possible" (p. 200).

The authentic therapeutic relationship is one of unfoldment: the counselor truly cares for the client, that is, the counselor cares about the client's growth and wants to bring something to life in the client from which the client is currently blocked. As the client's defensive blocks fall away, the client will naturally proceed in a constructive direction.

As stated earlier, the existential model of mental health allows for the reality that complete and constant authenticity is an ideal, a human impossibility. Therefore, the existential counselor burdens neither himself or herself nor the client with the expectation of perfect authenticity at all times. Rather, the counselor strives to maximize his or her own authenticity and encourage it in the client as well.

Stages and Techniques. Existentialists emphasize the relationship as the primary impetus for change, and therefore the stages of therapy and its techniques focus on the formation and development of the relationship. The technique of existential counseling is based on the therapeutic dialogue. As Deurzen-Smith (1997) pointed out,

> Existential therapists talk with their clients: they enter into dialogue, even into philosophical discussion and argument. They venture into the exploration of the other's world experience as if they were going into unknown territory. . . . This coming together is known as co-presence. (p. 218)

This dialogue is designed to create a space where client's can explore life issues. Deurzen-Smith (1997) noted several elements of this dialogue creation which resemble elements of techniques found in many other theories, but with a unique existential spin.

1. **Use of Silence**: In existential counseling, informed consent about the therapeutic process provides for a dialogue regarding the expectations of client and counselor within the therapeutic session. Once the ground rules are established, the existential therapist allows for periods of silence, inviting the client to take the step to share and work. "Welcoming silence will be one of the most significant interventions that the existential psychotherapist will use" (Deurzen-Smith, 1997, p. 227). From an existential perspective, overreliance on complex interpretation and questioning often directs the client in irrelevant directions. The existential therapist provides space for the client to explore.
2. **Constructive Questions:** Existential therapists ask questions to illuminate the underlying themes of the client's story and rarely use this device as a means for information gathering. Deurzen-Smith (1997) issued this basic rule for asking questions: "We ask the questions that are implied in the client's words, the ones already embedded in what they have said" (p. 228). In a sense, these questions are observations of the client's patterns with a question mark at the end to denote the tentative nature of the observations. For example, instead of asking, "How did that make you feel?" a counselor might note, "So, you were humiliated when your dad

showed up to your game drunk?" The constructive use of questions requires that the counselor listen between the lines of the client dialogue and formulate questions to make this content more explicit. For example, instead of asking a client, "How are you and your father alike?" a counselor can take the information that prompted that question and illuminate the subtext, "What you seem to be saying is that both you and your father have ways of escaping when you get anxious."

3. **Interpretation:** Contrary to popular belief, existential therapists make common use of interpretation. Interpretation is the tool for connecting various pieces of client dialogue in a way that promotes growth. The task of the existential counselor is to interpret elements of the dialogue in ways that are meaningful to the client. Lacing interpretation with theoretical jargon is viewed as an imposition of the counselor's framework onto the client. Granted, the theoretical conceptualization is helpful to the counselor ("This client is struggling with an *Eigenwelt* issue"), but is rarely useful to the client if given in that way. Counselors must honor the client's perspective and language in order to provide constructive interpretations.

The techniques described above briefly illustrate some existential methods for interacting with clients. In addition, May and Yalom (2000) described the *boundary situation*, in which one is urgently propelled into an acute encounter with one or more of the givens of life. Most people who seek counseling are involved in boundary situations: death, usually taking the form of loss of some type; a critical decision; a disturbed relationship; or a sense of meaninglessness in life. Yalom (1980) detailed the process of exploring the client's approach to confronting the givens of existence as well as how the givens are expressed within the therapeutic relationship. Through the following discussion of this process, you hopefully can get a sense of the flow and focus of existential therapy.

Death. The given of death and nonbeing can be explored both as it impacts the counseling relationship and as a personal struggle of the client. Through the discussion of both, the client and counselor will get a sense of how the anxiety associated with death is impacting the client's *Mitwelt, Umwelt, Eigenwelt,* and *Uberwelt.*

We will first examine how death affects the counseling encounter. Death is an automatic equalizer between counselor and client. Vontress (1983) noted that even if the client is vastly different from the counselor in ethnic background, gender, or beliefs, the common bond they share is that they will, one day, cease to be. In addition to the shared experience of death, every counseling situation has its one built-in death: termination. Clients will handle the anxiety that stems from termination in their own way. Some will no-show several weeks in advance of the termination session, others will return to old symptomatic complaints in hopes of cheating the death and prolonging the life of the relationship, and yet others may confront the end in a courageous manner, reflecting on the changes made and work still needing to be addressed. Counselors can explore this death anxiety by preparing the client for termination, beginning with the first session, and openly processing termination concerns.

As a personal issue, death anxiety is primary and exists throughout one's lifespan (May & Yalom, 2000). In therapy, evidence of anxiety over nonbeing may be more subtle than anxiety connected to the other givens, but it can most readily be accessed with clients who are grieving over life changes that involve loss, such as one's own terminal illness and impending death, the death or other loss of a loved one, or a change in careers or retirement. Existential counselors do not work to eliminate anxiety but to facilitate the client's use of anxiety as a stimulus to live life to its fullest, as defined by the client.

Isolation. In the therapeutic setting, the counselor encourages awareness of the anxiety involved in the unbridgeable gap between two people. Through the authentic relationship developed in counseling, a client gains valuable lessons on how to connect with, yet honor the separateness of, individuals one encounters in the *Mitwelt*. The authentic relationship, the counseling relationship, is psychologically intimate and intense by design. When clients begin to experience the warmth and acceptance of the authentic relationship, it is common for some clients to want to intensify the intimacy of the relationship, either through increased professional contact, such as additional telephone calls or sessions, or increased personal contact, such as taking the relationship to a social or sexual level. The counselor conceptualizes these actions as the client's attempt to merge with the counselor, to deal inauthentically with the anxiety of being separate or, even worse, alone. Existential counselors recognize the potency of the authentic relationship and use it to help the client deal constructively with the resulting anxiety.

Isolation as a personal issue calls for the client to become more comfortable spending time on the *Eigenwelt*. Clients who present with overdependence in their relationships need to experience time alone. Encouraging clients to engage in activities on their own can facilitate the clients confronting the anxiety of being by themselves in order to develop their sense of self. The following case excerpt illuminates how an exploration of isolation issues can help a client move from paralysis to creative fulfillment.

> When Karen and I got married, I thought that we had to spend every moment together. Up until a few months ago I would get so angry if she didn't want to watch TV with me or if she didn't want me to go with her to work out. I used to think, "If she loved me she would want to be with me all the time." I used to sit at home and get so angry and depressed that she was ignoring me so much. I began to believe that she must be having an affair or planning to leave me. A few weeks ago, I gradually started to spend that time by myself writing in a journal and working on household projects. I also started to jog everyday. I became aware that it was my fear

of being alone that was leading to all my misery. As I began to enjoy my time alone, I stopped noticing that she wasn't there. I mean, I stopped thinking she didn't love me because she was doing something else. I actually enjoy spending time with myself now and, to be honest, I also enjoy the time I spend with Karen a lot more, too. It feels less desperate.

Freedom. Freedom as a counseling concern is *the* counseling concern. The goal of counseling is to facilitate client awareness and to help the client gain courage to embrace the responsibility inherent in the freedom to choose. Existential counselors consistently explore and challenge their clients to access the courage needed to choose. Every situation in the client's life involves choice, so there is plenty of grist for the mill. Clients enact the same patterns of decision making within the counseling relationship as they do outside the therapeutic setting. Those who avoid choices outside of counseling will follow the therapist's lead and ask for direction during counseling. Those who resort to the defense of the ultimate rescuer will relate to the counselor as an all-knowing expert on the client's world, a situation incompatible with an authentic relationship. This phenomenon is especially precarious if the therapist lacks awareness of the dynamic at work. The lack of awareness and resulting inauthentic relationship can cement the client's avoidance of freedom and can be characterized as exploitation of the client by the counselor, however inadvertent.

A person unaware of one's choices is likely to feel trapped and restricted. The following case example demonstrates the subtle, yet powerful, impact the increased awareness of freedom of choice can have on someone.

Client: I don't want to be here. The court says I have to come, but I think it's crazy. I didn't do anything wrong.

Counselor: It seems you feel like you're being ordered here, like you have no choice.

Client: Yeah! I'm being pushed around, you know?

Counselor: Well, I can certainly understand why you wouldn't like being ordered around. I wonder if you actually do have some choices here, but are failing to see them.

Client: I don't get what you are saying. I don't have a choice to be here.

Counselor: I see three choices: You can choose to be here, you can choose to openly refuse the judge's order to her face and be sent to jail, or you can choose simply not to attend without letting the judge know and then take your chances with her finding out and sending you to jail. That's three choices as I count them.

Client: But jail is not a choice.

Counselor: I think it is. It might not be a comfortable choice, but it is an available one. You are choosing to come here because you do not want to choose to go to jail. Now, once you choose to come to counseling, your choices really expand. You can choose to discuss anything you wish or nothing at all; you can choose how you interact to me. Your way of being in counseling is up to you.

Client: I never thought about it like that. I mean, I still don't think coming here is the greatest thing, but I do see that I have some power in setting the agenda, you know, get my money's worth.

Counselor: It seems you're feeling more free in the process as you recognize that even in less than desirable circumstances, you have a few options open to you.

Meaninglessness: Counseling is a meaning-making journey. Clients are choosing to engage in a process that takes emotional endurance, time, and money. Clients will ask the question, "Is what we are doing making a difference in my life. Does this matter?" All of the existential counselor's responses to this question resonate with one theme: "To the extent that we connect, to the extent that you gain awareness of yourself and choose to face the anxiety that is a normal part of your existence, and to the extent that you develop courage to face the balance of life and death, this will matter." Existential counselors help the client experience meaning through the development and collaborative maintenance of the authentic relationship.

Meaninglessness as explored at a personal level means discovering how the client is creating meaning in life and then encouraging the client to create more. The exploration can address personal meaning and identity, the *Eigenwelt*, interpersonal relationships, the *Mitwelt*, or how one finds meaning in one's physical-biological and natural world, the *Umwelt*, but it should always attend to or have elements of the ideal, one's wishes and dreams, the *Uberwelt*. Existentialists believe that the cultivation of personal meaning is far from a selfish undertaking. Making meaning in an authentic manner inevitably involves others' well-being.

In summary, the method of extistential therapy is discovered not in techniques but in the process. The process begins and ends with the relationship. Everything in between focuses on gaining a true understanding of the client's way of being—*Dasein*—in the four spheres of the world and encouraging the client to confront the givens of existence in a creative versus an avoiding manner.

How do you know when existential therapy is over? The short answer is that when growth is evidenced outside of the counseling hour, counseling has been successful (Rychlak, 1981). The real answer is that counseling is a tutorial, a laboratory experiment in being. In that sense the process continues to expand and contract until termination.

CONTRIBUTIONS AND LIMITATIONS

Interface with Recent Developments in the Mental Health Field

The Effectiveness of Psychotherapy. Regarding research into the effectiveness of existential therapy, a systematic review of literature produced no specific research that addressed the efficacy of existential therapy. Many sources have reported anecdotes or case studies that discuss therapeutic outcomes (see Deurzen-Smith, 1988; Vontress, Johnson, & Epp, 1999; Yalom, 1989), but no publications appear to exist that report controlled studies. The lack of outcome studies is philosophically consistent with existentialism's emphasis on the subjective view of the client and the focus on being instead of specific necessary and sufficient elements of change. Existentialists maintain that the striving for authentic being cannot be broken down and measured, that research invariably diminishes the power of the process and vital dimensions of each participant's own journey.

The Nature/Nuture Question. Regarding the nature/nurture question, existentialism embraces the notion that everyone has biological and genetic limitations as experienced through one's *Umwelt*. If one is born with a disease such as leukemia, one cannot merely choose it away. The disease becomes a part of one's being. However, existentialists maintain that even with genetic or biological limitations, each individual will uniquely perceive and address the limitation. For example, one person may accept the fact that the disease exists but will continue to live a life that maximizes a sense of happiness. Another person may choose to conceptualize being diagnosed with a disease as already being dead and thus will live life as if it were over. From an existential perspective, genetics provide a boundary but do not determine the whole of a person's being; what determines that whole is the action and attitude choices the person makes in light of the boundary.

Similarly, as discussed in the development section, interactions that occur with others (*Mitwelt*) are meaningful only to the extent that one grants them importance or influence. One's *Mitwelt* can provide experiences, such as neglect, abuse, and poverty, that hinder the person's ability to develop authenticity, but even in these extreme situations, children have the ability to transcend these influences and choose the path they will take through and beyond these circumstances. From an existential perspective, both nature and nurture foster both growth and decay, but these biological and environmental factors are not as important as the individual's subjective interpretation of, and choices regarding, them. This existential view was succinctly summarized by Frankl (1988): "Man's [*sic*] freedom is not freedom from conditions but rather a freedom to take a stand on whatever conditions might confront him" (p. 16).

Pharmacotherapy. Regarding pharmacotherapy, existentialists take the position that medication is too often used as a means to escape a courageous confrontation of the normal anxieties of life. When one avoids the anxiety, instead of facing it and using it creatively, the client loses a piece of existence and, in effect, is living inauthentically. The painful symptoms are reminders to the client that one must face the givens of existence and experience the fullness of being. Nevertheless, existentialists acknowledge cases in which a client's symptoms are so paralyzing that medication is needed to reduce symptoms enough to make existential exploration possible. Frankl (1988) noted that he routinely used a combination of medication and existential therapy for cases of severe phobias, depression, and psychosis. Vontress remarked, "I do not think existentialists are against the prudent use of antidepressants as much as they are against the narcotizing of our existence" (Epp, 1988, p. 10). Within this approach medication may be used in extreme circumstances but should be viewed as a stepping stone to existential confrontation rather than as an escape from it that one relies upon throughout one's life. Medication may provide a person with a handhold out of the abyss, but existentialists would maintain that true health and authenticity requires a client to develop courage to face one's anxieties—one's individualized abyss—and fully experience one's being, free of medication or any other numbing agents.

Managed Care and Brief Therapy. The existential literature contains very little reference to the relationship between existentialism, brief therapy, and managed care. Existential therapy rests on the authenticity of the client–counselor relationship and on the choices the client makes regarding change. Theoretically, the authenticity of the relationship is not connected to the length of the therapy. May and Yalom (2000) asserted that many existential elements such as responsibility, identity exploration, and the creative use of anxiety can be utilized in a brief therapy approach. Although existential counselors may perceive compatibility, many elements of managed care are contrary to the philosophical underpinnings of the theory. Requirements of managed care companies, such as diagnostic labeling, contracts, a medical model philosophy based on pathology, and outcome assessment couched in behavioral terms (Davis & Meier, 2001), are incongruent with the existential approach.

Diversity Issues. Despite existentialism's roots in Europe, the givens of existence are applicable to all people across all cultures, regardless of race, gender, socioeconomic status, or sexual orientation. As Vontress stated, "Existentialism is not the provincial philosophy of a European elite, it is a universal philosophy of humankind" (Epp, 1988, p. 7). Within the philosophy of existentialism, each individual perceives the world in a unique way, striving for authenticity and dealing with the anxiety that arises from the givens. Because of differences in geography and cultural expectations, the specific circumstances that provoke existential anxiety may differ among various groups, but, at the most essential level of being, each person must confront death, freedom, isolation, and meaninglessness. This shared struggle cements the bond of humanity that transcends cultural, gender, or other differences.

Diversity issues can be explored from an existential perspective by considering not only the universal givens of existence, but also the four interactive dimensions of experience: *Umwelt, Mitwelt, Eigenwelt,* and *Uberwelt.* As discussed earlier, the *Umwelt* is the natural world of the individual and includes not only one's biology, but also the geographic area of the person's world. Understanding the individual's perception of the natural world is crucial to an authentic relationship with the client. Vontress (1983) remarked that failure to consider this element would negatively impact counseling outcome and lead to a distortion in the understanding of the client. *Mitwelt* is the interpersonal sphere of experience. Existential counselors expect and are open to interpersonal differences, because all individuals have their own perspectives regardless of background. Vontress (1983) contended that existential counselors should focus the *Mitwelt* exploration of the client's uniqueness that "transcends their developmental socialization" (p. 7). The *Eigenwelt* is the client's world of self. Existentialists believe that authentic counseling is a process of honoring the individual that therefore must avoid stereotyping and prejudging. Each client's view of self is much more important than objective facts that may be known about a cultural group, gender, or sexual orientation. For example, Vontress (1983) noted, "in counseling Blacks, anti-Black sentiments in society are not as important as each client's attitude toward them" (pp. 8–9). Simply put, we may all agree that hate crimes and discriminatory actions are prevalent against a certain minority group, but to assume the level of importance these factors may play in any client's life robs the client of their unique experience and perception. Intertwined with the other dimensions, one's *Uberwelt* makes up the spiritual world or world of the ideal as seen by the client. Appreciating that people have different definitions of "ideal" is crucial to understanding the client's *Uberwelt.* To further assess and apply a phenomenological cross-cultural approach to the explorations of the dimensions of experience, Ibrahim and Kahn (1987) developed the Scale to Assess World Views.

From the existential perspective, humans are vastly unique yet share a common bond of humanness that is displayed in our shared struggles with the givens of existence within the four dimensions of the world. Against this common backdrop of being runs the undercurrent of anxiety that issues from these concerns. In existentialism, diversity is a given, and understanding one's own individuality and seeing individuality in others is one dimension of an authentic way of being. In all of these spheres, considering the universality of the givens, the existential counselor is guided by one principle: to understand the client's unique way of being-in-the-world.

Spirituality. The concept of spirituality and its place in existentialism has taken an interesting historical ride. Existentialism's early beginnings were in Kierkegaard's Christian-based writings (1843/1954, 1844/1980). He used biblical stories to illustrate the existential condition and focused on sin, suffering, and encouragement to have faith in and loyalty to God. Since that time, existential writers have largely avoided the integration of religion or spirituality into the counseling or philosophical endeavor. However, existentialists avoid complete acceptance or rejection of spirituality due to the philosophical focus on understanding the individual, which may or may not include a spiritual life. Therefore, both strands of opinion are offered here with the understanding that the subjective experience of the individual is the primary factor in considering the spiritual realm, healthy or unhealthy.

As noted, openness to religion and spirituality as a part of being has played a part in the historical development of existentialism. In recent existential writings, Frankl has provided an extensive commentary on the role of spirituality in existence. Frankl (1988) noted that the *logos* in his logotherapy is translated as *spirit*, but that it should emphasize the human spirit, that is, the creative power and freedom inherent in humanity. Additionally, Frankl (1967) also remarked that religion and spirituality are of value to a person's health because they may provide an anchor to existence that facilitates courage to face the givens of existence.

Deurzen-Smith (1997) has made the most ambitious contribution to the integration of spiritual concerns to existential thought with her inclusion of the spiritual dimension—*Uberwelt*—as an addition to the other three dimensions of experience. The *Uberwelt* is the ideal world of the individual and inspires ultimate meaning when individuals surrender to an awareness that there is something larger than self in the universe. Far more than religion, the *Uberwelt* can include a multitude of belief systems. The main point of the *Uberwelt* is not to create a powerful superbeing to order our lives. Instead it is an encouragement to realize that there is much that we do not understand. We are neither the center of the universe nor helpless pawns of an omnipresent force. We are ultimately beings searching for meaning. The *Uberwelt* inspires humans to know their limits, accept their responsibilities, and understand that we will never know everything about the ways and means of the universe. This dynamic of responsibility and meaning/lack of meaning propels us to continually create a way of life that addresses our everyday concerns and encourages us to consistently and authentically connect to self and the world.

Just as existentialists conceptualize a positive and holistic conceptualization of spirituality, they also have comments on the inauthentic application of spiritual and religious concepts. The criticisms largely coalesce around the tendency for people to use spirituality as a means to avoid the anxiety of life. This avoidance is considered inauthentic and robs the individual of the opportunity to fully experience existence. In many cases, this avoidance manifests itself in the belief in an ultimate rescuer (Yalom, 1980) or in the absolution of responsibility for making poor choices or for attempting to make no choices at all. The following case example provides an illustration of how individuals can use spirituality to avoid the responsibility of daily life and its inherent anxiety.

> I know my world is crashing down around me but I just have to trust that the world has something better planned for me. I don't really believe in any religion, but I do believe that there is a guiding power in the universe. It is in the trees and air and out in space. It is all around us right now. I feel "It" watching over me and pushing me in certain directions. I believe that when the world wants something to happen, it will make it happen. If I am supposed to get a job, a job will come to me. Even though I am not a Christian, I pray on things. I believe that if I pray long enough, good things will start to happen. When I left my husband, I knew I hurt him, but I prayed on it and realized it must have been part of a bigger plan. I'm a pawn in this. Just a speck in the universe, waiting for my next break.

In this case, it is not one's spiritual beliefs that are inauthentic, it is how the person interprets and uses the belief system. If the beliefs are used to abdicate responsibility and hide from the anxiety that is a part of the human condition, then the beliefs are contributing to an inauthentic way of being. If the beliefs help facilitate courage to address the anxiety of everyday existence and add a sense of meaning and humility to a person's life, the person is using them in a way that promotes authenticity. In summary, existentialism allows for spirituality as an essence of being but not as the essence of one's entire being.

Technical Eclecticism. Existentialists believe that their philosophy of existence represents a unique and comprehensive approach to the human condition. Practitioners of existentialism hold that a firm grounding in this philosophy is fundamental to the development of an authentic approach to life and to the counseling situation. Theoretical eclecticism has been frowned upon by existentialists. Additionally, Bauman and Waldo (1988) proposed that the comprehensive nature of existentialism is a practical alternative to the chaos of a theoretically eclectic practice. Technical eclecticism may be appropriate to the degree that the adopted elements are consistent with existial philosophy (May & Yalom, 2000). May and Yalom noted, "The therapist's belief system provides a certain consistency. It permits the therapist to know what to explore so that the patient does not become confused" (p. 293). Theoretical eclecticism would be highly discouraged and in most cases would be conceptualized as the counselor's attempt to avoid the authentic relationship with the client by grabbing incompatible ideas desperately.

DSM-IV-TR **Diagnosis.** Regarding diagnosis, existentialists hold that focusing on symptoms and classifying individuals into a labeling system is destructive to the holistic view of the person. Existentialist practitioners would argue that a category such as "major depressive disorder" tells a counselor very little about the person and their unique way of being. Existentialism is a theory focused on the uniqueness and wellness of the client, a focus that is markedly different from the pathology foundation of most diagnostic symptoms. Bauman and Waldo (1988) pointed out that, "in fact . . . a focus on symptoms alone perpetuates the restricted being which probably brought clients into counseling" (p. 22). Bugental and Sterling (1995) strongly asserted that existential counselors have "relatively little need for such conventions as formal diagnosis" (p. 236). Although existentialists can and do use diagnostic systems as a means of communication with other professions and for insurance purposes, they may include an existential diagnosis that documents how the client is currently functioning in the four dimensions of the world and is addressing the givens of existence (Epp, 1988).

Weaknesses of the Theory

As illuminated in the discussion of research, the philosophy of existentialism makes it very difficult to study what is effective practice and what is not. Practitioners and students need to have some way to discern good practice from malpractice. Clients also deserve to know that the method of treatment has some merit. The lack of structure and distaste for objective measures places the practice of existential therapy behind a veil of mystery and vague practices. If existentialism is to survive in the world of validated approaches and patient's rights, the proponents of the theory might need to soften their resolve and use their anxiety about the meaninglessness of objectivity in a creative manner.

Another criticism that springs from the subjective nature of the theory lies in its ability to be transferred to new practitioners. In my (KAF) experience, students and instructors approach existentialism from two very different tangents. In one way, existentialism is taught as the theory of the intellectual, wealthy elite, steeped in deep philosophical jargon. The unspoken implication is, "This theory is too lofty and complicated, so let's move on to something more practical." This belief discourages many students from further exploration of the theory. The second interpretation of the theory is based on a belief that the theory is unstructured and is focused on listening and "being" with the client. Of course this "being" is translated as, "No one will know if I'm doing it right or not. It's all about sharing time and space with the client. I am beyond evaluation!" In this sense, the student is hiding within a simplified version of the theory and is avoiding the anxiety of being a counselor. One pattern makes existentialism too complicated; the other makes it too superficial. In either case, it is existentialism that loses.

Distinguishing Additions to Counseling and Psychotherapy

Existentialism has provided a bedrock philosophy that has helped shape many of the leading counseling theories of the 20th century. Theories that have existential roots include Adlerian, Gestalt, reality, person-centered, and rational emotive behavioral therapy (REBT). Out of this philosophical movement, mental health practitioners can include in their practice a greater understanding and emphasis on the humanity and uniqueness of each individual. The movement also can be credited with expanding the role of the counselor from blank screen to a feeling human being striving for authenticity, much like the clients we encounter. Just as existentialism broadened the role of the therapist, it also gave more responsibility and freedom to the client. The focus on choice and responsibility gave a new flavor to the therapeutic relationship that was vastly different from the prevailing psychoanalytic and behavioral approaches of the time.

RECOMMENDED RESOURCES

Books

Deurzen-Smith, E. van (1997). *Everyday mysteries: Existential dimensions in psychotherapy.* New York: Routledge. Emmy van Deurzen-Smith is the founder of the Society for Existential Analysis, and this book provides a very readable account of existential theory. The reader is given a comprehensive discussion of fundamental existential philosophy as well as a thorough overview of the existential approach to counseling complete with detailed case studies.

Frankl, V. E. (1988). *The will to meaning.* New York: Meridian. Excellent discussion of Frankl's logotherapy and applicable concepts. This book also provides nice coverage of the variety of thoughts regarding spirituality and religion as it applies to existential theory.

Yalom, I. D. (1980). *Existential psychotherapy.* New York: Basic Books and (1989), *Love's executioner: And other tales of psychotherapy.* New York: Harper. The first book is the most comprehensive discourse on his proposed givens of existence and how they apply to maladjustment and therapy. The second offering is a series of case studies treated from an existential perspective. The case studies are well written and provide insight into the inner thoughts of the therapist as he negotiated the counseling journey.

Video

Yalom, I. D., & Douglas, M. (1995). *Existential-humanistic psychotherapy in action : A demonstration*. San Francisco, CA: Jaylen Productions.

Websites

http://www.existential.mcmail.com/Society for Existential Analysis: This website is the official site for the Society for Existential Analysis based in London. The website contains helpful information about the application and theory of the existential approach and contains the links for additional materials and opportunities for training in existential therapy.

REFERENCES

Allers, R. (1961). *Existentialism and psychiatry.* Springfield, IL: Thomas.

Bauman, S., & Waldo, M. (1988). Existential theory and mental health counseling: If it were a snake it would have bitten! *Journal of Mental Health Counseling, 20,* 13–26.

Binswanger, L. (1963). *Being-in-the-world: Selected papers.* New York: Basic.

Bolling, M. Y. (1995). Acceptance and Dasein. *Humanistic Psychologist, 23,* 213–226.

Buber, M. (1970). *I and thou* (W. Kaufman, Trans.). New York: Scribner.

Bugental, J. F. T. (1965). *The search for authenticity.* New York: Holt, Rinehart & Winston.

Bugental, J. F. T., & Sterling, M. M. (1995). Existential-humanistic psychotherapy. In A. S. Gurman and S. B. Messer (Eds.), *Essential psychotherapies* (pp. 226–260). New York: Guilford.

Davis, S. R., & Meier, S. T. (2001). *Elements of managed care: A guide for helping professionals.* Belmont, CA: Wadsworth/Thompson Learning.

Deurzen-Smith, E. van (1988). *Existential counselling in practice.* London: Sage.

Deurzen-Smith, E. van (1997). *Everyday mysteries: Existential dimensions in psychotherapy.* New York: Routledge.

Epp, L. R. (1988). The courage to be an existential counselor: An interview with Clemmont E. Vontress. *Journal of Mental Health Counseling, 20,* 1–12.

Frankl, V. E. (1967). *The doctor and the soul: From psychotherapy to logotherapy.* New York: Bantam.

Frankl, V. E. (1988). *The will to meaning.* New York: Meridian.

Heidegger, M. (1962). *Being and time* (J. Macquarrie and E. S. Robinson, Trans.). New York: Harper & Row. (Original work published 1927)

Husserl, E. (1965). Philosophy as a rigorous science. In Q. Lauer (Ed.), *Phenomenology and the crisis of philosophy* (pp. 71–147). New York: Harper & Row.

Ibrahim, F. A., & Kahn, H. (1987). Assessment of world views. *Psychological Reports, 60,* 163–176.

Josselson, R. (1992). *The space between us: Exploring the dimensions of human relationships.* San Francisco: Jossey-Bass.

Keen, E. (1970). *Three faces of being: Toward an existential clinical psychology.* New York: Appleton/Century/Crofts.

Kierkegaard, S. (1954). *Fear and trembling.* Princeton, NJ: Princeton University. (Original work published 1843)

Kierkegaard, S. (1980). *The concept of anxiety* (R. Thomte, Trans.). Princeton, NJ: Princeton University. (Original work published 1844)

Maddi, S. R. (1967). The existential neurosis. *Journal of Abnormal Psychology, 72,* 311–325.

Maddi, S. R. (1976). *Personality theories: A comparative analysis* (3rd ed.). Homewood, IL: Dorsey.

May, R. (1939). *The art of counseling.* New York: Gardner.

May, R. (1950). *The meaning of anxiety.* New York: Norton.

May, R. (1961). *Existential psychology.* New York: Random House.

May, R. (1977). *The meaning of anxiety.* New York: Norton.

May, R. (1981). *Freedom and destiny.* New York: Norton.

May, R. (1983). *The discovery of being.* New York: Norton.

May, R. (1985). *My quest for beauty.* Dallas, TX: Saybrook.

May, R., & Yalom, I. D. (2000). Existential psychotherapy. In R. J. Corsini and D. Wedding (Eds.), *Current psychotherapies* (6th ed., pp. 273–302). Itasca, IL: F. E. Peacock.

Moustakas, C. (1994). *Existential psychotherapy and the interpretation of dreams.* Northvale, NJ: Jason Aronson.

Rabinowitz, F. E., Good, G., & Cozad, L. (1989). Rollo May: A man of meaning and myth. *Journal of Counseling and Development, 67,* 436–441.

Rychlak, J. F. (1981). *Introduction to personality and psychotherapy* (2nd ed.). Boston: Houghton Mifflin.

Sartre, J. P. (1965). Existentialism is a humanism. *Essays in existentialism* (H. E. Barnes, Trans.). Secaucus, NJ: Citadel.

Tillich, P. (1952). *The courage to be.* New Haven, CT: Yale University Press.

Vontress, C. E. (1983). An existential approach to cross-cultural counseling. *Counseling and Values, 28,* 2–12.

Vontress, C. E., Johnson, J. A., & Epp, L. R. (1999). *Cross cultural counseling: A casebook.* Alexandria, VA: American Counseling Association.

Yalom, I. D. (1980). *Existential psychotherapy.* New York: Basic.

Yalom, I. D. (1989). *Love's executioner: And other tales of psychotherapy.* New York: Harper.

CHAPTER 6

PERSON-CENTERED COUNSELING

BACKGROUND OF THE THEORY

Biographical and Historical Overview

Carl Rogers developed person-centered counseling and psychotherapy in the United States roughly between 1940 and 1990. His approach was born in an era when science pervaded Western thinking, when psychoanalysis dominated clinical psychology, and when progressivism challenged traditional education. His ideas matured concurrently with the emergence of behaviorism as a systematic approach to psychotherapy, with which his ideas differed fundamentally. One of the pioneers of the humanistic psychotherapy movement, Rogers expressed his humanistic views in his own summary statement of history:

> I am well aware that . . . one can place . . . a primary value upon society, and only a secondary value upon the individual. But only in the individual does awareness exist. Only in the individual can alternative courses of action be most deeply and consciously tested as to their enriching or destructive consequences. The whole history of mankind [sic], it seems to me, shows a gradually increasing emphasis upon the significance and worth of each individual. I not only observe this trend, I concur in it. (Rogers, 1989, p. 266)

Rogers himself lived through World War I, the Great Depression, World War II, the war in Vietnam, and much of the Cold War. He continued to refine his ideas throughout the turbulent social changes of the 1960s and 1970s, including the civil rights and women's rights movements. In these fertile times of social experimentation, Rogers and others subscribing to his views applied his principles to a variety of domains of human existence.

The last decades of Rogers' life occurred in a time of globalization that involved both enhanced awareness of areas of intense conflict around the world and relatively greater ease of contact between people of various cultures. Globalization provided Rogers an opportunity to apply tentatively his psychotherapeutic principles internationally to the arena of political conflict resolution. Also during his last decades, information and research increased regarding experiences of altered states of consciousness, including the intuitive, paranormal, and mystical domains both in life and surrounding death. Rogers used this information and, of course most importantly, his own experiences, to speculate on the ultimate nature of reality.

Founder's Biographical Overview

Carl Rogers was born in 1902 in Oak Park, Illinois, a middle to upper middle-class suburb just west of Chicago. He was the fourth of six children in a family he described as close and caring and, at the same time, strictly religious, ethical, and hard working. His family enjoyed their own company, neither socializing with others nor engaging in diversions such as card playing or dancing. Rogers accepted his parents' view that his family was different from other people. He described himself as a solitary, shy boy whose primary avocation was reading.

When Rogers was 12 years old, his family moved to a farm in the Chicago area, where he reportedly developed an appreciation for the scientific process. He began college in Wisconsin, majoring first in agriculture, then changing to history as preparation for the ministry. His attendance at an international Student Christian Federation Conference in China during his junior year prompted his development of his own religious beliefs independent from those of his parents.

During college he fell in love with fellow student Helen Elliott whom he had known prior to his family's move to the farm. Upon college graduation, he married Helen despite his parents' wishes that they delay until he was finished with schooling. Over the years, Rogers occasionally wrote in his characteristically personal and candid style about his marriage with Helen. They were still married when she died in 1979.

Beginning in 1924, Rogers spent 2 years studying at the doctrinally liberal Union Theological Seminary. During his second year, he and a small group of other students petitioned successfully to hold an instructor-less seminar in which they could explore their own questions about religion and life. Through this seminar he progressed substantially toward the development of his own unique philosophy and became aware that he was not suited to the ministry's requirement of allegiance to a specific religious doctrine.

Having enjoyed his exposure to psychology and psychiatry, he pursued these interests at Teacher's College of Columbia University, including a fellowship/internship at the Institute for Child Guidance. After graduation, he moved to Rochester, New York, to take a position as a psychologist in a child guidance center. During his 12 years there, he wrote his first book, *The Clinical Treatment of the Problem Child*. Soon after its publication in 1939, Ohio State University (OSU) offered him a full professorship in psychology.

Shortly after taking the position at OSU, he delivered a paper entitled "Some Newer Concepts in Psychotherapy," marking both the birth of client-centered therapy and Rogers' discovery that people could be very threatened by his ideas. Despite controversy, he expanded and published his views in the 1942 book, *Counseling and Psychotherapy*.

Rogers served 5 years at OSU, 12 years at the University of Chicago, and 4 years at the University of Wisconsin. During these two decades, he expanded and clarified his theory of psychotherapy, personality, and interpersonal relationships. He applied his theory to clinical populations beyond the individual and to settings beyond psychotherapy.

In 1964, Rogers moved to La Jolla, California, first taking a position at the Western Behavioral Sciences Institute and then, in 1968, helping create the Center for Studies of the Person. During the next 20 years, he expanded the application of his theory to education, marriage, administration, and politics. He was invited around the world to disseminate his views and to South Africa, Eastern Europe, the Soviet Union, northern Ireland, and Central America to engage in political conflict resolution.

Rogers' theory can be understood as having developed in three major phases. The first "nondirective" phase focused on how the nondirective counselor's conduct differed from that of more "directive" psychotherapists, such as psychoanalysts and behavior therapists. Rogers' 1951 publication of *Client-Centered Therapy* marked a shift in focus away from of the counselor and firmly onto the client as a responsible agent whose nature provided the rationale for the counselor's therapeutic conduct. The expanded application of Rogers' psychotherapeutic principles beyond the confines of traditional psychology marked the third, person-centered phase of his theory.

Rogers received numerous honors during his lifetime. Among his most valued was his receipt in 1956, with two other psychologists, of the American Psychological Association's first-ever Distinguished Scientific Contribution Award. It is interesting, also, to note Rogers' reception at the first Evolution of Psychotherapy Conference in Phoenix, Arizona, held in 1985. Virtually every leading figure in the field of psychotherapy was invited to make presentations; over 7,000 mental health professionals attended, representing every imaginable specialization within the field. One of the authors of this textbook (JMH) was privileged to be among those professionals and to attend numerous presentations by a variety of speakers. Only one speaker received a standing ovation, and he received one each of the three times he presented; that speaker was Carl Rogers. The accolades with which he was met reflected the ultimate esteem in which Carl Rogers was held. It is no wonder, then, that shortly before his death, Rogers was nominated for the Nobel Peace Prize.

At the close of his (1989) essay, "Growing Old: or Older and Growing," the 75-year-old Rogers reported that he had been a sickly child, predicted to die young, a prediction with which he had come to agree, albeit in a different sense than originally meant. That prediction and agreement proved equally accurate a decade later: At age 85, continuing, to the end, to add to his list of several authored books, hundreds of authored journal articles and presentations, several demonstration videotapes, and numerous international conflict resolution processes, Carl Rogers did, indeed, die young.

Rogers' theoretical beliefs are reflected in many of his life experiences. The reader, after learning the material that follows in this chapter, is encouraged to return to this biographical sketch and apply concepts from Rogers' theory to his life as described in the sketch.

To conclude this sketch, the reader is invited to partake of quotations from Carl Rogers regarding what he considered to be some of his most important learnings in life.

Rogers (1961):

> The more I am simply willing to be myself . . . and the more I am willing to understand and accept the realities in myself and in the other person, the more change seems to be stirred up. . . . It is a very paradoxical thing. (p. 22)

> I can trust my experience. . . . [M]y total organismic sensing of a situation is more trustworthy than my intellect. . . . [E]valuation by others is not a guide for me. . . . Experience is, for me, the highest authority. (pp. 22–23)

> I enjoy the discovery of order in experience. . . . I find it very satisfying to pursue. . . . [T]he reason I devote myself to research, and to the building of theory, is to satisfy a need for perceiving order and meaning. (pp. 24–25)

> The facts are friendly . . . so while I still hate to readjust my thinking . . . these painful reorganizations are what is known as learning [that] always lead to a more satisfying, because somewhat more accurate, way of seeing life. (p. 25)

> What is most personal is most general. . . . [T]he very feeling which has seemed to me most private, most personal, and hence most incomprehensible by others, has turned out to be an expression for which there is resonance in many other people. (p. 26)

> Life, at its best, is a flowing, changing process in which nothing is fixed. (p. 27)

Rogers in 1972 (from Rogers, 1989):

> The things in one's private life which cannot *possibly* be talked about *can* be talked about, easily and freely. (p. 23)

> I have come to value highly the privilege of getting away, of being alone. (p. 45)

Rogers in 1977 (from Rogers, 1989):

> I have found myself opening up to much greater intimacy in relationships . . . physically . . . psychologically. . . . I recognize how much I need to care deeply for another and to receive that kind of caring in return. . . . I can say openly what I have always recognized dimly: that my deep involvement in psychotherapy was a cautious way of meeting this need for intimacy without risking too much of my person. . . . Now I am more willing . . . to risk giving more of myself. (pp. 83–84)

> We are indeed wiser than our intellects . . . the nonrational, creative "metaphoric mind." . . . I am open to even more mysterious phenomena B precognition, thought transference, clairvoyance, human auras, Kirlian photography, even out-of-the-body experiences. These phenomena may not fit with known scientific laws, but perhaps we are on the verge of discovering new types of lawful order. (p. 83)

> Ten or fifteen years ago, I felt quite certain that death was the total end of the person. I still regard that as the most likely prospect. . . . My belief that death is the end has, however, been modified by some of my learnings of the past decade. . .near-death [experiences] . . . reincarnation . . . that individual consciousness is but a fragment of a cosmic consciousness. . . . [D]eath will be what it will be, and I trust I can accept it as either an end to, or a continuation of, life. (pp. 87–88)

Rogers in 1979 (from Rogers, 1989):

> In the eighteen months prior to my wife's death in March, 1979 . . . a series of experiences . . . decidedly changed my thoughts and feelings about dying and the continuation of the human spirit. . . . [My wife, Helen] and I visited a thoroughly honest medium. . . . The messages were extraordinarily convincing . . . involving facts that the medium could not possibly have known. . . . Helen also had visions and dreams of her family members, which made her increasingly certain that she would be welcomed on the other side. . . . [S]he "saw" evil figures and the devil by her hospital bed [whom] she dismissed [and they] never reappeared . . . visions of an inspiring white light which came close, lifted her from the bed, and then deposited her back on the bed. . . . All these experiences . . . have made me much more open to the possibility of the continuation of the individual human spirit. . . . I now consider it possible that each of us is a continuing spiritual essence lasting over time, and occasionally incarnated in a human body. (pp. 51–53)

Philosophical Underpinnings

Rogers (1957) noted that Walker (1956) had identified Rogers as "the successor to Rousseau [who observed] that every man comes from the hand of his

Maker a perfect being. This pristine splendor is corrupted, said Rousseau, by an imperfect society" (p. 89). Denying Walker's interpretation, Rogers cited evidence that his exposure to Rousseau had been extremely limited. Rather, he was adamant that his views were the product of his direct experience working with clients in psychotherapy.

However, Rogers (Raskin & Rogers, 2000) did acknowledge feeling supported by the theory of Otto Rank, which was quite similar in basic assumptions to his own. In particular, Rank believed in the creative power in each person, the importance of self-acceptance and reliance, the centrality of the client in the therapeutic process, the value in the counselor avoiding the role of educator, and the importance of the client experiencing the present moment in the therapeutic process. Rogers also noted similarities between his views and those of Søren Kierkegaard, who emphasized the importance of subjective experience, who believed that ultimate truth is never reached and that knowledge is always in a state of evolution, and who concerned himself with aspects of human experience such as alienation, anxiety, inauthenticity, and choice. Rogers also affirmed a similarity between his own views and those of Abraham Maslow, who postulated a self-actualizing tendency in humans—a tendency of humans to heal, grow, and fulfill their potential.

PERSONALITY DEVELOPMENT

Nature of Humans

The Function of the Psyche. Rogers did not see the core of human motivation as negative, that is, hostile, antisocial, destructive, or evil; nor as neutral, capable of being shaped into any form; nor as perfect in itself and corrupted only by an evil society. Rather, he saw humans at their deepest level to be essentially positive, having the fundamental, innate motive of all living organisms: the actualizing tendency to grow, to heal when injured, and to develop one's full potential. This actualizing motive renders people essentially forward-moving, constructive, and realistic. Rogers believed that, at the core, humans tend toward development, individuality, and cooperative relationships; toward movement from dependence to independence; toward a harmonized, complex, and fluid pattern of self-regulation; toward the preservation, enhancement, and further evolution of both self and the human species. Rogers considered humans, at their most essential level, to be trustworthy.

Rogers believed that everyone, to one degree or another, becomes alienated from the actualizing tendency. However, although the tendency can be thwarted, the only way to destroy it is to destroy the organism. In humans, the actualizing tendency is experienced as needs for phenomena that maintain or enhance the organism, such as affection, affiliation, aggression, and sex. Some needs are inborn; also inborn is the potential to acquire additional, learned needs.

To pursue the actualizing tendency, the infant is equipped with the capacity to perceive and to symbolize accurately in awareness both sensory and visceral experience. The infant is born also with the potential to deny experience by suppressing, selectively perceiving, or distorting how experience is represented in awareness. Experience that has been denied accurate conscious representation does not just "go away"; it is nonconsciously apprehended through the process of *subception*. Subception is illustrated by an adult encountering a specific situation and having a vague sense of uneasiness without initially knowing why. The newborn infant, however, having no reason to deny or distort experience from conscious awareness, engages exclusively in accurate symbolization of experience.

The infant's actualizing tendency interacts with perception in the *organismic valuing process*, whereby each object of perception is immediately experienced in terms of how well it actualizes the organism. Thus, each object of perception is experienced either positively as something that tends to actualize the organism, neutrally as something unrelated to the organism's actualization, or negatively as something that detracts from the organism's actualization. In other words, either an object fulfills a need, is unrelated to a need, or thwarts the fulfillment of a need.

The organismic valuing process is characterized by an *internal locus of evaluation*, in which the infant's preferences reflect the input of inner visceral and sensory perception and the assignment of value based on his own innate actualizing tendency. This process involves flexibility rather than rigidity, because a specific object may be perceived as actualizing at one moment and as contrary to actualization at another. For example, a nipple in the infant's mouth, rather than being rigidly valued as always positive or always negative, is likely to be valued positively when the infant is hungry (feels a need for food), but negatively when the infant is quite full or satiated (feeling a need for no additional food).

Also innate in infants is the capacity for behavior: holistic action aimed at the goal of satisfying needs. A person organizes activity to approach those experiences organismically valued positively and avoid those experiences organismically valued negatively. On the basis of feedback regarding how well a past behavior actually satisfied a need, a person will adjust future behavior to more nearly approximate the maximum possible need fulfillment.

The mechanism of feedback calls upon three innate conceptual capabilities of the self-actualizing tendency: memory of past experience, consideration of alternative behaviors, and prediction of possible future outcomes. Feedback also relies on the innate conceptual tendency to organize perceptions, including differentiating dissimilarities among experiences, identifying patterns of commonality among experiences, and seeking consistency and integrity among perceptions.

Perhaps the most important application of these conceptual capabilities is in the formation of the self-concept. The process begins when the infant comes to differentiate some aspects of her being and functioning as self-experience. In this process a crucial shift occurs: Rather than just simply and directly experiencing a need, the infant conceptualizes herself as experiencing the need; rather than just simply and directly valuing objects of her perception, she conceptualizes herself as valuing the object; rather than just simply and directly behaving in response to her values, she conceptualizes herself as behaving. In this way, what was formerly direct, organismic functioning now itself becomes an object of perception—actually a constellation of self-experiences—that become organized into her self-concept: who she thinks she is. As objects of perception, the self-concept as a whole and each of its contents become subject to evaluation. Whereas formerly she might simply cry when sad, now she observes herself crying; with that observation is born the potential to evaluate her crying as good, neutral, or bad, apart from her organismic valuation. How the child makes that secondary evaluation will be described in the next section. Once the evaluation is made, it becomes part of the *gestalt* or "whole picture" of the self-concept. Because of the human tendency to seek consistency and integrity in such perceptual gestalts, as a self-concept forms it will be defended psychologically against inconsistent information and experience. This process also will be more thoroughly described below.

The Structure of the Psyche. Rogers' view of the personality included several hypothesized psychic structures. He conceptualized the newborn infant's psyche as an undifferentiated, nonconscious whole consisting of all the infant's experience, also termed *organismic experience*, the total experience of the human organism. Gradually the infant comes to identify some of her organismic experience as "belonging to me" and thus develops a *self-concept*: a personal psychological representation of self. Initially, the self-concept and

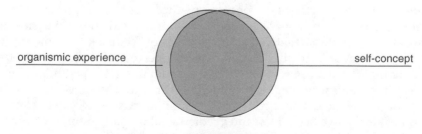

organismic experience ——————   —————— self-concept

FIGURE 6.1
Congruence between organismic experience and self-concept.

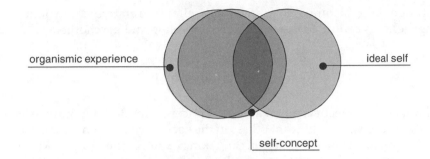

FIGURE 6.2
**Relationship between organismic experience, self-concept, and newly
forming ideal self.**

organismic experience are identical or *congruent*. This condition can be illustrated by a Venn diagram in which the circle representing self-concept and the circle representing organismic experience completely overlap (see Figure 6.1).

For reasons that will be explained in the next section, the infant's state of congruence changes. *Conditions of worth* develop: psychological representations of "what I must experience to be worthwhile." These conditions of worth form an *ideal self* that is inevitably different, at least to some degree, from the as-yet congruent self-concept and organismic experience (see Figure 6.2). The child alters the self-concept to bring it into closer alignment with the ideal self, thus creating a condition of *incongruence* between the self-concept and organismic experience. This incongruence can be illustrated by a Venn diagram in which the three structures of the psyche overlap only partially (see Figure 6.3).

The degree of incongruence varies among individuals. For the person-centered therapist, the ability to conceptualize the relative degree and the

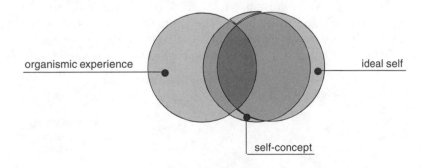

FIGURE 6.3
Incongruence between organismic experience, self-concept, and ideal self.

specific content of one's own and one's clients' relative congruence/incongruence is central to the process of counseling and psychotherapy.

Role of Environment

From Rogers' perspective, a human's self-concept is profoundly influenced by relationships with significant others in the social environment—especially primary caretakers but also others in caretaking or authoritative roles. Rogers believed that as a child's self-concept begins to form, the child develops a *need for positive regard* from significant others. Rogers considered it important not whether this need is innate or learned, but that it is universal among humans.

Each significant other can theoretically be placed on a continuum: at one end, the significant other feels and communicates to the child a totally *unconditional positive regard*, a complete empathic understanding, acceptance, and prizing of the child's being and inner experience; at the other end, the significant other feels and communicates to the child a totally *conditional positive regard*, empathically understanding, accepting, and prizing the child only when her being and inner experience matches some condition determined by the significant other (see Figure 6.4). Probably no one, in reality, exists at either extreme of the continuum. It is also important to note that unconditional positive regard does not involve total acceptance and prizing of all of the child's behaviors; rather, a caretaker can accept the child while setting limits on certain behaviors.

A significant other's regard for a child is reflected in all aspects of the relationship, but most notably in the forms of discipline. To say, "You're a bad girl for crying like that in the restaurant" is to reject the child's total being on the condition of worth that "I accept and value you as a whole person only if you behave in a certain way." To say, "You shouldn't get so upset when you can't have the exact drink you want" is to reject the child's inner experience on the condition of worth that "I accept and value your feelings only when they conform to what I think you should feel." To take the crying child to the car (or foyer), and to say, "I know you're upset they didn't have the exact drink you wanted, and I'm sorry for that. Because crying loudly doesn't change the situation, and because crying loudly is unpleasant for

X – X
unconditional   totally
positive   conditional
regard   positive
                                                                                 regard

FIGURE 6.4
The positive regard continuum.

other people in the restaurant, I'll wait here in the car (or the foyer) with you until you're finished crying. Then we'll go back inside" sets limits on the child's behavior without devaluing the inner experience that gave rise to the behavior or devaluing the child as a whole.

Caretakers inevitably express to children some degree of conditional positive regard. Subsequently, the child independently associates aspects of the self with gain or loss of positive regard; this is termed *self-regard*. She develops a learned need for positive self-regard. The more the child's significant others feel and communicate unconditional positive regard, the more likely the child will develop an ideal self consisting of unconditional self-regard: an acceptance and prizing of self in all experience. The more the significant others feel and communicate conditional positive regard, the more likely the child will develop an ideal self consisting of *conditions of worth*: an acceptance and prizing of self only when experience meets certain conditions. It is important to note that the ultimate source of the child's conditions of worth is not others' conditional positive regard but is one's own need for positive self-regard.

Rogers also believed that receiving positive regard from others is so potent, so compelling, that it becomes more important to a person than one's own organismic valuing process. In a sense, to receive positive regard from others, the person "sells out" her organismic valuing process. Feeling the need for positive self-regard, and then perceiving others' conditional positive regard, she creates internal conditions of worth which are then consolidated into an ideal self; she then redefines her self-concept to match that ideal. This process constitutes an intrapsychic trade-off: the person gains positive self-regard, but loses the guidance of the organismic valuing process, one's own inner wisdom.

An example of the process described above is a college student who is pursuing a pre-med curriculum despite the fact that she is not enjoying most of it and is getting only mediocre grades. She is very interested in law, but she perseveres in the study of medicine. The intrapsychic dynamics behind this situation are that, earlier in life, she perceived her father as communicating conditional positive regard: "I will be proud of you only if you are a physician." She created the condition of worth that, "I am worthwhile only if I am a physician." It became part of her ideal self, and she adjusted her self-concept to align with that ideal self: "I can become a physician." Although her organismic experience includes disliking and performing poorly in the study of medicine, she denies this experience to her awareness or, when it manages to break through, she distorts it to fit her self-concept: "Everyone struggles at times; I'm still in the process of adjusting to doing what I'm really meant to do: become a physician." Rogers termed this alienation between one's organismic experience and one's self-concept *incongruence*.

The Healthy/Adaptive versus Unhealthy/Maladaptive Personality. The relatively greater an individual's degree of congruence, the healthier and more adaptive the individual will be. Rogers called the person with a high degree of congruence a *fully functioning person*. Conversely, a relatively greater degree of incongruence characterizes the unhealthy or maladaptive personality.

To be a congruent, fully functioning person is not to be a conformist, nor always happy, nor in a fixed state of adjustment, homeostasis, fulfillment, or actualization. Rather, it is to be in an ongoing creative process. Being congruent, the person has no need for the defense of denial; the individual is open to and accurately symbolizes all experience. Existence is rich and varied as the person experiences deeply both fear and courage, both pain and ecstacy, both anger and love. Because all experience is perceived, subception is not needed. Feeling unthreatened by experience, the person does not need to control it or impose structure on it; thus, rigidity decreases. Self-structure in the fully functioning person is a fluid gestalt, changing as each new experience is sequentially assimilated. In each moment the person fully experiences the societal demands of the situation, one's own possibly conflicting needs, and associated relevant memories, and then openly trusts the inner wisdom of the total organism to respond holistically to all the available data with the most beneficial course of action.

Due to incomplete data from the environment, people will sometimes make choices that prove less than optimal, yet with that very feedback, future choices can be adjusted to be more optimal. Thus a congruent person is engaged in an ongoing, homeostatic process, using all physiological and psychological experience to find the greatest degree of intrapersonal and interpersonal harmony. In this way the person is exquisitely capable of adapting to novel information and to changing environmental conditions with both personally and socially constructive behavior.

Again, Rogers believed that humans move toward this evolutionary potential not by incorporating influences from the environment but by being in contact with their own deepest nature. In one of his eloquent passages, Rogers (1961) asserted that

> We do not need to ask who will socialize [a person], for one of his own deepest needs is for affiliation and communication with others. . . . We do not need to ask who will control his aggressive impulses, for . . . his need to be liked by others and his tendency to give affection will be as strong as his impulses to strike out or to seize for himself. [As he becomes more fully functioning] he will be aggressive in situations in which aggression is realistically appropriate, but there will be no runaway need for aggression. (p. 194)

The fully functioning person's relationships with others reflect overall harmony. Rogers (1961) concluded that to be fully functioning, what he termed "the good life," is "enriching, exciting, rewarding, challenging, meaningful . . . [T]he good life is not . . . for the faint-hearted" (p. 196).

Characteristics of the fully functioning person could be applied to the example of the pre-med student. If congruent, she would be open to her interest in the law and in becoming an attorney as well as to her disinterest and mediocre abilities in medicine, and she would act accordingly. Even if she perceived her father's approval of her as conditional on her being a physician, she would not turn that perceived conditional regard into an internal condition of worth. Rather, out of the organismic experience of her genuine interests, desires, and successes and failures, she would develop a self-concept ("I enjoy law and the process of becoming an attorney") that would be consistent with her ideal self: "I am worthwhile no matter what useful profession I pursue." She would be internally congruent and flowing unobstructedly in the process of becoming the person she has the innate potential to be.

Rogers believed that no one exemplifies the extreme of full functioning, that everyone, to some degree or another, is incongruent. With incongruence, a person encounters situations by including information that does not belong to the situation, such as rigid, usually unexamined values in the form of internal conditions of worth, and excluding information that does belong to the situation, that is, organismic experience that is defended against, and is denied to, awareness. One's behavior usually reflects one's self-concept, but the more incongruent one is, the more likely it is that one will manifest several reactions. First, the person subceives the incongruence, feels anxious, and is unable to maintain the defense of denial. With the weakening of the ability to suppress, selectively perceive, or distort organismic experience, that experience breaks into awareness and, because it contradicts the self-concept, shatters the gestalt of the self-concept. With the self-concept thus disorganized, behavior reflects organismic experience rather than the self-concept. In this case, one experiences one's behavior as alien to oneself. Sooner or later, the self-concept may regain organization, but the more one is incongruent or encounters circumstances that challenge lesser incongruence, the more one will experience anxiety and confusion and will vacillate between behavior consistent with the self-concept and behavior consistent with organismic experience.

Clearly, in this scenario, organismic experience is unable to function relatively consistently and holistically, which it must if its constructive potential is to be realized. Instead, one need is satisfied at the expense of another, then, at times, it gives way to the other need that has been previously denied. Thus, incongruence renders a person vulnerable to the feeling of anxiety and to behavior that is disorganized, inconsistent, and/or, to some degree, destructive.

In the case of the pre-med student, if she continues in incongruence, any of a number of results would be expected. To a great extent, to preserve the integrity of her self-concept, she would deny or distort her organismic experience of dislike for her studies, but at times that experience would break through the perceptual filter of denial or distortion. At those times, she would at least subceive distressing feelings and behaviors. For example, when anticipating studying or attending class, she may experience recurring lack of motivation and procrastination, and when forcing herself to study or attend class, she would at least subceive some degree of anxiety or other emotional distress. To preserve her self-esteem, her internal conditions of worth, she has psychologically waged war on herself, on her own inherent worth and on her own innate, perfectly constructive tendencies.

Rogers referred to incongruence in a variety of ways throughout his writings. He called the internal rift between immediate awareness based on intellectual values and unawareness of the deeper, organismic valuing a kind of divorce *of* oneself *from* oneself. Unable to recognize internally based aspects of oneself that do not correspond to externally based aspects of oneself, one no longer knows who one really is. Rogers considered this condition the fundamental estrangement of humans from ourselves. It is no wonder, then, that the internal disconnection from organismic experience and the reconnection with it are central concepts in Rogers' approach to counseling and psychotherapy.

The Personality Change Process

Basic Principles of Change. Incongruence develops in the context of a particular type of social environment, one characterized by conditional positive regard. Likewise, congruence can be created anew only in the context of a particular type of social environment, one characterized most importantly by *unconditional positive regard* along with *genuineness* and *empathy*. Rogers acknowledged that these latter three *core conditions of change* sometimes temporarily characterize everyday relationships, such as between friends, coworkers, parents and children, teachers and students, and bosses and employees. However, the consistent, persistent communication of these conditions over time is likely to occur reliably only in a special situation: psychotherapy.

In essence, when a person perceives one's existence and experience being valued unconditionally by someone else, one can prize and even reclaim suppressed aspects of oneself. In other words, when one feels no threat of external negative judgment regarding one's actual inner experience, one feels free to reconnect with and appreciate that inner, organismic experience and to trust it as a guide to making choices.

As organismic experience is acknowledged, it is integrated into the self-concept. As the self-concept aligns increasingly with organismic experience, the person "let's go" of conditions of worth she developed in response to external conditional positive regard, thus bringing her ideal self into alignment with her now more aligned self-concept and organismic experience (see Figure 6.5). She comes to believe that she "should be" who she "actually is." Thus, the person moves from the restricted and anxiety-ridden functioning of incongruence toward the full functioning of congruence; the funda-

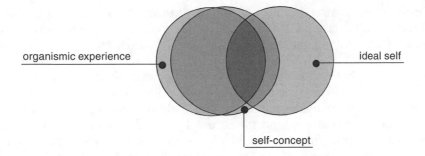

First, the person allows organismic experience into awareness, whereupon it is incorporated into the self-concept. When this incorporation occurs, it is as if the self-concept "moves" into alignment with organismic experience. The person perceives oneself increasingly as one really is.

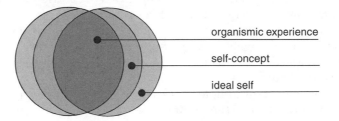

Then the person revises conditions of worth in the ideal self to align with the newly aligned self-concept and organismic experience. It is as if the self-concept/organismic experience alignment "pulls" the ideal self into alignment with them. The person believes one "should be" who one perceives oneself to be and who one really is.

FIGURE 6.5
The process of movement toward increased congruence.

mental intrapersonal alienation is repaired. With this inner reunification, the person is restored to greater internal harmony, manifests harmony in relationship with others, and moves in the direction of personal and evolutionary advancement.

For example, consider again the young pre-med student. She enters her pre-med studies with the condition of worth in her ideal self that "to be worthwhile, I must become a physician." Her self-concept includes "I am capable of becoming, and feeling fulfilled as, a physician." As she proceeds in her coursework, her lack of interest in, and even dislike for, her pre-med coursework is her organismic experience—her direct, "real" experience. To the extent that she perceives conditional positive regard from her social environment—parents, teachers, friends, and/or a counselor who convey approval only if she continues to pursue pre-med—she is likely to deny or distort her organismic experience, thus not allowing it into awareness and, consequently, not integrating it into her self-concept. To the extent that she perceives unconditional positive regard—parents, teachers, friends, and/or a counselor who convey approval for her to pursue whatever seems most fulfilling to her—she is likely to allow her organismic experience—her actual dislike of pre-med coursework—into her self-concept. "I really don't enjoy studying this material! This material does not interest me! I almost certainly would not feel fulfilled in a job that required me to use this kind of material on a daily basis!" At the same time, she would allow into awareness her actual attraction to the study of law: "I am interested in the law. I would probably be fulfilled in a job that required me to use law-related material on a daily basis." She most likely then would question, doubt, and then modify the condition of worth in her ideal self, "To be worthwhile, I must become a physician," into something like, "I will feel most worthwhile by pursuing a career that I find interesting and that makes a constructive contribution to society. Right now, the law seems to be my best bet for that kind of career." Based on her internal shift toward greater congruence, her actions also would reflect that congruence: She would change her major from pre-med to pre-law, would feel clear and decisive in doing so, and would feel enthusiastic about her new educational pursuit.

It is important to note that the reclaiming of congruence does not involve a mere return to the valuing process of infancy. Rogers pointed out that adult and infant organismic experience are similar in fluidity, flexibility, immediacy in the moment, capacity for differentiating the uniqueness of each situation, and internal locus of evaluation. He also highlighted crucial differences: that adult organismic experience involves greater complexity and scope, including relevant past memories, knowledge of a broader range of possible courses of action, more sophisticated hypothesizing about possible consequences of those courses of action, and more knowledge of, and ability to consider, external information. Rogers summarized that both the past and the future are included in each present moment of the ongoing adult valuing process.

Change Through Counseling. In Rogers' view, six conditions are necessary and sufficient for a client to move in the direction of constructive personality change. The first condition, two people in psychological contact, is dichotomous, either present or absent, and involves both counselor and client. The remaining five conditions are continuous, existing to a relatively greater or lesser degree; the greater the strength of these conditions, the greater will be the constructive personality change in the client. The second condition pertains exclusively to the client: a state of incongruence is present, usually experienced as vulnerability, anxiety, or other presenting symptoms. The third, fourth, and fifth conditions are the aforementioned core conditions of genuineness, unconditional positive regard, and empathy that the counselor must feel when in contact with the client. It is not enough for the counselor to believe that the core conditions are felt and met; the last condition requires that the client perceive and experience the genuineness, unconditional positive regard, and empathy coming from the counselor. These six necessary and sufficient conditions are fleshed out in the following section.

The Client's Role. *Motivation to change.* Client motivation is best understood by the second necessary and sufficient condition for constructive personality change. The incongruence experienced by the client causes significant distress manifested by any number of presenting symptoms. In other words, the client must at least subceive, if not actually perceive, some degree of tension, confusion, or feeling of being unsettled in some way. From the counselor's perspective, any inner sense of anxiety or vulnerability on the part of the client is the result of incongruence between the client's self-concept, ideal self, and organismic experience. Because of the innate human actualizing tendency to move toward inner consistency and harmony, the client feels a need to resolve the unsettling feelings.

Typically, the client has acted on that need by voluntarily seeking counseling. However, involuntary counseling also can result in constructive change if the client feels some inner sense of anxiety or vulnerability. Conversely, the client who has voluntarily sought counseling exclusively to achieve some ulterior agenda, such as convince a court of his qualifications to get child custody, cannot be expected to change. In other words, whether the client is voluntary or involuntary, perception and/or subception of inner turmoil motivates the client to change.

Capacity and responsibility for change. Ultimately only the client has the capacity to change, but the responsibility for change and the extent of change rest with the six conditions, only three of which involve the client directly. The first condition, as previously discussed, requires the client to perceive or subceive at least minimal psychological tension or vulnerability. Another condition, the one listed first by Rogers, is that the client be in psychological contact with a counselor who manifests certain characteristics. This statement underscores Rogers' belief that a client changes only in the context of a meaningful and nurturing relationship. In essence, the counselor is, at least to some minimal degree, a "significant other" to the client. Rogers did not clarify what factors might limit the client's perception of the counselor as psychologically important. Whatever the case, if no such person is available, or if a counselor who meets the other conditions is available but is not perceived by the client as important or significant, client change cannot be expected. A final condition is that the client must perceive and experience the counselor's communication of the three core conditions of genuineness, unconditional positive regard, and empathy. Again, Rogers was less clear about what factors might influence this client ability, but he offered some hints about how his views evolved over the course of his career.

In 1942, Rogers excluded from those who could benefit from nondirective psychotherapy the small minority of clients who are psychotic, cognitively defective, or unable to solve their own difficulties, even with assistance, as well as individuals faced with impossible demands from their environment. By 1957, he asserted, albeit tentatively, that the necessary and sufficient conditions for change applied to all clients, no matter what those clients' presenting problems might be. At that time, he acknowledged a contradiction to this assertion: the research finding that clients who externalize their problems, thus blaming others or outside circumstances and taking little self-responsibility, benefit from psychotherapy much less; he expressed openness to the possibility that such clients may need "something more" than the core conditions. Then, in 1977, he described Diabasis, an apparently successful residential treatment facility serving no more than six psychotic patients at a time and operating according to principles consistent with Rogers' core conditions. In this discussion, Rogers seemed to imply that the more severe the client's incongruence, the more pervasive, consistent, and persistent must be the relative core conditions 2 through 6. By 1986, he was hypothesizing, without qualification as to a person's degree of incongruence, that a person "has within himself or herself vast resources for self-understanding" and for changing one's own self-concept, attitudes, and behaviors (p. 135). Thus it might be inferred that someone experiencing a lesser incongruence; for example, a phobia—could benefit from a once-a-week experience of the core conditions, whereas someone experiencing a greater incongruence, for example, schizophrenia, would require the more prolonged and consistent experience of the core conditions available only in a residential environment.

Throughout his writing, Rogers did affirm the appropriateness of counselors defining the counseling situation to clients as an opportunity for client self-growth rather than for client receipt of answers from the counselor. This affirmation corresponds to his assertion that, in person-centered counseling, the locus of decision making and the responsibility for the consequences of decisions are centered unequivocally in the client.

Source of resistance. Though Rogers (1942) referred to "the usual slight amount of difficulty in getting the client to take the lead . . . and to talk freely and without restriction" (p. 273), he did not refer to this difficulty as "client resistance." Nevertheless, the person-centered counselor can, at times, experience the client resisting assuming initiative in counseling. This may be due to the client's lack of clarity about personal responsibility for self-growth in the counseling process, or it may be due to the client's wish, expectation, or even demand that the counselor provide answers.

Rogers (1989) did describe two types of resistance. One type is created by the client's wish to avoid "the pain of revealing, to oneself and another, the feelings that have hitherto been denied to awareness" (p. 133). The other is resistance created by the counselor, usually by rendering judgment on the client or her disclosures, but also by imposing direction on the counseling process that the client considers threatening or otherwise antithetical to the client's immediate needs. It is not as if person-centered counseling is without direction but, rather, that the direction in person-centered counseling is provided by the client's own actualizing tendency, and it is that direction alone, pursued in the client's own way and time, that the client ultimately will not resist.

The Counselor's Role. *Goals of counseling.* A person-centered counselor has one overarching goal: to create a psychological environment in which the client's actualizing tendency is free to resume its natural flow. The counselor moves toward achievement of this goal by cultivating certain attitudes toward, and attempting to communicate those attitudes to, the client.

The person-centered counselor believes that, if the core conditions are met, the client's psychological movement will be guided increasingly by the client's innately constructive actualizing tendency. Client movement will be toward increased congruence and thus full functioning.

Characteristics of an effective counselor. Five of Rogers' six necessary and sufficient conditions for constructive personality change speak to the characteristics of an effective person-centered counselor. The first condition, that the counselor and client be in psychological contact, implies not only sensory contact of some kind but also a sense that the relationship is vital to both client and counselor.

Rogers' third condition is that the counselor be genuine, real, congruent—not necessarily in every aspect of his or her life, but at least in the context of the relationship with the client. That is, the counselor accurately perceives anything experienced in relationship to the client and expresses any persistent experiences to the client. Genuineness reflects the counselor's attempt to be completely aware of his or her experience with the client and to give feedback to the client in an open and honest manner. For example, if the client is storytelling; giving a lot of information without seeming emotionally involved, and the counselor begins to feel bored, the counselor might say, "Bob, I am feeling distracted as you tell your story. I want to listen, and I also find I have trouble remaining attentive." Not attending to the felt sense of distraction and boredom and not communicating it to the client in a caring way might represent incongruence on the part of the therapist. As a result of the incongruence, the counselor would likely become more distracted, and the client would eventually pick up on the distraction and may even confront the counselor for "not listening to me."

Rogers' fourth condition is that the counselor experience unconditional positive regard for the client. In other words, the counselor feels a warm acceptance of all aspects of the client's experience, free of any evaluation that "I like and/or approve of you only if you are a certain way, only if your experiences meet certain conditions." Both "negative" and "positive" expressions by the client are equally valued. According to Mearns and Thorne (1997), consistency of the unconditional positive regard is the most distinctive characteristic of this person-centered attitude toward clients. Unconditional positive regard is more than acceptance; it is an unwavering respect for the humanity of the client that is not affected by the behavior demonstrated by the client. Because mental disturbances are an outgrowth of conditions of worth, unconditional positive regard acts as a counterconditioning process (Lietaer, 1984) whereby, in an environment conducive to self-prizing and growth, the client's conditions of worth are deconstructed and replaced, so to speak, by unconditional self-regard.

Rogers' fifth condition is that the counselor experience a moment-to-moment, accurate empathic understanding of the client's internal perspective. The counselor senses the client's inner world as if it were the counselor's own world, yet, at the same time, the counselor consistently maintains a separate sense of self. This experience of being understood is often extremely liberating to clients. As one adolescent male client remarked, "For the first time in my life, I feel like someone is in the game with me. Not calling the shots, just trying to figure out what it means to be me. It's weird but it's like I can see me more clearly through your eyes. It's weird."

The sixth and final condition is that the counselor succeed in communicating the previous three experiences: congruence, unconditional positive regard, and empathy, to the client. In other words, the effective counselor, through nonverbal and verbal behavior, endeavors to convey the experience of the three preceding conditions to the client, realizing that success in that conveyance also rests to some degree on the client, as discussed above. To the extent that the counselor succeeds, the client will perceive the counselor as consistent, dependable, trustworthy, sincere, accepting, and understanding, and the client will feel safe disclosing inner experiences and using inner resources for self-evaluation and -guidance.

For a counselor to consistently experience and convey the attitudes of genuineness, unconditional positive regard, and empathy can be extremely challenging at times. It is important to recall that probably no one succeeds perfectly in this goal. However, certain beliefs are crucial to a counselor's relative success. The person-centered counselor has an unshakable belief that each client is, at core, constructive and therefore trustworthy. The counselor believes that any destructiveness on the part of the client is the result of the client overriding the organismic valuing process of the actualizing tendency with conditions of worth based on values originally external to the client. The counselor, therefore, renounces the imposition of any evaluation, either positive or negative, onto the client, because such evaluation would constitute yet one more external value that has the potential to perpetuate the client's own intrapersonal alienation. The counselor strives to relinquish all control of the direction of counseling and to provide the client with absolute freedom to move in any direction, trusting firmly that the client will move in a positive direction. The effective person-centered counselor, when experiencing any lasting impediment to the achievement of these aims, would seek to resolve them by talking them over with the client, a colleague, a supervisor, or even his or her own counselor, as appropriate.

The person-centered counselor is best conceptualized as a fellow traveler on the client's journey of self-discovery. The counselor is a midwife of change rather than its originator. In his later years, Rogers (1986) alluded to a fleeting psychological state he sometimes observed in counselors and sometimes experienced himself that he associated with profound client healing and growth along with an enhanced sense of energy. He believed it occurs when one is close to one's inner, intuitive self, "in touch with the unknown [within] . . . perhaps . . . in a slightly altered state of consciousness . . . then simply [one's] *presence* is releasing and helpful" (p. 199). He suggested that this psychological state cannot be forced but can be facilitated by relaxing and being close to the "transcendental core" of oneself (p. 199). In this state, the counselor may behave in "strange and impulsive ways in the relationship" (p. 199), ways that cannot be justified rationally and that "have nothing to do with . . . thought processes" (p. 199), but that "turn out to be *right*" (p. 199). For himself, he concluded that "at those moments it seems that my inner spirit has reached out and touched the inner spirit of the other. Our relationship transcends itself and becomes a part of something larger" (p. 199).

Throughout his writings, Rogers made reference to counselors maintaining ethical standards. Presumably, his view of an effective counselor would include the counselor functioning within the limits of professional ethics.

Regarding the need for professional training, Rogers (1957) stated that the counselor's ability to experience and communicate the core conditions requires no specific intellectual knowledge but rather can be acquired through experiential training that may be, but unfortunately often is not, part of the professional training of mental health providers. Rogers was adamant that a counselor's views and values inevitably have consequences for her clients. He therefore believed that an effective counselor has clarified her views of human nature and her own value orientation and can explicitly state them. The clarification process could rightly be a part of professional training.

Stages and Techniques. Rogers delineated 12 steps in the person-centered counseling process. He emphasized that these steps are not actually separate, sequential events but, rather, represent a general trend consisting of an interwoven unfolding. Reviewing these steps, as described by Rogers (1942), can give the reader an overall sense of the person-centered counseling process.

1. The individual comes for help.
2. The helping situation is usually defined [as] an opportunity for self-growth, not answers.
3. The counselor encourages free expression of feelings in regard to the problem [that the client presents].

4. The counselor accepts, recognizes, and clarifies these negative feelings.
5. When the individual's negative feelings have been quite fully expressed, they are followed by the faint and tentative expressions of the positive impulses that make for growth.
6. The counselor accepts and recognizes the positive feelings which are expressed in the same manner in which he has accepted and recognized the negative feelings . . . which gives the individual an opportunity for the first time in his life to understand himself as he is . . . insight and self-understanding come bubbling through spontaneously.
7. This insight, this understanding of the self and acceptance of the self . . . provides the basis on which the individual can go ahead to new levels of integration.
8. Intermingled with this process of insight . . . is a process of clarification of possible decisions, possible courses of action.
9. Then comes . . . the initiation of minute, but highly significant, positive actions.
10. There is further insight.
11. There is increasingly integrated positive action on the part of the client . . . less fear . . . and more confidence in self-directed action.
12. There is a feeling of decreasing need for help, and a recognition on the part of the client that the relationship must end. (pp. 30–45)

The therapeutic relationship. In person-centered counseling, the client–counselor relationship that is characterized by the necessary and sufficient conditions for change is, itself, the instrument of change. Basic to this relationship is the strong valuing of psychological independence and integrity and the devaluing of conformity and the practice of having those who are seemingly more capable directing those who are seemingly less capable. In this relationship, a client discusses problems, but the focus is on the client rather than the problems because of the belief that clients psychologically equipped with congruence are able to handle reasonably well the problems that come their way. The counselor structures the therapeutic relationship by overtly or covertly reminding the client of the client's responsibility for the process. The counselor also sets and maintains ethical limits on the relationship.

In this relationship, a client will have feelings and emotions directed toward the counselor. Rogers noted two categories of such feelings. One consists of understandable reactions to the counselor's words and actions, such as positive feelings in response to a counselor's warmth, understanding, and concern, and negative feelings in response to a counselor's air of superiority, inaccurate or premature interpretation, or imposition of an agenda on the client and/or the process. A second category consists of projections transferred from another origin onto the counselor; whether or not triggered somehow by the therapist, they are identifiable by their disproportionate intensity. Rogers (1989) asserted that, from a person-centered perspective, distinguishing feelings as belonging to one of the two categories was unnecessary. "All," he said, "are best dealt with in the same way. If the therapist is sensitively understanding and genuinely acceptant and non-judgmental, therapy will move *through* these feelings" (p. 130). He believed that the therapeutic strategy of paying particular attention to transference feelings served only to create the new problems of fostering client dependency and prolonging therapy.

Assessment. Rogers' (1957) view of most psychological assessment in counseling was negative. He believed that practices such as diagnosis, analysis, and even taking a case history are not only unnecessary but also impede rather than facilitate the therapeutic process because they objectify the person of the client.

Rogers (1957) conceded only one case in which assessment, particularly diagnosis and case history, might be facilitative: when a counselor might feel more secure and therefore more accepting and understanding of the client if she has foreknowledge and/or diagnostic knowledge of the client. It would seem congruent with Rogers' thinking to believe that a counselor would be most therapeutically facilitative who, with no foreknowledge, felt secure meeting the client as an individual; however, Rogers did not state this explicitly.

Change strategies. As early as 1942, Rogers made clear his belief that the only "strategy" in his form of counseling was the attitude of acceptance. However, he conducted a comparison of directive and nondirective counseling sessions by analyzing the actual frequency of various types of verbal responses. The results are summarized in Table 6.1.

Some of the strategies listed in Table 6.1 are self-explanatory; others may require explanation. Reflections of feelings involve the counselor paraphrasing client emotions, as in responses that begin, "You're pleased that . . . ," "You're surprised to discover . . . ," or "You feel deeply sad when you consider. . . . " The counselor may reflect feelings in response to feelings the cli-

TABLE 6.1
The Seven Most Frequent Types of Verbal Responses in Directive and Nondirective Therapy, Beginning with Most Frequent

Directive	Nondirective
Closed-ended questions	Reflection of feelings directly expressed
Explanation and information giving	Reflection of feelings indirectly expressed
Open-ended questions	Open-ended questioning
Proposing an activity	Reflection of content
Reflection of content	Closed-ended questioning
Persuasion	Explanation and information giving
Identification of problem in need of correction	Defining the therapeutic situation in terms of client responsibility

ent expressed directly through a verbal statement, such as "I'm so mad!", or indirectly through nonverbal communication, such as body posture, facial expression, or tone of voice. Closed-ended questions can be answered by "yes" or "no," whereas open-ended questions cannot, thus requiring the client to elaborate. Both types of questions can redirect a client, but open-ended questions are less likely to do so. Reflections of content paraphrase the non-emotional content of a client communication.

Referring to questions that redirect the client, Rogers (1989) labeled them "unnecessary" and "clumsy" (p. 94), "much less profitable" (p. 101), and a "blunder" (pp. 101, 106). He labeled giving a homework assignment "un-wise" (p. 106). He labeled open-ended questions "productive" (p. 93). He labeled accurate reflections "helpful," (p. 89) "productive," (p. 95), "a better response" than a "direct question" (p. 97), and as promoting "clear progress in exploration at more than a superficial level" (p. 99). He labeled the avoid-ance of agreeing or disagreeing with the client "wise" (p. 100). He labeled avoidance of intellectual discussion and continued focus on client feelings "to [the counselor's] credit" (p. 94). He considered defining the client's re-sponsibility for the direction of the counseling interviews to be "helpful" (p. 106) and "defining . . . what counseling can mean . . . in terms of the client's symbols . . . using metaphors the client has offered—to be always a sound device" (p. 99). He made the point that if a counselor misses an aspect of experience important to the client, the client will express it again. In other words, the counselor need not feel pressured to reflect everything the first time; if the client perceives the core conditions, she will persist in expressing anything important to her (p. 127).

At the same time, Rogers (1989) vehemently objected to reflection of feelings being taught as a counseling technique. Although he acknowledged that many of his transcription responses could be so categorized, he stated adamantly that during counseling sessions, "I am definitely *not* trying to 're-flect feelings'" (p. 127). Rather, he asserted, "I am trying to determine whether my understanding of the client's inner world is correct," (pp. 127–128) and suggested that these responses be relabeled "testing understandings" or "checking perceptions." Nevertheless, he affirmed that, when accurate, such responses served as a mirror, a reflection, from which the client is likely to gain clarity and insight and to move toward greater congruence.

Addressing Client Resistance. The person-centered counselor perceives resistance as yet another dimension of client experience for the counselor to address as she addresses any aspect of client experience. To again quote Rogers (1989), "If the therapist is sensitively understanding and genuinely accep-tant and non-judgmental, therapy will move *through* these feelings" (p. 130).

CONTRIBUTIONS AND LIMITATIONS

Interface Between Theory and Recent Developments in the Mental Health Field

The Effectiveness of Psychotherapy. Rogers appeared to believe that virtually 100% of positive outcomes in psychotherapy could be attributed to the quality of the therapeutic relationship. He may have alluded very indirectly to client variables in his first and sixth conditions that addressed the client's being in psychological contact with the counselor and subceiving or perceiving the counselor's communication of core conditions. Nevertheless, Asay and Lambert's (1999) conclusion that only 40% of positive outcomes can be attributed to the quality of the therapeutic relationship, and that 55% of outcomes rest with variables that are predominantly or totally out of the counselor's realm of influence, represents a clearly different perspective than Rogers'. If the person-centered counselor is to achieve Rogers' own criteria of effectiveness, that is, taking in new information from the environment and integrating it into an internally consistent approach to counseling, the research results on positive outcomes must be reconciled with the traditional person-centered perspective.

Regarding research findings on the validated approaches to psychotherapy (Crits-Christoph, 1998), Rogers would probably have acknowledged those approaches as helpful to some people in some limited ways but not in the most important way: helping people to reconnect with their own inner wisdom. The validated approaches probably would have no place in person-centered counseling.

The Nature/Nurture Question. Rogers appears to have believed that personality is influenced powerfully both by the innate actualizing tendency and by the kind of environmental positive regard one experiences. In his early writing, Rogers (1942) made rare reference to innate factors that might limit one's capacity to benefit from psychotherapy, such as being cognitively "defective" (p. 128). However, in later writings he indicated that even the person with schizophrenia could come to function well in a psychosocial environment characterized by the core conditions.

Rogers died before the research on genetic origins of behavior became widely known. Because of his respect for scientific research, we can assume that he would have been open to integrating genetic research findings into his views. The contemporary person-centered counselor is faced with the task of reconciling the findings regarding genetics with the tenets presented by Rogers.

Pharmacotherapy. Rogers' references to pharmacotherapy were sparse. Presumably, he believed that it was rarely necessary, and he would have considered current practice in mental health to involve overmedication of clients. This presumption is substantiated by a reference he made to the success of the director of Diabasis, the in-patient facility for people with schizophrenia. He exclaimed, "Dr. Perry thinks he has given [only] two tranquilizers in the past ten months!" (1989, p. 393). In other words, he believed that the necessary and sufficient conditions alone could facilitate healthy functioning in most cases.

Managed Care and Brief Therapy. The managed care emphasis on brief therapy seems antithetical to person-centered philosophy. The focus of managed care is on resolution of the client's immediate problem and on returning the client to her previous level of functioning as expeditiously as possible, hence the managed care emphasis on validated approaches to psychotherapy. In a sense, setting a time limit on change is, in itself, a condition of worth. Rogers, on the other hand, never wavered from the position he established in 1940: that the individual, rather than the problem, is the focus of person-centered counseling. He elaborated that

> the aim is not to solve one particular problem but to assist the individual to grow, so that he can cope with the present problem and with later problems in a better integrated fashion. If he can gain enough integration to handle one problem in more independent, more responsible, less confused, better organized ways, then he will also handle new problems in that manner. . . . Therapy is not a matter of doing something to the individual, or of inducing him to do something about himself. It is instead a matter of freeing him for normal growth and development, of removing obstacles so that he can again move forward. (1942, p. 379)

As a review of the 12 steps typically experienced in counseling reveals (Rogers, 1942), the process of client integration is more likely to be gradual than rapid. The person-centered counselor must reconcile the philosophical perspective of the approach with practical considerations such as whether to seek third party payment through managed care as well as whether and how to work in a setting that values or requires a brief, problem-focused approach to counseling.

Regarding DSM-IV diagnosis, Rogers (1942) considered diagnostic labels to be "largely irrelevant" (p. 393) in the counseling process. As stated previously, in the case of the counselor whose empathy and genuineness would be enhanced by diagnosing a client, Rogers seemed to endorse diagnosis, albeit grudgingly. Extrapolating from that position, he might not have objected to rendering a diagnosis if it were required by managed care, although he probably would have suggested that the counselor, in her own mind, avoid objectifying the client and also that she be cautious in whether or how she communicated diagnostic information to the client.

Diversity Issues. Rogers (1989) believed that the same value directions, those that advance the individual, the people with whom the individual interacts, and the evolution of the entire species, are universal among humans regardless of culture, gender, or socioeconomic status. He believed that these universal values could be discovered only from inside each person rather than imposed from the outside. He believed these values would provide any person with "an organized, adaptive, and social approach to the perplexing value issues which face all of us" (p. 184).

However, Rogers did not address the fact that his beliefs represented a values position in and of themselves, a position with which some clients might fundamentally disagree at the outset, making person-centered counseling a poor fit for them. These include cultures in which people respect the wisdom of those in positions of authority, such as counselors, and look to authorities for guidance and "answers." Also included are subcultures in which a person's "inner authority" is believed to be vulnerable to influence by evil forces in the universe. In such subcultures, inner authority is highly suspect, and the only trusted source of guidance is external authority represented by the collective wisdom of the culture or by some other trusted external source.

Rogers occasionally addressed the issue of the counselor defining client responsibility in the counseling process. In light of the recognition that his approach itself represents a values position, a person-centered counselor would probably do well to seek informed consent from a client at the outset of counseling. The counselor could achieve this goal by using a Professional Disclosure Statement and discussion to explain the counselor's expectations regarding the process of counseling and the client's and counselor's respective roles in that process. A client informed of these expectations could decide whether or not the person-centered approach is consonant with her own values, goals, and expectations regarding counseling.

Regarding sexual orientation, at one point, Rogers (1957) made reference to homosexuals as one category of clients seeking change, presumably change of sexual orientation. Whether or not Rogers himself later integrated into his perspective the research that led to the depathologizing of homosexual orientation, the view that homosexual orientation is a natural variation characterizing a minority of humans seems highly compatible with the person-centered perspective.

Spirituality. Throughout his writings, Rogers made many interesting references to spirituality. He alluded, for example, to evidence indicating that, "a vast and mysterious universe, perhaps an inner reality, or perhaps a spirit world of which we are all unknowingly a part seems to exist" (Rogers, 1989, p. 424). Yet he never appears to have deviated from a radical assertion he made in 1961 that "no other person's ideas, and none of my own ideas, are as authoritative as my experience. . . . Neither the Bible nor the prophets . . . neither the revelations of God nor man can take precedence over my own direct experience" (p. 24).

Rogers (1989) asserted that the only reality a person could possibly know is the world as that person perceives and experiences it in the present moment. Consequently, each person's reality is inevitably different. He acknowledged a consensus reality held by a group of people, and he pointed out both its benefit, providing continuity for the continuation of culture, and its detriment, the persecution of those who deviated from it. Believing the detriments to outweigh the benefits, he called consensus reality "a myth we dare not maintain" (pp. 425–426). He continued:

> It appears to me that the way of the future must be to base our lives and our education on the assumption that there are as many realities as there are persons, and that our highest priority is to accept that hypothesis and proceed . . . to explore open-mindedly the many, many perceptions of reality that exist. . . . Might not such a society be a completely individualistic anarchy? That is not my opinion. . . . The natural human tendency to care for another would . . . be . . . "I prize and treasure you because you are different from me." . . . Idealistic? . . . It surely is. (pp. 426–427)

Yet, he believed, this process of mutual acceptance of unique subjective realities may be going on at an unconscious, collective level that could result, ultimately, in a shift in collective, and therefore each person's, consciousness. He concluded,

> If we accept as a basic fact of all human life that we live in separate realities; if we can see those differing realities as the most promising resource for learning in all the history of the world; if we can live together in order to learn from one another without fear; if we can do all this, then a new age could be dawning. And perhaps, just perhaps, humankind's deep organic sensings are paving the way for just such a change. (p. 428)

Rogers' statements on reality seem to indicate that he considered a spiritual domain separate from everyday reality to be a possibility; that he respected and valued each person's spiritual reality and beliefs, including the belief that no spiritual reality exists; and that he did not subscribe to any one view regarding the nature of spiritual reality. Rogers' quotes at the beginning of this chapter indicate that he was continually revising his own spiritual beliefs on the basis of new experience.

Clearly, the belief that everyone should accept one particular spiritual reality is not consonant with the person-centered philosophy nor, for that matter, with ethical and professional counseling standards. Rather, in the person-centered approach, the explicit respect for each individual's spirituality is consonant with ethical standards of the American Counseling Association and with the approach endorsed in the counselor competencies on spirituality created by a spiritually diverse group of counselor educators (Holden & Ivey, 1997).

From the perspective of at least one author of this text, Rogers' approach to spirituality seems quite consonant with many aspects of the creation spirituality of Matthew Fox. The interested reader is referred to http://www.creationspirituality.com and http://cti.itc.virginia.edu/~jkh8x/soc257/nrms/creation_spirituality.html.

Person-centered counseling also shares certain qualities with Buddhist mindfulness meditation. This meditation emphasizes openness to and awareness of all experiences "without wishing they were different or trying to change them" (Walsh, 1999, p. 194); paradoxically, it can result in powerful change, including powerful healing. One might think of person-centered counseling as a kind of interactive mindfulness meditation in which the counselor serves as an outside resource for enhancing client awareness.

Eclecticism. Each theory contains perspectives that distinguish it from every other theory. In the case of person-centered counseling, the unshakable belief in the unerring trustworthiness of the actualizing tendency and the absolute prohibition of the counselor from imposing any external evaluation or direction on the client represent its most salient distinguishing characteristics.

Not only do Rogers' six conditions represent what is necessary for constructive personality change and what is sufficient for such change, but any technique or strategy in addition to those conditions represents external direction, the phenomenon that perpetuates, rather than alleviates, the fundamental problem: the client's alienation from her own deepest experience. Thus person-centered counselors do not engage in technical eclecticism.

Weaknesses of the Theory

Some weaknesses of person-centered theory have been addressed above, such as the incompatibility of cultures that value collective wisdom with a psychotherapy that strongly values inner wisdom. In addition, from various other theoretical perspectives, person-centered counseling is seen as limited. In their unwavering belief in and exclusive enactment of the six conditions for constructive personality change, person-centered counselors reject the use of the validated approaches that indicate specific directive procedures for specific disorders. Critics object that a client who seeks counseling to solve a particular problem may not be well served by a counselor who pursues development of her person as a whole rather than addressing, in the most expeditious way possible, the problem she came to counseling to resolve.

Rogers conceded that some change techniques might be helpful to clients, but only to the extent that the techniques involved the six necessary and sufficient conditions. For counselors who use specific techniques, he endorsed their describing the technique and its purpose, asking the client if she wishes to use that technique, and permitting the client to opt out from its use, rather than prescribing the technique to the client. Yet he concluded that the general use of techniques makes counseling more counselor-centered than client-centered.

Rogers (1989) encountered strong opposition to his approach. At one point, he attributed that opposition to its novelty, to its founder being a psychologist rather than a psychiatrist, and to the way it undermined the counselor's power, rendering the counselor's role to that of a fellow traveler with the client rather than that of expert. It is interesting to note that he did not mention the possibility that some professionals objected because they believed his approach did not provide clients with the most expeditious and lasting relief from their suffering. Rogers criticized that, "new therapies . . . take a middle-of-the-road view. The expert is at times definitely the authority . . . but there is also a recognition of the right of the individual to be responsible for himself. . . . [T]hese [are] contradictions" (p. 384).

However, honoring both the subjective and the objective aspects of human functioning does not represent a contradiction but rather an acknowledgment and use of two distinct aspects inherent in human existence. The counselor who has expertise in techniques that many other clients have found helpful and who offers them to the client for the client to accept, modify to fit her own unique phenomenology, or refuse, both uses the objective domain to the client's benefit and respects the client's subjective domain. From this perspective, at a time in the history of psychology when objective approaches threatened to eclipse the subjective experience of the individual, Rogers' radical defense of the subjective domain served to ensure its survival as a theoretically and psychotherapeutically valid entity. However, the counselor who takes the subjective perspective to the exclusion of the objective may rob clients of the opportunity to partake of psychological technologies that clients might choose to use in the service of their actualization.

Distinguishing Additions to Psychotherapy

In tribute, Kirschenbaum and Henderson (1989) reviewed Carl Rogers' most salient contributions to the field of counseling and psychotherapy. In addition to the pioneering of nondirective/client-centered/person-centered counseling, they cited that Rogers

> . . . was the first person in history to record and publish completed cases of psychotherapy,

> . . . carried out and encouraged more scientific research on counseling and psychotherapy than had ever been undertaken anywhere,

> . . . spread . . . professional counseling and psychotherapy . . . to all the helping professions: psychology, social work, education, ministry, lay therapy, and others,

. . . was a leader in the development and dissemination of the intensive therapeutic group experience, sometimes called the "encounter group,"

. . . was a leader in the humanistic psychology movement,

. . . was a pioneer in applying the principles of effective interpersonal communication to resolving intergroup and international conflict, and

. . . was one of the helping professions' most prolific writers. (pp. 3–4)

In addition, Rogers was the first to record and transcribe counseling sessions for use in teaching and supervision. He introduced the term "client" to refer to the person utilizing psychotherapy as a responsible individual rather than as a sick "patient." And he, more than any mental health theorist before him, brought into focus the crucial role played by the therapeutic relationship, a perspective that has been substantially supported by research on positive outcomes in psychotherapy.

SUMMARY

Carl Rogers' person-centered approach to counseling and psychotherapy emerged during the mid-20th century as a major force in the humanistic psychotherapy movement. Through the humanistic perspective, person-centered counselors see humans as innately constructive at their deepest levels and also, as a result of the interaction of inner tendencies and factors in the social environment, psychologically alienated from that inner source of wisdom. The most helpful psychotherapy is the one in which the counselor provides a particular psychological climate in which the client can reconnect with her actualizing core. The person thus reconnected is able to use inner wisdom to live in harmony.

RECOMMENDED RESOURCES

Books

Kirschenbaum, H., & Henderson, V. (Eds.). (1989). *The Carl Rogers reader.* Boston: Houghton Mifflin. A collection of diverse readings from Rogers. The coverage of several different topics makes the book attractive.

Kirschenbaum, H., & Henderson, V. (Eds.). (1989). *Carl Rogers: Dialogues.* Boston: Houghton Mifflin. Much like the other suggested readings, the dialogues gives the reader information about the theory, and also illustrates the congruence between Rogers and the theory.

Rogers, C. R. (1961). *On becoming a person.* Boston: Houghton-Mifflin. In our opinion, any seminal work by Rogers would be a good read for those interested in the theory. *On Becoming a Person* provides a comprehensive discussion of the philosophical patterns that comprise the way of being that summarizes the therapeutic method.

Videotapes

Shostrom, E. T. (Executive Producer), Shostrom, S. K. (Producer), & Ratner, H. (Director). (1977). *Three approaches to psychotherapy II. Part 1. Carl Rogers. Client-centered therapy* [Videorecording]. (Available from Psychological and Educational Films, *PMB* #252, 3334 East Coast Highway, Corona Del Mar, CA 92625)

Websites

A good place to start is www.personcentered.com. This is the home site of Person-Centered International, an organization dedicated to the promotion and application of person-centered principles.

REFERENCES

Asay, T. P., & Lambert, M. J. (1999). The empirical case for the common factors in therapy: Quantitative findings. In M. A. Hubble, B. L. Duncan, & S. D. Miller (Eds.), *The heart and soul of change: What works in therapy* (pp. 33–55). Washington, DC: American Psychological Association.

Crits-Christoph, P. (1998). Training in empirically validated treatments: The Division 12 APA task force recommendations. In K. S. Dobson & K. D. Craig (Eds.), *Empirically supported therapies: Best practice in professional psychology* (pp. 3–25). Thousand Oaks, CA: Sage.

Holden, J., & Ivey, A. (1997, Spring). Summit on spirituality phase I, phase II, counselor competencies. *ACES Spectrum Newsletter*, 14–16.

Kirschenbaum, H., & Henderson, V. L. (Eds.). (1989). *The Carl Rogers reader.* Boston: Houghton Mifflin.

Lietaer, G. (1984). Unconditional positive regard: A controversial basic attitude in client-centered therapy. In R. Levant and J. Schlien (Eds.), *Client-centered therapy and the person centered approach* (pp. 41–58). New York: Praeger.

Mearns, D., & Thorne, B. (1997). *Person-centered counselling in action.* Thousand Oaks, CA: Sage.

Raskin, N., & Rogers, C. (2000). Person-centered therapy. In R. J. Corsini & D. Wedding (Eds.), *Current psychotherapies* (6th ed., pp. 133–167). Itasca, IL: F. E. Peacock.

Rogers, C. R. (1939). *The clinical treatment of the problem child.* Boston: Houghton Mifflin.

Rogers, C. R. (1942). *Counseling and psychotherapy.* Boston: Houghton Mifflin.

Rogers, C. R. (1951). *Client-centered therapy.* Boston: Houghton Mifflin.

Rogers, C. R. (1957). A note on "the nature of man." *Journal of Counseling Psychology,* 4(3), 199–203.

Rogers, C. R. (1961). *On becoming a person: A therapist's view of psychotherapy.* Boston: Houghton Mifflin.

Rogers, C. R. (1986). A client-centered/person-centered approach to therapy. In I. Kutash & A. Wolf (Eds.), *Psychotherapist's casebook* (pp. 197–208). San Francisco: Jossey-Bass.

Rogers, C. R. (1989). Growing old: Or Older and Growing. In H. Kirschenbaum & V. L. Henderson (Eds.), *The Carl Rogers reader* (pp. 37–55). Boston: Houghton Mifflin.

Walker, D. E. (1956). Carl Rogers and the nature of man. *Journal of Counseling Psychology,* 3, 89–92.

Walsh, R. (1999). *Essential spirituality: The seven central practices to awaken heart and mind.* New York: Wiley.

CHAPTER 7

GESTALT COUNSELING

BACKGROUND OF THE THEORY

Historical Context

Like many of the theories discussed in this text, Gestalt therapy grew from a reaction to the deterministic philosophy of classical psychoanalysis that permeated the psychological community of the early 20th century. The role of the analyst, cast as an anonymous blank screen, focused on the importance of interpretation of the client's unconscious drives. Consciousness was a small and insignificant portion of the client's psyche, while the unconscious was the vast entity responsible for psychological functioning. Because the client's unconscious was deemed inaccessible to the client, the analyst was seen as the only one who could unlock the mysteries of the unconscious and, through interpretation and analysis of transference, free the client from intrapsychic turmoil.

New York in the late 1940s provided the birthplace of what became Gestalt therapy. Yontef (1995) noted that the genesis of Gestalt thinking was in direct opposition to psychoanalytic thought and anything regarded as "authoritarian, mechanistic, or inflexible" (p. 262). Early Gestalt thinkers disagreed with the psychoanalytic emphasis on the analyst as the expert and did not believe that clients were helpless and incapable of change. They believed that the authoritarian position of the analyst not only afforded the analyst too much power, but also set up an inefficient and rigid method of psychotherapy.

> They (early gestaltists) wanted to construct a system oriented to fostering growth more than to remediating pathology, to actual experience more than to interpretations of an unexperienced reality, and to the most authentic contact possible more than replaying of experience in the transference neurosis. (Yontef, 1995, p. 262)

It was within this field of experience that the need for an active dialogue between therapist and client as an agent of change was perceived and honored.

Founders' Biographical Overview

I have often been called the founder of Gestalt Therapy.
That's crap.

—Fritz Perls, 1969

Frederick "Fritz" Perls, born in Berlin to a lower class Jewish family in 1893, was a child and adolescent full of energy and curiosity. His early life was filled with struggle, especially with his father. "His father humiliated him continually. Therefore he always had to prove that he wasn't as his father made him look" (Perls in Bernard, 1986, p. 370). After several years of less than stellar academic achievements (he failed the seventh grade—twice), he focused his energy on earning a degree in medicine, becoming a talented neurologist and psychoanalyst. For a more detailed account of Perls' early life, consult his autobiography, *In and Out of the Garbage Pail* (Perls, 1969b).

Perls' early career path included serving as a medic in World War I and working with Kurt Goldstein at the Goldstein Institute for Brain-Damaged Soldiers. Early experiences in both of these venues led him to appreciate the role of perception in psychological and physical problems. It was also during this time that Perls' professional career merged with his personal life in a very meaningful way. He met Lore (Laura) Posner, an assistant to Goldstein. Although 12 years his junior, Laura had developed an interest in psychology and was working on preliminary research for her dissertation. She had studied with the likes of Tillich and Buber and soon began psychoanalytic training supervised by Otto Fenichel. Laura and Fritz were both drawn to psychoanalysis, Fritz working with Wilheim Reich and Laura continuing her studies. In 1930 they were married, but only 3 years later, due to their activism in politics and the rise of Nazi Germany, they fled to South Africa.

In South Africa, the couple established a private practice and began the seminal writings that would become Gestalt therapy. While both worked on pieces for what would become *Ego, Hunger and Aggression*, they also led somewhat independent and busy lives, a trend that would extend throughout the life of the marriage. Sensing the impending political turmoil in South Africa, the couple decided to move once again, this time to the United States.

The move to the United States proved bountiful for Fritz and Laura Perls. Their book *Ego, Hunger and Aggression* was published in 1947. The fact that Fritz was credited as the sole author, although Laura helped with the book by writing two chapters, marked a pattern that would also endure for the life of the marriage: Fritz was the public face of gestalt while Laura chose the background. In 1951, *Gestalt Therapy: Excitement and Growth in the Human Personality* was written by Fritz Perls, Ralph Hefferline, and Paul Goodman. This work represented, and still represents, a comprehensive description of the theory and practice of Gestalt work.

Due to these two publications, the private practice activity of Fritz and Laura, and Fritz's lectures, Gestalt therapy began to attract a following. While in New York, Fritz explored the founding of the Institute for Gestalt Therapy. Laura was not enthusiastic about the formation of the Institute but became more involved when the primary interest in the group came from her own group therapy patients. The group that included such Gestalt therapists as Paul Weiss and Paul Goodman helped form the Institute in 1952 as a training center designed to apprentice those interested in Gestalt therapy (Humphrey, 1986).

The New York scene bustled and soon Fritz moved about the country, discussing and demonstrating Gestalt work. In the 1960s he settled in California, where he mainly held workshops at the Esalen Institute. This laid-back atmosphere seemed to be reflected in his writings, as later works such as *Gestalt Therapy Verbatim* (1969a), and the posthumously published *The Gestalt Approach and Eye Witness to Therapy* (1973) took on a more informal and playful tone.

After Fritz died in 1970, Gestalt therapy lost its dramatic public face. Laura Perls stepped more into the spotlight at that point, but many still see Fritz as the originator of Gestalt therapy. Laura Perls, in an interview by Bernard (1986), noted that Fritz's lack of recognition of her contributions had been a source of conflict between the two, but in true Gestalt form, she commented that any unfinished business between them had been worked out before his death and that although they often lived and worked apart, they were "on good terms" in the end.

Philosophical Underpinnings

Out of a reaction to their psychoanalytic training, Fritz and Laura Perls developed a theory of counseling that incorporated elements of psychoanalysis into an existential-humanistic therapy. The primary philosophical underpinning of Getsalt is the emphasis on a comprehensive phenomenological perspective of experience. Like many existential theories inspired by Husserl (1965) and Sartre (1956), Gestalt is grounded on the assumption that meaning is best derived and understood by considering the individual's interpretation of immediate experience. Perls emphasized "immediate" experience because this is the experience that is present and can be attuned to and impacted. "To me nothing exists but the now. Now = experience = awareness = reality" (Perls, 1970, p. 14). Therefore, the key phenomenological experience exists in the here-and-now and emphasizes all aspects of the individual's current perception. As Clarkson (1989) noted,

> The phenomenological method which pays total attention to the phenomenon (person, experience or object) as it presents itself, becomes the

method of choice in this counseling approach. Description is more
important than interpretation. Clients are able to find their own meaning
through this process. (pp. 13–14)

Unlike psychoanalysis, which counted on the analyst's interpretation of the
client's unconscious processes for change, Gestalt focuses on understanding
the world from the client's perspective, respecting the belief that each person has a unique perception of self, other, and environment. This individual
perception is the reality of the client, and understanding this reality is the
road to change.

Influenced by interactions with philosopher Jan Smuts in South Africa,
Gestalt theory is grounded in the holistic view of the human psyche. Perls
believed that the psychoanalytic view of the compartmentalization of the
psyche into id, ego and superego led to fragmented people. He viewed the
psyche as an integrated whole where a person's physical, emotional, and
spiritual elements are intertwined and inseparable to make the whole being.
The classic example of the whole being greater than the sum of its parts is
that of the cookie. What makes a cookie? A typical recipe for chocolate chip
cookies calls for flour, eggs, brown sugar, salt, chocolate chips, and heat.
Holism states that the individual nature of the collection of these ingredients
is different from the final cookie. Separating the ingredients and examining
them one by one and perhaps viewing one ingredient as the "essence of the
cookie" would not give you the same insight as if you looked at the finished
cookie as a whole. As with cookies, clients are encouraged to accept all aspects of self: pretty/ugly, smart/stupid, good/bad, productive/lazy; and attempts to ignore aspects of self, seen as splitting the whole, are considered
unhealthy.

Gestalt therapy draws philosophically from phenomenology and holism
and also forms concepts modified from scientific models, such as field theory
(Lewin, 1951) and elements of Gestalt psychology. Lewin's field theory is
also a phenomenological-holistic theory where the field exists in the hereand-now and represents the interaction between an organism and its environment. The field is described as containing the *ground*, all the
phenomenologically perceived information, and the *figure*, the part of the
ground that emerges and is of interest to the organism, most often experienced as a need. When a figure arises from the perceptual field (ground), the
organism then mobilizes energy to fulfill the need. If the need is fulfilled, the
figure recedes into the ground and a new figure can arise. If the need is not
fulfilled, the figure does not recede and becomes a distraction to the organism. This need fulfillment process is the basis for the Gestalt perspective on
the developing human being (Perls, Hefferline, & Goodman, 1951).

PERSONALITY DEVELOPMENT

Nature of Humans

Function of the Psyche. The basic function of the psyche is to fulfill needs. When the organism is functioning smoothly, needs arise, one at a time, as a figure from the ground. The organism mobilizes energy to satisfy the need and the figure recedes as a new figure emerges. Perls et al. (1951) asserted that all human beings strive for balance and self-regulation. The self-regulation potential emphasizes the ability of the organism to internally and spontaneously participate in need fulfillment in a natural free flowing manner. The important aspect of this potentiality is not that the organism remains balanced at all times—this would be viewed as either impossible or at least stagnant. In fact, the self-regulation tendency that moves toward balance stresses the movement aspect of the potentiality. That is, as a new need emerges, the organism is by definition unbalanced. The tendency is to be aware of the need and then fulfill the need, thus achieving balance once again until a new figure (need) arises.

The functioning of the psyche is such that one can experience only that which is in one's present awareness. The past is remembered and the future is fantasized, but neither can be directly experienced. One experiences oneself and the environment only in the now. The need that dominates the present moment also influences perception. To a hungry person, food looks attractive; to a satiated person, it can look uninteresting, even repugnant. Perception, therefore, reflects phenomenology. Objective reality cannot be known because one always perceives through the personal bias of one's current need.

Structure of the Psyche. One aspect of the structure of the psyche is the background, or simply ground, of awareness, and the foreground into which the current need (figure) emerges and becomes the focus of one's attention. As a need is met, or if the original need is unmet but another more pressing need emerges, the original need recedes into the ground and the new need takes the foreground. Personality structure is based on this ongoing interface between individual and environment and patterns that form from need fulfillment cycles. Korb, Gorrell, and Van De Reit (1989) explained:

> Out of the flow of experiencing, basic personality structures have coalesced in the ground of experience. These structures may be seen as a relatively constant set of constructs, attitudes, and beliefs about the individual and the environment which exists as part of the person's ground. (pp. 21–22)

The process of retaining elements of need fulfillment in the ground is the Gestalt explanation of learning. For example, if you need to start your car, you can be aware of past methods that satisfied this need (i.e., using your key) and utilize the recalled method with relative ease instead of experiencing the need fulfillment cycle of "starting the car" from scratch each time you get in your car. The patterns retained in a person's ground represent repetitive characterological strategies for attending to life's needs: one's personality. They also form the context for exploration that will become important as we discuss the therapeutic process.

Also structurally speaking, the psyche of the infant at birth is a unified whole that consists of a synergetic interaction between aspects such as feelings, thoughts, and actions; the psyche cannot be reduced to any one of these. Each person's psyche also contains the potential for every human quality such as both humor and seriousness, both selfishness and generosity, and both adventurousness and cautions. These qualities have the potential to become polarized, with one extreme of the polarity being disowned, that is, chronically reconciled to the ground of awareness, thereby limiting one's human potential to respond with all one's resources to the emergent need. At birth, the infant experiences himself or herself as undifferentiated from the environment. With experience, the infant comes to differentiate what is me from what is not-me. The border between the me and the not-me is the contact boundary, but a sense of not-me is never to be confused with being separate or isolated from one's environment. More accurately, self is the boundary of the organism that belongs to both the person and the environment. On the one side, the contact boundary is in relative contact with oneself, involving awareness of one's needs. On the other side, the contact boundary interacts with the environment.

Role of the Environment

For Gestalt therapy, the individual cannot exist without interacting with environment; the two are inextricably linked. Yontef (1995) explained, "There is no meaningful way to consider a person psychologically apart from the organism-environment field, just as there is no way to perceive the environment except through someone's observational perspective. Even the need to be alone is defined in relation to others" (p. 263). Individuals are acted upon by the environment and act upon the environment; a process that both fulfills needs and facilitates self-definition.

The phenomenological field is defined by boundaries between self and environment. "In Gestalt therapy theory, the sense of self is relational. There is no 'I', no person, no sense of self, isolated from interhuman environment" (Yontef, 1998, p. 89). Contact is the point of connection between that which is me (self) and not-me (environment). Awareness of me and not-me is vital to healthy contact; it allows an organism to have contact with the environment and maintain separation when the environment is deemed not healthy and also allows information to be exchanged when needed. Consider the experience of watching a movie. Throughout the movie you are in continuous contact with the environment (the film being projected on the screen, the seat in which you are sitting, the crowd around you, etc.). You are actively attending to some parts of your environment more intently than others—the film dialogue, for example. Attending to the crowd around you would be distracting, so you form a boundary around that contact and make the contact between self and the film dialogue more permeable. Focusing on the film, you are also aware that this is a movie, not real life that involves you, so although you could say you are "involved" in the movie, even experiencing emotion, you are aware of the boundary between self and the fictional aspect of the movie.

From a developmental perspective, the environment that comprises the infant's natural and social surroundings can be characterized as falling somewhere on a continuum between supportive at one extreme and toxic at the other, with neglectful in between. In the supportive environment, when the infant and young child attempt to meet a need, the environment provides whatever is needed. In the neglectful environment, the youngster's needs go unmet. In the toxic environment, the environment responds to the needing child with commodities antithetical to the child's well-being. For example, consider the child who needs food, experiences hunger, and is thus energized to meet that need through communication, such as crying or asking for food, and/or some other activity, such as finding commodities to put into one's mouth. The supportive environment consists of commodities, such as nutritious food, and people willing to provide those commodities. In the neglectful environment, such commodities and/or people are absent. In the toxic environment, the only available commodities are unhealthful, or people respond by punishing the child expressing the need, by providing the needing child unhealthy commodities to eat, or by coercing the child to eat when the child does not need to eat.

A poignant example of the child's vulnerability to assimilate toxicity under conditions of a nonsupportive environment is a scene from the movie *King of the Hill*, based on the memoirs of A. E. Hotchner. It is St. Louis in the Depression of the 1930s. Twelve-year-old Aaron is living alone in his family's apartment. In desperation, his father has taken a traveling sales job. His mother is in the hospital with tuberculosis. His parents have sent his sister away to live with a relative but have left him to fend for himself, believing him capable of self-support. Despite careful attempts to conserve, he runs out of food and money. He dares not leave the apartment because the unpaid landlord will take the first opportunity to lock him out, leaving him not only foodless but also homeless. After days without food, in desperation he creates a "meal" for himself by placing cut out magazine pictures of food onto a plate. Then, with fantasized savor, he eats the "meal," which actually ends up making him violently ill. Ultimately, he recovers and is saved from this situation, but his story illustrates how vulnerable people, and especially children, can be to assimilating what is toxic when the environment is neglectful or offers only toxicity in response to one's attempts to meet one's needs.

One should get a sense that the role of the environment is a two-way street in Gestalt therapy. Just as people must adjust to the field, experienced as familial or cultural expectations, laws, or rules, people also shape their environment to fulfill needs. Therefore, a balance between self-support and environmental support is encouraged. A good example is eating: We need food to survive, but the existence or presence of food in the environment is not enough to satisfy the need. One must actively be aware of the presence of food and take steps to ingest the necessary nutrients to survive. From a Gestalt perspective, this interactive process between environment and self is true for every need throughout the lifespan.

Interaction of Human Nature and Environment in Personality Development

View of Healthy Functioning. Healthy individuals approach life with vigor; experiencing and fulfilling one's needs as they arise in the here and now. The need fulfillment cycle discussed in the last section is completed consistently, with little disruption. To facilitate healthy functioning, Gestalt therapists believe individuals utilize awareness of self and environment, responsibility for self, a commitment to maturation, and a dedication to appropriate contact with the environment. To help flesh out these concepts, we will use Naranjo's (1970, p. 50) general principles formulated from his "injunctions for living the good life" as a method to provide a complete picture of healthy functioning from a Gestalt perspective.

1. *Valuation of actuality:* Within this principle, healthy individuals strive to live in the present, rather than the past or the future. Anxiety about what has already transpired or what might occur limits one's ability to focus on the needs at hand. Attending to the here-and-now enables the individual to experience each moment in its fullness and increases the probability of need fulfillment. As an added bonus, because one is fulfilling needs, there will be less to worry about regarding the past ("What did I miss?") or the future ("I am afraid of the unknown") because the attention is on what can be controlled (the present). The injunctions that go along with this principle include: "Live here. Live now. Stop imagining and experience the real" (Naranjo, 1970, p. 49).
2. *Valuation of awareness and acceptance of experience:* Healthy individuals embrace awareness of self and how self relates to and interacts with the

environment. As needs arise, one must first be aware of the need; without awareness, contact can never be made and need fulfillment will never take place. Without awareness of self and environment, one cannot fully accept experience or live in the here and now. The price for not being aware of needs as they rise from the ground includes discomfort, distraction, confusion, or other more serious symptoms depending on the denied need. For example, as I am writing this paragraph, I am aware that I am thirsty. I know this because I sense a dryness in my mouth and I am repeatedly engaging in behaviors such as licking my lips and swallowing. Although I have been aware of this need to drink, I have denied the need by trying to focus on finishing this section of the book. The result: The thirst and need to drink has become a distraction, an interference in my ability to work. In order to fulfill this need and value the awareness, I must both be aware of the need and take steps to fulfill it such as getting up and getting a drink of water. Having quenched my thirst, I am now prepared to focus on new needs as they emerge, for example, the need to finish this section.

Healthy individuals understand and accept all aspects of self. Realization that one can be both good and evil, healthy and unhealthy, right and wrong, at any given moment are essential to living a healthy existence. When one does not value all aspects of self, denial of self occurs, and thus limits full awareness. When this split occurs, polarities form. This concept will be discussed in more detail in the "View of Unhealthy Functioning" section. Specific injunctions that correspond to this principle include, "Stop unnecessary thinking. Rather taste and see. Express rather than manipulate, explain, justify, or judge. Give in to unpleasantness and pain just as to pleasure. Do not restrict your awareness" (Naranjo, 1970, p. 50).

3. *Valuation of wholeness, or responsibility:* Healthy people understand that life is a process, not separated or compartmentalized, but designed to be experienced as developmental in nature. As people mature, they shed old ways of being and become more self-sufficient, self-observing, and self-understanding. The valuation of wholeness requires a commitment to the maturation process and the struggles the process brings. Consider the challenges of your development from an infant to an adult. From a Gestalt perspective, the maturation process helps form the sense of personal identity and helps differentiate the individual from others in the environment. Healthy individuals are open to this process, embracing the possibilities of letting go of others and exploring self. I remember when my youngest child learned how to walk. One day, after months of crawling and walking with the aid of my finger, he let go and toddled out into space on his own. He fell, but tried again and again until he could walk competently. The look on his face, part terror, part astonishment, part wonder, is what Gestalt theory envisions as the experience we all encounter when we trust self and actively engage in maturation.

Responsibility is a key to maturation. Healthy individuals recognize that in order to think and feel on their own, to trust self, one must be willing to take responsibility for personal thoughts, actions, and feelings. Not only must one take responsibility for self, but one must also refrain from taking responsibility for other people's thoughts, feelings, and behaviors. The mantra "I am only responsible for myself. I am not responsible for others" fits the Gestalt principle of responsibility. When we refuse to accept responsibility for self or too willingly take on the responsibility of others, we blur the line between I and Thou and this blurring interferes with awareness and, ultimately, need fulfillment.

Even though we have broken down the aspects of healthy living into general principles to aid in understanding, hopefully the reader can appreciate the interconnectedness, the holism, of the principles. Without awareness we cannot be responsible for our thoughts, actions, and feelings. Without a here-and-now focus, we lose a sense of awareness and limit our ability to be actively responsible. Without a valuation of the wholeness of the life process and a commitment to maturation, awareness and responsibility become moot points and a here-and-now existence is impossible. Without responsibility, we lose the need to focus on the here-and-now or even be aware, because the locus of control lies outside of self. The three general principles intertwine to create a core of healthy living designed to maximize need fulfillment and healthy balance.

View of Unhealthy Functioning. All people develop methods for fulfilling one's needs and, as noted, continually and innately strive toward balance and need fulfillment. Even with the innate striving toward balance, no one grows up in a completely supportive environment. Therefore, everyone's needs sometimes go unmet. Everyone has the capacity to tolerate the inevitable occasional unfinished business. Yet if one's environment has been primarily supportive of need fulfillment, one is likely to have developed an appropriately permeable contact boundary, with the ability to process through the need fulfillment cycle on a regular basis, usually restoring homeostasis. Maladjustment occurs when one restricts awareness, and as a result, patterns develop that fail to fulfill needs or are destructive to self or other. In response to a persistently neglectful or toxic environment, one is likely to develop disturbance at the contact boundary. To avoid the anxiety of unfinished business, the child may disown awareness of unmet needs. If the people on whom the child depends communicate that the child should feel, think, or act differently than he or she is guided to by organismic self-regulation, the child may relegate the unacceptable aspect of self to the ground, where it is disowned from awareness. Only the polar opposite of this aspect is allowed into awareness, fragmenting the self and limiting the child's access to his or her full resources. At the same time, a disturbance develops at the contact boundary, rendering it overly permeable, overly impermeable, or vacillating between the two in an attempt to meet needs in the neglectful or toxic environment. If one manifests the contact boundary disturbance through the chronic use of contact boundary phenomena—introjection, confluence, projection, deflection, and/or retroflection—one's ability to contact oneself and the environment to meet one's needs is impaired.

One way to conceptualize the contact boundary is as a kind of psychological "skin" where self meets the environment. The "health" of the contact boundary is assessed by the size and shape of the "pores" of that skin. When the pores are moderately spaced and straight, the skin is, appropriately, both permeable and impermeable: assimilation of self-enhancing material and blocking out self-destructive material (toxins) from the environment is possible. In this condition, one is fully aware, and one's sense of self has integrity with an appropriate amount of openness and guardedness. This can be illustrated as:

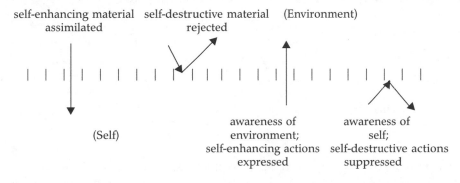

Contact boundary disturbances can be understood as the pores having deviated in some way, size or shape, accompanied by a disturbance in one's sense of self. In each case, the appropriate balance of exchange between self and the environment is upset. Each of the five contact boundary disturbances identified by Yontef and Jacobs (2000) can be understood in this way.

For example, in introjection, pores have become so open to the environment that the individual takes in both nutritious and toxic material. With pores too ingressly open and the contact boundary too permeable, one's sense of self is not well enough defined and is vulnerable to being defined by input from the environment, which is especially problematic if the input is toxic. This can be illustrated as:

One form of introjection is taking in rules that are rigidly held. Consider the man who learned as a child to stop and look both ways before crossing the street. One night at 3:00 a.m., the neighbor across the street calls asking the man for help with an urgent medical emergency. Approaching the curb, he neither sees nor hears any traffic on his quiet residential street, yet he stops at the curb and looks both ways before proceeding. His response-ability to his neighbor's emergency has been impaired by his unexamined, inflexible introjection. Another form of introjection is taking in self-concepts, such as the child who assimilates repeated messages from his father that he is stupid despite the child's own experience that he performs adequately in school work.

In projection, pores have become shaped such that one perceives personal qualities in the people and things of the environment. With one's pores too egressly open, one's sense of self is not adequately contained but is projected out into the environment. This can be illustrated as:

(Environment)

V V V V V V V V V V V／V

(Self)   awareness of self
                               not contained but
                               projected onto environment

An example of projection is the penny-pinching woman who always tries to get herself the very best deal, moneywise. In a business transaction, she is trying to manipulate the deal so that she gets more than her fair share. When others resist her strategies and persist in trying to get a fair shake, she angrily perceives them as trying to cheat her but is unaware that she began the conflict by trying to cheat them.

In confluence, pores have become so open that one does not distinguish between self and the environment, especially other people. Correspondingly, one's sense of self is quite diffuse. This can be illustrated as:

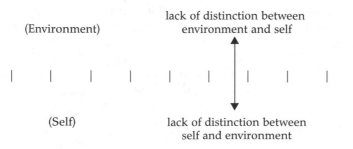

| | lack of distinction between |
| (Environment) | environment and self |

| | | | | | | | | |

| (Self) | lack of distinction between |
| | self and environment |

An example of confluence is the person who overidentifies with others' successes, failures, or problems. I (JMH) realized I was experiencing confluence when I became upset on my husband's behalf: He felt hurt by something his stepdaughter had done. What she had done did not involve me, but was entirely between him and her; I had lost my distinction between him and myself; I had become overly identified with him. With this awareness I transcended confluence by affirming that he is he and I am I; I "gave" him the problem, which was really his problem to begin with! Another example is the person who is so much what others expect that he has little sense of himself, such as someone who is excessively pleasing or excessively rebellious in response to others' expectations; such a person tends to be out of touch with his own needs and preferences.

In isolation and retroflection, the pores of the contact boundary become closed. One result can be that even nutritious material from the environment is rejected, leaving one quite isolated. Another is that even self-enhancing impulses are retroflectively turned back on oneself. These can be illustrated as:

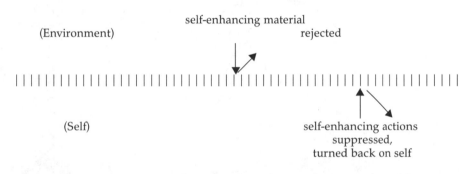

An example of isolation is the person in distress who cannot receive support or assistance offered by others. An example of retroflection is the person who feels angry but does not allow herself to express it and, instead, turns it back on herself and develops a stomach ulcer.

Disturbances in contact produce a stagnation or paralysis in the growth process, inhibiting the client from full awareness and maturation. Clients can avoid contact using one or more of the concepts discussed above, and symptomology will parallel the chosen disturbance strategy as discussed. Perls (1970) postulated five layers of psychopathology (see Figure 7.1), suggesting that working through these layers was much like peeling an onion. Each layer peeled not only helps the client strip away a false self, but also gets the client to be more aware of the true self. The specifics of how to work through these layers are discussed in the next sections.

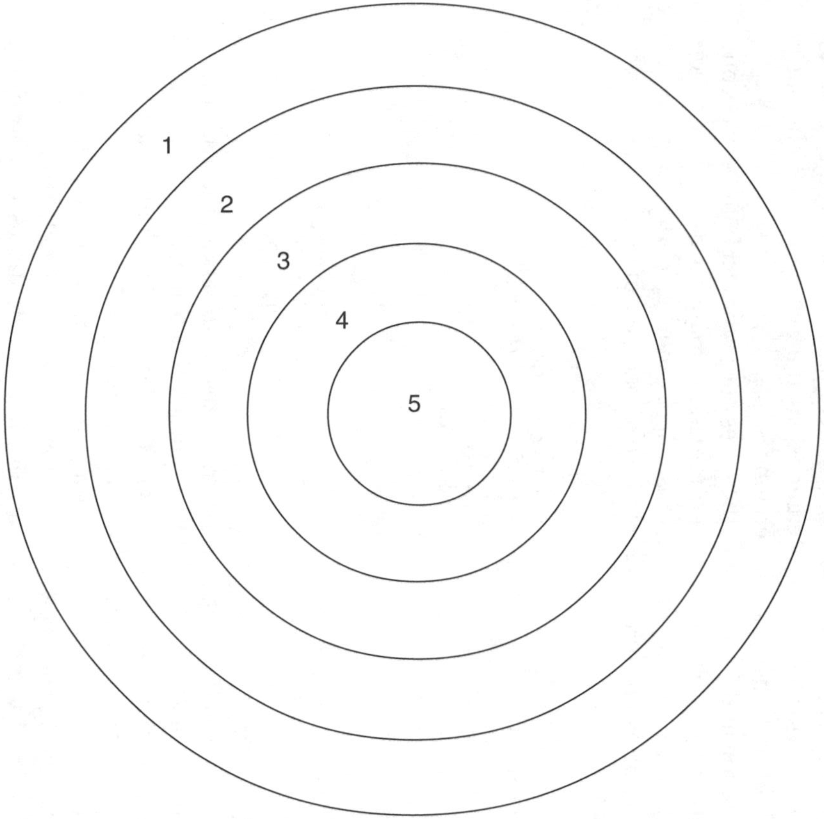

2. *The phobic*: If we manage to try to face all that we are, this level forces us to face the fear associated with being our whole self. Catastrophes such as, "My parents will not love me if . . ." or "My wife will think I am less of a man if . . ." arise to scare us back into the phony layer.

4. *Implosive*: We step into the abyss of the unknown as we begin to explore the blind spots in ourselves. The exploration often is awkward and scary, as we let go of our old ways of being and explore new ways.

1. *The phony*: Pretend to be something we are not. Social masks; real selves are hidden so we feel liked, feared, loved, etc. Much of the disowning of certain aspects of self (polarities) occurs here.

3. *Impasse*: The impasse is a point of paralysis where we face the dual terror of moving away from external support and of relying on self. Many people freeze at this layer or retreat because it is too difficult or the pain of avoiding contact or living a life of limited awareness is preferable to the pain and fear of change.

5. *Explosive*: Once we let go and embrace the responsibility of self in every here-and-now moment, we will feel truly alive. Perls likened this "a-ha" experience to an explosion of energy, wherein spontaneous expressions of intense anger, joy, grief, and sadness are common.

FIGURE 7.1

The Personality Change Process

Basic Principles of Change. From a Gestalt perspective, change occurs when the individual moves to a position characterized by more self-support/self-trust, insight, and, most importantly, awareness. Within the client–counselor dialogue, contact is created and experienced and blockages to awareness are explored phenomenologically, respecting the client's perspective of reality. Gestalt therapy adopts a paradoxical approach to change. That is, one can only change when one is truly oneself, and the more someone tries to be who she is not, the more stuck she will become (Beisser, 1970). Growth is inhibited by denying aspects of self, creating polarities, and causing disturbances in contact. As Perls (1969a) noted,

> the aim in therapy, the growth aim, is to lose more and more of your 'mind' and come more to your *senses*. To be more and more in touch with yourself and in touch with the world, instead of only in touch with the fantasies, prejudices and apprehensions. (p. 50)

The goal is to not buy into the curse of the ideal, where the client is seeking some dramatic improvement to be "better," but instead to be more fully aware of one's true self (Korb et al., 1989). As discussed in previous sections, if good health is characterized by an organism that self-regulates the fulfillment of needs as they arise, and if maladjustment is created through interruptions in that need fulfillment cycle, then change must address awareness of the blockages, and mechanisms that help return the organism to self-regulation and balance.

According to Yontef (1995) awareness is the primary principle for change and contains two vital elements: *microawareness*, which is awareness of a particular content area, and *awareness of the awareness process*. Microawareness is fairly easy for most counselors to grasp. For example, I am aware that I am writing about Gestalt therapy. You might be aware that you are reading about Gestalt therapy and learning about basic principles to change. Clients may be aware that they are discussing marital problems, listening to their child talk about the pain of the divorce, or hearing feedback from the therapist. Moment-to-moment content awareness plays an important role in the counseling process from all theoretical perspectives. Awareness of the awareness process, on the other hand, focuses on the client's ability to be aware that he has the power to choose to be aware of how needs are being met or being blocked, and that by being aware of this choice, one can focus awareness to choose differently. According to Yontef (1995), "Awareness of awareness strengthens the ability to choose to bring automatic habits into awareness as needed and use focused awareness and phenomenological experimentation for clarification, centering, and trying out new behaviors" (p. 275). Simply put, microawareness allows the client to track what is occurring in the field, while awareness of the awareness process is the key to the client taking responsibility for interacting with the field in a different way, thus promoting change.

The second aspect of change involves what happens after awareness is accessed. Awareness of the need, or of how the blockages occur in the cycle, is vital, but then the person must take steps to experiment with and experience new ways of fulfilling the need and completing the gestalt. As Korb et al. (1989) pointed out, merely talking about the issue will not fulfill the need, one must experience in the here-and-now a way of satisfying the need. As awareness increases, clients experience a "comfort with self" and begin to take steps to move from the reliance on external opinions and support to more internal support and trust in themselves. This transition, called maturity, is a hallmark of the Gestalt change process whereby the person can access awareness and facilitate healthy contact on one's own. Perls et al. (1951) stated that the end result of treatment is aimed at helping the client reach a point where "they can proceed without help . . . *natura sanat non medicus,* it is only oneself (in the environment) that can cure oneself" (p. 292). Methods for facilitating two important principles of change will be illustrated in the next three sections.

Change Through Counseling

The Client's Role. Because Gestalt therapy is active and focused on the here-and-now, the client plays a very important role in the therapeutic process. Greenwald (1976) outlined "ground rules for Gestalt therapy" that help conceptualize the role of the client (see Table 7.1). The author did not mean for the list of "rules" to be read as a list of commands and demands on the clients, but instead as an assortment of elements that "create an atmosphere and attitude toward working in therapy that lead to greater awareness of the reality of oneself and how one interacts with others and how one functions in the here-and-now" (Greenwald, p. 269).

The Counselor's Role.   Akin to other existential-humanistic approaches such as client-centered and existential therapy, Gestalt therapists are considered tools of change. The therapist is both supportive and confrontational, continuously working to encourage here-and-now awareness in the client through the direct experiencing of the I-Thou relationship. Gestalt therapists use feedback and immediacy to share their impressions and reactions to the client. This use of self by the therapist fosters contact and acts as the catalyst for here-and-now experiencing and awareness. As the client avoids contact with the therapist, the therapist challenges and brings the contact disturbances to the client's attention.

The role of the therapist is to ask "How?" and avoid the "Why?" with regard to client issues. Observing the client in the session, how she makes or avoids contact with the therapist, will provide important information about the client's perspective and function. How the client functions in the now is the most valid representation of the client's phenomenology available to the

TABLE 7.1
Ground Rules in Gestalt Therapy

1. **Attune oneself to the continuum of awareness:** Clients are encouraged to pay attention to the various modes of sensory awareness over the course of the session. Sensory awareness may include thoughts, feelings, emotions, bodily sensations—anything
   that is noticed internally or externally by the client.
2. **Commit to the here-and-now:** Because the focus of the therapy is the here-and-now,
   clients are expected to speak in the present tense. Even when one is discussing past
   material, dreams, or future expectations, the client will be encouraged to bring these
   into the now and discuss how the issue is impacting them in the present moment.
3. **Own everything:** In order to become more aware of self, clients must own all their
   thoughts, actions, feelings, and sensations. Just as clients are expected to speak in
   the present tense, they also use "I" language as an expression of self-responsibility.
   For example, instead of saying "You make me angry," clients may say "I feel angry."
4. **Commit to meaningful dialogue:** For a meaningful dialogue to occur, the rules discussed previously must be met. The ability to communicate to another person in a
   clear and responsible manner is just one aspect of the dialogue. In addition to communicating, one must be willing to listen to the other person's (the counselor's) perception of what was just shared. The openness to and assessment of environmental
   feedback is a vital aspect of the need fulfillment cycle and the maintenance of healthy
   contact.
5. **Avoid questions:** Questions of the counselor or even of oneself are largely seen as
   ways to avoid real contact. Questions elicit explanations or justifications and rarely
   get to the core issues. Gathering evidence to support a position removes the counselor–client dyad from the here-and-now.
6. **Take risks:** In Gestalt therapy, one must face one's fears and risk being rejected or
   humiliated in order to gain awareness into one's true self. Risks involve experimenting with all aspects of one's personality, especially the parts that are ignored or un-
   claimed. Clients who are not willing to explore those parts of self would not benefit
   from Gestalt therapy.
7. **Embrace personal responsibility:** Gestalt therapists believe that clients have the power
   to change and have the responsibility to decide when and how that change will occur.
   Therefore, there exists no "I can't" in Gestalt therapy, only the "I won't."

Adapted from "The Ground Rules in Gestalt Therapy," by J. A. Greenwald, in *The Handbook of
Gestalt Therapy*, edited by C. Hatcher and P. Himelstein, 1976, New York: Aronson.

counselor. Exploring the why only provides an explanation, a justification
for experience, but does not engage in experiencing. In fact, whys are distance-
makers and contact-breakers, while hows facilitate dialogue and contact.

Stages and Techniques. The most unfortunate aspect of Gestalt theory
is that, for many, it has been reduced to a collection of elaborate techniques.
Ask people about Gestalt therapy and many are likely to respond, "Oh yes,
the empty-chair therapy" or some variation on that. It is because of this association that we are reluctant to outline various techniques. However, experimentation is the method for facilitating awareness, and the techniques that
have been created are wonderful tools when used for the purpose of establishing a continuum of awareness. Therefore, a discussion of some Gestalt

experiments follows, but to make sure that the warning to not confuse Gestalt with a technique-only theory prevails, a message from Fritz Perls is provided as well:

> One of the objections I have against anyone calling himself a Gestalt Therapist is that he uses techniques. A technique is a gimmick. A gimmick should be used only in the extreme case. We've got enough people running around collecting gimmicks, more gimmicks, and abusing them. These techniques, these tools, are quite useful in some seminar on sensory awareness or joy, just to give you an idea that you are still alive . . . but the sad fact is that this jazzing-up more often becomes a dangerous substitute activity, another phony therapy that prevents growth. (Perls, 1969a, p. 1)

Although Gestalt therapy is an active, fluid process that emphasizes the here-and-now interaction between client and counselor, the traditional stages of therapy (rapport, defining the problem, exploring the problem, experimenting with change, and termination) seem to apply to Gestalt therapy. The first "stage" of therapy involves orienting the client to the Gestalt process of experiencing the here-and-now instead of there-and-then material. Within this orientation framework, the therapist is encouraged to get a sense of the reason the client has initiated counseling and assess the client's understanding of awareness, and any fear or resistance to change. A dialogue of the here-and-now develops at this stage as illustrated below. Notice the use of reflection and encouragement to experience the here-and-now.

Client: I really don't know why I am here. I mean, I feel bad all the time, but I am used to solving my own problems. My wife says I worry too much and should be able to handle life.

Counselor: You are feeling ambivalent about being here and are considering how other people feel about your current situation. Let's focus on you right now. Focus on what you are feeling right now. Tell me the first feeling that comes to your awareness.

Client: Well, nervous, I guess.

Counselor: You are not sure? Perhaps that is your feeling, unsure. What went through your mind as I said that?

Client: That I . . .

Counselor: You are editing, censoring yourself. Let it go and say it.

Client: OK, I do feel uncertain. I feel like that all the time and I feel like that now. I also feel like I should know, and I feel like an idiot when I don't. I feel like an idiot for being here.

Counselor: That's a great place to start.

The first stage focuses on initiating contact between counselor and client and provides an introduction to the experience of working with awareness within the therapeutic dyad. In Gestalt therapy, this characterizes what is known across theories as developing rapport or establishing a working relationship. If the first stage builds the foundation, then the second stage focuses on in-depth exploration of the contact disturbances and denied awareness experienced in the first stage. To help client and counselor address the need for contact in a here-and-now manner, Gestalt "experiments" were created. Each technique is designed to access and experience awareness in a free manner within the session and promote healthy contact between client and counselor. A few of the experiments are illustrated below.

Reversal. True awareness means experiencing and owning all aspects of self. All elements of personality exist on a continuum, but many people act as if they possess only the "good" side of a trait and possess none of the "bad" or vice versa. The reversal experiment asks the client to express the polar opposite of any feeling, thought, or action. The expression of these elements that have been kept out of awareness can only be integrated into the whole individual when openly disclosed. Consider the example below of a client who struggles with anxiety.

Client: I am anxious all the time. I cannot shake it.

Counselor: That is powerful language. Say the opposite and see how it feels.

Client: I can't.

Counselor: I am aware of the hopelessness inherent in the phrase, "I can't."
Let's start with "I can." Say that and tell me what you are aware of.

Client: I can. Hmm, that does feel different. I am aware of my body straightening out as I say it.

Counselor: OK, now try to the reverse of your earlier statement.

Client: I am not anxious all the time . . .

Counselor: What else are you?

Client: I am calm some of the time, peaceful.

Counselor: Your body and your voice resonate with that peace. It is inside of you after all. As witnessed here, you possess the capacity for anxiety and calm.

Dialogue. This experiment, commonly referred to as the "empty-chair technique," is designed to provide clarity to parts of self that have been unexplored or kept out of awareness. The aim is to provide a means for the integration of the denied aspects of self. The "parts" are played by the client, using two chairs. The client speaks as each part, moving from chair to chair in an ongoing dialogue. A common example of the experiment is the client dialogue between the internal "top-dog" and "underdog." Many people struggle between listening/obeying the moralistic, judgmental, demanding side (top-dog) and giving in to the side that claims helplessness, weakness, and powerlessness (underdog). Extreme manifestations of this conflict lead to clients exhibiting an overmanifestation of top-dog as evidenced by a controlling personality, or underdog as evidenced by helpless and victim-oriented personality traits. In the following dialogue, note the shift from there-and-then material to here-and-now material and the gradual integration of the elements of this client's personality.

Client: I am just so pissed that she won't get off her butt and do something with her life. I mean, she just wastes time!

Counselor: Perhaps this is not so much about her as about you and your own fear of being seen as lazy or unproductive. Would you be willing to examine this possibility?

Client: OK, I mean, I hate being seen as lazy. I am a hard worker.

Counselor: I want you to play both sides, the lazy part and the hard worker part, and I want you to act out a dialogue between these two entities. We will work with these two chairs. As you change parts, move to a different chair to begin the dialogue. Talk as if these two parts of yourself are speaking to each other. How would you like to begin?

Client: I'll start with my hard-working side.

Hard-working: I don't see why you are so damn lazy! I mean, I work hard all day. I'm doing things, and you just sit around and relax. You are useless.

Lazy: Well, I have to relax sometime or I'll be angry all the time like you. Relaxing is good too you know! You are always so stressed out. Wouldn't you like to take some time off?

Hard-working: No . . . yes! Yes, I would, but someone has to work around here. If I don't work nothing would get done.

Lazy: I think you could get more done if you took some time to rest.

Directed Awareness. Gestalt therapy emphasizes that blocks to awareness and contact are exhibited in a wide range of ways: behaviorally, emotionally, cognitively, spiritually, and physically. Directed awareness provides the atmosphere for the client to focus on any and all of these aspects while in the here-and-now.

Counselor: You seem tense, like you are anticipating something but are having a difficult time vocalizing it.

Client: Yeah, I have a lot going on right now; too many distractions.

Counselor: Let's practice some directed awareness. Try to sit in a comfortable position and close your eyes if you like. OK, as we have done before, as things come into awareness, verbalize with "I am now aware of . . . "

Client: (settling in) I am aware of tension in my back. I am now aware of moving my neck to pop it. I am aware of the thought, "I am overwhelmed." I am aware of the feeling of fear. (Sighs) I am aware that I just exhaled very deeply. I am aware that it felt good so I want to do it again. (Sighs) I am aware of the thought, "This is helping me to feel more relaxed." I am aware of my feet wiggling on the floor. I am aware of the thought, "I am not alone." I am aware that I am beginning to tear up. I am aware that the tension in my back has lessened. I am aware of the desire to open my eyes and talk about my feelings of not being alone.

As the client gains awareness, clarity, and integration of self through contact with the counselor and experimentation, insight learned in counseling is encouraged to be tested outside of the session. Clients take their comfort with aspects of self and experiment in other situations. For example, the person who had trouble relaxing could work on being aware of the top-dog/underdog struggle during the week and practice recognizing both. The ability to integrate self through recognition and elimination of blocks to contact and awareness both in and outside the therapy session can be an indication of completion of the therapy.

The fourth stage is the termination stage, where the counselor supports changes made by the client and continues to challenge the client in the here-and-now. Since these stages are not necessarily linear, one could view the fourth stage as an ongoing process. In fact, in keeping with the Gestalt idea of holism, the events and awareness that occur in any given "stage" could lead to movement into an earlier stage or to a later stage depending on the level of awareness. There is also no set time frame for stage progression. Change (awareness) can happen in an hour or it can take many years depending on the work that needs to be done and the intricate client and counselor variables in any given session. The key is for the counselor and the client to strive to be open to the moment and to be aware of the issues as they surface in the here-and-now.

CONTRIBUTIONS AND LIMITATIONS

Interface with Recent Developments in the Mental Health Field

Effectiveness of Psychotherapy. Regarding research and effectiveness, Gestalt therapy suffers from the same problems shared by other humanistic approaches discussed in this text. Many of the concepts do not mesh well with qualitative methodologies, and the phenomenology process of the client–counselor dialogue makes systematic descriptions and controlled studies near impossible. Reviews of research literature show mixed results for Gestalt therapy. Both Smith, Glass, and Miller (1980) and Greenberg, Elliott, and Lietaer (1994) reported that outcome studies show that Gestalt was more effective than no treatment. However Greenberg et al. (1994) also noted that when compared to other forms of treatment, Gestalt often demonstrated less favorable results. Although research is scarce in the qualitative arena, the recent interest in qualitative research methods may provide Gestalt therapy with needed tools to explore the efficacy of the theory.

Nature/Nurture. Regarding nature/nurture questions, Gestalt theory firmly believes in the dynamic interplay between self, biology, and environment. Philosophically rooted in holism and self-responsibility, Gestalt focuses not on the causal relationship between nature/nurture and behavior, but on the organism in the here and now. From a Gestalt perspective, a person is impacted by genetics and the environment while simultaneously impacting one's physiology and environment through the choices one makes. The individual's perception of the present moment becomes the context for understanding this interrelationship.

Pharmacotherapy. Regarding psychopharmacology, although modern Gestalt therapists recognize the latest research findings on the efficacy of medication in the alleviation of some symptoms, they would also argue that the client's problems do not end with the erasure of problematic symptoms. In fact, historically Gestalt therapists have criticized the medical model for focusing too much on what we would rather not see instead of working with what we are currently experiencing (Fagan & Shepherd, 1970). Clients who take medication as a quick fix would be seen as hiding in the phony layer of existence, unwilling to take the longer road to self-awareness. From a Gestalt approach, people who merely take medication run the risk of splitting self into the "Sick me" and "Not sick me" polarity. Taking medication as a means to correct a chemical imbalance and then proceeding to address personal issues that were once difficult to focus on would be seen as appropriate. For example, a client suffering from intense hallucinations and delusions takes medication to quell these symptoms but also seeks therapy to address underlying issues of self. For an excellent account of a schizophrenic client's struggle for self within the client–counselor dialogue, see Van Dusen (1975).

Managed Care and Brief Therapy. Regarding brief counseling and managed care, due to the holistic focus and here-and-now approach to the therapeutic encounter, Gestalt therapy has no definite length. Gestalt therapists would conclude that all therapy has the possibility of being brief, just as all therapy can be lengthy. The here-and-now focus avoids lengthy excursions into the past and the theory favors experiencing over analysis. The intense nature of the experiments and the immediacy of the counselor and client dialogue are designed to facilitate awareness in a short amount of time (Harman, 1995). Once awareness is achieved, conflicts can be readily resolved and if resistance to contact arises, it is addressed quickly as well. As Yontef (1995) noted, "Frequently, open-ended Gestalt therapy spontaneously concludes in a few sessions" (p. 273).

Diversity Issues. Regarding diversity issues of culture, gender, and spirituality, various views emerge of Gestalt's ability to encompass a wide variety of clientele perspectives. From a philosophical standpoint, the Gestalt's emphasis on phenomenology encourages therapists to understand the client's subjective perspective of the world as seen through the lenses of culture, gender, and spiritual beliefs. Every person is unique, so clients are diverse by definition, and respect of that individuality is crucial to the Gestalt experience. In fact, as noted previously, helping the client experience and become aware of all facets of his or her self is the primary goal of Gestalt therapy.

Because one's culture often reflects one's environment, internal and external, the self of the person is constantly influenced by one's perspective of culture. Gestalt therapy is not necessarily interested in the concrete specifics of the culture of the client, as in "You are an African American," but instead is more interested in what meaning is ascribed to the culture by the client, as in, "What does it mean for you to be African-American?" The literature contains examples of the use of Gestalt therapy in Latin American countries such as Argentina (Slemenson, 1998), Mexico (Munoz-Polit, 1998), and Brazil (Ciornai, 1998), and O'Hara (1998) commented that humanistic approaches such as Gestalt therapy represent credible examples of cross-cultural therapies that help people adapt to modern and postmodern crises.

On a more critical note, Saner (1989) proposed that Gestalt therapy, as practiced in the United States, has diverged from the true phenomenological base and has adopted an overemphasis on the Western value of individualism. "It is my assumption that most members of the American Gestalt therapy movement have over stressed 'I' ness because they are unaware of their cultural predisposition toward individualism with its corollary aversion or avoidance of lasting intimacy or committed 'we' ness" (p. 59). Saner contended that the emphasis on individualism profoundly distorts the therapy, as evidenced by the tendency to focus only on the client's awareness and not on how the client and counselor are making contact in the here-and-now. In an effort to promote the client's autonomy, the focus shifts away from the present relationship and moves more to creating techniques and experiments to "help the client." Counselors who stress individualism may neglect the dialogic relationship or fail to recognize its importance in the Gestalt process. American counselors who do not recognize this as a personal cultural issue run the risk of damaging the process in two important ways. First, the client may not share the perspective that individualism is the only way to operate. Individuals from Asian and Hispanic communities, to name a few, may value a greater emphasis on external support. Second, by only focusing on the client's change, the counselor robs the client of the most powerful element of the change process: the co-influencing nature and experience of the client to counselor contact.

Phenomenology provides a framework for understanding and honoring gender differences in Gestalt therapy. How the client perceives gender roles can be rich ground for exploring and becoming aware of disowned aspects of self. For many men, learning that the continuum of possible emotions extends beyond mad, sad, and glad can be a frightening yet liberating experience. Many men we have worked with firmly believe, "Emotions are not safe. If I show fear or sadness then people will think I am less of a man. They will try to take advantage of me. I'll be seen as weak." For some women, being assertive in decision making does not fit with their concept of femininity (Enns, 1987). The desire to get needs met on their own terms conflicts with their view of how women are supposed to act and feel. As one client commented, "I feel that if I stand up for myself, I will be labeled a bitch." From a Gestalt perspective, how one perceives gender roles can create polarities that provide obstacles to awareness and growth. Through therapy, these clients, regardless of gender, can access their inner assertiveness and emotionality, and claim and integrate them into everyday life. As Polster (1976) noted, "The basic human dimension of personhood is at stake in therapy—moving beyond stereotypes of man or woman into the full articulation and integration of everything any individual can be when all aspects of one's experience are available" (p. 562).

Spirituality. The role of spirituality in Gestalt therapy reflects the evolving and phenomenological approach of the theory. Perls (1969b) remarked that he grew disillusioned with religion early on in his family life and declared himself an atheist. Still confused and frustrated by trying to find himself in a chaotic universe, Perls delved into Zen Buddhism and was exposed to Tillich's perspective on Protestantism and Marcel's Catholicism, among others. The end result of these experiences amounted to an acceptance that one's faith could be a vital piece of one's identity and therefore could play an important part in understanding another person's view of the world. Ignoring this aspect of self, or denying it, inhibits awareness and maturation. Eynde (1999) explored the similarities between Gestalt and Buddhism, and many early Gestalt works, for example, Stevens (1970), integrated various spiritual paths such as Buddhism, Krishnamurti, and Native American views into the Gestalt approach.

Technical Eclecticism. Regarding eclecticism, Gestalt therapists encourage technical eclecticism, pulling techniques from a wide array of schools of thought in order to facilitate the awareness-enhancing dialogue between client and counselor. Zinker (1977) explained that Gestalt's emphasis on the creation of a here-and-now contact between counselor and client provides an opportunity for therapists to be creative in their approach. However, the use of techniques that deviate from the goals of Gestalt would be seen as counterproductive. In general, techniques that focus on the client's subjective experience, the counselor's experience of the client, facilitating awareness, and the dialogue between counselor and client would fit the Gestalt framework.

DSM-IV-TR Diagnosis. Similar to many of the holistic phenomenological approaches to counseling, Gestalt has traditionally avoided the use of diagnosis. Diagnosis is viewed as a compartmentalization of a being that is fluid and greater than the sum of its parts. Identifying a cluster of symptoms and labeling a person based on these limited aspects of self violates the basic philosophical underpinnings of the Gestalt approach. Many clinicians will remark, "My client has Major Depressive Disorder, Recurrent" or "My patient is suffering from an Anxiety Disorder." To focus on specific pieces of the client, cluster the pieces, label them, and then discuss them as if they were alien to the client is incongruent with the Gestalt notion of holism.

Having noted the traditional protests regarding diagnosis, Gestalt theory does appreciate the identification of repetitive maladaptive patterns of behavior in the form of dysfunctional methods of need fulfillment, poor boundary maintenance, or not owning all aspects of self. In fact, many authors describe the conceptualization of common diagnoses from a Gestalt perspective (Clemmons, 1997; Yontef, 1988). The key to the Gestalt perspective of diagnosis is that a diagnostic label and the symptoms that comprise the label are not static, but instead represent the person's present pattern of contact, and therefore, change is possible.

Weaknesses of the Theory

Gestalt theory emphasizes doing as a way of reaching the preferred state of awareness. Awareness is not a cognitive process as much as an experiencing process. From a Gestalt standpoint, too much thinking often gets in the way of true awareness and maturity. In the present time of mental health practice where cognitive-based therapies are often preferred by managed care companies, the lack of emphasis on the cognitive aspect of existence seems to be a limitation of the Gestalt approach.

In my (KAF) experience with Gestalt, I have found it to be a beginning counselor's worst nightmare. Many practitioners are attracted to the theory's active and dramatic experiments. In viewing tapes on Gestalt, viewers are in awe of Fritz Perls' charisma. As students get caught up in the excitement, they often fail to recognize the philosophical and therapeutic rationale for the techniques and instead use the experiments as "bail out techniques"— "things I do as a counselor when I feel stuck." During a live supervision session, I observed a student counseling an adolescent boy. The student had seen the boy three times and, working from a person-centered perspective, had done a nice job establishing rapport. But apparently, the therapy was not progressing fast enough for the counselor and she blurted out, "I think you have some issues with your father. Let's pretend he is sitting in the chair next to you. Tell him how you feel." The client looked perplexed and asked, "Why?" The counselor looked at the client blankly and changed the subject. After the session I processed the issue with the student. She stated that she felt the client needed some "pushing." I asked, "Where did the empty-chair idea come from?" She responded, "I saw it on a television show last night. It was a documentary on therapy." The technique failed not because the technique lacked efficacy, but because it was improperly applied. The counselor had no rationale for implementing the technique, and when confronted had to let it drop. Due to the active nature of Gestalt and its creative use of experiments, beginning counselors, and even seasoned practitioners, are likely to grasp at them without understanding the technique. This is more a weakness of the practitioner than of the theory, but one is wise to note this dynamic and make certain that one has adequate knowledge of the technique before integrating it into a system of counseling.

Distinguishing Additions to Counseling and Psychotherapy

Without a doubt, Perls integrated his personality into a theory that is exciting and compelling. Gestalt added the active element of client and counselor, a dynamic that is refreshingly different from the analyst-as-blank-screen role. Counselors who feel attracted to this theory appreciate the creativity and here-and-now aspect of the approach. The emphasis on emotional expression gave rise to many less comprehensive styles of therapy centered around the curative nature of emotional catharsis. As one practitioner related,

> More than any other theory, the aspect of contact truly brings a sense of aliveness to the counseling encounter for both counselor and client. The energy that is generated through the awareness of the moment is very powerful. I know that if I can be present and engage my client in the now, then therapy is fast moving and electric.

Current Status

Gestalt therapy remains a vital theory of practice in the United States and abroad. Gestalt institutes continue to provide training and supervision in major cities such as New York, Cleveland, and Los Angeles. In Mexico, many of the larger cities have training centers, and the University of Puebla offers a postgraduate specialty program in Gestalt therapy. Two journals, *The Gestalt Journal* and *Gestalt Review*, provide interested parties with articles strictly devoted to theoretical, practical, and research issues pertaining to Gestalt theory. The International Gestalt Association recently formed and held its first conference in Montreal, Canada in 2002. The organization also publishes the *International Gestalt Journal*.

SUMMARY

Gestalt theory, although often credited to Fritz Perls, owes its existence and development to a number of individuals. Without Fritz and Laura Perls, Goodman, Hefferline, the Polsters, and many others, the full figure of Gestalt would be fragmented and not whole. Gestalt theory is a humanistic-experiential therapy in which the goal of awareness and maturity is gained through authentic contact with one's environment. The therapeutic relationship provides an atmosphere for that contact. Through therapy clients experience, in the here-and-now, elements of their true selves and learn to continuously strive for that awareness and acceptance of self.

RECOMMENDED RESOURCES

Books

Perls, F., Hefferline, R. F., & Goodman, P. (1951). *Gestalt therapy*. New York: Crown. This is the seminal, and many say definitive, work on Gestalt therapy. It reads like many primary source materials, very dense, yet packed with good theoretical material.

Korb, M. P., Gorrell, J., & Van de reit, V. (1989). *Gestalt therapy: Practice and theory* (2nd ed.). New York: Pergamon. This text provides good theoretical information paired with practical examples and applications. Students find this text a good introduction to Gestalt work.

Videotapes

Good videotapes are difficult to find although the editors of the *Gestalt Review* are reportedly working on a demonstration video series. *What's Behind the Empty Chair* (contact LivEstrup@aol.com) provides a unique overview of the Gestalt therapy process. It is conceptual, and students may be disappointed in its lack of practical demonstrations.

Gestalt Therapy with Violet Oaklander: Child Therapy with the Experts Video (2002) is a quality video that demonstrates Gestalt with a child client. The series also includes pre- and postsession discussion with the counselor. Contact the publisher, Allyn & Bacon and reference ISBN # 0-205-33699-X.

Websites

www.gestalt.org: Gestalt Therapy Page: Excellent site covering historical, theoretical, and practical information and offering original transcripts of lectures by Fritz Perls and hard-to-find print resources.

REFERENCES

Bernard, J. M. (1986). Laura Perls: From ground to figure. *Journal of Counseling and Development, 64,* 367–373.

Beisser, A. (1970). The paradoxical theory of change. In J. Fagan & I. L. Shepherd (Eds.), *Gestalt therapy now* (pp. 47–69). New York: Harper.

Ciornai, S. (1998). Gestalt therapy in Brazil. *Gestalt Review, 2,* 109–118.

Clarkson, P. (1989). *Gestalt counselling in action.* Thousand Oaks, CA: Sage.

Clemmons, M. C. (1997). *Getting beyond sobriety: Clinical approaches to long-term treatment.* San Francisco: Jossey-Bass.

Enns, C. (1987). Gestalt therapy and feminist therapy: A proposed integration. *Journal of Counseling and Development, 66,* 93–95.

Eynde, R. (1999). Buddhism and gestalt. *The Gestalt Journal, 22,* 89–100.

Fagan, J., & Shepherd, I. L. (1970). *Gestalt therapy now.* New York: Harper.

Greenberg, L. S., Elliott, R., & Lietaer, G. (1994). Research on experiential psychotherapy. In A. E. Bergin & S. L. Garfield (Eds.), *Handbook of psychotherapy and behavior change* (4th ed., pp. 509–539). New York: Wiley.

Greenwald, J. A. (1976). The ground rules in gestalt therapy. In C. Hatcher & P. Himelstein (Eds.), *The handbook of gestalt therapy* (pp. 268–280). New York: Aronson.

Harman, R. (1995). Gestalt therapy as brief therapy. *Gestalt Journal, 18,* 77–85.

Humphrey, L. (1986). Laura Perls: A biographical sketch. *The Gestalt Journal, 9,* 5-11.

Husserl, E. (1965). *Phenomenology and the crisis of philosophy.* New York: Harper and Row.

Korb, M. P., Gorrell, J., & Van De Riet, V. (1989). *Gestalt therapy: Practice and theory* (2nd ed.). New York: Pergamon.

Lewin, K. (1951). *Field theory in social science.* New York: Harper & Row.

Munoz-Polit, M. (1998). Gestalt therapy in Mexico. *Gestalt Review, 2,* 119–122.

Naranjo, C. (1970). Present centeredness: Technique, prescription and ideal. In J. Fagan & I. L. Shepherd (Eds.), *Gestalt therapy now* (pp. 47–69). New York: Harper.

O'Hara, M. (1998). Gestalt therapy as an emancipatory psychology for a transmodern world. *Gestalt Review, 2,* 154–168.

Perls, F. (1947). *Ego, hunger and aggression.* Winchester, MA: Allen & Unwin.

Perls, F. S. (1969a). *Gestalt therapy verbatim.* Moab, UT: Real People.

Perls, F. S. (1969b). *In and out of the garbage pail.* Moab, UT: Real People.

Perls, F. (1970). Four lectures. In J. Fagan & I. L. Shepherd (Eds.), *Gestalt therapy now* (pp. 14–38). New York: Harper.

Perls, F. (1973). *The Gestalt approach and eye witness to therapy.* Palo Alto, CA: Science & Behavior Books.

Perls, F., Hefferline, R. F., & Goodman, P. (1951). *Gestalt therapy: Excitement and growth in the human personality.* New York: Crown.

Polster, M. (1976). Women in therapy: A gestalt therapist's view. In C. Hatcher & P. Himelstein (Eds.), *The handbook of gestalt therapy* (pp. 545–562). New York: Aronson.

Saner, R. (1989). Culture bias of Gestalt therapy: Made-in-U.S.A. *The Gestalt Journal, 12,* 57–72.

Sartre, J. P. (1956). *Being and nothingness.* New York: Philosophical Library.

Slemenson, M. (1998). Gestalt therapy in Argentina: Revolution, evolution, and contributions. *Gestalt Review, 2,* 123–130.

Smith, M. L., Glass, G. V., & Miller, T. I. (1980). *The benefits of psychotherapy.* Baltimore, MD: Johns Hopkins University Press.

Stevens, B. (1970). *Don't push the river.* Moab, UT: Real People.

Van Dusen, W. (1975). The phenomenology of a schizophrenic existence. In J. O. Stevens (Ed.), *Gestalt is* (pp. 95–115). Moab, UT: Real People.

Yontef, G. M. (1988). Assimilating diagnostic and psychoanalytic perspectives into gestalt therapy. *Gestalt Journal, 11,* 5–32.

Yontef, G. M. (1995). Gestalt therapy. In A. S. Gurman & S. B. Messer (Eds.), *Essential psychotherapies* (pp. 261–303). New York: Guilford.

Yontef, G. M. (1998). Dialogic gestalt therapy. In L. S. Greenberg, J. C. Watson, & G. Lietaer (Eds.), *Handbook of experiential psychotherapy* (pp. 82–102). New York: Guilford.

Yontef, G. M., & Jacobs, L. (2000). Gestalt therapy. In R. J. Corsini & D. Wedding (Eds.), *Current psychotherapies* (6th ed.). Itasca, IL: Peacock.

Zinker, J. (1977). Creative process in Gestalt therapy. New York: Brunner/Mazel.

CHAPTER 8

REALITY THERAPY AND CHOICE THEORY

BACKGROUND OF THE THEORY

Historical Context

In the years when Glasser first began formulating his views about the human change process, an important shift was beginning in the psychological community. Largely beginning with Adler and Jung in the 1940s, mental health professionals were noting that human experience seemed to involve more than had been explained by psychoanalysis. By the 1950s many practitioners and researchers were forming ideas that honored people's ability to choose and control their thoughts, feelings, and actions, thus freeing themselves from the chains of determinism. As the psychological zeitgeist moved toward existentialism, psychotherapy increasingly reflected a focus away from a client's internal drives and toward a client's perception of the world; from a deterministic view of the past toward free will in the present; and from the counselor as anonymous analyst toward the counselor as involved participant in a relationship that was, itself, a factor in healing. It was in the context of this psychocultural revolution, when such theories as person-centered, existential, and Gestalt were developing, that the genesis of reality therapy began.

Founder's Biographical Overview

William Glasser was born in 1925 in Cleveland, Ohio. His father was a small business owner who, as a young boy, had come to the United States with his Russian Jewish family to escape religious persecution. Glasser's mother emphasized education and encouraged young Glasser to read. Glasser's views about relationships, personality, and control were developed in his early years. "If the Olympics had an event in controlling, my mother could have gone for the gold medal. My father was totally choice theory. Never in the more than sixty years that I knew him did I ever see him try to control another person."

(Glasser, 1998, p. 90). Through his parents, Glasser experienced a continuum of behaviors that came to be reflected in his theoretical constructs: his mother's investment in controlling others and his father's intention not to control others but, rather, to specialize in self-control.

Glasser followed his older brother and sister to college and followed his father's advice that a major in engineering would be "practical" (Wubbolding, 2000a). Glasser worked as a chemical engineer for about a year, but he wanted to pursue a career in psychology. During one of his graduate psychology courses, the instructor encouraged Glasser to pursue psychiatry. Glasser doubted that he would qualify for medical school due to his poor undergraduate grades, but he decided to complete some foundational work and apply. He was accepted by Case Western Reserve and excelled in his studies.

During his internship, Glasser chose to spend 2 years at the Veterans Administration Center in Los Angeles and then moved to UCLA's outpatient division for his third year. Throughout his medical education, Freudian theory dominated the thinking of the time, but this theory never really fit for Glasser. During his time at UCLA, he was supervised by G. Harrington. The two became very close and shared views that were at variance with psychoanalysis. In a recent interview, Glasser (in Wubbolding, 2000a) recalled the moment when he chose to practice psychiatry in a different way: A client, who had been coming to the clinic for 4 years, met with Glasser and proceeded to discuss her problems with her grandfather, a topic discussed repeatedly with four other psychiatrists over the 4-year span. Glasser responded:

> I can tell you that if you want to see me, I don't have any interest in your grandfather. There is nothing I can do about what went on with him, nothing you can do about what went on with him. He's dead. Rest in peace. But if that's what you want, then you'll have to say that you want a new psychiatrist because I think you have some problems, but you have been avoiding them for a number of years by talking about your grandfather, and I want to talk about what is going on in your life right now. I have no interest in what was wrong yesterday. (Wubbolding, 2000a, p. 49)

When Glasser reported the confrontation to Harrington, Harrington was supportive and remarked, with a handshake, "Join the club" (Wubbolding, 2000a, p. 49).

While still in his third year of internship, Glasser began work at the Ventura School for Girls, a residential facility for delinquent girls. Glasser noted that the "school" was really run like a prison, where girls were routinely punished harshly and where little sense of community existed. Glasser sensed that because the girls were viewed as "losers," they came to believe they were losers. Glasser adapted the program to give each girl responsibilities, taught that each person was responsible for her own behavior, treated each girl with kindness and respect, and verbally praised the residents (Berges, 1976). With the implementation of Glasser's program, the school's effectiveness improved markedly.

From these two seminal experiences, Glasser's reality therapy began to take shape. In 1965, he wrote *Reality Therapy*, and several other books followed, including those written with his wife, Naomi, who was his personal and professional partner from the time of their marriage during his college years to her death in 1992. Glasser continuously lectured, taught, conducted private practice, and consulted with school systems during his early years of developing the approach. In 1977, Glasser used a work by Powers (1973), *Behavior: The Control of Perception*, as a theoretical backdrop for his therapeutic approach. The basic theoretical tenet was that people's choices are attempts to control their perception that their needs are being met in the world.

As reality therapy has evolved, so has its name. With the integration of Powers' ideas, Glasser began to call his approach control theory. In the late 1990s, Glasser modified the theory, largely to avoid the negative connotation of the word "control." Glasser wanted his theory to reflect the ideas of self-control and the power of choice. Therefore, he changed the name to choice theory. Choice theory provides the basis for the counseling model known as reality therapy.

Philosophical Underpinnings

Glasser maintained in several of his works that he developed choice theory primarily from his own experiences with patients. Unlike many of his predecessors who developed counseling theories, Glasser has not identified underlying ideas that may have contributed to his viewpoint. However, Glasser has noted that many of his ideas are similar to, and concur with concepts in, several other theories of counseling. Therefore, this discussion will focus on those similarities and points of divergence.

Reality therapy and Adlerian therapy seem to have many points of agreement. Adler viewed behavior as purposeful, and reality therapists concur with this teleological perspective. Adler posited that all humans strive for superiority and that this process could be healthy, striving for the betterment of humanity through cooperation with others, or unhealthy, striving for one's own superiority at the expense of others. This concept of motivation is similar to reality therapy's concept of responsible and irresponsible ways to fulfill one's needs. Glasser's recent focus on the central importance of the love and belonging need echoes Adler's emphasis on the need to belong as the primary goal of one's striving throughout life. The phenomenological stance of understanding the subjective worldview of the client is shared by both theories. The points of divergence that most clearly differentiate these two theories include respective views on the importance of attending to and having insight into past experience; in Adlerian therapy, these components are considered vital, whereas in reality therapy they are considered unhelpful.

Person-centered theory also shares similar philosophical beliefs with choice theory. Both include a belief in the purposefulness of all behavior.

Each theory also includes the contention that the client–counselor relationship, based on empathy, unconditional positive regard, and genuineness, is necessary for the client to change. However, whereas person-centered therapists believe that the relationship conditions are sufficient for change, reality therapists believe that more is needed. In addition, both theories emphasize different aspects of the psyche, although Glasser's concept of one's quality world and inner picture album is not too far removed from Rogers' organismic valuing system. Perhaps the largest philosophical difference is in the role of the counselor. In general, reality therapists are more active, directive, technique, and education-oriented than their person-centered counterparts.

Existential therapy and reality therapy also share many of the same philosophical constructs. Both theories emphasize the personal responsibility of the individual and the need for a constructive client–counselor relationship. The most interesting commonality rests within the similarity between reality therapy's needs and existential therapy's givens of existence. Existential theory maintains that every human must attend to the givens of meaninglessness, death, freedom, and isolation. Similarly, reality therapy states that all people must attend to five basic needs. Although the needs and givens differ at some points, they appear to overlap substantially.

PERSONALITY DEVELOPMENT

Nature of Humans

Function of the Psyche. According to choice theory, all humans are born with *five basic needs*: survival, love and belonging, power, fun, and freedom. Every human is genetically endowed with the motivation to seek fulfillment of these needs in order to avoid the pain that results when they are not fulfilled. However, the strength of each need varies among individuals. Additionally, although each need is distinct, several can interact and overlap in the same situation. For example, eating a good meal while on a date can serve the needs for survival, belonging, and fun.

Beginning at birth, a person has the potential to translate the needs into specific *wants*—the people, objects, or circumstances that the person desires because they meet one or more of his needs—and to revise those wants throughout life. Also beginning at birth, to get the wants that meet the needs, a person has the potential to generate *total behavior*: thinking, doing, feeling, and physiology. In this context, thinking refers to the cognitive processes of voluntary and involuntary thought. Doing refers to observable actions. Feeling refers to emotions, and in choice therapy feelings are discussed not in the passive terminology of "getting" angry, depressed, or relieved, but in the active—and distinctive—verbiage of "angering," "depressing," or "relieving." Finally, physiology includes biological processes such as heart rate and perspiration. From a choice theory perspective, a person's every behavior—thinking, doing, feeling, and physiology—constitutes the current best effort to meet one or more basic needs.

Every human also is born with the potential to fulfill his or her needs with total behavior that is either *responsible or irresponsible* and *effective or ineffective*. In responsible behavior, one fulfills one's own needs without preventing others from fulfilling theirs. Irresponsible behavior fulfills one's own needs in a way that prevents others from fulfilling theirs.

The various needs sometimes come into conflict as each person attempts to find a balanced fulfillment of the needs. To clarify understanding of these concepts, each need is defined below along with examples of wants that arise from the needs and of total behaviors—both responsible and irresponsible— that people generate to satisfy their needs.

The *survival* need is the one need that is not purely psychological. Our biological imperative is to survive and to procreate to ensure future survival. Behaviors that increase an individual's chance for survival, such as eating healthfully, exercising, and paying the electric bill, and those that increase the chance of survival of the human species, such as sexual behavior, fall into the category of survival needs. An example of responsible fulfillment of the survival need is the child who, having forgotten her lunch money, borrows from a friend and, the next day, pays it back. Irresponsible fulfillment would involve something like stealing another child's lunch money. An example of the survival need coming into conflict with another need is eating a half-pint of rich ice cream: This action may fulfill the fun need but, for many people, runs counter to the survival need. A responsible way to resolve this conflict is to exercise regularly and eat the half-pint only occasionally.

Human beings are social creatures who have a need for *love and belonging*. The desire to congregate, to have friends, and to engage in sexual intimacy are all manifestations of this basic need. Infants seek nurturing and approval from their caretakers. Beginning in childhood, people seek the comfort of friendship. In adolescence, peer groups become even more important, not only as a means to belong but as an extension of and a laboratory for a developing sense of personal identity. Also in adolescence, a new kind of belonging emerges: intimate relating. The need for this blend of love and sex is very powerful; people feel both plagued by the desire for it and fulfilled by the satisfaction of it throughout life. Wubbolding (2000a) noted that in a society where survival needs are largely met, the need for love and belonging will be in the forefront of client concerns. Glasser (2000) went a step further and stated that forming relationships with others and meeting the need for love and belonging is the barometer of healthy and unhealthy behavior. As Glasser (2000) remarked, "To satisfy every other need, we must have relationships with other people. This means that satisfying the need for love and belonging is the key to satisfying the other four needs" (p. 23).

The need for *power* is satisfied by a sense of accomplishment and competence. This need also can be understood as a desire for a felt sense of personal worth to others. As one client remarked, "It means so much to be needed in my marriage, to know I am valuable to him." "How do you know you are needed?", the counselor asked. "Because he listens to my opinions and ideas," the client stated firmly. Responsible fulfillment of this need includes getting good grades in school or a raise at work. Gaining power at the expense of others, through such actions as bullying, unethical business practices, or gossip, constitutes irresponsible fulfillment of this need. As infants, power is realized the moment crying leads to instantaneous comfort from caretakers. As any parent would attest, temper tantrums are a powerful tool. As adolescents, the struggle for independence from parental bonds is a prime training and battleground for the meeting of power needs. The adolescent carries into adulthood the pictures—mental images of successful strategies—of how to attain power, whether those strategies involved irresponsible or responsible behavior.

The need for *fun* is defined as the quest for enjoyment. Wubbolding (2000a) affirmed that the need should not be construed as shallow silliness but, instead, as a feeling of invigorating playfulness and deep intimacy. According to Glasser (1998), "fun is the genetic reward for learning" (p. 41). Through the meeting of the fun need, people not only learn about self and others but also build more satisfying relationships with others. Infants and children spend most of their time pursuing fun by playing. Through play, infants learn to define themselves, and through play with other children, children learn valuable lessons about how to connect interpersonally and thus fulfill the belonging need. Adolescents pursue fun in both childlike and newer adult ways. Through this pursuit, the teenager learns about more complex relationships. Play also continues into adult life—or should anyway! Having fun in relationships creates intimacy and forges a "pleasure bond" between the people that helps maintain the relationship. This process is nowhere more important than in couple relationships.

The need for *freedom* is expressed in the human desire for autonomy: to be able to make a choice, relatively unrestricted, from among several options. Like other needs, it may be identified most clearly through the pain one experiences when the need is thwarted: No one relishes the idea of working under a tyrannical boss or being imprisoned. In both cases, the opportunity to fulfill one's remaining needs is restricted, for example, one has no chance to go a friend's house for a party when one is in jail. Or one can meet a particular need only at the expense of another need; for example, with a boss who forbids socializing during work, one's love and belonging need is met only at the expense of one's survival need: job insecurity. It is important to note a core belief in choice theory: that every human at every moment *is* free to choose. The *need* for freedom is reflected in the innate human desire to expand one's options and to seek circumstances whereby one can fulfill each need without thwarting the fulfillment of the others.

The need for freedom can be seen in the infant's desire to explore the environment unrestricted, the adolescent's desire to choose his own friends, the adult's desire to pursue the career that she finds satisfying. According to Glasser (1998), responsible behavior that meets the freedom need often involves creativity, a defining human characteristic. Someone unjustly imprisoned can either irresponsibly and uncreatively withdraw into despair or responsibly and creatively take every legal action to establish his innocence and secure his release, in the meantime using creativity to maximize the responsible satisfaction of his other needs. Someone with a tyrannical boss can respond irresponsibly and uncreatively with hostility or can responsibly and creatively seek both to influence the boss to become more humane and also to find alternative ways to responsibly meet her other needs. In choice theory, at the heart of responsible fulfillment of the freedom need—indeed, all the needs—is a central tenet: One can influence but not control others; one can control only oneself.

Structure of the Psyche. In choice theory, the central structure is the brain: the controlling system for the organism. Glasser (1990a) conceptualized the function of the psyche, or the need fulfillment process, through the metaphorical structure of an automobile. In this example, the basic needs represent the car's engine, while the individual's unique wants steer the vehicle. The wheels of the car are connected to the elements of total behavior. The front wheels are represented by thinking and doing, while the rear wheels are feeling and physiology. The car model represents the philosophical belief that behavior, total behavior, is purposeful. All four components work together to one end: fulfilling the needs as directed by the navigation of the person's inner picture album.

In Glasser's theory, humans are front-wheel drive vehicles, which ascribes importance to the thinking and doing aspects of total behavior. Glasser maintains that people have much more control over thinking and action than feeling and physiology. It is easier to adjust one's thinking about a situation, for example, to stop dwelling on the difficulty of a situation and start thinking about possible solutions, or to run faster or slower than it is to make yourself instantly feel differently or make yourself spontaneously sweat or digest your food more quickly. People have the innate potential to control their thoughts and actions directly, but to control their feelings and physiology only indirectly, through changing their thoughts and actions. For example, to sweat less, stop running or, in the case of anxious sweating, think calming thoughts. This assumption has important implications for change. Namely, if one wants to have the highest probability of successful change, one needs to target those areas of total behavior that one can control: thinking and doing; then the car (organism) will move in a new direction.

People are born with the potential to develop several psychic structures. Among these are the *quality world*, also known as the *inner picture album*. Out of all a person has ever perceived, the quality world consists of the perceptions of all the phenomena that have fulfilled—and we believe can continue to fulfill—one or more basic needs. According to Glasser (1998), the pictures in this mental album represent three main categories: "the people we most want to be with; the things we most want to own or experience; and the ideas or systems of belief that govern much of our behavior" (p. 45). Although most people are only dimly aware of the basic genetic needs and the many ways they seek to fulfill them, each person has an internal feeling of what works—what fulfills needs—and what does not. People single out mental pictures of satisfying phenomena to store them in the picture album for future reference. This dynamic explains the wide variety of likes and dislikes of people and, even more importantly, the vastly wide array of choices different people make to fulfill the basic needs.

As each person grows and develops, the innate tendency is to continually assess the mental pictures in the quality world and, when encountering more satisfying pictures, replacing the old, less satisfying with the new, more satisfying. Although people may keep pictures that are ineffective due to a lack of more need fulfilling pictures, most people routinely update the inner picture album. Consider the person who plays soccer to fulfill the needs for fun, survival (physical fitness), and belonging. As she gets older or suffers an injury, playing soccer may cease to be a realistic option. She then can replace the picture of soccer with another or a combination of others that work to fulfill these needs. For example, she might have fun watching soccer on television, achieve a sense of belonging by coaching a team, and stay fit by adopting a less strenuous exercise regimen. If she chooses to keep the picture in the album, need fulfillment will be frustrated, and she may begin to choose symptoms as ineffective means to fulfill her needs. This process will be further explained in the unhealthy functioning section.

Role of the Environment

Familial. Many of the writings on reality therapy avoid discussing familial impact because the focus on change is always on present relationships. Dwelling on how one's pictures of need satisfaction were constructed is not as important or useful as exploring new ways of fulfilling needs. With that caveat, reality therapy holds that family factors supply the initial need fulfilling opportunities for the growing child. As the child develops and begins to choose behaviors that fulfill needs, the family is largely the source of need fulfilling people, things, and ideas. The family does not determine behavior, but familial interactions tend to play a significant role in impacting the child's picture album.

Extrafamilial. Just as a person's family provides opportunities for need fulfillment, the environment outside the home—church, school, neighborhood, culture, and geographic location—all influence the person by providing unique environmental opportunities and limitations for need satisfaction. For example, I (KAF) grew up in a South Texas town that was close to the beach. My geographic surroundings provided a means for me to place "going to the beach" in my internal picture album as a way to fulfill my need for fun. My son, Dylan, has lived in the South all of his life and has never seen snow. This environmental factor limits his ability to choose "playing in the snow" as an effective way to fulfill any of his basic needs.

As mentioned earlier, environment is obviously more than just geography. Using the examples mentioned above, one's school decides on the means and topics of instruction—how and what one is taught; one's church encourages certain values and explores a collectively held belief of the difference between "good" and "evil"; one's neighborhood can provide examples of social living; and one's culture provides a foundation for everything from community rituals to language and what foods are appropriate to eat. With all of the possible environmental opportunities every individual encounters, it is important to note that, from a reality therapy perspective, it is not the environment itself, but how the individual perceives and chooses what the environment provides, that is most important.

Interaction of Human Nature and Environment in Personality Development

View of Healthy Functioning. From the perspective of choice theory, healthy functioning is characterized by responsible behavior: the ability to meet one's own needs without preventing others from meeting theirs. It follows, then, that healthy people are able to build relationships with others and are able to develop and maintain vital connections to fulfill needs. As stated previously, Glasser (1998) identified the love and belonging need as the key to meeting the other needs. One is not likely to sustain relationships with others if one is meeting one's own needs at the expense of others. In addition, choice theory includes the tenet that a good balance of the other needs is necessary for healthy adjustment. Although the need for love and belonging is primary, one must attend to all the needs to achieve a sense of well being.

Wubbolding (2000a) outlined a stage model of achieving the basic needs in a balanced manner. He called the model "effective life direction" (p. 70), and its stages are outlined as follows:

1. *"I Want to Change and I Want to Grow"* (p. 71): This stage requires that a person desire a change in current lifestyle. This statement of change is necessary before any concrete change in behavior can occur. Healthy individuals are not immune from choosing unwisely and hurting self and others, but these individuals make the commitment and are open to making more effective choices.

2. *"Effective Behaviors"* (p. 71): After verbalizing or thinking about a commitment to change, healthy individuals take action. Their commitment to more effective living does not exist within insight alone; it must be put into action. Behaviors discussed by Wubbolding (1988) that indicate a choice for a healthier lifestyle include:

   A. Assertive and Altruistic Behaviors: Healthy people are goal oriented and take responsibility in setting and achieving long- and short-term goals. Choosing actions that help the individual connect in positive ways with others is a hallmark characteristic of these behaviors. Such actions might include participating in charitable activities, conducting oneself in an ethical manner at work, and contributing to one's family and intimate relationship.

   B. Positive Thinking Behaviors: In the total behavior model, cognitions are vital, constituting one of the two wheels of the front-wheel drive system. Healthy individuals utilize positive inner statements to help steer life. For example, thinking thoughts such as, "I can control only myself and not others"; "I am responsible for my actions"; "I am free to make my own choices"; and " I can and will choose positively and effectively" are all thoughts that help facilitate effective living.

   C. Effective Feeling and Physiological Behaviors: Healthy people also use the back wheels of the total behavior system for effective living. They cultivate feelings that facilitate need fulfillment, and those feelings manifest in the rest of their total behavior. For example, being patient, trusting, and hopeful all radiate specific behaviors characterizing each emotion. Healthy individuals also enact behaviors that enhance physiology. Such behaviors might include eating a balanced diet and getting regular exercise and an appropriate amount of sleep.

3. *Positive Addictions:* According to Wubbolding (2000a), very few people are able to achieve and maintain this third stage. To develop a positive addiction, a person must engage daily in a behavior that produces a natural high and requires little concrete concentration so the mind is free from the minutiae of the day-to-day existence. The behavior must not take up so much time that it creates obstacles in the person's relationships, yet the behavior is not merely a trend but is an activity to which the person is dedicated. In his book, *Positive Addiction,* Glasser (1976) proposed jogging as an example that fits the criteria listed above. Many runners jog daily and report the "runner's high" that accompanies a good run. Many jog early in the morning, so as not to interfere with work or family and report that the brain goes on auto-pilot as they run. Finally, to achieve the high, one must jog for many months so the exercise becomes ingrained into the physical and mental regimen of the runner's life. Another example of a positive addiction is meditation. Running and meditation are obviously not the only positive addictions. The reader is encouraged to think of examples and realize that any behavior that enhances effective living is a positive step.

View of Unhealthy Functioning. As early as 1965, Glasser's view was that people exhibiting maladjustment are not "crazy" and should not be considered mentally ill. Glasser contended that people are responsible for their own behavior, and the range of behaviors that mental health professionals call "abnormal" are just more examples of the ways people choose to behave when they feel thwarted in the attempt to satisfy any of their five basic needs.

Beginning in 1998 with the book *Choice Theory*, but more clearly defined in *Reality Therapy in Action* (2000), Glasser precisely defined the root of almost all human maladjustment: "the lack of satisfying present relationships" (p. xvii). Glasser posited that maladjustment is a disconnection between the person and others. According to Glasser (2000), "What is called mental illness is a description of the ways in which huge numbers of people . . . choose to deal with the pain of their loneliness or disconnection" (p. 1). In other words, maladjustment involves choosing one form of pain to avoid an even greater form of pain.

But why would clients choose to be miserable at all? And wouldn't anyone suffering from depression or an anxiety disorder be highly offended at the notion that they are somehow responsible for their pain? Glasser (1985) cited three main reasons why people create and endure misery. The following reasons have been adapted to fit the current notion of maladjustment.

1. Choosing intense symptoms such as depression and anxiety helps keep angering under control. Because angering may lead to relatively more painful consequences, such as being arrested or injured, one chooses instead to depress, which tends to bring about less painful consequences.
2. By choosing intense symptoms, one brings other people into one's service. As a client stated, "If I am not depressed, you will not see me in therapy." When a person chooses to depress, other people begin to comfort and take care of that person. The person is enduring the pain of loss of power, freedom, and fun that accompanies intense symptoms in order to avoid the even greater pain of loneliness. Glasser would contend that a person who was not coddled when choosing to depress would quickly give the behavior up because it would not fulfill any need for love and belonging.
3. Choosing intense symptoms enables people to avoid doing what they are afraid of doing. An adolescent who sees himself as inept may choose to depress so he can avoid relationships or academic challenges at school. He chooses the pain of depression to avoid the even greater pain of embarrassment, rejection, or humiliation.

In all three cases, by choosing the symptom, the individual thwarts any possibility for truly satisfying relationships. Despite great discomfort, the person will likely report feeling paralyzed or trapped in the symptom and, from a choice theory perspective, will choose to persist in the symptom because it is the best way the person knows to meet his needs, even if only partially and self-defeatingly.

Reality therapists' framing of symptoms not as the nouns "depression" and "anxiety" but as the verbs "depressing" and "anxietying" constitutes a semantic shift consistent with the theory's emphasis on self-responsibility. In reality therapy, clients are not depressed without a choice in the matter but are, instead, choosing to depress. This terminology is not meant to blame or criticize the client. The word change is designed to demonstrate to the client that the control to change lies within and that the choice of any behavior is an attempt to satisfy a need or needs using the best strategy in the client's awareness. With the responsibility for change resting within the client, the foundation for therapy is laid.

The Personality Change Process

Basic Principles of Change. Reality therapists view change as just another series of choices. To change, people must be willing to take responsibility for their choices and the direction of their lives. *Choosing new total behavior is the primary mechanism for change.* For the behavior change process to be most effective, one must begin to realize the multitude of options in any given situation. Glasser (1992) noted that people change when they realize that present behavior is not getting them what they want and that other behavior has a greater probability of success. Once one takes an active and responsible role in the choice process, assessment of the effectiveness of any behavior can begin to take shape. It is this process (choice and assessment) that is at the heart of the change process from a reality therapy perspective. Although this process can and does occur outside of counseling, the more restricted the pictures in a person's internal picture album, the more likely the person will require the organized resources of counseling to supplant less effective pictures with more effective ones.

Change Through Counseling
The Client's Role. The client in reality therapy must be willing to focus on and change behavior. Some clients enter into therapy wanting and expecting to explore past relationships and family dynamics. Reality therapists do not spend time focusing on these phenomena because they perceive such time to be wasted. Clients must be willing to accept the here-and-now focus and be open to being educated about choice theory. Glasser (2000) remarked that he expects his clients to be motivated and encourages them to read *Choice Theory* as homework.

In reviewing the case study books on reality therapy, *Control Theory in the Practice of Reality Therapy* (N. Glasser, 1989) and *Reality Therapy in Action* (W. Glasser, 2000), a pattern emerges among the case study clients. In the beginning of therapy, as the relationship is forming, most clients seem offended at the notion of choosing symptoms. For example, Jerry, in Glasser

(2000), makes statements such as, "I don't choose [obsessive-compulsive behaviors]. What are you talking about? I'm sick" (p.18). Lucy, also in Glasser (2000), retorts, "What do you mean I choose to be depressed? What are you talking about? I don't want to feel this way" (p. 31). As the relationship develops, the clients respond to Glasser's challenges, and they begin to take responsibility for making more effective choices. Clients in reality therapy must be open to building a relationship with the therapist and have the strength to maintain the relationship and persist in the process even when challenged by the counselor.

The Counselor's Role. The role of the counselor and the relationship between counselor and client are closely tied to the primary goal of counseling. Glasser (2000) asserted that "the continuing goal of reality therapy is to create a choice theory relationship between client and counselor" (p. 23). By experiencing a satisfying relationship, clients can learn a lot about how to improve the troubled relationship that brought them into counseling. Thus, in many ways, the client–counselor relationship becomes the cure agent for the client; a laboratory for learning how to forge relationships based on the tenets of choice theory.

The client–counselor relationship is so important that Glasser believes if the counselor fails to connect with the client, change will not occur. The first stage in the counseling process is known as "making friends." The cycle of reality therapy that will be further discussed in the next section, clearly outlines the dos and don'ts of the "making friends" stage. This friendship is based on respect, boundaries, and choices, and it contains many facets. Wubbolding (1988) and Wubbolding and Brickell (1998) listed some of the characteristics of good therapists:

- Continuously Practicing the AB's (Always Be): Wubbolding (1988) summarized the first collection of counselor characteristics by using an easy-to-remember ABCDEFG approach. The AB stands for *always be*, while the other letters remind the therapist to be *courteous* to the client, even in the face of anger, *determined* that the client can change and that change comes through making different choices, *enthusiastic* toward the client, *firm* regarding the plans and commitments that the client has made in therapy, and *genuine* with the client, thus treating each client with openness and honesty.
- Focusing on the Present: Glasser has contended that the road to change lies within the client making new choices in the here-and-now. Reality therapists use the client–counselor relationship as it is occurring in the present and spend little time discussing past issues.
- Using Humor: Fun is one of the basic needs, and laughter is not only an excellent way to fill the fun need, but it also leads to greater psychological intimacy between therapist and client. Counselors should model the use of responsible humor as a relationship-enhancing agent.

- Use of Empathic Confrontation: The primary task of the counselor is to influence the client to make more effective choices. The foundation of influence is the ability to connect with and understand every client. As an outcome of this understanding, the counselor will effectively confront the client and encourage action in the direction of more responsible need satisfaction. Thus the effective counselor is able and willing to connect with and confront clients.

In addition to the above characteristics, Wubbolding (1988) included several behaviors an effective counselor avoids:

- Don't Accept Excuses: Many therapists from other schools of thought are interested in the reasons behind client behaviors. From a reality therapy perspective, asking or even wondering why a client behaved in a particular manner invites the client to excuse her behavior rather than take responsibility for it: "I am depressed because my wife is angry at me," "I am anxious because I did not study for my test and I am afraid I will fail and have to repeat the class." It can also invite the counselor to make excuses for the client, thus failing to encourage the client to take responsibility for her choices: "He is depressed because he has a chemical imbalance," " She is an addict because she grew up in a troubled family." Reality therapists posit that all behavior is a choice that represents the client's best attempt to satisfy needs at the present time. Figuring out the why's of behavior is more than useless; it counterproductively draws both client and counselor away from the essence of healing: making more responsible choices.
- Don't Argue or Criticize: Counselors often feel frustrated to see clients make ineffective choices over and over again. However, if the counselor fully understands choice theory, then she will also respect the client's freedom to make any choice. Arguing with the client or criticizing the client represents an unhealthy need fulfilling behavior on the part of the counselor. Concentrating on the AB's and the advice in the next paragraph will help the counselor refocus.
- Don't Give Up Quickly: Clients will not give up behaviors, ineffective or effective, quickly. Change is difficult. If the overarching goal is to form a choice theory relationship with the client, then the client–counselor relationship will have highs and lows like any other relationship. The task of the counselor is to maintain an empathic and challenging attitude toward the client and never give up on the client's ability to change.

Stages and Techniques. Although reality therapy, when used correctly, is designed to both challenge and encourage the client to make new and better choices, Wubbolding (1988, 1991, 2000a) outlined the "WDEP" system as a way to describe the stages of reality therapy. The system is discussed below but should not be used as a lockstep method of therapy. Instead, the system should be viewed as a web of skills and techniques, all aimed at helping the client choose more effective, healthy, responsible behavior. Space considerations limit the depth of our discussion of each step. For further explanation of the WDEP system, the reader is encouraged to consult Wubbolding (1988, 2000a).

W (Wants). In this first part of the system, the counselor assesses the client's wants, needs, and perceptions with regard to self, others (spouse, children, boss, the counselor, etc.), and the environment. Counselors help the client more clearly identify the core components of the quality world and inner picture album. This exploration is not as nebulous as it sounds. Asking a series of questions such as, "What do you want?", "What are you not getting from your relationship that you would like to get?", and "What is preventing you from getting what you want?" all provide the counselor and client with a better picture of the client's quality world. This process of exploring is neither as inexact as trudging through an ill-defined internal picture album, nor as simple as merely asking a multitude of questions. As Wubbolding (2000a) noted, "As with any list or series of questions, making them unique to the client constitutes the art of Reality Therapy" (p. 99). Consider the following case excerpt as an example of how elegant questioning can elicit quality world information.

Client: I am just so unhappy in my relationship with my wife.

Counselor: What do you want in your marriage?

Client: What all people want, to be happy and loved.

Counselor: How would you know you were being loved? (This question clarifies the client's specific picture of "love in a relationship.")

Client: I guess we would spend more time together. The more we are apart the more depressed I get.

This response provides information about the picture in his quality world: being with, spending time with, his wife. This information provides the foundation for new choices. It gives the counselor a view of the purpose of the choice to depress: It might spark attention from his wife. The answer also provides a possible solution to his problem: Choose behaviors that increase the probability of spending time with his wife.

D (Direction and Doing). This component involves exploring the client's current life direction. Direction can best be assessed through observable behavior. Using the automobile model of total behavior, this stage seeks to illuminate how the wheels are guiding the client's direction. Counselors can ask clients, "What are you doing?" Wubbolding (2000b) provided an interesting analysis of the significance of each word in this important sentence.

- "What" directs the client to be specific. It moves the client away from excuses and vague answers that why questions could produce. Reality therapists are interested in helping the client pinpoint specific behaviors to retain or modify.
- "Are" is the verb that signifies present tense. The here-and-now is the domain of change, according to reality therapy, and all questions and explorations should reflect this focus. What a client "was" doing is relatively unimportant unless the past behavior is having a direct impact on the present.
- "You" puts the focus on the client and not on others. The philosophical root of personal responsibility is found in this word and demonstrates to the client that change will not be found by hoping others will act differently. One can control only one's own behavior and, therefore, the new direction must begin with self.
- "Doing" provides the focus on behavior, which the client is likely to interpret only as action, but which opens the door to educating the client about the concept of total behavior. Through counseling, clients learn that they have more control over their total behavior, especially cognitions and actions, than they previously realized, and, as stated earlier, the true assessment of change can be found only in doing something different in one or more of the four domains of total behavior. As the client makes better choices—particularly thinking and acting in new ways—the emotional and physical life of the client will also improve, thus yielding an improvement in total behavior.

E (Evaluation). In the previous two components, the counselor and client have discovered what the client wants and what the client is currently doing. The E step puts these two pieces of information together and asks, "Is what you are doing getting you what you want?" If the answer is "yes," then there is probably not a problem. If the answer is "no," then the client can either make the same choices and get the same response or the client can choose differently and then reassess to determine the relative success of the new choice. Let us revisit the case excerpt illustrated under the W step:

Counselor: It seems as though you want to spend more time with your wife and that you are currently choosing to depress. Behaviorally this choice is demonstrated through sleeping most of the day, not going to work, and complaining about how bad you feel. Is this behavior getting you what you want in your relationship?

Client: Hell no! It did in the beginning, when she was worried about me. Now it seems to repel or exhaust her.

Counselor: By "it" you mean your behavior.

Client: Yeah.

Counselor: If this set of behaviors is not working, wouldn't it make sense to choose some others?

At the Evaluation stage, the counselor's main task is to facilitate the client's assessment of the effectiveness of any chosen behavior. The counselor should remember and convey to the client that current ineffective behavior does not make the client a bad person, but represents the best choice the client could make at the given time. Counseling is about learning that new choices are possible and learning a process to evaluate future choices.

P (Plan). Reality therapists hold that insight regarding effective and ineffective behaviors is not enough to create new behaviors. Action is needed, and the highest probability that the effective behavior will become consistent requires the use of a comprehensive plan. Plans are physical—written-down—representations of decisions to adopt new, more effective behaviors. In reality therapy, to be more effective, the behaviors must meet the criteria of responsibility: need fulfillment that does not infringe on the rights or well being of others. Once the chosen behaviors pass this litmus test, the plan can be scripted. Reality therapists can assess client plans using the $SAMI^2C^3$ system, which means that plans need to be:

- Simple: The plan needs to be straightforward and easy for all parties to understand.
- Attainable: The plan needs to be within the grasp of the client. Some clients, infused with energy over the decision to change, will make plans that exceed reality. For example, a student who decides, after failing three out of four grading periods, that he will get all A's and pass for the year, may have a positive plan, but not a very realistic one.
- Measurable with regards to outcome and timeline: The specifics of the plan need to be as detailed and concrete as possible. For example: "I will tell my husband 'I love you' every night" is more measurable than, "I will show my husband love throughout our marriage."
- Immediate: The execution of the plan needs to be as soon as possible. The quick turnaround avoids any procrastination on the part of the client and allows for prompt evaluation of the new behavior.
- Involves counselor: The inclusion of the counselor provides a layer of support and objective feedback for the client. The level of support should be dictated by the client.
- Controlled by the client: The formation and execution of the plan should be the responsibility of the client. This idea honors the focus on personal accountability for one's decisions.
- Commitment: As stated before, for change to occur, the client must decide to do something differently and then choose to enact this decision behaviorally. The counselor does not accept excuses for not committing to the plan and does not accept "I will try." Commitment to change is demonstrated through "I will" statements coupled with follow-through on the part of the client.
- Consistent: For true change to take place, the behavior must become a pattern in the client's life. Symptoms that the client reports are ineffective

behavior patterns used by the client to consistently attempt to meet the basic needs. Healthy behaviors must also be used consistently to have the desired result.

Once the plan is carried out on a consistent basis, other issues can be explored and the WDEP process can start over. More than a linear process, therapy is likely to address many issues that the client is processing at various levels in the WDEP system. Likewise, the counselor will move among the components of the process, encouraging the client to let go of behavior that is not need-fulfilling and to choose new total behavior that helps the client get what the client wants.

Contributions and Limitations

Interface with Recent Developments in the Mental Health Field

Effectiveness of Psychotherapy. Regarding the relationship between the reality therapy perspective and the conclusions from research on the effectiveness of psychotherapy, several conclusions can be inferred. Reality therapy appears to be in alignment with the research findings that the therapeutic relationship, specific therapeutic interventions, the client's expectation for improvement, and certain extratherapeutic factors, such as the client's motivation to improve, play a determining role in a positive psychotherapeutic outcome. However, reality therapists would probably weigh these factors somewhat differently than research has suggested. Reality therapists would probably give more weight to the therapeutic relationship, the client's motivation, and the counselor's specific interventions, along with less weight to certain extratherapeutic factors, such as the severity and chronicity of the client's problem; the client's capacity to relate to other people; ego strength and psychological mindedness; and the quality of the client's social support system. Some reality therapists might see these latter factors as irrelevant, capable of being influenced by the therapist, or under the choice control of the client. Indeed, from a reality therapy perspective, many of these factors smack of being "excuses" that clients use to avoid responsibility for the choices that actually are under their control.

Researchers have examined the validity of reality therapy concepts, such as the basic needs (Deci, 1995; Harvey and Retter, 1995), as well as the effectiveness of reality therapy with a variety of populations, such as students (Comiskey; 1993; Dryden, 1994; Edens & Smryl, 1994), reality therapy trainees (Cullinane, 1995), clients with addictions (Honeyman, 1990), and perpetrators of domestic violence (Rachor, 1995). Radtke, Sapp, and Farrell (1997) analyzed the outcomes of over 20 studies on reality therapy and concluded the therapy produced a medium effect.

Murphy (1997) and Wubbolding (2000a) criticized reality therapy research and encouraged future research to focus on the following:

- Use theoretically pure forms of reality therapy as provided by Glasser (1998) and Wubbolding (2000a). Many of the studies use mutated forms of the therapy which confounds results about the theory's effectiveness and hampers replication studies.
- Use practitioners who are trained and certified in reality therapy. Many of the studies failed to assess the level of expertise of the counseling or training providers. Because the development of a choice theory relationship is crucial to success in therapy, inexperienced or untrained therapists could adversely impact results.
- Both agreed that future research should be longitudinal in nature. Many of the studies were conducted over brief time periods, a condition that could have negatively affected the results.

Nature/Nurture. Regarding the nature/nurture questions reality therapists posit that every person is genetically endowed with the five basic needs. Apart from the fundamental genetic predisposition to meet these needs, reality therapy contends that the remainder of development is largely dictated by each person's perception and choice of direction within her given environment. A person is responsible for the unique choices she makes to fulfill her genetically based needs within the ranges of options she perceives in her environment. Simply put, genes and environment impact but do not dictate behavior. *Choice* dictates behavior.

This perspective seems to ignore recent research findings that several phenomena addressed in counseling have a known or a strongly suspected genetic influence. Indeed, choice theory has been criticized for not giving at least a nod to the possibility that, for a person whose brain is deficient in certain neurochemicals, the ability to make certain admittedly more healthy choices may be extremely challenging, at best. However, reality therapists are in agreement with mental health practitioners who acknowledge genetic influence in psychological distress and who nevertheless conclude that "biology is *not* necessarily destiny" (Baker & Clark, 1990, p. 599). Such practitioners assert that when a genetic influence is known to exist, environmental accommodations often can maximize or minimize the genetic influence. Reality therapy constitutes just such an environmental accommodation.

Pharmacotherapy. Regarding pharmacotherapy, Glasser has consistently and adamantly opposed the use of medication for mental problems. He (2000) reported never having to use medication with any of his clients. Reality therapists posit that clients choose all four components of their total behavior as their best attempt to meet their five basic needs. Because all behavior is chosen, a biochemical rationale for behavior and its associated medical remedy take the responsibility away from the client. Glasser believes that all parties—pharmaceutical company, insurance company, client, and mental health professional—enjoy a relief from responsibility when medication is prescribed for psychological reasons.

Glasser (2000) proposed that money is a prime reason why the psychiatric and pharmaceutical companies propagate the medical cure for mental distress. He observed that, "Since our society will never run out of disconnected people and as long as we believe in mental illness, the industry will never stop producing new drugs to treat it" (p. 229). Glasser contends that prescribing medicine not only is ineffective, but also serves purposes either that are not associated with client care or that run counter to the basic principles of change as outlined in reality therapy. Clearly, from the perspective of mental health professionals who believe that pharmacotherapy sometimes actually saves lives and frequently contributes to the quality of life for people debilitated by genetically faulted neurochemistry, Glasser's position is radical though theoretically consistent. Glasser's strict opinion is somewhat peripheral to the theory, in that it would be possible to hold a more liberal view on the use of medication and maintain the basic tenets of reality therapy.

Managed Care and Brief Therapy. Regarding brief therapy and managed care, reality therapy poses some interesting advantages and disadvantages. Insurance companies routinely require a DSM-IV diagnosis and approve of medication used in conjunction with therapy. Both of these approaches run contrary to the pure version of reality therapy. However, as the previously cited quote by Glasser indicates, at least he is pragmatically flexible on the issue of diagnosis. A practical reality therapist most likely uses diagnosis as a tool to help the client get what both client and counselor want—reimbursement for therapy expenses—while they proceed with reality therapy.

Reality therapy seems to be well suited for the time-limited framework appreciated by managed care as well as for being characterized as the kind of cognitive-behavioral approach that many insurance companies prefer or even require. Glasser stated that changes can be made in 1 session, while 10 to 12 sessions are often enough to start seeing changes in the client's behavior. These figures correspond roughly to those cited in chapter 1 from research on psychotherapy at large (Asay & Lambert, 1999).

Wubbolding (2000a) asserted that although reality therapy can be time limited, it is by no means a quick cure. Wubbolding cited Sleek (1994), who concluded that 16 weeks is the minimum time needed for results within a cognitive behavioral approach. Glasser emphasized that the therapy system does not determine the length of therapy as much as the ability to form a choice theory relationship between counselor and client coupled with the client's own motivation to change. Without these two elements, therapy will not only take longer but also most likely fail.

Diversity Issues. Regarding diversity issues, probably more than any other theory discussed in this book, reality therapists have made a significant effort to adapt choice theory to a wide array of cultures and study these applications of the theory. Wubbolding (2000a) provided an excellent overview of the multicultural applications of reality therapy to a variety of populations: Japanese, Chinese, Koreans, Singaporeans, Puerto Ricans, Native Americans, African Americans, and Irish. In addition, reality therapy has been utilized with Jewish and Arabian students (Renna, 1998), as well as Eastern Russians (Bogolepov, 1998).

Reality therapists believe that choice theory is flexible and can and should be modified to incorporate the client's cultural worldview. One's quality world is formed within the context of one's culture, and therefore to consider the client without respect to culture would result in a failure to understand the world of the client. Without this clear understanding, a choice theory relationship could not be formed, and therapy would fail. Wubbolding (2000a) encouraged reality therapists to obtain knowledge about the client's culture and to adapt the WDEP system to fit the needs of the client. Wubbolding asserted that the WDEP system is flexible. A good example of its possible cultural adaptation involves modifying its typically liberal use of direct questioning. People from many Eastern cultures view direct questioning as intrusive and rude. Reality therapists can honor this perspective by asking more indirect forms of the traditional direct question. For example, Wubbolding (2000a, pp. 185–186) suggested that instead of asking, "What do you want?" the therapist could ask, "What are you looking for?" And instead of asking, "How hard do you want to work at solving the problem?" ask, "What would happen to your life if you decided to do things differently?" Because such clients are likely to find the results of these subtle semantic shifts more acceptable, therapy is likely to be more effective.

Unlike the impressive attention to cultural issues, little reference to gender or sexual orientation issues can be found in the reality therapy literature. Because gender represents a genetic given that both restricts and expands possible behavioral choices, the absence of attention to such issues represents a deficit in the theory's literature. Additionally, the choice and genetic aspects of sexual orientation beg to be addressed by choice theorists. Glasser (2000) discussed a case where a man wanted to become a woman, but the case failed to fully explore sexual orientation issues. The absence of a thorough treatment of both gender and sexual orientation represents a deficit that, hopefully, will be addressed in future choice theory/reality therapy literature.

Spirituality. Within the context of reality therapy, spirituality is best viewed through each client's pictures in his quality world. In fact, the number of different spiritual denominations can be interpreted as evidence that there is no singly correct spiritual direction, merely the direction chosen by the individual that best fulfills that person's needs. Often through spirituality, people acquire pictures and values regarding the nature of an afterlife and how to conduct oneself in life. In light of these internal factors, people choose ways to fulfill needs that are in accordance with their chosen spiritual belief system. Many of the tenets of reality therapy are similar to various spiritual principles. For example, responsibility, defined as the fulfilling of needs in a way that does not hinder or hurt others, is quite similar to the Golden Rule— to do to others only what one would want done to oneself—that is believed by many spiritual scholars to be universal among spiritual systems.

Linnenberg (1997) and Mickel and Liddle-Hamilton (1996) further detailed how to incorporate spiritual components into the reality therapy perspective. Like any behavior, spiritual behavior can be responsible or irresponsible. For example, attending Mass can fulfill the belonging need responsibly. Conversely, believing that one need not change because one's deity has caused one's circumstances or because one's deity will bring about any needed change, are irresponsible cognitions. Therapists are encouraged to treat the spiritual domain as a vital component in many clients' chosen quality worlds and also to assess the extent to which it promotes or impedes clients' responsible fulfillment of their needs.

Technical Eclecticism. Regarding eclecticism, reality therapy is, by design, a flexible system of psychotherapy that easily incorporates any techniques from other theories that help clients choose more effective behavior in the present. To accomplish this feat, counselors must have a firm understanding of the principles of choice theory or run the risk of employing techniques that contradict the goals of the therapy. Insight techniques, dream work, focusing on the past, or any other technique that focuses more on awareness and insight than immediate commitment to behavioral change is usually avoided. Therefore, theoretical eclecticism would certainly be discouraged, while technical eclecticism practiced by a theoretically informed practitioner would be encouraged.

DSM-IV-TR Diagnosis. Regarding DSM-IV diagnosis, reality therapists, from a theoretical standpoint, view diagnostic labeling as inappropriate or unnecessary within the therapeutic environment. Diagnoses are clusters of symptoms, and symptoms, from a reality therapy perspective, represent ineffective choices in the process of fulfilling one's needs. Providing a diagnostic classification for a person's choices often gives the client and the therapist relief from the responsibility for change. As one client stated, "If I just knew I had ADHD, then I would feel better. I would know it was not my fault." Although reality therapy is not designed to blame and criticize clients for their difficulties, the theory does stress responsibility as the basic ingredient of change. Glasser (2000) summarized this view from a practical and theoretical position: "Clients should not be labeled with a diagnosis except when necessary for insurance purposes. From our standpoint, diagnoses are descriptions of the behaviors people choose to deal with the pain and frustration that is endemic to unsatisfying present relationships" (p. 24).

Weaknesses of the Theory

One potential weakness of the theory is that upon a superficial reading, the therapy seems very easy to execute. Before writing this text, I (KAF) would routinely ask my graduate students, "As you end your first 'Theories of Counseling' course, what are some of your general impressions of the theories covered in the text? (I was using another theories text.) A large portion of the responses indicated that both person-centered and reality therapy seemed very elementary in terms of procedures, with many responses indicating that reality therapy seemed like "just asking a bunch of questions." Keep in mind, these results are by no means empirically validated and the sample was of beginning graduate students. However, this limitation has been pointed out in reviews of the research on reality therapy (Murphy, 1997; Wubbolding, 2000a). The critique is that many practitioners are conducting reality therapy without a full understanding of what reality therapy really looks like. This weakness has more to do with how people are educated about the theory and less with the theory itself, but partial responsibility lies with the authors who write about reality therapy. Several of the seminal works are written in self-help format with little attention to key clinical detail. Hopefully, books that eloquently explore clinical issues, such as *Reality Therapy for the 21st Century* by Wubbolding (2000a), will help clarify this misconception.

Distinguishing Additions to Counseling and Psychotherapy

Reality therapy has made a significant contribution to the field of education. In *Schools Without Failure* (1968) and *The Quality School*, Glasser (1990b) outlined the application of choice theory to an educational setting. Since his first work at the Ventura School for Girls, Glasser and other reality therapists have trained teachers, parents, and school counselors to work effectively with children using the principles of reality therapy. In a quality school, all participants are trained in choice theory. Currently over 262 schools have begun the quality school process (Wubbolding, 2000a). The action-oriented, short-term focus is appealing to the hectic schedule of the school counselor and the issues of instilling responsibility are appealing to teachers, principals, and parents.

Glasser's formulation of the basic genetic needs and the quality world are unique to reality therapy, as is Wubbolding's WDEP system. Each of these concepts helps add depth and definition to the theory and also provide constructs for future research. The WDEP model provides students and practitioners with a structure to explore the principles and process of reality therapy. The fluid model is easy to understand, theoretically consistent, and flexible enough for advanced practitioners to expand. The model is also fairly easy for clients to comprehend and integrate into their own lives.

CURRENT STATUS

Currently, Glasser continues to teach the evolving nature of reality therapy through lectures, writing, and private practice. Glasser remarried, and his current wife, Carleen, is very active in the application of reality therapy in the schools. Robert Wubbolding is a current reality therapist who has contributed greatly to the practice and research on reality therapy and is the director of the Center for Reality Therapy in Cincinnati, Ohio. Training and certification in reality therapy can be attained through the William Glasser Institute in Chatsworth, California. Reality therapy also has a journal, *The International Journal of Reality Therapy*, devoted to ongoing research and practice ideas. Whatever the name of the underlying theory, reality therapy continues to impact the psychological and educational community, especially in the school counseling arena.

SUMMARY

Reality therapy is a present-oriented therapy that focuses on ways clients can make more effective choices in their lives. People behave to fulfill the basic genetic needs of fun, freedom, power, love and belonging, and survival, in the most effective ways they know at any given time. Therapy involves assessing current behavior. If current strategies are not meeting the needs of the client, the client is encouraged to adopt new behaviors that are more effective. This process requires the commitment of the client to do something differently and continuously evaluate behavior in terms of need fulfillment. The change process is also predicated on the ability of the counselor to form a choice theory relationship with the client based on empathy, respect, a here-and-now focus, and honest confrontation to adopt new and more effective ways of forming relationships and fulfilling needs. Although the theory has undergone several revisions since its conception in the 1960s, the clarifications act to refine the basic underlying structure of the theory.

RECOMMENDED RESOURCES

Books

Glasser, W. (2000). *Reality therapy in action*. New York: Harper Collins. This is Glasser's most recent conceptualization of the theory and several adjustment have been made. The application of reality therapy is completed through case studies. This format is illuminating, but the reader is encouraged to have some background in reality therapy before reading this book. Otherwise reading the cases in the book may give the reader the impression that treating serious issues can be fairly simple.

Glasser, W. (1998). *Choice theory*. New York: Harper Collins. This book provides the reader, practitioner, or client with all the basic information about choice theory. Each theoretical concept is explained using understandable language and many examples. Reality therapists often assign this book as homework for clients.

Wubbolding, R.E. (2000). *Reality therapy for the 21st century*. Philadelphia, PA: Brunner-Routledge. This book is by far the most comprehensive piece on reality therapy available. The book provides an overview of basic theoretical concepts, several in-depth chapters on the specifics of treatment application, a whole chapter on multicultural issues, and an informative interview with Glasser. The writing style and content are appropriate for a clinical audience and the liberal use of case examples is helpful.

Videotapes

Wubbolding, R. (2001). *Reality therapy in family counseling*. North Amherst, MA: Microtraining Assoc., and Chatsworth, CA: The William Glasser Institute.

Wubbolding, R. (1999). *Psychotherapy with the experts: Reality Therapy*. Needham Heights, MA: Allyn and Bacon.

Websites

www.wglasserinst.com: This website of the William Glasser Institute is an excellent source of information about the newest ideas and applications of reality therapy. Visitors can also get information on how to get certified in reality therapy through the institute's 18-month program.

www.realitytherapywub: This website contains up-to-date information about the current use and special applications of the WDEP system.

REFERENCES

Asay, T. P., & Lambert, M. J. (1999). The empirical base for the common factors in therapy: Quantitative findings. In M. A. Hubble, B. L. Duncan, & S. D. Miller (Eds.), *The heart and soul of change* (pp. 23–55). Washington DC: American Psychological Association.

Baker, L. A., & Clark, R. (1990). Introduction to special feature. Genetic origins of behavior: Implications for counselors. *Journal of Counseling and Development, 68*, 597–605.

Berges, M. (1976). A realistic approach. In A. Bassin, T. E. Bratter, & R. L. Rachin (Eds.), *The reality therapy reader: A survey of the work of William Glasser*. New York: Harper & Row.

Bogolepov, S. (1998). From Russia with love. *International Journal of Reality Therapy, 17*, 30.

Comiskey, P. (1993). Using reality therapy group training with at-risk high school freshmen. *Journal of Reality Therapy, 12*, 59–64.

Cullinane, D. K. (1995). The influence of Glasser's control theory and reality therapy on educators. *Dissertation Abstracts,* 56-09A, 3546.

Deci, E. (1995). *Why we do what we do.* New York: Penguin.

Dryden, J. (1994). The quality school consortium: Insights into defining, measuring, and managing for quality schools. *Journal of Reality Therapy, 16,* 47–57.

Edens, R., & Smyrl, T. (1994). Reducing classroom behaviors in physical education: A pilot study. *Journal of Reality Therapy, 13,* 40–44.

Glasser, N. (Ed.). (1989). *Control theory in the practice of reality therapy: Case studies.* New York: Harper & Row.

Glasser, W. (1965). *Reality therapy: A new approach to psychiatry.* New York: Harper & Row.

Glasser, W. (1968). *Schools without failure.* New York: Harper Collins.

Glasser, W. (1976). *Positive addiction.* New York: Harper & Row.

Glasser, W. (1985). *Control theory: A new explanation of how we control our lives.* New York: Harper Collins.

Glasser, W. (1990a). *The basic concepts of reality therapy.* Canoga Park, CA: Institute of Reality Therapy.

Glaser, W. (1990b). *The quality school.* New York: Harper Collins.

Glasser, W. (1992). Reality therapy. *New York State Journal for Counseling and Development, 7,* 5–13.

Glasser, W. (1998). *Choice theory: A new psychology of personal freedom.* New York: Harper Collins.

Glasser, W. (2000). *Reality therapy in action.* New York: Harper Collins.

Harvey, V. S., & Retter, K. (1995). The development of the basic needs survey. *Journal of Reality Therapy, 15,* 76–80.

Honeyman, A. (1990). Perceptual changes in addicts as a consequence of reality therapy based on group treatment. *Journal of Reality Therapy, 9,* 54–58.

Linnenberg, D. (1997). Religion, spirituality and the counseling process. *International Journal of Reality Therapy, 17,* 55–59.

Mickel, E., & Liddle-Hamilton, B. (1996). Black family therapy: Spirituality, social constructivism and choice theory. *Journal of Reality Therapy, 16,* 95-100.

Murphy, L. (1997). Efficacy of reality therapy in schools: A review of research from 1980–1995. *Journal of Reality Therapy, 16,* 12–20.

Powers, W. (1973). *Behavior: The control of perception.* New York: Aldine Press.

Rachor, R. (1995). An evaluation of the first step PASSAGES domestic violence program. *Journal of Reality Therapy, 14,* 29–36.

Radtke, L., Sapp, M., & Farrell, W. (1997). Reality therapy: A meta-analysis. *International Journal of Reality Therapy, 17,* 4–9.

Renna, R. (1998). Israel: Conflict and the quality world. *International Journal of Reality Therapy, 18,* 4–7.

Sleek, S. (1994). Merits of long, short term therapy debated. *Monitor, 25,* 41–42.

Wubbolding, R. E. (1988). *Using reality therapy.* New York: Harper & Row.

Wubbolding, R. E. (1991). *Understanding reality therapy.* New York: Harper Collins.

Wubbolding, R. E. (2000a). *Reality therapy for the 21st century.* Philadelphia, PA: Brunner-Routledge.

Wubbolding, R. E. (2000b). *Reality therapy training manual* (11th ed.). Cincinnati, OH: Center for Reality Therapy.

Wubbolding, R. E., & Brickell, J. (1998). Qualities of the reality therapist. *International Journal of Reality Therapy, 17,* 47–49.

CHAPTER 9

BEHAVIORAL COUNSELING

BACKGROUND OF THE THEORY

Historical Context and Founder's Biographical Overview

The roots of contemporary behavioral counseling go back to the first half of the 20th century (Spiegler & Guevremont, 2003). Ivan Pavlov, a Russian physiologist, discovered a learning process that came to be known as *classical conditioning*. This process fit with the views of John B. Watson, a Johns Hopkins University experimental psychologist. Watson "rejected mentalist concepts such as consciousness, thought, and imagery" (Spiegler & Guevremont, 2003, p. 15) and emphasized instead the objective study of observable behaviors. He came to be known as the father of behaviorism, the theory upon which behavior therapy and behavioral counseling are based (Spiegler & Guevremont, 2003). Other clinicians successfully applied the principles of classical conditioning to problems of phobias, bedwetting, and tension-related disorders. Meanwhile, Columbia University psychologist Edward Thorndike and Harvard University psychologist B. F. Skinner developed the principles of operant conditioning, the other learning process in behaviorism (Spiegler & Guevremont, 2003).

Prior to 1950, despite developments in behaviorism, psychoanalysis dominated the field of psychotherapy. Only after World War II was the length of psychoanalytic treatment found unsuitable for the masses of people traumatized by the war, as well as the effectiveness of psychoanalysis brought into question. These conditions provided a fertile ground for the simultaneous, and apparently independent, development of behavior therapy in the United States, South Africa, and Great Britain during the 1950s (Spiegler & Guevremont, 2003).

By the 1960s, behaviorists had conducted a great deal of research substantiating the effectiveness and efficiency of behavior therapy. During the 1960s, Stanford University psychologist Albert Bandura developed and researched *social learning theory* that included the principles of classical and operant conditioning as well as social (modeling and imitation) and cognitive (thought, image, and expectation) factors in learning (Bandura, 1977, 1986). Other clinicians developed *cognitive-behavior therapy* (see chapter on Cognitive Counseling).

Beginning in the 1960s, behaviorists developed numerous professional organizations and journals. In subsequent decades, they expanded the research and applicability of behavioral strategies. By the 1970s, "behavior therapy emerged as a major force among psychotherapy approaches" (Spiegler & Guevremont, 2003), a position it has maintained to the present. Some current behaviorists are "radical," focusing only on observable behavior, but most consider cognitive concepts and procedures important, if not vital, to their theory and practice (Wilson, 1995).

Philosophical Underpinnings

Western philosophical thought from the 1600s through the end of the 20th century has been dominated by the assumptions of modernistic science (Richards & Bergin, 1997). Like Freud and his psychoanalytic followers in the early 20th century, Watson and other early behaviorists were committed to developing psychology as a science. In this pursuit, they subscribed to "naturalism, determinism, universalism, reductionism, atomism, materialism, mechanism, ethical relativism, ethical hedonism, classical realism, positivism, and empiricism" (Richards & Bergin, p. 24). Monte (1999) classified the philosophical underpinnings of behaviorism into four main areas: evolutionary continuity, reductionism, determinism, and empiricism.

Evolutionary continuity refers to the view that animal behavior is identical to human behavior. This assumption is important, as it allows inferences about humans to be made from animal experiments. The only difference is one of complexity (Watson, 1967). Human behavior is seen as infinitely more complex than rat behavior, but both comprise the same building blocks. Thus, we can extrapolate our more complex behavior by watching the rat.

Reductionism is the process of shrinking behavior to its smallest, final source: electrons and atoms. Behavior is the final product of glands, nervous systems, organs, cells, molecules and atomic particles. The position of the behaviorist rests on the assumption that behavior can be reduced to biopsychology, and thus has nothing to do with intrapsychic processes.

The assumption of determinism holds that all behavior has a direct physical cause and is never unpredictable or random. Present behavioral responses are determined by previous shaping, reinforcement, and conditioned responses. Determinism, in the radical behaviorist sense, obviously focuses on physical determinants and thus views cognitive events as inferior, if not unimportant. Cognitions—beliefs and thoughts—have no concrete place in the physical structure and therefore are not significant in producing behavior. After Bandura's work (1969, 1977, 1986, 1997), many behaviorists softened from this radical stance. They gave credence to symbolic processes in learning, and with their view of people's ability to self-regulate, they moved away from extreme determinism toward a view of people as agents with at least some degree of free will.

Empiricism emphasizes the observable, the testable, and the measurable. Early behaviorists endorsed a more rigorous positivism and empiricism than was employed by the other leading theory of the time, psychoanalysis. Behaviorists eschewed inferences, such as the psychoanalytic inference about unconscious processes, and they endorsed the view that an accurate formulation of the laws of behavior would result from considering only directly observable phenomena, namely, behaviors.

PERSONALITY DEVELOPMENT

The following discussion of personality development will tend to reflect a radical behaviorist perspective with some reference to social learning theory.

Nature of Humans

Function of the Psyche. Regarding function, at birth each person is like a *tabula rasa*, a blank slate, with no presumed innate motives, drives, needs, or tendencies except the capacity to learn behavior. The person learns all behavior as a result of environmental contingencies. Each person is a passive product of his or her environment.

Structure of the Psyche. The structure of personality reflects the structure of the human peripheral nervous system with its two major divisions. The sensory-somatic division essentially mediates voluntary behavior, and the autonomic nervous system essentially mediates involuntary behavior. Each person is born with several involuntary responses, such as the orienting and sucking reflexes. The person learns all the rest of behavior, both voluntary and involuntary. Behaviorists, taking an aggregate view, consider personality to be the sum total and the interaction of voluntary and involuntary behaviors in one's response repertoire at any given time.

Role of the Environment

Aside from several inborn reflexes, a person's behavior consists of the voluntary and involuntary behaviors one learned as a result of experience in the environment. Learning is defined as a relatively permanent, observable change in behavior that results from experience or practice. "Relatively permanent" means the person tends to repeat the behavior under the same environmental conditions, or antecedents. "Observable change" means that the person is behaving differently in some measurable way than he or she used to behave; it includes doing either more or less of a particular response than previously. "Results from experience or practice" means that an environmental event that preceded or followed the previous occurrence of the behavior apparently caused the subsequent occurrence of the behavior. This definition is sometimes characterized as "ABC"—antecedent, behavior, consequence (Spiegler & Guevremont, 2003)—reflecting the notion that current behavior is the result of the events that occurred before and after that behavior.

A particular learning process corresponds to each branch of the peripheral nervous system. A person learns voluntary behavior through *operant conditioning* and involuntary behavior through *classical conditioning*. The basic principle behind each of these forms of conditioning is that a person tends to repeat behavior that is reinforced and tends not to repeat behavior that is not reinforced. In a circular definition, reinforcement is any environmental contingency related to a response that is followed by an increase in the response.

Operant Conditioning. The basic principle behind operant conditioning is that when a person makes a voluntary response of any kind, if it is followed fairly quickly by some form of reinforcement, the person is likely to make that response again under the same or similar environmental conditions. Phenomena that often serve as positive reinforcers include attention, praise, and money.

Before addressing what maintains or decreases the frequency of a voluntary behavior, we will first address how a voluntary behavior occurs for the very first time. Being voluntary, the behavior presumably is not inborn. Rather, a person emits a voluntary response initially through one of three processes.

Consider a person who is learning a new computer program. In *random* or *accidental* emission of a novel response, the person involved in one maneuver stumbles onto another maneuver that is followed by some form of reinforcement. In *trial and error*, the person tries one maneuver and then another until one is found that is followed by reinforcement. In *imitation of a model* the person does something new by following the instructions in the manual or following the example of someone who knows the program. Of these three phenomena, modeling through demonstration and prompting is most often involved in a process specific to operant conditioning called *shaping*, whereby a complex behavior is broken down into simpler components, and the person sequentially acquires and is reinforced for each component until the entire complex behavior is learned. Anyone who has successfully taught a child to tie her shoes is familiar with this process ("First take this shoelace in this hand like this, and this other shoelace in this other hand like this . . .").

From a behavioral perspective, once a voluntary behavior occurs for the first time, the subsequent presence, absence, strength, and frequency of the behavior is the result of one of the four processes listed in Table 9.1.

TABLE 9.1

	To *increase* the frequency/strength of a voluntary response		To *decrease* the frequency/strength of a voluntary response	
Using a(n) . . .	*Pleasant* consequence		Positive reinforcement	Extinction
	Unpleasant consequence		Negative reinforcement	Punishment

From "Cognitive-behavioral theories," by J. M. Holden, 2000, in *Handbook of Counseling*, edited by D. C. Locke, J. E. Myers, and E. L. Herr. Newbury Park, CA: Sage.

In *positive reinforcement*, a person in a particular environmental circumstance emits a voluntary response, fairly quickly some reinforcement occurs in the environment, and thereafter the likelihood increases that the person under the same or similar environmental conditions will emit a similar voluntary response. For example, in a classroom in which the teacher asks a question (specific environmental condition), a child answers the question (voluntary response), and the teacher praises the child (reinforcement), after which the child is more likely to offer answers to the teacher's future questions.

In the case of positive reinforcement, a person emits some observable voluntary response because in the past it has been followed by something pleasurable. In the case of *negative reinforcement*, the person emits an observable voluntary response because it has been followed by the avoidance of something aversive. For example, as midnight of April 15 approaches in the United States, many people converge on their local post offices to get their tax returns in the mail (voluntary response), not because they will get anything like attention, praise, or a financial bonus (positive reinforcement), but because they will avoid losing money as a result of a late charge penalty (negative reinforcement).

One factor in reinforcement is the *schedule of reinforcement. Continuous reinforcement* occurs each time the person emits a particular response. *Intermittent reinforcement* occurs only some of the time the person emits the response. *Regular* intermittent reinforcement occurs either at the end of a particular *interval* of time in which the person emitted the response (such as monthly payment of salary) or in *ratio* to a specific number of times the person emitted the response (such as a salesperson getting a bonus for every tenth sale). *Irregular* intermittent reinforcement occurs at irregular times, a schedule of reinforcement that results in the most frequent and long-lasting response pattern (as seen with gambling, in which the gambler persists in gambling despite winning only some of the time and usually unpredictably).

Another interesting phenomenon regarding reinforcement is illustrated by superstitions. Consider Pat who, dressing for a ballgame, puts on a particular pair of new socks, then proceeds to win the game. True to the irregular intermittent reinforcement principles of operant conditioning , Pat insists upon wearing those same socks for each subsequent game that season, even though Pat does not always win. Pat's superstition illustrates not only the endurance of voluntary responses that are intermittently reinforced, but also the fact that there need not be a causal connection between a response and a reinforcement for the response to be reinforced Pat herself may agree that her socks cannot actually have an influence over the outcome of her ballgame, yet she will continue to insist upon wearing those socks for each game because wearing them has been followed, even if irregularly, by victory.

Reinforcement and Me

Take a sheet of paper and divide it vertically down the middle. In the left column, list 20 voluntary behaviors you do. Be sure to list only things you *do, not* things you *don't do* or purposely *avoid doing.* Begin with routine daily behaviors, but be sure to include any behaviors you wish you didn't do or would like to stop doing. Then in the right column, list positive or negative reinforcement(s) you have experienced following each behavior, even if only once. See the examples below. If you're unable to identify a reinforcement for any behavior, consult with someone else to try to identify at least one. Here are some examples:

Voluntary behavior	*Reinforcement* (positive (+) or negative (−))
Brush teeth	Look attractive (+), avoid rejection from others due to bad breath (−), avoid pain of cavities and dentist's drill (−)
Wear "in" clothes	Approval from others (+), avoidance of criticism and rejection (−)
Eat too much chocolate	Tastes good (+), supposedly releases endorphins, the "natural opiates" in the human body (+)

After completing your list, ask yourself, "What is the role of reinforcement in my life? Did I list any behavior for which I couldn't identify a reinforcer?"

Once a person has emitted a voluntary response, that response likely will reduce or discontinue if the response either is no longer followed by positive reinforcement (*extinction*) or is followed by an aversive event (*punishment*). Certain phenomena accompany each of these processes.

For example, in extinction, a person will likely display some or all of the reactions associated with grief identified by Elisabeth Kübler-Ross (1997):

denial (persist in the behavior temporarily), anger, bargaining (increase the behavior or associated behaviors in an attempt to regain the reinforcement), and acceptance (discontinuation of the behavior). Consider Francis, who talks on the phone while his sister often interrupts him. Employing extinction, Francis ignores his sister's interruptions, that is, withdraws the reinforcement of attention. Francis can expect his sister to persist at first, to show signs of anger, and actually *increase* the interruptions before she finally stops interrupting. (However, if he even once responds to an interruption, he probably will have inadvertently powerfully reinforced interruption through intermittent reinforcement! In extinction, consistency is vital.) Finally, even after his sister discontinues interrupting, at some future time she may suddenly interrupt again, a phenomenon termed *spontaneous recovery*; if Francis continues to ignore her, she will again discontinue interrupting.

Whereas a person experiencing extinction tends to reduce gradually the behavior being extinguished, the person experiencing punishment, as in the case where a behavior is followed by physical pain, tends to discontinue the behavior rapidly. The recipient of punishment may exhibit some of the same behaviors associated with extinction, such as intense anger. In addition, the recipient may display anxiety and may subsequently avoid the punisher. The recipient may imitate punishing behavior in relationships with others, such as the abused child who becomes abusive to others.

Extinction, Punishment, and You

Take a sheet of paper and divide it vertically down the middle. In the left column, list 20 voluntary behaviors you have done but no longer do, or could do but don't do. Include both behaviors you're glad you don't do and those you regret you don't do. Then in the right column, list examples of extinction (discontinued pleasurable event following the behavior), and label them "e," and/or punishment (aversive event following the behavior), and label them "p." See the examples below. If you're unable to identify a reinforcement for any behavior, consult with someone else to try to identify at least one. Here are some examples:

Decreased/discontinued voluntary behavior	Extinction (e) or punishment (p)
Stopped calling Fred	He stopped returning my calls. (e)
Reduced dessert-eating from every day to weekends only	I was gaining weight. (p)
Reduced how often I work out	I was losing sleep and feeling crabby all day from getting up early to work out. (p)

Then ask yourself, "What is the role of extinction and punishment in my life? Did I list any behavior for which I couldn't identify an extinction or a punishment?"

A final disadvantage accompanies both extinction and punishment. Both serve only to decrease a response rather than to increase the likelihood of an alternative, more desirable response.

Extinction and punishment are pervasive in human experience. Because of less distressing or destructive side effects, extinction is considered preferable to punishment. In addition, where possible, *prompting*, that is, instructing someone in a more desirable response, and then reinforcing that response is considered preferable to extinction or punishment of the undesirable response. For example, which of the following alternatives seems to be the most constructive way to teach a child to wait her turn in conversation: slapping or humiliating her when she interrupts (punishment); ignoring her when she interrupts (extinction); warning her that if she interrupts again, she will be sent to her room until she is prepared to wait for a pause before speaking during conversation (negative reinforcement; she can avoid the confinement by waiting for a pause in conversation); or telling her it's polite to wait for a pause before beginning to speak and then giving an approving nod when she does so (prompting and positive reinforcement)? Behaviorists would generally agree that the foregoing examples are provided in an order from least to most constructive.

Once an operant response is learned, two other process come into play. A person may *generalize* a response from the original situation in which the response was learned to a new, similar situation. Going back to the computer program example, the person learning the new program might transfer a learned response from an old program to the new one. In *discrimination*, when the person makes a generalized response, she is not reinforced, and she ends up continuing the response with the old computer program but discontinuing it with the new, thus discriminating between the old and the new.

From a behavioral perspective, the processes described in the foregoing discussion of operant conditioning can explain the part of personality comprised of voluntary responses. As a person interacts with the environment, the person acquires new voluntary responses. As the environmental conditions either continue or change, so too will the person's voluntary responses that result from those conditions either continue or change.

Classical Conditioning. Each person is born with a host of involuntary responses to innately eliciting environmental conditions. Classical conditioning is the process by which we learn to emit those involuntary responses to new, rather than only to the innately eliciting, environmental conditions.

Ivan Pavlov is credited with the discovery of classical conditioning while studying digestion in dogs. The reader can have a similar experience by following the instructions in the box.

Classical Conditioning

Read the following imagery, then take about 3 minutes to close your eyes and engage in the imagery. Imagine you are at home in your kitchen, standing at a counter. On the counter is a freshly cut, juicy half grapefruit and an empty juice glass. Squeeze the grapefruit juice into the glass. Rotate the grapefruit and squeeze again until most of the juice is squeezed out into the glass. Pick up the glass and take some of the grapefruit juice in your mouth, not swallowing but rather holding it in your mouth. Swish it around. When you feel compelled to swallow, do so. Take another mouthful and repeat the holding and, finally, swallowing.

Now close your eyes and, in as much detail as possible, imagine this scenario. When you open your eyes, answer the following questions:

- Did you find that you salivated during the imagery, or even as you read the description of the imagery?
- If so, are you aware you were salivating to mental pictures or words in the complete absence of any actual grapefruit?
- Do you believe you were born salivating to the mental image or written description of drinking grapefruit juice? If you had never experienced anything like a grapefruit, and on your first sight of a grapefruit, before actually tasting or smelling it, had imagined squeezing it and drinking its juice, do you think you would have salivated to that imagery?
- Did you intend to salivate or did it happen involuntarily?
- Try vividly imaging the scene again and *not* salivating. How successful are you?

If you were to engage in an experiment, and every day for a week you were to spend 10 minutes imagining a grapefruit, and during that week you were to have no exposure to any citrus fruit, what do you think would happen to your amount of salivation throughout the week?

Classical conditioning begins with an *unconditioned* (unlearned) *stimulus*, in this case the taste of grapefruit juice, and an *unconditioned* (unlearned/ innate involuntary) *response*, in this case salivation. If someone put a drop of grapefruit juice in a newborn's mouth, the baby would salivate (though, of course, it's actually not appropriate to feed newborns anything but mother's milk or formula). A third ingredient in the classical conditioning process is a *conditioned* (learned) *stimulus*, in this case the sight of a grapefruit. If someone merely showed a grapefruit to a child who had never seen or tasted anything like it, the child would not salivate. But if the child saw or imagined the grapefruit (conditioned stimulus) while tasting the grapefruit juice (unconditioned stimulus), the child would salivate (unconditioned response). And after a few experiences like this, the child would salivate to the sight of the grapefruit alone (*conditioned response*). Salivation to the sight alone of the grapefruit has been learned/conditioned: Whereas he did not formerly salivate to the sight of a grapefruit, now, as a result of experience, he does. And salivation is an *involuntary* response to the sight of the grapefruit; it occurs without the child's intention, and it occurs, at least soon after being conditioned, even if the child intends that he *not* salivate.

Some of the same processes that apply to operant conditioning also apply to classical conditioning. In *generalization*, a person responds similarly to a similar conditioned stimulus. For example, if the child was originally conditioned with the sight of a yellow grapefruit, he will also salivate to the sight of a pink grapefruit. In *extinction*, the conditioned response dies out if the person is exposed repeatedly to the conditioned stimulus without the unconditioned stimulus. For example, salivation to the sight or mental image of a grapefruit would reduce and discontinue if one were repeatedly to see or imagine a grapefruit without actually tasting any grapefruit juice during that time. The process of *discrimination* involves repeated exposure to one conditioned stimulus along with the unconditioned stimulus, and repeated exposure to a similar conditioned stimulus without the unconditioned stimulus, resulting in a conditioned response to the one conditioned stimulus but not to the other. In the example, it would involve the person repeatedly tasting grapefruit juice while seeing yellow grapefruit but never while seeing pink grapefruit, resulting in salivation to the sight or image of the former but not the latter.

From a behavioral perspective, the processes described in the foregoing discussion of classical conditioning can explain the part of personality comprised of involuntary responses. As a person interacts with the environment, the person acquires involuntary responses to various conditioned stimuli. As the environmental conditions either continue or change, so too will the person's learned involuntary responses that result from those conditions either continue or change.

The Relationship of Operant and Classical Conditioning. As stated previously, a person's personality consists of the voluntary behaviors the person learned from operant conditioning and the involuntary behaviors he learned from classical conditioning. However, almost any observable behavior the person emits has both operant and classical conditioning components. Thus, one's personality is actually a complex interconnection of these two processes.

Consider the man who is seen sitting under a tree, daydreaming, and who reports he was thinking about his beloved. A behaviorist would speculate the following. In the presence of his beloved (unconditioned stimulus), he feels physical pleasure as the hormone phenylethylamine (Love &

Robinson, 1994) is released in his body (unconditioned response). Any reminder of his beloved (conditioned stimulus) results in similar hormone release and pleasurable feelings (conditioned response). So he takes himself to a quiet spot under a tree (voluntary response) where he can purposely indulge in thoughts of her (voluntary response, conditioned stimulus) and feel pleasure (conditioned response, reinforcement). Note that the pleasure he feels is both a classically conditioned response to the thoughts *and* an operant reinforcement for purposely engaging in the thoughts and purposely placing himself in a situation where he had a good chance of being able to think about her without being distracted.

Consider the person with a phobia of water that began after the person nearly drowned. Water (conditioned stimulus) has become associated with drowning (unconditioned stimulus), which elicited fear (unconditioned response); now, at the sight or even thought of a body of water, the person becomes fearful (conditioned response). Because going near water (voluntary response, conditioned stimulus) results in powerfully aversive feelings of fear (conditioned response, punishment), the person avoids being in proximity to bodies of water.

People reportedly experience the involuntary responses of the autonomic nervous system as painful or pleasurable. These feelings both are involuntary, classically unconditioned and conditioned responses and also are reinforcers and punishers of our voluntary behavior. From the viewpoint of the radical behaviorist, a person's personality is the sum total and the complex interaction of these processes of operant and classical conditioning.

Impact of the Familial Versus Extrafamilial Environments. Behaviorists acknowledge the important role the family plays in personality development. A child's first conditioning experiences occur in the family environment and can have a relatively lasting effect on the child's behavior. Therefore, parents can have a direct impact on the shaping and reinforcement of both positive and negative behaviors. For children, many studies have indicated that behavioral training of the parents can lead to the improvement of many childhood problems such as conduct disorder (Graziano & Diament, 1992), fire setting (Kolko,1983), and phobias and fears (D'Amico & Friedman, 1997; Friedman & Campbell, 1992).

However, the behaviorist view is that one's *current* environment primarily maintains one's current behavior. Therefore, behaviorists emphasize the contingencies in one's present environment as crucial in understanding and influencing one's present behavior.

The Healthy/Adaptive Versus Unhealthy/Maladaptive Personality. From a behavioral perspective, all learned behavior, both functional and dysfunctional, is acquired through the same two processes of classical and operant conditioning. A person's "dysfunctional" behavior is viewed from the behavioral perspective not as pathology but as "problems in living." These problems arise from the failure to learn needed behaviors or from having learned behaviors that, in one's current environment, result in a lack of reinforcement or in punishment.

Noteworthy primary sources on behaviorism, such as Nezu and Nezu (1989), Spiegler and Guevremont (2003), and Wilson (1995), do not include reference to any model of optimal human functioning. However, the behavioral notion of optimal functioning one would gain from a survey of behavioral journals would include *painlessness and competency to solve problems and obtain reinforcement.* It would posit no common characteristics of the "healthy" person, but would focus only on the outcomes obtained by that individual's behavior (italics in original; Jones, 1988, p. 165).

The Personality Change Process

In general, a person's behavior changes when the environmental contingencies that control one's behavior change. The prime mover of change is the environment that controls one's observable actions. In classical behaviorism, feelings and thoughts, being impossible to observe directly, were not considered appropriate foci of attention.

Change Through Counseling
The Client's Role. A radical behaviorist would not speculate about a person's motivation to seek counseling, because motivation cannot be directly observed. From the counselor's perspective, a person who sought counseling could be expected to report that one's current behavior yielded a dearth of reinforcement and/or a spate of punishment.

From a behavioral perspective, a client's behavior is maintained entirely by the current environment. To the extent that the current environmental contingencies that control one's behavior can be changed, the client's behavior will change. Thus the client is theoretically capable of extensive change in personality.

In behavioral counseling, the client, in collaboration with the counselor, determines the goal(s) of counseling; the counselor, in collaboration with the client, determines the process. The client's "responsibility" is to follow the process the counselor recommends. With each step in the process, the client keeps the counselor informed about behavior changes and continues to collaborate with the counselor as the counselor modifies and refines change processes.

Apparent resistance on the client's part, that is, failure to follow the counselor's directives, is understood like any other response or lack of response. For example, a client will continue to make undesirable responses if those responses continue to be reinforced. Conversely, a client will tend to not make a desirable response heretofore absent from the client's response repertoire if that response has not been modeled for the client, if the client has never experienced reinforcement for making the response, and/or if the response is too complex for the client to enact all at once.

The Counselor's Role. The counselor's goal in counseling is to arrange current environmental contingencies such that the client's behavior changes in accordance with the client's wishes. In Wilson's (1995) words, the behavioral counselor asks, "'What is causing [the client] to behave in this way right now, and what can [the client and I] do right now to change that behavior?'" (p. 209). The behavioral counselor focuses less on the client's past and more on the *present* and the future. While acknowledging and addressing client emotion, the counselor considers *behaviors* and *cognitions* to be the appropriate foci of change. Through an *aggregate* view of personality, the counselor focuses on specific behaviors and cognitions rather than the whole of the client's personality.

The effective behavioral counselor can listen to client complaints and translate them into goals consisting of observable changes in behavior. This process involves detailed analysis of the target behaviors and the application of classical and/or operant conditioning principles to the plan for behavioral change. The behavioral counselor is active and directive in guiding the client through new conditioning experiences.

The therapeutic relationship is as important in behavioral counseling as it is in other approaches to counseling. Behavioral counselors acknowledge research results indicating the vital role a good counseling relationship plays in positive client outcome. Wilson (1995) used several words to describe the behavioral counselor's demeanor in relationship with the client: "understanding, warm, sincere, and interested, . . . concerned—a problem solver and a coping model, . . . open, . . . genuine, and . . . disclosing" (p. 209). The counselor employs positive reinforcement; typically this includes paying attention to the client, acknowledging the client's existing strengths (adaptive responses), acknowledging and/or praising any client changes that constitute progress toward the counseling goals, being generally pleasant and patient. The skillful counselor is also observant of what each client finds uniquely reinforcing and adapts accordingly; for example, some clients respond well to joking and kidding while others respond well to businesslike seriousness.

In addition to using positive reinforcement, when confrontation is necessary to the achievement of counseling goals, the behavioral counselor addresses client discrepancies with the client and challenges the client to tackle somewhat difficult behaviors or procedures in the service of goal achievement. John Gottman (1999) has found that in lasting, satisfying marriages, the couple exhibits a ratio of at least five positive interactions to every negative one. Behavioral counselors consider the possibility that this ratio may characterize any satisfying relationship, including the therapeutic one. The counselor who maximizes the use of positive reinforcement along with the occasional use of well-timed confrontation increases the likelihood that clients will experience both the counseling process and progress as reinforcing and thus will persevere to a positive outcome.

Assessment. Behavioral counselors make extensive use of a variety of assessment methods. From most to least frequently used, these include interview by the counselor, direct self-report inventory completed by the client, self-recording of the frequency of and conditions surrounding a particular behavior, checklist or rating scale completed by someone other than the client, systematic observation of the client in a natural and/or a simulated setting, role playing during counseling, and physiological measurement in the counseling or a naturalistic setting (Spiegler & Guevremont, 2003).

Spiegler and Guevremont (2003) identified several ways in which behavioral assessment differs from traditional assessment. One difference is a narrow focus on target behaviors rather than a global assessment of personality, based on the behavioral belief that specific behaviors can be singled out for lasting change. Another difference is identifying the antecedents and consequences that currently maintain target behaviors rather than seeking to determine the past origin of the behaviors.

The behavioral counselor's goal in the initial assessment is to devise an individualized treatment plan that specifies observable behavioral goals and the means to achieve them. The counselor also uses assessment throughout the counseling process to ascertain progress toward the goals and to use new or additional information to adjust the treatment plan as needed. Client termination—or recontracting for a new set of goals—is clearly indicated when the client achieves the original treatment plan goals.

Change Strategies. Behavioral change strategies are numerous. They can be categorized as based on operant or classical conditioning principles. In most cases, behavioral counselors assist clients to acquire new responses in the actual counseling setting. In addition, through assignment of homework, they encourage clients to practice newly acquired responses and to acquire further new responses in the environment outside the counseling setting. Although behaviorists typically work with individuals, they also work with couples (Jacobson, 1998), families, and groups.

Strategies Based Primarily on Operant Conditioning. The following discussion addresses the best known of the numerous operant change strategies described in the clinical behavioral literature. The discussion first describes strategies to help a client increase desirable, adaptive voluntary behavior, then describes strategies designed to decrease unwanted voluntary behavior.

In *modeling*, someone demonstrates a voluntary behavior that the client reports wanting to do but never having done, and the client imitates the model. Models can include other people from the client's life, the counselor, actors in film or on television, or even a videotape of the client rehearsing the behavior oneself. Behavioral counselors use modeling extensively to help people develop social skills and assertiveness (Jakubowski & Lange, 1978; Lange & Jakubowski, 1976). A related use is when a client avoids an adaptive behavior, reportedly because of anticipating a negative consequence; if the client observes a model performing the behavior without negative consequences, the client is more likely to imitate the model's behavior.

In *behavioral rehearsal/role play*, a client first practices a new voluntary behavior in the counseling setting and then performs it outside of counseling. The counselor often provides prompting—suggestions and directions to help the client refine the behavior and responds to each improvement with positive reinforcement. If the behavior is too complicated for the client to perform all at once, the counselor and client can use shaping to break the behavior down into "smaller response pieces" and then to progress systematically from simpler to more complex or from easier to more difficult pieces, mastering each piece before moving on to the next.

The previous strategy, termed *graded task assignment*, is one of a group of strategies termed *guided discovery* that cognitive counselors (see chapter 10) have developed employing the principles of operant conditioning. Two additional strategies can be helpful when a client, particularly one exhibiting depression or anxiety, reports low motivation to engage in adaptive behavior. In *activity scheduling*, the counselor and client chart the client's daily activities for the near future. This structure helps the client with depression stay active rather than lapse into inactivity and helps the client with anxiety not avoid activities the client reportedly fears, on the assumption that once the client engages in the activities, the client likely will experience reinforcement. In *mastery and pleasure rating*, the client rates anticipated pleasure prior to engaging in adaptive behavior and actual pleasure after engaging in it. For the client whose preactivity scores are consistently lower than postactivity scores, this exercise helps the client learn to take action despite negative anticipation—and reap the reinforcement.

To decrease or eliminate unwanted voluntary behavior, behaviorists prefer some strategies over others. In *reinforcement of a competing response*, whenever the client begins to engage in the undesired behavior, he stops and engages instead in another behavior that he finds reinforcing and that makes it impossible for him to engage in the undesirable behavior. Cognitive counselors employ *diversion* as a form of competing response. This strategy is exemplified by the Alcoholics Anonymous (AA) practice that when one feels the urge to drink, one instead calls one's sponsor or attends an AA meeting; one cannot easily drink while talking under these circumstances, and the social interaction provides reinforcement such as attention, sympathy, and/or amusement.

When reinforcement of a competing response is not a viable option for reducing an unwanted behavior, the counselor next explores the possibility of using extinction. Only if extinction also is not viable does the counselor consider punishment. The client who can self-administer punishment might snap a rubber band on her wrist each time she begins to engage in the un-desired behavior. For example, a client with trichotillomania who wants to stop pulling out her hair snaps the rubber band on her wrist each time she finds herself reaching for her hair.

Counselors also use therapeutic punishment with children with devel-opmental disabilities whose self-injurious behaviors threaten their health or their very lives (Spiegler & Guevremont, 2003). Using a mild electric shock comparable in discomfort to having a rubber band snapped on one's wrist, the counselor delivers the shock whenever the child engages in the self-injurious behavior, and the child quickly stops the dangerous behavior.

In most cases, counselors can use less aversive strategies to help clients decrease unwanted behavior. In *time out*, whenever the client engages in an unwanted behavior, she separates herself—or is separated—from any possible source of positive reinforcement for a previously specified brief period of time. In *response cost*, the client loses something valuable each time he enacts an undesired behavior (punishment); conversely, when he engages in activi-ties other than the undesired behavior for a specified period of time, he not only avoids losing the valuable thing (negative reinforcement), but actually regains it (positive reinforcement). An example of response cost is the client who wants to stop fighting with classmates. She gives her school counselor six $5 bills and the name and address of the person she most dislikes. Each time the client reports or is reported having fought, her counselor arranges for the disliked person to receive one of the $5 bills. In addition, if the client engages only in nonfighting behavior, first for a few days and then for in-creasing periods of time, at the end of each time period not only does the disliked person not receive one of the $5 bills, but also the client herself gets one back.

In structured settings, such as schools and psychiatric hospitals, coun-selors employ operant conditioning principles in the form of *token economies*. When students or patients behave in appropriate ways, the staff reinforce those behaviors with tokens that can be traded for goods or privileges. When students or patients behave inappropriately, the staff, whenever possible, use less aversive strategies, such as time out, to decrease the inappropriate behaviors. Because of the potential for staff abuse of power, ethical (profes-sional) and moral (personal) guidelines are vital components of token economy programs.

Strategies Based Primarily on Classical Conditioning. For client prob-lems involving anxiety, the behaviorist employs a category of interventions involving *exposure and response prevention*. The client comes to counseling distressed and/or debilitated by classically conditioned anxiety. The client also has been negatively reinforced for certain operant responses; for ex-ample, the client has learned to escape from anxiety by operantly avoiding the source of anxiety, as in the case of phobia, or by repetitious behavior, as in the case of obsessive-compulsive disorder. The operant response of avoidance or repetition has, itself, become a problem.

To stop the problematic operant behavior, the counselor must help the client reduce the anxiety from which the client is seeking to escape. The counselor achieves that reduction by arranging for the client to expose herself repeatedly or prolongedly to the anxiety-producing situation (conditioned stimulus) while preventing herself from making the anxiety-reducing operant response. Assuming that the unconditioned stimulus (frightening circumstance) that elicited the unconditioned response (anxiety) is consistently absent, according to the principle of extinction, the client's repeated exposure to the conditioned stimulus without the unconditioned stimulus will result in reduction of the conditioned response (anxiety).

One procedure of this type is *systematic desensitization*. Counselor and client first collaborate to develop a stimulus hierarchy: a list of anxiety-eliciting conditioned stimuli, ranked from least anxiety-producing to most anxiety-producing. For example, a person with a water phobia might list hearing the sound of the ocean, seeing the ocean, putting a toe in the ocean, and immersing one's entire body in the ocean. The counselor–client team then puts the list aside while the client learns relaxation, most typically progressive relaxation of the muscle groups of the body by progressively tensing and relaxing them, starting at the head and ending at the toes. When, after practice, the client can quickly become relaxed, the client encounters the least frightening stimulus from the list, either in imagery or *in vivo*—in real life. The client uses a SUDs scale (subjective units of distress) from 1 (low) to 10 (high) to report his level of anxiety. If the client reports a SUDs of 3 or more, the counselor guides him temporarily to relax; when a SUDs of 1 or 2 is reported, the counselor guides him to refocus on the anxiety-eliciting stimulus. With each repetition of this process, the client remains more and more relaxed in the real or imagined presence of the conditioned stimulus, at which point the next stimulus on the hierarchy is encountered. Ultimately, the client can focus on the previously most frightening stimulus and remain relaxed, reporting a SUDs of 1 or 2. Applying the constructs of classical conditioning, the person encountering the conditioned stimulus now elicits the conditioned response of relaxation rather than anxiety.

A second procedure involving exposure and response prevention that a counselor might use is *flooding*. The client, instead of gradually encountering increasingly frightening conditioned stimuli, attends a long counseling session during which he continuously encounters the most frightening conditioned stimulus. Again, with prolonged exposure to the conditioned stimulus without the unconditioned stimulus (something that innately elicits the unconditioned response of anxiety), the conditioned response of anxiety extinguishes. Of the two exposure and response prevention procedures, counselors favor systematic desensitization (Spiegler & Guevremont, 2003), a kinder, gentler approach to the extinction of anxiety.

The counselor and client also can employ classical conditioning principles in the *treatment of enuresis*. Bedwetters typically have no trouble controlling urination while they are awake. The problem seems to be that while deeply asleep, they do not awaken to the rather subtle sensations of a full bladder and urination. Awakening is an involuntary response to an unconditioned stimulus such as a loud noise. If a loud noise, such as an alarm, could somehow occur just as the client experiences the sensation of a full bladder (conditioned stimulus) and begins to wet the bed, within a few nights, when the client has the sensation of a full bladder (conditioned stimulus), he would awaken (conditioned response). To achieve this, the counselor and client arrange for the client to sleep on a special mattress pad that, at the moment of contact with moisture, sets off an alarm. Once the client is conditioned to awaken to the sensation of a full bladder, he goes to the bathroom, an operant response that had been conditioned prior to the intervention.

Another counseling intervention based on classical conditioning principles is *aversion therapy*. When a client has had a strong positive association to something, the pursuit of which has brought about negative consequences for the client, aversion therapy can help the client develop a negative association to that thing. Examples include addictions to alcohol, cigarettes, food, and illicit substances as well as sexual attraction to things or people that are deemed illegal or inappropriate. In aversion therapy, the counselor and client use an aversive unconditioned stimulus and unconditioned response, such as discomfort from a painful but not harmful electric shock, or nausea induced by the counselor graphically describing something disgusting or by injection of the drug apomorphine. The client experiences the aversive reaction (unconditioned response) while she attends to the conditioned stimulus, for example, seeing, smelling, and smoking a cigarette, or imagining the sexual object. After repeated trials, whenever she encounters the conditioned stimulus in reality or imagery, she experiences the aversive reaction (conditioned response). According to the operant principle of negative reinforcement, the client then avoids the conditioned stimulus so she can escape from the aversive response.

For a number of reasons, counselors and clients use aversion therapy only when the client faces potentially catastrophic negative consequences from the original condition and when other less distressing change interventions are not viable or have failed. The use of aversion therapy in certain cases, such as clients seeking to change their homosexual orientation to heterosexual, has generated a great deal of controversy in the professional mental health literature (Donaldson, 1998).

Addressing Client Resistance. From the behavioral perspective, client reluctance or unwillingness to use a change strategy offered by the counselor is the result of the same dynamics as any other behavior. For example, the client who wants a romantic relationship but feels anxious and lacks social skills to develop such a relationship will probably resist being thrown into an intense social situation without preparation. The preparation might include the counselor modeling and prompting the client in the nonverbal and verbal skills of social conversation, systematic desensitization of anxiety while imagining making conversation, and graded task assignment accompanied by a behavioral record that enables the client to observe a general trend of success.

Behavioral counselors avoid resistance through a number of strategies. One is agreement with the client on the goals of counseling and explanation of how each change strategy has the potential to bring the client closer to those goals. Another is the maintenance of a balance of more pleasant to fewer aversive contingencies throughout the counseling process.

CONTRIBUTIONS AND LIMITATIONS

Interface with Recent Developments in the Mental Health Field

Nature/Nurture. Regarding the nature/nurture question, radical behaviorist John B. Watson once claimed he could take any three healthy children and, through manipulation of their environments, make them into any three different professionals (doctor, lawyer, Indian chief) one might wish to specify. In stark contrast to Watson, Bandura (1997) emphasized self-efficacy beliefs of the individual and demonstrated how high self-efficacy could impact physiological (genetic) processes and control or improve neurotransmitter secretions, stress levels, and blood pressure. Current behaviorists, valuing empirical evidence as they do, are more likely to accept research results on the genetic origins of behavior. Consequently, they would accept the notion that genetics set the range of possible responses, and environmental conditions strongly influence exactly which response the person will manifest within that range.

Pharmacotherapy. Regarding pharmacotherapy, again, behaviorists value the empirical literature that endorses the use of psychoactive medication in certain cases. However, "it is noteworthy that behavior therapy fares well in comparison to drug therapy" (Spiegler & Guevremont, 2003, p. 491). Behaviorists are likely to use psychoactive medication only as a temporary assist in behavior therapy rather than as a long-term solution.

Regarding research on the effectiveness of psychotherapy, "behavior therapy arguably has the broadest and strongest empirical base of any form of psychotherapy" (Spiegler & Guevremont, 2003, p. 491). In one meta-analytic study of therapeutic outcomes, behavior therapy was found to be effective with every psychological problem reviewed (Sadish & Sweeney, 1991). On the American Psychological Association's list of treatments, approximately 75% of empirically validated treatments and 65% of probably effective treatments are cognitive, behavioral, or cognitive-behavioral.

Managed Care and Brief Therapy. Behavior therapy is, by philosophy, a brief therapy aimed at changing specific, current behaviors. Norcross and Wogan (1983) reported that among theoretical approaches, behavioral therapists saw their clients less in both frequency and duration. Managed care emphasizes brief treatments that demonstrate observable changes with a wide variety of client issues. The growing reliance on managed care for payment coupled with managed care's interest in behavior modification has made behavioral therapy very popular (Bloom, 1992), and often *the* favored psychotherapeutic approach.

Diversity Issues. Although it would seem that behaviorism would not recognize an individual's subjective view or perspective on his or her culture or gender, many behaviorists have attempted to integrate culture and gender factors as variables that could influence behavioral outcomes. Regarding diversity issues, Spiegler and Guevremont (2003) have observed that "behavior therapists have paid very little attention to issues of race, gender, ethnicity, and sexual orientation" (p. 498). These authors discuss considerations and challenges in this regard and conclude by charging behavior therapists with the task of developing greater clinical sophistication around issues of diversity.

The impact of culture and ethnicity on behavior has best been addressed by the social behaviorists, such as Bandura. They view culture as another medium for enhancing or diminishing efficacy beliefs. Thus, a culture can influence behavior in the following way: "cultural context shapes how efficacy beliefs are developed, the purposes to which they are put, and the social arrangements through which they are best expressed (Bandura, 1999, p. 185).

Regarding sexual orientation in particular, at one time behavioral technology was at the center of a controversy: Should aversion therapy be used to alter a client's sexual orientation from homosexual to heterosexual? More recently, the focus of the controversy has shifted from aversion therapy itself to the broader questions discussed in chapter 1. Mental health professionals continue to debate the appropriateness as well as the relative effectiveness, especially as it relates to duration, of various approaches aimed at changing sexual orientation.

Spirituality. Behaviorists view religion and spirituality through the lenses of observable phenomena. Skinner (1953) discussed "religious control" (p. 350) with regard to how certain religious agencies use religion to extinguish and reinforce certain behaviors.

> Traditional descriptions of Heaven and Hell epitomize positive and negative reinforcement. The features vary from culture to culture, but it is doubt-

ful whether any well-known positive or negative reinforcer has not been used. Only the electric shock of the psychological laboratory is missing. In actual practice a threat to bar from Heaven or to consign to Hell is made contingent upon sinful behavior, while virtuous behavior brings the promise of Heaven or a release from the threat of Hell. (Skinner, 1953, p. 353)

As early as 1979, behaviorists addressed the integration of spiritual and behavioral approaches to counseling (Elkins, Anchor, & Sandler, 1979; Miller & Martin, 1988). More recently, Richards and Bergin (1997) have shown how the assumptions of modernistic science that underlie behaviorism contradict the assumptions underlying theistic religious (Western) traditions, though some assumptions may be compatible with the objective idealistic (Eastern) religious worldview (see Balodhi & Mishra, 1983; de Silva, 1984; Mikulas, 1981). Although major texts on behavior therapy may make virtually no reference to spirituality or religion (cf. Spiegler & Guevremont, 2003), integration of behavioral principles into an integrated theory of counseling and psychotherapy is possible (Richards & Bergin, 1997; Wilber, 1999). In fact, Martin and Booth (1999) outline practical behavioral methods for enhancing one's spiritual development.

Technical Eclecticism. The term "technical eclecticism" was coined by Arnold Lazarus, originally a behavior therapist who remained true to behavioral theory yet adopted and adapted techniques from other psychotherapeutic approaches to develop his *multimodal therapy*. Lazarus apparently is not alone. According to Spiegler and Guevremont (2003), other behavior therapists, valuing empirical evidence as they do, have increasingly included validated nonbehavioral approaches in their psychotherapeutic repertoires. True to the spirit of theoretical purity and technical eclecticism, the authors challenged behavior therapists "to incorporate non-behavioral treatments without violating the fundamental behavioral approach, which would preserve the integrity of behavior therapy" (p. 501) and expressed hope but uncertainty that this challenge can be met.

DSM-IV-TR Diagnosis. "Most behavior therapists . . . assign DSM-IV diagnoses" (Spiegler & Guevremont, 2003, p. 80), primarily because work settings and third party reimbursers require it. Although "philosophically, diagnosis is antithetical to the fundamental premises of behavior therapy and behavioral assessment" (p. 80), if the therapist remains mindful of avoiding the pitfalls of diagnosis, it can serve a constructive role in a comprehensive and "detailed description of a client's problem and the antecedents and consequences that are maintaining it" (p. 81). Despite the theory's seemingly antidiagnosis stance, the diagnostic community seems very probehaviorist. The evidence for this lies in the diagnostic criteria (symptoms) being mostly behavioral in nature, which in turn are most amenable to behavioral interventions.

Weaknesses of the Theory

Regarding limitations of the approach, former charges that the behavioral approach is impersonal and mechanistic have mostly been allayed. However, behaviorists have not addressed, or have downright discounted, certain domains of experience that many people have found useful, even compelling. These include the domains of dreams and of spiritual experiences. For example, numerous studies have highlighted the profound transformation that many people manifest in the aftermath of near-death experiences; behavioral theory accounts for neither the experiences nor their aftermath. Although philosophically behavior therapy cannot incorporate the spiritual domain, a spiritual perspective can incorporate much of what is good and useful from behavior therapy.

Distinguishing Additions to Counseling and Psychotherapy

Regarding contributions of the approach, behavior therapy, more than any other psychotherapeutic approach, has provided specific treatment procedures for many specific counseling issues. These include anxiety disorders, unipolar depression, sexual disorders, interpersonal and couple problems, developmental disabilities, psychosis, childhood disorders, and stress-related disorders (Wilson, 1995). Specific procedures make standardization of treatment possible through the development of treatment manuals, while attention to the subjective dimension of each client enables the counselor to customize and individualize treatment to the particular needs and conditions of each client. Behaviorists' commitment to scientific research has resulted in both validation and expansion of the theory and therapy.

Current Status

Since becoming an established approach to counseling and psychotherapy, behaviorism has changed. As a result primarily of the work of Albert Bandura, most behaviorists acknowledge the role of "cognitive mediational processes" in human behavior (Wilson, 1995, p. 198). Behaviorists consider that peoples' thoughts, expectations, appraisals, hypotheses, and symbolic representations influence their behavior, sometimes even more than objective environmental conditions do.

Also as a result of Bandura's work, behaviorists no longer view an individual as the passive product of the environment. Increasingly, they view behavior as the product of one's active regulation of oneself: "People are not only knowers and performers guided by outcome expectations—they are also self-reactors with a capacity for self-direction. This capability is grounded in a self-regulatory structure" (Bandura, 1999, p. 175). This structure includes the ability to self-observe, make judgments based on values, and react to the observations and judgments.

Even the distinction between classical and operant conditioning has become blurred with the phenomenon of biofeedback. Using feedback on some biological function formerly believed to be entirely involuntary, such as heart rate, blood pressure, or skin temperature, one can develop considerable voluntary control over such processes.

The addition of cognitive and self-regulatory processes in the understanding of behavior have led to the use not only of biofeedback but also of such therapeutic strategies as guided imagery, self-monitoring, and cognitive restructuring. Consequently, most behaviorists now refer to themselves as cognitive-behaviorists.

SUMMARY

Since 1950, behavior therapy reached prominence in the 1970s, at which time it became closely affiliated with cognitive therapy. Cognitive-behavior therapy is arguably the most influential approach to counseling and psychotherapy today, backed by the most empirical evidence for effectiveness and efficiency and, consequently, the treatment modality preferred by managed care. Behavior therapy continues to develop as its proponents, believing strongly in empirical evidence, incorporate and integrate nonbehavioral strategies that have been shown to be effective.

RECOMMENDED RESOURCES

Books

Kanfer, F. H., & Goldstein, A. P. (Eds.). (1991). *Helping people change* (4th ed.). New York: Pergamon.

Spiegler, M. D., & Guevremont, D. C. (2003). *Contemporary behavior therapy.* Pacific Grove, CA: Brooks/Cole.

Media

Krumboltz, J. (1998). Cognitive-behavior therapy [videorecording]. In J. Carlson & D. Kjos, *Psychotherapy with the experts.* Boston: Allyn & Bacon.

Lazarus, A. A. (1994). Multimodal therapy [videorecording]. In T. Plott (Ed.), *APA psychotherapy videotape series*. Washington, DC: American Psychological Association.

Websites

www.aabt.org: Association for Advancement of Behavior Therapy. This site posts publications, conference information and various fact sheets that apply to the practice of behavior therpy.

www.bfskinner.org: BF Skinner Foundation. This site provides biographical information on BF Skinner, important publications, and a self-instruction program designed to teach the principles of behavior analysis.

server.bmod.athabascau.ca/html/Behaviorism/: This site features a three-part behaviorism tutorial that teaches the differences in two behavioral approaches. It even includes multiple choice questions to test your knowledge.

REFERENCES

Balodhi, J. P., & Mishra, H. (1983). Pantanjala yoga and behavior therapy. *Behavior Therapist, 6*, 196–197.

Bandura, A. (1969). *Principles of behavior modification*. New York: Holt, Rinehart & Winston.

Bandura, A. (1977). *Social learning theory*. Englewood Cliffs, NJ: Prentice-Hall.

Bandura, A. (1986). *Social foundations of thought and action*. Englewood Cliffs, NJ: Prentice-Hall.

Bandura, A. (1997). *Self efficacy: The exercise of control*. New York: Oxford.

Bandura, A. (1999). Social cognitive theory of personality. In L. A. Pervin & O. P. John (Eds.), *Handbook of personality: Theory and research* (2nd ed., pp. 154–196). New York: Guilford.

Bloom, B. L. (1992). *Planned short-term psychotherapy*. Boston, MA: Allyn and Bacon.

Crits-Christoph, P. (1998). Training in empirically validated treatments: The Divison 12 APA Task Force recommendations. In K. S. Dobson & K. D. Craig (Eds.), *Empirically supported therapies: Best practice in professional psychology*. Thousand Oaks, CA: Sage.

D'Amico, P. J., & Friedman, A. G. (1997). Parents as behavior change agents in the reduction of children's fears. In L. VandeCreek, S. Knapp, & T. L. Jackson (Eds.), *Innovations in clinical practice: A sourcebook* (vol. 15, pp. 323–339). Sarasota, FL: Professional Resources Press.

de Silva, P. (1984). Buddhism and behaviour modification. *Behaviour Research and Therapy, 22*, 661–678.

Donaldson, S. M. (1998). Counselor bias in working with gay men and lesbians: A commentary on Barret and Barzan (1996). *Counseling and Values, 42*(2), 88–91.

Elkins, D., Anchor, K. N., & Sandler, H. M. (1979). Relaxation training and prayer behavior as tension reduction techniques. *Behavioral Engineering, 5*, 81–87.

Friedman, A. G., & Campbell, T. A. (1992). Children's nighttime fears: A behavioral approach to assessment of treatment. In L. VandeCreek, S. Knapp, & T. L. Jackson

(Eds.), *Innovations in clinical practice: A sourcebook* (vol. 2, pp. 139–255). Sarasota, FL: Professional Resource Press.

Gottman, J. M. (1999). *The marriage clinic: A scientifically based marital therapy.* New York: W. W. Norton.

Graziano, A.M., & Diament, D.M. (1992). Parent behavioral training: An examination of the paradigm. *Behavioral Modification, 16,* 3–38.

Jacobson, N. (1998). *Acceptance and change in couple therapy : A therapist's guide to transforming relationships.* New York: W. W. Norton.

Jakubowski, P., & Lange, A. J. (1978). *The assertive option: Your rights and responsibilities.* Champaign, IL: Research Press.

Jones, S. L. (1988). A religious critique of behavior therapy. In W. R. Miller & J. E. Martin (Eds.), *Behavior therapy and religion: Integrating spiritual and behavioral approaches to change.* Newbury Park, CA: Sage.

Kanfer, F. H., & Goldstein, A. P. (Eds.). (1991). *Helping people change* (4th ed.). New York: Pergamon.

Kolko, D. J. (1983). Multicomponent parental treatment of firesetting in a six year old boy. *Journal of Behavior Therapy and Experimental Psychiatry, 21,* 349–353.

Kübler-Ross, E. (1997). *On death and dying* (reprint ed.). New York: Simon & Schuster.

Lange, A. J., & Jakubowski, P. (1976). *Responsible assertive behavior: Cognitive/behavioral procedures for trainers.* Champaign, IL: Research Press.

Love, P., & Robinson, J. (1994). *Hot monogamy: Essential steps to more passionate, intimate lovemaking.* New York: Penguin.

Martin, J. E., & Booth, J. (1999). Behavioral approaches to enhance spirituality. In W. R. Miller (Ed.), *Integrating spirituality into treatment: Resources for practitioners* (pp. 161–175). Washington DC: American Psychological Association.

Mikulas, W. L. (1981). Buddhism and behavior modification. *Psychological Record, 31,* 331–342.

Miller, W. R., & Martin, J. E. (Eds.). (1988). *Behavior therapy and religion: Integrating spiritual and behavioral approaches to change.* Newbury Park, CA: Sage.

Monte, C.F. (1999). *Behind the mask: An introduction to the theories of personality* (6th ed.). New York: Harcourt Brace.

Nezu, A. M., & Nezu, C. M. (1989). *Clinical decision making in behavior therapy: A problem-solving perspective.* Champaign, IL: Research Press.

Norcross, J.C., & Wogan, M. (1983). American psychotherapists of diverse persuasions: Characteristics, theories, practices and clients. *Professional Psychology, 14,* 529–539.

Richards, P. S., & Bergin, A. E. (1997). *A spiritual strategy for counseling and psychotherapy.* Washington, DC: American Psychological Association.

Sadish, W. R., & Sweeney, R. B. (1991). Mediators and moderators in meta-analysis: There's a reason why we don't let dodo birds tell us which psychotherapies should get prizes. *Journal of Consulting and Clinical Psychology, 59,* 883-893.

Skinner, B. F. (1953). *Science and human behavior.* Toronto: Free Press.

Spiegler, M. D., & Guevremont, D. C. (2003). *Contemporary behavior therapy* (4th ed.). Pacific Grove, CA: Brooks/Cole.

Watson, J.B. (1967). *Behavior: An introduction to comparative psychology.* New York: Holt, Rinehart and Winston.

Wilber, K. (1999). Integral psychology. In *The collected works of Ken Wilber, Vol. 4.* Boston: Shambhala.

Wilson, G. T. (1995). Behavior therapy. In R. J. Corsini & D. Wedding (Eds.), *Current psychotherapies* (5th ed., pp. 197–228). Itasca, IL: F. E. Peacock.

CHAPTER 10

COGNITIVE COUNSELING

BACKGROUND OF THE THEORY

Historical Context

The two decades following World War II were characterized in the United States at large by both the optimism of economic expansion and the anxiety of the Cold War, with its issues of nuclear threat and deterrence. The relative social conservatism of the 1950s, with an emphasis on conformity, gave way to the social liberalism of the 1960s, with an emphasis on dissent. The trend was toward valuing independence of thought and having the intellectual integrity to "tell it like it is" (Landon, 1998).

The domain of clinical psychology also was undergoing change. By 1960 in the United States, behaviorism had begun to displace psychoanalysis, the Rogerian approach was gaining momentum, and the treatment of mental disorders with psychoactive medication was becoming well established. Nevertheless, many clinicians who had become dissatisfied with psychoanalysis also found behavioral approaches too narrow, the Rogerian approach too inefficient, and the medical approach too mechanistic to produce meaningful change.

In this social and professional climate of the early 1960s, Aaron Beck developed cognitive therapy. Through his own research and clinical experience, he detected client psychological dynamics that had gone unidentified by psychoanalysts, behaviorists, and Rogerians. Moving beyond his own psychoanalytic training and the growing trend to treat mental disorders with medication, Beck "called it as he saw it," thus pioneering a unique theory and therapy. He asserted that each of the various mental disorders was characterized by a particular cognitive pattern and that the most effective, efficient, and lasting psychotherapy involved intervention in that cognitive pattern. His autonomous stand in reference to the psychological "establishment," including a principled willingness to dissent and even rebel (Weishaar, 1993), paralleled the social tenor of the times. Despite his breaking free of the constraints of the prevailing psychological perspectives, his was not a rejecting stance but one that retained what was useful about those perspectives and also moved beyond them (Beck & Weishaar, 2000; J. S. Beck, 1995).

Throughout history, two or more people have virtually simultaneously pursued the same innovations. It is as if the time is ripe for the innovation, and more than one individual picks up on the "readiness" for the development to emerge. Such was the case with the cognitive revolution of the 1970s in psychology, in which Beck was a key figure (Leahy, 1996; Weishaar, 1993). During the same period, Albert Ellis developed Rational Emotive Behavior Therapy also as a cognitively based psychological theory and therapy. However, the two theorists worked independently, unaware for some time of each other's work. Although both approaches are cognitively based, the similarity practically ends there, with the two innovators taking substantially divergent perspectives and approaches (Beck & Weishaar, 2000; Ellis, 2000).

Founder's Biographical Overview

Aaron Temkin Beck was born on July 18, 1921, the youngest child of Harry and Elizabeth Temkin Beck. Both of Aaron's parents were Jewish Russians who had migrated to the United States as older teenagers in the early 1900s. The first and third of their five children died, to which Elizabeth responded with a year-long depression that mostly abated with Aaron's birth. Beck "smiles at the notion that he was able to cure his mother's depression at such an early age" (Weishaar, 1993, p. 9).

At age 7, Beck had an accident in which he broke his arm. A complication developed when the bone became infected and the infection spread to Beck's blood. He underwent a traumatic surgery, and for 2 months, he was expected to die. He survived, but he developed anxieties and phobias related to his health, and he missed so much school that he was held back in first grade. He concluded that he was stupid, but, disliking being behind his friends in school, he devised a plan to catch up. He ended up not only succeeding but actually exceeding his peers, an experience that contributed to his reformulated belief that he actually was quite bright and could "dig [himself] out" of a hole (Weishaar, 1993, p. 10).

Beck has attributed a lifelong "sensitivity to others' unexpected mood changes" (Weishaar, 1993, p. 11) to his childhood experiences with an emotionally erratic mother and an emotionally abusive first grade teacher. His interests during his school years included science and nature, Scouts, and editorship of his high school newspaper. In reference to Beck's middle name, a high school friend nicknamed him "Tim," the name that Beck's wife and close associates still call him (Weishaar, 1993, p. 11).

Beck graduated first in his high school class. After beginning the study of liberal arts at Brown University, and despite being discouraged by a dean from pursuing medical school because of a "quota system enforced against Jews" (Weishaar, 1993, p. 12), Beck pursued a pre-med curriculum and graduated *magna cum laude* in 1942.

Over the next decade, Beck became a psychiatrist—by circumstance more than purposeful design (Weishaar, 1993)—and a reluctant, but ultimately convinced, recruit to psychoanalysis. Wanting to correct the absence of research demonstrating the effectiveness of psychoanalysis, Beck embarked on studies of his own. However, rather than finding corroboration, he found substantial evidence that psychoanalytic concepts neither accurately predicted nor explained how depressed people actually functioned. Rather, he found that these patients had constructed a distorted view of reality that involved inaccurately pessimistic views of themselves and their capacity to achieve success and happiness. From these roots, Beck went on to create the innovation of cognitive therapy for the treatment of depression, anxiety, and numerous other mental disorders (Leahy, 1996; Weishaar, 1993). Since his groundbreaking book in 1976, *Cognitive Therapy and the Emotional Disorders*, he has gone on to publish prolifically. His most recent book is his 1999, *Prisoners of Hate: The Cognitive Basis of Anger, Hostility, and Violence.*

While he was a student at Brown University, Beck met fellow student Phyllis Whitman. The two married in 1950. Her career developed from newspaper reporter to Pennsylvania Superior Court judge, and his career development culminated in a psychiatry professorship at the University of Pennsylvania and directorship of the Beck Institute in Pennsylvania. During that time, the Becks had four children, all of whom are now adults with children of their own. Their daughter, Judith, is a major figure in her own right in the field of cognitive therapy (J. S. Beck, 1995).

Throughout Beck's professional development, he achieved mastery over phobias and anxieties that he traced back to childhood traumas (Weishaar, 1993). In particular, he overcame a blood/injury phobia that originally caused him to faint at the sight of movie hospital scenes, as well as a public speaking phobia. Some of his students believe a residue of performance anxiety causes him to come across in filmed psychotherapy demonstrations as much less warm and engaging than he is with patients in real life.

The extent of Beck's mastery over these impediments makes Beck's professional honors even more impressive. In 1982, the prestigious journal *American Psychologist* conducted a survey of clinical and counseling psychologists who identified Aaron Beck as one of the "Ten Most Influential Psychotherapists." Today, he "is the only psychiatrist to have won the highest research awards from both the American Psychiatric and the American Psychological Associations" (Weishaar, 1993, p. 43). With his distinguishing head of white hair, his trademark bow tie, his intellectual autonomy, and his personal humility, Aaron Beck continues to solidify and further the cognitive revolution that currently dominates U.S. psychology and psychotherapy.

Philosophical Underpinnings

Beck and Weishaar (2000) named three conceptual foundations of cognitive therapy, two of which specifically involve philosophy. The first is phenomenology. This perspective dates back to the Greek Stoics who asserted that the mind is analogous to a blank slate; that through sensory experience, one develops concepts; and that although concepts constitute one's "reality," they are subjective formulations that were "interpreted" through the senses and, thus, are actually only approximations of "reality." (see http://www.utm.edu/research/iep/s/stoicism.htm). Beck and Weishaar (2000) also cited the 18th century philosopher Immanual Kant as having emphasized the importance of conscious subjective experience. It is noteworthy that both Aristotle and the Stoics advocated achieving happiness by the control and the annihilation, respectively, of irrational passions through the use of reason (see http://www.utm.edu/research/iep/s/stoicism.htm).

The second philosophically related "pillar" of cognitive therapy was "the structural theory and depth psychology of Kant and Freud, particularly Freud's concept of the hierarchical structuring of cognition into primary and secondary processes" (Beck & Weishaar, 2000, p. 245). As you may recall, primary process refers to the mind's unconscious, irrational workings, whereas secondary process refers to its conscious, rational workings. Elsewhere in this book, see the chapter on psychoanalysis for a more in-depth refresher on these processes. As you read this chapter on cognitive counseling, you will see continuous reference to these Stoic and Kantian concepts.

A third component in the foundation of Beck's cognitive therapy is empiricism and its brainchild, the scientific method. The influence of empiricism on cognitive therapy is seen in two ways. One is the use of hypothesis testing in the therapeutic process itself. Client and counselor first identify the cognitive conclusions about life to which the client has come, collaboratively consider them not as conclusions but as hypotheses, and then test the validity of those hypotheses. True to empirical procedure, hypotheses that are not supported by evidence are rejected and replaced by other hypotheses that the evidence better supports.

The other influence of empiricism on cognitive therapy has been Beck's own research on psychotherapy, which spawned cognitive therapy. Yet another is others' research and theory in cognitive psychology (Beck & Weishaar, 2000). An early contemporary influence was George Kelly (1955), whose cognitive model of personality was based in the concept of "personal constructs." Kelly's model never achieved widespread application in the United States, however, due in part to its incompatibility with prevailing views of the 1950s (Leahy, 1996). Other contributors to a shift in focus toward the cognitive domain were Magda Arnold (1960) and Richard Lazarus (1984), who pointed to the role of cognition in emotion and behavior; Albert Bandura (1977), who demonstrated how, even more than environmental reinforcement conditions, cognitive processes such as expectancy and belief predicted behavior; structuralists like Piaget (1954, 1965, 1970) and Chomsky (1965), who demonstrated that, cross-culturally, people cognitively structure reality in predisposed and evolving ways (Leahy, 1996); Loftus (1980), who showed how cognitive structures, once formed, actually limit further cognitive innovation and change by modifying and directing attention and memory; and researchers who studied the factors to which people attributed their relative successes and failures and how those attributions influenced future success and failure (Leahy, 1996).

PERSONALITY DEVELOPMENT

Nature of Humans

Function of the Psyche. At birth, an infant is endowed with the motive to survive. Later in life, another "evolutionary derived objective" will emerge: to procreate (Beck, 1996, p. 5). To accomplish these aims, the individual must process information, that is, perceive, interpret, and learn from experience; draw conclusions, make predictions, and formulate goals. Information processing is, itself, informed innately by pleasurable feelings and emotions, which are crude indications that survival and procreation are being served, and painful feelings and emotions, which are crude indications that survival and procreation are not being served and which motivate corrective action.

To process information, the infant is endowed with a variety of functions: not only sensation and emotion, but also memory and the potential for increasingly voluntary motor movement. Crucial to information processing is cognition, the ability to form sensory images and verbal thoughts. The cognitive aspect of information processing in the infant is quite primitive, involving nonverbal visual, auditory, tactile, olfactory, and gustatory images. As the child develops cognitively, information processing becomes increasingly verbal, abstract, and subject to growing ability to reason, though always retaining its sensory basis. At every stage of development, "the processing of information is crucial for the survival of any organism" (Beck & Weishaar, 2000, pp. 241–242).

From a cognitive counseling perspective, experience does not fall on a mind that, endowed with the above functions, is otherwise a metaphorical blank slate. Cognitive theorists acknowledge the extensive research indicating "different temperaments at birth. Temperamentally, [a person] may tend to be more frightened, active, outgoing, or shy. . . . [T]emperaments push us in certain directions" (Young, n.d.a). Thus, even shortly after birth, two infants are likely to perceive the same event differently, and perceptual differences can become only more idiosyncratic as individuals move through their unique life experiences. In addition, related to research on innate temperament is research on innate genetic/neurochemical predisposition to psychopathology, which cognitive therapists also acknowledge.

However, despite their affirmation of innate predispositions, cognitive therapists do not see individuals as passive victims of inborn tendencies but as "active participants in their environment, judging and evaluating stimuli, interpreting events and sensations, and [ultimately] judging their own responses" (Beck & Weishaar, 2000, p. 244). People actively create and seek to achieve goals they believe to serve both their vital and their less-than-vital interests.

It is, therefore, only natural that individuals become distressed when they experience a threat to their interests (Beck & Weishaar, 2000). From the infant who cries in hunger to the teen who fears failure on an exam to the adult who grieves the death of a spouse, psychological upset is tied to the perception of a threat to one's well being—ultimately, one's ability to survive and procreate. The more vital to one's perceived well being, the more intense the upset. In other words, the perception of threat to one's vital interests results in a more highly *charged* or energized response than does the perception of threat to less-than-vital interests. A newborn infant is more likely to become more emotionally upset from extreme hunger than from mild hunger. As adults, most people are more likely to become more intensely upset at the loss of a beloved spouse than at the loss of a valued piece of jewelry.

Structure of the Psyche. From a cognitive perspective, the human psyche consists of schemas, systems, and modes. Together, these components comprise the personality.

The fundamental building block of the psyche is the *schema*. Schemas are core phenomena that comprise five survival-supporting *systems*: cognitive, emotional, physiological, motivational, and behavioral. Cognitive schemas are core beliefs, such as those about perceived danger, violation, loss, and gain. Emotional schemas are the core emotions, such as anxiety, anger, sadness, and joy. Motivational schemas are the core impulses: to escape or avoid, to lash out, to grieve, or to seek and approach. Behavioral schemas are core actions, including shaking, scowling, crying, and smiling. Physiological schemas refer to the core ways that the body's autonomic, motor, and sensory systems are energized along with the emotional arousal.

Perhaps you have noticed the parallel construction of the examples in the previous paragraph. For example, the cognitive perception of danger is accompanied by the emotion and physiology of anxiety, the motive to escape or avoid, as well as the behavior of shaking. Likewise, the cognitive perception of having been violated in some way is accompanied by the emotion and physiology of anger, the motive to lash out, and the behavior of scowling. The cognitive perception of loss is accompanied by the emotion and physiology of sadness, the urge to grieve, and, typically, the actual behavior of crying. The perception of gain is accompanied by the emotion and physiology of joy, the urge to seek and approach, and the behavior of smiling. Each of these cases exemplifies a *mode*, a subpersonality structure comprised of a network of interrelated cognitive, emotional, physiological, motivational, and behavioral schemas.

During waking life, one mode is dominant at a given time, while others lie dormant, awaiting activation and temporary—or prolonged—dominance. How modes emerge and recede as the dominant "player" in a person's immediate experience is clarified by understanding the three types of modes. The *orienting mode* is the network involved in the almost constant process of scanning the environment for threats and opportunities related to one's interests, both vital and otherwise. The cognitive schema within an orienting mode contains a virtual template of threat or opportunity, such as one's perception of potential danger, failure, rejection, or benefit. When one perceives no match between the template and current environmental circumstances, one is likely to be in a *minor mode* (Beck, 1996, p. 10), pursuing less-than-vital interests. Minor modes include working at one's job or in one's garden, conversing with a friend or playing a computer game, and experiencing mild emotional states such as concern, irritation, disappointment, and satisfaction. When a perceived environmental circumstance matches the template of threat or opportunity to one's *vital* interests, it activates a related cognitive schema that, in turn, powerfully and simultaneously energizes the emotional, physiological, motivational, and behavioral components of a *major* or *primal mode* such as the anxiety, anger, sadness, or joy mode. The word "primal" refers to the primitive, universal, survival-related nature of these modes (Beck, 1996; Beck & Weishaar, 2000, p. 242).

For example, a driver is driving along on an errand one day; he is, in effect, in his minor "driving mode." Suddenly, a dog darts out in front of his car. The driver's orienting mode perceives a match between the template of danger and these circumstances. Instantly he thinks, "I must not hit the dog!" (automatic thought), which activates his anxiety mode: Frightened (emotion), his body is energized (physiology), he feels the impulse to avoid hitting the dog (motivation), and he follows that impulse by swerving the car (behavior). He misses the dog, which happily darts out of sight between some parked cars. The driver's orienting schema no longer perceives a match between the template of danger and existing circumstances, and he gradually returns to the minor mode of driving. The potential to develop modes and shift from mode to mode is an innate endowment.

A difference between major/primal and minor modes is that major/primal modes are more intensely charged with energy, and the charge lingers for some time after the template-matching external event has passed. In the above example, the driver will need some time to calm down.

Another crucial difference involves the one remaining aspect of the psyche, the *conscious control system.* This system "is separate from, and relatively independent of, [modes]. When activated, this control system has the potential . . . to de-energize the mode" (Beck, 1996) by thinking about and acting on one's cognitive and behavioral systems. The driver who averted disaster can facilitate the calming process by purposely enacting the behavior of relaxing his muscles and purposely engaging the cognitions, "Everything is OK. The dog wasn't hurt. Everything is fine." However, *while* a primal mode is activated, access to the conscious control system is limited. The automatic thoughts of the cognitive system, in particular, are characterized by narrowed focus, selective attention, and extreme, absolutistic evaluation, and the remaining components of the mode instantaneously "shift into gear." The driver thinks only about how he *must* avoid hitting the dog and only about the features of the environment relevant to that goal. Unlike the cognitive rigidity of the major/primal modes, cognitive flexibility characterizes the minor modes that, in turn, are more easily influenced by the conscious control system.

Cognitive therapists are so named because they are particularly interested in the cognitive component of modes. The basic contents of the cognitive system—its specific schemas—are not in place at birth. Rather, an infant is endowed with *protoschemas,* the basic, general structures pertaining to broad, survival-related themes such as danger, failure, rejection, and benefit. With experience, these protoschemas become specific schemas. In other words, humans are innately endowed with the basic potential to recognize circumstances signaling danger, violation, loss, and gain. Specific schemas, however, such as the core belief in anxiety disorder that one is continuously vulnerable to serious harm, result from specific learning experiences.

Schemas are not the only level of cognition in the psyche. Cognitive therapists view cognitions as *hierarchically organized* based on their *availability to awareness* and their *stability* (Beck & Weishaar, 2000). The least available to awareness and most stable cognitions are the cognitive schemas, one's core beliefs about self, others, the world, and the future. These beliefs are formed in early childhood while the child is at a preoperational level of cognitive development—when the child is not yet able to reason abstractly (Leahy, 1996). Consequently, cognitive schemas can be reasonable or can reflect some degree of error in logic.

Each cognitive schema involves a specific theme. Jeffrey Young (n.d.b) has identified 18 maladaptive schemas, each with a one- or two-word name, such as abandonment/instability. We believe that these schemas cover the gamut of what clients address in counseling. Theoretically, each person, based on innate predisposition and life experiences, has formed a schema for each of these themes. For each theme, each person's specific schema can be understood as falling somewhere on a continuum between extremes. For example, regarding the abandonment/instability theme, each person has a cognitive schema that falls somewhere in the range from the extreme belief that other people are always completely stable and reliable sources of support and connection, to the extreme belief that other people are always completely unstable and unreliable sources of support and connection.

Right now, you might be thinking, "Where do I fall on that continuum?" If that is the case, you are experiencing, right now, how core beliefs are normally completely out of awareness. As fundamental as this single belief is to your basic approach to any relationship with another person, it was formed at such an early age that it became part of the foundation from which you operated rather than a conclusion that you periodically questioned or re-evaluated. Nevertheless, cognitive therapists do not believe that cognitive schemas are *deeply* buried in the unconscious but that they are rather readily available to consciousness, though not the *most* available type of cognition.

Schemas remain relatively stable because, once formed, a schema acts like a pair of tinted glasses. For example, the person who believes people are completely unstable and unreliable sources of support and connection is likely to have an orienting mode that "sniffs out" any hint of abandonment. Conse-quently, the person more readily *notices* abandoning behavior in others, more readily *interprets* even neutral behavior as abandonment, and thus *remembers* more of such behaviors. Thus, once a schema is formed, it further influences the processing of information. In addition, this person probably inadvert-ently *perpetuates* abandoning behavior in others. To understand this last point, imagine that the person perceives abandonment in a series of neutral ac-tions on the part of a friend. The person is likely to shift into "abandonment mode," including reacting with emotional intensity, such as sadness, anger, or withdrawal. The friend is likely to find these frequent overreactions un-pleasant and to break off the friendship—thus abandoning the person with the abandonment schema. We will return to Young's schema taxonomy in a later section of this chapter.

Moving up the hierarchy, somewhat more available to awareness and less stable are the cognitions that arise out of schemas: *assumptions* (Leahy, 1996) or *intermediate beliefs* (J. S. Beck, 1995) consisting of rules. These rules take the form of *if-then* propositions and *shoulds* that apply generally across situations. Someone toward the more secure end of the abandonment/insta-bility continuum might hold the assumption that "If I am reasonably consid-erate to others, I am not likely to be abandoned" and "I should be reasonably considerate to others." Someone toward the insecure end might believe, "If I take care of others, they will never leave me" so "I should make every effort to take care of others," and "If I focus exclusively on others' needs, I don't have to think about my own needs and how I might be abandoned" so "I should put all my attention on what others need" (Leahy, 1996, p. 198).

Further up the hierarchy, most available to awareness and least stable are *automatic thoughts,* the cognitions—verbal thoughts and sensory images—that arise from the intermediate beliefs in the context of specific situations. The secure person who sees his partner scowl might think, "She must have had a bad day." He is likely to remain in a minor mode and might actually tell her, sympathetically, that she looks like she might have had a rough day. The insecure person might think, "Oh, no! She must be upset with me!" He is likely to shift into a major mode and ask with some emotional desperation, "What's wrong? Did I do something to upset you?"

Summary. An infant is born with the innate disposition to survive and procreate. Throughout life, the individual fulfills that disposition through processing the information that arises from experience, using innate feelings of pleasure and pain as a guide. Each person is equipped to process information using the four psychological systems of cognition, emotion, physiology, motivation, and behavior. Certain innate connections exist between these systems, which comprise modes, such as between the cognition of danger, the emotion of fear/anxiety, the motivation to escape or avoid, and the behavior of fleeing, which comprise the anxiety mode. The personality consists of several modes—the orienting mode that operates continuously in waking life; the minor modes that, for most people, operate most of the time; the major/primal modes that are activated when one perceives threats or opportunities related to one's vital interests of survival and/or procreation—along with the conscious control system that has the ability to de-activate primal modes.

The cognitive system comprises sensory images and verbal thoughts that exist in a hierarchy: the most accessible, unstable, and situation-specific automatic thoughts; which arise from the less accessible and more stable and general intermediate thoughts that take the form of rules, which arise from the least accessible (though still accessible), most stable, and most fundamental beliefs about self, others, the world, and the future: core beliefs or schemas. Newborn infants are endowed with protoschemas that, through experience, become content-specific. Most cognitive schemas form during early childhood when the child is developmentally prone to make errors in reasoning. The cognitions with which people appraise their circumstances powerfully influence their emotional-motivational-behavioral responses. In particular, some cognitive systems, right down to the schemas, are more reasonable and functional than others. In addition to the role of innate temperament and predisposition, how some people develop more reasonable, functional schemas, and yet others develop less reasonable and more dysfunctional schemas, is the subject of the next section.

Role of the Environment

For the cognitive therapist, "environment" refers to both the physical and social environments (Beck & Weishaar, 2000, p. 241). The goals of survival and procreation are served by processing information about the earth's gravity and the behavior of plants and other animals as well as processing information about one's interactions with other humans.

Cognitive therapists subscribe to social learning theory. That is, they believe that, even more than people's behaviors themselves, people's *cognitions,* their beliefs, their conclusions, expectations, and predictions *that underlie* their behaviors, are influenced by modeling, by the presence and form—or absence—of reinforcement and punishment, and by vicarious learning from significant others. Whereas cognitive therapists acknowledge innate predispositions to perceive stimuli in particular ways, they more strongly "[emphasize] the individual's learning history, including the influence of significant life events" (Beck & Weishaar, 2000, p. 249) on the development of personality. Whereas personality results from the interaction between innate disposition and environmental factors, the greater influence is considered to be the environment.

Because schemas develop in early childhood (Young, n.d.b), the single greatest influence on the development of one's schemas is the aspect of the environment that most frequently and powerfully provides modeling, reinforcement, and punishment during one's early years: That environment typically is one's family. As the child seeks to adapt in the pursuit of survival, the messages one perceives from one's early caretakers, both behavioral and verbal, contribute most to one's core beliefs about self, others, the world, and the future. So, for example, a child is likely to develop an abandonment/instability schema if, when he or she was young, a parent "died or left the home permanently . . . was moody, unpredictable, or an alcoholic . . . withdrew or left [one] alone for long periods of time" (Young, n.d.c), failed to protect one from abuse, or the like.

Additional influences include the extrafamilial domains of the larger social environment—one's culture—and, as previously stated, the physical environment. At the same time that these environmental factors impinge strongly on one's development, the environment is not solely responsible for one's schemas. The individual's innate predispositions play a role in how one perceives environmental contingencies. In addition, with cognitive development comes the increasing ability to engage one's conscious control system to deactivate dysfunctional major/primal schemas, and even to access and modify them.

The Healthy/Adaptive Versus Unhealthy/Maladaptive Personality

Beck and Weishaar (2000) offered a succinct summary of the cognitive perspective on personality development. Cognitive therapists, they asserted, view "personality as reflecting the individual's cognitive organization and structure, which are both biologically and socially influenced. Within the constraints of one's neuroanatomy and biochemistry, personal learning experiences help determine how one develops and responds" (p. 249).

The individual with adaptive cognitive schemas exhibits a kind of modal flexibility. Under normal life circumstances, she spends most of her time in minor modes with easy access to her conscious control system. When circumstances call for a shift into a major/primal mode, she makes that shift, and when those circumstances end, she shifts back to minor mode functioning.

This pattern is made possible by schemas that are reasonable and functional. Her schemas probably go something like, "I'm pretty competent. Others are usually trustworthy and supportive. The world is usually a safe place where I can usually achieve my goals. The future looks essentially bright."

The individual with maladaptive schemas exhibits a kind of modal rigidity. Under normal life circumstances, she spends much or virtually all of her time in major/primal modes. Probably almost everyone has one or more schemas that stray from the ideal range on the schema continuum. However, when schemas are located rather far, or very far, from that ideal range, *DSM-IV-TR* (American Psychiatric Association, 2000) Axis I disorders and Axis II personality disorders, respectively, are manifested. For example, in depression, cognitive schemas about self, the world, and the future contain themes of *exaggerated and relatively persistent* loss. In anxiety-related disorders such as generalized anxiety, panic disorder, phobia, obsession, compulsion, anorexia, and hypochondria, cognitive schemas contain themes of *exaggerated and relatively persistent* danger. In hypomania, cognitive schemas contain themes of *exaggerated and relatively persistent* gain. Though chronic hostility is not an official DSM-IV disorder, Beck (1996) asserted "that it should be included . . . to account for individuals' excessive reactions leading to violence and homicide" (p. 13). In these disorders, the cognitive schemas contain themes of an *exaggerated and relatively persistent* sense of being violated. In personality disorders, such as narcissistic and borderline, cognitive schemas are at such an extreme end of the continuum range that the person spends virtually all of her time in major/primal modes.

The exaggerated and persistent nature of distorted schemas renders their associated modes distinct from the primal modes from which they originate. The primal sadness mode, with distorted schemas, becomes depression mode; primal anxiety mode becomes anxiety disorder mode, phobic mode, or the modes of any other of the anxiety-based disorders; primal anger mode becomes violent mode; and joy mode becomes hypomanic mode.

Beyond the general themes of loss, danger, violation, and gain, Beck (1996; Beck & Weishaar, 2000) has hypothesized an even more specific *cognitive profile* for each psychological disorder, consisting of characteristic cognitive schemas. Though each client's schemas will be unique, the cognitive counselor expects to find this profile in some form in a client presenting with the specified disorder. For example, depression, the mode of exaggerated and persistent loss, is accompanied by the profile of the *cognitive triad:* an exaggerated and persistently negative view of oneself, the world, and the future. The depressed client sees oneself as incapable, abandoned, and valueless; the world as overwhelmingly demanding with huge obstacles to goal achievement and complete absence of satisfaction; and the future as holding no improvement over the present negative conditions. This latter perception is associated with the emotion of hopelessness, which Beck and other researchers (Beck, 2000) have found to be a highly reliable predictor of suicide. Other symptoms include the motivational component of "paralysis of will"

(Beck & Weishaar, 2000, p. 251) and the behavioral components of inactivity and eating and/or sleeping too little or too much. These other symptoms and the cognitive component mutually feed back to each other to maintain the depressive mode. For example, believing himself incompetent, he feels unmotivated to set and achieve even a simple goal, spends several hours sleeping; having accomplished nothing, he then is reinforced in the belief that he is incompetent.

The cognitions that comprise psychological disorders' cognitive profiles both reflect and perpetuate *a systematic bias in information processing* (Beck & Weishaar, 2000, p. 250). This bias takes several characteristic forms, called *cognitive distortions,* that can be detected in the client's cognitive system—his automatic thoughts, intermediate thoughts, and core beliefs. The forms are:

- Arbitrary inference: Jumping to a conclusion in the absence of supporting evidence or even despite evidence to the contrary. For example, a teacher who struggles with a particularly difficult class concludes, "I'm a horrible teacher."
- Selective abstraction: Conceptualizing an entire situation based on taking one detail out of context and ignoring other aspects of the context. For example, a husband who, along with his wife, enjoys fairly frequent sex, describes in counseling a recent night when his wife declined to make love. He states, "My sexual needs are *not* getting met."
- Overgeneralization: "Abstracting a general rule from one or a few isolated incidents and applying it too broadly and to unrelated situations" (Beck & Weishaar, 2000, p. 250). For example, a successful store owner is robbed one day and concludes, "People can't be trusted. I'll never get ahead."
- Magnification and minimization: Attributing much more or less importance to something than is warranted. Magnification is often manifested in catastrophizing, such as the man who believes, "If my date sees my anxiety on our first date, she'll want nothing more to do with me." Minimization is often manifested in denial, such as the woman who believes her husband's frequent bouts of physical abuse are "not the real him."
- Personalization: Attributing the cause of external events entirely to oneself without evidence supporting a causal connection (Beck & Weishaar, 2000). For example, a child's parents divorce, and the child concludes, "It's all my fault."
- Dichotomous thinking: Conceptualizing shades-of-gray phenomena in black-or-white categories. For example, a student believes, "If I don't get the best grade in the class, I'm a total failure."

David Burns (1980, 1999) offered different terms for some of these cognitive distortions, and he has added a few to Beck's list.

- Jumping to conclusions: Burns' term for arbitrary inference.
- Mental filter: Burns' terms for selective abstraction.

- Blame: listed by Burns with, and as a converse to, personalization: attributing internal responsibility entirely to external events. For example, a student who is failing a class attributes his poor performance entirely to the teacher's "bad teaching."
- All-or-nothing thinking: Burns' term for dichotomous thinking.
- Disqualifying the positive: Akin to minimization, this distortion specifically involves arbitrarily concluding that positive experiences "don't count" in an evaluation process.
- Emotional reasoning: The assumption that emotions reflect reality. For example, in procrastination, one thinks, "I don't feel like doing [a particular task] right now, so it's actually not a good time to do it."
- Should statements: Distorted attempts to motivate oneself and others by psychological force.
- Labeling and mislabeling: A form of overgeneralization and all-or-nothing thinking in which one labels a total phenomenon based on one experience. This distortion can be directed at oneself, as when a salesman loses one account and thinks of himself as incompetent; at someone else, as when a friend forgets a lunch date and is labeled inconsiderate; or at a thing or activity, as when a word processing program uncharacteristically quits and is labeled totally worthless.

As previously stated, Young (n.d.b) has identified 18 maladaptive schemas that underlie most psychological disorders. Though we have space here to describe only a few, see if you can generate some distorted intermediate and automatic thoughts that might arise from these dysfunctional schemas: *vulnerability to harm or illness*, the exaggerated fear that imminent catastrophe will strike at any time and that one will be unable to prevent it; *entitlement/grandiosity*, the belief that one is superior to other people, entitled to special rights and privileges, or not bound by the rules of reciprocity that guide normal social interaction; *self-sacrifice*, an excessive focus on voluntarily meeting the needs of others in daily situations, at the expense of one's own gratification; and unrelenting standards/hypercriticalness, the underlying belief that one must strive to meet very high internalized standards of behavior and performance, usually to avoid criticism. (Young, n.d.b)

The problem with distorted cognitions is that they are associated with unnecessarily distressing emotions and nonadaptive behaviors that often serve as a feedback loop, perpetuating further distorted thinking and associated self-defeating feelings and behaviors. The person who thinks, "I'm boring; if I talk to people, they'll reject me," is likely to feel anxious at a party and avoid social interaction. In this social phobia mode, he experiences *cog-*

nitive deficits: His ability to access his conscious control system, which has the potential to "turn off idiosyncratic thinking, to concentrate, recall, . . . reason . . . [engage] reality testing and refine global conceptualizations" (Beck & Weishaar, 2000, p. 248), is reduced. Failing to find evidence that disputes the cognition, he is likely to come away from the party believing even more firmly that, indeed, he must be boring.

A final note on the maladaptive personality is that, in the case of dysfunctional modes, the associated intermediate beliefs—rules—reflect themes of *avoidance* or *overcompensation* (Leahy, 1996, pp. 193–194). Consider, for example, the person with social phobia whose schema reflects "defectiveness/shame: The feeling that one is defective, bad, unwanted, inferior, or invalid in important respects" (Young, n.d.b). One might avoid experiencing the schema by avoiding social situations in which conversation is necessary ("If I avoid parties, I won't be seen as boring, so I should avoid all parties"). One might overcompensate by becoming a center-of-attention clown ("If I am always clowning around, people won't see how boring I am, so I must be the perpetual clown at parties"). When one is avoiding and/or overcompensating for a schema, one is responding to the schema rather than stopping to examine it. Thus, the schema continues unchallenged.

In summary, distorted schemas are, by nature, self-perpetuating, and people tend to respond to them with avoidance or overcompensation. For all these reasons, distorted schemas themselves tends to go unidentified, unexamined, and, therefore, unchanged.

The Personality Change Process

Basic Principles of Change. Lasting change consists of the ability to neutralize a dysfunctional mode, that is, to use the conscious control system to shift into a more functional, minor mode. Unfortunately, dysfunctional modes tend to be self-perpetuating and to go unidentified and unexamined. Consequently, a shift is not likely to occur spontaneously in the course of normal life. It is much more likely to occur under the special conditions of the therapeutic situation.

Change Through Counseling. The cognitive therapist seeks to help a client learn how to shift himself or herself out of dysfunctional mode[s] into more functional mode[s]. Because a mode operates holistically and is maintained through feedback between the various components, theoretically an intervention targeting any component—cognitive, emotional, motivational, or behavioral—should achieve a shift. However, some components are more amenable than others to change; for example, the motivational and emotional components are less accessible to direct influence than are the cognitive, behavioral, and physical components. It is not effective to suggest that a client "just feel more motivated" or "just feel less sad." However, those components can be affected indirectly through direct intervention with the other components: inviting a depressed person to consider a different perspective, to participate in a behavioral experiment, or to take an antidepressant medication. A further consideration is that research shows intervention with the physical component—by taking antidepressants—tends to be effective only as long as one takes the medication; when medication is discontinued, one is likely to experience relapse. Furthermore, behavioral experiments such as, upon awakening in the morning, getting up and accomplishing a simple task rather than languishing in bed, affect the physical mode via cognition: "I will (and do) feel better if I get up and accomplish something easy." Ultimately, therefore, effective, lasting change occurs through a fundamental shift in the cognitive component of a mode, whether addressed through cognitive or through behavioral strategies.

In the process of cognitive therapy, the counselor relies on the client's desire to change. The counselor invites the client to collaborate by learning some of the basic principles of cognitive therapy. With that knowledge, the client can then join the counselor in a process of coinvestigation that can result in change. With the counselor's help and in response to guiding questions, the client identifies situations in which he felt extreme or undue emotional reactions and/or behaved in some undesirable, self-defeating way; identifies the cognitions—thoughts and/or images—related to the extreme emotions or unwanted behavior; considers the cognitions not as self-evident conclusions but as testable hypotheses; tests those hypotheses for their reasonableness and usefulness; finding any that are unreasonable and/or not useful, modifies them in the direction of more reasonable and/or useful cognitions; and practices the modified cognitions and, often, the new behaviors that the new cognitions potentiate. As the client learns these skills, he becomes increasingly active and directive during sessions and the counselor less so, until he is reasonably well equipped to discontinue therapy and proceed on his own.

Beck and Weishaar (2000) summarized that "cognitive therapy employs a learning model" (p. 255) that "teaches patients to use conscious control to recognize and override maladaptive responses" (p. 242). "The shift to normal cognitive processing is accomplished by testing the erroneous inferences that result from biased [information] processing. Continual disconfirmation of cognitive errors, working as a feedback system, gradually restores more adaptive functioning" (p. 244).

Leahy (1996) noted that "cognitive therapy is the *power of realistic thinking, not the power of positive thinking*" (p. 24). Beck concurred and added that, similarly, the concept that client problems are essentially "cognitive" is not meant to imply that their problems are "all in their head"—imaginary. Quite the contrary,

> Patients may have serious social, financial, or health problems as well as
> functional deficits. In addition to real problems, however, they have bi-

ased views of themselves, their situations, and their resources that limit their range of responses and prevent them from generating [effective] solutions. (Beck & Weishaar, 2000, p. 254)

It is those biased views that cognitive therapy targets to create lasting, constructive change in all aspects of functioning.

The Client's Role. Motivation to change. Clients usually come to counseling complaining of persistent, intensely distressing emotions or painful consequences to such emotions and associated behaviors. From the cognitive perspective, those distressing emotions and behaviors are components of major/primal modes activated by distorted cognitions. When in pain, people naturally seek corrective action. Because of the self-perpetuating nature of the modes, the person is unable to generate a corrective alternative for himself, so he seeks counseling in an attempt to find less painful, more pleasurable alternative ways of being.

Indeed, the client's pain is the counselor's ally. "[A mechanism] of change common to all successful forms of psychotherapy [is] . . . the patient's emotional engagement in the problem situation" (Beck & Weishaar, 2000, p. 259). Without that engagement, as is often the case with mandatory clients such as those referred by the court, counseling is much less likely to be successful.

Capacity for change. Beck and Weishaar (2000) described the characteristics of the client most likely to benefit from cognitive therapy. Socioeconomically, "cognitive therapy is effective for patients with different levels of income, education, and background" (p. 260). Attitudinally, it works best with clients who can accept the client role and who take responsibility for actively coping with their problems. Emotionally, the ideal client can tolerate the anxiety of carrying out experiments and can persist to complete the counseling process. Cognitively, clients can best benefit if they "have adequate reality testing (i.e., no hallucinations or delusions), good concentration, and sufficient memory functions. . . . As long as the patient can recognize the relationships among thoughts, feelings, and behaviors and takes some responsibility for self-help, cognitive therapy can be beneficial" (Beck & Weishaar, 2000, p. 260).

Responsibility for change. The client in cognitive therapy is expected to join the counselor in sharing equal responsibility for client change. The client must be active, collaborating with the counselor to set the session agenda, describing situations in which problems occurred, and providing information about distressing emotions and behaviors and associated cognitions—picture images and/or verbal thoughts—that occurred during those situations. The client actively learns how to mentally convert convictions into hypotheses and test them for validity as well as how to modify invalid hypotheses into more functional cognitions. The client must be willing to carry out homework assignments after each session, consisting of activities like keeping thought records, conducting behavioral experiments to test the validity of cognitions, and practice thinking reformulated cognitions and doing new behaviors that they make possible (Beck & Weishaar, 2000). The client also is best served who is willing to give the counselor honest feedback after each session about what was and was not helpful.

Source of resistance. Cognitive therapists (Beck, 1996; Beck & Weishaar, 2000; J. S. Beck, 1995) tend not to refer to client "resistance" to change, perhaps because of the adversarial connotation of the phrase that seems inconsistent with a collaborative approach, and tend more to speak simply in terms of why a client in cognitive therapy *does not change*. Before embarking on possible reasons, it is important to note that the feedback a counselor solicits at the end of each session, inquiring into what the client found helpful or not helpful, is designed to help the counselor continuously tailor counseling specifically to the client's needs and therefore avoid "resistance." Nevertheless, even with the routine solicitation and use of client feedback, clients sometimes still do not change (Beck & Weishaar, 2000).

Perhaps the most fundamental reason is that the client does not perceive herself to have a problem, or does not perceive her problem to be a real threat to her vital interests. In either case, she will lack the emotional involvement to carry her through the risks and challenges of changing her basic beliefs (Beck & Weishaar, 2000).

Even if she sees her problem as a vital threat, changing her thinking and staying with the therapy process involve effort, some discomfort, and perseverance. Her tolerance for discomfort may be insufficient to the challenge of change (Beck & Weishaar, 2000). Other client factors in the absence of change include dysfunctional beliefs about therapy, such as that it requires no effort on the client's part, or about the therapist, such as that he or she will be controlling.

Some reasons clients do not change have less to do with the client than with the therapist. "The therapist may lack rapport or may have failed to provide a rationale for a procedure; an assignment may be too difficult for the patient . . . there may be a lack of consensus on the aims and goals of therapy" (Beck & Weishaar, 2000, p. 260). Therefore, when clients do not change, counselors look to themselves as much as to their clients for causes and solutions.

The Counselor's Role. *Goals of counseling.* "The goals of cognitive therapy are to correct faulty information processing and to help patients modify assumptions that maintain maladaptive behaviors and emotions" (Beck & Weishaar, 2000, p. 254). The counselor seeks to engage the client's conscious control system to meta-cognize: think about the cognitive system involved in the client's problematic mode; inquire into the reasonableness and usefulness of the automatic thoughts, intermediate thoughts, and, ultimately, the core beliefs, that underlie her distressing, self-defeating emotions and be-haviors

"Cognitive therapy initially addresses symptom relief, but its ultimate goals are to remove systematic biases in thinking and modify the core beliefs that predispose the person to future distress" (Beck & Weishaar, 2000, p. 254). It also aims to arm the client with the skills to address future distress if and when it does occur.

Characteristics of an effective counselor. Cognitive therapists affirm the research on the critical role the counseling relationship plays in positive out-come in psychotherapy (Asay & Lambert, 1999). Therefore, the cognitive counselor is, first and foremost, warm, empathic, and genuine (Beck & Weishaar, 2000; Burns, 1992). These attitudes, and their associated skills such as nonverbal attending and verbal reflection, are considered absolutely nec-essary for client change.

However, they are not sufficient. In addition to the essential therapeutic qualities, a cognitive counselor must have expertise in the theory and tech-niques of cognitive therapy. She is collaborative, working *with,* not *on,* the client. She respects the client as the expert on his own experience, and "does not regard the patient's self-report as a screen for more deeply concealed ideas" (Beck & Weishaar, 2000, p. 243). She provides a rationale for each procedure she uses, demystifying the counseling process. She has interest and aptitude in investigation, joining the client in discovering his own idio-syncratic manifestations of the cognitive profiles of psychological disorders.

"The cognitive therapist eschews the word 'irrational' in favor of 'dys-functional' because problematic beliefs are nonadaptive rather than irratio-nal. They contribute to psychological disorders because they intervene with normal cognitive processing, not because they are irrational" (Beck & Weishaar, 2000, p. 244). Similarly, once a client identifies a dysfunctional belief, the cognitive therapist does not employ "disputation" strategies but invites the client to collaborate in "co-investigation" strategies. In this pro-cess, she is able to use logic and to question skillfully, guiding the client through the reasoning process. She opts for co-investigation on the assump-tion that a client will more easily accept, and more likely put to use, conclu-sions he arrives at through his own conscious control system rather than arguments forcefully asserted by an external authority.

The effective cognitive therapist is observant and flexible, able to notice and respond to changing client needs. If the client needs support, she pro-vides it. If the client seems ready to learn, she can competently teach the client the principles of cognitive therapy. As clients express cognitive distor-tions in their normal course of speech, she can identify them. When clients are first learning how to identify and evaluate cognitive distortions, they often need considerable guidance; the effective cognitive counselor can then take the lead. Toward the end of counseling, clients usually have become quite able to move on their own through the process of identifying, examining, and reformulating cognitive distortions; the counselor is able to relinquish the lead and, instead, follow. Another aspect of the cognitive counselor's flexibility is the ability to use self-disclosure when it serves the client's counseling goals.

> Flexibility in the use of therapeutic techniques depends on the targeted symptoms. For example, the inertia of depression responds best to behavioral interventions, while the suicidal ideation and pessimism of depression respond best to cognitive techniques. A good cognitive therapist does not use techniques arbitrarily or mechanically, but with sound rationale and skill and with an understanding of each individual's needs. (Beck & Weishaar, 2000, p. 255)

The effective cognitive therapist also displays flexibility by being open to client feedback. Receiving and incorporating client feedback affirms the counselor's respect for the client as expert on his own well being and strengthens the collaboration between counselor and client.

Finally, the effective cognitive therapist has received formal, supervised training in cognitive therapy (Beck & Weishaar, 2000). She takes responsibility for continuing education to fortify and add to her therapeutic skills.

Stages and techniques. Regarding overall structure, cognitive therapy is designed to be short term. Most clients with DSM-IV-TR Axis I disorders achieve their counseling goals within 12 to 16, and up to 25 weeks. Clients with personality disorders may require longer duration. Cognitive counselors usually meet with clients weekly for 45-minute sessions. Some will conduct longer intake sessions, and in the case of moderate to severe client problems, they will see the client twice a week for a few weeks and then move to weekly sessions. After clients have met their therapeutic goals, they typically return once a month for 2 months for follow-up/booster sessions (Beck & Weishaar, 2000).

A cognitive counselor usually see clients in her office, but in the case of clients with phobias, the counselor will meet with the client in a real-life setting relevant to the phobia, such as, in the case of an elevator phobia, a building with elevators. "Cognitive therapists give their patients their home phone numbers in case of emergency" (Beck & Weishaar, 2000, p. 264).

> Whenever possible, and with the patient's permission, significant others, such as friends and family members, are included in a therapy session to review the treatment goals and to explore ways in which the significant others might be helpful. This is especially important when family members misunderstand the nature of the illness, are overly solicitous, or are behaving in counterproductive ways. Significant others can be of great assistance in therapy. (Beck & Weishaar, 2000, p. 264)

Regarding the therapeutic relationship, as previously stated, it is collaborative (Beck & Weishaar, 2000). The cognitive counselor seeks to convey warmth, empathy, and genuineness. As fits the client's needs, at some times the counselor is directive, and at other times the client takes the lead.

Throughout counseling, the counselor enacts several roles. As necessary, the counselor serves as *nurturer*. Some clients benefit from little or none, others from nurturance around the beginning of counseling when they are severely distressed and have not yet begun stable improvement, and yet others, usually clients with personality disorders, may require intense nurturance well into the process of therapy. On a related note, Burns (1992) distinguished between the counselor's *relationship establishment and maintenance skills*, including nonverbal attending; reflection of feeling, content, and meaning; and gentle, open-ended questioning, and *specific change strategies* that enable the client to shift modes by intervening in the cognitive system, including Socratic questioning (further explained below), designing behavioral experiments, and assigning relevant homework. He estimated that he spends, on average, 50% of therapeutic time enacting each of these two skill sets. With clients who arrive at therapy functioning relatively well, he might spend 5% of time on relationship and 95% on change; with poorly functioning clients, such as those with personality disorders, he might spend 90% on relationship and 10% on change.

During the change strategies portion of the therapeutic process, all cognitive counselors generally progress through a series of roles that begin more directive and end nondirective: teacher of cognitive principles, guide for how to apply the principles in the client's unique case, catalyst of corrective experiences in which clients experience change and its benefits, and consultant who responds to requests for points of refinement by increasingly self-reliant clients (Beck & Weishaar, 2000).

Regarding assessment, cognitive therapists use both objective and subjective approaches to conduct "a thorough examination of the client's developmental history and his or her own idiosyncratic meanings and interpretations of events" (Beck & Weishaar, 2000, p. 249), to determine initial severity of client distress, to specify problems and related goals, to assess progress toward goals, and to solicit feedback from the client throughout the course of counseling. Clients are asked to complete objective data prior to the first session, and before and after each session. Prior to the first session, cognitive clients are likely to complete a background questionnaire. One of us (JMH) has adopted Arnold Lazarus' *Multimodal Life History Inventory* (Lazarus & Lazarus, 1991) for this purpose. Depending on the client's presenting problem, he might complete one or more self-report inventories at the beginning, and periodically throughout, counseling to assess initial severity of, and progress in overcoming, those specific problems. At Beck's Center for Cognitive Therapy, the instruments used most frequently are the *Scale for Suicide Ideation*, the *Anxiety Checklist*, and the *Dysfunctional Attitudes*

Scale (Beck & Weishaar, 2000, p. 260) the *Beck Depression Inventory* (BDI), the *Beck Hopelessness Scale*, and/or the *Beck Anxiety Inventory*. Also useful in identifying clients' vulnerable schemas is Young's (n.d.c) *Schema Questionnaire*.

To learn about the client's subjective perspectives, the cognitive counselor uses the clinical interview at the beginning of counseling and clinical inquiry—both verbal and through some routine forms—throughout counseling. The counselor uses the initial clinical interview

> to obtain background and diagnostic data; to evaluate the patient's stress tolerance, capacity for introspection, coping methods, . . . to obtain information about the patient's external situation and interpersonal context; and to modify vague complaints by working with the patient to arrive at specific target problems to work on. (Beck & Weishaar, 2000, p. 256)

The interview also enables the counselor to learn the client's expectations of the counselor and the counseling process and, when necessary, negotiate and modify those expectations (Beck & Weishaar, 2000, p. 260).

Verbal forms of clinical inquiry throughout counseling include the counselor opening each session with a question about how homework went. The counselor supplements clients' verbal reports with their completion of routine forms. These include the Daily Record of Dysfunctional Thoughts, in which the client identifies an upsetting event; the specific emotion(s) involved; the strength of those emotions using a scale from 1 (lowest the client ever experienced) to 100 (highest the client ever experienced); the automatic thoughts—verbal thoughts and/or pictorial images—that seemed to "feed" the distressed emotions; the cognitive distortions evident in those thoughts; more realistic and useful reformulated thoughts; and, upon substitution of the original thought(s) for the reformulated thought(s), the strength of one's emotions, from 0 to 100. Another routine form for feedback purposes is Burns' (1989) Client's Report of Counseling Session. The form includes the Empathy Scale that asks the client to rate 10 items addressing the "health" of the therapeutic relationship, and it provides a place for the client to write anything that bothered them about the last session, what they found helpful from the last session, and what they might want to address in their next session.

> In general, relief from symptoms is indicated by changes in scores on standardized inventories such as the BDI, changes in behavior as indicated through self-monitoring and observation by others, and change in thinking as evident in such measures as the Daily Record of Dysfunctional Thoughts, . . . by the outcome of the [weekly] homework assignments, . . . in the relative ease with which a patient challenges automatic thoughts, the decrease in frequency of maladaptive cognitions and behaviors, the increase in ability to generate solutions to problems, and improved mood. (Beck & Weishaar, 2000, p. 261)

Regarding change strategies, cognitive therapists always employ verbal and behavioral strategies to help clients develop the skills to identify, evaluate, and reformulate dysfunctional cognitions. Though cognitive therapists reflect the general counseling profession's preference for "skills over pills" in combating dysfunction, they are not averse to employing medication under certain circumstances. Those circumstances conform to the general standard of care: when the client is a serious danger to himself (suicidal) or someone else (homicidal), when the client is so distressed that he is unable to benefit from talk/action therapy, or when the client is strongly in favor of medication, even after experiencing in the first counseling session how cognitive techniques can relieve distressing symptoms. The cognitive counselor sees medication as only a short-term solution and believes that long-term improvement and reduced chances of relapse result from change in the client's schemas/core beliefs and the client's acquisition of skills to shift to, and maintain, more functional modes.

One of the counselor's goals in the first session is to give the client a "taste" of how cognitive therapy can relieve distressing symptoms. Enabling the client in the first session to experience how cognitive therapy can bring relief can instill hope—particularly important if the client is feeling hopeless/suicidal—and help the client feel motivated to carry out the first homework, which usually involves self-monitoring of feelings, behaviors, and thoughts. For example, a client with depression mentioned in his first session that he worried that his difficulty concentrating might indicate a brain tumor.

Counselor: So when you think you might have a brain tumor, you feel worried or anxious. On a scale from 1 (low) to 10 (high), how worried or anxious do you feel when you think about the possibility of having a brain tumor?

Client: I don't know. (Pauses to think.) Probably a 7.

Counselor: OK. A 7. Now, actually, you've described several symptoms of depression, such as your feeling sad a lot of the time, feeling low energy, not feeling hungry, feeling like sleeping a lot more than usual, and feeling worthless. I notice you haven't mentioned any typical symptoms of brain tumor like a rather sudden increase in severe, prolonged headaches; loss of the actual ability to move or speak; or loss of actual physical sensation. Is that right that you haven't noticed any symptoms like that?

Client: No, not those kinds of things.

Counselor: Well, actually, difficulty concentrating is a well-known symptom of depression. Because you haven't had any of the more typical symptoms of brain tumor, but you have several symptoms of depression, and difficulty concentrating is one of those, it's fairly certain that your difficulty concentrating is just part of your depression, which we can address here, and isn't a brain tumor.

Client: Huh (appears to be thinking about what the counselor said).

Counselor: You look a bit relieved. When you think about the evidence that your difficulty concentrating is much more likely an aspect of your depression than an indication of a brain tumor, how anxious do you feel on that scale from 1 to 10?

Client: Not as much. Probably about a 2 or 3.

Counselor: OK. So, when you examined the actual evidence, and revised your original thought accordingly, your worry and anxiety went down from a 7 to a 2 or 3. It's a lot less distressing to feel a 2 or 3 than a 7. This is pretty much the process that we'll be doing, and that you'll be learning how to do on your own, with other troubling feelings you're having, like your sadness and lack of motivation.

After the initial session, later sessions follow a kind of formula (Burns, 1980; Greenberger & Padesky, 1995; Padesky & Greenberger, 1995). The client brings in situations that occurred since the last session in which he felt distressed and/or acted in some self-defeating way. This specificity of concerns sets the agenda for the session. Then, together, counselor and client move through a series of steps. Early in counseling, the counselor guides the client through the steps; later, as the following description will illustrate, the client moves through the process virtually independently.

The client prioritizes the situations. Focusing on the top priority, he describes the upsetting event, identifies what emotion(s) he was experiencing and what actions he took, and specifies how strong the emotion(s) were by rating from 1 to 100. Thinking back, the client "takes himself back" to the moment in the situation when he first realized he was emotionally upset, and he or the counselor asks what Beck has called "the fundamental cognitive probe for identifying automatic thoughts" (Dattilio & Padesky, 1990, p. 29): "At the moment I first realize I am upset, *what is going through my mind* in the way of thoughts or images?" He jots down what usually is a list of verbal thoughts and/or picture images, stopping when he has gotten them all down. Out of this list, one thought usually stands out as the "hot thought" (Greenberger & Padesky, 1995)—the one that seems most to "feed" the distressing feeling. He identifies the hot thought and then examines it for cognitive distortions. Finding some, he examines the evidence for and against the thought. If he finds that the evidence is not very strong, he reformulates the thought into a form that the evidence *better* supports. Thinking that thought, he again rates the strength of his emotion.

During the early and middle phases of counseling, when the client is learning the process described above, the counselor and client spend a large abount of time with the counselor asking questions—a particular type of question—and the client responding. This special question-and-answer dialogue is called *Socratic dialogue*. The counselor carefully forms questions to facilitate new client learning. Though Socratic dialogue is used at every stage of the process, it is especially important during the phase of "examining the evidence." Socratic questions are not "leading questions" that imply a predetermined answer. Socratic questions are asked in a truly open manner, with the counselor prepared to hear the client respond differently than she expects. With client and counselor truly in agreement on, and both invested in, therapeutic goals, a good therapeutic relationship in place, a relevant hot thought identified, and the counselor's open attitude and skillful posing of questions, the client is highly likely to examine his automatic thoughts—and eventually his intermediate thoughts and core beliefs—nondefensively and, in the process, discover something new and useful.

Following is a Socratic dialogue between counselor and client. The client is the husband in couple counseling during an individual session. He is describing a situation that occurred 2 days previously in which his wife declined to have sex with him. He responded with angry hostility, and she had not spoken with him since. As he describes the incident and his reactions to it, he becomes increasingly upset and concludes by declaring, "My sexual needs in this marriage are *not* getting met!"

Counselor: Zero!

Client: That's right: Zero!

Counselor: And how angry are you feeling right now, on a scale from 1 (low) to 10 (high)?

Client: An 8!

Counselor: OK. So you're pretty angry! You tell yourself that your sexual needs are getting met at a zero level, and you feel really mad! (Counselor pauses.) I wonder if you're willing to stop and examine this situation a little more closely.

Client: (Calming down slightly, says begrudgingly) I guess.

Counselor: OK. Let's take a look at that automatic thought. (Pauses briefly to give the client a little more time to shift into his conscious control system.) Let's review what you and your wife have told me during our conjoint sessions so far. The two of you have sex once or twice a week. Is that right?

Client: Yes.

Counselor: And both of you enjoy sex when you have it?

Client: Yes.

Counselor: You also have some complaints. You would like sex somewhat more often, sometimes within a day or two of the last time, and with more variety and novelty, not just the same routine. Is that right?

Client: Exactly.

Counselor: In fact, your wife has responded to some of your requests for novelty from time to time?

Client: That's right—on occasion.

Counselor: So taking everything into account that we've just reviewed—the frequency of your sexual encounters and the quality of them—both the extent that you enjoy them and the ways you'd like them to change, overall, how satisfied do you feel with your sex life, on a scale from 1 to 10?

Client: Well, usually around a 5 or 6.

Counselor: What's the lowest you've experienced?

Client: Probably a 5.

Counselor: And the highest?

Client: Probably a 7 or 8.

Counselor: So your average satisfaction is a 5 or 6, ranging from 5 to 7 or 8.

(*Client* nods)

Counselor: So, then, how true is it that your sexual needs are being met at a zero level?

Client: It's not true. But I'm not really satisfied.

Counselor: Yes, I understand that you'd like more frequency and novelty. Let's do a cost/benefit analysis of telling yourself zero and generating a lot of anger in yourself. What are the advantages of that?

Client: I get my point across. I get to let her know how frustrated I feel.

Counselor: OK! You can feel pretty confident that she knows how much you're hurting. Anything else?

Client: I guess when I'm angry, I don't notice my frustration so much. I'd rather feel angry than frustrated.

Counselor: OK! The power of anger feels better to you than the powerlessness of frustration. Anything else?

Client: (Introspects for a moment.) No, I guess that's it, mainly.

Counselor: OK. How about the costs?

Client: She hasn't talked to me for 2 days. That's been pretty miserable. That tension all the time.

Counselor: So you don't like the feeling of tension and isolation between the two of you. Anything else?

Client: It will probably be *more* than a week before things calm down enough that she'll want to have sex again.

Counselor: So you actually end up having sex *less* often. Anything else?

Client: I have to apologize and make it up to her. That takes extra effort and is uncomfortable.

Counselor: So you end up spending a lot of mental and emotional energy repairing things between the two of you. Anything else?

Client: No, those are the main things.

Counselor: OK. So on the plus side, you get your point across that you're hurting and you get to feel powerful rather than powerless—at least for awhile. On the negative side, you end up putting up with the tension and isolation, having sex *less* often, and spending a lot of mental and emotional energy repairing things between the two of you.

(*Client* nods)

Counselor: So, if you had to distribute 100 points between the two sides, the benefit side and the cost side, like 50/50 or 60/40, what does the proportion feel like to you, of which side weighs out heavier, the benefits or the costs?

Client: I'd say, 35/65.

Counselor: So the costs outweigh the benefits. So let's review. When your wife declines to have sex with you, you tell yourself your sexual needs are getting met at a zero level, and you feel really angry and say something hostile. In fact, you feel satisfied at about level 5 or 6, ranging from 5 to 8. And getting angry and saying something hostile ends up costing you about twice as much as it gains you. So what would be a more accurate thought that might save you from that cost?

Client: I guess to keep a perspective and remind myself that one "no" doesn't make my sexual satisfaction a zero; it's actually a 5 or 6 overall, even with the "no's."

Counselor: And when you do think "I'm satisfied overall at a level 5 or 6," how angry do you feel, 1 to 10?

Client: About a 3.

Counselor: So thinking "zero" is less accurate and less useful, and reminding yourself that you're satisfied at a 5 or 6 level is more accurate and more useful and helps you feel less angry: from an 8 on the anger scale to a 3. And when you're less angry, you're less likely to be hostile. And it doesn't change the fact that you still have requests of her that you still want to pursue. So that "5 to 6" thought sounds like a good thought to rehearse mentally.

Client: (noticeably more calm) Yeah, but what am I supposed to do? She's never going to change.

Counselor: Never?

Client: (chuckles, catching himself in his automatic thought) OK! But you have to admit, the evidence isn't very promising!

Counselor: (smiling) I hear you. And I think you posed a great question: What else *could* you do that holds more promise in getting you what you want than getting angry and hostile does? Let's look at that. [Counselor proceeds to the topic of effective communication.]

You may have noticed that the Socratic questions employed some purposeful strategies. In the example, the counselor used *scaling* and *cost/benefit analysis.* She chose scaling—asking him to look at the evidence and rate his sexual satisfaction—as an antidote to his all-or-nothing thinking ("zero"). Scaling is a form of "thinking in shades of gray" (Burns, 1980). She chose the cost/benefit analysis as an antidote to what she perceived as emotional reasoning; when her client said, "Yes, but I'm not really satisfied," it was as if he was saying, "If I *feel* dissatisfied, it follows that I *act on* what I'm feeling." The cost/benefit analysis helped the client evaluate the *actual* advantages and disadvantages of acting on his hostile impulse.

Other cognitive strategies include what Leahy (1996) called "examining criteria" and what Burns called "define terms": The client is asked to define key terms and labels such as "worthless," "success," and "failure," which often results in the client moving from global, overgeneralized concepts to specific, often achievable goals. On a related note is Burns' (1992) "semantic method." He gave the example of the client who believed, "I am a defective human being." After trying a few cognitive strategies unsuccessfully, Burns suggested that the client try the slightly semantically different thought, "I am a human being with defects." The client reported a noticeable shift: Being a defective human being meant he was essentially "wrong," whereas being a human being with defects meant he was essentially OK with identifiable problems he could potentially improve upon.

The "double standard technique" involves the client applying his own beliefs about himself to someone he loves. A client who was sexually abused as a child and believes he is "damaged goods" is invited to imagine that his best friend was similarly abused as a child and imagine telling his friend that the friend is damaged goods. Clients usually recoil at such a suggestion. They then can be invited to role play what they would say to the friend who believed that about himself, and then to practice saying the same things to himself.

Reattribution (Beck & Weishaar, 2000) is an antidote for the cognitive distortions of personalization and blame. In the case of personalization, the client reduces excessive guilt by identifying factors besides himself that contributed to some occurrence. In blame, the client reduces anger at others for their role in some occurrence by taking appropriate responsibility for his own contributions.

In externalization of voices (Leahy, 1996), the client who has successfully challenged a distorted belief is invited to switch roles with the counselor. The counselor tries to convince the client of the *distorted* beliefs, and the client argues how the beliefs are inaccurate and not useful and argues in favor of more accurate and useful beliefs.

Sometimes, clients' automatic thoughts are realistic, yet their responses seem excessive. For example, the client who became despondent when she heard her mother's cancer diagnosis reported the automatic thought, "My mother might die soon." Under the circumstances that thought was true. In such cases, the cognitive counselor uses the "downward arrow technique": Proceeding from that automatic thought, the counselor asks, "What if that were true? What would that mean to you?" In this case, the client said, "I will be all alone in the world." Taking the arrow one level further, the client said, "I'll be miserably lonely for the rest of my life"—most likely a cognitive distortion, and one that explained her despondency.

According to Beck and Weishaar (2000), cognitive therapists also use behavioral strategies

> to modify automatic thoughts and assumptions, . . . also . . . to expand patients' response repertoires (skills training), to relax them (progressive relaxation) or to make them active (activity scheduling), to prepare them for avoided situations (behavioral rehearsal), or to expose them to feared stimuli (exposure therapy). Because behavioral techniques are used to foster cognitive change, it is crucial to know the patient's perceptions, thoughts, and conclusions after each behavioral experiment. (p. 263)

Burns (1999) listed more than 50 techniques for inquiring into the functionality of a cognition. Obviously, it is beyond the scope of this introductory chapter to describe them all. The interested reader is referred to the recommended resources at the end of this chapter.

As therapy progresses, a counselor looks for, and invites the client to look for, themes among similar and recurring automatic thoughts that suggest rules and, ultimately, schemas by which the client lives. Because particular phrasing seems to "really fit," the counselor is open to the client taking time to search for and find the most fitting words, and to reword phrases offered by the counselor. Because a client's deepest beliefs are tied modally to his deepest feelings, clients often are deeply moved when a schema is empathically identified. In fact, a client's tears are often an indicator that a core belief has been identified. Of course, the display of emotion in cognitive therapy is not an end in itself; lasting change results from modification of cognitions. That modification also can be deeply touching; consider the client abused in childhood at the very moment when he first *truly grasps* that he *is not* "damaged goods."

Regarding client "resistance," Beck and Weishaar (2000) affirmed that some clients cannot tolerate the anxiety of giving up old ways of thinking and do not progress in cognitive therapy. Others, who leave counseling as soon as they experience some symptom relief but before they have modified core beliefs, are prone to relapse. Even with clients committed to change, difficulties can occur. When they do, the counselor applies cognitive principles to the situation. If she has erred, she accepts responsibility without engaging in the distortion of personalization, and she takes corrective action. If the problem arises from a cognitive distortion on the part of the client, such as mistaken expectations of the counselor, the counseling process, or the process or consequences of change, she invites the client to identify and examine those expectations as he would any cognition (Beck & Weishaar, 2000).

Judith Beck (1995) noted that cognitive therapy is present-focused. However, she clarified that the cognitive therapist shifts attention to the client's past in three situations: "if the client strongly desires it, if the focus on the present produces no change, and/or if the counselor believes that a client's understanding of how he developed his cognitions will significantly facilitate the counseling process" (p. 7). Thus, cognitive therapists believe that a failure to explore past origins of clients' cognitions can sometimes contribute to an absence of change in counseling.

Like all counselors, cognitive counselors feel challenged when working with challenging diagnoses such as personality disorders and with clients who have histories of unsuccessful therapy. For such cases,

> Beck, Rush, Shaw, and Emery (1979) provide [the following] guidelines . . . 1) avoid stereotyping the patient as *being* the problem rather than *having* the problem; 2) remain optimistic; 3) identify and deal with your own dysfunctional cognitions; 4) remain focused on the task instead of blaming the patient; and 5) maintain a problem-solving attitude. By following these guidelines, the therapist is able to be more resourceful with difficult patients. The therapist also can serve as a model for the patient, demonstrating that frustration does not automatically lead to anger and despair. (Beck & Weishaar, 2000, p. 265)

CONTRIBUTIONS AND LIMITATIONS

Interface with Recent Developments in the Mental Health Field

Effectiveness of Psychotherapy. Among the American Psychological Association's list of empirically supported approaches to the treatment of mental disorders, the number of cognitive and cognitive-behavioral treatments is second only to that of behavioral treatments (Crits-Christoph, 1998). A structured approach, it is amenable to description in treatment manuals that enable clinicians to follow standardized procedures that increase consistency in the care provided to clients.

Cognitive therapy is well established as an effective treatment for unipolar depression, with or without medication. Similarly, clients with anxiety-related problems, whether or not they begin counseling using anti-anxiety medication, can be expected to learn to function well without medication. Additional "controlled studies have demonstrated the efficacy of cognitive therapy in the treatment of panic disorder, . . . social phobia, . . . substance abuse, . . . eating disorders, . . . marital problems" (Beck & Weishaar, 2000, p. 247) and health problems such as irritable bowel syndrome and chronic pain (Crits-Christoph, 1998). Though not empirically supported, cognitive therapy is used along with medication in the treatment of bipolar disorder, psychotic depression, and schizophrenia (Beck & Weishaar, 2000).

Nature/Nurture. Probably more than any other approach to psychotherapy, cognitive therapy explicitly incorporates recent research on genetic origins of behavior as expressed in innate temperament and predispositions to psychopathology. Whereas current research indicates a slightly greater influence of environment than heredity in personality development, cognitive therapists attribute a much greater influence on one's learning history to personality development.

Pharmacotherapy. Probably more explicitly than other therapeutic approaches, with the possible exception of behavioral, cognitive conceptualization specifies the conditions in which the use of psychotropic medication is affirmed. Though the cognitive therapy goal is to arm the client with cognitive techniques instead of medication whenever possible, cognitive therapists do not eschew the use of medication, especially in the acute conditions that characterize the beginning of therapy and, as stated above, as an ongoing resource in cases of bipolar disorder and psychoses.

Managed Care and Brief Therapy. Cognitive therapy is the darling of managed care. It is inherently a brief approach. By virtue of the consistency of service provided by practitioners' use of treatment manuals, the quality of client care is enhanced.

Diversity Issues. Many of the well-known cognitive therapy sources (Beck, 1976; Beck & Weishaar, 2000; Burns, 1980) have not explicitly addressed diversity issues such as ethnicity, gender, and sexual orientation. In part, this may be due to the strong emphasis in cognitive therapy on understanding the client's subjective perspective, through which diversity issues are expressed. Beck and Weishaar (2000) did state that cognitive therapy is effective with clients from a variety of backgrounds and socioeconomic statuses.

A refreshing exception to the pattern described above is Padesky and Greenberger's (1995) *Clinician's Guide to* "Mind Over Mood." In a section entitled "Adapting Mind Over Mood to a Client's Culture," the authors address specific ethnic groups, socioeconomic status, religious/spiritual affiliations, and gender and sex-role values, including sexual orientation.

One of us (JMH) has been intrigued by the similarity between basic cognitive precepts and the very first of the sayings of the Buddha: "We are what we think; all that we are arises with our thoughts; with our thoughts, we make the world" (Byrom, 1976). Websites of two cognitive therapists, David Burns (www.feelinggood.com) and Jeffrey Young (www.schematherapy.com), have explicitly addressed the relationship of cognitive therapy to religion and spirituality.

Technical Eclecticism. Though explicit cognitive strategies are clearly cognitive and behavioral in nature, Beck and Weishaar (2000) clarified that any technique consistent with the cognitive theory of emotional disorders is, essentially, fair game. This technical eclecticism includes the use and adaptation of experiential techniques such as the empty chair technique that grew out of Gestalt therapy (J. S. Beck, 1995). In essence, any technique is endorsed that a counselor employs to help a client modify dysfunctional cognitions and acquire self-help skills.

Though none of the best-known resources on cognitive therapy alludes to dreamwork, an excellent text, Hill's (1996) *Working With Dreams in Psychotherapy*, describes in detail a cognitively based approach. In brief, Hill asserted that recurrent and other salient dreams that people recall upon awakening reflect the psyche's attempt to accommodate incongruent experience into existing schemas. By discovering the meaning of dream symbols, which are idiosyncratic to the dreamer, the accommodation process can be facilitated.

For example, you may recall from the chapter on psychoanalysis the dream of an adult female client. This dream was very simple. It began with a baked potato with a lengthwise cut and the white part of the potato "plumped up" through the opening. A single green pea came and landed in the potato. The potato was dry, and the pea was supposed to moisten it, but the pea was completely inadequate to the job.

Using Hill's (1996) approach, the client explored associations to the dream, such as peas being her husband's favorite vegetable, "pea" associating with "penis." At one point, after several associations, the meaning of the dream became absolutely clear to her. Over the past several months, her husband had become increasingly impotent (im-potato-ant?), and she had become increasingly frustrated, sexually. But her frustration was more than sexual. Over the past couple of years, she'd had the increasing sense that she was continuing to grow, to be psychospiritually "fertile," while her husband seemed to be languishing, remaining in a familiar but "small" and, for her, inadequate and unsatisfying lifestyle. Up to the time of this dreamwork, she had had very vague feelings that now became crystal clear to her. Her marriage, which had been extremely satisfying for many years, had gradually over the past couple of years become unsatisfying. This shift in her basic perception of her marriage was only the beginning of an important chapter in this client's counseling, but it was major catalyst in her forward movement.

DSM-IV-TR Diagnosis. Along with behavior therapy, cognitive therapy explicitly references DSM-IV-TR diagnoses. Whereas DSM-IV-TR descriptions of mental disorders do not speculate beyond descriptive criteria for various diagnoses, Beck has supplemented cognitive therapists' concepts of mental disorders by offering cognitive profiles for many of the diagnostic categories.

Weaknesses of the Theory

Until the mid-1990s, Beck's theory was based on a linear model of cognitions, emotions, and behavior. To accommodate recent research, he modified his model (Beck, 1996), adding the holistic concepts of modes and the energetic concepts of charges to his personality theory. The theory has become more accurate, but less elegant. It continues to evolve, and elegance may still be in its future.

Considering the extent to which cognitive therapists are willing to modify the theory in light of research, one of us (JMH) finds it curious that a particular, seemingly salient research finding has not been incorporated. Several researchers have found that "[nondepressed] people are highly vulnerable to illusions including unrealistic optimism, overestimation of themselves, and an exaggerated sense of their capacity to control events. The same research indicates that depressed people's perceptions and judgments are often less biased" (Alloy, 1995, p. 4). These findings suggest that the extent to which one's cognitions fit the evidence, that is, the extent to which they are "realistic," is not as adaptive as the extent to which cognitions help people achieve their goals, that is, the extent to which they are "useful." Regarding Leahy's (1996) assertion that cognitive therapy is not the power of positive thinking but of realistic thinking, we wonder if it is not better said to be the power of *useful* thinking.

Distinguishing Additions to Counseling and Psychotherapy

Before cognitive therapy, person-centered therapists honored the client's phenomenological perspective and respected the client's wisdom about his own well being, but it lacked structure and efficiency. Behavior therapy, on the other hand, brought to psychotherapy specificity and a systematic approach to problem identification and treatment, but many practitioners found it mechanistic. Cognitive therapy has combined the best of both approaches: the humanity and respect of the person-centered approach with the structure and efficiency of the behavioral approach.

The cognitive profiles of mental disorders offer a foundation for the conceptualization of clients. The use of treatment manuals has improved the quality of client care, specifying what works and enabling uniform application of those specifications. Extensive research in cognitive therapy has established its usefulness.

CURRENT STATUS

Cognitive therapy is a major, if not the major, force in current psychotherapy. The Center for Cognitive Therapy at the University of Pennsylvania, affiliated with the University of Pennsylvania Medical School; the Beck Institute in Bala Cynwyd, Pennsylvania; and 10 other centers in the United States offer training in cognitive therapy. Several publications, including a newsletter and several professional journals, are devoted to the dissemination of information about ongoing developments in cognitive therapy. Cognitive therapy is well represented among presentations at conferences of mental health professionals.

One assessment instrument, in particular, "the Beck Depression Inventory . . . has been used in hundreds of outcome studies and is routinely employed by [mental health professionals] to monitor depression in their patients and clients" (Beck & Weishaar, 2000, p. 247).

SUMMARY

Since the 1960s Beck and his associates have been developing cognitive therapy, an active, problem-focused approach to psychotherapy that targets the cognitive aspect of the personality to affect constructive change in all aspects: emotional, behavioral, motivational, and physical. Extensive research has supported the effectiveness of cognitive therapy across a wide variety of mental disorders. As research continues to be conducted, the cognitive approach to counseling will continue to evolve.

RECOMMENDED RESOURCES

Books

Beck, A. T., & Weishaar, M. E. (2000). Cognitive therapy. In R. J. Corsini & D. Wedding (Eds.), *Current psychotherapies* (pp. 241–272). Itasca, IL: F. E. Peacock. An excellent overview of the theory and therapy.

Beck, J. S. (1995). *Cognitive therapy: Basics and beyond.* New York: Guilford. An extremely clear presentation, replete with clinical examples of specific techniques.

Greenberger, D., & Padesky, C. A. (1995). *Mind over mood: Change how you feel by changing the way you think.* New York: Guilford. An excellent client introduction to cognitive therapy and step-by-step workbook.

Padesky, C. A., & Greenberger, D. (1995). *Clinician's guide to* Mind Over Mood. New York: Guilford. Indispensable counselor's accompaniment to the client workbook.
Frieberg, R. D., & McClure, J. M. (2002). *Clinical practice of cognitive therapy with children and adolescents: The nuts and bolts.* New York: Guilford. Outstanding guide for counselors who specialize in work with children.
Dattilio, F. M., & Padesky, C. A. (1990). *Cognitive therapy with couples.* Sarasota, FL: Professional Resource Exchange. Good introduction to work with this special population.
Hill, C. E. (1996). *Working with dreams in psychotherapy.* New York: Guilford. An unparalleled guidebook for working with dreams, period. Bonus: Her approach is based in a cognitive perspective.

Media

Beck, A. (1986). Cognitive therapy. *Three approaches to psychotherapy III,* Part 3 [Motion picture]. Corona Del Mar, CA: Psychological & Educational Films, 3334 East Coast Highway, #252, Corona Del Mar, CA 92625. Dr. Beck works with a depressed client, Richard.
Gladding, S. (Director), & Holden, J. M. (Featured Counselor and Editor). (2002). *Cognitive counseling* [videotape]. Produced by Association for Counselor Education and Supervision and Chi Sigma Iota. Available from Microtraining Associates, 25 Burdette Ave., Framingham, MA 01702. One counselor demonstrates her "10 steps of the cognitive counseling routine" with three clients: a young, middle-aged, and older adult. Accompanied by a 20-page student workbook.
Padesky, C.: Dr. Padesky has developed five extremely good videotapes for training mental health professionals in cognitive therapy. She also has numerous audiotapes. They are available at her website: http://www.padesky.com/tape_pdf_cat.htm

Websites

Jeffrey Young has an excellent website at www.schematherapy.com
David Burns also has an interesting website at www.feelinggood.com
Aaron Beck's webpage is at http://mail.med.upenn.edu/~abeck/index.html
Another excellent website is Robert Leahy's at the American Institute for Cognitive Therapy: http://www.cognitivetherapynyc.com/problemsaddressed.html

REFERENCES

Alloy, L. B. (1995, April). Depressive realism: Sadder but wiser? *The Harvard Mental Health Letter,* pp. 4–5. (74 Fenwood Road, Boston, MA 02115)
American Psychiatric Association. (2000). *Diagnostic and statistical manual of mental disorders* (4th ed., text rev.). Washington, DC: Author.

Arnold, M. (1960). *Emotion and personality* (Vol. 1). New York: Columbia University.

Asay, T. P., & Lambert, M. J. (1999). The empirical case for the common factors in therapy: Quantitative findings. In M. A. Hubble, B. L. Duncan, & S. D. Miller (Eds.), *The heart and soul of change.* Washington, DC: American Psychological Association.

Bandura, A. (1977). *Social learning theory.* Englewood Cliffs, NJ: Prentice-Hall.

Beck, A. (1976). *Cognitive therapy and the emotional disorders.* New York: Meridian.

Beck, A. (1996). Beyond belief: A theory of modes, personality, and psychopathology. In P. Salkovskis (Ed.), *Frontiers of cognitive therapy* (pp. 1–25). New York: Guilford.

Beck, A. (1999). *Prisoners of hate: The cognitive basis of anger, hostility, and violence.* New York: HarperCollins.

Beck, A. T., Rush, A. J., Shaw, B. F., & Emery, G. (1979). *Cognitive therapy of depression.* New York: Guilford.

Beck, A. T., & Weishaar, M. E. (2000). Cognitive therapy. In R. J. Corsini & D. Wedding (Eds.), *Current psychotherapies* (pp. 241–272). Itasca, IL: F. E. Peacock.

Beck, J. S. (1995). *Cognitive therapy: Basics and beyond.* New York: Guilford.

Burns, D. (1980). *Feeling good: The new mood therapy.* New York: New American Library.

Burns, D. (1989). *The feeling good handbook: Using the new mood therapy in everyday life.* New York: William Morrow.

Burns, D. (1992). *Feeling good: Fast and effective therapy for anxiety and depression and the resistant client.* Paper presented at the 24th Annual North Texas Counseling Conference, Denton, TX, February 28.

Burns, D. (1999). http://www.feelinggood.com/tutorials/full_distortion_list.htm

Byrom, T. (1976). *Dhammapada: The sayings of the Buddha.* Boston: Shambhala.

Chomsky, N. (1965). *Aspects of the theory of syntax.* Cambridge, MA: Massachusetts Institute of Technology.

Crits-Christoph, P. (1998). Training in empirically validated treatments: The division 12 APA task force recommendations. In K. S. Dobson & K. D. Craig (Eds.), *Empirically supported therapies: Best practice in professional psychology.* Thousand Oaks, CA: Sage.

Dattilio, F. M., & Padesky, C. A. (1990). *Cognitive therapy with couples.* Sarasota, FL: Professional Resource Exchange.

Ellis, A. (2000). Rational emotive behavior therapy. In R. J. Corsini & D. Wedding (Eds.), *Current psychotherapies* (pp. 168–204). Itasca, IL: F. E. Peacock.

Frieberg, R. D., & McClure, J. M. (2002). *Clinical practice of cognitive therapy with children and adolescents: The nuts and bolts.* New York: Guilford.

Greenberger, D., & Padesky, C. A. (1995). *Mind over mood: Change how you feel by changing the way you think.* New York: Guilford.

Hill, C. E. (1996). *Working with dreams in psychotherapy.* New York: Guilford.

Kelly, G. (1955). *The psychology of personal constructs.* New York: W. W. Norton.

Landon, P. J. (1998). Review of The History Channel Presents The Fifties, *Film&History*, H-Net Reviews. Retrieved March 18, 2003, from http://www.h-net.msu.edu/reviews/showrev.cgi?path=118.

Lazarus, A. A., & Lazarus, C. N. (1991). *Multimodal life history inventory* (2nd ed.). Available from Research Press, 2612 Mattis Avenue, Champaign, IL 61822.

Lazarus, R. (1984). On the primacy of cognition. *American Psychologist, 39,* 124–129.

Leahy, R. (1996). *Cognitive therapy: Basic principles and applications.* Northvale, NJ: Jason Aronson.

Loftus, E. (1980). *Memory.* Reading, MA: Addison-Wesley.

Padesky, C. A., & Greenberger, D. (1995). *Clinician's guide to Mind Over Mood.* New York: Guilford.

Piaget, J. (1954). *The construction of reality in the child.* New York: Basic.

Piaget, J. (1965). *The moral judgment of the child.* New York: Free.

Piaget, J. (1970). *Genetic epistemology.* New York: W. W. Norton.

Weishaar, M. E. (1993). *Aaron T. Beck.* Thousand Oaks, CA: Sage.

Young, J. (n.d.a). Coping styles. Retrieved April 15, 2003, from http://www.schematherapy.com/id62.htm

Young, J. (n.d.b). Early maladaptive schemas and schema domains. Retrieved April 15, 2003, from http://www.schematherapy.com/id73.htm

Young, J. (n.d.c). Schema therapy YSQ-L2. Retrieved April 15, 2003, from http://www.schematherapy.com/id53.htm

CHAPTER 11

RATIONAL EMOTIVE BEHAVIORAL THERAPY

BACKGROUND OF THE THEORY

Historical Context and Founder's Biographical Overview

Albert Ellis, the father of Rational Emotive Behavior Therapy (REBT) was born in Pittsburgh in 1913. When Ellis was 4 years old, his family moved to New York, where he since has made his home. Ellis was the oldest of three children and struggled with serious kidney problems that continue to this day. In addition to the physical ailments, Ellis learned to survive on his own, as his father was a traveling businessman and Ellis perceived his mother to be emotionally absent. To deal with his physical and family issues, young Ellis developed a philosophy of viewing life that later became REBT. A famous example of his early application of REBT ideas is how a teenage Ellis confronted his reluctance to approach girls. He approached 100 girls in a 1-month period to test his fear that rejection would lead to some personal catastrophe. The experiment proved to be a "success": He was rejected, and the horrible tragedy that he feared never occurred.

Ellis received his bachelor's degree from City College of New York in 1934, and 8 years later, decided to pursue a graduate degree in clinical psychology. He received his Ph.D. in 1947 from Teachers College, Columbia. Heavily influenced by psychoanalysis, for 6 years Ellis practiced psychoanalytic therapy and wrote in the areas of personality assessment and marriage and family therapy.

In the early 1950s, Ellis became increasingly dissatisfied with the impact of analytic forms of therapy. Having personally undergone analysis for over 3 years and being seemingly perplexed and uncertain of its long-term impact, he began to experiment with briefer forms of analysis, adding components that were more congruent with his personal philosophy of change. Time after time, he found the passive approach of the analyst to have little effect on the belief systems that seemed to sustain symptom reformation in clients.

Why, when I seemed to know perfectly well what was troubling a patient, did I have to wait passively, perhaps for a few weeks, perhaps for months, until he, by his own interpretive initiative, showed that he was fully ready to accept my own insight? Why, when patients bitterly struggled to continue to associate freely, and ended up by saying only a few words in an entire session, was it improper of me to help them with several pointed questions or remarks? (Ellis, 1962, p. 7)

In an attempt to find a more permanent solution for his clients, Ellis explored several modes of therapy and philosophy. In 1956, at the American Psychological Association's conference, Ellis introduced the psychological community to his philosophy of change. Labeled Rational Therapy, Ellis constructed a method for change that largely resembled his own experiments as a child and adolescent. This form of therapy directly confronted clients' irrational belief systems and taught and encouraged clients to learn how to dispute and conquer their maladaptive ways of thinking.

Since the theory's inception, it has undergone several modifications and name changes. Unhappy with the interpretation that Rational Therapy meant ignoring emotion, Ellis changed the name to Rational Emotive Therapy. Finally, in 1993, Ellis again modified the name to Rational Emotive Behavior Therapy to honor the theory's "highly cognitive, very emotive, and particularly behavioral" elements (Ellis, 1993, p. 1). Throughout the various name changes of his therapeutic approach, Ellis has remained a prolific writer and presenter. His abrasive and energetic presentation style is as unique as his philosophy of therapy. He has written over 60 books and 700 scholarly articles on the theory and practice of REBT and continues to refine and expand his approach. He continues to train individuals at the Albert Ellis Institute in New York and encourages research through the *Journal of Rational-Emotive and Cognitive Behavior Therapy*. In addition to his research agenda, Ellis also sees clients weekly in both individual and group sessions.

Philosophical Underpinnings

REBT, like every other theory of counseling, is formed on the foundation of the philosophical leanings of its creator. According to Bernard and Joyce (1984), REBT's philosophical underpinnings deal with questions such as, "how we know what we know (epistemology), the role of logical thought and human reason in the acquisition of knowledge (dialectics), goals for which individuals strive (values), and the criteria and standards for deciding how to relate to others (ethics)" (p. 39).

Epistemology and Dialectics. REBT rests on the assumption that our knowledge is based on our selective interpretations of our world. In other words, how a person perceives events and people will largely impact how that person thinks, feels, and behaves. This constructivist philosophy has its roots with the first century A.D. Roman slave philosopher, Epictetus, who wrote, "humans are disturbed not by things, but by the views they take of things" (1955, p. 19). Consider the following scenario: A professor hands back graded exams to her students and announces, "Everyone did very well on this exam." As she gives each exam to a student, she notices various facial expressions, some positive, some distraught. Below are some of the internal interpretations based on identical stimuli.

Professor: Everyone made above an 80 on this exam. Therefore, everyone
  did great.
Student #1: I made an 85. That's horrible. I always make A's. Maybe I'm not
  cut out for graduate school. I guess I didn't study enough.
Student #2: I made an 85. That stinks. The professor did not teach us the
  material very well. I feel cheated. The test was so unfair.
Student #3: I made an 85. That's so cool. I've never made above a C before on
  an exam. I am going out to celebrate!

The philosophy underlying REBT also can be considered relativistic, because it assumes that no absolute truth or reality exists but that each person's truth or reality is internally defined and experienced. Believing that reality exists only as one perceives it might be comforting, but it also carries a co-existing belief that other realities are just as appropriate as one's own. Therefore, being understanding of others' subjective views and being flexible in one's own would be essential within the REBT philosophy.

The role of logic in the acquisition of knowledge is central to REBT. Rationality and logic dictate that individuals consider all pertinent evidence before drawing a conclusion. At the very least, a rational thinker would understand that no conclusion can be based on all information, so the conclusion/ belief may need to be modified or changed as new evidence is discovered. However, most people fail to be flexible or logical in their thinking. In fact, people typically make judgments based on very little data. For example, the adolescent girl who believes, "He hates me" when her boyfriend does not call her one evening; the father who thinks his son is not interested in spending time with him because the son has something else planned on one particular date; or the employee who believes the boss is angry at him because she did not say hello to him in the hall are all examples of how people are impacted emotionally and behaviorally when they draw conclusions based on limited information. Because REBT holds that rational thinking is the mediator between the world and the individual, teaching people how to identify irrational thinking and how to produce rational thinking is the primary thrust of REBT.

Responsible Hedonism. According to REBT philosophy, enjoying life is a primary goal and rational individuals strive to maximize pleasure. Pure hedonism would involve achieving pleasure at any cost, but REBT adherents, who emphasize personal responsibility, advocate responsible hedonism. A person who is responsibly hedonistic is able to create short- and long-term goals that maximize pleasure potential. Practitioners of this philosophy use "hedonic calculus" to determine the relationship between short-term pleasure and long-term goals (Bernard & Joyce, 1984). A pure hedonist would sacrifice long-term goals for short-term pleasure, while a responsible hedonist would forgo short-term pleasure if it meant achieving long-term pleasure goals. Consider the example of marriage. For many people the decision to get married means commitment to a long-term goal that includes a multitude of individually perceived pleasurable components, including consistent companionship, lack of loneliness, support, caretaking when ill, a sexual partner, children, and financial support. When a casual sexual encounter becomes available, a pure hedonist would participate in the affair with the justification, "Pleasure is the goal. I'm not going to consider how this fling might destroy my marriage. I want to have fun now." A responsible hedonist, using hedonic calculus, would see that a moment of pleasure that the affair might produce would greatly jeopardize the long-term pleasure goals that marriage might produce. Therefore, participating in the affair would be viewed as irrational, and the affair would be avoided to maximize future pleasure potential.

Humanism. REBT embraces the humanistic philosophy of appreciating the individuality, creativity, and autonomy of the person. REBT proponents believe in the innate worth of every individual and believe that dysfunction arises out of a need to criticize self and make comparisons between self and others. Ellis views these comparisons and self-evaluations as thoroughly destructive and irrational. No universal criteria exist regarding right and wrong, pretty and ugly, or good and bad. Therefore, all such criteria are arbitrary, and to criticize oneself for not living up to some arbitrary standard sets one up for unnecessary distress. Self-evaluations that arise out of the comparisons are equally harmful. Ellis believes that rational beings have unconditional self-acceptance and have no need or desire to put themselves down. REBT proponents hold that all of these comparisons and evaluations contradict the ability to rationally experience a situation and degrade the inherent worth of every human being.

Personality Development

Nature of Humans

Function of the Psyche. According to REBT, humans have the innate desire to survive, feel pleasure, and attain self-actualization. Ellis contends that humans are largely influenced by two innate biological tendencies. One is the overwhelming tendency for individuals to think and behave irrationally. According to Ellis, the need to self-evaluate and self-criticize seems to be inborn, as is the need to accept assumptions about self, others, and the world that cannot be empirically validated. Ellis believes that even when raised in the most rational of environments, a person will still construct irrational beliefs about self, others, and the world (Ellis, 2000b).

The other biological tendency is to think rationally and be pro-active in identifying and disputing irrational beliefs in order to live a more rational, self-actualized life. Ellis contends that, because of this biological capacity, each person has power over, and responsibility for, one's own change process. As one chooses to dispute irrationality and be more logical and flexible, one is actively self-actualizing. Although the slip into irrationality may be natural, Ellis believes it is equally natural for each person to live a rational life. In essence, every person chooses to succumb to the innate tendency to be emotionally disturbed and can choose at any time to follow the equally innate tendency to become undisturbed again.

Structure of the Psyche. The basic structure of the personality according to REBT is parsimoniously summarized in Ellis' ABC model. The ABC model is traditional in that it includes specific internal structures of the psyche like those hypothesized by Freud. However, unlike Freud's three parts of the personality, Ellis' structural model is comprised of a universal processing system. In this system, the A is the *activating* event or activating experience, which may be external, such as one's beloved spouse filing for divorce, or internal, such as a sharp pain in the abdomen. The C represents the emotional and/or behavioral *consequence*. After hearing of the divorce plans, one might feel depressed or angry and might not go to work for awhile. After noticing the sharp pain, one might feel anxious and contact one's physician.

Most people reading the scenarios above would assume that A, such as the divorce, caused C, the feelings of depression and anger and the behavioral withdrawal. However, from the REBT perspective, A does not cause C; instead, one's *beliefs* about A cause C. In other words, one's emotions and actions are not the consequences of internal or external activating events; they are the consequences of one's beliefs about those activating events. In the scenario described above, the belief about divorce that led to depressed and angry feelings and behavioral withdrawal were probably something like, "My spouse is the only one I could ever love. Without my spouse, I'll never be happy. My spouse has 'done me wrong' by initiating divorce and should have been more loyal." According to REBT, the belief about the activating event, not the activating event itself, causes the emotional and behavioral consequences.

Some readers might conclude that the person in the above scenario is rational: that divorce would always cause the kinds of feelings and behavior that were described. The ABC model demonstrates that how one thinks about

TABLE 11.1

A	B	C
Divorce	"That is unfortunate, but not the end of the world. She is free to make her own choices, and I can move on with life."	Brief mourning Resume dating
Divorce	"That is horrible! I must be a complete loser. No one will ever love me again! I am all alone, unlovable, and I can't live without her."	Intense depression Hopelessness Extensive withdrawal Suicide
Divorce	"Who cares? I can find someone else. I never really loved her anyway and am definitely better off without her; think of all the money I'll save! I can't wait to start dating again!"	Apathy Excitement Relief

a stimulus is the greatest predictor of how one will react to the stimulus. In addition, because beliefs are individually constructed by individual experience and perception, no belief is universally applied to the same stimulus. Consider the different beliefs applied to the activating event of divorce with the corresponding emotional/behavioral consequences, listed in Table 11.1.

If A *caused* C, the same C would always follow a given A. But this is not the case; different Cs follow the same A. As the ABC model clearly demonstrates, the different Cs are the result of different Bs. It is beliefs, not activating events, that cause emotional and behavioral consequences in the aftermath of activating events. As the reader will soon see, REBT practitioners utilize this dynamic ABC model to assess and change clients' irrational beliefs into more rational beliefs that produce more satisfying consequences.

Role of the Environment

Although Ellis affirmed a biological basis for irrational and rational living, he also viewed one's environment as having an impact on personality development. Specifically, Ellis (1979) listed the following possible environmental influences that have been updated to include modern examples: instruction from parents, teachers, other relatives, and coaches; media, such as radio, music, television, books, magazines, and the internet; environmental rewards such as wages, honors, or anything else that fits a societal definition of success; environmental consequences such as legal sanctions, social sanctions, and anything that does not fit a societal definition of success; organized groups such as churches, athletic teams, gangs, socioeconomic status, political affiliation, and occupation; peer groups and romantic affiliations. All of these (and this list is not exhaustive) influence an individual's thoughts, emotions, and behaviors. In terms of dysfunction, Ellis believed that many beliefs involving absolutistic musts and shoulds emanate directly from environmental injunctions, such as "You must make all A's to be a good son"; "You should marry before age 25 or you are unlovable"; "You must do what you are told or you are bad"; or "Life should be fair."

Overall, Ellis hypothesizes an interdependent relationship between biology and environment. "REBT holds that people's environment . . . reaffirms but does not always create strong tendencies to think irrationally and to be disturbed. . . . People naturally and easily add rigid commands to socially inhibited standards" (Ellis, 2000b, p. 179). Demonstrating a stance consistent with REBT philosophy, Ellis declines to identify either influence as absolutistically causative. Instead, he affirms the influence of both heredity and environment, along with the individual's responsibility for perceiving, interpreting, and believing in a uniquely personal way.

Interaction of Human Nature and Environment in Personality Development

View of Healthy Functioning. In REBT philosophy, the rationality of one's belief system is directly related to one's level of mental health. A rational individual is "pragmatic, logical and reality based" (Dryden & DiGiuseppe, 1990, p. 3). Rational people are flexible in their approaches and conclusions, are willing to make mistakes and learn from them, and base interpretations and conclusions on realistic data. When faced with situations they find difficult, rational people interpret the events as hurtful or disappointing but not catastrophic. For example, a rational person who is confronted with a disagreement with a friend will form beliefs about this activating event that are characterized by a *rational evaluation of badness* ("I do not like fighting with Justin, but it is not the end of the world"); a sense of *tolerance* (being open to other points of view, understanding that disagreements are a part of every relationship, and actively pursuing other aspects of life while attending to the disagreement); and a sense of *acceptance* ("I am human, so I can make mistakes. I might be wrong about this, and that is fine. I can live with being wrong. If this relationship ends because of this disagreement, I can move on, too").

Expressing a philosophical kinship with the existential writers of his time, Ellis (1962) considered the work of Braaten (1961) to be a fitting summary of rational health. The main themes are described below, as cited in Ellis (1962, p. 124), along with added commentary on how they fit within a rational life, including movement toward self-actualization.

1. **You are free; define yourself.** A rational person accepts both the privilege and responsibility of free will. With the knowledge that one is free comes

an understanding that "I alone" am accountable for personal feelings, thoughts, and behaviors.

2. **Live in dialogue with your fellow human beings.** REBT maintains that the environment holds many opportunities for feedback about reality. Isolation breeds belief stagnation and raises the risk of reindoctrination of irrational beliefs. An open dialogue with others, free of negative comparisons and self-evaluations, is the essence of self-acceptance and self-actualization. A rational person is open to receiving input from others and weighing it while keeping in mind the next theme.

3. **Your own experiencing is the highest authority.** Taken in isolation, some might view this theme as being inherently selfish and possibly contradictory to the preceding theme. However, this theme directly addresses the dynamic of being responsible for self and not blaming others and/or putting too much credence in other people's views and opinions of your life. Overall, intertwined with the other themes, this theme is the heart of self-actualization: unconditional self-acceptance of strengths and weaknesses.

4. **Be fully present in the immediacy of the moment.** For REBT practitioners, one cannot be rational and live in the past or the future. Both worrying and moping about what happened 10 years ago, and being consumed with anxiety about what might happen tomorrow, are ineffective and do not maximize the potential for long-term happiness. Confronting current ways of thinking and collecting information from the present provides the road to change and, ultimately, to effective, satisfying living.

5. **There is no truth except action.** As discussed in the biographical overview, Ellis became disillusioned with psychoanalysis because of its emphasis on insight over action. Ellis believes that in order to change, one needs to actually do something different. Merely understanding why a behavior or belief developed will not necessarily lead to change. Active disputation of irrational beliefs and consistent participation in new ways of thinking, feeling, and behaving are hallmarks of a rational life.

6. **You must learn to accept certain limits in life.** Ellis maintains that rational individuals recognize personal strengths and weaknesses, and although it is appropriate, even courageous, to continuously try to improve, one must recognize that no one is perfect. Perfection is an impossible goal; therefore, believing that perfection is or should be attainable is irrational. Accepting personal fallibility as a condition of life and not as a catastrophe is a key element to rationality and thus self-actualization.

View of Unhealthy Functioning. Unlike many schools of therapy that focus on why and how maladjustment develops, REBT is more concerned with how individuals maintain psychological disturbance. As noted previously, all people have a biological predisposition to act and think irrationally. Biology coupled with experience provides a level of vulnerability to disturbance that is then solidified when individuals reindoctrinate irrational beliefs in the present. Basically put, all people are vulnerable to "crooked thinking," and the only way to remediate the problem is to work passionately to "think straight."

Although REBT espouses psychological interactionism, wherein a person's thoughts, feelings, and behaviors are seen as interdependent and overlapping, the core of maladjustment is seen to rest with the belief system. REBT holds that humans tend to think absolutistically about activating events. These absolute conclusions tend to take the form of three basic musts, shoulds, and oughts (Dryden & DiGiuseppe, 1990), outlined below.

1. **Musts about self:** These beliefs are statements about one's worth and expected success. Examples include, "I must be liked by others, and if someone does not like me, then I am horrible" or "I can't stand it when I am not picked first for the team. I am a failure if I am not the best." Self-directed musts typically lead to consequences of guilt, shame, inferiority, and underachievement.
2. **Musts about others:** These beliefs are directed at others and make demands on others' behavior. "You must treat me with respect, because when you don't, I fall apart" and "You mustn't get angry with me, because if you do, it means you do not love me, and I can not handle that" are common examples. Anger, resentment, jealousy, passive-aggressive behavior, and acts of violence are consequences of beliefs based on these musts.
3. **Musts about the world:** These beliefs make demands about how life should be at all times and under all conditions. Examples include, "Life must be fair, and if it is not, then I am a victim" and "Life should be happy, and if I'm not completely happy, then I am miserable." Helplessness, hopelessness, procrastination, and suicide are all possible consequences of these beliefs.

When used individually or as a collection or theme of beliefs, these musts construct a "musturbatory" belief system or ideology that is considered, at its core, irrational, because it increases the probability that the beliefs will interfere with goal achievement and personal satisfaction (Ellis, 1977a).

Individuals who adhere to an irrational philosophy based on the core "musturbatory" beliefs typically derive specific types of beliefs based on the three core musts. These irrational "musturbatory" derivatives, contrasted with rational beliefs, are characterized by rigid belief systems and typically occur in the following patterns:

1. **Awfulizing:** The situation is perceived as more than 100% bad. "I missed my bus, and that is horrible. My whole week is ruined!"
2. **I-Can't-Stand-It-itis:** These beliefs indicate a low tolerance for frustration and a belief that a catastrophe will occur if life maintains the current level of perceived stress. "I can't stand my job. It's too mundane and stupid. I will explode if I have to work there one more day."
3. **Damnation:** This pattern is characterized by intense criticism of self,

other(s), or the environment. "I am such a complete loser. No wonder I can't get dates. I'm worthless."

4. **Always and Never Thinking:** This irrational style uses a small amount of evidence to make sweeping conclusions about self, others, or the environment. "My mom won't take me to the movies. She never does anything for me."

Reindoctrination and perpetuation of the irrational belief cycle can take many forms. One common example is becoming disturbed about a primary disturbance. These "secondary disturbances" not only make the symptoms of the primary problem worse but also make the primary problem more difficult to treat because the secondary disturbance acts as a barrier between rational disputation and the primary problem. Common examples of secondary disturbances include becoming anxious about being anxious (see APA, 2000, section on "Panic Disorder with Agoraphobia"), feeling hopeless about depression, and worrying about insomnia. In each example the secondary disturbance prevents treatment of the primary disturbance, increases the level of irrationality, and thus increases the amount of psychological disturbance.

Before leaving the topic of mental health and unhealth, it is important to realize that not all negative emotions are unhealthy. Crawford and Ellis (1989) discussed how rigid beliefs about activating events yield self-defeating consequences, while flexible beliefs about activating events yield self-actualizing consequences. Even "negative" emotions can be either inappropriate or appropriate (Table 11.2). In this way, REBT parallels existential theory by differentiating inappropriate from appropriate negative emotions based on their impact on the individual.

Table 11.3 outlines Ellis' view of common irrational and rational beliefs.

The Personality Change Process

Change Through Counseling

The Client's Role. REBT is an active and directive form of therapy and demands a high level of interaction and cooperation on the part of the client. The client needs to be motivated to learn about the REBT philosophy, to be open to exploring the belief system as the point of change, and to possess

TABLE 11.2

Inappropriate negative emotions	Appropriate negative emotions
Experienced as emotional pain	Experienced as a warning, an alert
Motivate self-sabotaging behaviors	Motivate self-actualizing behaviors
Paralyze; inhibit goal achievement	Energize; facilitate goal achievement

TABLE 11.3

Ten major irrational beliefs	Ten major rational beliefs
1. I must have love or approval from all people I find significant.	1. While it is desirable for me to be approved of and loved, I do not need it to survive. It is most desirable to concentrate on self-acceptance and on loving instead of being loved.
2. I must be thoroughly competent, adequate, and achieving.	2. It is more advisable to accept myself as an imperfect creature with human limitations and fallibilities.
3. When people act obnoxiously and unfairly, I should blame and damn them and see them as bad, wicked, or rotten individuals.	3. People often behave unfairly, stupidly, and inconsiderately and it would be better if they were helped to change their ways rather than to be severely damned and punished. It is not legitimate to rate their total worth on the basis of their individual acts.
4. Things are awful, terrible, and catastrophic when I get seriously frustrated, treated unfairly, or rejected.	4. While it is undesirable to fail to get what I want, it is seldom awful nor is it intolerable.
5. Emotional misery comes from external pressures and I have little ability to control or change my feelings.	5. Because I mainly create my own emotional upsets, I can change them by thinking more rationally.
6. If something seems dangerous or fearsome, I must preoccupy myself with and make myself anxious about it.	6. Worrying will not magically make things disappear. I will do my best to deal with potentially distressful events and when this proves impossible, I will accept the inevitable.
7. It is easier to avoid facing many life difficulties and self-responsibilities rather than to undertake more rewarding forms of self-discipline.	7. In the long run, the easy and undisciplined way is less rewarding than is the longer range approach to pleasure and enjoyment.
8. My past remains all-important and because something once strongly influenced my life, it has to keep determining my feelings and behavior today.	8. Continual rethinking of my old assumptions and reworking of my past habits can help minimize most of the pernicious influences from my childhood and adolescence.
9. People and things should turn out better than they do and I must view things as horrible and awful if I do not find good solutions to life's grim realities.	9. Whether I like it or not, reality exists and I'd better accept its existence before I set about changing it.
10. I can achieve maximum happiness by inertia and inaction or by passively and uncommittedly "enjoying myself."	10. I will tend to be happiest if I get involved in long-term, challenging work which requires the taking of risks and forces me to act against my own inertia.

From *A New Guide to Rational Living* by A. Ellis and R. A. Harper, 1997, North Hollywood, CA: Powers.

enough cognitive sophistication to grasp the process. Clients who enter therapy expecting to explore past experiences and have their feelings extensively validated will be disappointed within the REBT framework. Dryden (1990, p. 14) outlined the following that describes the numerous responsibilities the client must adhere to when working in collaboration with a REBT therapist.

1. Acknowledge the problem.
2. Identify and overcome any secondary disturbances about this problem.
3. Identify the irrational belief that underpins the primary problem.
4. Understand why the irrational belief is irrational (illogical, inconsistent with reality, and will give them poor results in life).
5. Realize why the rational alternative to this irrational belief is logical, is consistent with reality, and will give them better results in life.
6. Challenge the irrational belief to strengthen the conviction in the rational alternative.
7. Learn to use a variety of cognitive, emotional, imaginal, and behavioral assignments to strengthen the conviction in the rational belief and weaken the conviction in the irrational belief.
8. Identify and overcome obstacles to therapeutic change using the above structure, while simultaneously accepting the tendency to personally construct such obstacles.
9. Keep working against the tendency to think and act irrationally.

   The Counselor's Role.   Although the client–counselor relationship is important in REBT, it differs from the relationship endorsed in many of the other theories discussed in this textbook. Unlike Rogers, Ellis disagrees with the notion that a warm relationship provides the necessary and sufficient conditions for change. In fact, Ellis believes that devoting energy to developing warmth between counselor and client could actually interfere with and distract from the therapeutic goals. Furthermore, it could feed into a client's irrational belief that "I must be loved by everyone I find important." However, Ellis stresses that unconditional acceptance of the client is essential to promoting change, and the literature on REBT suggests that effective REBT counselors learn how to actively dispute and reject the client's behavior while unconditionally accepting the client as a striving, yet fallible, human being (Dryden & DiGiuseppe, 1990; Ellis, 1962; Ellis & Dryden, 1997; Weinrach, 1995). This "despise the behavior but embrace the person" dynamic might be difficult for novice therapists to grasp. The example below demonstrates the process.

Client: I don't know. It's just that I feel so stupid, like everybody is judging me.

Counselor: Based on that statement, you are saying that you feel stupid because everyone is judging you?

Client: Yeah, I guess.

Counselor: I don't think "everyone" has anything to do with it. I think you believe that you are stupid and are using other people to take the blame for your feelings. Let's take "everyone" out of the picture. Let's stick with you. Say "I am stupid" and then prove to me why you are "stupid."

Client: Well, I don't know.

Counselor: Sure you do. That self-evaluation that concluded that you were stupid comes from within you, so let's hear it. Convince me.

Client: Well, I'm not doing a very good job here. I feel confused.

Counselor: Is it such a catastrophe to feel confused? Is it so horrible? Confusion is part of the human condition. It seems that the only failure here today was in your ability to convince me, part of the "everyone," that you are stupid. What's your take on that failure?

Client: (laughing) It's not so bad.

In this example the counselor attacks the irrational label of "stupid" by pushing the client to personalize and define the term. The counselor normalizes the feelings of the client while demonstrating that the belief is not only internally based but also lacks empirical support. In the end, the counselor disputes the conclusion that the client is stupid and conceptualizes the original irrational belief as a mistake (failure).

Ellis (1997) maintained that effective REBT therapists are active and directive; are skilled teachers, communicators, and problem solvers; have a good sense of humor that is appropriately used in session; are not afraid to take appropriate therapeutic risks such as confronting clients; are energetic and forceful; and accept themselves as imperfect and have the courage to work on their imperfections. REBT practitioners focus primarily on the present, actively exploring, disputing the client's irrational beliefs, and instructing clients in the art of REBT. Therefore, counselors do not concentrate on taking lengthy histories and put little weight on childhood and unconscious factors when considering present dysfunction. Although REBT counselors are present oriented and typically move quickly, they may find therapeutic benefit in moving more slowly in the case of certain client styles and presenting problems, for example, trauma such as rape or incest (Dryden, 1990; Ellis, 2000b; Zachary, 1980).

Practitioners of REBT need to be aware of how their own absolutistic belief may interfere with the client's work. Ellis (1983, pp. 4–7) outlined several common irrational beliefs that therapists need to modify to work effectively with clients.

1. I have to be successful with all of my clients all of the time.
2. I have to be respected and loved by all of my clients.
3. I must be a great counselor and be more competent than any other counselor I know.

4. Because I am working so hard, my clients must also work hard and listen to what I say.
5. Because I am human, I must be able to have a good time in the session and use these sessions to get something useful for myself such as emotional satisfaction or learning how to solve my own problems.

As behavioral consequences of any of these beliefs, a counselor may inappropriately push the client to change. For example, a counselor who believes that his worth is linked to client change may push the client to change before she is ready or may develop feelings of resentment toward the client when she is not moving at the counselor's pace: "That client is just stuck. She's resistant to therapy." Conversely, a therapist who believes the client must like him at all times may not confront the client enough for fear that the client may dislike him. It is vital for REBT practitioners to explore their own belief systems and actively dispute irrational beliefs that may interfere with therapy. Seeking supervision as well as personal counseling are two ways to monitor one's beliefs and thus one's practice.

Stages and Techniques.   Although Ellis never specified a stage progression of REBT, several authors have outlined steps or stages of the therapeutic process (Dryden, 1990; Dryden & DiGiuseppe, 1990). The main stages—beginning, middle, and ending—will be discussed, followed by a brief overview of common techniques.

The beginning stage can be characterized as a time of building rapport with the client and teaching the client about the basics of REBT. Although Ellis believed that a warm relationship was not a necessary or sufficient condition for change, he did believe that the counselor and client need a working relationship to make progress. Dryden (1990) characterized a good working relationship as including: setting the parameters of counseling (fees, length of sessions, frequency of sessions), collaborating on goals, encouraging discussion of issues, demonstrating unconditional acceptance, and establishing therapeutic credibility by adopting a problem solving approach. As the therapeutic alliance solidifies, the client will be more open to confrontations and disputations on the part of the therapist.

REBT therapists take an active-directive approach from the start of therapy. Assuming that the client knows nothing about the therapeutic process and specifics of REBT, the therapist acts as an instructor in the art of irrational belief disputation. Working through the ABC model of intervention, the counselor can follow the steps outlined in Figure 11.1. By working through the disputation process using several personal issues, the client begins to internalize the therapeutic process. The client is encouraged to maximize learning by completing homework assignments that can be found in a variety of REBT-oriented workbooks (Dryden & Gordon, 1990; Ellis, 1988). The therapist's goals for the end of the beginning stage are for the therapeutic alliance to be formed and for the client to have a working knowledge of the basics of REBT.

A (Activating Event):
My father yelled at me and grounded
me for the weekend.

↓

B (Belief About A): —————————→ **Disputation**
"He is unfair. He should be more   1) What evidence supports these
caring."   beliefs?
"I am always a victim."   2) Are these beliefs helping or hurting
                                           me?
"He must understand me. Because he 3) Is it really as awful as I believe?
doesn't, my life is ruined."

↓   ↓

Consequences   **New Effect**

Unhealthy negative emotions: Healthy emotions:
Rage   Frustration
Shame   Regret
Betrayal   Disappointment

Self-defeating behaviors: Self-actualizing behaviors:
Denies responsibility for actions   Accepts responsibility for own actions
Refueses to build relationship w/dad Communicates directly with father
Sneaks behind dad's back

FIGURE 11.1
ABC Model of Intervention.

The middle stage is characterized by the client's utilization of the ABC
model to dispute core irrational beliefs. While disputing the target problem
irrational beliefs will lead to a remediation of the target problem, identifying
and disputing core irrational beliefs will also result in changes in other aspects of life. For example, a person who was having problems at work because of the irrational belief, "I must always be liked by my coworkers" can
identify a core irrational belief, such as, "I must be liked by everyone, or I am
a complete loser." Disputing the target problem irrational belief and, later,
the core irrational belief, can have an impact on the target problem site, work,
and also on the client's other relationships, such as with the intimate partner
and children.

During this stage, the therapist often employs a wide range of techniques
to help the client engage in a rational existence and integrate new rational
beliefs. The techniques are broken down into cognitive, emotive, and behavioral techniques.

Cognitive Techniques
1. **Rational self-statements:** The client is encouraged to create a list of rational statements that dispute common irrational beliefs. "It is normal to
   make mistakes. It means I am human." "I would like to make my husband

happy, but if I don't, it is not the end of the world." "Smart people do not have to say smart things all of the time." These are examples of some client-created self-statements that are connected to their disputation work.

2. **Becoming a REBT teacher:** Others' irrational beliefs are usually much easier to identify than one's own. By encouraging clients to actively teach the principles of REBT to others, each client gains extra practice in the REBT process. The personal impact of learning through teaching is an important aspect of REBT homework and of REBT-oriented groupwork (Ellis, 1997; Ellis & Dryden, 1997).

3. **Semantic precision:** An important piece of disputing irrational beliefs is paying attention to and correcting irrational language (Dryden, 1990). For example, a client can change, "I can't possibly speak to that professor" to "I am choosing not to speak to that professor because I am afraid"; or "It would be devastating if my girlfriend did not call me this evening" to "It would be disappointing, but bearable, if my girlfriend did not call me this evening." Inherent in this precision is the recognition that expecting catastrophic outcomes is irrational and that distinguishing between needs and preferences—and fostering the latter over the former—is rational.

Emotive Techniques

1. **Imagery:** The use of imagery can take many forms in REBT. One method is to fix an image of an unpleasant activating event (A) and mentally switch from an irrational belief about A to a rational thought about A and feel the difference in the sensation of the emotional consequence (C). The goal is for the client to experience the change in emotion simply by changing the thought. In another method, the therapist uses imagery to follow the client's irrational thought to its catastrophic consequence, as illustrated below.

> *Client:* If Melissa breaks up with me, my life will be over.
>
> *Counselor:* Let's take a trip through time and get snapshots of your life assuming that Melissa breaks up with you right now. What will you look like in 2 hours?
>
> *Client:* I would be a wreck, crying and alone in my room.
>
> *Counselor:* That sounds pretty sad. Let's take a look 2 weeks from now. What will you be doing?
>
> *Client:* I don't know. Probably still sad.
>
> *Counselor:* But you will still be here, right?
>
> *Client:* Yeah.
>
> *Counselor:* Good. What about 6 months from now?
>
> *Client:* Wow, that's a long time. I guess I would be working, and dating someone else.

Counselor: You are a fast mover! What about 10 years from now?

Client: I'll be out of college. I'll have my degree and hopefully a job. Who knows, I might even be married.

Counselor: So, getting back to Melissa. You will be sad if she breaks up with you, but it is NOT the end of the world. Right?

Through imagery, the client is able to work past the catastrophe that is tied to the irrational belief about the break up.

2. **Humor:** The use of humor can be an excellent way to demonstrate the irrationality of a client's beliefs. When extended to its illogical end, the inherent nature of an irrational belief is that it is unbelievable, and sometimes even funny. One way Ellis uses humor is through constructing humorous songs that can be sung by both client and therapist. If the therapist (or client) is very creative, the songs can be tailored to the client's personal irrational beliefs. A couple constructed the following song during their time in therapy:

I Hate Me, You Hate You
(Sung to the tune of "I love you, you love me" the Barney song)

I hate me, You hate you
Now there is no one to be mean to
I am so bad, You could not love me
We're the worst example of matrimony

I hate me, You hate you
Now there's nothing left to do
But sit in the house and cry our life away
No one would miss us anyway

3. **Shame-attacking exercises:** These experiments are designed to help clients feel less intimidated and impacted by how others feel about them. Counselors can encourage clients to break minor social mores, such as skipping down the street, singing to yourself, or asking silly questions, while making note of how others respond. One of two things will happen: Either people will not notice or will respond neutrally or positively, or they will respond negatively. In the first scenario, clients will learn that they put too much pressure on themselves worrying that others will notice them making mistakes. In the second scenario, clients will learn that even when people actually think they are weird, clients can think differently. As one client put it, "You cannot imagine how liberating it was to act completely goofy. This one guy thought I was nuts. He said, 'Cut it out you freak'. The old me would have been humiliated, but I just walked away and continued my day. I was fine!" Shame-attacking exercises can

be fun and freeing for clients who obsessively worry about others' negative reactions to them, but it is emphasized that the experiments need to be legal and need not to include actions or events that could lead to injury of self or others.

Behavioral Techniques. REBT therapists realize that, to be effective, attacking irrational beliefs needs to be a consistent process and therefore must occur outside of the therapy session as homework assignments. To maximize the integration of a rational lifestyle, REBT therapists routinely assign activity-oriented homework based on in vivo desensitization and flooding models. Many of these activities are designed to help the client tolerate discomfort or encourage them to avoid procrastination (Grieger & Boyd, 1980). For example, a husband who is afraid that his request for affection may result in rejection from his wife may be assigned to ask her 10 times a day for various levels of affection, such as holding hands, hugging, and kissing, and to record the outcome. The results of his "experiment" are discussed at the next session, and the client very likely will realize that he gets more affection when he is assertive and that although he will be turned down some of the time, the rejection is not catastrophic.

The last part of the REBT counseling process is called the ending stage. The ending stage is marked by a resolution of presenting problems and, more importantly, the client's demonstrated ability to utilize the REBT disputation process as a method for problem solving. Along with termination of the therapeutic relationship, counselors can expect irrational beliefs to surface within the client regarding future success without counseling (i.e., "I must have therapy to cope. Without therapy I will go back to the way things were"). Ellis (1996, pp. 96–100) encourages clients to maintain their therapeutic gains by considering the following:

1. Reinforce therapeutic learning by reviewing what worked in counseling.
2. Continuously risk and try new behaviors. The success will add to a success mentality, and the mistakes will demonstrate that one can survive poor decisions.
3. When you do not get what you want, continuously experience and note the difference between appropriate negative feelings, such as sadness, disappointment, and/or frustration, and inappropriate negative feelings, such as panic, depression, shame, and/or extreme guilt.
4. Encourage self-motivation and dispute procrastination.
5. Practice using REBT, and teach it to friends. Practicing reinstills rational living, and the more members of a client's social system know about REBT, the more support the client is likely to receive.
6. Find pleasure in life. Developing new interests provides intrinsic and extrinsic rewards that give the person something to strive to attain.

CONTRIBUTIONS AND LIMITATIONS

Interface with Recent Developments in the Mental Health Field

Effectiveness of Psychotherapy. In 1977, Ellis (1977b) wrote an exhaustive review of studies that support the use of REBT. More than just outcome studies, Ellis outlined the key philosophical underpinnings of the theory and included over 950 citations that supported the various elements. DiGiuseppe and Miller (1977) conducted a review of empirical outcome studies and reported substantial support of the efficacy of REBT with a wide range of problems and populations. Since these two overviews, hundreds of other articles have been published citing the effectiveness of REBT when compared with other forms of therapy or with no therapy (see Engels, Garnefski, & Diekstra, 1993; Lyons & Woods, 1991; Silverman, McCarthy, & McGovern, 1992).

Nature/Nurture. When Ellis first developed REBT, he posited that disturbance was largely learned from one's environment as a child. After working with clients for many years, Ellis changed his view to incorporate the growing evidence of the role that heredity plays in psychological dysfunction. Ellis now believes that the ability to be rational and irrational is not determined by any one source but instead is the outcome of intertwining biological and environmental variables. In REBT theory, neither nature nor nurture holds ultimate sway over an individual's thought processes. Although Ellis believed that everyone has irrational thoughts and is born vulnerable to irrationality, all humans have an innate tendency toward both irrationality and rationality, one's environment encourages both, and each person has the capacity to reinstill rational or irrational belief systems.

Pharmacotherapy. Consistent with most theories of therapy, REBT supports the adjunctive use of medication for disorders where empirical studies validate a pharmacological treatment. Ellis (2000b) commented that among numerous client complaints, REBT is appropriate for "overt psychotics . . . when they are under medication" (p. 191). For REBT practitioners, the beliefs about the medication would be as instructive and important as the chemical outcome. For example, a client who believes that medication is a "magic bullet" or an "instant cure" would probably forgo therapy and thus remain irrational. REBT encourages disputation of all absolutistic beliefs, even those regarding treatment.

Managed Care and Brief Therapy. Consistent with its directive, high-energy style, REBT seems well suited for brief therapy. As noted previously, Ellis developed REBT out of his dissatisfaction with the slow and arduous process of analysis. Even when Ellis was experimenting with more active forms of psychoanalysis, he reported cutting analysis time from 100 sessions to around 35 sessions, often with better results (Ellis, 1962).

Research analyzing treatment length yielded the finding that the average number of sessions for REBT was 16.5 (DiGiuseppe, 1991). Meanwhile, Ellis has written extensively about applying REBT to even shorter time frames: from 1 session to as many as 20 structured sessions (Ellis, 1992, 1996). Ellis (2000b) outlined several approaches that can accelerate the REBT therapeutic process. For example, during the time between sessions, clients can listen repeatedly to the audiotapes of previous sessions. New insights, learning, and reindoctrination of disputed irrational beliefs can occur outside the weekly session and thus reduce the overall time spent in therapy. Additionally, the use of homework and worksheets specifically designed for REBT can be used between sessions. Such written activities also can help the client rely less on the therapist for disputation and more on individual skills after counseling has been terminated.

REBT approaches the use of diagnosis as necessary in this age of managed care. Ellis believes that, regardless of diagnosis, REBT can be helpful to the client by uncovering and disputing the irrational beliefs that contribute to the reporting of catastrophic symptomatology. However, Ellis has noted that REBT is more effective with single-issue clients than with more seriously disturbed clients, as is the case with other psychotherapeutic approaches (Ellis, 1998). Outcome studies demonstrate a correlation between clusters of certain irrational beliefs from Ellis' original list and certain specific diagnostic mental disorders (Woods, 1992).

Diversity Issues. As discussed in chapter 1, U.S. culture is quickly moving in the direction of increasing diversity. The basic tenets of REBT support flexibility in thinking and attitudes about self and others. In considering cultural diversity, counselors are encouraged not to assume that clients share the same worldview as the counselor. It is equally important for counselors to realize that cultural beliefs can be irrational, rigid, and absolutistic or rational, flexible, and preferential. Clients who believe that all people must respect their culture are likely to feel angry, frustrated, and victimized when a counselor—or anyone else—does not appreciate their diversity. Internally, if clients feel they must absolutely adhere to their cultural rules at all times, they will constantly evaluate themselves and denigrate themselves for the slightest infraction of the rules. Within the REBT theory, all clients, regardless of culture, are encouraged to replace the demandingness of musts and shoulds with preferential beliefs. It should be noted that this encouragement could violate some cultural values. REBT therapists are advised to discuss the therapeutic philosophy with the client and include it in a Professional Disclosure Form, similar to what was discussed in chapter 6.

Congruent with its underlying humanistic philosophy, REBT can help both men and women lead rational lives and move beyond rigid, stereotypical gender roles. Ellis firmly believes in the right of all individuals to live the type of lives they desire and opposes having one set of standards for men and another for women. REBT proponents recognize that women in the past have experienced gender roles that stress dependence and inferiority and currently experience gender roles containing musts and shoulds regarding independence and power. Ellis and other REBT proponents have been extremely active in designing programs for women to explore and dispute irrational beliefs related to gender roles. These programs are built around various components such as consciousness raising through group counseling; bibliotherapy emphasizing other women's struggles and successes; assertiveness training; encouraging and developing female relationships; developing positive self-messages, such as, "I am making a valuable contribution as a full-time mom"; disputing culturally based irrational relationship demands, such as "I need a man to survive" or "I should be married by the time I am 28"; and self-pleasuring assignments, including the belief, "I have a right to have fun" (Bernard, 1991, Wolfe & Russianoff, 1997).

Ellis' view of sexual orientation rests on the belief that we are born bisexual, with the ability to enjoy sexual relationships with any partner. Individuals exhibit irrationality in believing, "I must have sex only with women" or "I must have sex only with men." Ellis' 1965 book, *Homosexuality: Its Causes and Cure*, although laced with terminology linking homosexuality to dysfunction as was customary at that time, stressed that homosexuality was not inherently problematic or abnormal. However, Ellis did believe that homosexuality could be viewed as irrational because the social costs of the supposed choice of homosexual orientation are high. Faced with constant opposition, the freedom of the homosexual is reduced, so choosing to continue such behavior when it is obviously harmful would be, by definition, irrational. Mylott (1994) outlined 12 irrational beliefs that "drive gay man and women crazy" (p. 61). True to Ellis' conceptualization, many of the irrational beliefs are not gay specific and could easily apply to heterosexual men and women, such as "I need to have sex with another person" (p. 62) and "I need to be loved" (p. 63). However, a few pertain exclusively to a homosexual lifestyle: "People shouldn't be homophobic" (p. 66); "I can only accept my homosexuality if I know for certain that it is genetically determined, or that God made me gay. Otherwise, I cannot accept myself" (p. 67).

Spirituality. The issue of spirituality is an excellent example of the flexibility and growth of REBT over time. In early formulations of his theory, Ellis saw religious beliefs as irrational and contributory to emotional disturbance (Ellis, 1960, 1971, 1973). He contended that spiritual beliefs in higher powers, ultimate dictums of right and wrong, and eternal damnation or punishment usually lead people to surrender self-direction or to engage in constant self-evaluation in the form of assessment of sin, which leads to self-criticism, guilt, and shame. As Ellis (1980) concluded, "devout faith in supra human entities and powers always leads to poor emotional health and long range unhappiness" (p. 327).

Over time, numerous REBT practitioners and researchers have studied the integration of REBT philosophy with spiritual and religious ideas and philosophies (DiGiuseppe, Robin, & Dryden, 1992; Johnson, 1993; Johnson, Ridely, & Nielsen, 2000; Nielsen, Johnson, & Ridley, 2000). While much of the literature focuses on organized forms of religion, basic philosophical similarities have been found between REBT and common religious beliefs and traditions. Some of the common ground between REBT and religious/spiritual philosophies discussed in the literature (Ellis, 2000b; Johnson, 1994; Johnson, Ridley, & Nielsen, 2000; Nielsen, 1994; Nielsen, Johnson, & Ridley, 2000) includes:

• The view that all people are worthy of forgiveness and that imperfection is a part of the human condition.
• The use of education as a change agent.
• The perspective that all people have free will and thus largely create their own health or disturbance and are responsible for behaving and thinking differently ("God helps those who helps themselves").
• The encouragement of high frustration tolerance (in spiritual terms, this may be discussed as faith).

Ellis reviewed these discussions and research and, consistent with his philosophy of flexibility, integrated the new ideas into REBT. He was most persuaded by the studies that demonstrated that people who viewed their chosen God as supportive, loving, and caring were more likely to lead healthier lives than those who viewed their God as vengeful or angry (Gorsuch, 1988; Hood, Spilka, Hunsberger, & Gorsuch, 1996; Kirkpatrick, 1997). Upon considering these writings, Ellis moderated his earlier view and admitted that some absolutistic spiritual beliefs could be healthy, but he continued to believe firmly that devout, dogmatic, rigid beliefs still contribute to irrational thinking. "My view now is that religious and nonreligious beliefs in themselves do not help people to be emotionally 'healthy' or 'unhealthy'. Instead their emotional health is significantly affected by the kind of religious and nonreligious beliefs they hold" (Ellis, 2000a, p. 30).

Technical Eclecticism. Although REBT shares many similarities with person-centered, Adlerian, existential, Gestalt, cognitive, behavioral, and other theories of change, REBT is a unique theory with a distinctive approach to treatment. REBT practitioners would engage only in a technique or process that was specifically designed to illuminate and dispute the client's irrational beliefs. Therefore, theoretical eclecticism would be viewed as distracting from the elegant process of disputation. However, REBT practitioners can utilize a broad range of techniques from various schools of thought that help with the disputation process. In this regard, REBT supports and encourages technical eclecticism.

Distinguishing Additions to Counseling and Psychotherapy

Ellis' contribution to the field rests primarily in three areas: his ability to translate Adler's ideas into a more present-oriented and focused approach, his ABC model, and his forceful personality. First, he readily credits Adler with being the pioneer of cognitive forms of therapy and with contending that people generate their own disturbance via personally created beliefs about the stimuli. Ellis integrated Adler's core ideas and stripped away the childhood, family, and life task concepts, thus producing a theory based strictly on waging active war on present irrational beliefs. This here-and-now, nononsense approach makes even the "common sense" psychology of Adler seem complicated. REBT's simplified cognitive approach represented a divergence from thick intrapsychic theories, such as self-psychology, psychoanalysis, and Adlerian, and proved more scientific than some of the "touchy feely" theories of Ellis' time, such as person-centered or Gestalt.

The ABC model, developed by Ellis for specific application within REBT, represents a distinguishing characteristic. The ABC structure provided an innovative way to demonstrate not only the change process but also the basic workings of the personality. The ABC model is used as a tool for in-session demonstration and education as well as for homework and ongoing learning by the client.

Although some might debate whether a theorist's personality could be a contribution to the field, Ellis' instructional and therapeutic manner has had an impact on the world of therapy. His abrasive, humorous, and confrontational style represented a stark contrast to past and contemporary theorists and practitioners. His personal style not only contributed to the directive ideas found in his theory, but it also demonstrated to a world of therapists that not all therapists were warm and cuddly. Counseling students often respond strongly to Ellis' handling of clients in video demonstrations. One therapist (Johnson, 1980) has responded to Ellis' therapeutic style by publishing a journal article titled, "Must the Rational Emotive Therapist Be Like Albert Ellis?" (His answer to the title question, in a nutshell: No!) Whatever one's viewpoint, Ellis' personality has been a primary contribution to his theory and thus to the field.

SUMMARY

Albert Ellis created REBT as an active/directive/educational theory in which a therapist could address and dispute a client's irrational belief system. REBT includes an ABC model of personality, whereby a person's beliefs about events lead directly to emotional and behavioral consequences. Beliefs can be irrational or rational. Although everyone is influenced biologically and environmentally to think both rationally and irrationally, most people lean toward the irrational. Irrational beliefs are characterized by rigidity, self-evaluation, and absolutistic demands. These beliefs lead to magnified emotional and behavioral consequences, whereas rational beliefs, characterized by flexibility, lead to moderate consequences or no consequences.

Working within these basic therapeutic premises, REBT counselors do not rely on a warm relationship or uncovering of past experiences as change agents but, instead, focus on actively disputing irrational beliefs in the here and now. To facilitate effective disputation, REBT therapists use a variety of cognitive, emotional, and behavioral techniques. In therapy, clients and counselors work together to dispute irrationality, and clients learn the REBT process and integrate the methods so they can continue to use the techniques long after the formal therapy has terminated.

RECOMMENDED RESOURCES

Books

Dryden, W. (1990). (Ed.). *The essential Albert Ellis: Seminal writings on psychotherapy*. New York: Springer. This edited work is very thorough and contains many of the most important written contributions of Ellis. The text's two main sections, Theory and Practice, provide the reader with a broad scope of information that is easily accessed and utilized.

Ellis, A. (1962). *Reason and emotion in psychotherapy*. Secaucus, NJ: Lyle Stuart. This classic text is comprehensive and gives the reader an excellent theoretical and historical flavor of REBT.

Videotapes

Interested viewers will be impressed by most of the tapes available from the Albert Ellis Institute. The videos include taped sessions with real clients presenting with a wide variety of issues. Below are four that students seem to like the best. Except for the first, the remaining tapes can be ordered directly from the Institute by calling 212-535-0822.

Baxley, N. (Producer) and Ferraro, E. (Director). (1982). *Rational emotive therapy* (videorecording). Champaign, IL: Research Press. Though dated, this video still provides an excellent overview of REBT as demonstrated by Ellis and others at Ellis' institute in New York City.

Ellis, A. *Coping with the suicide of a loved one.* New York: Albert Ellis Institute.

DiGiuseppe, R. *Coping with anger.* New York: Albert Ellis Institute.

Wolfe, J. *Woman coping with depression and anger over teenagers' behavior.* New York: Albert Ellis Institute.

Websites

The best choice is the official website for the Albert Ellis Institute: www.rebt.org. This site contains valuable information about REBT and the application of the theory. Readers have access to catalogues and informational resources, and the site even has an "Ask Ellis" feature where interested parties can submit questions; Ellis answers one question per month.

REFERENCES

American Psychiatric Association. (2000). *Diagnostic and statistical manual of mental disorders—Text revised* (4th ed.). Washington DC: Author.

Bernard, M. (1991). *Staying rational in an irrational world.* New York: Lyle Stuart.

Bernard, M. E., & Joyce, M. R. (1984). *Rational emotive therapy with children and adolescents.* New York: Wiley.

Braaten, L. J. (1961). The main theories of "existentialism" from the viewpoint of a psychotherapist. *Mental Hygiene, 45,* 10–17.

Crawford, T., & Ellis, A. (1989). A dictionary of rational-emotive feelings and behaviors. *Journal of Rational-Emotive and Cognitive Behavior Therapy, 7,* 3–27.

DiGiuseppe, R. (1991). A rational-emotive model of assessment. In M. E. Bernard (Ed.), *Using rational-emotive therapy effectively: A practitioner's guide* (pp. 151–172). New York: Plenum.

DiGiuseppe, R., & Miller, N. J. (1977). A review of outcome studies on rational-emotive therapy. In A. Ellis & R. Grieger (Eds.), *Handbook of rational-emotive therapy* (pp. 72–95). New York: Springer.

DiGiuseppe, R., Robin, M. W., & Dryden, W. (1992). On the compatibility of rational emotive therapy and Judeo-Christian philosophy: A focus on clinical strategies. *Journal of Cognitive Psychotherapy: An International Quarterly, 4,* 355–368.

Dryden, W. (1990). *Rational emotive counselling in action.* London: Sage.

Dryden, W., & DiGiuseppe, R. (1990). *A primer on rational emotive therapy.* Champaign, IL: Research Press.

Dryden, W., & Gordon, J. (1990). *How to be a happier you: Solving your emotional problems by rational thinking.* London: Sheldon Press.

Ellis, A. (1960). There is no place for the concept of sin in psychotherapy. *Journal of Counseling Psychology, 7*, 188–192.

Ellis, A. (1962). *Reason and emotion in psychotherapy*. Secaucus, NJ: Lyle Stuart.

Ellis, A. (1965). *Homosexuality: Its causes and cure*. New York: Lyle Stuart.

Ellis, A. (1971). *The case against religion: A psychotherapist's view*. New York: Institute for Rational Living.

Ellis, A. (1973). *Humanistic psychotherapy: A rational-emotive approach*. New York: Institute for Rational Living.

Ellis, A. (1977a). The basic clinical theory of rational-emotive therapy. In A. Ellis & R. Grieger (Eds.), *Handbook of rational-emotive therapy* (pp. 3–34). New York: Springer.

Ellis, A. (1977b). Research data supporting the clinical and personality hypotheses of RET and other cognitive-behavior therapies. In A. Ellis & R. Grieger (Eds.), *Handbook of rational-emotive therapy* (pp. 35–71). New York: Springer.

Ellis, A. (1979). Toward a new theory of personality. In A. Ellis & J. M. Whitely (Eds.), *Theoretical and empirical foundations of rational-emotive therapy* (pp. 33–60). Monterey, CA: Brooks/Cole.

Ellis, A. (1980). Psychotherapy and atheistic values: A response to A. E. Bergin's Psychotherapy and religious values. *Journal of Consulting and Clinical Psychology, 48*, 635–639.

Ellis, A. (1983). How to deal with your most difficult *client:* You. *Journal of Rational Emotive Therapy, 1*, 3–8.

Ellis, A. (1988). *How to stubbornly refuse to make yourself miserable about anything—yes, anything!* Secaucus, NJ: Lyle Stuart.

Ellis, A. (1992). Brief therapy: The rational-emotive method. In S. H. Budman, M. F. Hoyt, & S. Friedman (Eds.), *The first session in brief therapy* (pp. 36–58). New York: Guilford.

Ellis, A. (1993). RET becomes REBT. *IRETletter, 1*, 4.

Ellis, A. (1996). *Better, deeper, and more enduring brief therapy: The rational emotive behavior therapy approach*. New York: Brunner/Mazel.

Ellis, A. (1997). REBT and its application to group therapy. In J. Yankura & W. Dryden (Eds.), *Special applications of REBT: A therapist's casebook* (pp. 131–161). New York: Springer.

Ellis, A. (1997). The evolution of Albert Ellis and rational emotive therapy (REBT). In J. K. Zeig (Ed.), *The evolution of psychotherapy* (pp. 69–78). New York: Brunner/Mazel.

Ellis, A. (1998). *How to control your anxiety before it controls you*. Secaucus, NJ: Carol Publishing.

Ellis, A. (2000a). Can rational emotive behavior therapy (REBT) be effectively used with people who have devout beliefs in God and religion? *Professional Psychology: Research and Practice, 31*, 29–33.

Ellis, A. (2000b). Rational emotive behavior therapy. In R. J. Corsini & D. Wedding (Eds.), *Current psychotherapies* (6th ed., pp. 168–204). Itasca, IL: F. E. Peacock.

Ellis, A., & Dryden, W. (1997). *The practice of rational emotive therapy*. New York: Springer.

Ellis, A., & Harper, R. A. (1997). *A guide to new rational living*. North Hollywood, CA: Melvin Powers.

Engels, G.I., Garnefski, N., & Diekstra, R. F. W. (1993). Efficacy of rational-emotive therapy: A quantitative analysis. *Journal of Consulting and Clinical Psychology, 61*, 1083–1090.

Epictetus. (1955). *The enchiridion* (trans. T.W. Higginson). Indianapolis: Bobs-Merrill.

Gorsuch, R. L. (1988). Psychology of religion. *Annual Review of Psychology, 39*, 201–221.

Grieger, R., & Boyd, J. (1980). *Rational-emotive therapy: A skills-based approach.* New York: Van Nostrand Reinhold.

Hood, R.W., Spilka, B., Hunsberger, B., & Gorsuch, R. (1996). *The psychology of religion* (2nd ed.). New York: Guilford.

Johnson, N. (1980). Must the rational emotive therapist be like Albert Ellis? *The Personnel and Guidance Journal,* 49–51.

Johnson, W. B. (1993). Christian rational emotive therapy: A treatment protocol. *Journal of Psychology and Christianity, 12,* 254–261.

Johnson, W. B. (1994). Albert Ellis and the religionists: A history of the dialogue. *Journal of Psychology and Christianity, 13,* 301–311.

Johnson, W. B., Ridley, C. R., & Nielsen, S. (2000). Religiously sensitive rational emotive behavior therapy: Elegant solutions and ethical risks. *Professional Psychology: Research and Practice, 31,* 14–20.

Kirkpatrick, L. A. (1997). A longitudinal study of changes in religious belief and behavior as a function of individual differences in adult attachment style. *Journal for the Scientific Study of Religion, 36,* 207–217.

Lyons, L. C., & Woods, P. J. (1991). The efficacy of rational-emotive therapy: A quantitative review of outcome research. *Clinical Psychology Review, 11,* 357–369.

Mylott, K. (1994). Twelve irrational ideas that drive gay men and women crazy. *Journal of Rational Emotive and Cognitive Behavioral Therapy, 12,* 61–71.

Nielsen, S. L. (1994). Rational-emotive therapy and religion: Don't throw the therapeutic baby out with the holy water! *Journal of Psychology and Christianity, 13,* 312–322.

Nielsen, S. L., Johnson, W. B., & Ridley, C. R. (2000). Religiously sensitive rational emotive behavior therapy: Theory, techniques, and brief excerpts from a case. *Professional Psychology: Research and Practice, 31,* 21–28.

Silverman, M. S., McCarthy, M., & McGovern, T. (1992). A review of outcome studies of rational-emotive therapy from 1982-1989. *Journal of Rational-Emotive and Cognitive-Behavior Therapy, 10,* 111–186.

Weinrach, S. G. (1995). Rational emotive behavior therapy: A tough-minded therapy for a tender-minded profession. *Journal of Counseling and Development, 73,* 296–300.

Wolfe, J., & Russianoff, P. (1997). Overcoming self negation in women. *Journal of Rational-Emotive and Cognitive Behavior Therapy, 15,* 81–92.

Woods, P. J. (1992). A study of belief and non-belief items from the Jones irrational beliefs test with implications for the theory of RET. *Journal of Rational-Emotive and Cognitive- Behavior Therapy, 10,* 41–52.

Zachary, I. (1980). RET with women: Some special issues. In R. Grieger & J. Boyd (Eds.), *Rational emotive therapy: A skills based approach* (pp. 249–264). New York: Van Nostrand.

CHAPTER 12

SYSTEMS APPROACHES

BACKGROUND OF THE THEORY

Historical Context

The accepted paradigm of mental health counseling until the 1930s focused primarily on conceptualization and treatment of dysfunctions resting within the individual. All of the preceding theories discussed in this book were founded on this individual-based paradigm, and although most proponents of those theories treated families, the focus remained on how to ameliorate the symptoms of individual members of the family.

The historical road to the inclusion into the mental health field of a very different paradigm—the systemic paradigm—has been a bumpy one (Nicholls & Everett, 1986). Interestingly, the systemic orientation in mental health grew primarily out of the public's need and demand for more socially holistic approaches to child guidance, marriage counseling, and the treatment of schizophrenia than were provided by the prevailing theories of the time. Particularly in the United States, the tide of support from the public met with opposition from the psychoanalytic community committed to the idea that psychological healing was exclusively the domain of the inner workings of the individual. Until the years following World War II, the ideologically and politically powerful psychoanalytic community largely choked out forms of therapy that involved conjoint sessions, in which two or more clients attend together, and that involved a conceptualization of client concerns that included the social context (Nicholls & Everett, 1986).

Unlike systemically oriented clinicians in the United States, those in Europe encountered little opposition when, in the early 1900s, they began treating marital concerns by working conjointly with the marital dyad. In the 1920s, Abraham and Hannah Stone emigrated from Europe to New York, where they began one of the earlier marriage therapy practices in the United States In the 1930s, U.S. therapists such as Paul Papanoe and Emily Mudd began treating couples together and conceptualizing problems within the marriage as being of a mutual rather than individual nature (Broderick & Schraeder, 1991). The field of marriage counseling defined itself as a unique treatment approach in 1945 with the establishment of the American

Association of Marriage Counselors, which later became the American Association for Marriage and Family Therapy (AAMFT).

The most important historical event in the family therapy movement came in the 1950s. In Palo Alto, California, a group known as the Mental Research Institute (MRI) conducted therapy and research with hospitalized patients with schizophrenia and their families. What they discovered profoundly changed the way many people viewed the process of therapy and the road to change. Bateson, Jackson, Haley, and Weakland (1956) presented what is known as the double-bind hypothesis involving a consistent and contradictory pattern of communication from parent to schizophrenic child. According to this hypothesis, the parent would place the child in a double bind by giving the child an either/or choice and then responding negatively no matter which way the child responded. For example, the parent would communicate that the child should be more loving and affectionate; if the child did not exhibit more affection, the parent would express disapproval, yet if the child did, the parent would ignore or demean the child. In essence, this no-win situation was "crazy-making."

The importance of these findings were that they demonstrated the systemic nature of symptoms—that not all pathology was rooted in the individual but, rather, could be caused by patterns of communication and behavior within the family, and that pathology could be reduced or eliminated by addressing those interpersonal communication and behavior patterns rather than addressing the intrapsychic dynamics of the individual. Bodin (1981) stated that these findings and the research that emerged as a result constituted the "definitive landmark in the revolutionary shift from individual to systems focus in concepts of pathogenesis" (p. 281).

Although research since that time has not supported the double-bind hypothesis, it has revealed a different systemic dynamic. People with schizophrenia typically have periods of relative stability, in which their symptoms are chronic but less severe, punctuated with periods of relapse, in which their symptoms become severe. Research has revealed that persons with schizophrenia who stabilize in an extrafamilial setting, such as the psychiatric hospital, run a much greater risk of relapse if they return to a family with at least one member who is high in "expressed emotion," showing "signs of hostility or emotional overinvolvment or speak[ing] critically of the patient when interviewed or answering a questionnaire" (Relapse and Expressed Emotion, 1999, p. 6). Similar patterns have been observed for patients with mood and eating disorders. Thus, although the specifics of the original double bind hypothesis are no longer widely accepted, the systemic conceptualization of dysfunction has remained intact.

Early family systems theorists drew upon several threads of emerging scientific knowledge to synthesize their new findings. From Norbert Weiner's (1948) cybernetics, they drew the concept that through continuous feedback loops, a system maintains and corrects itself. From anthropologists such as Talcott Parsons and Robert Bales (1955), they drew the concept of psychological and functional boundaries within a family. And they drew from the biologist Ludwig von Bertalanffy (1950, 1968) his formulation of general systems theory that seemed to tie together several concepts, including feedback and boundaries. Out of the work of these pioneers emerged a new way of thinking about the human change process.

Founders' Biographical Overviews

Whereas each of the other theories in this textbook arose primarily from the thinking of one person, systems theory arose from the thinking of several people. In fact, the term "systems theory" is an umbrella term that includes numerous unique theories that address mental health issues from a shared perspective.

Throughout the reading of this chapter, you will notice references to Table 12.1. This table outlines the theories subsumed under the systems perspective, each with its own points of emphasis, founder of the theory, and view of maladjustment and change. Because each of these systems-oriented approaches is a theory in its own right, it seems superficial to try to explain each in one chapter. Instead, this chapter is designed to provide an introductory overview of systems thinking. The current standard of practice in mental health calls for a counselor to approach an understanding of each client by using several perspectives, including intrapersonal/individual, interpersonal/systemic, and biological. For this reason, we encourage you to build on the knowledge you gain in this chapter by enrolling in at least one course devoted to couple and family counseling.

Philosophical Underpinnings

Understanding systems theory requires making a shift in thinking from an individual to a system focus. Understanding and actually making that philosophical shift can be facilitated by understanding its origin: scientific work explaining the nature of biological and cybernetic systems. Readers who are interested in seminal work on general systems theory should consult Bertalanffy (1968). Family therapists drew upon the work of, among others, Bertalanffy, adapting his general systems theory and applying it to family systems. Minuchin (1985) provided a comprehensive yet understandable outline of the basic principles of systems theory. Two of the principles specifically address core philosophical assumptions and are detailed below.

Any System Is an Organized Whole, and Elements Within the System Are Necessarily Interdependent (Minuchin, 1985, p. 289). This one statement is the philosophical core of systems theory. In other holistic theories, the

TABLE 12.1

Comparison Chart of Major Family Therapies

	Bowen	Framo	Boszormenyi-Nagy
Name of Founder			
Name of therapy	Family multigenerational therapy	Object-relations/family of origin therapy	Contextual family therapy
View of family	The family is an emotional unit–a network of interlocking relationships, best understood when viewed from a multigenerational framework.	The family is an intricate system with its own unique bonding, rules, homeostatic mechanisms, secret alliances, communication network, myths, regressive features, and dynamic influences from previous generations.	The family understanding is based on the principle of "reciprocity"–having received and having to reciprocate. Each spouse brings the heritage and loyalties of previous generations into the context of the new family.
The healthy family	Emotional detachment in the form of separation from the intellect is the hallmark of the healthy family. Members have learned to establish their own identities, to differentiate themselves from the family of origin.	In the healthy family: parents are well differentiated; generational boundaries are clear; the loyalty of the spouses is greater to the family of procreation than the family of origin; spouses view the marital subsystem as primary; and autonomy for all is encouraged.	Spouses who experienced a high degree of relational equitability in the families of origin bring to the marriage a ledger of indebtedness and entitlements that is balanced. Thus they are able to focus on the mutual welfare interests of the entire family.
Dysfunction	Members of the marital dyad have poor differentiation of self and are emotionally "stuck-together" to their families of origin. Styles of origin are repeated in marital relationships and are passed on to the children.	Intrapsychic conflicts derived from the family of origin are replicated with spouse and/or children. Efforts at the interpersonal resolution of the inner conflict are at the heart of the kinds of distress found in troubled couples and families.	Dysfunction occurs when the adult child is not able to transfer loyalty from the family of origin to the new marital relationship; loyalty owed to previous/subsequent generations tends to always conflict with loyalty owed to spouse, siblings, friends, and peers.

Role of therapist	The therapist is a "coach"—an active expert who educates family members (primarily the marital dyad) but remains disengaged from the family system: detached, objective, and neutral.	The therapist is active and very structured, moving from empathy to confrontation. The therapist usually works with a cotherapist who is of the other gender. The therapist works primarily with the marital dyad only and has a strong "educative" function.	The therapist is an active, encouraging guide. Using "multidirectional partiality" he/she is an advocate for all persons involved in therapy, moving from gentle exploration to a more confrontive style while holding participants responsible for their own movement.
Goal of therapy	The basic overarching goal is to assist family members (primarily the marital dyad) toward a better level of differentiation of self. Growth in differentiation will facilitate reduction of anxiety and relief from symptoms.	The two major goals for the marital dyad are: to discover what issues/agendas from the family of origin impact the current family and to have a corrective experience with parents and siblings from the families of origin.	The goal is to enable participants to move toward relational integrity, relational commitments, and balances of fairness, and to enable family members to gain trust in one another's increasingly trustworthy input.
Primary techniques	Genograms; therapist detachment as a primary technique; defining the roles/relationships in the family system; teaching the "I" position; defusing emotion and avoiding blame; examining/reestablishing contact with the family of origin.	Male–female cotherapy team; standard techniques of *Couples Therapy; Couples Group Therapy; Family of Origin Sessions*—bringing in the family of origin with individual members of the marital dyad to deal directly with unresolved attachment issues.	Three-generational assessment; conjoint family therapy as the norm; multidirectional partiality; self-disclosure; guiding; confrontation; instruction in building trusting & equitable relationships; suggestions; directives; loyalty framing; exoneration; some use of cotherapy.

(Continued)

TABLE 12.1
Continued

Name of Founder	Satir	Mental Research Institue	Haley
Name of therapy	Process/communications approach	Brief family therapy	Strategic family therapy
View of family	Families are balanced, rule-governed systems which, through the basic components of communication and self-esteem, provide a context for growth and development.	The family is an interacting communications network in which every member from the newborn to the elderly grandfather influences the nature of the entire system and is in turn influenced by it.	The family is a system which involves power relations and has rules by which it operates. The power struggle is not a question of who controls whom but rather of who controls the definition of the relationship and by what maneuvers.
The healthy family	In the healthy family, members are in touch with their own feelings; communicate in a congruent manner; accept others as different from themselves; and view those differences as a chance to learn and explore rather than as a threat.	The healthy family is able to maintain its basic integrity even during periods of stress. Changes are accommodated as needed. Communication is handled in a clear and logical manner.	Functional families develop suitable up-front methods of dealing with conflict/control struggles. In addition, they have clear rules and a balance of stability and flexibility.
Dysfunction	Dysfunctional families consist of persons whose freedom to grow/develop has been blocked. Dysfunctional behavior results from the interplay of low self-esteem, incongruent communication, poor system functioning, and dysfunctional family rules (overt and covert).	Incongruent communication—contradictions between verbal and nonverbal communication—is at the heart of dysfunction. Family problems develop by the mishandling of normal life difficulties; attempted solutions often maintain or exacerbate family difficulties.	Symptoms are understood as an attempt to control a relationship. The maneuver to control is understood as dysfunctional if one or both participants deny the issue of control and/or exhibit symptomatic behavior in the process of doing so.

Role of therapist	The therapist is a facilitator, a resource person, an observer, a detective, and a teacher/model of congruent communication and warmth and empathy. And the therapist is highly active, personally involved in the system, yet able to confront when necessary.	The therapist is actively in charge of the case and all aspects of the case, including who is seen for treatment. The therapist is a data collector, case planner, treatment hypothesis tester, communications teacher/model. The therapist is actively in charge of therapy.	The therapist takes an active, directive, and authoritative "take-charge" approach to the power struggle that is therapy. The therapist assumes the role of family change-maker–he or she assumes temporary leadership of the family.
Goal of therapy	Three overarching goals: (1) persons will grow in understanding of self and in the ability to communicate congruently; (2) increased respect for the uniqueness of family members; and (3) the family members will view individual uniqueness as opportunity for growth.	The basic goal of therapy is symptom abatement; to bring about change in behavior and/or view the problem that reduces the client's/family's pain sufficiently that treatment is no longer desired by the client/family. The focus is entirely on action and problem solving.	Change in the system is the basic goal of therapy. Therapy is focused on altering behavior patterns maintaining the presenting problem
Primary techniques	Family Life Chronology; conjoint family therapy is the norm (marital dyad seen first); family reconstruction; psychodrama; guided fantasy; family sculpting; therapist as communications model/teacher.	A variety of managerial techniques to maintain control over the therapy process; focus on the marital dyad or one person from the system; extensive data collection; reframing; the "one-down" position; homework; paradoxical injunctions (therapeutic double-blind).	Focuses on behavior and communication patterns; one therapist, with one or more therapists behind a one-way mirror; uses "straightforward" advice, directives, etc., with compliant families; uses paradoxical interventions with noncompliant families.

(Continued)

TABLE 12.1
Continued

	Minuchin	Whitaker	White and Epston
Name of therapy	Structural family therapy	Symbolic/experiential family therapy	Narrative therapy
View of family	A family is more than the individual biopsychodynamic of its members. Family members relate according to certain arrangements which govern their transactions. These arrangements form a whole: the structure of the family.	The family is an integrated whole and through a sense of belonging to the whole the freedom to individuate and separate from the family is derived. The power of the family–for good or for ill–is the key to individual growth and development.	A family is a small social system nested in larger cultural systems. Although the family has its own set of beliefs and values, these are largely influenced by cultural beliefs and values.
The healthy family	The well-functioning family has an underlying organizational structure that allows for fluid and flexible responses to changing conditions through the family life cycle. Thus the family provides both for mutual support and for autonomy of its individual members.	Health is a process of perceptual becoming. The healthy family: has a sense of wholeness; maintains generational boundaries along with role flexibility; is creative and playful; encourages expression of autonomy; and grows in spite of adversity and resultant stress.	Healthy families adventurously re-author their life stories to build on strengths and successes. When problems emerge, healthy families consider the outside threat and work to write a life story that overcomes the negative influence.
Dysfunction	Symptoms are believed to arise when family structures are inflexible, whether enmeshed or disengaged, and appropriate structural adjustments are not made; the family responds in an inflexible manner to changing conditions in the family life cycle.	Dysfunctional families are characterized by interactional rigidity and emotional deadness. The specific symptom is often related to the preestablished roles and triangles of family members. Symptoms serve to maintain the status quo.	Dysfunction is seen as a force existing outside the family that oppresses or keeps the family stuck. Families that fail to recognize their strengths and successes fall into the pattern of internalizing the problem and develop system defeating stories.

Role of therapist	The therapist's role is paradoxical: supportive while challenging; attacking while encouraging; being *for* the family yet *against* the dysfunctional system. The therapist is an active, authoritative agent of change: an actor, director, and producer in family change.	The therapist focuses on *being* fully with the client/family; to use him/herself to help family members fully express/communicate what they are experiencing. The therapist is very active but usually not very directive—a coach or a surrogate grandparent; cotherapy is normative.	Therapist actively asks questions of the family to assess how the problem is influencing the family. Therapist works with family to focus on strengths and shifts the problem focus from inside the system to outside the system. Therapist acts as editor and reader of family's new story.
Goal of therapy	The basic goal is the restructuralization of the family's system of transactional rules, such that interactions become more flexible, with expanded availability of alternative ways for family members to relate to one another.	The goal is growth and creativity rather than reduction of symptoms because individual growth and creative freedom will reduce the need for the symptom: growth occurs when family members are able to experience the present moment and communicate that experience with other family members.	The goal is for the family to re-author the problem saturated story and create a story that empowers the family members to continuously author growth-oriented life narratives.
Primary techniques	Structural/Family Mapping: "joining" techniques: maintenance, tracking, accommodation, mimesis; "disequilibriating" techniques: reframing, use of metaphors, enactment, boundary marking, blocking, punctuation, unbalancing.	The therapist as a person as a primary technique; conjoint family therapy and the use of a cotherapist is the norm; reframing; modeling; therapeutic absurdity; affective confrontation; fantasy; paradoxical intentions; "as if" situations.	Externalization of the problem, deconstruction of the problem and the reconstruction or re-authoring of new story, letter writing, the client's identification of unique outcomes, and specific questioning techniques.

Compiled by Richard Watts, personal communication, 1996. Used by permission.

individual is the system whose dimensions of feeling, thinking, and acting are inseparably interrelated and can be understood only in the context of the interaction of all dimensions: the whole person. By contrast, in systems theory, the social group is the system whose individual members are inseparably interrelated and can be fully understood only in the context of the interaction of all members: the whole social group. In other words, when considering the social group of the family from a systems perspective, individual members of the family can be completely understood only in the context of the entire family. More accurately, individual members can be understood outside their social contexts, but a great deal of understanding is lost without that contextual information.

By way of illustration, Satir (1972) used the analogy of a mobile—a hanging art piece consisting of various components suspended in balance by threads. Movement of component A results in the movement of other components. If an observer focused only on component B, trying to understand its movement outside of its relationship to component A, the observer's understanding would be incomplete. Likewise, in the family, a change in the functioning of one person is considered a reflection of a change in the family system to which that person belongs.

Systems theorists maintain that by understanding *the interactive, interdependent relationships* of the members of a family system, a counselor can more fully both understand and address the systemic factors in the family's functioning as a whole and each family members' relative functioning and satisfaction. For example, in the case of schizophrenia described above, the goal of therapy becomes a family goal: how the family can maintain a relatively consistently supportive family atmosphere—neither hostile nor overinvolved—and how they can respond most effectively if the supportive family atmosphere is disrupted. The focus is not merely shifted from the schizophrenic to the emotionally expressive family member(s); it is shifted to the role that *each* family member plays in influencing each other and the overall functioning that characterizes the family atmosphere.

Patterns in a System Are Circular Rather than Linear (Minuchin, 1985, p. 290). According to traditional therapies, one person's dysfunctional symptoms can be traced back to a cause within that person. In the case of schizophrenia, for example, linear causality yields the conclusion that the schizophrenic's biological disorder causes her relapses. Systemic thinking does not merely shift the focus of responsibility from the "identified patient" to someone else in the patient's system: For example, it also would be linear thinking to conclude that the emotionally expressive family member(s) are "responsible" for the schizophrenic's relapses.

Circular causality involves the concept that mutual interaction means *mutual influence*. One of the challenges in talking about circular influence is that one must start somewhere in the circle, and starting in one place can mistakenly imply linear causality. To transcend any tendency toward linear thinking, notice what you experience as you read the following two sentences that pertain to the family containing a member with schizophrenia.

- The stress of living with the symptoms of a person with schizophrenia contributes to emotional expressiveness on the part of other family member(s); at the same time, the stress of other family member(s)' emotional expressiveness exacerbates the symptoms of a person with schizophrenia.
- The stress of other family member(s)' emotional expressiveness exacerbates the symptoms of a person with schizophrenia; at the same time, the stress of living with the symptoms of a person with schizophrenia contributes to emotional expressiveness on the part of other family member(s).

Notice that both sentence sequences make sense. No one factor is "the" cause of a schizophrenic's relapse. Both factors "cause" each other and result in relapse. Relapse is a development of family members' mutual influence on each other. However, rarely is the family interaction pattern this simple. For example, another family member may provoke emotional expressiveness by such behaviors as teasing the "emotionally expressive" member who, in turn, expresses hostility toward the schizophrenic member. By focusing on the entire family interaction pattern, the counselor can reframe the problem as one in which every family member plays a role in, and thus shares responsibility for, the quality of the family atmosphere.

Another more ubiquitous example illustrates the concepts of interdependency and circular causality. A pervasive systemic dynamic among couples is one variously named the pursuer/avoider, pursuer/distancer, or critic/ stonewaller. This dynamic can be observed most clearly when a couple argues.

Consider the case of Justin and Kelly, whose arguments usually end without resolution of the issue of disagreement. In traditional counseling, the goal would depend in part on who came for counseling. If Justin came, the following linear pattern might emerge (the arrow, $\rightarrow$, means "causes"): During arguments, Justin immediately becomes defensive and then increasingly withdraws, both emotionally and physically $\rightarrow$ The issue of disagreement remains unresolved.

The counseling goal might be to help Justin understand intrapsychic reasons for his defensiveness and withdrawal, be accountable for his responses, and work on ways to be less defensive and remain engaged in problem solving with Kelly.

If Kelly came for counseling the linear pattern might be: During arguments, Kelly diffuses focus from the issue at hand by bringing up numerous other issues and by blaming Justin and criticizing his personality $\rightarrow$ The issue of disagreement remains unresolved.

In Kelly's counseling, the focus may be on the reasons for and/or purpose of Kelly's diffusive and critical, blaming attitude and style. Kelly and her counselor might address how she can communicate in a way that more productively leads to problem solving of the original issue.

In both of these counseling sessions, the focus is on individual responsibility and largely ignores what the other person is doing or not doing to contribute to the problem. In fact, the problem is not diagnosed as an interpersonal problem but as an intrapersonal one.

In systems theory, because of belief in the mutual influence of the members of the system, causation is assumed to be circular. Using the principle of circular causality, a systemic counselor would understand Justin and Kelly's arguments as follows: Kelly brings up an issue of dissatisfaction → Justin responds defensively by minimizing her complaint, arguing his innocence of any fault, or countercriticizing Kelly → Kelly intensifies her complaint by bringing up additional dissatisfactions → Justin begins to withdraw by folding his arms and looking away → Kelly turns the focus to a criticism of Justin's personality—by describing him in derogatory terms, describing how he "always" and "never" does certain things, etc. → Justin retreats in stoney silence to his lounge chair → Kelly stomps out of the room → When the issue resurfaces, Kelly brings it up again in a critical, blaming way → Justin is quick to respond defensively → and so on.

The temptation of linear thinking is to conclude that if Kelly just wouldn't complain or would just be consistently gentler, Justin would not be so defensive and withdrawing. However, it's equally possible that if Justin didn't immediately respond defensively, Kelly would not escalate into diffusion, criticism, and blame. In fact, research (Gottman, 1994) has shown both conclusions to be accurate: Both the pursuer's criticism and blame and the distancer's defensiveness and stonewalling, especially when they go unchecked by repair mechanisms such as listening to the other's point of view and affirming the validity of the other's perspective, contribute to a pattern of communication associated with relationship distress and a high likelihood of relationship dissolution. In addition, the longest and happiest relationships were characterized by the wife complaining (but not criticizing) *early and often* in the relationship (Gottman & Krokoff, 1989)!

The system perspective's philosophical principle of circular causality provides a foundation for assessment and change. "Change must be directed toward the cycle, although the point of entry and the manner of interrupting the cycle are matters of choice" (Minuchin, 1985, p. 290).

THE THEORY

Development and Characteristics of Family Systems

Nature of Family Systems. Family systems are ubiquitous. Most children are born into or, soon after birth, enter a family system, their *family of origin*.

Most humans also participate in the creation of at least one family system, their *family of creation*, which may or may not produce children of its own. Family systems take many forms across cultures: monogamous (two spouses) or polygamous (more than two spouses); nuclear (the core of which is one set of parents and possibly their children living together) or extended (the core of which is three or more generations living together). The following discussion will address characteristics of systems that are universal and, for ease of explanation, will sometimes make particular use of the form of family system most strongly associated with prevailing U.S. culture, the heterosexual, monogamous, nuclear family.

Function of Family Systems.   This section will be organized around two motivational functions of systems: *goal-directedness* and *the maintenance of dynamic equilibrium.* In the process of discussing these two motivational functions, we will also discuss several operational functions of systems. Also, it is customary in systemic thinking to make little or no reference to intrapsychic processes, such as awareness. However, as you read the following information, you will be thinking—an intrapsychic process—and one of the things you may be thinking is, "In all my years of membership in family systems, I never really noticed what is being described here." The systems literature does occasionally make reference to the fact that members of a system function within the system largely nonconscious of the operating principles in which they are participating—principles that they themselves are, in fact, enacting. For that reason, we will frequently remind you of the largely nonconscious nature of systemic functioning.

   Goal-Directedness.   Every system, including the family system, has a goal or purpose. Regarding the human family in particular, consider the fact that some form of family is found in every culture (Bestor, 2001). It stands to reason, therefore, that the family, a universal social institution, serves some universal purpose. Although some systems theorists object to the concept of purposefulness, considering it a culturally based assumption (Becvar & Becvar, 2002), others consider purposefulness—more specifically, *goal-directedness*—to be inherent in systems, particularly cybernetic systems (Heylighen & Joslyn, 2001; Weiner, 1948). Because we have found the concept of teleology not to detract from, but rather to enhance, our understanding of systems theory as it applies to families, we will proceed on the assumption that the family system exists for the purpose of facilitating the greatest overall survival, health, and development of its members. Indeed, the same theorists who decried the concept of purposefulness offered a definition of family as "individuals operating . . . *in support of* the mutual welfare of all and the individual development of each" (Becvar & Becvar, 2002, p. 84; italics added). The phrase "in support of" implies a purposeful goal of the system.

   However, we argue with the phrase "mutual welfare of all and . . . individual development of each." Although these are the *ideal* aims of the family system, several phenomena show that such aims are not *defini-tive* of families. Among the most salient examples are geriatricide and infan-ticide: the practice in some cultures of killing elderly parents and newborn children perceived as a liability rather than an asset to the overall family's welfare. Even in the current United States, infanticide occurs; some people believe geriatricide does, as well. Clearly, the victim's welfare—and very life—is sacrificed for the overall welfare of the family; thus, welfare is hardly mu-tual or supportive of the individual development of each member. More commonly, family systems theorists have postulated that some families bol-ster their existence by *scapegoating* one family member, beating them down psychologically or even physically. Clearly, the "scapegoat's" welfare and de-velopment are sacrificed, rather than supported, in the service of maintain-ing the soundness of the family system. Even more salient is the case of an *abusive* family in which a spouse—in a heterosexual couple, almost always the wife—and, often, the children subject themselves to psychological and physi-cal violence out of the perception that these circumstances constitute their best chance at their greatest welfare overall.

In all these cases, the family is still a family—their definition remains in tact—although the ideal, the *mutual* welfare of all and *maximal* development of each, is far from achieved. On a hopeful note, family therapy has demon-strated that, for example, regarding the practice of scapegoating, a family can develop ways to maintain its soundness through alternative strategies. When a family functions in such a way that the ideal—mutual welfare and maximal development of each member—is realized, the family might be said to be maintaining its integrity in *both* senses of the word.

Thus, one motivational function of a system is teleology, purposeful-ness, goal-directedness, intentionality. The purpose of the family system is, by our definition, to facilitate the greatest overall survival, health, and devel-opment of its members and, ideally, to support the mutual welfare of all fam-ily members and to advance maximally the individual development of each family member. The fact that you may not have actually thought about the purpose of the family points up the mostly nonconscious nature of the fam-ily purpose. An additional example of the goal-directedness of families comes from Gottman, Driver, and Tabares' (2002) work with couples. Gottman, Driver, and Tabares noted that, through skillful questioning by a counselor, each member of a couple will uncover a "dream"—a subjective, desired goal that the member perceives the marriage will help to achieve. Chronic con-flict can be reframed—understood in a more positive light—and thus better managed in light of both members' conscious awareness of each one's "dream." For the purpose of understanding systemic thinking, suffice it to say that the family system is purposeful.

Maintenance of Dynamic Equilibrium. John and Mary meet. The pur-pose of their interactions at first may or may not be a "family purpose." On the one hand, one or both of them may be seeking to pair-bond and may perceive the other as a potential partner; on the other hand, one or both of them may be seeking something else, such as friendship or sex. In either case, as they interact, two fundamental operational functions come into play, which are the mechanisms of the creation and maintenance of a social system: *morphogenesis* and *morphostasis*. *Morphogenesis* is *the tendency arising out of interaction for a system to create and recreate its own structure* (morph = structure, genesis = creation). In other words, *systems self-organize and reorganize into their own characteristic patterns of interaction.* More specifically, John and Mary's goal-directed interactions form into patterns of interaction that uniquely characterize their relationship; as they continue to interact, they continue to create and recreate such patterns. It is this mostly nonconscious self-organization into unique patterns, rather than any particular pattern itself, that is universal among family systems.

For example, Gottman (1979) has found that equally lasting, happy marriages can be, in our terms, high, medium, or low volume. High-volume couples have frequent, passionate debates and arguments; medium-volume couples have occasional discussions characterized by open communication of thoughts and feelings; and low-volume couples spend relatively less time together and spend much of their "together time" in silence or with minimal interaction. By way of another example, I (JMH) recall an overnight stay at my cousin's house when I realized how her family's way of frequently cutting up and teasing each other contrasted with my family's way of being relatively quiet and serious. The fact that her family's interaction pattern was a "realization" to me underscores the nonconscious nature of such patterns: It had never occurred to me that a family could function any differently than my own did. All of these examples illustrate the self-organization of systemic interactions into *some* form of patterns through which it fulfills its purpose, though the specific pattern in one system may vary significantly from the pattern in another.

If systems operated only on the basis of morphogenesis, they would be constantly recreating themselves, constantly changing, and thus would lack a sense of continuity. Another fundamental operational function provides for a system's continuity: morphostasis. *Morphostasis* is *the system's fundamental tendency to keep its structure the same, stable* (morph = structure, stasis = no movement). Actually, the above examples also illustrated morphostasis: Once a couple morphogenetically creates their interactional volume level, that level tends to remain a stable, unique pattern of interaction; once a family establishes its level of seriousness, it tends to maintain that level.

Like all systems, family systems establish and maintain characteristic levels of interaction around myriad aspects of the systemic relationship: not only the levels of "volume" and "seriousness" but also levels of such things as openness/privacy, dominance/submission, generosity/selfishness. Virtually any aspect of systemic functioning revolves around a level of functioning that characterizes that systemic relationship. It is as if the members of the system calibrate, that is, establish particular set points, for each aspect of systemic functioning.

To maintain functioning within an acceptable range around a particular set point, family members establish mostly nonconscious family rules, such as, "Thou shalt remain within a certain range of seriousness." Then family members mostly nonconsciously monitor deviation from the set point/rule. When members detect deviation, they perceive a perturbation of the system's dynamic equilibrium—*dynamic* referring to the fact that the system is always "in motion" as people continuously act and interact, and *equilibrium* referring to the maintenance of balance around a set point. When family members detect disequilibrium, they mostly nonconsciously employ corrective strategies to decrease disequilibrium. Technically, we could speak of the family seeking either to "restore equilibrium" or to "decrease disequilibrium." For reasons that will become clear in a moment, we are purposely speaking in the latter terms.

For example, in a high-volume couple, if interactions drift away from emotional intensity, one member of the couple will provoke a debate that the other member is likely to join willingly; in a low-volume couple, if interactions drift toward emotional intensity, both members are likely to nonconsciously cooperate in a way to create a more comfortable distance. The joking family that drifts toward seriousness instigates jokes; the serious family that drifts toward levity instigates calming strategies. Now that I (JMH) understand systemic thinking, I find it not at all surprising that one trigger of my childhood asthma was laughing long and hard; nothing aborts levity like an asthma attack. What a creative way to maintain a serious family atmosphere! Notice that anyone, child or adult, can be involved in the maintenance of a family rule.

Perturbations—those changes that provoke or threaten to provoke disequilibrium—can take a few different forms. They may arise from *inside* or *outside* the system; they may be *passive*, such as the "drifts" just discussed, or *active*, such as some acute event; and they may actually have *already occurred* or merely *threatened to occur*. Examples of active perturbations include a member of the system being added (birth or adoption of a child, grandparent or other person comes to live with the family) or taken away (death, marriage, imprisonment, off to college); a member becoming unable to perform a certain role (due to illness, additional employment, or additional responsibilities at school or work) or for the first time, becoming able to perform a certain role (due to reduced employment or outside responsibilities or to developmental progress such as the ability to do household chores or to drive a car); a member stepping outside a given role (a child begins swearing, a spouse at work develops a best friend of the other sex). Notice that some of the examples involved perturbations that arose from outside the family (more responsibilities at work) and others from inside (developmental progress of a child). Examples of *threats* of a challenge to the system's equilibrium include when a teenage child starts *talking about* getting a driver's license or a job, a couple *learns* they are expecting a child, or a spouse *begins researching* a new, potentially time- or finance-consuming hobby.

The *corrective strategies* family members employ when they detect disequilibrium can have one of two effects: they can decrease the disequilibrium or increase it. For example, if a parent notices a child has begun to swear, and swearing violates a family rule that "thou shalt not swear," the parent (and probably the child, as well) will experience a sense of systemic disequilibrium. If the parent uses the corrective strategy of frowning at the child, and the child stops swearing, disequilibrium has been decreased. If the parent frowns and the child continues, swears more, makes a hostile remark to the parent—all of which children sometimes do in response to parental corrective strategies and all of which constitute further family rule violation—disequilibrium has been increased. Information about the effect of a corrective strategy on the system's disequilibrium is termed *feedback.* Information that a corrective strategy has *decreased disequilibrium* is termed *negative feedback*, and information that a corrective action has *increased disequilibrium* is termed *positive feedback*. See why we worded it this way? It's harder to think of *negative* feedback as information that *equilibrium has been restored;* it's easier to remember it in terms of *disequilibrium being decreased.* In addition, our wording conveys the "feel" that family (and all systemic) interaction is "all about" monitoring and managing *dis*equilibrium.

We want to clarify a few key points about corrective strategies and negative and positive feedback. First, any single corrective strategy can result in either negative or positive feedback. We already illustrated this in the case of the swearing child. Consider also the wife who develops a new best friend at work—a friend of the other sex, violating the family rule that "thou shalt not have sexually intimate or even very emotionally intimate relationships with members of the other sex," and thus disequilibrating the couple system. The husband might employ any of a number of corrective strategies. He could protest the friendship; if the wife agrees and acts accordingly by "cooling" the outside friendship, disequilibrium is reduced, and the husband's protest yielded negative feedback. However, if she responds to his protest by disagreeing, they argue, and they refuse to speak to one another, disequilibrium was increased, and his protest yielded positive feedback. He might employ a different corrective mechanism: lavishing attention on her. If she responds positively and they become emotionally closer, disequilibrium has decreased: negative feedback. If she recoils from his "smothering" attentiveness and retreats increasingly to the friendship, disequilibrium in the couple relationship has increased: positive feedback. It may be surprising to you to learn that even the husband's *saying and doing nothing different* can constitute a corrective strategy. If he says nothing and the wife's friendship remains simply a platonic one and the marital relationship continues undisturbed, his nonresponse constituted negative feedback, whereas if the friendship evolves such that the marital relationship deteriorates, his nonresponse constituted positive feedback.

As the examples illustrate, the words "negative" and "positive" do not clearly correlate with "unpleasant" and "pleasant." The parent's unpleasant frown and the husband's pleasant attention have the potential to function as either negative or positive feedback. A related point is that, as the above examples also illustrate, whether a particular response will *actually* function as negative or positive feedback *cannot always be predicted,* but it *can almost always be observed*, a point to which we will return.

Another point regarding feedback is that "negative" and "positive" do not mean "good" or "bad." Both types of feedback are constructive to the extent that they succeed in restoring dynamic equilibrium. The family systems literature represent negative feedback as always constructive, and positive feedback as sometimes destructive but sometimes constructive, the latter when it results in the restoration of dynamic equilibrium by establishing a new set point that is more functional for the evolving system (Goldenberg & Goldenberg, 2000). Whereas these principles may accurately reflect mechanical cybernetic systems, we believe it makes sense in the case of human systems to consider the possibility that both negative and positive feedback can also be destructive: Negative feedback—deceleration or decrease in deviation from the set point—is not good if the rigid system actually needs to respond to current perturbation by morphogenetically reorganizing itself around a new set point, which it can discover only by "creatively" deviating from the current set point. Positive feedback—accelerating or increasing deviation from the set point—is not good if the chaotic system actually needs to revert to functioning around an established set point enough to morphostatically stabilize itself.

The overuse of negative feedback is illustrated by the parents who become increasingly controlling in response to an older teen's increasing bids for independence; they may succeed temporarily in restoring equilibrium, but the teen is highly likely at some point to rebel "big time." The parents are like the heating system in a home that turns on more and more frequently in response to the slightest deviation from the set point; that system is likely to burn out and be unable to regulate the temperature at all. The overuse of positive feedback involves a family responding to perturbation with increasingly intense deviation from the "old way," as in the case of an argument that spins out of control, resulting in destruction to property or people. The arguers are like a lady I (JMH) knew who, at the slightest temperature discomfort, reset her thermostat several degrees—up and down, and then even more extremely up and down—resulting in chaotic temperature fluctuations rather than the slight adjustments she actually needed. Thus, both negative and positive feedback, that serve respectively to decrease or increase deviation from a given set point, have the potential to constructively restore dynamic equilibrium or destructively upset dynamic equilibrium even further—either by squelching its dynamism or disrupting its equilibrium. The ways a family manifests positive and negative feedback and the extent to which those manifestations result in restoration or further disruption of dynamic equilibrium are the foci of the family therapist.

A final point regarding feedback is that, to define the concepts of negative and positive feedback, we resorted to linear causality (did you notice?): Cause (perturbation and deviation from set point): effect (response). Although our examples did avoid determinism by illustrating that a parent or jealous husband might respond in any of a number of ways, we still invoked linear causality by specifying a starting point. In fact, in systemic thinking, even the "cause" is seen potentially as an effect. For example, a child starting to swear can be a response to the perturbation of not enough connectedness in the parent–child relationship (a bid for attention) or of too much connectedness (a bid for independence). Similarly, a wife developing a best friendship at work with a member of the other sex can be a response to not enough closeness in the marital relationship (a bid for attention and more intimacy with husband) or to too much closeness (a bid for distance from husband). Systemically speaking, every response is a response to a response, and the function of any one response—its effect on the system—can be understood only in the context of the systemic relationship.

Two final operational functions should round out your understanding of the function of systems: the two types of change. Related to morphostasis, first-order change involves the family *adapting* their *current* mode of operation; related to morphogenesis, second-order change involves a family *adopting* a *new* mode of operation. When a young child begins swearing, first order change is illustrated by the parents who devise a new penalty relevant to the child's current interests: A child who recently developed an interest in video games is prohibited from playing video games for a specified period of time. This kind of change may or may not succeed in restoring equilibrium. By contrast, when an adult child begins swearing, second-order change is exemplified by the parents deciding that swearing is to be tolerated, even if they still do not like that kind of language. The young child's parents who do not consistently enforce the rule against swearing facilitate second-order change; the adult child's parents who intensify enforcement of the rule exemplify first-order change. Again, both types of change are potentially helpful and/or harmful to a system, depending on such factors as the context of the situation, such as the child's age, and whether a family makes excessive use of either type of change in response to perturbations. A system so morphostatically rigid that it cannot adapt is in danger of collapsing in on itself, a kind of "implosion," whereas a system so morphogenetically changable is in danger of falling apart, a kind of "explosion."

In summary, from a systemic perspective, *the members of a system are always monitoring and regulating the dynamic equilibrium of their system*. To apply the concepts addressed in this section, consider that all family systems, in the course of the *family life cycle*, experience some common challenges/

perturbations. Work through the box on this page to explore your own family system's approach to the maintenance of dynamic equilibrium through morphostasis/morphogenesis, feedback, and change. Remember: Very different strategies can be effective in the face of perturbation.

Consider the events listed below that occur in a typical family during its life cycle. Make note of how your family responded to the change. You may use your *family of origin* (the one, or one of the ones, in which you were raised) or your *family of creation* (the one, or one of the ones, you have created). If you have experienced two or more families, work through the events using at least two of the family systems. What changes did you note after the event? What new patterns emerged?

- Marriage
- Birth of a first child
- First child goes to school
- Birth of second child
- Child goes to high school, starts dating, gets driver's license
- Death of parent/grandparent
- 18-year-old child leaves home to establish separate residence or attend college
- Child gets married

What other challenges, perturbations, or disequilibrating circumstances did your family(s) face, for example, serious or chronic illness, unemployment, or unwanted pregnancy? What strategies did your family employ to cope with the perturbation? How effective was the strategy in maintaining the family system's equilibrium?

Structure of the Family Systems. Family system theorists postulate that every system contains *subsystems*, those smaller than and contained within it, and that virtually every system exists within *supersystems*, those larger than it. These various contexts comprise multiple layers (see Figure 12.1). Because it would be overwhelming to consider all systemic contexts involved in a therapeutic situation, family therapists have bracketed the following as the systems of focus: the family system, the family subsystems; and, to some degree, the extended family, community, and cultural systems.

Beginning with the family itself, family systems theorists honor the family's own definition of itself. Consider the Jackson family:

Mr. and Mrs. Jackson have two children, Iesha, 12, and Ben, 8, and they live in downtown New Orleans, Louisiana. Mr. Jackson's mother, Grandma, also lives in the house. Both Mr. and Mrs. Jackson work full time outside the

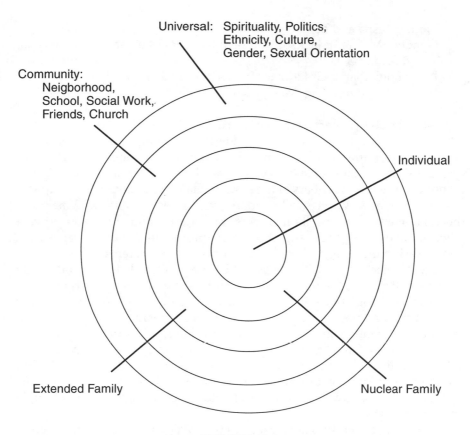

FIGURE 12.1
Systemic levels.

home, so Grandma fulfills most of the parenting duties. Grandma, Mr. Jackson, and Iesha all play the piano. Mrs. Jackson is a former ping-pong champion, and Ben, in particular, likes playing ping-pong with her and learning competitive tips. The members of this family system are Mr. Jackson, Mrs. Jackson, Iesha, Ben, and Grandma.

A system's subsystems are structures that distribute and carry out all functions within the larger system. Subsystems in a family include the spousal subsystem, which is monogamous or polygamous, depending on the cultural context, and may include the parental subsystem, meaning all those who caretake the children; the sibling subsystem, which in some cultures may mean brothers and sisters, whereas in others, brothers, sisters, and cousins; gender subsystems; and other subsystems. In the Jackson family, the most salient subsystems are:

Spousal: Mr. and Mrs. Jackson
Parental: Mr. and Mrs Jackson and Grandma

Sibling: Iesha and Ben
Gender: (Male) Mr. Jackson and Ben; (Female) Mrs. Jackson, Grandma, and Iesha
Avocation: Piano: Grandma, Mr. Jackson, and Iesha
             Ping-pong: Mrs. Jackson and Ben

At all levels of supersystem, system, and subsystem, systemic structures are differentiated by *boundaries*. Boundaries are comprised of the mostly nonconscious, "unwritten" *rules* about who belongs and does not belong to a system (or supersystem or subsystem); what the members of a system do and do not do; and how members of the system relate to nonmembers (members of other systems). A system's boundaries and rules establish and maintain the uniqueness of it and its members. Boundaries and rules also provide guidance about how the system processes internal information, carries out system tasks, and integrates information from other systems.

I (KAF) had an explicit discussion about a family rule just the other day with my son, Dylan, the 6-year-old. He came home from school and wanted to know what the "F-word" meant. I said, "We don't talk that way in our family. You don't need to know what the F-word means. If someone is talking like that around you, just walk away." In that single, brief interchange, I communicated a family rule: "We don't use the F-word or curse in this family"; a firm boundary between outside information and the family: "Don't use that word; You don't even need to know what it means"; and a rule or method for handling such information should it come up again: "Ignore people who talk like that."

Boundaries and rules are structures that play a role in every interaction within the system. Examine the following interaction within the Jackson system and identify the boundaries and rules around the issue of grades. Note the boundaries/rules that differentiate the subsystems pertinent to this issue.

Iesha: Here's my report card. I didn't do so hot this quarter, but my math teacher stinks.

Grandma: Well, your other grades are pretty good, mostly A's and a few B's, but you are right, a C in math in not acceptable. When your parents come home we will discuss it.

(Parents come home.)

Mr. Jackson: Well, Iesha this is really disappointing.

Iesha: But, dad, the teacher is such an idiot.

Mrs. Jackson: No excuses! Your grade has nothing to do with your teacher. We don't make excuses, Iesha.

Grandma: You know, if we saw you studying more, then we wouldn't be so upset. You don't do your homework until late, and you're on the phone for half the evening. That has to stop.

Mr. Jackson: I agree. You will do your homework first thing when you get home. I or your mom will check it when we get home. Phone time will be from 7:00–7:30, if you have your homework done, no exceptions.

Mrs. Jackson: If you bring your grades up, we will consider expanding your privileges.

By examining the dialogue, the parental subsystem—Mr. Jackson, Mrs. Jackson, and Grandma—is identifiable. In this case the parental subsystem is in charge of assessing the child's grades and providing consequences for any deviation from the norm. A member of the child subsystem is represented, Iesha. There are clear boundaries between the subsystems as evidenced by the parent's holding the power of assessment and consequence. In other words, there is no mistake who is in charge and who is in trouble in this scenario. The rule being discussed is the value or expectation of academic performance. Inferring from the discussion, the boundary/rule is something like, "Only grades of A or B are acceptable for members of the sibling subsystem." Iesha's breaking of that rule constitutes a perturbation that is a experienced as disturbance of the family's equilibrium, to which the parental subsystem responds with a corrective strategy. Iesha also seemed to break a family rule by blaming her teacher for her unacceptable grade. The parental subsystem seeks to regain equilibrium by enforcing the rule, that is, issuing consequences for the rule violation.

Iesha complains briefly, then sullenly accepts the stipulations laid down by the parental subsystem. Thus, this situation exemplifies negative feedback, in that further deviation from the norm pertaining to grades is decelerated. If positive feedback had occurred, it could have taken any of several forms. For example, the parental subsystem could have altered the rule right away, on the basis that, "Because junior high work is more challenging, one 'C' is acceptable as long as the other grades are 'A's' and 'B's.'" Another positive feedback scenario might have been Iesha persisting in her protest: "He really *is* a jerk; I've tried going early and staying late to get help from him, and he's always impatient and mean." After Mr. Jackson talks with the teacher and finds him rather uncooperative, he puts a call in to the principal. In the meantime, he consults with the parental subsystem which concludes that, under the circumstances, they will lift the phone restrictions they had imposed.

The flexibility or rigidity of the rules and boundaries are important to the structure of the system. Systems thinkers refer to the degree of *openness or closedness* of the boundaries/rules to describe the extent to which a system lets external information in or internal information out. Akin to the concept of dynamic balance between morphostatsis and morphogenesis is the delicate balance between openness and closedness. Neither is healthy all the time. In this state of balance between openness and closedness, "the system is allowing in information and permitting change as appropriate, while screening out information and avoiding changes that would threaten the survival of the system" (Becvar & Becvar, 2002, p. 74). In order to adapt and change, the system must have boundaries and rules that are flexible and allow for new information. Without new knowledge, the system could not survive. Likewise, systems must have boundaries and rules stable enough to provide a consistent identity for the family. Imagine how chaotic it would be if expectations, values, and rules were constantly changing.

The last ubiquitous systemic structure we will discuss is the *triangle*. In systems thinking, a two-person system, like a two-legged stool, is relatively unstable; as with the addition of a third leg to the stool, a dyadic system is stabilized by the inclusion of a third person. In times of relative equilibrium, the third person can serve to provide a sense of togetherness for the twosome. For example, consider the two possible triangles in Figure 12.2.

Each of the third persons, mother-in-law and secretary, can serve to strengthen the couple's sense of togetherness. When either the husband talks with the wife's mother or the wife talks with the husband's mother, each of the spouses' membership in the marital system is affirmed. When either husband or wife talks with their respective secretaries about such things as upcoming events the couple will be attending, the spouses' "coupleness" is affirmed.

In times of relative disequilibrium, the third person can serve to decrease the intensity experienced within the twosome. Intensity is usually defined as conflict within the twosome that escalates to the point at which the system is threatened. For example, if a spouse feels neglected or pressured by the partner, he or she may call a friend in whom to confide and from whom to receive consolation and support. Having been supported, the intensity of the conflict between spouse and partner would likely be reduced. If the reduction in conflict helps the couple resolve the issue, the triangulation has been constructive. If it promotes a bypassing of the issue, leaving the issue unresolved, it has been destructive.

Guerin, Fogarty, Fay, Kautto, and Kautto (1996) described four common family triangles, as shown in Figure 12.3. In each of these triangles, conflict within the twosome intensifies the triangulation. For example, in the first

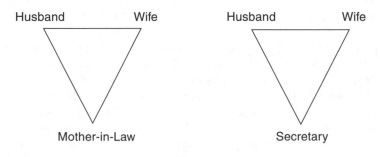

FIGURE 12.2

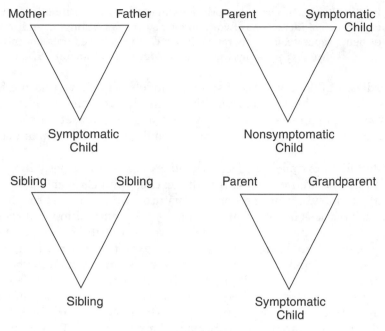

FIGURE 12.3

triangle the husband and wife are having marital problems and fight frequently. The child begins failing in school. As the parents join in solving the
child crisis, the conflict between them abates. In the same scenario, the parents may pull the child in by being critical of the child's work at home or
school. The "shared enemy" of the child gives the subsystem an avenue for
ventilation so the marriage does not disintegrate. It is in this way that the
identified patient, in this case the child, may not be the "source" of the problem; rather, the child is (usually nonconsciously) expressing for the family
the unresolved conflict between the parents.

Again, triangulation is an equilibrating force that is not inherently good
or bad. If it results in too much conflict reduction, the incentive to resolve
the issue is temporarily lost, and the issue goes unresolved, only to recur in
the future. If it results in some conflict reduction—enough for the dyad to
resolve the issue, usually through a form of second-order change—the triangulation has been constructive. The latter illustrates the intended role of the
therapist: to be constructively triangulated into the family system.

Role of the Environment

Familial. The family is the system of focus for family therapy, so its influence and importance is primary.

> In all cultures, the family imprints its members with selfhood. Human experience of identity has two elements: a sense of belonging and sense of being separate. The laboratory in which these ingredients are mixed and dispensed is the family, the matrix of identity. (Minuchin, 1974, p. 47)

Regardless of the variability of systems models, all believe that the foundation of behavior, healthy or unhealthy, is closely associated with the interactions among members of the family system. The information contained in this chapter details the influence of the family system on its members.

Extrafamilial. Extrafamilial factors include everyone and everything outside the family system: neighbors, friends, teachers and classmates, bosses and coworkers, members of one's church, nature, and culture. Through contact with each of these factors, family members gain information that they bring into the family system and that may serve to contribute to or perturb the family equilibrium. Iesha's grades were an example of perturbing information. Another example: Consider the family system in which the boundary/rule regarding sexual activity among the unmarried has been "abstinence only." If a child learns at school about safe sex and brings that information into the family system, the family's equilibrium may be perturbed. To regain equilibrium, the parental system may take corrective action by providing counterinformation. They may be sure to attend their religious institution at the next opportunity to interact with like-minded others and to hear a sermon on the sin of premarital sex and the value of abstinence before marriage. If the child "returns to the fold" regarding this issue, the family-generated information has served as negative feedback; equilibrium has been restored. If the child revolts, the information has served as positive feedback and the equilibrium of the family continues to be challenged.

Interaction of Human Nature and Environment in Personality Development

View of Healthy Functioning. Answering the question "What is a healthy family?" proves to be a daunting task. Each specific theory under the umbrella of systems thinking includes its own answer (see Table 12.1).

Consider the following examples of how three separate families respond to perturbations and strive to reestablish equilibrium. Look for examples of the various concepts introduced so far in this chapter.

The Browns are a very close family. All family members live within 50 miles of each other, and most work in the family business. Jill, upon graduation from high school, decides to attend a university 5,000 miles away. One week before she leaves for college, her father becomes very depressed and refuses to go to work. Her mother and older siblings become very angry with

Jill and repeatedly tell her, "You are killing your father." Jill decides to stay home and attend a community college nearby. Within a week, her father is feeling much better, though the family has taken on an atmosphere of uneasiness.

The Garzas also are a close family. Mr. Garza loses his job and feels as if he is letting his family down. Feeling ashamed and guilty, he becomes irritable, losing his temper more often. The other members are sensitive to his feelings. They realize that he needs support and a way to know that he is contributing to the family, but they are unsure how best to respond. Although he cannot provide financially like he used to, the family discovers that in addition to other things he used to do, such as yardwork, Mr. Garza can cook for the family, easing the burden on his full-time-employed wife, and that he can help the children with their schoolwork such that their teachers report they are doing noticeably better at school, both academically and socially. Understanding that, due to the economy and the nature of Mr. Garza's work, it may be some time before he finds work again, the family also has agreed on strategies to conserve money while Mr. Garza continues to seek work. In the meantime, Mr. Garza and his family appreciate his contributions. The stress within the family subsides.

The Smith's also are a close family until their fourth child is born with Down's syndrome and requires fairly intense and continuous care. Mrs. Smith responds by focusing her attention almost exclusively on the youngest child. When Mr. Smith expresses dissatisfaction, they argue, and Mrs. Smith becomes depressed. Mr. Smith gradually spends more and more time at work. Meanwhile, the other three children develop various health and school-related problems. Eventually, Mr. Smith has an extramarital affair, remaining half-heartedly in the role of husband and father; more and more frequently, he contemplates divorce.

While reading the three vignettes, you may have an internal reaction that one family is "healthier" than the others. One employs excessive morphostasis, one balances morphostasis and morphogenesis, and one exercises excessive morphogenesis. It is worth repeating that, from a systems perspective, various strategies to maintain equilibrium are neither good nor bad, though some are more functional than others, that is, some actually serve to maintain the system, whereas others threaten the system. For example, in the case of the Smiths, Mr. Smith may have undertaken the affair to meet his emotional and sexual needs without placing further stress on the marriage/family system—an attempt to maintain the system—yet it ended up threatening the system as he increasingly contemplated divorce. However, the strategy might have worked: In Sonya Friedman's (1994) book *Secret Loves: Women with Two Lives,* she described women she interviewed who had sustained long-term affairs—some as long as 20 years and still going—that reportedly enabled them to *maintain* their marriages and families by compensating for what they felt was lacking in their marriages and perceived their spouses unable to provide. From a family systems perspective, even a phenomenon as charged as an extramarital affair is evaluated in light of its effect on the system: Although affairs often threaten the system, they apparently, at times, can serve to stabilize it. Fortunately, most strategies families use to maintain their system's existence are less morally controversial. The seminal works of Prigogine (1973) and Maruyama (1963) described how systems can respond to disequilibriating forces by exploring new alternatives, creating new patterns, and thus reaching a new sense of balance and stability that is appropriate to the new circumstance.

Walsh (1993) provided an excellent collection of literature intended to define and describe "normal family processes." Fenell and Weinhold (1997) succeeded in transcending the variations in families and theories by outlining the following general characteristics of healthy families.

Clear Subsystem Boundaries and Clear Family Roles. A colleague of mine is fond of saying, "In families, you need to be able to tell the difference between the kids and the parents." His advice points up the importance of establishing clear subsystem boundaries and member roles. Most systemic theorists believe that well-differentiated subsystems are keys to healthy functioning because they make the roles and rules easier for system members to define and fulfill; thus the system is less chaotic, that is, equilibrium is more easily maintained. A number of approaches advocate defined hierarchies: a prioritizing of subsystems based on power (Framo, 1992; Minuchin, 1974). In particular, a well-defined parental subsystem is vital; for example, by and large, parents care for children, not vice versa. Another important challenge many families face is distinguishing the parental subsystem from the spousal subsystem. In healthy families, the members of the spousal subsystem spend time with each other and apart from the rest of the family system in order to nurture the spousal relationship as separate and distinct from their roles in the parental subsystem. "The [spousal subsystem] is especially important to the family: Any dysfunction in the spousal subsystem is bound to reverberate throughout the family [and spill over into the parental subsystem], resulting in the scapegoating of children or co-opting them into alliances with one parent against the other" (Goldenberg & Goldenberg, 2000, p. 378).

Clear Family Rules with Consistent and Fair Enforcement. Healthy families also have rules that are known and understood by all members of the system; when infractions occur, consequences are fair and consistent. The idea is that if the members know what to expect, they have a higher probability of maintaining equilibrium and are less likely to erupt in rebellion if a consequence is warranted and enforced. A client in a group counseling session shared the story of how his teenage daughter missed curfew; as a consequence, she was not allowed to attend a party the following night. He stated, "When she came home, I laid down the law [well defined parental and child subsystem]. I told her that because she missed curfew, she would be staying in the next night. It's on her, as far as I'm concerned. She knew she had done wrong, so she just went to her room to sulk." His story provides a good example of how rules are handled in a manner that is known to all, with minimal surprises in expectations or outcomes.

Respect for Individual Autonomy Coexisting with a Respect for Family Connection. Healthy families also respect the individuality of their members while encouraging membership in the system. The concept of *differentiation* can be helpful in understanding this characteristic of a healthy family. Kerr and Bowen (1988) defined differentiation as "the ability to be in emotional contact with others yet still autonomous in one's emotional functioning" (p. 145). Healthy systems encourage members to form distinct identities and voice beliefs and knowledge gained through interaction with other systems without being threatened by members' distinct ways of thinking and functioning. Different points of view are honored within healthy systems and can actually form the basis of the cohesion experienced by the members. The operating belief in this type of system might be, "I can speak my mind and not fear losing my place in the family or expect intense coercion from other members." At the same time, "I listen to others' points of view and, if differences exist between our perspectives, I express my position and do not coerce them." A useful strategy in such cases is to "agree to disagree."

Clear and Direct Communication. The last aspect of a healthy family is clear and direct communication patterns. A number of systemic thinkers (Alexander & Parsons, 1982; Beavers & Hampson, 1990; Minuchin, 1974; Olsen, 1993; Satir, 1983) have concurred that effective communication includes good listening skills, the sending of direct messages, using "I" language (e.g., "I would like for you to hug me" instead of, "You never want to be around me"), a willingness to share personal feelings about the relationship and oneself, the ability to stay on the topic at hand, and the willingness to be open to alternatives.

View of Unhealthy Functioning. Trying to clearly define what constitutes an "unhealthy family" is as problematic as attempting to define a healthy one. Table 12.1 offers descriptions of how different family therapies address the characteristics of a dysfunctional system. For the sake of consistency, we used Fenell and Weinhold's (1997, p. 34) elements of family dysfunction.

Subsystem Boundaries Are Either too Rigid or too Diffuse. In dysfunctional systems the boundaries that differentiate one subsystem from another can be conceptualized along the following continuum:

Diffuse-----------------(--------------Healthy------------)------------------Rigid

When the boundary is too diffuse, one cannot tell one subsystem from the other, and members have difficulty identifying the various subsystems in their own family. Families with diffuse boundaries may have adults and children who alternate between acting like adults and acting like children. The impact of diffuse boundaries on the family is confusion and chaos. The family belief or motto is, "We have no beliefs or mottos." Conversely, when boundaries are too rigid, the system becomes paralyzed and incapable of change. Families with rigid boundaries fear the disequilibriating effect of outside information and, as a result, become very insular in their interactions. The family mottos are "We fear change," and "This is the way it has always been done."

Rules and Enforcement Are Either too Rigid or Very Inconsistent. When subsystems are poorly or rigidly organized, one can expect that the rules governing these systems will follow suit. In diffuse systems, the only consistent rule is that there are no rules. Rules are arbitrary, open for constant revision, and inconsistently enforced. Any attempt to challenge the chaotic balance is met with fierce resistance. Consider a true story from therapy in which one parent recounted a feeble attempt to set a rule and establish a new pattern in a diffuse system.

Mrs. Jones heard on a talk show that families should eat together every evening. She thought about her own family: Dad worked crazy hours, often eating out and then going to bed upon getting home; daughter was 16, had just earned her driver's license, and often stayed out with friends, even on school nights; son was 13 and played on three different soccer teams—when did he eat, anyway? Mrs. Jones announced that starting tomorrow, "We will eat together as a family." The family's reply? Dad said, "OK" and then did not come home until 11:45. Daughter left a post-it note on the refrigerator saying, "Went on a date with Ricky. C-ya!" Mom herself got caught up at work on a project and forgot to come home. Son showed up at appointed time but left when no one else arrived.

Rigid subsystems follow rigid rules in which the appropriate behavior is often narrowly defined and deviations are countered with extreme prejudice. The rules in the system are designed to keep all members within a narrow homeostatic range; even the smallest perturbance leads to extreme reactions by the system—often over what most people would consider "small" issues. Consider the following case, and see if you can detect the rule and the extreme reaction.

George knew his parents liked to keep the house clean, so before he went to play, he made sure his room was spotless. He hung up his clothes and put all of his toys away. One day George was playing at a friend's house when his mother called on the telephone, saying, "You need to come home right away." George told his friend goodbye and walked home. When he arrived, he found his mother in his bathroom. She said, "You left the cap off of the toothpaste again! You need to learn to keep your room clean, and when you don't, you embarrass the whole family. Now clean this mess up, and you can stay in your room for the rest of the day."

The rigid rules tend to be static and fail to change over time. As time passes, contexts change. If the system is unable to adapt to the changes by adopting new rules, disequilibrium occurs increasingly frequently, and the system must become increasingly rigid to withstand it.

Roles and Expectations of Members Are Either too Rigid or Not Clearly Defined. Dysfunctional roles operate with the same effect as dysfunctional rules. Diffuse roles fail to help the individual members forge personal or family identities. Members feel very confused, often not knowing what they are supposed to be doing in the family. The following case excerpt demonstrates the chaos of a diffuse boundary between parent and child subsystems and the corresponding role confusion.

"I don't know what to do. Six months ago, my husband and I divorced, and my 12-year-old son and 15-year-old daughter have been punishing me ever since! I am a nervous wreck, so I started smoking again. I wasn't sure if I should, so I asked my son. He said that I should not start smoking, but I started last week. When he caught me, he ripped the cigarette out of my hand and threw it on the ground. I just cried. My daughter is now failing biology, so I grounded her, but she won't listen. I am going to stick to my guns though. I'm her mother! In addition to all this mess, I am dating someone but keeping it a secret from the kids. They would die if they found out. I don't think they would let me if I told them."

Individual Identity Is Not Encouraged or Even Recognized. Minuchin (1974) discussed the difference between enmeshed and disengaged families; correspondingly, Bowen (1978) spoke in terms of a lack of differentiation within families. Both were addressing the dysfunctional system's approach to individuality and autonomy. In *enmeshed families* or systems with low differentiation, autonomy is a threat to the system. All members must think the same thoughts, feel the same feelings, and behave in similar ways. It is as if all the members of the system share the same brain; whoever possesses the lead brain dictates the identity of the system. Decision making is a very trying process in which the typical response is, "I don't care. I'll do whatever you want to do." Guilt, the message that one did something wrong, and shame, the message that one is inherently faulty, are two frequently used enforcement strategies.

Disengaged families have little sense of system identity, so the individual identity is virtually all the person has to work with. The system's balance revolves around an "I'll do my thing, you do yours" mentality. Members are emotionally distant from one another and fail to provide support when needed. Because the affection and support is not found within the family and is even resisted, members typically find it within another systemic level such as school, work, church, or friends.

Communication Is Unclear, Indirect, Abusive, and/or Coercive. In systems characterized by diffuse structures and inconsistency, communication is vague, confusing, and often limited. Simply put, it is common for these systems to fail to communicate, and when they do, the signal is often very weak or full of static. In rigid systems the message is clear—LOUD AND CLEAR—delivered in an authoritarian or abusive manner. Consider the father who tells his college-bound daughter, "You don't need to stay out past 11 o'clock when you are at school. There is nothing going on after 11. If you want to stay out past 11, then you will just be hanging around with low-lifes and whores. If you are going to be doing that, then you can just come back home and live with us." He is using threats and derogatory terms to enforce a rigid family belief that fails to recognize the changing context of his daughter's life.

Theories vary widely in their concepts of what is healthy and what is not in families. How particular theorists answer the question of what is healthy guides their interventions. The next section builds on this foundation and addresses the elements of change.

The System Change Process

Basic Principles of Change. From a systems perspective, for a therapist to facilitate constructive change, the family must be able to see the problem as a systemic issue and not an individual one. For many families, this means that the first step toward change is to redefine the problem. Once the systems focus has been established, the emphasis becomes quite different from other nonsystems approaches in which the focus is on restoring order or returning the client to a previous state of healthy functioning. Instead, systems therapists believe that systems enter therapy when negative or positive feedback has proven ineffective in restoring dynamic equilibrium. The system must change how it addresses change; the existing strategies, intended as they are to restore equilibrium, are not doing so.

Although Table 12.1 highlights the variety of methods and approaches found among the different family therapies, a few common threads of systems thinking weave through those various approaches. Goldenberg and Goldenberg (2000, p. 389) highlighted those common threads:

1. People are products of their social connections, and attempts to help them must take family relationships into account.
2. Symptomatic behavior in an individual arises from a context of relationships, and interventions to help that person are most effective when they address and alter the faulty interactive patterns from which the symptomatic behavior arises.
3. Individual symptoms are maintained externally in current family system transactions.
4. Conjoint sessions in which the family is the therapeutic unit and the fo-

cus is on family interaction are more effective in producing change than attempts to uncover intrapsychic problems in individuals by therapy via individual sessions.

5. Assessing family subsystems, including the permeability of boundaries within the family and of those between the family and the outside world, offer important clues regarding family organization and susceptibility to change.

6. The goal of family therapy is to change maladaptive or dysfunctional family interactive patterns—those that maintain dysfunctional symptoms.

By putting these ideas into practice, a family counselor emphasizes the mutual causality of symptoms and, along the same lines, the mutual nature of change. Consider the following situation that counselors frequently see:

Mr. and Mrs. Smith bring their 8-year-old son and only child, Damien, into therapy. Both parents claim Damien is a hell-raiser; he is failing in three subjects, and he bullies other children. Mom and Dad fight over how to handle Damien. Dad gets frustrated and stays at work until Damien goes to bed. Mom coddles Damien and resents Dad.

How would a systems thinker conceptualize this problem? Obviously there are many directions to go and avenues to pursue, but, generally speaking, a systems perspective would view Damien's school problems as a family issue, not solely a Damien problem. A possible hypothesis of the circular causality within this system is visualized in Figure 12.4. From a systems perspective, each response is connected to the other, and no method of communication—verbal or nonverbal—exists in isolation.

Within the systems perspective, *change* means *altering the method of solving a problem*. As previously stated, change can be of the first or second order (Becvar & Becvar, 2002). A first-order change involves *clarifying and following the system's existing rules*, whereas second-order change involves *creating and implementing new rules*. In the case of Damien, if the existing family rule is

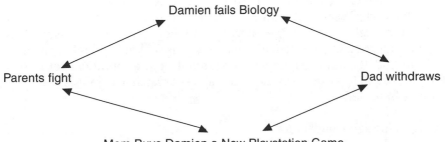

FIGURE 12.4

that each parent independently does what (s)he believes will promote their child's achievement, Mr. Smith may decide to spend regular study time with Damien; although Mrs. Smith continues to exercise her "right" to buy Damien special treats such as the Playstation, she is less likely to do so if she no longer perceives Damien to be "abandoned" by his father.

First-order change may seem simplistic, and often it is the overuse of first-order change that, from a systems perspective, constitutes "the problem." However, first-order change often *is* an effective strategy, and some families too quickly implement second-order change, thereby promoting more chaos than order in the family's functioning. In the latter case, less second-order change and more first-order change is needed.

If first-order change does not restore equilibrium, the Smiths and their counselor might seek second-order change in a variety of ways. For example, Dad and Mom may agree that it is better for them to collaborate on the problem than fight. Dad may come home and take a walk with Mom to discuss the day and any problems/challenges that face the family. The family may decide that Damien is responsible for his school work and his behavior at school and that he is also responsible for any consequences that arise from his choices. Mom and Dad may provide support through helping Damien study or hiring him a tutor. They may agree to make special treats, such as a Playstation, contingent on Damien's reasonable success in school, as reflected in his grades and other aspects of his school record. These second-order changes represent vast revisions in the philosophical approach to the problem when compared to the former methods. As Becvar and Becvar (2002) noted, "By changing the rules, we change our perception, or the way we view the problem, and new behavioral alternatives become possible in the process" (p. 94).

Most often, by the time most families get to counseling, they have tried numerous first-order changes and, in some cases, second-order changes without succeeding in restoring equilibrium in the family. Less often, a family presents as chaotic due to repeatedly seeking second-order change, in which case first-order strategies—the establishment of reasonable rules and their consistent, fair enforcement—is more likely to restore (or create) equilibrium. As Watzlawick, Weakland, and Fisch (1974) commented, "a system which may run through all its possible internal changes (no matter how many there are) without effecting a systematic change, . . . is said to be caught in a Game Without End. It cannot generate from within itself the conditions for its own change" (p. 22). It is exactly in these moments of systemic paralysis that counseling is indicated.

Change Through Counseling

The Client's Role. Members of a system usually enter therapy with the expressed desire for the therapist to fix the identified client. Families routinely view the problem as individually based and rarely have a strong desire to explore the mutual causality of the symptoms. In the most basic of forms, the system is asking the therapist to return the identified client to the way he or she was before the symptoms spiraled out of control. The role of the client in systems thinking is the willingness to view the problem as systemically, rather than individually, based.

Resistance is a predictable and normal part of the therapeutic process that arises from the system's natural homeostatic function: The therapist perturbs by suggesting new perspectives and behaviors; the system resists. Ineffective as are the family's existing change strategies, they are likely to find the change strategies facilitated by the counselor to be new, alien, and unknown—potentially *further* threatening to the family's equilibrium. The role of the family member is to express the resistance so the therapist can be aware of it and seek ways to help the family get past it.

The Counselor's Role. From a systems perspective, the moment the family enters counseling is the moment the counselor becomes a part of the system. The counselor presents new information into the system and acts as a disturbance to the balance of the system. The nature and method of the disturbance depends on the personality of the counselor and the specific theory of operation (see Table 12.1). However, regardless of theoretical orientation, systems approaches all see the therapist as less a change agent and more of a dispenser of new information that perturbs the system to action. As Becvar and Becvar (2002) noted, "By virtue of our presences, we help define a new context and thus a new family within which the members behave differently. . . . [W]e must provide new information, which the system may choose to incorporate into a self-corrective process that at the same time facilitates self-maintenance" (p. 100).

In my (KAF) attempts to think of a metaphor for the role of the systems therapist, I consulted a colleague. He likened the role of a systems practitioner to that of an agitator in a washing machine. The agitator is the pole-like mechanism in the middle of the machine drum that rotates the clothes and churns them in the water and soap solution. The really good ones are shaped with screw-like ridges that not only push the clothes from side to side, but also move them up and down. A systems therapist is like an agitator, the system is the clothing, and the therapy is the machine. The therapist's job is to move the system in various directions and agitate/perturb them enough to facilitate change. Perhaps at the end of the "cycle" of therapy, the system is a little "cleaner" than when it started.

Stages and Techniques. Each of the different models of family therapy offers a different model of the stages of therapy. For overview purposes, we refer to the general stage model proposed by Nicholls and Schwartz (2001). The stages in this model include the initial contact, the first interview, the early phase of treatment, the middle phase, and termination.

The initial contact. The goal of the first contact, usually over the telephone, is to set up an appointment with the entire system. The therapist needs to get only a brief overview of the reason for therapy; any in depth discussion begins the formation of an alliance with the caller. After hearing the presenting problem, the focus shifts to structural concerns such as time and place of appointment and who should attend.

The most difficult task is getting the caller, who often views the issue as an individual problem, to consider bringing in the entire family for the session. Nicholls and Schwartz (2001) maintained that resistance is normal and that an understanding yet firm approach on the part of the therapist generally works through most resistance. The therapist conveys understanding of the caller's perspective and simultaneously asserts that a meeting with everyone for informational purposes is a vital first step. Although there are many ways to wrangle entire systems into therapy, the following conversation should provide an example of the delicate balance of empathy and insistence.

Caller: Yes, I need to make an appointment to bring my son into therapy.

Therapist: OK, can you tell me a little about the reason for seeking counseling?

Caller: Sure, the school counselor told me to call. He's failing math and he's just not trying. I mean . . .

Therapist: How has the family responded to his grades?

Caller: Oh, we are very angry. Especially his father! I mean, Billy, that's my son, just doesn't try.

Therapist: I think I have enough information for now and will certainly have time to learn all about the issue when you come in. For the first session, I would like for the whole family to come.

Caller: Oh, I don't think that's possible. His father is very busy and his sister has basketball practice.

Therapist: I understand that everyone is very busy, but to get the best information possible and to formulate the best way to help you, I really need to talk with everyone, especially during this first session. When would be the most convenient time? How about Thursday at 7:00?

In the dialogue, the counselor gathers quite a bit of information about the family. The counselor can note that the mom is calling to make the appointment, that Billy is the identified client who has seemingly broken a family rule regarding grades and "trying," that the father is "busy" and "angry," and the sister is "busy" as well. The therapist gently but firmly insists that meeting with the family is the ideal way for treatment to proceed at this point. Nicholls and Schwartz advised that because families might be reluctant to come to therapy, a reminder call the day before the first session might cut down on "accidental" no-shows.

The first interview. The goal of the first interview, rapport building, is no different from many of the individual-based theories discussed in this text. The difference is that instead of connecting with an individual client, the counselor is forming a relationship with the system. The counselor orients the family to the therapy experience and, with Mom's consent, briefly discusses what was disclosed during the phone conversation. Counselors make sure to give each member a fair share of the time to discuss their view of "the problem" while also spending some time discussing the family's strengths. While the family is detailing various views of the problem, the therapist is gathering information about the family dynamics by paying attention to who speaks and in what order, who sits next to whom, how differences in opinion are tolerated, who is the identified client, how the family has tried to handle this problem before, and any other systemic dynamics. Each dynamic observed provides an additional piece to the family puzzle. Counselors may use graphic representations of generational patterns, such as family maps or genograms, to gain a perspective on family dynamics. Let us continue to follow the case of Billy's family during the first session.

The counselor greets the family in the waiting room. The counselor notes that Dad and Brianna, the daughter, are sitting side-by-side on the couch, and that Billy and mom are squeezed into a loveseat across the room. Dad looks frustrated, Mom looks worried, Brianna looks disgusted, and Billy looks defeated. The counselor collects the paperwork the family has completed while waiting and invites the family into the counseling room. Dad and Brianna choose the loveseat, while Billy sits in an oversized chair. Mom moves a chair from across the room to sit next to Billy.

Therapist: Welcome. I spoke to you (Mom) on the phone and you stated there was some concern about Billy's recent grade in math. That is about all I know about this situation, so I would like to give each of you an opportunity to discuss what you see as the important issues in your family at this time. Who would like to start? [The therapist lets the family know what she knows from the first contact so everyone knows where to begin. The initial invitation to discuss "important issues in your family" is a subtle message that emphasizes the system rather than the presenting individually based problem. Although it is doubtful the family will shift this soon, building a gradual transition to a systems perspective is often more effective than a quick jump.]

Brianna: I'll start. Billy just needs to try a bit more. All he does is hang out with his creepy friends and play video games. Me, I study 4 or 5 hours a day and still manage to play varsity basketball.

Therapist: It seems as though you are very disciplined as well as talented. How did you learn self-discipline? [The therapist avoids focusing on the presenting problem and instead connects with a resistant family member by focusing on her strengths. Her statement and next answer begin to illuminate some key family rules about self-discipline.]

Brianna: I guess I just do it, you know. Mom is real good at helping me when I need help, but you have to ask.

Dad: Well I think this is a load of crap. He's lazy and needs to pull himself up and work. I tell him that but he just ignores me.

Therapist: It sounds like you have a pretty good idea of what you want to have happen, but your current strategies are not helping you get there. [Once again, instead of focusing on the specific issue, the therapist personalizes each person's unique role.]

The dialogue continues and at the end of the session, the therapist is able to construct a genogram based on information gathered (see Figure 12.5).

Through examination of the genogram, counselor and family can learn about patterns within the system. Common triangles can also become apparent. For example, the following patterns emerge from Billy's family genogram.

- The three lines connecting Mom and Billy denote an enmeshed, or overinvolved relationship. This pattern is multigenerational, as evidenced by the same pattern between Mom and maternal grandmother.

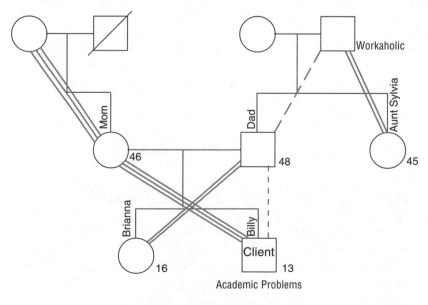

FIGURE 12.5
Billy's family genogram.

- The two lines connecting Dad and Brianna denote a close relationship. This pattern is also replicated in dad's family of origin between paternal grandfather and Dad's sister, Sylvia.
- The dotted line between Dad and Billy represents a distant or diffuse relationship. Dad reported a similar type of relationship with his father.

An abundance of useful information can surface from a well-constructed genogram. A counselor can add other demographic information and additional generations to further illuminate family patterns. For a more in-depth discourse on genograms consult McGoldrick and Gerson's (1985) book *Genograms in Family Assessment.*

The early phase of treatment.   The early phase of treatment is marked by a shift in focus characterized by a move away from rapport building and toward a stance of perturbing the system so change can occur. Remember, the system usually enters counseling because its dynamic equilibrium has been disrupted and its self-correcting method of feedback is not reestablishing equilibrium. The system might be experiencing a negative feedback loop that is restricting the possibility of constructive reorganization or a positive feedback loop that is stuck in only amplifying the deviation. The good news is that the system will act out its pattern in real time during the sessions, which is one reason why it is important to have the entire system in the room. One of the easiest ways to challenge the system is to concentrate on the system's conceptualization of the problem.

Tasks in this phase of treatment include the emphasis on circular or mutual causality of the family's problem and influencing the family to work for change within the session and at home. Homework assignments that target changes in patterns are most effective. Billy's family has now entered the early phase of treatment and their struggles are described below.

After working and connecting with the family, the counselor generated the following hypothesis about the system: When the system is perturbed, the members use the following strategies to restore balance: Dad uses anger and shame and then withdraws; Mom uses nurturing and, to some extent, "babying"; Brianna uses aloofness and often follows Dad's lead, and Billy hits his "shut down" switch. When the usual strategies fail to work, the system intensifies its strategies, creating a positive feedback loop that has served only to amplify the disequilibrating forces: The family is caught in a cycle. The therapist knows that because of mutual causality, it does not matter where the intervention occurs within the cycle, as long as the cyclical nature of the interactional dynamics is addressed. The following dialogue provides one example of a systemic challenge.

Therapist: It seems to me that this family is a little stuck. All families get stuck, but I am wondering about your perspective about *how you* are stuck.

Dad: Well, he just won't listen to me, and he is so damn lazy.

Mom: Oh, honey, you are being too hard on him. [The therapist hypothesizes that the tension between Dad and Billy leads to a triangulation of Mom to cool off the conflict.]

Therapist: It seems like the two of you are going in two different directions. Dad, you try the hostility thing, and Mom, you try to smooth it over. When they do that, what do you think of all that, Billy?

Billy: They usually start fighting, and I walk away.

Therapist: Dad, when you yell, Mom jumps in to break it up, and Billy walks away. The problem never gets resolved. Because each of you plays a role in the stuckness, each of you will need to do something different to get a different result. [The therapist is noting the mutual causality of the problem and challenges each member to change.]

The middle phase of treatment. Once the therapist has succeeded in formulating a hypothesis regarding the patterns with the family system and has begun work on perturbing the system to facilitate change, the middle phase is largely devoted to encouraging interactions among members and testing out new ways of being. Once the family gets used to the process, the therapist can move to the periphery of the system and be less directive and challenging. The therapist becomes a system process observer, pointing out interactions that experiment with new ways of relating and alerting the family to interactions that reflect a return to old patterns. Homework is especially important in this phase so that learning can be experienced and generalized to the "real world."

Therapist: Well, it has been 6 weeks since we started therapy. Billy, how are things going?

Billy: OK, I guess. My grades in math are getting better.

Therapist: What is different?

Billy: Well, since we've been coming here, my family listens a little more to me.

Therapist: You seem very observant. Can you provide me with an overview of changes you have seen in everyone in your system? [Here the therapist turns the table on the family. The person who initially was labeled as "the problem" is now providing guidance. The risk of the family shutting the process down or reacting in a negative way is minimized because the focus is on positive change.]

Billy: Hmmm. . . . Well, Mom is not hovering as much. You know, coming by my room every 5 minutes checking to see if I'm all right. I think that homework where she kept a log of her "fly bys" really helped her. I actually go ask her stuff more often now because I have more room to breathe. [Note the new pattern that has developed.] Brianna has been around more and seems happier. She's really smart and has taken a lot of the classes I am in right now. She is less bossy and more helpful. Dad has really changed! Instead of yelling at me, he spends a half-hour with me every night just going over stuff. That's been pretty cool. I try to get my homework done so we can just hang out some of the time instead of spending it all on math.

Therapist: Wow, very nice! That is a lot of change in 4 weeks. It sounds as if you have made changes, too. Without your willingness to be open to doing something different, this whole new pattern could not have developed.

Termination. Termination occurs when the family decides that change is not necessary or has modified the system's rules enough to have reached a new sense of balance. In a sense, termination begins with the first contact, so therapists must be mindful and honor the process of ending the therapy. Termination issues can be discussed as family functioning is assessed. Questions such as, "What are you doing differently?", "How have things changed?" and "How will you know if you are sliding back into the old pattern?" are important to the process of termination. Highlighting the changes that have been made and the skills used to make them provide the family with resources upon which to draw when future problems occur.

Although some techniques were discussed in the stages sections, systems theorists have created a vast number of innovative techniques that focus on illuminating and modifying interactional patterns within the system. A few are discussed to give the reader a taste of what is out there, but you are encouraged to consult specific books on the subject for a more comprehensive discourse on techniques (see Sherman & Fredman, 1986; Watts, 1999).

Reframing. Reframing is a verbal technique designed to alter the system's perspective of the problem and allow for the generation of alternatives. In a sense, it means looking at the issue at hand from a different viewpoint, often putting a less negative spin on the issue. For example, the father of two sons, ages 5 and 8, complains that his sons do not listen to authority. The therapist notices that the sons do have conflicts but work hard to figure problems out for themselves. The therapist reframes disobedience as "independent thinkers who like to solve problems on their own" and explores with the father the parenting skills that encouraged such healthy behavior in his sons. The outcome: Instead of getting into a power struggle within the family, the therapist helped the system see the problem in a productive way.

Sculpting. Sculpting is an experiential technique that illuminates each member's perspective of the dynamics of the system. The therapist encourages each member to be the "sculptor," physically arranging the members of the family in the room, creating a symbolic structure representing the interaction patterns within the family. Consider the case example of a 10-year-old boy named Sam, sculpting his family.

Sam: I would put my brother, Ben, right here in the middle of the room.

Therapist: How would he look? Arrange his body in some gesture that demonstrates his role in the family.

Sam: I don't understand.

Therapist: Ok, how would you describe Ben?

Sam: Oh, I guess he's all right, but he thinks he is real great and knows a lot more than me.

Therapist: I see. So if I walked in the room and saw your sculpture, how would Ben be posed so I would look at him and say, "Oh, that guy thinks he's pretty smart"?

Sam: I get it. I'm going to have Ben smirking and raising his finger and saying over and over, "I'm number 1!"

Therapist: I think you've got a handle on this.

Sam: My Mom would be standing with her arm around Ben looking proud.

Therapist: Does she have something to say?

Sam: How about, "Ben is number 1!" My Dad, hmmmm, well, he is so worried all the time. I think I'll have him walking around in circles saying, "Where is all the money?" I guess that's it.

Therapist: Not yet, Sam. Where are you in this sculpture?

Sam: Oh, I forgot me. I am in the corner. I think I would look sad. Maybe I would wave every once in a while to get people to look at me, but no one notices.

Therapist: OK, everyone, take your places, and when Sam says, "Go," everyone act out their roles.

Just reading the preceding dialogue, you might have a sense of the vivid and powerful family dynamics at play in sculpting. After the sculpture is arranged and experienced, family members process new insights and emerging patterns.

Prescriptions. Prescriptions are instructions given to the family by the counselor that are designed to disequilibrate the system and give the family an alternative to the current pattern. In a sense, the therapist is creating a positive feedback loop to amplify any noted deviation. There are many types of prescriptions, and some are noted below.

Paradoxical: With this type of prescription, the therapist may instruct the system to create and/or maintain the symptom for a specific period of time. For example, if the problem is anger, the assignment might be to refrain from fighting until a prescribed time and duration (i.e., 7:00–7:30 p.m. on Wednesday nights). The effect of this type of prescription often results in an increase in awareness about the futility of the dysfunctional pattern and, even more importantly, that the system controls the pattern.

Countersystemic: This prescription provides a direct contradiction to the system's ordinary pattern. For example, a mother who complains about the irresponsibility of the children—but also cleans up after them—is told that she has been fired from maid duty for the rest of the week. During the next session, the therapist processes changes that occurred in the system. Did the Mom find it hard to stay off the job (this highlights Mom's role in the pattern)? How did the other members try to get Mom back on the job? How did other members respond over time to the vacant job and the responsibilities left open by the vacancy?

Restructuring: This prescription injects new skills or new patterns into the system. For example, the counselor may prescribe parenting classes for the parents with the plan that the classes will provide new information to the parental subsystem that may perturb the system and lead to constructive change. The therapist may prescribe responsibilities in the family that may elicit cooperation among disengaged members (cleaning the yard together) or an individual sense of responsibility among enmeshed members (each person is responsible for waking themselves for school or work).

CONTRIBUTIONS AND LIMITATIONS

Interface with Recent Developments in the Mental Health Field

Effectiveness of Psychotherpy. Regarding effectiveness of the systems perspective, a large amount of outcome research exists on this topic despite the relative newness of the practice of family therapy. Although very few studies exist that compare different forms of family therapy, outcome research supports the efficacy of family therapy when compared to no treatment or individual-focused forms of therapy (Baucom, Shoham, Mueser, Daiuto, & Stickle, 1998; Dunn & Schwebel, 1995; Pinsof, Wynne, & Hambright, 1996; Shadish, Ragsdale, Glaser, & Montgomery, 1995).

Friedlander, Wildman, Heatherington, and Skowron (1994) provided an excellent overview of the literature on family therapy research and concluded that although much is known about the process and efficacy of family approaches, much is also not known. They encouraged future researchers to focus on the family members' cognitive, emotional, and behavioral experience in therapy, how change occurs in more experiential forms of family therapy, and the role of cultural issues in therapy.

Nature/Nurture. Regarding the nature/nurture question, systems theory postulates that a person's identity and personality are formed through the dynamic interplay of one's genetic makeup, environment, and one's perception of both. One's genes and environment provide the individual with numerous opportunities and limits, and if one fails to perceive the given opportunities or limits, then they hardly matter. Family systems theory holds that people are proactive beings, neither predetermined by genes nor completely determined by the environment. Instead, a system perspective focuses on the interaction among the variety of influences within the system

Pharmacotherapy. Regarding the prescription of medication, systems purists may consider medication as treating the symptom instead of dealing with the family dynamics that create the dysfunction. However, to ignore the research on the benefits of medication for a number of disorders exposes the client to unneeded suffering and opens the counselor's door to malpractice suits. Ethical systems clinicians are encouraged to form cooperative relationships with psychiatrists when a family enters counseling with a preexisting psychiatric relationship and to refer families to psychiatrists who understand and respect the systems perspective (Brock & Barnard, 1999). Just as a diagnosis and medication can be a distraction from what systems counselors consider to be the relevant therapeutic focus, a turf battle between therapist and psychiatrist can be equally distracting from and disruptive to treatment. Therapists can work with clients taking medication as long as all parties understand that the medication is not a cure-all for the problems within the system.

Managed Care and Brief Therapy. Overall, systems approaches are time-limited, problem solving forms of therapy that lend themselves to brief treatment. One could conclude from the literature that the systems approach was a brief-oriented modality from the inception of the theory. When systemic thinkers were trying to gain a foothold in the professional therapeutic community, the battle was with the lengthy treatment regimen of psychoanalysis, so shortening the span of treatment was one way to differentiate the systems perspective. While some approaches outlined in Table 12.1 (strategic, structural, or MRI's brief therapy) are more time-limited than others, most forms of systems therapy treat the system by perturbing the system, exploring new alternatives to dealing with the challenge, and then letting the family terminate therapy and work on the changes themselves. The literature contains many examples of brief family systems applications (Berg & deShazer, 1993; Epstein, Bishop, Keitner, & Miller, 1990; O'Hanlon & O'Hanlon, 2002).

Diversity Issues. Systems theorists have devoted a substantial literature to exploring cultural factors in couple and family therapy. Excellent books by

Ho (1987) and McGoldrick, Giordano, and Pearce (1996) give readers an overview of specific cultural outlooks and how to integrate different cultural perspectives into a systems framework. Systems practitioners appreciate that cultural influences are complex forces that must be examined from the family's context to fully appreciate the dynamics of the system. McGoldrick and Giordano (1996) encouraged therapists to adopt the role of a "culture broker, helping family members to recognize their own ethnic values and to resolve the conflicts that evolve out of different perceptions and experiences" (p. 21).

Gender issues have been a concern historically for systems approaches. At the inception of systems thinking, the family system was set up to include a "model" nuclear family: husband, wife, and child. Times have changes from the early days of family therapy, the 1950s and 1960s when model families were of the "Leave It to Beaver" and "Father Knows Best" variety. From a gender perspective, many of the foundational ideas of systems thinking pathologized the roles of women and obviously fail to take into account modern family manifestations. Early writings in systems thinking linked mother behaviors to dysfunction, discussing concepts like "the schizophrenogenic mother" (Fromm-Reichmann, 1948) and stereotyping mothers as being overprotective and fathers as being distant.

Although many people would note that gender bias predominantly hurts women, systems theory has made a concerted effort to demonstrate that gender bias injures all members of the system, both male and female. Lewis (1992) provided excellent guidance to system therapists by encouraging them to practice gender-sensitive therapy. Some of the guidelines include:

- treating male and female clients equally,
- avoiding gender stereotypes in diagnosis and treatment,
- being aware of one's own gender beliefs and biases,
- monitoring the use and misuse of power within the therapeutic relationship,
- understanding the system's definition of gender roles.

For those interested in further reading on gender issues in family therapy, Luepnitz (1983) conducted a feminist critique of the major family system theories.

Spirituality. Regarding spirituality, a content analysis of the major marriage and family journals revealed only 13 articles related to spirituality and/or religion (Stander, Piercy, McKinnon, & Helmeke, 1994). This led the researchers to conclude that the profession of family therapy viewed spirituality as being outside the scope of therapeutic practice. However, in the past 10 years, the amount of literature exploring the role of spirituality in the context of systems practice has increased dramatically (Frame, 2000; Hodge, 2000; Joanides, 1996; Walsh, 1999). The overall conclusion from the theoretical and practical literature is that spirituality plays a potentially significant role in the family system that presents for therapy. Therapists who dismiss or ignore the role of spirituality run the risk of operating with less than complete information regarding that system.

Technical Eclecticism.   Regarding eclecticism, the systems perspective serves as the unifying force that connects all theories outlined in Table 12.1. Systems practitioners could be drawn to one approach based on personality of the therapist and, once proficient in that approach, could conceivably draw from the techniques of other approaches and still maintain theoretical consistency due to the shared assumptions of systems thinking. As a product of the unifying theme of systems thinking, these approaches have a much better chance at developing an integrative approach when compared to the struggle and diversity faced by the numerous individual-based theories. In fact, a number of theorists and practitioners have already advocated for an integrative approach that encompasses and unites all the systems approaches (Lebow, 1984; Nichols and Everett, 1986; Pinsof, 1995). It will be interesting to observe the growth of systems theory over the next few decades to see if the dream of integration can be realized.

DSM-IV-TR Diagnosis.   Regarding diagnosis, the traditional diagnostic process of the DSM is rooted in labeling individually based pathology. Rendering a diagnosis for an individual within a system using a classification that does not take the system into account is, therefore, categorically inconsistent with systems thinking. Furthermore, the diagnostic "symptom as bad" connotation does not mesh well with the system perspective that views symptoms only as a piece of the greater systemic balance. Becvar and Becvar (2002) posed the question as to whether diagnosis is even an ethical behavior for a systems practitioner. We gathered a few quotes on diagnosis from prominent systems thinkers who have generated their own systems-based perspectives:

> Part of the difficulty in beginning therapy properly has been the confusion between diagnosis for institutional reasons and diagnosis for therapy reasons. For an institution and for medical insurance reasons, it was necessary to see a person alone and classify him or her as a diagnostic type according to some scheme, such as the DSM. That procedure was irrelevant to therapy and could even handicap the therapist. (Haley, 1987, p.11)

> An individual diagnosis is a static label, which emphasizes the individual's most salient psychological characteristics and implies that these are resistant to changes in the social context. In family therapy, individuals and families are seen as relating and changing in accordance with their social context. The advantage of an evolving diagnosis related to context is that it provides openings for therapeutic intervention. (Minuchin, 1974, p.131)

> There are three problems with making concrete diagnoses. First, is that our language is not structured to describe process. The result is that a diagnosis may have iatrogenic effects on the life of the family by reifying

the problems. The second is that diagnostic terms are expended meta-phor, an attempt to make one kind of reality conform to another type of reality. The third problem is that each family has a private culture and language system to which the therapist has only partial access. The diagnostic process may be crippling to the family and/or mystifying (Whitaker & Keith, 1981, p. 197).

Obviously, traditional diagnosis does not fit well within the systems approach. However, systems practitioners do make use of what they call interactional or relational diagnosis (Kaslow, 1996). Each system's approach will emphasize different aspects of the system, but most will look for the general characteristics of the healthy family and will also assess how the family responds to the therapeutic encounter, especially toward the entrance of the therapist into the system. Minuchin (1974) pointed out that interactional diagnosis comprises every information-gathering technique necessary for the therapist to get an accurate read on the context of the family's functioning. This can include communication patterns, subsystems, boundaries, nonverbal cues, the family's reaction to questioning and probing (a systemic perturbance), and multigenerational patterns. The last important piece concerning interactional diagnosis is that it is always changing. As the family changes, usually experiencing morphogenesis, new boundaries and rules form, and a new dynamic equilibrium is established. Systems counselors understand that interactional diagnosis involves ongoing assessment of the system. Fortunately for systems practitioners, the DSM committees have agreed to consider interactional diagnosis for the next edition of the DSM.

Weaknesses of the Theory

The most glaring weakness of systems thinking is derived from its philosophical grounding in mutual causality. As an outcome of the theory's emphasis that behavior is not linearly caused and that interactions among members of a system produce systemic behavior, researchers and practitioners in the field of family violence have historically criticized systems theorists as participating in victim blaming. As one of those family violence researchers and clinicians, I (KAF) am concerned about many systems thinkers who continue to conduct family therapy with violent families despite well-established therapeutic contraindications and despite the potential risks to the family members.

The literature suggests that the dynamics of domestic violence do not follow the mutual or circular causality model and, instead, are much more linear in nature. The batterer co-opts the power in the system, and this dynamic of control becomes the pattern which is dictated by the batterer (Jacobson & Gottman, 1998; Jackson & Oates, 1998; Jones, 1994). Avis (1992) asserted that as long as we train therapists in systemic theories without balancing that training with an understanding of the non-neutrality of power dynamics, we will continue producing family therapists who collude in the maintenance of male power and are dangerous to the women and children with whom they work. (p. 231)

Because family violence is a concern that has reached epidemic proportions in the United States (United States Department of Justice, 1998), family therapists will routinely confront issues of spousal physical and sexual abuse and child neglect and physical and sexual abuse. Until systems thinkers consider some of the issues inherent in situations of family violence, the treatment may not only be ineffective with these populations, but may also lead to more violence. Readers interested in treatment of domestic violence can consult Pence and Paymar (1993), Fall, Howard, and Ford (1999), and Wilson (1997).

In our view, another weakness of the systemically oriented professional organizations is their retention of the term "marriage" in their title. That retention not only reflects heterosexism—failing to recognize homosexuals as legitimate consumers of relationship therapy—but also therapeutically disenfranchises dating couples who may manifest even the most distressing of systemic symptoms, such as physical and sexual abuse. It is our personal, and probably improbable, dream that AAMFT change its name to AART: the Association for Relationship Therapy.

Distinguishing Additions to Counseling and Psychotherapy

Most notably, systems thinking represents a paradigm shift in the way mental health professionals view the human change process. Systems thinking spawned numerous independent theories based on the common philosophical assumptions of the systems approach. The shift in conceptualization from an identified client to a family-based perspective on pathology and growth has produced a lasting impact on the treatment of families and couples and has led to the establishment of a distinct profession centered around the systems perspective. The next section details the gains made in this area over the past 60 years.

CURRENT STATUS

The practice of family therapy has come a long way since the first clinics opened in Europe and later in the United States. The AAMFT oversees the credentialing of family therapists and has established training guidelines that include attention to theory (systems and developmental concepts), practice, research, and ethics (AAMFT, 1994). Many marriage and family training programs required 60 hours of graduate coursework at the master's level, with additional coursework required for a doctorate. AAMFT's Commission on Accreditation for Marriage and Family Education (COAMFTE) accredits master's and doctoral degree programs, and, to date, 37 states have accredited institutions. In addition to university degrees, numerous training institutes, such as the Philadelphia Guidance Center, the Minuchin Center for the Family, and the Menninger Foundation, all provide advanced training in family therapy. Most states offer the Licensed Marriage and Family Therapist (LMFT) credential that recognizes the practice of family therapy as a field with distinct training requirements.

To guide the practice of family therapists, numerous journals address continuing education needs. Some of the more popular include *American Journal of Family Therapy, Family Process, International Journal of Family Therapy, Journal of Marital and Family Therapy, The Family Journal, and Journal of Marriage and the Family*. Professional organizations at the national, regional, and state levels routinely hold conferences devoted to the discussion of the latest research and practice trends in couple and family therapy. AAMFT has also written a code of ethics specific to the practice of marriage and family therapy (AAMFT, 1998).

Do you have to hold a LMFT licence to do family or couple's therapy?

The answer to this question is more a question of competency than what license one holds. A person with a LMFT has met the curriculum, exam, and supervision requirements and is deemed competent to treat couples and families. However, many graduate programs in counseling, psychology, social work, and psychiatry do not meet the AAMFT requirements, and yet their graduates can be competent to treat couples and families. The primary concern is whether your license allows you to practice with this population. In most areas, it is extremely rare to be excluded from treating a population based on license type, so the real question becomes, "Are you competent to treat this population?" A safe and ethical way to answer the question is to consider the triad of competency. The triad consists of three basic questions: (a) Do you have graduate coursework training in this area? (b) Do you have supervised experience with this population? and (c) Do you regularly seek out continuing education in this area? If these three criteria are met, one could conclude basic competency to treat the population.

SUMMARY

Systems theory represents a shift in thinking about human growth and dysfunction from the individual to the larger systems in which the individual is embedded. Systems thinking rests on a set of assumptions about the mutual causality of behavior and the interdependence of members of any given system. The systems approach is actually an umbrella term that connects many diverse approaches to this type of therapy. Family and couple therapy has blossomed into a distinct professional identity represented by professional organizations, training centers, and licensure requirements.

RECOMMENDED RESOURCES

Books

Due to the vast amount of material devoted to general systems theory and each theory under its umbrella, we decided to do something a little different with this chapter's recommended print resources. Resources are included for most of the systemic approaches.

General Systems
Bertalanffy, L. V. von (1968). *General systems theory*. New York: Braziller. This seminal work on general systems theory provides an in-depth description of the theory applied to various types of systems. The reader can really get a sense of the roots of family therapy when reading this book.

Becvar, D. S., & Becvar, R. J. (2002). *Family therapy: A systemic integration* (5th ed.). Boston: Allyn & Bacon. This text is great for an introduction to systems thinking, but also goes into depth on several applications and descriptions. It serves as a very nice resource book.

Bowen's Multigenerational Theory
Kerr, M. E. (1988). *Family evaluation*. New York: Norton. This is an amazing book that describes every facet of this theory in detail. It is very easy to read and provides case examples to facilitate the comprehension of the theory's more complex concepts.

Structural Theory
Minuchin, S. (1974). *Families and family therapy*. Cambridge, MA: Harvard. This book comprehensively outlines Minuchin's structural approach with liberal use of case examples and detailed descriptions of the core techniques.

Minuchin, S., Lee, W., & Simon, G. M. (1996). *Mastering family therapy*. New York: Wiley. This book both provides a good overview of the theory and takes the reader behind the scenes and into supervision sessions facilitated by Minuchin.

Communications Theory

Satir, V. (1983). *Conjoint family therapy* (3rd ed.). Palo Alto, CA: Science and Behavior Books. This book presents a basic overview of Satir's approach. The concepts are fleshed out through case excerpts, but the list/outline structure of the book may be distracting to some readers.

Strategic Therapy

Haley, J. (1987). *Problem-solving therapy* (2nd ed.). San Francisco: Jossey-Bass. This book serves as the primary resource for the strategic approach. Particularly helpful are the clarity with which the role of the therapist is discussed and the ample use of case dialogue.

Videotapes

Allyn and Bacon produced an entire series titled, *Family Therapy with the Experts,* narrated by Jon Carlson and Diane Kjos. This excellent set of videotapes provides you with a session facilitated by a proponent of a family therapy approach and commentary about the session and the theory.

Websites

www.aamft.org: This site is the home page for the American Association for Marriage and Family Therapy. The site contains great information on licensure and credentialing as well as a number of helpful print resources. The site is lacking in theoretical detail but does a nice job of directing you to places to get that type of material.

REFERENCES

Alexander, J. F., & Parsons, B. V. (1982). *Functional family therapy.* Pacific Grove, CA: Brooks/Cole.

American Association for Marriage and Family Therapy. (1994). *Membership requirements and applications.* Washington, DC: Author.

American Association for Marriage and Family Therapy. (1998). *Code of ethics.* Washington, DC: Author.

Avis, J. M. (1992). Where are all the family therapists? Abuse and violence within families and family therapy's response. *Journal of Marital and Family Therapy, 18,* 225–232.

Baucom, D., Shoham, V., Mueser, K. T., Daiuto, A. D., & Stickle, T. R. (1998). Empirically supported couple and family interventions for marital distress and adult mental health problems. *Journal of Consulting and Clinical Psychology, 64,* 333–342.

Bateson, G., Jackson, D. D., Haley, J., & Weakland, J. (1956). Towards a theory of schizophrenia. *Behavioral Sciences, 1,* 251–264.

Beavers, W. B., & Hampson, R. B. (1990). *Successful families: Assessment and intervention.* New York: W. W. Norton.

Becvar, D. S., & Becvar, R. J. (2002). *Family therapy: A systemic integration* (5th ed.). Boston: Allyn & Bacon.

Berg, I. K., & deShazer, S. (1993). Making numbers talk: Language in therapy. In S. Friedman (Ed.), *The new language of change* (pp. 5–24). New York: Guilford.

Bertalanffy, L. V. von. (1950). An outline of general systems theory. *British Journal for the Philosophy of Science, 1,* 139–164.

Bertalanffy, L. V. von. (1968). *General systems theory.* New York: Braziller.

Bestor, T. C. (2001). Cultural universals (a partial list): A list of elements of culture and society that are found in some form or other in ALL human cultures. http://icg.harvard.edu/~anth110/Overheads/What_is_Culture/Cultural_universals.htm

Bodin, A. M. (1981). The interactional view: Family therapy approaches of the Mental Research Institute. In A. S. Gurman & D. P. Kniskern (Eds.), *Handbook of family therapy* (pp. 267–309). New York: Brunner/Mazel.

Bowen, M. (1978). *Family therapy in clinical practice.* New York: Jason Aronson.

Brock, G. W., & Barnard, C. P. (1999). *Procedures in marriage and family therapy* (3rd ed.). Boston: Allyn & Bacon.

Broderick, C. B., & Schraeder, S. S. (1991). The history of professional marriage and family therapy. In A. S. Gurman & D. P. Kniskern (Eds.), *Handbook of family therapy* (Vol. 2, pp. 5–38). New York: Brunner/Mazel.

Butzlaff, R. L., & Hooley, J. M. (1998). Expressed emotion and psychiatric relapse. *Archives of General Psychiatry, 55,* 547–552.

Dunn, R. L., & Schwebel, A. I. (1995). Meta-analytic review of marital therapy outcome research. *Journal of Family Psychology, 9,* 58–68.

Epstein, N. B., Bishop, D. S., Keitner, G. I., & Miller, I. W. (1990). A systems therapy: Problem centered systems therapy of the family. In R. A. Wells & V. J. Gianetti (Eds.), *Handbook of brief psychotherapies* (pp. 405–436). New York: Plenum.

Fall, K. A., Howard, S., & Ford, J. (1999). *Alternatives to domestic violence.* Philadelphia, PA: Accelerated Development.

Fenell, D. L., & Weinhold, B. K. (1997). *Counseling families* (2nd ed.). Denver, CO: Love.

Frame, M. W. (2000). The spiritual genogram in family therapy. *Journal for Marital and Family Therapy, 26,* 211–216.

Framo, J. (1992). *Family-of-origin therapy: An intergenerational approach.* New York: Brunner/Mazel.

Friedlander, M. L., Wildman, J., Heatherington, L., & Skowron, E. A. (1994). What we do and don't know about the process of family therapy. *Journal of Family Psychology, 8,* 390–416.

Friedman, S. (1994). *Secret loves: Women with two lives.* New York: Crown.

Fromm-Reichmann, F. (1948). Notes on the development of treatment of schizophrenics by psychoanalytic psychotherapy. *Psychiatry, 11,* 253–273.

Goldenberg, I., & Goldenberg, H. (2000). Family therapy. In R. J. Corsini & D. Wedding (Eds.), *Current psychotherapies* (6th ed., pp. 375–406). Itasca, IL: F. E. Peacock.

Gottman, J. (1979). *Marital interaction: Experimental investigations.* New York: Academic Press.

Gottman, J. (1994). *What predicts divorce?* Hillsdale, NJ: Erlbaum.

Gottman, J., Driver, J., & Tabares, A. (2002). An empirically derived couple therapy. In

A. S. Gurman & N. Jacobson (Eds.), *Clinical handbook of couple therapy* (3rd ed., pp. 373–399). New York: Guilford.

Gottman, J., & Krokoff, I. (1989). Marital interaction and satisfaction: A longitudinal view. *Journal of Consulting and Clinical Psychology, 57,* 47–52.

Guerin, P. J., Fogarty, T. F., Fay, L. F., Kautto, J., & Kautto, J. G. (1996*). Working with relationship triangles.* New York: Guilford.

Haley, J. (1987). *Problem-solving therapy* (2nd ed.). San Francisco: Jossey-Bass.

Henggeler, S. W., & Borduin, C. M. (1990). *Family therapy and beyond.* Pacific Grove, CA: Brooks/Cole.

Heylighen, F., & Joslyn, C. (2001). Cybernetics and second order cybernetics. In R. A. Meyers (Ed.), *Encyclopedia of Physical Science & Technology, Vol. 4* (3rd ed., pp. 155–170). New York: Academic Press.

Ho, M. K. (1987). *Family therapy with ethnic minorities.* Thousand Oaks, CA: Sage.

Hodge, D. (2000). Spiritual ecomaps: A new diagrammatic tool for assessing marital and family spirituality. *Journal of Marital and Family Therapy, 26,* 217–228.

Jackson, N. A., & Oates, G. C. (Eds.). (1998). *Violence in intimate relationships.* Woburn, MA: Butterworth-Heinemann.

Jacobson, N., & Gottman, J. (1998). *When men batter women.* New York: Simon & Schuster.

Joanides, C. (1996). Collaborative family therapy with religious family systems. *Journal of Family Psychotherapy, 7,* 19–35.

Jones, A. (1994). *Next time, she'll be dead.* Boston: Beacon.

Kaslow, F. (Ed.). (1996). *Handbook of relational diagnosis and dysfunctional family patterns.* New York: Wiley.

Kerr, M. E., & Bower, M. (1988). *Family evaluation.* New York: Norton.

Lebow, J. L. (1984). On the value of integrating approaches to family therapy. *Journal of Marital and Family Therapy, 19,* 127–138.

Lewis, J. A. (1992). Gender sensitivity and family empowerment. *Topics in Family Psychology, 1,* 1–7.

Luepnitz, D. A. (1988). *The family interpreted: Feminist theory in clinical practice.* New York: Basic.

Maruyama, M. (1963). The second cybernetics: Deviation-amplifying mutual causal processes. *American Scientist, 51,* 164–179.

McGoldrick, M., & Gerson, R. (1985). *Genograms in family assessment.* New York: W. W. Norton.

McGoldrick, M., & Giordano, J. (1996). Overview: Ethnicity and family therapy. In M. McGoldrick, J. Giordano, & J. K. Pearce (Eds.), *Ethnicity and family therapy* (pp. 1–27). New York: Guilford.

McGoldrick, M., Giordano, J., & Pearce, J. K. (Eds.). (1996). *Ethnicity and family therapy.* New York: Guilford.

Minuchin, P. (1985). Families and individual development: Provocations from the field of family therapy. *Child Development, 56,* 289–302.

Minuchin, S. (1974). *Families and family therapy.* Cambridge, MA: Harvard University.

Nicholls, W. C., & Everett, C. A. (1986). *Systemic family therapy: An integrative approach.* New York: Guilford.

Nicholls, M. P., & Schwartz, R. C. (2001). *Family therapy: Concepts and methods* (5th ed.). Boston: Allyn & Bacon.

O'Hanlon, S., & O'Hanlon, B. (2002). Solution oriented therapy with families. In J. Carlson & D. Kjos (Eds.), *Theories and strategies of family therapy* (pp. 190–215). Boston: Allyn & Bacon.

Olsen, D. H. (1993). Circumplex model of marital and family systems. In F. Walsh (Ed.), *Normal family processes* (2nd ed., pp. 104–137). New York: Guilford.

Parsons, T., & Bales, R. F. (1955). *Family, socialization, and interaction processes.* New York: Free Press.

Pence, E., & Paymar, M. (1993). *Education groups for men who batter: The Duluth model.* New York: Springer.

Pinsof, W. M., Wynne, L. C., & Hambright, A. B. (1996). The outcomes of couple and family therapy: Findings, conclusions, and recommendations. *Psychotherapy, 33,* 321–331.

Pinsof, W. M. (1995). *Integrative problem-centered therapy.* New York: Basic.

Prigogine, I. (1973). Can thermodynamics explain biological order? *Impact of Science on Society, 23,* 159–179.

Relapse and expressed emotion. (1999, February). *Harvard Mental Health Letter, 15*(8), 6.

Satir, V. (1972). *Peoplemaking.* Palo Alto, CA: Science and Behavior.

Satir, V. (1983). *Conjoint family therapy* (3rd ed.). Palo Alto, CA: Science and Behavior.

Shadish, W. R., Ragsdale, K., Glaser, R. R., & Montgomery, L. M. (1995). The efficacy and effectiveness of marital and family therapy: A perspective from meta-analysis. *Journal of Marital and Family Therapy, 21,* 345–360.

Sherman, R., & Fredman, N. (1986). *Handbook of structured techniques in marriage and family therapy.* New York: Brunner/Mazel.

Stander, V., Piercy, F. P., MacKinnon, D., & Helmeke, K. (1994). Spirituality, religion and family therapy: Competing or complementary worlds? *American Journal of Family Therapy, 22,* 27–41.

United States Department of Justice. (1998). *Crime statistics.* Washington, DC: Author.

Walsh, F. (1993). *Normal family processes.* New York: Guilford.

Walsh, F. (1999). *Spiritual resources in family therapy.* New York: Guilford.

Watts, R. E. (1999). *Techniques in marriage and family counseling.* Alexandria, VA: American Counseling Association.

Watzlawick, P., Weakland, J. H., & Fisch, R. (1974). *Change: Principles of problem formation and problem resolution.* New York: Norton.

Whitaker, C., & Keith, D. V. (1981). Symbolic-experiential family therapy. In A. S. Gurman & D. P. Kniskern (Eds.), *Handbook of family therapy* (pp. 187–225). New York: Brunner/Mazel.

Weiner, N. (1948). Cybernetics. *Scientific American, 179,* 14–18.

Wilson, K. J. (1997). *When violence begins at home.* Alameda, CA: Hunter House.

CHAPTER 13

INTEGRAL COUNSELING: THE PREPERSONAL, PERSONAL, AND TRANSPERSONAL IN SELF, CULTURE, AND NATURE

Integral: the word means to integrate, to bring together, to join, to link, to embrace. Not in the sense of uniformity, and not in the sense of ironing out all the wonderful differences, colors, zigs and zags of a rainbow-hued humanity, but in the sense of unity-in-diversity, shared commonalities along with our wonderful differences

—Wilber, 2000c, p. 2

BACKGROUND OF THE THEORY

Historical Context

For much of his career, Ken Wilber developed his ideas in association with the field of transpersonal psychology, although he has not called himself a transpersonal thinker, per se, for nearly 20 years. Yet one of the outstanding features of his theory, which he has termed *integral*, is its explicit inclusion of a transpersonal dimension of psychological and spiritual experience. The following section will begin with an explanation of the term "transpersonal," provide a brief overview of the history of the field of transpersonal psychology, and conclude with a discussion of the relationship between transpersonal psychology and integral psychology and counseling.

Throughout history and across cultures, many people have reported transpersonal experiences, and many of these people have manifested *transpersonal* levels of development. The term transpersonal means "beyond the personal," that is, beyond the sense of oneself as a separate entity who functions in the space/time world of earthly existence to achieve individual survival.

Expanding on a definition offered by Stanislav Grof (1998), a *transpersonal experience* can be defined as a spontaneous, transient experience involving perception or action that *transcends* the ego boundaries of space and/or time yet, paradoxically, is perceived as authentic or potentially authentic *by* the experiencer's ego with consensus reality testing in tact (Holden, 1999). Intuitive, paranormal, and mystical experiences are included among transpersonal experiences.

Intuitive experiences can be understood as those moments of direct, immediate, holistic knowing that involve more than merely one's sensory input and one's reasoning. An example was provided by Judith Orloff, MD (1996), who one day received an answering machine message from a woman, Robin, who wanted to make an appointment. Knowing no more than this, Judith proceeded to have a strong, distinctively negative feeling about Robin—to the point that she hesitated to return Robin's call and schedule an appointment. A few hours later, Judith received a call from her local district attorney's office.

> He told me that he'd been assigned to a suit filed against Robin. "Robin is under a court order to receive psychotherapy and treatment for drug addiction and alcoholism," he explained. "You should also know the district attorney is processing a complaint against her by two of her former psychotherapists, both women. Is seems she became obsessed with them. They're charging her with harassment."
>
> Mr. Young went on to describe how Robin would show up at the therapists' offices unscheduled and call them at all hours of the day and night. A restraining order was finally issued by the Superior Court. Now, learning from Robin that she was planning to start treatment with me, Mr. Young advised that I not take her on, suggesting that she would do better with a male therapist.
>
> I agreed and thanked him. . . . (pp. 118–119)

Paranormal experiences involve the everyday, earthly world and also include phenomena that appear to defy the known physical laws of that world. One category of paranormal experiences is extrasensory perception (ESP), knowledge a person has gained without the mediation of the physical senses, of which several types exist. In *precognition,* one inexplicably knows the future, such as when a person, in a wakeful "flash" or a dream, foresees a car accident involving a loved one and, before he can contact the loved one to warn them, the accident occurs. In *telepathy,* one inexplicably shares the thoughts, feelings, or physical experience of someone out of physical contact, such as the father who, driving down the road one day, clutches his chest in excruciating pain and thinks of his son on active duty in the Middle East. The pain passes, but he goes to a nearby hospital emergency room, where they admit him for 24-hour observation. Finding nothing wrong, they send him home. The next day, a knock comes at the door; it is military personnel coming to inform him that his son died of a chest wound during a military operation 2 days before. In *clairvoyance,* one is able to envision things out of visual range, as in the case of the successful CIA training in remote viewing whereby a trainee was given latitude and longitude coordinates and was able to accurately visualize in detail what was located at that site (Targ & Katra, 1999).

Another category of paranormal experiences involves influencing the physical world without normal means, such as by thoughts and intention alone. One type, telekinesis, involves moving objects with the mind alone. A closely related type within this category is illustrated by the increasing evidence that prayer can influence growth and healing. In one double blind, randomized, clinical trial, for example, U.S., Canadian, and Australian prayer groups prayed for a group of Korean women undergoing in vitro fertilization/embryo transfer, and the group for whom they prayed had significantly higher success rates than did the control group for whom they had not prayed (Cha, Wirth, & Lobo, 2001).

In *mystical experiences*, one encounters a perceived reality beyond the everyday earthly world in which one's sense of self expands to include such phenomena as all of humanity, the world, deity, or the entire universe. Near-death experiences are fairly well-known phenomena that often include mystical features. One such feature is reunion with deceased loved ones and communing with a deific being of light. Another is experiencing a life review in which one reexperiences one's own thoughts and feelings while also experiencing the thoughts and feelings of others with whom one interacted: It is as if one is both oneself and the other. With one's identity thus expanded, one fully experiences how it felt to be on the receiving end of one's actions throughout one's lifetime.

Transpersonal development involves transformation into a new, relatively stable mode of functioning beyond a merely healthy self. One concept of the farther "stages" of transpersonal development is "enlightenment," presumably involving levels of wisdom and compassion that transcend what is achievable by a separate self whose purpose is individual or collective physical survival. In Wilber's (2000b) view, a transpersonal experience is a temporary *state* of consciousness, whereas transpersonal development involves the integration of such states into an enduring *trait* of consciousness.

Thus, "transpersonal" refers to the expression of the transcendent in, through, and as the person. It is a basic assumption of transpersonal psychology that if one looks within one's being deeply enough, one paradoxically finds that which is far greater than and beyond the person: the transpersonal.

Wilber (2000b), in summarizing the work of numerous scholars, presented a strong argument that, historically, Western psychology has attended almost exclusively to the domain of personal development—the ego and self— whereas Eastern psychology has attended almost exclusively to the domain of transpersonal development. Nevertheless, Wilber (2000b) credited several pioneers with having contributed to a vision of human development that integrates both domains. Foremost was Prussian psychologist Gustav Fechner

(1801–1887), often credited as the originator of experimental psychology but whose belief was clearly that the material world is an expression of divine consciousness. Also important was the American James Mark Baldwin (1861–1934), upon whose conceptual foundation current developmental psychology is substantially built and whose concept of development included a hyperlogical domain that, in contemporary terms, is clearly transpersonal. Wilber also credited the East Indian philosopher sage Sri Aurobindo (1872–1950), and the American psychologist Abraham Maslow (1908–1970). He also affirmed the invaluable contributions of contemplatives from every major religion including, as will interest many of you, Christianity.

One hallmark in the development of the transpersonal perspective was William James' 1901 classic book, *The Varieties of Religious Experience*. In it, the eminent American psychologist referred to religion as an individual's apprehension of himself or herself in the presence of the divine (p. 42) and as "the belief that there is an unseen order, and that our supreme good lies in harmoniously adjusting ourselves thereto" (p. 58). He described numerous experiences that, today, would fall into the category of the transpersonal. He argued that psychologists should approach the understanding of such phenomena not by reducing them to more basic, materialistic psychological dynamics but rather by nonreductionistically acknowledging them in their own right as valid subjective human experiences and inquiring into their meaning and function.

James' transpersonal experience-affirming attitude was echoed by Carl Jung. Over the first half of the 20th century, Swiss psychiatrist Jung developed a psychological and psychotherapeutic theory called analytic psychology. He both agreed substantially with Freud and also hypothesized psychological structures and processes that Freud did not address in his published works.

Regarding the unconscious, for example, Jung hypothesized in each person's psyche not only a personal unconscious but also a collective, or universal, unconscious. The collective unconscious is the repository of the sum total of human experience, and it consists of archetypes, or preexisting forms (Singer, 1972, p. 118). For example, it is now known in the field of linguistics that children all over the world learn language in a specific, predictable sequence. They appear to be innately endowed with psychological "deep structures" that provide the form and pattern to acquire the "surface structures" of their specific language (Chomsky, 1969). Decades before this fact was discerned, Jung hypothesized such deep structures—archetypes—as underlying not only language acquisition but all aspects of human functioning. Examples include the Hero's Journey, the Inner Child, the Mother, the Goddess, the Victim, and the Wise Old Man (Douglas, 2000). Thus, a person's unique unconscious and conscious patterns arise from the collective unconscious that is every person's birthright. Jung agreed with Freud's hypothesis of the Oedipus complex, but he saw it as only one archetype among many in the collective unconscious. Other archetypes, Jung believed, included those pertaining to spirituality that were equally valid and powerful in their own right and that could not, as Freud believed, be reduced to the mere sublimation of more primitive, basic motivations.

Jung also embraced the nonrational quality of the unconscious as sometimes regressively irrational, as Freud had identified, but also as sometimes progressively transrational—fostering development through processes that did not involve, and could not be understood by, linear reasoning. An example was Jung's hypothesis of synchronicity, "meaningful coincidences that cannot be explained through linear causality" (Grof, 1998, p. 91). In a famous clinical example, Jung (1969) was in session one day with a patient who had dreamt that she had been given a golden scarab, a beetle. During dream analysis, Jung brought up the point that, since ancient times, the scarab has been symbolically associated with transpersonal phenomena. As had been the case with this patient, she was resistant to the idea of the transpersonal domain, in general, and a transpersonal aspect of her own psyche, in particular. Their dream work was interrupted by a distracting clicking at Jung's window. When he went to the window, he found a rare specimen of beetle, one he had never seen before. He brought it to the patient, who was profoundly affected by this highly unlikely but extremely meaningful coincidence.

Wilber (2000b, pp. 248–249) noted that a misinterpretation of Jung has contributed to confusion in thinking about the relationship between the prepersonal stages of development, the first few years of life prior to the emergence of a clear sense of self, and the transpersonal stages, those occurring, if at all, after the emergence, consolidation, and elaboration of the self. Wilber called this confusion *the pre-trans-fallacy*, which has both reductionistic and elevationistic forms. In the former, the transpersonal realm is misinterpreted as prepersonal (Freud was guilty of this); in the latter, the prepersonal realm is misinterpreted as transpersonal (Jung was guilty of this). For a better understanding of Jung, you are encouraged to read Joseph Campbell's (1972) *The Portable Jung* and June Singer's (1972) *Boundaries of the Soul: The Practice of Jung's Psychology*.

Despite the dominance of psychoanalysis and behaviorism in the field of psychology for almost its first 100 years of existence, eminent figures such as James and Jung, along with other lesser known figures, carried the thread of the transpersonal through the 20th century. One such lesser known figure was Italian psychiatrist Roberto Assagioli (1965, 1991), whose humanistically and transpersonally oriented approach he called *psychosynthesis*. His psychological perspective included concepts of a higher self, a higher unconscious or superconscious, and spiritual awakening. It was not until the late 1960s, however, that modern-day transpersonal psychology began to grow out of the humanistic psychology movement.

In the early 1960s, Abraham Maslow and Anthony Sutich, noteworthy figures in both the humanistic and transpersonal movements (Walsh, 1993b), first joined other likeminded professionals in establishing humanistic psychology, the "third force" after psychoanalysis and behaviorism. These professionals aimed to study and nurture an understanding of some of the more healthful and meaningful, as opposed to pathological and reductionistic, aspects of human nature, such as the human capacity and tendency to fully actualize one's inherent potential.

Eventually, Maslow and Sutich joined others like Assagioli in realizing that the concept of self-actualization seemed inadequate to capture the full essence of humans' developmental potential. They struggled to find a term that captured the transcendent essence of this emerging "fourth force" in psychology. Then Stanislav Grof, an experimental and clinical psychologist who studied higher states of consciousness with individuals under the influence of LSD, proposed to Maslow the term "transpersonal" that apparently first had appeared in a syllabus that William James prepared in 1905–1906 (Perry, 1936, pp. 444–445). Maslow believed that the term captured the transcendent quality he and his cohorts sought: "beyond individuality, beyond the development of the individual person into something which is more inclusive" (cited in Schwartz, 1995, p. 345). In 1967, Maslow presented a paper titled, "The Farther Reaches of Human Nature," in which he proposed his ideas regarding a

> "higher" Fourth Psychology, transpersonal, transhuman, centered in the cosmos, rather than in human needs and interest, going beyond humanness, identity, self-actualization and the like. . . . Without the transcendent and the transpersonal, we get sick, violent, and nihilistic, or else hopeless and apathetic. (Malsow, 1968, pp. iii–iv)

In the past three decades, the field of transpersonal psychology has been bolstered by numerous key figures and cultural developments. Among the key figures was Ken Wilber, whose prolific writings included numerous articles in the *Journal of Transpersonal Psychology* and other transpersonally oriented publications. However, for a number of reasons, including atheoretical and contradictory theoretical perspectives associated with the transpersonal movement, Wilber has disassociated himself from that movement, notwithstanding his affirmation of the fundamentally transpersonal orientation of his theory.

Founder's Biographical Overview

The man who, for many years, has been acknowledged by colleagues as the leading theoretician of consciousness and transpersonal psychology, Ken Wilber, was born in Oklahoma City to two devoted parents. Largely due to his father's career as an Air Force officer, Wilber's family moved frequently. Thus, at an early age, long before he knew of Buddhism, Wilber realized the Buddhist insight of impermanence. Eager to be liked, and sorrowed by frequently having to say goodbye to friends, the young Wilber "learned to get involved with people very quickly and intimately, but also to hold everything lightly. It was a genuine Buddhist education: to be open, and yet to know that everything comes and goes" (Wilber, cited in Schwartz, 1995, p. 347). Although Wilber reported feeling overprotected, smothered, and a bit overwhelmed by his mother, he deeply appreciated the support and intellectual freedom his parents gave him.

Since childhood, Wilber has been passionate about science. "I fashioned a self that was built on logic, structured by physics, and moved by chemistry. . . . My mental youth was an idyll of precision and accuracy, a fortress of the clear and evident," wrote Wilber (cited in Schwartz, 1995, p. 348). With bachelor's and master's degrees in chemistry, Wilber was working toward his Ph.D. in that same subject when he began to realize that science was not "wrong" but profoundly narrow and limited in its scope, and silent with regard to the meaning of life. As always, he was spending far more time in his self-education than in his formal schooling. Mentally devouring numerous disciplines within philosophy, religion, and psychology, he was trying to reconcile what appeared to be contradictory views from such diverse geniuses as Einstein, Freud, and the Buddha. "I felt they were all saying something true," wrote Wilber, "but that *none* of them had it entirely figured out. . . . It slowly dawned on me that these people weren't all addressing the same *level* of consciousness" (cited in Schwartz, 1995, p. 351). Thus, the question was no longer "Whose view is correct?" but "How do these differing insights fit together in such a way that they don't contradict one another?" What Wilber (1977) called his "Grail search" culminated in his leaving chemistry studies and his writing *The Spectrum of Consciousness* (1977), which the 23-year-old wrote in longhand for 12 hours each day over a 3-month period (Schwartz, 1995).

Since then, Wilber has written more than 20 books that have been translated into as many as 25 languages, making Wilber the most widely translated academic writer in America. His books have been used as texts at Harvard and numerous other universities and have received critical acclaim from renowned thinkers in fields as diverse as business and philosophy.

Wilber's own development is of utmost importance to him. He has extensively practiced transcendental meditation, Zen, and Tibetan Buddhism as well as participated in psychoanalytic and Gestalt therapies. Thus, although he is not himself a clinician, he has first-hand and in-depth familiarity with the terrain of human change processes. He also has devoted himself consistently to a "full-spectrum" approach by attending to each of the broad domains of physical, emotional, mental, and spiritual work. Physically, he lifts weights regularly and labored manually as a dishwasher throughout his early years as a writer. Emotionally, he has undergone extensive psychotherapy and continues to explore this domain via his personal relationships. Mentally, he reads, studies, and writes voraciously. Spiritually, he has developed what many people from diverse spiritual traditions recognize as a rare and precious realization of many of the most sublime and exalted religious truths.

Currently living in Denver, Colorado, Wilber reportedly spends his time mostly writing, reading, or meditating. Although he has declined most offers to teach or speak and rarely grants interviews, he is increasingly recognizing that devoting some of his time to personally educating people about his work would be valuable indeed. He prefers to live a nonpublic and contemplative life surrounded by a circle of brilliant, loving friends (Schwartz, 1995).

> The main work I do in the world is writing. I average six to ten hours a day, seven days a week, 365 days a year. On intense writing days, I go up to fifteen to eighteen hours. When I first started meditating, I sat for three to four hours a day. Once a week, I'd take a whole day and sit ten or twelve hours. I still sit every day for at least two hours. These are my two main practices: meditating and writing. They are very solitary, and what I do is very cognitive. My strong point is my mind, no question. That's the talent I was given. (Schwartz, 1995, p. 362)

Wilber's intellect has been hailed as truly extraordinary in its penetrating, synthesizing, and discriminative capacities. His knowledge of psychology, philosophy, sociology, comparative religion, mysticism, anthropology, and even "hard" sciences such as biochemistry and physics is virtually encyclopedic, but, most importantly, he has personal experience with the states and levels of consciousness about which he writes (Schwartz, 1995; Wilber, 2000b, vol. 8). Wilber has commented that without his meditative practice, his work, which involves reading literally hundreds of books each year and writing, on average, a book each year, would be "severely limited" (Walsh & Vaughan, 1994, p. 19).

Although he certainly should not be viewed as only an intellectual, his affinity for the mental and spiritual realms, as opposed to the bodily and emotional realms, is clear. Likewise, although his passion is greater for transpersonal than prepersonal and personal stages of development, he has nonetheless consistently emphasized the dire need to recognize and embrace a full-spectrum view of consciousness and humanity's place therein.

Philosophical Underpinnings

Our normal waking consciousness, rational consciousness as
we call it, is but one special type of consciousness, whilst all
about it, parted from it by the filmiest of screens, there lie
potential forms of consciousness entirely different.
—James, 1993, p. 94

Integral counseling probably represents the most inclusive point of view of any system presented in this book. Because all the other systems address the ego or self almost exclusively and make no reference to the transpersonal domain, integral counseling provides a unique perspective on the nature of one's ultimate identity and on what constitutes "reality." Upon reading this material, you may feel anything from powerful disconcertion to a deep, familiar resonance.

Integral psychology is not a subset of psychology but rather an integration of many disciplines including psychology, philosophy, spiritual traditions, anthropology, cognitive sciences, consciousness studies, and neuroscience. It is the product of an integrative quest spanning the entire spectrum of human possibilities as manifested in both the individual and the collective, from both subjective and objective perspectives. Integral psychology honors both ancient wisdom and modern knowledge, East and West.

Perennial Philosophy. The philosophical foundation of integral counseling is generally known as the *perennial philosophy* (Huxley, 1946; Schumacher, 1977; Smith, 1976, 1992), the "common core of the world's great spiritual traditions" (Wilber, 2000b, p. 5). "Perennial" refers to the remarkable consistency with which this philosophical perspective has emerged throughout human history, across both time and culture, suggesting its universality.

Among the essential claims of the perennial philosophy is that the phenomenal, material, "gross" world—what is consensually agreed to be "real"— is a secondary manifestation of a divine ground, spirit, or consciousness. Thus, this *spiritual ground*, rather than its manifestation as matter, is primary and irreducible; the Spiritual Ground is what is "really" real. Perhaps even more important, humans not only can know *about* this realm but also can experience and know it *directly*; such mystical experiences involve the knower *communing with*, and then *identifying as*, divine spirit itself (Huxley, 1946/ 1993). Ultimately, identification with the divine does not deny the existence, at one level, of one's separate self-sense, nor does it inflate that self-sense with self-importance, -omniscience, -omnipotence, or -superiority over other humans; it merely affirms experientially the *ultimate* nature of *each* human. From the perspective of the perennial philosophy, realization of one's own identity as God, Atman, the self, Buddha, nature, or whatever name one may use "is the *summum bonum*: the highest goal and greatest good of human existence" (Walsh, 1999, p. 8). It is important to bear in mind that the perennial philosophers have not claimed these ideas as dogmatic assertions to be blindly believed. Rather, every major religion has its mystical tradition consisting of a set of contemplative or esoteric practices; if ardently undertaken, these practices will allow one's own consciousness to become a personal laboratory within which these claims may be experimentally tested for oneself.

Another of the core concepts of the perennial philosophy, and a central one for Wilber's integral psychology, is the *great chain of being*. The great chain is a model of the *kosmos*, a word used by the ancient Greeks to refer to the patterned nature of the entire universe rather than simply the physical universe or "cosmos." In this model, the kosmos is seen as comprised of different but continuous "levels of existence—levels of being and of knowing—ranging from matter to body to mind to soul to spirit" (Wilber, 2000b, p. 5). In other words, these levels emerge in an invariant order, from the most gross, fundamental, nonconscious, and limited, characterized by a relative reality of ever-changing conditions, to the most subtle, significant, conscious, and inclusive, characterized by realization of an absolute, eternal reality.

More accurate than the metaphor of a chain or ladder is that of a series of nested, concentric spheres with each successive sphere both including and exceeding the preceding sphere: a *great nest of being* (see Figure 13.1). Thus, out of matter emerges life, out of life emerges mind, and so forth. Each successive stage includes the qualities of the previous stage: Life includes matter; mind includes life. At the same time, each stage adds its own unique and emergent qualities to the previous stage: Whereas matter cannot repro-

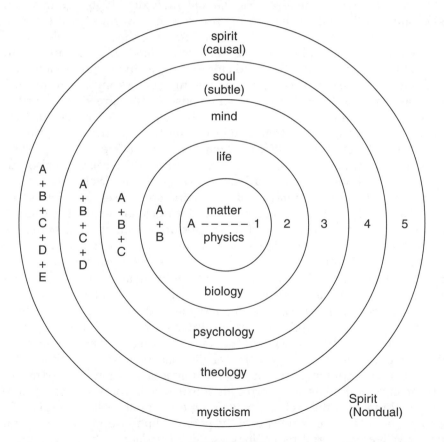

FIGURE 13.1
The great nest of being. Spirit is both the highest level (causal) and the nondual ground of all levels. Reprinted from *Integral Psychology: Consciousness, Spirit, Psychology, Therapy*, by K. Wilber, 2000, with permission.

duce itself, usually is not mobile, and is unaware of its environment, life has these capabilities; whereas the merely enlivened body, like someone in a coma, cannot reflect on its own life and activity, the mind can (Wilber, 2000a, vol. 6).

The great nest of being constitutes a particular kind of hierarchy. Each sphere is a *holon:* a complete *whole* at one level and, simultaneously, a *part* of the next level. Thus, the sequence of spheres is a *holarchy,* a hierarchy composed of holons. Holarchies exist everywhere in nature: Atoms are wholes that are parts of molecules, which are wholes that are parts of cells, which are wholes that are parts of organs, and so forth. Wilber (2000a, vol. 7) posited that "all developmental and evolutionary sequences that we are aware of proceed in large measure by hierarchization, or by orders of increasing holism" (p. 454).

The concept of hierarchy is currently out of favor, largely because many people equate normal, "actualization" hierarchies found everywhere in nature and complex systems with what Wilber (2000a, vol. 6) has called "pathological" or "domination" hierarchies, in which "one holon assumes agentic dominance to the detriment of all. This holon doesn't assume it is *both* a whole and a part[;] it assumes it is the whole, period" (p. 31). It may help readers to know that the term "hierarchy" was introduced originally by the Christian contemplative Saint Dionysius and referred to "governing one's life by spiritual principles"; *hiero* means sacred or holy, and *arch* means rule or governance (Wilber, 2000a, vol. 7, p. 453). Inherent in this original meaning is the constant reminder that one's current developmental level is both a whole and a part of a larger whole that is the spiritual ground of everything. More spirit/reality/consciousness is incorporated or *enfolded* into the structure of each successive level, which is simultaneously a greater revelation or *unfolding* of spirit/reality/consciousness.

Four Quadrant Model. Early in Wilber's professional development, he recognized that various influential people in human history, such as Freud, Piaget, Marx, Newton, and the Buddha, each appeared to offer a valid but partial truth regarding humanity and the universe (Wilber, 1999b, vol. 1). In grappling with the question of how the diverse and seemingly contradictory views of these people might fit together in complementarity rather than in opposition, Wilber (2000a, vol. 6) incorporated the perennial philosophy into an encompassing *four quadrant model.* Considering various perspectives such as those offered by Western psychology, the natural sciences, spiritual traditions, economic structures, technological modes, linguistics, and cultural worldviews, he discovered that each fit into a model formed by the intersection of two axes: interior-exterior and individual-collective (see Figure 13.2).

The interior domain consists of that which is subjective, which is unequivocally experienced but cannot be objectively observed and measured. By contrast, the exterior domain consists of that which can be observed and measured independent of subjective experience. The individual domain in-

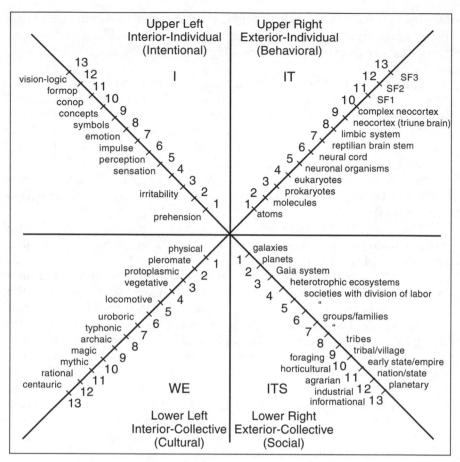

FIGURE 13.2
Reprinted from *The Collected Works of Ken Wilber* (Vols. 1–4), by K. Wilber,
1999, Boston: Shambhala, with permission.

cludes phenomena pertaining to an individual person/holon, whereas the collective domain refers to phenomena shared by two or more persons/holons. All four quadrants are inextricably related to each other but cannot be reduced to each other.

Take, for example, being in love. The upper left individual-interior quadrant includes the unmistakable subjective feeling of having fallen in love. The upper right individual-exterior quadrant includes the objective fact that, when in love, one's bloodstream shows increased levels of phenylethylamine and other endogenous chemicals. Notice that, inextricably linked as the feelings and the chemicals are, the subjective experience of being in love could never reveal knowledge of the endogenous chemicals, nor does knowledge of the chemicals inform the subjective experience; the two phenomena are inseparably related to, but irreducible to, each other.

Moving to the collective quadrants, the lower left collective-interior quadrant contains the cultural meaning of falling in love. Consider, for example, that most people in Western culture perceive falling in love to be a basis for the decision to marry, whereas many people in Eastern culture perceived falling in love to be irrelevant to that decision. Indeed, it has been said that Westerners love, then marry, whereas Easterners marry, then love. The lower right collective-exterior quadrant includes such social phenomena as, for example, how the couple in love makes contact with each other: whether they visit as a result of a long ride on horseback or a short drive in the car; whether they communicate by telegram or by e-mail.

In essence, a complete understanding of any phenomenon requires all four quadrants: the *intentional, behavioral, cultural,* and *social perspectives.* The following summary provides a more complete overview of the model. In your reading of it, we suggest that you worry not about "getting" all the details but rather about getting the overall point of the model: the necessity of considering all four very different perspectives that cannot be reduced to one another without distorting the significance of each view.

Upper left, interior-individual (intentional): The subjective, phenomenological dimension of individual consciousness: one's experience "from the inside." This quadrant includes sensations, perceptions, feelings, and thoughts that can be subjectively described in "I" language. Prominent theorists include Freud, Jung, Piaget, Aurobindo, Plotinus, and the Buddha. It is on this quadrant that the perennial philosophy concentrated. Clinically, as pertains to a client, this quadrant addresses the client's subjective experience: her sensations, feelings, thoughts, values, and so on.

Upper right, exterior-individual (behavioral): The objective, "scientific" perspective of individual structure and/or behavior as viewed "from the outside." This quadrant includes individual structures and processes that can be objectively described in "it" language. Prominent theorists and approaches include Skinner, Watson, Locke, empiricism, behaviorism, physics, and biology. Clinically, as pertains to a client, this quadrant involves appraisal of objective aspects of her such as her sensory, physical, and mental functioning; medical conditions and any medications she is taking; her diet, including drug and alcohol use; patterns of exercise, sleep, and rest; and diagnoses for which her symptoms meet specified criteria.

Lower left, interior-collective (cultural): The intersubjective dimension of collective consciousness: the group's experience "from the inside." Understanding the contents of this perspective requires a sympathetic resonance to the shared worldviews, linguistic semantics, symbolic meanings, and communal values shared by the members of a community, phenomena that are subjectively described in "we" language. Prominent theorists include Kuhn, Dilthey, Gebser, Stolorow, Atwood, and Habermas. Clinically, as pertains to the client, this quadrant addresses *what it means to the client* to be a member of one's ethnic group; to be a member of one's community of friends, family, neighborhood; and to have one's socioeconomic status and one's political, religious, and sexual affiliations.

Lower right, exterior-collective (social): The interobjective, "scientific" perspective of the collective as viewed "from the outside." This quadrant includes objective aspects of a society, such as architecture, transportation systems, governmental systems, and communication systems, as exemplified by buildings, subways, democracy, and the internet, respectively. These phenomena are objectively described in "its" language. Prominent theorists and approaches include Comte, Marx, Lenski, and systems theories/studies of complexity. Clinically, as pertains to the client, the social quadrant involves understanding the client's socioeconomic status and other objective conditions of the client's social system, such as the condition and layout of the client's household, neighborhood, and educational or work environments.

The reader should appreciate that each quadrant provides a *different* perspective on a given phenomenon, each of which is *valid* for that quadrant. Implications of this model are far more complex and far-reaching than is appropriate to explore in this chapter. Suffice it to summarize that each holon within a given holarchy exists not only in relationship with the holons within and beyond it, but also interdependently with holons in the other three quadrants. In a comprehensive integral vision, individual human development is understood as it relates to all four quadrants. No holon exists in isolation. Rather, each holon is always in relational exchange, both within its own quadrant and with other quadrants. Each person and phenomenon has a subjective, an objective, an intersubjective, and an interobjective aspect. Even the simple process of feeling hungry and planning what to eat (intentional) involves certain brain structures and neurochemistry (behavioral); occurs in a context indicating when, what, and how to eat (cultural); and utilizes some technological means to produce and ingest the meal (social) (Wilber, 2000a, vol. 6).

Complete a four-quadrant assessment of the following two phenomena relevant to contemporary psychotherapy:

1. A client with clinical depression
2. A highly empathic counselor (End inset)

PERSONALITY DEVELOPMENT

Wilber's writings explicitly address many, but not all, of the topics addressed for each theory described in this text. Where his own work does not provide an explicit answer, we have drawn on the writings of psychotherapists who have explicitly identified themselves as integral, including Robert Kegan, Michael Mahoney, Frances Vaughan, Jenny Wade, and Roger Walsh, and those whose techniques are theoretically compatible with integral counseling, such as Seymour Boorstein.

Nature of Humans

Function of the Psyche.

> *By their own theories of human nature, psychologists have the power of elevating or degrading that same nature. Debasing assumptions debase human beings; generous assumptions exalt them.*
> —Allport, cited in Walsh & Vaughan, 1994, p. 18

No theorist of counseling holds a more optimistic and elevating view of human nature than Ken Wilber, for he has conceptualized humans as divine in nature, despite the fact that most people are unaware of their ultimate identity as spirit, the source and ground underlying all manifestation. In fact, Wilber has contended that human nature is inseparably interconnected with the entire kosmos and that our core is essentially spiritual, loving, and positively directed. Likewise, Adi Da, perhaps the most integral of spiritual teachers and an influential figure in Wilber's developmental model, declared that spiritual transformation is a potential for "every human being. It is only more consciously activated or served in extraordinary or more perfectly awakened individuals. But it is present in everyone. . . . [T]he human individual is natively or structurally disposed . . . to grow beyond his present limits" (Da, 1980, pp. 50–51).

From an integral perspective, the underlying motivation of all humans is *to realize their divine nature:* a condition of original perfection, unity, and happiness—not a pleasurable or pain-free existence but a deep and profound peace and a complete and eternal freedom from the binding power of exclusive identification with any one thing. Wilber (1999b, vol. 2) called the yearning for and struggle toward realization of one's true nature "the Atman project": "All things are driven, urged, pushed and pulled to manifest this realization" (p. 60).

Rather than a discovery, realization of one's true nature is actually a *remembering*: "the Buddhist *smriti* and *sati-patthana*, the Hindu *smara*, the Sufi *zikr*, Platos' *recollection*, Christ's *anamnesis*: all of those terms are precisely translated as remembrance" (Wilber, 1999b, vol 2, p. 268). Thus, it may be inferred that assuming human form and developing psychological structures such as the ego tends to severely limit awareness and experience of the divine light of one's true nature; yet shining at first as a very faint beacon, it is the light toward which all life movement is aimed. Each phase of development constitutes an increasing realization of that light, which is experienced as a recognition or remembering of what always has been, and realizing union with that beacon constitutes divine awakening: enlightenment.

The process of realization is one of *development,* which involves several functions. First, throughout life, people experience the yearning for realization as the felt motivation of *needs*. If development proceeds well, fulfillment of needs at one level provides the foundation for fulfillment at the next level. The following discussion distills multiple, nuanced needs into four major categories.

The newborn and very young infant is dominated by *physical needs.* Through the course of normal development, the infant's emerging capacity for interpersonal relationship is accompanied by the emergence of *emotional needs*. Throughout childhood, mental faculties develop accompanied by the emergence of *mental needs*, such as for knowledge, for "making sense of things," and for other forms of mental stimulation. Finally, *spiritual needs* emerge, "to be in relationship with a Source and Ground that gives sanction, meaning, and deliverance to our separate selves" (Wilber, 2000b, p. 118). Thus, from an integral perspective, each level of need fulfillment, of development, is an increasingly exquisite expression of, and progression toward fulfilling, the ultimate human desire for divine realization.

At each level, the inability to meet the emerging need is experienced as painful, disruptive, even potentially lethal. Being motivated to avoid this pain, disruption, and death, humans create increasingly complex psychological structures. At first unequipped to satisfy the newly emergent need and overwhelmed by the onslaught of need-related experiences, ideally the person gradually *metabolizes experiences*—incorporates them through organization and mastery—thus creating the capacity to meet the new need in a systematic way. With each newly emerging need, this process involves adding qualitatively different structures or functions to the previously existing one. Thus, the process of development is a recapitulation of the cycle of *identification* with and consolidation of a level of functioning; then, as new needs emerge, *disidentification,* that is, transcendence of exclusive identification with that level, which enables *realization* of a broader mode of functioning than the previous level had allowed; then *integration,* the inclusion of the previous level with the new one, resulting in a qualitatively different and broader level of functioning.

This process, however, is not entirely smooth. Leaving the familiarity and security of the old structure and entering the unfamiliarity and uncertainty of the new is, in itself, an experience of pain, disruption, even death—a letting go of the only way of life one has known in order to be born into a new, more satisfying way. Consequently, as a function of the same underlying motives—to seek happiness and to avoid pain, disruption, and death—people both seek and resist development.

An analogy of the developmental process is upgrading one's living quarters. The realization can be painful and unsettling that one's formerly secure haven has recently become inadequate. At first one might try to rearrange the furniture in an effort to make the existing quarters satisfactory, a process Wilber called *translation*. As the inadequacy of translation to meet emergent needs is increasingly acknowledged, one must confront the pain, disruption, and death involved in *transformation*. The resources for upgraded housing must be found, the stressful process of searching for adequate housing must be undertaken, and the disruptive process of moving, resettling, and reorienting must be accomplished. The best possible new housing will have the useful features of the old but also more features that better meet the emerging needs. Yet, to leave the security and familiarity of the old house can feel like a kind of death. If the move is successfully resolved, one looks back on the old home with nostalgia—appreciating what it provided at one time—while simultaneously looking on the new home with excitement and some well founded trepidation, for, as anyone knows who has ever moved, the new home brings with it both new satisfactions and new challenges all its own.

A key structure in the process of development is the self, or self-sense, or self-system, the seat of a host of functions. Some of these have already been described, such as identification, gaining identity by associating with a level of functioning; organization, providing a sense of cohesion to experiences; and metabolism, psychological digestion that transforms one's discrete experiences, or one's *states*, into enduring modes of functioning and levels of development, or one's *traits*. Also involved are *will*, exercising choice and initiating action; *defense*, nondevelopmental strategies that mitigate against pain, disruption, and death; and *navigation*, wending one's way through the developmental labyrinth. Thus the self is an agent capable of choice regarding how to respond to "givens" such as heredity and environment, mostly within the limits of one's current developmental capabilities. Yet one can exceed even those limits at times through *creativity*. Whereas creativity as a human capacity is addressed in other systems of psychology, it is understood in those systems to be a kind of "wild card" inherent in human nature, having no clear source. From an integral perspective, creativity involves temporary access to that which is beyond one's prevailing developmental level, a reach into the *all that is* that seems beyond one's purview but actually is the ground of all, the essence of one's own nature that, therefore, is always potentially available.

To summarize thus far, each human is innately endowed not only with a motivation to meet physical, emotional, and mental needs but also with an impulse, however faint, to meet spiritual needs that ultimately involve transcendence of the separate self-sense and identification with spirit, the source of everything. Ultimately, this transcendental, transformational disposition does not involve a detached avoidance or abandonment of the material world but rather an involvement in the world along with a transcendence of it into its source. To transcend and transform is both to include and to go beyond.

Wilber (1999b, vol. 2) wrote also about the human potential to fail to develop:

> prior to . . . divine awakening, all things seek Spirit in a way that actually prevents the realization. . . . We seek for Spirit in the world of time; but Spirit is timeless. . . . We seek for Spirit in this or that object . . . but Spirit is not an object. . . . In other words, we are seeking for Spirit in ways that prevent its realization, and force us to settle for substitute gratifications. (p. 60)

Thus, people are often more absorbed in such substitute gratifications as money, food, sex, power, or fame, all of which can bring temporary and imperfect peace and none of which, therefore, can quench the thirst for ultimate freedom. "All our desires, wants, intentions, and wishes are ultimately 'substitute gratifications' for unity consciousness–but only half satisfying, and therefore half frustrating" (Wilber, 1999b, vol. 1, p. 569).

Thus it is that humans are prone to be misguided, seduced by half-satisfactions that "feel like" development, "feel like" they meet peoples' deepest needs. By seeking happiness in the phenomenal realm of eternally changing conditions that can never provide lasting happiness, by seeking peace in the inertia of routine and the placation of the familiar, people actually maintain the peaceless status quo of half-satisfaction. When combined with the fact that developmental progress involves taking on the very phenomena of pain and disruption from which one seeks to escape, the difficulty of development becomes clear. This, then, is the condition of tension in which humans face the purpose of life: spiritual development (Holden, 1993; Marquis, 2002; Walsh, 1999). Again, it is worth stressing that achievement of the ultimate level of development as a trait of consciousness does not mean a life of exclusive peace and bliss but rather an ongoing, underlying sense of peace and bliss that, in essence, gives the individual an ultimate resource with which to meet the vicissitudes of life.

Structure of the Psyche. Wilber has addressed both *conscious* and *unconscious* aspects of the human psyche. The conscious aspect includes the totality of which one is aware, and the unconscious aspect includes those potentials that have yet to become conscious as well as phenomena from past experience that have been defensively relegated out of awareness (Wilber, 2000b, p. 101). Wilber has addressed several other psychological structures more explicitly.

Self. The above discussion of function alluded to a central structure in integral psychology: *the self.* Interestingly, Wilber, along with many prominent transpersonal theorists, conceptualized human development prior to the transpersonal stages from a predominantly psychodynamic perspective. Thus, structures such as the ego and self are central to transpersonal and integral psychology.

Wilber (2000b) described the *overall self* as consisting of several aspects. The ground of the self is "pure Consciousness . . . the Spirit that transcends all...the transcendental Self, antecedent Self" (p. 34), what Wilber termed the ultimate *witness.* The witness manifests in each individual as a *proximate self,* your immediate *felt-sense of* yourself, and a *distal self,* everything you *know about* yourself. In addition, the self contains lines/streams and subpersonalities, both of which will be discussed below, and it is the self that performs the functions of identification, organization, metabolism, will, and defense. Whereas the overall self does not undergo development, it navigates the sequence of developmental levels while one aspect of itself, the proximate self, proceeds through that same sequence. It is to the developmental levels that we now turn.

Levels. In Wilber's view, the great nest of being manifests in humans as levels or stages of development. "Levels" connotes the qualitatively distinct nature of each stage of development. Wilber has also referred to stages as "structures" to underscore the integrated, holistic nature of each stage, and as "waves" to emphasize the fluidity with which the stages flow into one another. Another important point is that, although the following discussion will focus on the development of the self, "the basic structure or basic waves themselves are devoid of a sense of self. . . . [T]he basic structures are simply the waves of being and knowing that are available to the [proximal] self as it develops toward its highest potentials" (Wilber, 2000b, p. 35). It is accurate to speak of a given individual at a given time as "functioning primarily at a particular level of development," that is, as having realized one's developmental potentials to a particular extent, a type of developmental center of gravity. It is even more accurate, however, to focus primarily on one's full developmental potential and only secondarily on the extent to which one has realized that potential. In other words, from an integral perspective, awareness of any individual's full developmental potential is never eclipsed by focusing on the current prevailing level of one's realization of that potential.

Preparatory activity: Describing a rainbow. How many colors are in a rainbow? Most people would say a rainbow contains an infinite number, covering the full spectrum of visible color. Yet, if you were to meet someone who was familiar with colors but had never seen a rainbow, how would you describe it? Take a moment to write down your answer.

Probably your answer included something like, "an infinite blending of one color into another, from red to orange to yellow to green to blue to purple."

Though arbitrary, the identification of three primary and three secondary colors from among the infinite number present in the rainbow provides a structure for at least a preliminary understanding of what constitutes a rainbow. Likewise, Wilber (1999b, vol. 4) noted the arbitrariness of separating the continuous process of development into any particular number of stages, yet affirmed the explanatory value of doing so. Consequently, he conceptualized the levels of human development as 10 holarchical spheres clustered into three realms: *prepersonal, personal,* and *transpersonal.* The prepersonal realm, corresponding roughly to the great nest spheres of matter and life, and the personal realm, corresponding roughly to the great nest sphere of mind, are corroborated by Western academic psychology (Freud, 1971; Kohut, 1977, 1984; Mahler, Pine, & Bergman, 1975; Piaget, 1977). Empirical evidence for the transpersonal realm, which corresponds to the Great Nest spheres of soul and spirit, rests primarily in the developmental mappings of the contemplative traditions, both Eastern and Western (Aurobindo, 1970; O'Brien, 1984). With transformation into each progressive level of development, the individual retains the resources afforded by the previous level and acquires additional resources to use in the process of living.

When referring to the line of identity/self-sense development (lines of development will be subsequently discussed), Wilber (1999a) used the terms *level* and *fulcrum* synonymously. At any given time, one's self identifies primarily with one of the 10 levels of development yet accesses adjacent levels and, to an increasingly lesser degree, more "distant" levels. As such, one's sense of self often "teeters," identified primarily with the predominant level of functioning, sometimes dipping slightly backward, but increasingly reaching slightly forward, until transformation renders a deep-structure, forward shift in one's fundamental sense of self: the fulcrum "jumps" to the next, broader level of identification and functioning. Wilber used the designation "F-" to refer to each of the 10 levels of identity development, F-1 through F-10.

Each human typically spends the first 7 years of life proceeding through three fulcrums or basic structures of development that, together, comprise the *prepersonal* realm, during which a stable, coherent, individuated self-sense is, as yet, only in the process of emerging. Psychological functioning in this realm is *prerational.* At birth, the infant enters the *sensoriphysical level* (F-1) in a state of psychological undifferentiation from her environment. During her first 18 months of life, she takes her first tentative steps toward individuation by developing an identity as a *physical self,* a body separate from the environment. Then, in the *phantasmic/emotional level* (F-2), the toddler develops a sense of her *emotional self* that feels different emotions than other people do and, therefore, feels separate from others. Between the second and third years of life, at the *representational mind level* (F-3), the *mental self* emerges: What the child previously knew only through the senses, she now is capable of representing mentally. Piaget (1977) classified this third level as the preoperational period in which the capacity for symbols and language provides the child access to an entirely new world of objects and ideas in both the past and the future.

Because levels 4 through 6 involve the stabilization and elaboration of a coherent, autonomous self, they comprise the *personal realm*. Psychological functioning in this realm is relatively *rational*. The 7-year-old typically enters the *rule/role mind level* (F-4), a stage that corresponds to Piaget's (1977) concrete operations. The child at this stage develops the capacity to take the perspective (role) of others and assumes an identity as a *role self*, learning the rules associated with various social roles. The dawn of adolescence is accompanied by the *formal-reflexive level* (F-5), corresponding to Piaget's (1977) formal operations: The young teenager becomes capable of thinking about thinking. This development enables the person for the first time to introspect, marking the emergence of a *conscientious self*. Many people continue into and through adulthood at this fifth level of functioning. However, around age 21, the potential develops for the young adult to emerge into the *vision-logic level* (F-6). Whereas the fifth level involved dichotomized, either/or thinking, the sixth is integral-aperspectival: The individual can simultaneously hold multiple, apparently contradictory perspectives in her attention and, through synthesis and integration, can conceptualize networks of interactions among the various perspectives. At this level, existential concerns characterize the self that Wilber called the *centaur*, borrowing the term Erikson used "to denote a mature mind-and-body integration, where 'human mind' and 'animal body' are harmoniously one" (Wilber, 2000b, p. 44).

Whereas the first four or five levels tend to emerge without intentional effort, progressive emergence of the higher order structures tends to require increasingly purposeful pursuit of contemplative practice. Because the last four levels involve increasing disidentification from a sense of self as isolated, separate, and individual, these structures are termed *transpersonal,* including as well as transcending the personal. Psychological functioning in this realm is deemed *transrational* in that it involves direct and immediate apprehension without sensory or mental mediation. You should be forewarned that you may have difficulty fully grasping the following description of any transpersonal realm that you have not experienced directly.

In the *psychic level* (F-7), psychic or other paranormal experiences, which, as described above, include references to the natural, "gross" world, often—but not always—occur as one's identity expands to include all of cosmic nature; thus, one experiences *nature mysticism*. One's identity emerges as a *universal self* that transcends the individual self's sense of limited space and time. This oneness with the universe is not to be confused with the undifferentiated state of a newborn infant who has not yet developed a clear sense of self. Rather, the universal self includes a sense of oneself as an individual, and the sense of self also expands to include all natural phenomena.

Experiences of the *subtle level* (F-8) involve the transcendence of gross referents; that is, the contents of these inner experiences transcend the everyday physical world and typically involve archetypal forms and patterns, interior luminosities and sounds, and subtle currents of bliss. One's identity expands in a union of one's soul with deity; thus, one experiences *deity mysticism*. For example, some near-death experiences include a state of union with a being of light that a Christian experiencer is likely to interpret as Jesus or God. If one metabolizes the experience, one will report that every waking moment, as one moves through the day, one experiences a trait of union: the ongoing/constant/continuous feeling of inseparable connection with God. Again, the person retains a separate self-sense while that self-sense also has expanded to include union with deity.

In experiences of the *causal level* (F-9), one realizes the formless ground from which all phenomena, of both the exterior and interior worlds, arise. These are experiences of pure consciousness, devoid of all content, in which attention—the root-essence of mind—abides without effort, strategic manipulation, or "self-consciousness." In this witness-consciousness (Avabhasa, 1985), one does not merely know about, but directly experiences/realizes the unmanifest source, ground, support, and *cause* of all of the previous levels. When such experiences are metabolized, one's identity abides as the unmanifest source of all arising phenomena.

By contrast, in the *nondual level* (F-10), the experiencer transcends even the distinction between the formless ground and the phenomena that arise from the ground. This level actually is not a discrete level apart from other levels but, rather, is the reality, suchness, or condition of *all* levels. In other words, in this ultimate state of unity consciousness, spirit and its manifestations, consciousness and its display, emptiness and form, nirvana and samsara—the ultimate reality or truth and the conditional realm of suffering in which most people are engrossed—are all realized to be "not-two." When such experiences are metabolized, the self has retained and integrated all its previous forms into the stable realization and experience of its true nature as the all.

Wilber's developmental model, which he has termed the spectrum of development, is summarized in Table 13.1.

Lines. In addition to navigating through the levels of development, the self also contains *lines* or "streams" of development. A line of development can be thought of as an *aspect* of the individual's overall development. Each line or stream proceeds sequentially, yet quasi-independently, through the 10 waves or levels. Empirical research indicates that at least two dozen of these relatively independent lines exist, including cognitive, affective, moral, empathic, creative, worldview, and spiritual.

Each line manifests in an identifiable way at each wave or level; however, the lines can and do develop at different rates. Consequently, a person may be relatively more developed in some lines and less developed in others (see Figure 13.3). Thus, although *specific* developmental lines and levels unfold sequentially, "*overall development* . . . is far from a sequential, ladder-like,

TABLE 13.1

Ken Wilber's Spectrum of Human Development

Realm	Great nest sphere	Psychological functioning		Developmental fulcrum/level	Age in years	Identity
Prepersonal	Matter/life	Prerational	F-1	Sensoriphysical	0–1.5	Physical self
			F-2	Phantasmic/emotional	1.5–3	Emotional self
			F-3	Representational mind	3–7	Mental self
Personal	Mind	Rational	F-4	Rule/role mind	7–12	Role self
			F-5	Formal-reflexive	12–21	Conscientious self
			F-6	Vision-logic	21 (potential)	Centaur
Transpersonal	Soul	Transrational	F-7	Psychic	(potential)	Universal self (nature mysticism)
			F-8	Subtle	(potential)	Includes union with deity
	Spirit		F-9	Causal	(potential)	Witness-consciousness/unmanifest source
			F-10	Nondual	(potential)	Unity consciousness

From *Integral Psychology: Consciousness, Spirit, Psychology, Therapy,* by K. Wilber, 2000, Boston: Shambhala, with permission.

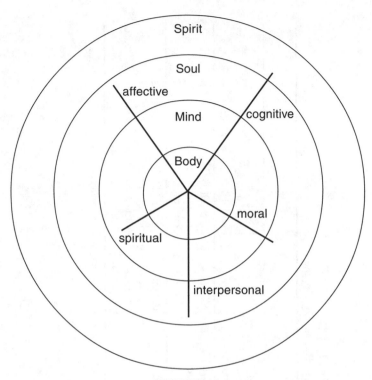

FIGURE 13.3
Example of an "integral psychograph" demonstrating the relationship
between developmental lines and levels. Reprinted from *Integral Psychology:
Consciousness, Spirit, Psychology, Therapy,* by K. Wilber, 2000, Boston:
Shambala, with permission.

clunk-and-grind series of steps, but rather involves a fluid flowing of many
waves and streams in the great River of Life" (Wilber, 2000a, vol. 6, p. xvii).

Reflection
Using only the lines identified in Figure 13.3, sketch your own integral psychograph, knowing that it will be your "best guess" or approximation. Then sketch the psychographs of two other individuals
you know well. How do these lines help to bring out a person's
individuality? How might lines of development help one to understand how a spiritual authority, such as a minister, priest, or guru,
might engage in behavior such as sexual or other exploitation of
one or more followers?

States. Wilber (2000b, p. 35) noted that although the self at any given time mostly reflects the structure of one level of development, it is not confined only to experiences associated with that level. Rather, in addition to predominant functioning at the current level, the self can temporarily regress to an earlier level of functioning or temporarily progress to a later level of functioning through a range of states of consciousness that are *potentially* available. Thus, virtually anyone can have a temporary transpersonal experience or state.

Wilber (2000b, p. 13) identified two general categories of temporary states of consciousness. *Natural* or ordinary states include waking functioning at one's current developmental level; dreaming, the nightly, mostly unconscious excursion into the subtle domain; and deep sleep, the nightly unconscious excursion into the causal domain. *Altered* or nonordinary states include those regressive or progressive experiences induced by a variety of conditions including fasting, fever, drugs, EEG biofeedback, contemplation, prayer or meditation, or profound stressors such as intense exercise or being near death.

Temporary altered *states* of a transpersonal nature, rather than their metabolism into relatively stable transpersonal *traits*/levels/waves of development, have sparked much of the interest in the transpersonal field. However, Wilber (1999b, vol. 4; 2000a, vol. 7) has contended that although anyone at any level of development can have a temporary experience, or state, of any of the other levels, whether that state will be metabolized into an enduring trait depends on certain factors. These factors include the frequency and duration of the temporary states, the "distance" between one's current fulcrum or level of development and the level from which the experience or state arose, the degree of awareness that is brought to the process of metabolism, and the amount of intentional practice one devotes to integrating the new awareness into one's daily life.

Consider, for example, a young child in the fourth rule/role level/wave of concrete operations who has a spontaneous seventh-level psychic experience, such as precognition of a disastrous event. Because psychic-level understanding is, as yet, developmentally unavailable to her, she is unlikely to conclude that she temporarily gained access to a transpersonal source of information. Rather, she is likely to interpret the experience with rule/role thinking and conclude that she caused the event, that is, thought it into existence—a conclusion that is likely to be distressing. Another example is an adult in the fifth formal/reflexive level of functioning who has an eighth-level mystical experience. He might dismiss the experience or deny its reality because it is incongruent with his current worldview. In these cases, distress and denial will likely impede the integration of the experience. The individual is, so to speak, developmentally unprepared to metabolize the experience into a quasi-permanent realization, mode of functioning, level or wave of development. The more isolated and short-lived the temporary state or experience and the more advanced the wave from which it arose, the less likely the self will consolidate it into a new level or wave of functioning. The greater the frequency, duration, and awareness brought to the temporary state or experience—as results most reliably from a regimen of contemplative practice—and the more "adjacent" to one's current level is the level from which the state or experience arose, the more likely it is that the self will consolidate the experiences into the next level of development: stable functioning at a more inclusive level of being and knowing.

Types and Subpersonalities. At any level of any line, a person might be characterized by any of a number of *types* of orientations, such as those assessed by the Myers-Briggs Type Indicator or the Enneagram. Wilber (1999c) has even hypothesized gender to be a kind of "type." It is important to recognize that whereas levels can be thought of "vertically" and are universal structures through which all individuals must pass, types are "horizontal" phenomena that may or may not be present at any of the levels. Thus, types add to the fluid and nonlinear appearance of overall self-development.

The self also contains *subpersonalities*, which Wilber (2000b) defined as "functional self-presentations that navigate particular psychosocial situations" (p. 101). In other words, a subpersonality is a particular thought/feeling/action/physiology mode that "kicks in" to cope with certain types of situations. A common example is the harsh critic who, when confronted with her own and/or others' fallibility, responds with judgmental thoughts; with angry, superior feelings; with critical words and punitive actions; and with tense physiology.

Wilber (2000b) cited authorities who have contended that the average person has about a dozen subpersonalities. A person can form one or more subpersonalities at any level of development and often does form at least one at each level. Consequently, some relatively common subpersonalities have been identified in various systems of psychology as personality parts: psychoanalysis' id, ego, and superego; transactional analysis' child, parent, and adult ego states; Gestalt's top-dog and underdog; focusing's critic. Subpersonalities revolve around particular archetypal forms and can include social roles such as the father role or wife role. Wilber noted that people can even form subpersonalities associated with the soul levels of development. The crucial issue for healthy functioning is the extent to which the self can disidentify from a subpersonality so that the self can "take charge" of it—have choice as to when and how the subpersonality is engaged—rather than being taken over by it.

In summary, the primary structures of the human psyche are the self, the 10 levels of development with their various states and traits, the approximately 24 lines of development, the types, and the approximately 12 subpersonalities. The universality of these structures accounts for commonality among humans; the combinations and permutations of these numerous factors as they are creatively expressed by each person in each culture accounts for the uniqueness of each human.

To close this section on a philosophical note, Wilber (2000b) repeatedly asserted that the psychological structures that humans have manifested "can better be understood as formative habits of evolution, 'Kosmic memories', . . . and not pregiven modes into which the world is poured" (p. 145). In other words, out of emptiness, the creative ground of all that is, humans could have created any of a myriad of habitual patterns. The levels, lines, and so on, that scholars, both Eastern and Western, have identified constitute the particular forms that not only humans but all consciousness, all sentience, have constructed out of that creative ground.

Role of the Environment

From an integral perspective, the existence of every holon at every level depends on *interrelationship* with its environment. In particular, an individual and his or her environment are constantly engaged in an ongoing system of relational exchange involving the needs associated with one level of development and the environmental provision of the "food" that meets those needs. Indeed, Wilber (2000b, p. 118) has characterized the environment as consisting of a *holarchy of "food"* that corresponds to the needs at each level of the holarchy of individual development. Physical "food" includes nutrition and physically safe surroundings. Emotional "food" includes emotional nurturing and, when developmentally appropriate, sexual intimacy. Mental "food" includes the psychological stimulation of communication and ideas. Spiritual "food" includes opportunities "to be in relationship with a Source and Ground that gives sanction, meaning, and deliverance to our separate selves" (p. 118). You may have noticed that Wilber did not specify social needs, although need fulfillment often occurs through relationship with other people. This is because individual holons are *always* members of social holons; therefore, social interaction is inherent in the system of relational exchange throughout life.

The environment can provide the various forms of food or can fail to provide them or even provide seemingly toxic experiences. In particular, Wilber (2000b, p. 101) mentioned three environmental conditions that can be detrimental to developmental progress, although he did not elaborate on them. "Developmental miscarriages" probably refers to conditions of *chronic deprivation* that preclude normal development, for example, starvation, lack of contact comfort, or any other absence of "food" at any level. *Repeated trauma* probably refers to actual assaults on the developing organism, that is, multiple exposures to conditions for which one is not developmentally prepared to cope, for example, ongoing childhood sexual abuse. *Recurrent stress* probably refers to conditions with which one is developmentally prepared to cope except for the chronicity of the conditions that "wear away" at one's coping resources, for example, trying to find work in a chronically depressed economy. As the examples show, these conditions can exist in either or both the familial and/or extrafamilial environments, both of which are represented by the bottom two quadrants of Wilber's four quadrant model.

Familial. In accordance with psychodynamic principles, Wilber has identified the familial environment as a crucial factor in early development. In his view, object relations and self psychology have provided the best explanations of the first four levels of development, both of which include the fundamental contention that the quality of early child–caregiver relationships greatly influences the quality of the child's sense of self.

The family can continue to exert influence on a member throughout that member's life. Yet, as an individual progresses through the spectrum of development, influence shifts increasingly from familial to extrafamilial, particularly to one's cultural group.

Extrafamilial. An individual's inextricable embeddedness in, and interrelationship with, his or her culture and society plays a crucial role in development. The collective provides the background without which a self-sense—the felt sense of being an "I"—would not even emerge (Wilber, 2000a, vol. 7). The culture itself can be understood as having its own developmental structure around which it is centered that reflects its collective level of development within the great nest of being. This collective "center of gravity" exerts powerful pressures on individual development.

> The center of gravity of a given culture tends to act as a 'magnet of development': if you are below that average, the magnet pulls you up; if you try to go beyond it, it pulls you down. . . . [T]hus, with any postformal and post-postconventional developments, not only are you on your own, you are sometimes actively discouraged. (Wilber, 2000a, vol. 7, pp. 730–731)

In particular, a culture that does not include belief in the realities of development beyond the separate, individual self will certainly not foster such development.

> Cultures seem to function . . . as collective conspiracies to constrict consciousness. . . . [S]ociety may encourage development up to societal norms but hinder development beyond them . . . [which] explain[s] the fate of all too many saints and sages who throughout human history have ended up poisoned, crucified, or burned. The net result is that our latent capacities and geniuses may be covertly suppressed rather than encouraged and expressed. (Walsh & Vaughan, 1993, pp. 110–111)

Another developmentally restrictive aspect of Western culture, in particular, is what anthropologists such as Laughlin, McMaus, and Shearer (1993) termed its *monophasic* quality: valuing and deriving a worldview from a single state of consciousness, the normal waking state. In contrast, most cultures are *polyphasic* in that their values and worldviews reflect an appreciation of multiple states of consciousness, including waking, dreaming, and numerous mystical or contemplative states. Because of *state-specificity*, insights and understandings derived from a given state of consciousness are likely to be incomprehensible to those who have not experienced that state (Tart, 1983; Walsh, 1989). This phenomenon may explain why contemplative or mystical experiences and disciplines have been so widely misunderstood in the West.

Thus, one's culture, and how it is expressed in one's social environment of family, friends, coworkers, and so forth, plays a powerful role in one's development. Maslow (1968) encouraged people to create optimal environments to facilitate personal and spiritual growth. These "euspychian environments" involve sharing the company of those who value personal and transpersonal development, who are practicing their cultivation, and who provide conditions of safety that allow each other the opportunity to reduce defenses and emerge into new ways of being. More specifically, Wilber (2000b) has repeatedly emphasized the necessity for a person to have an ongoing relationship with a spiritual teacher to facilitate transpersonal development.

Interaction of Human Nature and Environment in Personality Development

From an integral perspective, a comprehensive view of development includes reference to all developmental levels as they manifest in all four mutually influencing quadrants: interior and exterior, individual and collective. Nevertheless, the integral treatment of the subject of human development focuses more on the individual-interior—the upper left quadrant. In addition, although the environment provides both opportunities and limits, the individual can choose what meaning she makes of circumstances she cannot control and can use her creativity to generate new opportunities and exceed external limits. However, her choices and creativity are probabilistically related to her level of development: She is most likely to choose from the resources available to her at her current prevailing level, and to this extent her free will is limited, though, again, in only a probabilistic rather than an ultimate way, because all humans, at all times, at the deepest level of being, have access to—in fact, *are*—all that is. Indeed, the history of human development is highlighted by the creative acts of people who exceeded the limits of both exterior, and even seemingly interior, conditions. The point to keep in mind in the following upper-left-quadrant-focused discussion is that human development is actually a highly complex, all-quadrant affair.

View of Healthy Functioning. Integral counselors consider optimal human functioning to be far more than the absence of symptoms of mental disorder. A substantial amount of research accumulated in the last 30 years strongly suggests that average adults have by no means realized their developmental potentials (Alexander, Druker, & Langer, 1990; Assagioli, 1991; Maslow, 1968, 1971; Wade, 1996; Wilber, 2000b, vol. 4; Wilber, Engler, & Brown, 1986). As Maslow (1968) asserted, "what we call 'normal' in psychology is really a psychopathology of the average, so undramatic and so widely spread that we don't even notice it" (p. 16). Even in the absence of diagnosable mental disorders, people may suffer from a host of what Maslow (1971) termed "metapathologies": "failure[s] to recognize and satisfy our transpersonal nature and needs," wrote Walsh and Vaughan (1993), "[that] may underlie much of the individual, cultural, and global suffering that surrounds us" (p. 137).

An integral view of optimal functioning involves at least four notions. First, *the broader one's developmental level,* the more resources one has to bring to the process of living. With each subsequent level of development, one retains the abilities of the previous levels and adds to them. This does *not* mean that someone at a higher stage of development is *better* than someone at a lower stage, any more than an oak tree is better than an acorn: Given its stage of development, the acorn is just as perfect as the oak. The acorn, however, is more vulnerable to environmental dangers, such as fires or hungry squirrels, than is the oak tree. Similarly, even though each individual is a radiant expression of the divine, those who experience themselves as only their bodies and minds have fewer resources with which to meet life than do those who have awakened to their identities beyond the separate self-sense. In a sense, the more developed one is, the freer one is of previous limitations.

Second, healthy functioning is associated with the *completeness of identification with one's level* of development, whatever that level is. Healthy developmental progress involves the individual disidentifying with one level, identifying with the next level, and integrating the preceding level within the new level. Pathology involves either/both a failure to disidentify from, or entirely from, the previous level, resulting in developmental arrest or fixation, respectively, and/or failure to integrate the previous level, resulting in repression, fragmentation, and alienation (Wilber, 1999b, vol. 4).

Third, given that the self includes numerous *lines* that can develop rather independently of each other, an integral notion of health involves a relative *balance among the lines*. For example, an individual with high cognitive and moral development but low interpersonal development is likely to feel isolated and lonely, whereas one with high cognitive and interpersonal development and low moral development may be manipulative and exploitive. Thus, the more similarly developed one's various lines of development are, the less distressed one is likely to feel and the less distressing to others one is likely to be.

Finally, integral health includes a *balance among the quadrants* within one's level of development. For example, regardless of one's level, excessive emphasis on the I (intentional quadrant) leads to egocentrism, inordinate concern for "we" (cultural quadrant) results in conformity, and too much focus on "it" (behavioral and social quadrants) produces dissociation (from I and we). Thus, the integral view of optimal functioning includes one's "place" among the 10 levels of development, one's completeness of identification with one's current prevailing level, balance among one's 24 lines of development, and balance among the four quadrants.

Healthy people are happy people, but remember that this does not imply hedonism or a pain-free life. In fact, pain is not to be avoided but, rather, fully experienced and explored (Puhakka, 1994; Walsh, 1995). When one understands pain and suffering, one knows that attachment to certain desirable conditions are their source. In the words of T. S. Eliot (1943), "Desire itself is movement not in itself desirable" (p. 20). Unhappiness is essentially a discrepancy between what one desires and what one has. "Happiness lies not in feeding and fueling our attachments but in reducing them and relinquishing them. Nowhere is this summarized more succinctly than in the Buddha's Third Noble Truth: 'Freedom from attachment brings freedom from suffering'" (Walsh, 1999a, p. 41). This message was also expressed by the Christian mystic, Meister Eckhart: "the greatest and best virtue with which man [sic] can most completely and closely conform himself to God . . . [is] a pure detachment from all things" (cited in Walsh, 1999a, p. 41). Thus, healthy people address their physical, emotional, mental, and spiritual needs while giving relatively less energy and attention to the fulfillment of specific desirable conditions and giving relatively more energy and attention to the realization of peace and happiness in the midst of whatever conditions arise or pass away.

In many ways, healthier people appear to be more developed beings (Vaughan, 1985; Walsh, 1999a). Such people are more loving, compassionate, and serving than most; they appear less motivated by fear and greed and more concerned with living in harmony with all beings; they experience more inner peace, gratitude, reverence for life; and they appreciate both unity and diversity; such people are humorous, generous, forgiving, wise, accepting, and more open—and, therefore, more vulnerable. Finally, health demands wholeness, which requires integration of not only the "shadow"—disowned aspects of ourselves that are unacceptable to us—but also the integration of the physical body, emotionality, mental ego, existential self, and spiritual self. "Thus, while mental and existential identifications represent essential stages of human growth, healthy maturation and wholeness require growing beyond them" (Vaughan, 1985, pp. 30–31).

View of Unhealthy Functioning. Conversely, the integral view of suboptimal functioning includes a relatively "lower" prevailing level of development, incomplete identification with one's current prevailing level, imbalance among one's 24 lines of development, and/or imbalance among the four quadrants. More specifically, Wilber (1999a, vol. 4) has posited that each stage of development, if unsuccessfully navigated, will produce its own specific pathology. For each of the 10 stages respectively, these pathologies are psychoses, borderline/narcissistic personality disorders, neuroses, script pathologies, identity neuroses, existential pathologies, psychic disorders, subtle disorders, and causal disorders (the nondual stage is pathology-free).

Within the prepersonal realm, *psychoses* represent "a failure to differentiate and integrate the physiosphere" (Wilber, 1995, p. 211). Reflecting "the most profound and primitive lack of psychological organization" (Marquis, 2002, p. 19), they include such diagnostic entities as schizophrenia and psychotic depression. In *borderline/narcissistic personality disorders*, having differentiated from others physically but not emotionally, people

> feel overwhelmed or engulfed by their emotional environment (borderline disorders), treat their environment as an extension of their own feelings (inflated narcissism), or derive their sense of self-worth from their perceptions of how others feel about them (fragile narcissism) . . . [and] employ primitive defenses such as splitting and denial. (Marquis, 2002, p. 20)

Neuroses involve "the more mature defenses such as repression or displacement" such that "the mental self [dissociates] from the emotional self or [remains] fixated upon certain bodily or emotional impulses"; as a result, "that which was repressed returns in the form of 'disguised symptoms' forcing themselves into consciousness (Wilber, 1995; Wilber et al., 1986)" (Marquis, 2002, pp. 21–22).

Within the personal realm, *script pathologies* refer to a broad array of manifestations that have as their source role confusion (Erikson, 1963); rule confusion, distortion of the rules of logic in one's thinking (Beck & Weishaar, 1989); and/or duplicitous transactions. In the latter, overt messages mask hidden agendas or covert messages (Berne, 1961), such as the boss who asks her late-arriving secretary, "What time is it?", a message overtly seeking information but covertly expressing hostile criticism. *Identity neuroses* refer to a broad array of manifestations that have as their source "the vulnerabilities and distresses of the emerging introspective self" (Marquis, 2002). These include obsession over possible losses and the struggles of resisting social pressure in order to emerge as one's own person. *Existential pathologies* have as their source questions about the ultimate meaning of life in general and one's own life in particular and can manifest in a broad array of concerns including the givens of life—death, meaninglessness, freedom, and responsibility (Yalom, 1980)—and issues of personal autonomy, authenticity, self-actualization, and existential isolation.

Proceeding to the transpersonal realm, the reader is again alerted to the fact that transpersonal pathologies may seem alien, not "making sense" if someone has not had experiences from the level in question. Indeed, the transpersonal realm cannot "make sense" precisely because it is transpersonal: beyond the senses—trans-sensational, and beyond reason—trans-rational.

Psychic disorders fall into three main groups.

> First are the spontaneous awakenings of unsought spiritual energies and capacities, such as kundalini, which 'can be psychological dynamite'. Next

are the spiritual crises that, during severe stress, invade the lower levels of development . . . psychotic-like episodes [that can be differentiated from actual psychosis] . . . Third are the many problems of those beginning a contemplative life, such as psychic inflation—attributing the transpersonal energies to the individual self/ego, structural imbalances—resulting from improper employment of spiritual disciplines, and the 'dark night of the soul'—having tasted unity with the Divine and then to have it fade, one enters a profound state of despair [that can be differentiated from personal-realm depression]. (Wilber et al., 1986, cited in Marquis, 2002, p. 37)

Subtle disorders take many forms, two of the most common of which will be described here. One is a kind of fragmentation in which one *observes* rather than *is* archetypal awareness (Wilber et al., 1986, p. 123). Another is mistaking the phenomena of subtle level experiences—archetypal forms, interior luminosities and sounds, and currents of bliss—as enlightenment itself.

The *causal* disorders involve either a failure to differentiate or a failure to integrate. Either the person fails to

differentiate from, or die to, "the subtlest level of the separate self-sense," or, having differentiated itself from all objects of awareness—to the extent that no objects arise to consciousness—one fails to *integrate* the causal unmanifest with the manifest realm of forms. (Marquis, 2002, p. 44)

For each pathology, Wilber (1999b, vol. 4) proposed treatment modalities consisting of widely practiced psychotherapeutic approaches, alternative therapies, and practices from the world's mystical traditions. His spectrum of treatment brings order and harmony to the cacophony of psychological theories and treatment options available to mental health professionals. It is to the psychotherapy process that we now turn.

The Personality Change Process

The Self is integral; so is counseling.

Basic Principles of Change. According to Wilber (1999b, vol. 4), people change in two ways: translation and transformation. *Translation* involves change *within* one's level of development, maintaining the same deep structure of functioning but changing surface structures. *Transformation* involves change *of* one's level of development, a fundamental shift in the deep structure of one's functioning in the direction of greater complexity. As previously stated, translation is analogous to rearranging one's furniture, whereas transformation is analogous to moving to upgraded living quarters (Wilber, 1999b, vol. 3).

Translation and transformation recur in the process of human development; to this extent, change is a naturally occurring, indeed, an unavoidable phenomenon that people manifest in response to emerging needs: physical, emotional, mental, and spiritual. At the same time, because of people's tendency to avoid pain and disruption, and because of chronic deprivation, repeated trauma, and recurrent stress in the environment, virtually everyone, at one time or another, has become "stuck" in the process of developmental change. Wilber (2000b) asserted that, in every case,

> the curative catalyst . . . is bringing *awareness* or *consciousness* to bear on an area of experience that is (or has been) denied, distorted, falsified, or ignored. Once that area enters (or reenters) consciousness, then it can rejoin the ongoing flow of evolutionary unfolding, instead of remaining behind, stuck, . . . sending up painful symptoms. . . . Encountering (or reencountering) these disturbed or ignored facets [of experience] allows them to be differentiated (transcended) and integrated (included) in the ongoing waves of ever-expanding consciousness. (p. 99, italics added)

Like the process of becoming "stuck," the process of becoming "unstuck" can and does occur naturally. However, the latter process is more elegantly achieved in the special circumstance of counseling, an environment specifically aimed at the development of consciousness. The exceptional caring and expertise that characterizes the counseling environment can facilitate the "unearthing" and overcoming of impediments to development.

Change Through Counseling

The Client's Role. From the client's perspective, he seeks counseling because he wants relief from pain. From the integral counselor's perspective, the client's pain is a manifestation of his being stuck in the process of development; it is a kind of feedback from the proximal self that one is not progressing as one's deepest nature intends. Thus, from the counselor's perspective, the client's felt motivation is to alleviate pain, and his deeper motivation is to continue in the process of development.

Although clients may seek counseling for any of the nine pathologies corresponding to the first nine fulcrums of development that Wilber has posited, most clients seek counseling to alleviate suffering that arises from "a few levels: mostly fulcrum-3 (which involves uncovering and integrating repressed feelings and shadow elements), fulcrum-4 (which involves belongingness needs and cognitive reprogramming of harsh scripts), and fulcrums 5 and 6 (which involve self-esteem and self-actualization)" (Wilber, 1999b, vol. 4, pp. 17–18).

Integral therapists acknowledge that, at the same time that clients seek relief, they also resist change. The process of transformative change, in particular, involves the disruption and death of exclusive identification with the previous fulcrum, mode of functioning, or self. "The self, at every level, will attempt to defend itself against pain, disruption, and ultimately death" (Wilber, 2000b, p. 94). As Adi Da put it, the separate self is "at war with its own Help" (cited in Murthy, 1990, p. 31). Wilber (1996b, vol. 1, p. 563) posited that every level of the spectrum of development contains its own forms of defense and resistance. For example, whereas a client at F-3 representational-mind resists and disowns bodily impulses such as sex and aggression, someone at F-6 vision-logic has accepted and integrated those impulses, but now is resistant to experiencing the immediate here-and-now. Likewise, at the transpersonal levels, individuals do not resist the present moment but resist fully surrendering to unity consciousness. At any level, "people will sometimes opt for the known pain of the old adaptive pattern rather than endure the pain of transcendence, disintegration, and reintegration" (Holden, 1993, p. 15).

Because counseling involves the "threat" of development, a client must be willing to endure the temporary discomfort of transformation to alleviate the chronic discomfort he sought counseling to relieve. Evolutionarily, what Mahoney (2003, ch. 12) called "core ordering processes"—emotionality, personal identity, one's sense of reality, and power/control—have been "given special protection against changing. . . . [S]uch resistance reflects basic self-protective processes that serve to maintain the coherence of the living system" (p. 2). The problem from an integral perspective is that one ultimately is more than simply the living system. Thus, what is most adaptive for the biological organism (great nest sphere of life) may not serve one's deepest nature (great nest spheres of soul and spirit).

An effective counselor can facilitate a client's willingness to change and the process of change itself. However, the primary responsibility for change rests with the client. This notion is corroborated by substantial research (Asay & Lambert, 1999; Bohart & Tallman, 1999; Lambert & Bergin, 1994; Mahoney 1991, 2003) suggesting that client variables, such as motivation, presenting concern, and the assumption of responsibility, are more predictive of counseling success than are counselor variables such as theoretical orientation and techniques employed. In addition, integral therapists believe that to each successive fulcrum of development, one must bring increasing intentionality that is expressed in action. In particular, for one to proceed through the transpersonal fulcrums, one must engage in a program of spiritual practice. Regarding both counseling and spiritual practice, Walsh (1999) wrote that what is necessary is "an open mind and a willingness to experiment. . . . It takes courage to examine yourself and your life carefully. It takes effort, . . . commitment. . . . Fortunately, the more you practice, the more these essential qualities grow" (p. 15).

In the end, Wilber's view of the human capacity to change is exalted indeed: Each human being has enfolded within her being the entire great nest, from dirt to divinity, from matter to spirit. Thus, like transpersonalists in general, integral therapists believe in each person's "wealth of inner resources and an innate capacity for self-healing" (Vaughan, 1993, p. 160).

The Counselor's Role. The counselor's role in integral counseling could be stated most basically as helping clients be happier and suffer less (Walsh, 1999) by promoting clients' development, that is, their translative and transformative change. Because most clients will seek translation rather than transformation (Wilber, 1999b, vol. 4), most counselors will pursue what Wilber has termed the *prime directive:* helping clients maximize their functioning at their current prevailing level of development. Thus, analogously speaking, the goal is not necessarily to live in the building's penthouse but to live as happily as possible on one's own floor, with some access to the entire building.

To prepare for both translative and transformative work, integral counselors fulfill certain prerequisites. One prerequisite is the ability to conceptualize his clients, himself, and life in terms of integral theory. Another is the counselor's pursuit of his own development. A final prerequisite is the counselor's mastery of the psychotherapeutic techniques associated with the developmental levels of clients with whom he works.

Regarding the first prerequisite of integral conceptualization, studying this chapter is an excellent beginning. Reading primary sources on integral counseling also is necessary, as is supplementary reading of sources that address transpersonal counseling and spirituality in counseling. Seeking out continuing education through conferences, workshops, and university coursework is also essential. Integration of integral concepts will also be advanced by revisioning one's own life and experience in the world in terms of integral theory. A specific manifestation of this perspective is that the counselor grasps the counseling process as a sacred journey that involves "[joining] another person in an extraordinarily intimate way . . . trying to become a helpful part of [a client's] very evolution" (Kegan, 1982, p. 278). As such, integral counselors *care* for clients such that they are moved by their experiences with clients—a quality potentially as helpful to clients as the counselor's professional knowledge. Another manifestation of the counselor's integral perspective is an appreciation of the mutual influence of the counselor's personal and professional life (Mahoney, 2003). This appreciation leads naturally to the second prerequisite.

Regarding the second prerequisite, pursuit of one's own development, Walsh and Vaughan (1993) quoted the Buddha: "To straighten the crooked, You must first do a harder thing—Straighten yourself" (p. 154).

It is an axiom in transpersonal counseling that one can elegantly facilitate others' achievement of only those developmental levels that one has achieved in oneself. To say it another way, one must have "been there and done that" in order to help others "be there and do that" (or something similar to that). "The depth of [counseling] is necessarily limited by the [developmental] stage of the therapist. . . . [T]he further the therapist has evolved through the stages of Self-awareness at various levels of consciousness, the more effective he or she is likely to be as a healer" (Vaughan, 1985, pp. 184–185). For transpersonally oriented therapists, including integral therapists, "undergoing their own in-depth, transpersonally oriented psychotherapy and long-term practice of transpersonal disciplines such as yoga or meditation are invaluable . . . part of a lifetime practice" (Walsh & Vaughan, 1993, p. 154). From an integral perspective, the counselor's presence, being, unconditional positive regard, empathy, and compassion are believed to be largely a function of the counselor's own spiritual work (Boorstein, 1997; Epstein, 1995; Ram Dass, 1973). In general, "to whatever degree my personal [spiritual] practice keeps *me* loving, keeps *me* compassionate and empathic, to that degree therapy proceeds most effectively" (Boorstein, 1997, p. xvi). In particular, to work with clients in the transpersonal domain, one must undertake some form of spiritual practice to facilitate a direct and greater understanding of what were, at first, merely cognitive assertions (Vaughan, 1985, 1995; Wittine, 1993).

The third prerequisite, mastery of the psychotherapeutic techniques associated with the developmental levels of clients with whom one works, calls for the counselor to become technically eclectic. As will be discussed below, Wilber's spectrum of development and pathology are associated also with a spectrum of treatment. The integral counselor first decides which developmental levels of client concerns he will work with, then he develops the skills of the psychotherapeutic approaches that most appropriately address those levels. For levels with which he does not work, he identifies qualified practitioners to whom he refers clients with concerns involving those levels. For example, a counselor might be competent to work with clients whose concerns fall primarily into the personal domain but refer clients whose concerns fall primarily within the prepersonal or transpersonal domains. An implication of integrally based technical eclecticism is that any integral counselor will have mastered the psychotherapeutic skills common to all psychotherapeutic approaches, such as the basic counseling skills that provide the foundation for establishment and maintenance of the therapeutic relationship, session management skills, professional ethics skills, and so forth. Always at the foundation of integral counseling, even more primary than an understanding of the client in terms of quadrants and level of development, is the counselor's valuing of the client as another human being, another manifestation of spirit.

Stages. "Just as life is complex, so too, is counseling" (Mahoney, 2003).

Relationship. The integral counseling process begins with the therapeutic relationship. From an integral perspective, any relationship constitutes a small culture of its own, represented within Wilber's four quadrant model in the lower left quadrant. When that culture is healthy, when it is pervaded by intentions of well being and by mutual vulnerability and influence, it provides for the client "a 'secure base'—a safe, accessible, and compassionate human bond—the therapeutic relationship becomes a context in and from which the client can explore, experiment, and express" (Mahoney, 2003, ch.

2, p. 14). The therapeutic relationship is thus the primary vehicle of change—the culture in which clients grow (Kegan, 1982).

At its best, the therapeutic relationship provides a client with the security to transform, to dis-integrate so that aspects of one's self may be reintegrated at a higher level. Winnicott described this type of relationship as "an environment in which one can safely and easily be in bits and pieces without the feeling of falling apart" (cited in Epstein, 1995, p. 206). When therapy is proceeding well, both counselors and clients can tolerate the discomfort—sometimes terror—of disintegration by seeing it in its place in the developmental process. "More than anything else," wrote Wittine (1993), "our clients need to be seen and felt as the Self they truly are, which is no different from the true Self we are" (p. 169). Thus, beyond the positive regard of person-centered therapy is the positive regard of integral counseling in which the client is regarded at her core as an embodiment of the ultimate goodness, beauty, and truth of the divine.

Assessment. A critical aspect of integral counseling is an accurate and comprehensive assessment of a client's four quadrant profile, level of development, and lines of development. Only with this information can appropriate counseling goals and processes be established and mutually agreed upon.

A client's four quadrant profile can be assessed using the Integral Intake (II; Marquis, 2002). The II is a self-report, short-answer instrument that a client can complete prior to the first counseling session. The counselor can assemble a conceptual snapshot of the client's intentional quadrant by noting client responses to items addressing self-image, self-esteem, concerns, and what the client deems meaningful and valuable. The counselor can ascertain the behavioral quadrant through client responses regarding more objective phenomena such as medical disorders, medications, diet, alcohol and/or drug use, aerobic and/or strength exercise, and patterns of sleep/rest. The client's cultural quadrant is reflected in the client's reported cultural experience, from ethnicity, family dynamics, and vocational relationships to political, environmental, and religious or spiritual beliefs. Finally, the counselor constructs an understanding of the client's social quadrant through client responses regarding the more objective aspects of the client's environment, such as socioeconomic status, work environment, conditions of one's neighborhood, layout or state of household, and other environmental stressors and conditions.

The counselor can use this holistic assessment to formulate an integral profile, including prioritized phenomena to be addressed, to present to the client as a way to initiate collaborative goal setting. A unique feature of integral counseling is reflected in how the II formally assesses every client's culture, the lower left quadrant. Thus, multicultural considerations are given substantial, structured attention from the outset of integral counseling. Also unique to integral counseling and reflected in the II is the attention paid to the objective domains. Client drug dependence, lack of exercise, or chemical

imbalance (upper right quadrant) or unemployment or abusive or other un-
safe living conditions (lower right quadrant) are addressed in integral counseling prior to or along with upper left quadrant concerns that constitute the
priority, if not sole concerns, of traditional psychotherapy.

The upper left quadrant is given its due in the assessment of a client's
developmental level. From an integral perspective, people at different stages
of development face different struggles, the resolution of which calls for different counseling approaches and practices. The spectrum of development,
pathology, and corresponding treatment modalities and, in some cases,
contraindications, are summarized in Table 13.2. Wilber stressed that

> the nine general levels of therapy that I outlined are meant to be sugges-
> tive only; they are broad guidelines. . . . There is, needless to say, a great
> deal of overlap between these therapies. For example, I list "script pathol-
> ogy" and "cognitive therapy" as being especially relevant to fulcrum-
> 4. . . . Cognitive therapy has excelled in rooting out these maladaptive
> scripts and replacing them with more accurate, benign, and therefore
> healthy ideas and self-concepts. But to say cognitive therapy focuses on
> this wave of consciousness development is *not* to say it has no benefit at
> other waves, for clearly it does. The idea, rather, is that the farther away
> we get from this wave, the less relevant (but never completely useless)
> cognitive therapy becomes. (Wilber, 1999b, vol. 4, p. 16)

Currently, no single instrument exists that assesses developmental level
in a full spectrum context. A variety of instruments exist that assess psychopathology in the prepersonal and personal realms, and the DSM-IV-TR can
be helpful in this regard. However, even some levels within these domains
may not be adequately addressed by existing instruments. At the current
time, integral counselors must rely on existing instruments, observation, and
interview along with their knowledge of the spectrum of development and
pathology to come to a diagnosis—perhaps in some cases a tentative one.
One aid in this regard is alertness to signs of developmental arrests or fixa-
tions. For example, patterns of highly unstable relationships and the use of
primitive defense mechanisms suggest borderline (F-2) disorders; repression
of sexual and aggressive impulses resulting in "disguised symptoms" suggest
neurotic (F-3) disorders; issues pertaining to role confusion, distorted thinking, "duplicitous transactions"—in which hidden agendas or covert messages
are masked by different overt messages—or overly harsh and rigid internal
scripts suggest role or script (F-4) disorders.

Finally, various *lines* of development should be explored. This can be
done in a relatively informal way or with the use of assessment instruments
such as Kegans' subject–object interview, Loevinger's scale of ego development, and/or Kohlberg's and Gilligan's assessments of moral development.
Using results from line-of-development assessment, the counselor formulates
an "integral psychograph" (see Figure 13.3) that reveals to what level each of
the client's lines have developed.

TABLE 13.2

Ken Wilber's Spectrum of Human Development, Pathology, Treatment, and Contraindications*

Realm		Developmental Fulcrum/Level	Pathology	Treatment	Contraindications
Prepersonal	F-1	Sensoriphysical	Psychoses	Pharmaceutical, physiological, possible psychotherapy as adjunct; perhaps Holotropic Breathwork and/or Primal Scream	Contemplative practice; notion of oneness with God
	F-2	Phantasmic/emotional	Borderline and narcissistic personality disorders	Structure-building psychotherapy: object relations, psychoanalytic ego psychology, self psychology (behavior therapy)	Vipassana meditation; notion of oneness with God
	F-3	Representational mind	Neuroses	Uncovering techniques: psychoanalysis, Gestalt, Jungian, Ego and Self Psychologies, Focusing, (Person-Centered)	
Personal	F-4	Rule/role mind	Script pathologies	Collaboration between student and therapy, (Adlerian, Choice Therapy, Multimodal, systems approaches)	
	F-5	Formal-reflexive	Identity neuroses	Introspection, philosophizing, Socratic dialogue	
	F-6	Vision-logic	Existential pathologies	Existential psychotherapy	
Transpersonal	F-7	Psychic	Psychic disorders	Path of yogis (sometimes temporary suspension of contemplative work)	
	F-8	Subtle	Subtle disorders	Intensification of contemplative practice, increased contact with spiritual teacher	
	F-9	Causal	Causal disorders	Collaboration between student and spiritual teacher	
	F-10	Nondual			

*Approaches appearing in parentheses are extrapolations made by the text authors.
Wilber, K. (2000.) *Integral Psychology: Consciousness, Spirit, Psychology, Therapy,* by K. Wilber, 2000, Boston: Shambhala, with permission.

Treatment plan. Reflecting upon the client's four-quadrant profile, level of development, and integral psychograph, the counselor then tailors integral therapeutic approaches most appropriate to this particular client. At the heart of these approaches are *integral transformative practices* (ITPs): practices that honor and nurture the entire human being, from the body, emotions, and mind, all the way to soul and spirit, as *each* unfolds in self (I), culture (we), and nature (it and its). Thus, regardless of one's level of development, one attempts to be as "all-quadrant, all-level" as one can be (Wilber, 2000c, p. 136). The basic premise is that one is most likely to transform if one exercises and cultivates as many aspects of one's being as possible. It is not sufficient merely to think differently. "Truly, adopting a new holistic philosophy, believing in Gaia, or even thinking in integral terms—however important those things might be, they are the least important when it comes to spiritual transformation" (Wilber, 2000c, p. 137). It is through the actual and consistent engagement of ITPs that one transforms. Wilber recommended that one

> start with the self: the waves of existence . . . can be exercised by a spectrum of practices: physical exercises (weightlifting, diet, jogging, yoga), emotional exercises (qi gong, counseling, psychotherapy), mental exercises (affirmation, visualization), and spiritual exercises (meditation, contemplative prayer).
>
> But these waves of existence need to be exercised—not just in self ([a narcissistic affliction Wilber termed] boomeritis!)—but in culture and nature as well. Exercising the waves in culture might mean getting involved with community service, working with the hospice movement, participating in local government, working with inner-city rehabilitation, providing services for homeless people. It can also mean using *relationships in general* (marriage, friendship, parenting) to further your own growth and the growth of others...
>
> Exercising the waves of existence in nature means that nature is viewed, not as an inert and instrumental backdrop to our actions, but as participating in our own evolution. Getting actively involved in respect for nature, in any number of ways (recycling, environmental protection, nature celebration) not only honors nature; it promotes our own capacity to care.
>
> In short, integral transformative practice attempts to exercise all of the basic waves of human beings—physical, emotional, mental, and spiritual—in self, culture, and nature. . . . [T]his is the most powerful way to trigger transformation to the next wave—not to mention simply becoming as healthy as one can be at one's present wave, whatever it might be (no small accomplishment!). (Wilber, 2000c, pp. 138–139)

In addition, essential to such a lofty endeavor is some sort of communal support, whether that be a formal institution or a group of family and friends who encourage and inspire such practice (Murphy, 1993; Wilber, 2000c).

Regarding specific treatment plans, Wilber (2000a, vol. 7, p. 643) offered these examples:

- A client with borderline pathology, impulsive ego, preconventional moral-ity, and splitting defense mechanism might be offered structure building therapy, bibliotherapy, weight training, nutritional supplements, pharma-cological agents (as required), verbalization and narrative training, and short sessions of a concentration-type meditation (no awareness-training medi-tation, which tends to dismantle psychological/self-structure, which the borderline does not yet adequately possess).
- A client with anxiety neurosis, phobic elements, conventional morality, repression and displacement defense mechanisms, belongingness needs, and persona self-sense might be offered uncovering psychotherapy, bioen-ergetics, script analysis, jogging or biking (or some other individual sport), desensitization, dream analysis/therapy, and vipassana meditation.
- A client with existential depression, postconventional morality, suppres-sion and sublimation defense mechanisms, self-actualization needs, and a centauric self-sense might be offered existential analysis, dream therapy, a team sport (e.g., volleyball, basketball), bibliotherapy, t'ai chi chuan (or prana circulating therapy), community service, and kundalini yoga.
- A client who has been practicing Zen mediation for several years, but suf-fers life-goal apathy and depression, deadening of affect, postconventional morality, postformal cognition, self-transcendence needs, and psychic self-sense might be offered uncovering therapy, combination weight training and jogging, tantric deity-yoga (visualization meditation), tonglen (com-passion training), and community service (p. 643).

Wilber (2000a, vol. 7) acknowledged the untested nature of integral therapy. Research is currently in progress to assess its effectiveness (Wilber, 2000a, vol. 7, p. 642).

Techniques. Integral counseling employs interventions that arose from the various approaches that constitute the spectrum of psychotherapy. Due to space considerations, only those techniques that are unique to transpersonal and integral counseling will be discussed here. The integral counselor uses these techniques when, and only when, they are appropriate to a client's concerns, goals, and spiritual worldview.

In general, transpersonal practices were developed within the world's wisdom, or spiritual, traditions. "Spiritual practice" usually refers to the mani-festing or rehearsal of desired qualities or ways of being, which eventually become natural and spontaneous, whereas "spiritual techniques" are the spe-cific methods or exercises employed in such practice (Walsh, 1999). In general, counselors should recommend only those techniques that they have person-ally experienced or practiced. Also important to bear in mind is that enjoy-ing solitude in nature, participating in art, meditating, or anything else that is a potential spiritual practice "can serve either the ego or the soul, depend-ing on the intention with which they are pursued" (Vaughan, 1995, p. 253).

Bibliotherapy. Boorstein (1997) reported that recommending spiritual reading material is often helpful to clients, even for those who are severely disturbed. He posited that not only are they empowered by their perception that he views them as able to do spiritual work, but that his recommending to them spiritual literature that is personally meaningful to him bolsters their self-esteem and ego strength through identification with him. Boorstein (1997) noted that *A Course in Miracles* (Foundation for Inner Peace, 1975), also know as "The Course," was written in the tradition of Christian mysticism and stresses genuine forgiveness as a powerful means of eradicating barriers that separate us both from others and our own divine nature. Some other books to recommend to clients include Vaughan's (1985) *The Inward Arc*, Hixon's (1978) *Coming Home*, and Walsh's (1999) *Essential Spirituality*.

Great questions. The intense pondering of profound questions can be powerful in promoting both insight and the disintegration of rigid, limiting, and illusory preconceptions regarding the nature of self and reality. A few of these questions are, "Who am I?" "How shall I live?" "Who or what is always already the case before 'I' do anything at all?" "Am 'I' the one who is 'living' (animating/manifesting) me (the body-mind) now?" (Avabhasa, 1985).

Prayer/contemplation. Because people from the Judeo-Christian tradition are sometimes put off by the word "meditation," recommending contemplative prayer may be helpful in eliciting a sincere, authentic, contemplative response. In fact, Christian contemplatives such as Father Thomas Merton (1969), Father Thomas Keating (1986), and Brother David Steindl-Rast (1983, 1984) frequently used the words "prayer," "contemplation," and "meditation" interchangeably. They also agreed that petitionary prayer, in which one asks for some desired condition for oneself, is the lowest form of prayer, while contemplation, or communing with God's presence or experiencing union with Godhead, is the highest form.

In essence, contemplation and meditation are the same, although the aim of contemplation is usually said to be communing with the presence of God and, ultimately, union with God, which is only possible when one has quieted and emptied one's mind such that one is capable of resting in silence. Merton's (1956) Christian views sometimes seem indistinguishable from a Buddhist perspective: "We find god in our own being" (p. 134); "God Who is at once infinitely above us and Who yet dwells in the depths of our being" (p. 135); "Then will I truly know Him, since I am in Him and He is truly in me" (p. 139). Keating (1986) and Steindl-Rast (1983, 1984) offered superb descriptions of contemplative practices within the Christian tradition.

Meditation.

> *We must close our eyes and invoke a new manner of seeing, a*
> *wakefulness that is the birthright of us all, though few put it to use.*
> —Plotinus, in O'Brien, 1984

The training of attention is probably as good a definition of meditation as any. Meditative practices fall into one of two categories.

Concentrative meditation increases the mind's ability to focus, analogous to the intense power of a laser compared to the diffused and relative weakness of scattered light. This ability to maintain a concentrated focus on a single object is a prerequisite to awareness types of meditation. Although description of all the different types of concentrative practices would fill volumes, they all have in common the goal of single-pointed attention, regardless of the object of one's attention. Such single-pointed absorption is experienced as inherently joyous: the "oceanic feeling" of union and bliss.

Meditating on a mantra is a common form of concentrative practice. A mantra is a spiritually meaningful word or phrase that is repeated, either softly or silently, as the object of one's attention. *Metta* (lovingkindness) meditation or prayer involves silently repeating one's hope that all beings feel happy, peaceful, and free from suffering. While visualizing the person(s) to whom these wishes are intended, one silently repeats something along the lines of "May you be at peace; may you be happy; may your heart remain open and sensitive to the light and love of your true nature." This is particularly effective with people who are angry or critical of themselves or others (Boorstein, 1997).

In Tibetan Buddhism, one can find meditations designed to promote almost any virtuous quality. One example of this is *Tonglen*, an extremely powerful meditation of compassion. Tonglen is Tibetan for "giving and receiving," and essentially involves the taking in of others' pain and suffering and the giving to them of one's love, happiness, and healing energy. Briefly, the practice is to invoke as much compassion within oneself as possible and then to visualize another's pain, suffering, and distress in the form of dark, grimy, tar-like smoke. On the in-breath, the practitioner visualizes breathing in this great mass of suffering to the core of one's being, where it is purified and dissolved. On the out-breath, one visualizes the giving of a radiant, pure, white light of love, joy, and happiness to the one who is suffering. Some people are put off by the intensity of this practice. For them, less extreme versions of Tonglen are available (see chapter 12 of Sogyal Rinpoche's [1993] *The Tibetan Book of Living and Dying*). "No other practice I know," wrote Rinpoche (1993), "is as effective in destroying the self-grasping, self-cherishing, self-absorption of the ego, which is the root of all our suffering and the root of all hard-heartedness" (p. 193).

Awareness/insight meditation in its classic form is called *vipassana*. After having developed the ability to maintain a concentrated focus, one applies "bare attention" or "choiceless, nonjudgmental awareness" to all that arises in and passes out of one's present field of attention. One practices simply being as aware as possible of everything experienced, from one's breath to sensations, emotions, thoughts, and eventually the felt sense of "I," taking care to notice the difference between what arises and how one experiences what arises. The aim is not to search for anything in particular, not to hold on to or cling to any images or feelings; nor to avoid or deny anything that arises. With arduous practice, one realizes that literally everything that arises also passes, and that one's suffering is due to one's desire to cling to pleasurable, satisfying experiences that will inevitably be lost, while trying to avoid unpleasant experiences. When one truly realizes that everything is constantly in flux, one relaxes one's attachments and the illusion of control and is thus able to be more fully present in each moment. One develops a greatly deepened capacity to tolerate and accept unpleasant conditions. In this disposition, one can see that one is not as much of an active, conscious entity, but rather a *process* of identifying, automatically and unconsciously, with patterns of *re*activity. "It is *the* fundamental tenet of Buddhist psychology," maintains Epstein (1995), "that this kind of attention is, in itself, healing" (p. 110).

Many vipassana practitioners claim that this type of meditation, more than dreams, is the "royal road to the unconscious" (Vaughan, 1985; Walsh, 1999; Washburn, 1988; Wilber, 1999b, vol. 3), because its potential to uncover repressed psychological material is enormous. This practice should be recommended only for those individuals who have an already established, strong ego, because, unlike the goal of concentrative meditations—to facilitate the experiences of peace and bliss—one goal of vipassana is the dissolution of ego boundaries and defenses. For an excellent overview of a wide variety of meditative practices, from the Jesus prayer of Christianity to the zazen of Zen Buddhism, the reader is referred to parts I and II of Goleman (1972), Epstein's (1990) "The Psychodynamics of Meditation," and chapter 10 of Wilber's (1997a) *The Eye of Spirit*.

Silence. Frequently, the most powerful therapeutic moments are those of silence—not awkward, dead, or paralyzing silence, but healing silence pregnant with meaning and possibilities. "This healing silence, which is an untouched natural resource for the practice of psychotherapy" (Epstein, 1995, p. 187) is possible only when the counselor can be with a client without an agenda, simply being present to the intersubjective field arising between counselor and client. This capacity is greatly augmented by the counselor's meditative or contemplative practice.

Yoga. The word *yoga* derives from the word "yoke" and thus involves a set of disciplines designed to consciously yoke or unite the practitioner with the divine. Yoga is not simply a postural endeavor but a family of practices and technologies of transformation more than 4 thousand years old that includes ethics, meditation, breathing, postures, movement, intellectual study, devotion, service, sex, lifestyle, and work (Feuerstein, 1997a). Interested readers are referred to Feuerstein (1996).

Visualization. Visualization can be a powerful aid in the healing process. Although different religions suggest visualizing different forms (Jesus, Shiva, Chenrezig), they all attest to the efficacy of this method. In addition to visualizing deities, Assagioli (1991) recommended visualizing the unfolding of a beautiful rose with the potential of the bud symbolizing our potential to realize our hidden, true nature and beauty. For a detailed description of a 12-step transpersonal visualization technique called the "Power Within," the reader is referred to Chapin (1989).

Service, forgiveness, and devotion. In daily life, authentic spirituality demands some form of service, a service motivated not by a sense of duty or obligation but by the felt need to help others. "If we are awake to our true nature and aware of self and soul, service seems to be a natural expression of who we are" (Vaughan, 1995, p. 287).

Forgiveness has long been emphasized in Christianity for its transformative power. *A Course in Miracles* even states that "forgiveness is the key to happiness" (Foundation for Inner Peace, 1975, vol. 2, p. 210) and that the inability or unwillingness to forgive is an unwillingness to let go of the past (Boorstein, 1997).

Devotion is not a simple issue. Although it has always been emphasized in Christianity and has long been an integral element of Hinduism and Tibetan Buddhism, in modern America, the ideal of the autonomous individual and the emphasis on the equality of each person is greatly at odds with such practice. Even though it is certainly not the appropriate practice for everyone, "when it is done right, Guru Yoga [the practice of devotion to a Spiritual Teacher] is the most powerful yoga there is" (Wilber, 1999c, p. 224); it is a practice reminiscent of Jesus' disciples' devotion to him. Moreover, for individuals working with transpersonal issues, an authentic spiritual teacher, or master, is probably more important than a transpersonal counselor, although working with both would be ideal. For an overview of contemporary spiritual teachers, see Rawlinson (1997).

Addressing Resistance. Therapeutically responding to a client's resistance is the art, and heart, of integral counseling. Balancing the dialectical tension of a client's desires and fears of developing into the unknown, counselors must walk a razor's edge between support and challenge. This is a fancy way of saying *counselors work with, not against, clients' resistance* (Mahoney, 1991, 2003; Wilber, 1999b, vol. 1). How does one do this?

First, the counselor adopts the perspective that the client's resistance to change is not an opponent to be conquered but an ally to be honored: Resistance is the self's protection against pain, disintegration, and death. The problem is that in protecting against *all* forms of pain, disintegration, and death, the self can block those forms that are part of the process of developmental progress. Consequently, "the therapist doesn't try to get rid of the resistances, by-pass them, or ignore them. Instead, he [sic] helps the individual see how, and secondarily, why he is resisting" (Wilber, 1999b, vol. 1, p. 564). Thus the counselor is, again, implementing the primary process goal of integral counseling: to bring awareness or consciousness to experience. The integral counselor does not pursue this process initially by facilitating the client's direct contact and acceptance of that which he is resisting. Rather, the counselor skillfully employs what Wilber termed *special conditions* for the purpose of frustrating the client's resistance. The client is most likely to become aware of resistance when that resistance is frustrated. Only when a client becomes aware that he is actively, even if unconsciously, resisting will he be free to choose to continue, to increase, or to decrease his resistance.

Consistent with his full-spectrum model, Wilber (1999b, vol. 1) posited a specific technique, or "special condition," to work with the unique type of resistance encountered at each level of development. For example, for an F-3 client with neurosis who is repressing and resisting his sexual and aggressive impulses, the special condition is the technique of *free association*, in which the client is asked to freely tell the counselor everything that enters his mind. If resistant, the client will have difficulty freely relating his fantasies and associations. At the moment when the client stops associating freely, rather than confronting the client with what the counselor thinks the client is resisting, the counselor simply points out that the client hit a snag of some sort, and, together, they explore the client's experience in the moment, which likely will facilitate the client's awareness of how and why he was resisting. Thus, free association is a special condition that reveals F-3 clients' resistances.

By contrast, consider a centauric (F-6) client. Because she has developed beyond the neurotic level, she has integrated the bodily and emotional aspects of her being with her cognitive/role self and thus is not resistant to the same impulses to which the neurotic client is resistant. Rather, the centauric client is dealing with issues such as meaning and authenticity, and as such, she is resistant *not* to memories of the past or fantasies of the future but to being immediately and authentically present. The special condition at this level is the client's concentration on

> the immediate present in all its forms and the bodymind which discloses it. . . . The therapist will watch—not for blocks *in* thought—but for any flight from present awareness *into* thought. . . . In ego-level therapy a person will be encouraged to explore his past; in centaur-level therapy, he will be prevented from it. (Wilber, 1999b, vol. 1, p. 565, italics added)

Such special conditions are also available for each of the transpersonal levels of development. The spiritual practice of such conditions discloses that "although the only thing a person fundamentally wants is unity consciousness, the only thing he is ever doing is resisting it" (Wilber, 1999b, vol. 1, p. 569).

CONTRIBUTIONS AND LIMITATIONS

Interface with Recent Developments in the Mental Health Field

Wilber has always demonstrated a great openness to new evidence and therefore to revising his theory. Since 1973, his work has evolved through four distinct phases, each demanding either revision or additional concepts.

Effectiveness of Psychotherapy. Because of its newness, integral counseling itself has not been the subject of much research. However, because integral counselors employ established therapeutic approaches for the majority of clients who are seeking change in the personal domain, and because they concur with research on factors in the effectiveness of psychotherapy, their work in the personal domain probably reflects the best practices indicated by psychotherapy outcome research. In addition, recent research suggests that "expert" counselors and psychologists evaluate the Integral Intake as the most comprehensive, efficient, and helpful published idiographic assessment instrument (Marquis, 2002).

Integral counselors also employ strategies that address the transpersonal domain. Some of these strategies have been researched and found effective. For example, since 1970, beginning with Wallace's groundbreaking publication of "The Physiological Effects of Transcendental Meditation" in *Science*, more than a thousand experiments have been performed studying meditation and its effects. The consensus is that meditation accelerates psychological development without altering the sequence of developmental stages (Alexander, Druker, & Langer, 1990; Haruki & Kaku, 2000; Haruki, Ishii, & Suzuki, 1996; Richards & Commons, 1990; Walsh, 1993a).

Transcendental meditation (TM) is one type of mantra meditation which has been extensively studied with prison inmates, children, young adults, and the elderly. The results have consistently shown numerous benefits, ranging from purely physiological, to emotional, cognitive, and spiritual (Alexander, Davies, et al., 1990; Brown & Engler, 1986a, 1986b). For example, physically, stress, cholesterol, muscle tension, and blood pressure levels drop (Benson, 1975; Murphy & Donovan, 1989); psychologically, anxiety, post-traumatic stress, phobias, insomnia, and mild depression decrease; intelligence, creativity, and academic achievement are enhanced; and self-control, empathy, peace, and joy increase (Walsh, 1993a, 1999a). Another study found that with regard to Loevinger's scale of ego development, only 1 percent of a sample of college students appeared to have reached one of the two highest levels, whereas 38 percent of a similarly-matched sample of TM meditators reached those levels (Alexander, Davies, et al., 1990). Numerous studies corroborate this notion; the interested reader may consult the Research Appendix in Alexander, Druker, and Langer (1990), and Shapiro and Walsh (1984).

Several studies have measured brain wave activity through the use of the electroencephalograph (EEG), demonstrating with objective, quantitative data that meditation positively affects one's brain. Not only do meditators' brain waves slow down, but also various cortical regions show increased synchronization and coherence (Walsh, 1993a, p. 63).

Research has revealed a great deal about meditative technologies, but not much is known regarding which ones are most efficacious for specific types of people at varying stages of life. The question remains: Which types of ITPs best facilitate transformations in which lines of development for which types of people? Also, no research has been performed to assess the validity of Wilber's spectrum of treatment modalities. A major goal of the newly established Integral Institute is to fund just such research. Currently, the Integral Institute's primary research project is *Human Change Processes* named after Mahoney's 1991 classic, a comprehensive literature and meta-analysis of everything that has been studied relative to transformational technologies, from bodywork and journaling to psychotherapy and meditation.

Readers interested in transpersonal research methodologies are referred to Braud and Anderson (1998).

Nature/Nurture. Wilber has written little about the specifics of how genetics influence one's capacity to realize one's developmental potentials. However, by acknowledging heredity as a component in the upper right, individual-objective, behavioral quadrant, he has probably addressed it more explicitly than most counseling theorists. His four quadrant model also provides an elaboration on the theme of genetic propensities that is virtually absent in other theories. The upper left quadrant addresses how genetic propensities *feel* to the individual. The lower left quadrant addresses the meaning that such propensities are given by the individual's culture, for example, whether shyness is perceived as sensitivity or as cowardice. The lower right quadrant addresses the environmental factors that interact with heredity and greatly influence the extent to which a genetic propensity will actually be expressed—factors such as diet, drugs, physical traumas, and the ways the individual and others have adapted the environment to "fit" the individual's tendencies. Returning again to the upper left quadrant, one is believed to have some degree of ability to be conscious of—to witness—one's genetic tendencies and thus to assume at least some degree of agency over those tendencies.

Wilber's view of the relative importance of genetics in the grand scheme of things is reflected in his notion of "tetra-evolution": that the evolution both of the individual and of humanity at large is not predetermined but, rather, is a function of all four quadrants as they manifest and interact with each other (Wilber, 2000b). Referring to the Human Genome Project, the $3 billion undertaking to systematically map the entire sequence of human DNA, Wilber (1997a) wrote that

> this spectacular project promises to revolutionize our ideas of human growth, development, disease, and medical treatment, and its completion will surely mark one of the great advances in human knowledge. Not as well known, but arguably more important, is what might be called the Human Consciousness Project, the endeavor, now well under way, *to map the entire spectrum of the various states of human consciousness.* (p. 30)

Pharmacotherapy. From Wilber's perspective, pharmaceutical treatment should be limited *primarily* to those with the severe fulcrum-1 disorders such as schizophrenia, autistic disorder, depressive psychoses, and so forth. This is *not* to say that pharmaceutical treatment is never appropriate for other psychiatric problems, because Wilber (2000a, vol. 7, p. 642) also included pharmaceuticals within the physical realm, the most fundamental of all levels. When something is wrong with one's body, whether it is pain, illness, or fatigue, the body is that much harder to transcend. However, the prominence of pharmaceutical use is a reflection of our culture, which still focuses primarily on the behavioral quadrant. In response to depression, administering a pill is primarily a behaviorally objective endeavor, as opposed to inquiring into the meaning that the client's depression has for them, a primarily subjective endeavor. For further discussion of this topic, the reader is referred to Victor's (1996) *Psychopharmacology and Transpersonal Psychology.*

Managed Care and Brief Therapy. Integral counseling has only recently emerged, and not much regarding brief integral counseling has been written. From an integral perspective, brief therapy most likely addresses translative change, whereas long-term therapy is most likely necessary for transformative change. Most clients seek translative change, and most are addressing issues related to fulcrums F-3 through F-6; in many such cases, approaches endorsed by managed care are, from an integral perspective, quite appropriate. However, "Core [transformative] change is more often hard work requiring patience, persistence, and devoted practice that spans years, if not a lifetime" (Mahoney, 2003, ch. 12, pp. 27–28). When a client is pursuing transformative change, especially involving the transpersonal domain, brief therapy is not applicable, and thus managed care is not likely to be a viable option.

Diversity Issues. The cultural quadrant reveals that *a person absolutely cannot be adequately understood without also considering the cultural context within which she has lived and lives.* Thus, cultural issues are central to integral counseling. In addition, Wilber's incorporation and integration of traditions as diverse as Tibetan Buddhism, the !Kung African tribal spirituality, and Vedantic Hinduism encourage integral counselors to be relatively free of

Western ethnocentrism. Likewise, his exposition of the perennial philosophy has revealed that rather than one culture having the doorway to salvation, each major religion has, at its contemplative core, a unique and valid pathway to truth, God, or spirit. The reader is referred to "In a Modern Light: Integral Anthropology and the Evolution of Cultures" in Wilber (2000a, vol. 7).

In several of his works, Wilber has considered issues such as whether men and women have different, even if complementary, types of morality and spirituality. Discussing more than a dozen different forms of feminism, particularly that of Carol Gilligan and Peggy Wright, Wilber (2000a, vol. 7) summarized his view: Men and women *transform* (develop) through the same gender-neutral basic stages of development, "but men tend to *translate* with an emphasis on *agency*, women with an emphasis on *communion*" (p. 588). Neither is "better" than the other, and, in fact, both genders exist, as do all holons, as agency-in-communion.

As always, Wilber's criticism is not that the various feminist perspectives are "wrong" but that they tend to be limited and exclusionary, usually focusing on only one of the quadrants and often only on one level within that quadrant. "I believe," wrote Wilber (2000a, vol. 7)

> that what we need is a much more integral approach, an approach that, in acknowledging the truly different perspectives of a dozen or so different feminist schools, might actually find a scheme that would be more accommodating to each of them. This more integral approach is indeed part of what *Sex, Ecology, and Spirituality* attempts to develop, at least in rough outline form. SES is volume 1 of the Kosmos trilogy; in the forthcoming volume 2 (tentatively entitled Sex, God, and Gender: The Ecology of Men and Women), I expand and fill in the details of this general model of sex and gender. (p. 591)

The interested reader is referred to "Integral Feminism: Sex and Gender on the Moral and Spiritual Path" in Wilber (2000a, vol. 7).

Spirituality. It should be clear by now that no other theorist of counseling places spirituality in such a central role as does Wilber. He (1999d) has dealt with the perplexing issue of defining spirituality by identifying the five more common definitions found in the broad spiritual literature: (a) Spirituality pertains to the highest level of each of the developmental lines; (b) spirituality is the sum total of the individual's development in all the developmental lines; (c) spirituality is itself a separate developmental line; (d) spirituality is an attitude, such as openness or love, that one can have at any developmental level; and (e) spirituality involves peak experiences rather than developmental levels. He concluded that each of these definitions has value and that no one definition yet incorporates the useful aspects of each of the five definitions.

Wilber also has postulated both translative/legitimate/exoteric and transformative/authentic/esoteric aspects of spirituality. Examples of *translative spirituality* include elaboration of one's exoteric system, such as reading more or attending workshops related to one's belief system, or conversion from one belief system to another within the same developmental wave. According to Wilber (1997b) and Feuerstein (1997a), translative spirituality is the more commonly observed function of religion: to fortify the self. Through an *exoteric* system of beliefs and rituals, people are helped to understand and perhaps minimize the inherent suffering of the separate self; thus, translative spirituality fosters feelings of security, comfort, consolation, and perhaps protection or fortification. Translative spirituality is *legitimate* because it provides a certain sense of legitimacy to one's beliefs about the world and one's place therein.

An example of *transformative spirituality* involves someone who, after sustained contemplative practice or in the wake of a well-integrated near-death experience, expands from the vision-logic wave of development into the subtle wave, and perhaps beyond. According to Wilber (1997b), transformative spirituality constitutes a less commonly observed function of religion: *to deconstruct the self*. Rather than consoling, fortifying, or legitimizing the self, it uses *esoteric* practices to dismantle, transmute, transform, and liberate the self, ultimately from its illusion of separateness through a series of deaths and rebirths of the self into ever more inclusive developmental waves, all of which constitutes the process of *authentic* spirituality. Authentic spirituality inquires into legitimate spirituality and concludes that the latter tends to entrench a person in the current wave of development and thus prolong, even if more comfortably, the illusion of separateness that is, ironically, the actual source of suffering. In his glib way, Wilber (2000a, vol. 8) summarized that, in transformative spirituality, "the self is not made content. The self is made toast" (p. 305). From the integral psychology perspective, both translative and transformative functions of spirituality are vitally important. Equally important is discrimination between the two because of their different goals and processes. Readers interested in addressing spiritual issues in counseling are referred to Marquis, Holden, and Warren (2001).

Technical Eclecticism. Also obvious to the reader by now is the extent to which technical eclecticism is inherent in integral psychology. In fact, the integral approach offers the practitioner a rationale for utilizing the broadest range of possible techniques within a theoretically consistent context. Rather than assuming a traditional theoretical position and "imposing" it on every client, the counselor identifies and employs the approach that addresses the level of development with or within which the client is struggling.

Along with this wide embrace of a variety of techniques comes an equally weighty responsibility: for the integral counselor to be competent in the techniques she uses. Ethically speaking, competence is based not only on study but on supervised practice. Therefore, it is possible that an integral counselor might practice only within a narrow band of techniques—those in which she is competent—while maintaining the broad integral perspective.

DSM-IV Diagnosis. Similar to psychodynamic assessment, integral assessment focuses more on *levels* of development than *specific disorders within a given level*. However, in keeping with his goal of expanding the orthodox perspective by working within it, Wilber suggested including DSM-IV diagnoses, when appropriate, with the integral psychograph. Although attempting to be comprehensive, the DSM-IV disorders are all right-quadrant perspectives: Axes I, II, III, and V are objective descriptions of the individual, the upper right, behavioral quadrant; and Axis IV is an objective description of the individual's system, the lower right, social quadrant. References to the left, subjective quadrants appear in the text of DSM-IV-TR, but only sporadically. Until the DSM gives the subjective quadrants what, from an integral perspective, is the attention they are due, it behooves the integral counselor who uses DSM-IV-TR diagnosis to rectify the diagnostic neglect of the subjective quadrants by devoting particular attention to them.

Weaknesses of the Theory

The most common criticism of Wilber's work is that it has emerged from a nonclinician and therefore that some of his elegant theory is less-than-elegant at the practical level. A common example of this criticism is the spectrum of treatment modalities: A few therapists have claimed that although it makes a tremendous amount of sense, it is too rigid. However, this criticism may stem from a misunderstanding. As pointed out earlier in this chapter, Wilber never meant the spectrum of treatment modalities to be a rigid prescription dictating that only one approach was appropriate for a given individual; but that is how some critics have framed it.

Another glaring weakness of the approach is the lack of research. Because integral psychology and psychotherapy are so new, as long as research is undertaken with the urgency Wilber has expressed, this weakness currently may be forgiven. Indeed, research assessing the utility of a newly developed integral intake instrument has recently been completed (Marquis, 2002).

Distinguishing Additions to Counseling and Psychotherapy

Wilber's contributions to psychotherapy are numerous, and psychotherapy is just one of many, many disciplines his work addresses. Wilber's three most significant, unique contributions to psychotherapy are the "all-quadrant, all level perspective"; his spectrum of development, pathology, treatment, resistance, and special conditions for the resistance; and his emphasis on the necessity of counselors' and clients' commitment to integral transformative practices. Many counselors have found his spectrum of development to be immensely helpful in their understanding of the "full spectrum" of clients. Understanding developmental hierarchies allows the integral counselor to more fully join, understand, and communicate with clients as they are.

Wilber was also the first to discern and recognize many dynamics that seem increasingly obvious: the need to conceptually separate *lines* and *levels* of development; the difficulties involved with defining a "spiritual" line of development; that geniuses such as Freud and the Buddha—the former claiming the goal of mental health was a strong ego, the latter claiming the goal was transcendence of the ego, the source of suffering—were not contradicting each other, but rather addressing different levels of the great nest of being. His all-quadrant, all-level model, with its honoring of and demand for both objective and subjective approaches to knowledge at both the individual and collective levels, is the most likely candidate to lend credibility in the eyes of orthodox thinkers to unorthodox notions such as transpersonal levels of development.

CURRENT STATUS

Currently, the field of transpersonal psychology is not a unified discipline but consists of three main, and largely incompatible, camps: (prerational) magic-mythic-astrological adherents ("New Age"), those who focus on nonordinary *states* of consciousness, and those who devote attention to transpersonal *levels* of development. Not only because they were unable to agree with one another, but also because they failed to be genuinely comprehensive, Wilber in 1983 disaffiliated himself from the transpersonal community. Nevertheless, he continues to express respect for transpersonal scholars such as Stan Grof, Michael Washburn, Peggy Wright, Donald Rothberg, and many others, to whom he still refers as gifted and brilliant (see Ken Wilber Online, http://wilber.shambhala.com).

In 2000, Wilber founded the Integral Institute, an "all-quadrant, all-level" organization with branches in business, ecology, psychology, politics, medicine, art, law and criminal justice, education, religion, and the university student outreach. He hopes that his theoretical model, which honors the importance of objective, conventional disciplines and approaches and integrates them with the interior, subjective domains of existence at all levels, including transpersonal levels, will foster the building of bridges to the conventional world that the transpersonal field has been unable to achieve. In its inaugural year, the Integral Institute produced an extraordinarily rich cross-fertilization of ideas from these diverse fields. Some of the scholars who have identified themselves as integral include Michael Murphy, George Leonard, Roger Walsh, Frances Vaughan, Michael Mahoney, Robert Kegan, Allan Combs, Bert Parlee, Jenny Wade, Sean Hargens, and Don Beck. They, together with numerous other gifted people from diverse fields, are doing all-quadrant, all-level research and applications, ranging from effects of ITPs to how to help inner city "at-risk" children.

SUMMARY

This chapter is only an introduction to the richness of integral counseling, yet, hopefully, readers who resonate with integral counseling and find it a candidate for their guiding theory are inspired to pursue further study, both intellectual and experiential.

In the words of Walsh and Vaughan (1994), Ken Wilber

> has forged a systematic, broad-ranging, multidisciplinary, integrative, visionary yet scholarly worldview based in psychology, grounded in philosophy, spanning sociology and anthropology, and reaching to religion and mysticism. . . . The scope of his synthesis is perhaps unparalleled. (p. 18)

Ultimately, Wilber's integral philosophy, with its quadrants, lines, and levels, is, like all other theories, just a map. Its purpose will have been fulfilled if it encourages and helps both counselors and clients live more integral lives. Never before in human history has so much wisdom, ancient and modern, Eastern and Western, been available to all. An integral life puts that wisdom to use. Such a life is not intended to be rigid or ascetic. Rather, an integral life embodies health, joy, love, humor, wisdom, and compassion. In Wilber's words:

> I don't suggest the mere study of maps. What I actually recommend is finding and engaging a practice that speaks to your potentials and shows you the actual territory. . . . [T]he practice could be anything – art, community service, raising sane kids, writing novels, sports—so long as it also pulls you out of yourself and into a larger being. The point is that each of us has to take the actual journey, in our own way, in our own time, at our own pace. (Schwartz, 1995, p. 374)

RECOMMENDED RESOURCES

The complete body of Wilber's writings is now available in his eight-volume *Collected Works*. We suggest that the interested reader begin with *Integral Psychology*, then proceed to *A Brief History of Everything, A Theory of Everything, One Taste*, and *The Eye of Spirit*. An excellent reference site for information regarding Wilber's books, key concepts, criticism, and so forth, is www.worldofkenwilber.com.

Leonard and Murphy (1995) provided detailed descriptions of how to tailor ITPs so that they become an integral part of one's daily life. If you are interested in joining one of the approximately 40 ITP groups that have begun across the country, Murphy and Leonard can be contacted at: www.itp-life.com.

Out of the vast transpersonal literature, we most highly recommend Scotton, Chinen, and Battista (1996), Walsh and Vaughan (1993), and Schwartz (1995). Walsh (1999) is an excellent introduction to central spiritual practices and techniques. Also, Vaughan (1985), in which each chapter concludes with an experiential exercise, may prove helpful to counselors. A wealth of videotaped interviews of persons prominent in transpersonal psychology is available in the Thinking Allowed television series: www.thinkingallowed.com.

REFERENCES

Alexander, C., Davies, J., Dixon, C., Dillbeck, M., Druker, S., Oetzel, R., Muehlman, J., & Orme-Johnson, D. (1990). Growth of higher stages of consciousness: Maharishi's Vedic psychology of human development. In C. Alexander & E. Langer (Eds.), *Higher stages of human development* (pp. 286–341). New York: Oxford University.

Alexander, C., Druker, S., & Langer, E. (1990). Introduction: Major issues in the exploration of adult growth. In C. Alexander & E. Langer (Eds.), *Higher stages of human development* (pp. 3–32). New York: Oxford University.

Almaas, A. H. (1988). *The pearl beyond price: An integration of personality in being: An object relations approach*. Berkeley, CA: Diamond.

Almaas, A. H. (1996). *The point of existence: Transformations of narcissism in self-realization*. Berkeley, CA: Diamond.

Asay, T. P., & Lambert, M. J. (1999). The empirical case for the common factors in therapy: Quantitative findings. In M. A. Hubble, B. L. Duncan, & S. D. Miller (Eds.), *The heart and soul of change* (pp. 23–55). Washington, DC: American Psychological Association.

Assagioli, R. (1965). *Psychosynthesis*. New York: Penguin.

Assagioli, R. (1991). *Transpersonal development: Dimensions beyond psychosynthesis*. San Francisco: Aquarian.

Atwood, G. E., & Stolorow, R. D. (1984). *Structures of subjectivity: Explorations in psychoanalytic phenomenology*. Hillsdale, NJ: Analytic.

Aurobindo, S. (1970). *The life divine* (vols. 1 & 2). Pondicherry: All India Press, Sri Aurobindo Ashram.

Avabhasa, D. (1985). *The dawn horse testament*. Clearlake, CA: Dawn Horse.

Battista, J. (1996). Offensive spirituality and spiritual defenses. In B. Scotton, A. Chinen, & J. Battista (Eds.), *Textbook of transpersonal psychiatry and psychology* (pp. 250–260). New York: Basic.

Beck, A. T., & Weishaar, M. (1989). Cognitive therapy. In A. Freeman, K. M. Simon, L. E. Beutler, & H. Arkowitz (Eds.), *Comprehensive handbook of cognitive therapy* (pp. 21–36). New York: Plenum.

Benson, H. (1975). *The relaxation response.* New York: Avon.

Berne, E. (1961). *Transactional analysis in psychotherapy.* New York: Grove.

Berzin, A. (2000). *Relating to a spiritual teacher: Building a healthy relationship.* Ithaca, NY: Snow Lion.

Bohart, A. C., & Tallman, K. (1999). *How clients make therapy work: The process of active self-healing.* Washington, DC: American Psychological Association.

Boorstein, S. (1997). *Clinical studies in transpersonal psychotherapy.* Albany: State University of New York.

Braud, W., & Anderson, R. (1998). *Transpersonal research methods for the social sciences: Honoring human experience.* Thousand Oaks, CA: Sage.

Brown, D., & Engler, J. (1986a). The stages of mindfulness meditation: A validation Study. Part I: Study and results. In K. Wilber, J. Engler, & D. P. Brown (Eds.), *Transformations of consciousness: Conventional and contemplative perspectives on development* (pp. 161–191). Boston: Shambhala.

Brown, D., & Engler, J. (1986b). The stages of mindfulness meditation: A validation Study. Part II: Discussion. In K. Wilber, J. Engler, & D. P. Brown (Eds.), *Transformations of consciousness: Conventional and contemplative perspectives on development* (pp. 193–217). Boston: Shambhala.

Campbell, J. (Ed.). (1972). *The portable Jung.* New York: Viking.

Cha, K. Y., Wirth, D. P., & Lobo, R. A. (2001). Does prayer influence the success of in vitro fertilization-embryo transfer? *Journal of Reproductive Medicine, 46*(9), 781–787.

Chapin, T. (1989). The power within: A humanistic-transpersonal imagery technique. *Journal of Humanistic Psychology, 29*(4), 444–456.

Chomsky, N. (1969). *Deep structure, surface structure, and semantic interpretation.* Bloomington, IN: Indiana University Linguistics Club.

Da, Free John (1980). *Scientific proof of the existence of God will soon be announced by the White House!* Middletown: Dawn Horse.

Davis, J. (1999). *The diamond approach: An introduction to the teachings of A. H. Almaas.* Boston: Shambhala.

Douglas, C. (2000). Analytical psychotherapy. In R. J. Corsini & D. Wedding (Eds.), *Current psychotherapies* (pp. 99–132). Itasca, IL: F. E. Peacock.

Eliot, T. S. (1943). *The four quartets.* New York: Harcourt Brace Jovanovich.

Epstein, M. (1990). Psychodynamics of meditation: Pitfalls on the spiritual path. *Journal of Transpersonal Psychology, 22*(1), 17–34.

Epstein, M. (1995). *Thoughts without a thinker: Psychotherapy from a Buddhist perspective.* New York: Basic.

Erikson, E. (1963). *Childhood and society* (2nd ed.). New York: Norton.

Feuerstein, G. (1996). *The philosophy of classical yoga.* Rochester, NY: Inner Traditions International.

Feuerstein, G. (1997a). To light a candle in a dark age. *What Is Enlightenment? 12,* 34–43.

Feuerstein, G. (1997b). *The Shambhala encyclopedia of yoga.* Boston: Shambhala.

Foundation for Inner Peace. (1975). *A course in miracles* (vols. 1–3). Tiburon, CA: Author.

Fox, M. (2000). *Passion for creation: The earth-honoring spirituality of Meister Eckhart*. Rochester, NY: Inner Tradition.

Freud, S. (1914). Further recommendations in the techniques of psychoanalysis: Recollection, repetition, and working through. In Philip Rieff (Ed.), *Freud: Therapy and technique* (pp. 157–166). New York: Collier.

Freud, S. (1971). *A general introduction to psychoanalysis*. New York: Pocket.

Goleman, D. (1972a). The Buddha on meditation and states of consciousness. Part I: The teachings. *Journal of Transpersonal Psychology,* 4(1), 1–44.

Goleman, D. (1972b). The Buddha on meditation and states of consciousness. Part II: A typology of meditation techniques. *Journal of Transpersonal Psychology,* 4(2), 151–210.

Grof, C., & Grof, S. (1993). Spiritual emergency: The understanding and treatment of transpersonal crises. In R. Walsh & F. Vaughan (Eds.), *Paths beyond ego: The transpersonal vision* (pp. 137–144). Los Angeles: Jeremy P. Tarcher.

Grof, S. (1967). *Realms of the human unconscious: Observations from LSD research*. New York: E. P. Dutton.

Grof, S. (1998). *The cosmic game: Explorations of the frontiers of human consciousness*. Albany: State University of New York.

Hargens, S. (2002). Intersubjective musings: A response to Christian de Quincey's "The promise of Integralism." *Journal of Consciousness Studies,* 8(12), 35–78.

Haruki, Y., & Kaku, K. T. (Eds.). (2000). *Meditation as health promotion: A lifestyle modification approach*. Delft: Eburon.

Haruki, Y., Ishii, Y., & Suzuki, M. (Eds.) (1996). *Comparative and psychological study on meditation*. Delft: Eburon.

Hixon, L. (1978). *Coming home: The experience of enlightenment in sacred traditions*. Burdett, NY: Larson Publications.

Holden, J. (1993). Transpersonal counseling. *Texas Counseling Association Journal, 21*(1), 7–23.

Holden, J. M. (1999). *Introduction to the transpersonal perspective in counseling*. Paper presented at the 48th Annual World Conference of the American Counseling Association, San Diego, CA.

Holden, J. M., VanPelt, P. T., & Warren, S. (1999). Spiritual emergency: An introduction and case example. *Counseling and Values, 43,* 163–177.

Huxley, A. (1946). *The perennial philosophy*. New York: Harper & Brothers.

Huxley, A. (1993). The perennial philosophy. In R. Walsh & F. Vaughan (Eds.), *Paths beyond ego: The transpersonal vision* (pp. 212–213). Los Angeles: Jeremy P. Tarcher.

James, W. (1950). *The principles of psychology* (vols. 1 & 2). New York: Dover. (Original work published 1890)

James, W. (1901). *The varieties of religious experience*. New York: Holt, Rinehart & Winston.

James, W. (1993). The varieties of consciousness: Observations on nitrous oxide. In R. Walsh & F. Vaughan (Eds.), *Paths beyond ego: The transpersonal vision* (pp. 94–95). Los Angeles: Jeremy P. Tarcher.

Jung, C. G. (1969). Synchronicity: An acausal connecting principle. In G. Adler, M. Fordham, W. McGuire, & H. Read (Eds.) and R.F.C. Hull (Trans.), *The collected works of C. G. Jung* (vol. 8, pp. 419–519). Princeton, NJ: Princeton University Press.

Kapleau, P. (1980). *The three pillars of zen*. New York: Doubleday.

Keating, T. (1986). *Open mind, open heart: The contemplative dimension of the gospel*. Amity: Amity House.

Kegan, R. (1982). *The evolving self: Problem and process in human development*. Cambridge, MA: Harvard University.

Kohut, H. (1972). *The analysis of the self*. New York: International Universities.

Kohut, H. (1977). *The restoration of the self*. New York: International Universities.

Kohut, H. (1984). *How does analysis cure?* Chicago: University of Chicago Press.

Kornfield, J. (1993). Even the best meditators have old wounds to heal: Combining meditation and psychotherapy. In R. Walsh & F. Vaughan (Eds.), *Paths beyond ego: The transpersonal vision* (pp. 67-69). Los Angeles: Jeremy P. Tarcher.

Lambert, M.J., & Bergin, A.E. (1994). The effectiveness of psychotherapy. In A.E. Bergin & S. L. Garfield (Eds.), *Handbook of psychotherapy and behavior change* (4th ed., pp. 143–190). New York: Wiley.

Lauglin, C., McMaus, J., & Shearer, J. (1993). Transpersonal anthropology. In R. Walsh & F. Vaughan (Eds.). *Paths beyond ego: The transpersonal vision* (pp. 190–194). Los Angeles: Jeremy P. Tarcher.

Leonard, G., & Murphy, M. (1995). *The life we are given: A long-term program for realizing the potential of body, mind, heart, and soul*. New York: G. P. Putnam's Sons.

Lukoff, D. (1985). The diagnosis of mystical experiences with psychotic features. *Journal of Transpersonal Psychology, 17*, 155–182.

Magai, C., & McFadden, S. (1995). *The role of emotions in social and personality development*. New York: Plenum.

Maharshi, R. (1985). *Be as you are: The teachings of Sri Ramana Maharshi*. London: Penguin.

Mahler, M., Pine, F., & Bergman, A. (1975). *The psychological birth of the human infant*. New York: Basic.

Mahoney, M. (1991). *Human change processes: The scientific foundations of psychotherapy*. New York: Basic.

Mahoney, M. (2003). *Constructive psychotherapy: A practical guide*. New York: Guilford.

Marquis, A., Holden, J. M., & Warren, E. S. (2001) *"An Integral Psychology Response to Helminiak's (2001) 'Treating Spiritual Issues in Secular Psychotherapy'." Counseling and Values, 45*(3), pp. 218–236.

Marquis, M. (2002). *Mental health professionals' comparative evaluations of the Integral Intake, Life-Style Introductory Interview, and the Multimodal Life History Inventory*. Unpublished doctoral dissertation.

Maslow, A. H. (1968). *Toward a psychology of being* (rev. ed.). New York: Van Nostrand Reinhold.

Maslow, A. H. (1971). *The farthest reaches of human nature*. Oxford: Viking.

Merton, T. (1969). *Contemplative prayer*. New York: Herder and Herder.

Murphy, M., & Donovan, S. (1989). *The physical and psychological effects of meditation*. San Rafael, CA: Esalen Institute.

Murphy, M. (1993). Integral practices: Body, heart, and mind. In R. Walsh & F. Vaughan (Eds.), *Paths beyond ego: The transpersonal vision* (pp. 171–173). Los Angeles: Jeremy P. Tarcher.

Murthy, T. S. (1990). *The life and teaching of Sri Ramana Maharshi*. Clearlake, CA: Dawn Horse.

O'Brien, E. (1984). *The essential Plotinus*. Indianapolis: Hackett.

Orloff, J. (1996). *Second sight*. New York: Warner.

Perry, R. B. (1936). *The thought and character of William James*. New York: Harper & Row.

Piaget, J. (1977). *The essential Piaget*. H. E. Gruber & J. J. Voneche (Eds.). New York: Basic.

Puhakka, K. (1994). The cultivation of wisdom: An interview with Roger Walsh. *Humanistic Psychologist, 22,* 275–295.

Puhakka, K. (2000). An invitation to authentic knowing. In T. Hart, P. Nelson, & K. Puhakka (Eds.), *Transpersonal knowing: Exploring the horizon of consciousness.* Albany: State University of New York Press.

Ram Dass. (1973). *Love, serve, remember* (audiotape). Santa Cruz, CA: Hanuman Foundation.

Rawlinson, A. (1997). *The book of enlightened masters: Western teachers in Eastern traditions.* Chicago: Open Court.

Richards, F., & Commons, M. (1990). Postformal cognitive-developmental theory and research: A review of its current status. In C. Alexander & E. Langer (Eds.), *Higher stages of human development* (pp. 139–161). New York: Oxford University.

Rinpoche, S. (1993). *The Tibetan book of living and dying.* San Francisco: Harper Collins.

Rothberg, D. J., & Kelly, S. (Eds.). (1998). *Ken Wilber in dialogue: Conversations with leading transpersonal thinkers.* Wheaton, IL: Theosophical Publishing House.

Schumacher, E. F. (1977). *A guide for the perplexed.* New York: Harper & Row.

Schwartz, T. (1995). *What really matters: Searching for wisdom in America.* New York: Bantam.

Scotten, B. W., Chinen, A. B., & Battista, J. R. (Eds.). (1996). *Textbook of transpersonal psychiatry and psychology.* New York: Basic Books.

Shapiro, D., & Walsh, R. (Eds.). (1984). *Meditation: Classic and contemporary perspectives.* New York: Aldine.

Singer, J. (1972). *Boundaries of the soul: The practice of Jung's psychology.* New York: Doubleday.

Smith, H. (1976). *Forgotten truth: The primordial tradition.* New York: Harper & Row.

Smith, H. (1992). *Forgotten truth: The common vision of the world's religions.* San Francisco: HarperCollins.

Steindl-Rast, D. (1983). *A listening heart: The art of contemplative living.* New York: Crossroad.

Steindl-Rast, D. (1984). *Gratefulness, the heart of prayer: An approach to life in fullness.* New York: Paulist.

Stolorow, R. D., Brandchaft, B., & Atwood, G. E. (1987). *Psychoanalytic treatment: An intersubjective approach.* Hillsdale, NJ: Analytic.

Targ, R., & Katra, J. (1999). *Miracles of mind: Exploring nonlocal consciousness and spiritual healing.* New York: New World Library.

Tart, C. (1983). *States of consciousness.* El Cerrito, CA: Psychological Processes.

Trungpa, C. (1988). *Shambhala: Sacred path of the warrior.* Boston: Shambhala.

Vaughan, F. (1985). *The inward arc: Healing and wholeness in psychotherapy and spirituality.* Boston: Shambhala.

Vaughan, F. (1991). Spiritual issues in psychotherapy. *Journal of Transpersonal Psychology, 23*(2), 105–119.

Vaughan, F. (1993). Healing and wholeness in psychotherapy. In R. Walsh & F. Vaughan (Eds.), *Paths beyond ego: The transpersonal vision.* Los Angeles: Jeremy P. Tarcher.

Vaughan, F. (1995). *Shadows of the sacred: Seeing through spiritual illusions.* Wheaton, IL: Quest.

Victor, B. (1996). Psychopharmacology and transpersonal psychology. In B. Scotton, A. Chinen, & J. Battista (Eds.), *Textbook of transpersonal psychiatry and psychology* (pp. 327–334). New York: Basic.

Wade, J. (1996). *Changes of mind: A holonomic theory of the evolution of consciousness.* Albany: State University of New York.

Wallace, R. (1970). Physiological effects of transcendental meditation. *Science, 167,* 1751–1754.

Walsh, R. (1989). Can Western philosophers understand Asian philosophies? *Crosscurrents, XXXIX,* 281–299.

Walsh, R. (1993a). Meditation research: The state of the art. In R. Walsh & F. Vaughan (Eds.), *Paths beyond ego: The transpersonal vision* (pp. 60–66). Los Angeles: Jeremy P. Tarcher.

Walsh, R. (1993b). The transpersonal movement: A history and state of the art. *Journal of Transpersonal Psychology, 25,* 123–139.

Walsh, R. (1995). The problem of suffering: Existential and transpersonal perspectives. *Humanistic Psychologist, 23,* 345–357.

Walsh, R. (1999). *Essential spirituality: The seven central practices to awaken heart and mind.* New York: Wiley.

Walsh, R., & Vaughan, F. (1993). Introduction. In R. Walsh & F. Vaughan (Eds.), *Paths beyond ego: The transpersonal vision.* Los Angeles: Jeremy P. Tarcher.

Walsh, R., & Vaughan, F. (1994). The worldview of Ken Wilber. *Journal of Humanistic Psychology, 34*(2), 6–21.

Washburn, M. (1988). *The ego and the dynamic ground: A transpersonal theory of human development.* Albany: State University of New York.

Washburn, M. (1994). *Transpersonal psychology in psychoanalytic perspective.* Albany: State University of New York.

Wilber, K. (1977). *Spectrum of consciousness.* Wheaton, IL: Theosophical.

Wilber, K. (1995). *Sex, ecology, spirituality: The spirit of evolution.* Boston: Shambhala.

Wilber, K. (1997a). *The eye of spirit: An integral vision for a world gone slightly mad.* Boston: Shambhala.

Wilber, K. (1997b). A spirituality that transforms. *What Is Enlightenment?, 12,* 22–32.

Wilber, K. (1999a). An approach to integral psychology. *Journal of Transpersonal Psychology, 31*(2), 109–136.

Wilber, K. (1999b). *The collected works of Ken Wilber* (vols. 1–4). Boston: Shambhala.

Wilber, K. (1999c). *One taste: The journals of Ken Wilber.* Boston: Shambhala.

Wilber, K. (1999d). Spirituality and developmental lines: Are there stages? *Journal of Transpersonal Psychology, 31*(1), 1–10.

Wilber, K. (2000a). *The collected works of Ken Wilber* (vols. 5–8). Boston: Shambhala.

Wilber, K. (2000b). *Integral psychology: Consciousness, spirit, psychology, therapy.* Boston: Shambhala.

Wilber, K. (2000c). *A theory of everything.* Boston: Shambhala.

Wilber, K., Engler, J., & Brown, D. P. (1986). *Transformations of consciousness: Conventional and contemplative perspectives on development.* Boston: Shambhala.

Wittine, B. (1993). Assumptions of transpersonal psychology. In R. Walsh & F. Vaughan (Eds.), *Paths beyond ego: The transpersonal vision.* Los Angeles: Jeremy P. Tarcher.

Yalom, I. (1980). *Existential psychotherapy.* New York: Basic Books.

Yalom, I. (1985). *The theory and practice of group psychotherapy.* New York: Basic Books.

Yalom, I. (1989). *Love's executioner and other tales of psychotherapy.* New York: Harper Perennial.

AUTHOR INDEX

SUBJECT INDEX

Adlerian psychology, 249 *See Also* Individual psychology
Aggression, 62
Aggressive drive, 48, 62, 72
Analyst:
   characteristics, 57
Analytic psychology, 422–423
Anger management, 62
Anticathexis, 37–38, 40–41
Anxiety, 12–13, 20, 25, 38, 45, 48, 50, 52–55, 57, 82, 86, 89, 95, 99, 125, 151–159, 161–168, 170–171, 173, 175–180, 188, 195–196, 198–199, 224, 226, 235, 241, 257–258, 279, 287–289, 291, 294, 301, 304–306, 308, 310–311, 315, 319–320, 322, 327–328, 344, 460, 466;
   as struggle against nonbeing, 158–159;
   response to, 163
Anxiety Checklist, 319
Awareness:
   as self-consciousness, 158;
   as vigilance, 158;
   of givens in life, 158

Beck Anxiety Inventory, 320
Beck Depression Inventory (BDI), 320, 332
Beck Hopelessness Scale, 320
Behavior:
   genetic origins of, 19
Behavioral counseling:
   activity scheduling in, 287;
   assessment methods in, 286;
   aversion therapy in, 290;
   behavioral rehearsal/role play in, 287;
   behavior change in, 284–286;
   brief therapy in, 292;

classical conditioning in, 276, 280–283, 288–290, 295;
client's role in, 284–285;
contributions to psychotherapy, 294;
counselor's role in, 285–286;
current status of, 294–295;
determinism, 274;
diversion in, 287;
diversity issues in, 292;
effectiveness of, 291–292;
empiricism, 275;
evolutionary continuity, 274;
exposure and response prevention in, 288–289;
extinction in, 278–280, 282, 287–289;
extrafamilial impact in, 283;
familial impact in, 283;
flooding in, 289;
function of psyche in, 275;
graded task assignment in, 287;
guided discovery in, 287;
healthy/adaptive personality in, 283–284;
historical context, 273–274;
involuntary behaviors, 275–276, 280–283, 290, 295;
managed care in, 292;
mastery and pleasure rating in, 287;
modeling in, 286–287;
nature/nurture in, 291;
negative reinforcement in, 277;
operant conditioning in, 276–280, 282–283, 286–288, 295;
pharmacotherapy in, 291–292;
philosophical underpinnings, 274–275;
positive reinforcement in, 277, 284–287;
prompting in, 280;